Transport

Transport

An economics and management perspective

David A. Hensher

Ann M. Brewer

OXFORD

UNIVERSITY PRESS

This book has been printed digitally and produced in a standard specification
in order to ensure its continuing availability

OXFORD
UNIVERSITY PRESS

Great Clarendon Street, Oxford OX2 6DP

Oxford University Press is a department of the University of Oxford.
It furthers the University's objective of excellence in research, scholarship,
and education by publishing world-wide in

Oxford New York

Auckland Bangkok Buenos Aires Cape Town Chennai
Dar es Salaam Delhi Hong Kong Istanbul Karachi Kolkata
Kuala Lumpur Madrid Melbourne Mexico City Mumbai Nairobi
São Paulo Shanghai Taipei Tokyo Toronto

Oxford is a registered trade mark of Oxford University Press
in the UK and in certain other countries

Published in the United States
by Oxford University Press Inc., New York

ISBN 0-19-877641-1

Printed in Great Britain by
Antony Rowe Ltd., Eastbourne

Dedication

We dedicate this book to our families Johanna, Andrew, and Danielle Hensher, Robert and Michael Case for their support and patience and understanding about all the long hours needed to bring this work to fruition. We also dedicate the intellectual contribution to Michael Beesley, a very special friend and one of the most influential transport economists of the twentieth century who passed away on 24 September 1999.

Preface

In writing this book we had a desire to recognize the broadening of the management framework within which many transport decisions are made, hoping to attract those who promote the mainstream views of transport practice to expand their thinking in this regard.

This book is the product of many years of lecturing in graduate programmes in transport economics, transport planning methods, organizational behaviour, human resource management, and strategic thinking. Students provide the best sounding board for the relevance of material. The hours of feedback have materially improved the structure and content of this book. The sequence of chapters is the result of testing differing orderings of material only to find time and time again that the big strategic picture and institutional setting always wins as the starting position before introducing important themes such as demand and costs.

Acknowledgements

To Phil Goodwin, Daniel McFadden, and the late Michael Beesley we owe a special debt for their contribution to the literature and for their inspiration to the authors. Graduate students read earlier versions of the book and guided us in revisions. The influence of other colleagues has been substantial in our appreciation of the topic. We thank Bill Greene, Jordan Louviere, Joffre Swait, Chris Nash, John Dodgson, Ken Small, Charlie Lave, Tu Ton, Bill Waters, Tae Oum, Alan Fels, the late Simon Domberger, Tom Golob, Axel Boersch-Supan, Stephen Glaister, Stephen Potter, John Bates, Andrew Daly, Hugh Gunn, John Taplin, Ted Kolsen, Truong Truong, Mark Bradley, Juan de Dios Ortuzar, and Sergio Jara Diaz.

Contents

Part 1   The institutional environment

Part 2 The cornerstones of transport economics

Part 3 The cornerstones of organizational management

About the authors

DAVID A. HENSHER is Founding Director of the Institute of Transport Studies (a Commonwealth Key Centre) and Professor of Management in the Faculty of Economics and Business at the University of Sydney. David is a Fellow of the Academy of Social Sciences in Australia, immediate Past President of the International Association of Travel Behaviour Research, and a Vice-Chair of the International Scientific Committee of the World Conference of Transport Research. David is on the editorial boards of nine of the leading transport journals (such as *Transportation Research, Journal of Transport Economics and Policy, Transport Policy*), and Area Editor of *Transport Reviews*. He has published extensively (over 240 papers) in the leading international transport journals and key journals in economics and marketing (such as *The Economic Journal, Review of Economics and Statistics, Journal of Business, Journal of Econometrics, Journal of Consumer Research, Marketing Letters*) as well as five books. His most recent books are on the *Demand for Automobiles*, published by North-Holland, *Operating a Bus and Coach Business* (with Ann Brewer published in 1997 by Allen and Unwin) and *Stated Choice Methods and Analysis* (with Jordan Louviere and Joffre Swait published by Cambridge University Press). His particular interests are transport economics, transport strategy, sustainable transport, productivity measurement, traveller behaviour analysis, stated choice experiments, privatization, and institutional reform. David has advised numerous government and private sector organizations on matters related to transportation.

ANN M. BREWER is the Foundation Professor of Organizational Logistics at the University of Sydney which draws on cognate areas of organizational behaviour, work organization, and human resource management to provide an overall framework for the organization that integrates theory and applications into a new structure of understanding for practice. Ann's research is based on relevant industry issues and problems across a range of sectors with a recent focus on transport, logistics, and supply chain management. As the Director of the Institute of Transport Studies Logistics Management Group, Ann initiated and designed the Masters of Logistics Management. She has designed a portfolio of industry certificates that are offered to those entering tertiary study for the first time. Ann has published in leading international transport journals including *Transportation, Journal of Transport Policy, Transport Reviews, Transportation Research, Journal of Public Transport, Journal of Air Transport Management*, as well as more broadly in *Gender, Work and Organisation* and *Journal of Managerial Psychology*. She is the author of five books including *Managing Employee Commitment, The Responsive Employee, Change Management*, and co-authored with David Hensher, *Operating a Bus and Coach Business*.

List of figures

List of tables

List of abbreviations

ABARE	Australian Bureau of Agricultural Economics
ACCC	Australian Consumer and Competition Council
ACT	Australian Capital Territory
AIC	average incremental cost
AKC	average capital cost per annum
ASC	average social cost
asv	alternative-specific attributes
AVI	automatic vehicle identification
BIE	Bureau of Industry Economics
BPP	best practice programme
BPR	business process re-engineering
BTCE	Bureau of Transport and Communication Economics
CEO	chief executive officer
CER	cargo exchange ratio
CF	competitive franchising
CH_4	methane
cif	cost inclusive of freight charges
CLRs	competitive line rates
CO_2	carbon dioxide
COAG	Council of Australian Governments
COP1	First Conference of the Parties to the Convention
CPI	consumer price index
CS	consumer surplus
CSOs	community service obligations
CT	competitive tender
CV	compensating variation
CWW	compressed work week
DGT	Director-General of Transport
DTSs	direct transport services
d.w.t.	dead-weight tonnage
EDI	electronic data interchange
EEO	equal employment opportunities
EJRCF	East Japan Railway Corporate Finance
EPP	employee participation programme
ERG	existence, relatedness, and growth needs
ESOs	environmental and social obligations
ETC	electronic toll collection
FCCC	Framework Convention on Climate Change
f.o.b.	free on board
FWS	flexible work scheduling
GGE	greenhouse gas emissions
GRT	gross registered tonnage

GST	goods and service tax
HFCs	hydrofluorocarbons
HR	human resource
HRP	human resource planning
IER	inverse elasticity rule
iff	if and only if
IID	independently and identically distributed
IMO	International Maritime Organization
IPART	Independent Pricing and Regulatory Tribunal
IPCC	Intergovernmental Panel on Climate Change
IT	information technology
JIT	just-in-time
JNRSC	JNR Settlement Corporation
k.p.h.	kilometres per hour
KPI	key performance indicators
LBL	London Bus Limited
LBO	learning by organizations
LD	long distance
LGA	local government area
LIO	learning in organizations
LRMC	long-run marginal cost
LRT	London Regional Transport
LTL	less-than-truckload
MC	marginal cost
MEC	marginal environmental external costs
MIS	management information systems
MLE	maximum-likelihood estimation
MNL	multinomial logit model
MPSE	multi-product scale economies
MR	marginal revenue
MRP	materials requirement planning
MSB	marginal social benefit
MSF	Management Stabilization Fund
NAASRA	National Association of Australian State Road Authorities
nAch	need for achievement
nAff	need for affiliation
N_2O	nitrous oxide
nPow	need for power
NRT	net registered tonnage
NSB	net social benefit
NSW	New South Wales
NT	Northern Territory
NTSSs	non-transport support services
OC	organizational outcomes
OD	origin-destination
OFFER	electricity regulator

OFGAS   gas regulator
OFRAIL   rail regulator
OFTEL   telecommunications regulator
OFWAT   water regulator
OL   organizational learning
OP   organizational performance
OPRAF   Office of Passenger Rail Franchising
ORR   Office of Rail Regulation
pcu   passenger car units
PDM   physical distribution management
PFCs   perfluorocarbons
pkm   passenger kilometre
PT   public transport
PTRC   Passenger Transport Research Corporation
QLD   Queensland
RAC   Rail Access Corporation
RAY   ray average cost
RC   road congestion costs
Ro/Ro   roll-on/roll-off vessels
RP   revealed preference
RSE   ray scale economies
RUM   random utility model
SA   South Australia
SC   supply chain
SCM   supply chain management
SF_6 sulphur hexafluoride
SQI   service quality index
SRA   New South Wales (Australia) State Rail Authority
SRAC   short-run average cost
SRMC   short-run marginal cost
TAS   Tasmania
TCT   telecommunications technology
TFP   total factor productivity
TMSC   total marginal social costs
TOCs   Train Operating Companies
TQM   total quality management
TUE   20-foot equivalent unit
UNEP   United Nations Environment Programme
VEHOP   vehicle operating cost
VIC   Victoria
VFR   visiting friends and relatives
vkm   vehicle kilometres
VMI   vendor-managed inventory
VTTS   valuation of travel time savings
WA   Western Australia
WMO   World Meteorological Organization

Transport economics and strategic management: an introduction

1.1 Introduction

Improving management performance and making 'good' decisions involves an ongoing understanding of the influences that impact on an organization and the broader sphere of stakeholder responsibilities. Equally important are internal and external influences. There is a tendency in transportation to emphasize the external environment and to treat the organization as a physical entity that can be manipulated with ease through the composition of its constituent inputs such as labour, capital, and energy. Such a perspective may be the product of the dominant focus of economics and engineering. The recognition that an organization is much more complex than the economic interpretation is a strong motivation for this book. It is also a challenge for transport specialists with backgrounds in economics, planning, and engineering who often struggle to understand the relevance of qualitative and complex relationships between people, culture, mindsets. They are more than just another set of influences to quantify and include in an optimization program.

There are three major themes throughout the book. The practice of transport management needs to be placed in a wider setting than that conventionally offered in transport economics while recognizing the continuing importance of a focus on economic performance. We see the wider focus being promoted by the idea of the supply chain and its constituent parts, of which transportation is an

important contributor. An aspect of the supply chain that deserves particular emphasis is the role of people, work, and organizations that we refer to as organizational logistics. It is also an important component of transport management. The incorporation of organizational logistics in a book with a strong focus on transport economics provides the licence to promote the book as a contribution to the practice of transport and organizational management. The importance of mindsets, economics, and people pervades the book.

The remaining sections of this chapter overview the key themes of the book. These include the importance of a strategic focus to decision-making but within a framework in which there are linkages between objectives at the tactical and operational levels. The strategic level sets reference points (through goals such as efficiency, equity, and environmental sustainability) against which more practical objectives can be assessed (e.g. affordability). At the tactical level, the emphasis is on planning with actions driven by policies emanating from a strategic focus which have definition, interpretation, and specification. The operational level focuses on implementation (e.g. outsourcing and insourcing), involving all parties in the supply chain such as the provider of a final transport service, the regulator, the suppliers of inputs, and the end user.

1.2 Strategic decision-making

A major theme in transport management is strategic decision-making. The loss of dissatisfied customers, market share, profitability, and competent workers, and (in the public sector) increasing subsidy result in huge costs for a business enterprise but are arguably relatively insignificant compared to the cost of poor strategic decision-making. If industries today were facing more predictable contexts, management could address competitors by a generic strategy of cost leadership, differentiation, and focus (Porter 1985). However, today the focus is on total value management of the supply chain by exploiting supply chain (interorganizational) relationships and alliances in both the passenger and freight sectors, which establishes and, at the same time, modifies the competitive context in which each business operates. Strategic decision making in this sense represents a complex set of trade-offs of key challenges and associated (perceived) benefits and costs to the business. Active market and institutional forces changing at a fast pace present challenges to the fields of transport and logistics management.

A strong focus of this book is on understanding how to enhance quality management performance, particularly in relation to decision-making, business and market strategy against a background of operational activity including demand forecasting, costing, pricing, people, work, and organizations. Improving managerial performance occurs within the context of the organization, its culture, work organization, and workforce. Few would contest the proposition that managers today operate within a climate of change, both internal and external to their organizations. Managerial performance occurs within a context of environmental change. There are a number of key external influences impacting businesses including increased global competition, changing customer demands, technological change, and institutional reforms such as privatization, economic deregulation, and contracting out. We will comment briefly on some of these themes prior to outlining the structure of the following chapters.

1.2.1 Competitive challenges and increased global competition

Fast changing competitive conditions often create persistent environmental changes for businesses that are not always consistent with past practices. These discontinuous forces lead to a paradox for management that requires them to address the contradictions between current practices, management lore, and customer demands (Handy 1994). These forces can be labelled performance drivers (e.g. customer demands), performance enablers (e.g. strategic alliance and integrated logistics), and performance inhibitors (e.g. economic regulation, formation of an economic bloc) depending on who the stakeholders are and their perceptions of these changes. In the past many of these changes occurred as single one-off events but today they are more likely to be clustered in novel ways. These changes include manufacturing, information and telecommunications technologies; economic reforms such as privatization and economic deregulation; demographic changes; and social changes such as greater flexibility at work, career restructuring, education, and training. These changes lead to shifts in global competition, customer demand, technological change, and work redesign, as well as new economic and people challenges.

1.2.2 Global competition

Competing globally focuses on which markets to enter and the process used to achieve this, for example, joint venturing. The key factors that have emerged include knowing your markets and which ones to serve, understanding entry and exit barriers, and accepting cross-cultural values. All transport and logistic businesses compete with each other on some level, either directly or indirectly. Competitive challenges consist of the ways by which management attempt to gain a competitive advantage over others through the planning and acquisition of scarce resources. The key factors that have emerged include increased productivity, quality, technological change, and innovation. The capacity to innovate in products and services is a major factor in performance management if the business is to gain market share (Pisano 1997). It is often the mixture of simple initiatives that creates uniqueness and competitive advantage.

1.2.3 Changing customer demands

Customer expectations for time, place and possession utility, service quality, and price continue to grow. Greater investment is needed in market research to analyse and anticipate customer preferences and reactions to new products and hence determine end-user demand for products and services. These customer service requirements can be partially addressed by analysing economic, technological, demographic, and social trends. Increasingly, however, we are investigating the demand for products which have not been experienced in particular markets (e.g. high speed rail, tollroads, mega container ships) and whose demand is difficult to forecast using information on past behavioural responses. Importantly, customer demands are derived from the culture in which they reside and are shaped by perceptions of time, space, and distance. When thinking strategically it is important that management do not overlook these cultural trends (Hammond and Morrison 1996).

1.2.4 Technological change

Without exception, all enterprises have been influenced in some way by immense technological change, principally in the area of information technology and telecommunications. This trend means that most businesses are performing quite differently to the way they were even five years ago and which many would have thought impossible ten years ago. In almost every business context, public or private sector, new technology has either lessened the entry barriers, enhanced cross-national investment, streamlined the supply chain, integrated logistics functions, enhanced or replaced transportation, improved transit and transaction time, led to new service and product innovations, and improved service delivery.

1.2.5 Economic challenges

Risks and opportunities, challenges and rewards pressure the economic world of transport and logistics management. Economic challenges are the dynamics linked to the production and distribution of resources among transport organizations. At the macroeconomic level, economic factors such as inflation, unemployment, interest rates, budget deficits or surpluses, and the international balance of trade influence transport management. At the microeconomic level, economic trends have evolved such as downsizing, cutbacks, the burgeoning service and tourism sectors, and changes in corporate ownership, including the separation of responsibilities for infrastructure and the use of such infrastructure (e.g. rail access and rail use).

Economic and associated institutional reforms have reinforced the importance of transport organizations knowing their costs, knowing their markets and which ones to serve, and the evolution of prices and service quality in line with the pricing strategy, be it profit maximization, social welfare maximization, or constrained (or cost recovery) social welfare maximization (i.e. Ramsey pricing). Economic regulators and industry associations also have a vested interest in such knowledge in order to promote the broad goals and objectives of their brief in managing the respective transport sectors.

One of the most dramatic changes is the economic and institutional reform of the transport sector. Privatization, economic deregulation, competitive tendering, and national competition policy, the latter accompanied by new economic regulation and a watchdog regulator, are increasingly creating new challenges and opportunities. The reform process in general is slow, but ongoing and in some sectors at its infancy or even embryonic stage. Industries and businesses are now confronting the evolution to less direct government intervention, which, in turn, has influenced global competition dramatically. This trend has impacted consumer demand providing greater choice over services and products. This is a pervasive theme throughout the book.

1.2.6 People, work, and organization

The interrelationship between business strategy, management, and workers gives rise to an increasing number of issues such as adjusting business processes and work practices to use resources productively, whether these are people, capital, energy, or materials. These topics are covered in this book under the headings of organizational structure, business culture, work design, and people management. Never has it been so important to concentrate on managing people so that they are committed to the delivery of high quality customer service. There are many factors involved in developing people to maximize the capacity of a transport or logistics business. Effective communication is an essential facet of people management, be it communication of the business strategy, vision, or information and data. Empowerment is also an important process in management of worker commitment which requires managers facilitating workers in defining their own goals against the business strategy as well as evaluating their own performance and the processes they manage. Training and development provide a key link between the performance of the overall business and individual workers. Team working is also an important tool for managing people in transport and logistics businesses as a way of placing value on workers, for integrating logistics functions, developing quality and commitment.

1.3 The structure of the book

The themes presented above define the focus of the book. We recognize the role of all stakeholders in the supply chain, internal and external to each business. A hierarchy of critical success factors such as productivity gain, organizational learning, financial improvement, and quality enhancement represents some of the many dimensions by which one might judge the performance of decisions made throughout the supply chain. Measures of customer satisfaction, patronage, response flexibility, and productivity, for example, provide useful indicators to link the strategic vision of a transport business to a set of underlying operational measures such as quality, delivery, process time, and cost.

Throughout the book, we offer a range of conceptual frameworks and analytical tools to assist in providing ways of thinking about and quantifying the practice of transport and organizational logistics within a framework designed to capture the commitment of a business to multiple objectives, goals, and a vision. Each reader will raise many questions, many of which cannot be investigated without reading further material from the extensive set of references to the wider literature.

The following chapters have been organized into three parts: the institutional environment (Chapters 2 and 3); the fundamental cornerstones of transport economics: knowing your market (Chapter 4), knowing your costs (Chapter 5), and knowing your prices (Chapters 6 and 7); and the fundamental cornerstones of organizational management: knowing your organization from a supply chain perspective (Chapter 8), knowing your business culture (Chapter 9), knowing your work design (Chapter 10), and knowing your people (Chapter 11). The themes of each chapter are introduced briefly here.

1.3.1 Part 1: the institutional environment

The practice of transport and organizational logistics does not and never will be able to be pursued in isolation from the institutional environment. Where the market is unable to act efficiently and effectively as the watchdog, governments use regulatory instruments. The mixture of market and regulatory forces exists in all sectors of transport and logistics operations, and impact to varying degrees. Chapters 2 and 3 introduce the major features of the spectrum of what has become known as 'competition and ownership' options under which individual transport businesses, private and public, operate. Privatization, economic deregulation, competitive regulation (e.g. competitive tendering), and competition policy are dominating themes. Case studies are presented in Chapter 3 to illustrate the way in which nations have tackled the process of economic reform of transport markets.

1.3.2 Part 2: the cornerstones of transport economics

Chapter 4 ('Knowing your market') introduces principles and practice for understanding and predicting travel choice and demand for passenger and freight transport services. The literature is extensive and highly analytical; however there are some very simple and powerful principles which can guide the specification of analytical models capable of studying the phenomenon of choice and demand. We concentrate on the entry-level toolkit necessary to appreciate the very precise meaning of travel demand appropriate in determining market opportunities in all transport sectors, be they passenger or freight. Single cross-section and time series methods are presented as frameworks within which to empirically analyse data.

Chapter 5 ('Knowing your costs') takes a close look at the costs of operating a transport business at the level of the individual firm and for an industry sector as a whole. The great majority of transport firms are interested in how they can be more cost efficient in the delivery of services. However, transport firms do not exist in a vacuum; their future is very much influenced by the performance of their industry as a whole and its interfaces with the rest of the economy. Regulators require information on the health of a transport sector (e.g. ports, rail, shipping, airports, roads) in making judgements on the performance and obligations of that sector. This information includes knowledge of the extent of economies of scale, density, scope, and network integrity. With such information, arguments are advanced as to the legitimacy of specific market practices, especially in respect of the impact on consumers and the community and the cost to government where subsidy and/or direct ownership are entailed. The tools used by industry watchers to monitor structure, conduct, and performance are presented in a way that highlights their practical value, avoiding the complexities which economic theory has imposed on many such useful empirical constructs.

The chapter begins with the individual transport business, introducing the way in which costs should be viewed if managers think strategically. A case study for the bus and coach sector illustrates how the ideas are translated into good practice. We then introduce the industry-level perspective, and draw on examples in coastal shipping, urban car use, and long-distance trucking to illustrate how costs are assessed sectorally. Further details on the operating costs of cars and trucks are given in Chapter 7 in the context of an evaluation of transport subsidy.

Chapter 6 ('Knowing your prices') brings together the knowledge of demand and costs to establish a pricing regime for transport services. The prices to be charged in a transport market should have strong links with the costs of delivering services and the responsiveness of the market to such prices. This includes recognition of the role of subsidy under conditions of community service obligation (CSO). The functional relationship between prices, costs, and demand will be influenced by the pricing strategy of a particular transport business in either the public or private sector, for both the provision of infrastructure (e.g. airports, roads, railways, ports) and operations (e.g. travel on airlines, buses, trains, ships). We devote a considerable amount of space to the principles and practice of transport user charges including the ways in which externalities such as traffic congestion should be handled given a commitment to economic efficiency, distributive justice, and environmental sustainability.

Developments in the reforms of urban public transport in the 1980s and 1990s have highlighted the extent to which it is possible to deliver public transport without subsidy. In countries where market reforms have been most active, such as the UK and New Zealand, local urban bus and rail services continue to attract subsidy, albeit to a lesser extent than previously. In most other developed and developing economies, subsidy is a 'way of life' for public transport. The justification for subsidy must rest with obligations to deliver a specific level of service deemed to have community value that would not be guaranteed through the forces of commercial activity in a competitive market. Consequently, we see the need for minimum subsidy (or net) competitive tenders where there is a commitment to use the market to its limit, and direct negotiated subsidy where a service is delivered in a protected public or private monopoly setting. Chapter 7 presents a method for establishing the justification for subsidy to all forms of public transport, utilizing a benefit-cost framework.

1.3.3 Part 3: the cornerstones of organizational management

Businesses today compete on a world platform. The question is how can business leverage all of its resources to improve customer service, operate more efficiently and cost effectively, and ensure competitive success. Almost instinctively, managers consider their enterprise as competing for success and survival in an adversarial rather than a collaborative arena. Management's task is to match the business's capabilities with the forces imposed by the competitive context such as expanded markets and the proliferation of services and products, to provide an advantage in the marketplace. Issues including supply

chain management, organization design, and strategic alliance are discussed in Chapter 8.

Perhaps the most important development is the customer-driven change in service standards. How are these changes being addressed? Are they being rejected, resisted, or welcomed into the business? Some organizations habitually take refuge in denial while others want to explore what they can learn and how they can develop from these changes. What makes these organizations different in terms of accepting change? The ways people think, feel, and act in organizations do not occur by chance and are strongly influenced by 'how the organization does things'. Chapter 9 ('Knowing your business culture') considers culture, the 'black box' of organizations in terms of both structural and operational characteristics in leading to business outcomes.

Increasingly management is playing a key role in shaping industry, the labour market, and industrial relations through the way it structures its business, designs work and work practices, and human resource management. Due to the complex interplay of strategies and its implications on a larger industry platform, work design is no longer viewed as an isolated strategy, but needs to be seen in the context of the market, industry, and business strategy. Chapter 10 ('Knowing your work design') discusses the linkage between work and organizational design as a way of focusing on how effectively the design of the organization is in the attainment of its business strategy.

The future of work lies in understanding the design of the internal organization, work routines and capabilities, telecommunications and information technologies, together with the market context. The flexibility associated with information technologies presents a number of people-related challenges. The essential flexibility of these technologies means that they need to be implanted in the cultural organization of the workplace in order to achieve a competitive blending of worker commitment, performance, and high quality customer service. These developments are reshaping work, skill, and organizational structures presenting two key challenges for managers that are discussed in Chapter 11 ('Knowing your people').

Case studies are introduced at the conclusion of Chapters 8 to 11 as an opportunity for reflective practice. Each case study focuses on a particular issue related to one of the themes covered in the chapter. When confronted with the case, the reader as learner will draw upon a deep source of previously learned patterns and information as well as new learning from the chapter itself. Compared to experienced learners and practitioners, novice learners produce fewer interpretations and potential options for action due to less well-defined pattern recognition skills. Expertise is based on well-defined pattern recognition skills that enable learners to relate problems to principles, concepts, and theories (personal and others). The principles for displaying expertise include all the processes included in a case study such as:

- defining and interpreting problems,
- setting goals for problem-solving,
- utilizing principles and 'theories-in-use',
- reinterpreting the problem,
- appreciating constraints,
- prescribing solution processes and consequences of each,
- taking action.

Discussion issues for Chapter 1

1 Discuss the importance of broadening the mindset to incorporate organizational logistics in the practice of transport management.

2 A strategic focus to all transport problems adds insights that are missed when too much emphasis is placed on tactical and operational activity. Discuss.

3 A knowledge of institutional reform in the economy as a whole is important to all organizations—public and private. Why might this be so?

4 It is often the mixture of simple initiatives that creates uniqueness and competitive advantage. Discuss.

5 The greatest resource an organization can have is its human capital. Give examples to support this view.

6 Precision in the use of concepts such as efficiency and effectiveness will enable you to communicate appropriately in a debate on matters of relevance to good decision-making in the transport sector. Even before you study the chapters that address these constructs, why do you think such precision is crucial?

Part 1

The institutional environment

2 Institutional and market environment: privatization and competitive tendering

2.1 Introduction

Transport businesses, whether in the public or private sector, are subject to a range of regulatory and market forces, which mould the way in which they go about their daily business and plan their future. Even in markets where there is freedom of entry and exit and where individual organizations are 'free' to set prices and levels of service, regulatory agencies acting in the interests of consumers are watching to ensure that the principles of competitive efficiency and fairness are being complied with. This is designed to ensure that consumers do indeed have the opportunity to purchase goods and services at prices deemed to be in the 'public interest'. Anti-competitive behaviour is frowned on and, since the 1990s and beyond, is increasingly not tolerated and subject to sanctions in various forms such as fines, compensation, and termination of business.

The practice of transport management and organizational logistics does not and never will be able to be pursued in isolation from the institutional and market environment. Where the market is unable to act efficiently and effectively as the watchdog, governments use regulatory instruments. The mixture of market and regulatory forces exists in all sectors of transport operations and impacts to varying degrees. This chapter and the following chapter introduce the major features of the competition and ownership options under which individual transport businesses, private and public, operate. In recent times, there has been a growing interest in moving away from protected highly monopolized markets served by the public sector towards competitive markets served by both public and private agencies, selected on the basis of their competitive advantage rather than who owns them.

We have found that the best way to introduce the range of institutional and market environments is to consider the debate on ownership, and in particular the notion of a public sector supplier being replaced (through privatization) with a private sector supplier. The arguments developed to evaluate the potential strengths and weaknesses of privatization provide a nice lead into the discussion of the spectrum of market environments, covering monopoly, competitive regulation (often referred to as competitive tendering or competitive outsourcing), and economic deregulation. Even with transport businesses that have always been in the private sector (e.g. trucking companies, airlines, taxis, shipping companies), there is still much that can be learned from the experiences surrounding the privatization of previously public sector organizations (e.g. bus and rail operators, ports, airports, and airlines).

The discussion of privatization, interpreted as the sale of assets to the private sector, opens up a debate on the (additional) gains from exposing businesses to competition through encouraging competition in the delivery of services by competitive tendering or outright economic deregulation. This raises the question of whether there is more to gain in introducing competition in various ways rather than changing the ownership of a transport business from public to private control. Figure 2.1 summarizes the possibilities, illustrated in the context of shifting a publicly owned supplier into various ownership and market regimes.

After establishing the arguments for and against privatization, we consider in some detail the role of competitive tendering, described in many different literatures as outsourcing or contracting out. The focus is on *competitive* tendering *per se*; *negotiated outsourcing* is still widespread and has always occurred in transport and logistics businesses. What is different with competitive tendering is that both in-house and external bids can be made to deliver a service under pre-defined conditions and it is open to anyone who is deemed eligible on a set of pre-agreed competitive terms (see Sect. 2.5). The links with privatization are very strong, in that competitive tendering is often seen as a way of privatizing the delivery of services (i.e. operations) without the outright sale of the assets of the business. The best examples are organizations that have historically owned infrastructure and operated services on this infrastructure, such as railways, ports, and airports. There are arguments for separating infrastructure from services utilizing the infrastructure; treating the infrastructure (e.g. rail track, port terminals) as a

natural (spatial) monopoly under the control of government, and setting up an access regime for anyone to competitively bid for time on the network (see Sect. 3.3 for more details). The service dimension is seen as a competitive market. There are also arguments for retaining the combined entity.

The remaining topic area of economic deregulation is discussed in Chapter 3, where the role of the market becomes the dominating force in setting prices, output, and quality levels. The reality of markets is such that there are many 'impurities' which act to prevent the efficient working of market forces. Consequently a regulatory regime is commonly in place as a way of encouraging market operators to behave competitively. Any evidence of wasteful competition, collusion, cartel formation, and predatory pricing which can be shown to be inconsistent with the efficient workings of the market can lead to prosecution and a whole host of penalties. We use the arguments for economic deregulation as an appropriate context within which to introduce the idea of *competition policy*. We contrast the competition laws of Europe, the USA, and Australia/New Zealand as a representative set of international frameworks within various countries to determine the nature of competitive compliance. Empirical examples are used throughout the chapter to illustrate the way in which institutional and market reforms are treated.

2.2 Privatization: concepts, issues, and arguments

Transport businesses throughout the world are increasingly exposed to the economic elements of competition, private ownership, and tendered operations as part of a strategy by governments to improve the efficiency of service provision and reduce the level of explicit subsidy from the State. The experience with increasing exposure to competition and privatization is not limited to the transport sector. In a growing number of countries, electricity, telecommunications, water and gas utilities, and postal services have been privatized and opened up

to competition. To gain an appreciation of the debate on privatization, and especially the lessons for government, the main topics to address are:

- the role of efficiency objectives,
- exposure to capital markets,
- the weak bankruptcy constraint in the public sector,
- exposure to competition in the product market,
- price control, and
- the promotion of competition.

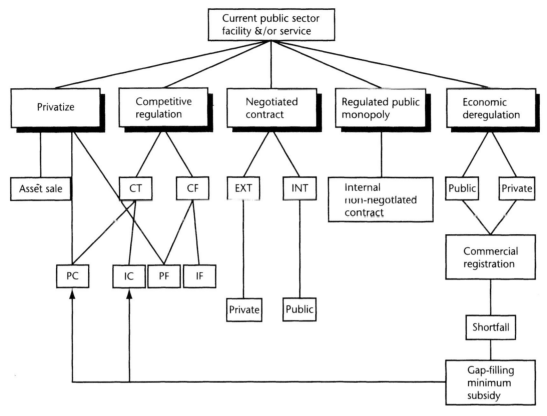

Fig. 2.1 Competitive and ownership contexts

Notes: PC = private contract   IC = internal contract   PF = private franchise   IF = internal franchise   CT = competitive tender   CF = competitive franchise

The evidence has a direct bearing on future strategies for all transport agencies, public and private.

Privatization and increased competitiveness in all its manifestations continue to be attractive options for governments who seek greater efficiency (see Sect. 2.2.1 and App. 2A for definitions of efficiency). Governments recognize that they ultimately have responsibility for ensuring that socially necessary services are provided and that 'fair play' ensures the continuity of supply at prices (and quality) that are consistent with pre-defined objectives set for suppliers, such as profit maximization and (constrained) social welfare maximization (defined in detail in Ch. 6). But this ultimate responsibility does not require government to own the services; indeed an effective umpire is one who has no vested interest in any of the players but an overriding commitment to ensuring that the game is executed efficiently, effectively, and equitably. Any decision by government to provide direct financial support (albeit a subsidy) must be justified on the basis of community service obligation. There is a strong view that it is transparently easier to do this where there is an unambiguous separation between ownership, operation, and regulation.

Privatization and increased competitiveness is a learning process for governments and analysts, as is the relationship between the utility regulators and the more general pro-competitive institutions and legislation. The lack of experience and information acts as an inhibitor to change. The experiences since the mid-1980s provide a rich base of evidence to draw on as a springboard for ongoing debate.

2.2.1 Objectives for change

Underlying the overt process of privatization are two ideological objectives and a set of economic efficiency objectives. Ideology centres on the desire to shrink the direct state influence on economic affairs (including the reduction of government debt) and the spreading of share ownership more widely within the population. 'Shrinkage' has become a synonym for reducing the influence of labour in State enterprises both in respect of the direct bargaining with unions and the incidence of labour in overall expenditure. Spreading share ownership either through listed acquisition or worker buy-outs is seen to be incentive-compatible, giving much more explicit links between principals and agents.

The great motivation for privatization is the belief that more productive efficiency must be introduced into (public) enterprises. *Productive (or cost) efficiency* is a very precise economic concept which is satisfied if a business is able to use inputs such as labour, capital, energy, information, and materials to supply a *given level of service* at the lowest cost. It is different to cost minimization, which is a meaningless objective (since the zero-cost 'solution' is to close down). In recent years the idea of corporatization has embodied the fulfilment of the cost efficiency objective. References to commercialization imply compliance with cost efficiency, although such efficiency is a necessary but not sufficient condition for commercialization. Consideration of prices is also required, and is known as the fulfilment of allocative efficiency with respect to output (i.e. levels of service), according to the agreed pricing strategy of the business (e.g. profit maximization or social welfare maximization—see Ch. 6 for this link).

A central feature of the privatization debate is the idea of effective incentives. The 'owners' of public organizations are in a sense the taxpayers, who 'appoint' politicians to represent their public interests. Unfortunately, from a business perspective, the loose association between taxpayers ('principals') and governments ('agents') is usually shown to have limited if not negative incentives. The privatization process is designed to bring an organization closer to its financial owners, which will, in most cases, create the right set of incentives for management and staff to perform in a cost-efficient manner.

Privatization often removes the Central Treasury capital rationing constraint, which in the case of public utilities often inhibits profitable development. While it is true to suggest that sourcing capital under the protective cloth of government in many Western countries does produce more attractive risk profiles (given the stability of government), it stifles the opportunities for greater reward under increased financial risk. There has been recognition that just because the market does not work optimally, this is not a sufficient reason for government ownership. Government failure can be more serious than market failure. Privatization also lessens substantially (if not solves entirely) the problem of multiple objectives imposed on public enterprises. Chief executives of government authorities often complain that they are not given an unambiguous brief with clear mandates and a single objective. This results in continuous 'battles' between them and government. The introduction of a single commercial objective and an independent decision-making framework eliminates the hassles of dealing with government ministers and provides a more transparent basis for identifying cost structures if government imposes or seeks a community service obligation (CSO).

The manner in which privatization has been implemented in most countries has also exposed enterprises to market forces in various forms. The two major sets of market forces are exposure to the capital market and exposure to more product market competition. The former has not been given as much attention as the latter. Creating market competition has promoted a number of economic paradigms. These range from economic deregulation to franchised 'competitive' operating areas, with a number of variations on competitive tendering at spatial levels of activity such as the route (e.g. truck, bus, coach, and rail) and network (e.g. rail, airline, port, and bus). Competitive tendering in its various guises is a softer form of privatization in which a service may be supplied by the private sector under a government-determined set of operating requirements such as minimum levels of service. Specifically, competitive tendering forgoes the direct test for the existence of new or changed markets, available through free entry and exit.

2.2.2 Exposure to capital markets

The capital market discipline exposes a business to bankruptcy, to the possibility of takeover, and has a direct influence on the supply of capital. In the context of promoting efficiency and competition, the bankruptcy threat within a public enterprise is a very weak constraint. Although accountability for public money is never absent, the limits on behaviour when managing someone else's money (especially where 'someone else' is not the transparent shareholder) are likely to be less binding. Exposure to capital markets also provides a real continuous market test of the value of an enterprise. Privatization without flotation on the stock market means either a management buy-out or sale by tender. The market is tested at the time of buy-out or tender, but there is no continuous test of the value of assets or of the appropriate opportunity cost of capital as there is in the case of a stock market flotation. But a private firm is always subject to the possibility of non-sustainable losses and hence the increased threat of takeover and merger. The incentives to be more efficient are very clear.

Exposing a business to the possibilities to takeover is closely allied to exposing an industry to managerial competition. Takeover is very largely a matter of one set of managers using the corporate vehicle to supplant another set of management. This increased rivalry among top management has an accompanying paradox—you cannot replace too many managers in a takeover otherwise you would have little to sell. The emphasis must be on top management—the individuals who receive the corporate gains and who are put at risk differentially in this process. There is strong evidence of a higher degree of turnover of top management in the lead up to and after privatization than is usual. Governments in many countries have progressively moved from a 'chauvinistic' position in respect to takeovers (e.g. foreign shareholding restricted to 15%) to a more open policy, which can lead to sizeable amounts of takeover. This is not necessarily undesirable from an efficiency point of view. There appears to be no basis on ideological grounds for imposing artificial 'golden shares' for a fixed period that limit the powers of shareholders to change the direction of a business. The 'normalization' of a company needs to be open from the first day.

When there is a direct exposure to the capital market, a business's cost of capital is dictated by the required rate of return from shares of an equivalent risk class (or in the case of the absence of a trading market, by the opportunity cost of capital invested elsewhere). This strategically places a business in its correct risk spectrum, having an effect on the direct cost of raising capital at the margin. This has to be justified. Exposing an enterprise to stock market performance measures enables an assessment of share price behaviour relative to the market. This information feeds directly into the rating of managerial performance. Falling stock prices are an indication of poor management and the beginning of exposure to takeover. Unfortunately the absence of a stock market indicator for many transport businesses and the difficulty of creating a shadow market (given the problems of identifying the nature of risk due in part to the small amount of transacting) result in the use of a rate of return criterion based on an average return from alternative investments without due consideration of relative risk. Access regimes, where infrastructure such as rail track has been separated from utilization of the track, rely on an implicit rate of return for the owners as the criterion for establishing access prices in competitive downstream markets (King 1997).

An additional advantage of participation in capital markets is that an effective monitoring system is created. There is an entire industry developed around financial advice that has a fiscal incentive to monitor performance and to take an interest in the affairs of the privatized enterprise.

The UK has been privatizing longer than any other Western country and is a rich bed of experience for newcomers. In the UK, experience with progressive privatization of utilities—beginning with British Telecom, then gas, airports, buses, water, electricity, and rail—has demonstrated the wisdom of increasing the potential for the market's influence over successive flotations by having smaller units to privatize. The number of privatized entities out of each utility has increased over time. For example, British Telecom and British Gas were kept intact, later there were 10 water entities, 12 electricity distributors, 25 rail companies, and 70 bus companies. The need for more effort in restructuring before privatization is essential. Why three English electricity generators when there are 72 generating sets? The answer must be guided by a combination of supply-side considerations such as economies of scale, estimates of the potential number of bidders under alternative packaging scenarios, and any potential benefits to consumers through economies of network integrity (i.e. economies of scope—see Sect. 5.6.4).

Privatization requires a track record of at least five years of accounts to put in the prospectus. Where an enterprise needs more preparatory time, corporatization as an intermediate stage may have some appeal providing an opportunity to undertake the restructuring required for eventual privatization. In the water and electricity authorities in the UK, for example, information and accounts were readily formed into several enterprises. In contrast, British Telecom prior to privatization had a very inefficient accounting system and managerial structure resulting in it having little idea of business conducted with its largest customers. This top end of the market is where the greatest degree of competition is occurring (from Mercury in particular). It took six years after privatization to establish suitable accounting systems to identify the relationship with British Telecom's 350 largest customers.

2.2.3 Exposure to competition in the product market

A desirable feature of a strategy to change the ownership profile of a business from public to private is to remove or lower barriers that have previously restricted competition. The private sector has a long history of presence in a competitive market. Critics have argued that not nearly enough has been done to lower entry barriers at the same time as privatiza-

tion. Consequently the gains from privatization are not fully extracted, notably in the product market. The essential issue here is the extent to which a desirable condition for privatization is economic deregulation. A key issue is the determination of what the government should accept for selling 'its property'? This increasingly relates to the degree of competition *ex post*. The receipts could be negative—with the government putting money in or donating property. In the larger utilities the political issue of selling the family silver cheap and the Treasury's desire to use the proceeds for macroeconomic purposes requires careful consideration of the timing of free entry for competitors.

Timing is especially important when government wishes to secure maximum value from a sale—the risk of the privatized entity losing market share through accompanying economic deregulation is sufficient reason for government to throw caution to the wind while opening up the market. This has, however to be balanced against the gains in internal efficiency which result from competitive pressures. It appears on balance that potential investors often prefer the monopoly outcome, at least for a number of years after privatization. The recognition of open competition down the track is sufficient incentive to improve performance. There is a rather different story for buses in the UK, for example. The Treasury was content to have 'claw-back' rights to profits from property put into the management buy-outs, since it could not hope for the cash flow associated with selling a big utility.

In interpreting the 'evidence' on economic deregulation, one has to be extremely careful to distinguish situations of ultra-free entry from situations with imposed conditions of entry. Evans (1990a), for example, concluded on the basis of monitoring the performance of the local commercial bus route service market outside London that a natural (private) monopoly on the supply side has evolved, leading him to suggest that there is a practical case for competitive tendering. However, entry was not ultra-free—the commercial registrant had to provide a minimum level of service, preventing in most situations the possibility of entry by the single vehicle owner-driver or other smaller units of service. Low fares and subsidy have also been shown to be barriers to entry (Beesley 1992). Any restriction on entry in a partially deregulated market makes it extremely difficult to replicate the level of service supplied by an operator under a fully deregulated market. Regardless of the nature of economic deregulation, competition as a servant and not a master must be used to best advantage together with a clear specification of subsidy arrangements (where appropriate) and tendering conditions. This is considered in more detail in a later section on competitive tendering.

Despite the attraction of securing greater efficiency gains through exposure to capital and product markets, there is potential conflict between exposure to the capital market and increased exposure to product market forces. You cannot sell anything to the capital market without selling something. What is it that is being offered to the capital market to attract funds? Even when a business has been dismembered, potential shareholders must have an incentive to invest. The incentive in a government enterprise with an unknown or very uncertain rate of return and risk portfolio is some *value of a government right.* This is some value of protection from entry—you have to sell the entity for something, so inherently if you want to get the capital market involved you have to pay the capital market for its participation.

The premium is usually based on some arbitrary estimate linked to the historical value of assets. Thus the practical privatization process requires providing the capital market with some rents of the government position, including current barriers to entry for a period of time. Some analysts have described this as the price that government has to pay for stifling the organization's performance in the past by over-regulation and protective monopoly. The fundamental point is that there must be some demonstrated positive value for someone to consider investing in the enterprise. Without an appropriate market to reveal these rents (for example, what is the cash flow and profitability profile for a private supplier operating in the current catchment area of the public supplier of rail services?), government rights for a negotiated period become the carrot. This procedure has also been applied in competitive tendering in New Zealand where a 15% cost advantage was given in 1991 to the incumbent bus bidder in Auckland in the first round of three-year tenders to enable them to gain the necessary experience in delivering competitively regulated services.

The process of establishing an attractive investment involves establishing the required rate of return by identifying an equivalent risk class. The value of what is being sold should be converted to present value terms. A firm with a present value of zero is a commercially viable firm but not an attractive investment. The capital market needs a present value greater than zero. If the present value is to be greater than zero, the terms of sale have to be improved. This can and often is improved by a more generous price capping (see Sect. 2.2.4). Since government both sets the *price cap* and wants security for the assets, there is no given solution to the trade-off. Hence an arbitrary value, such as historical cost, is usually selected.

2.2.4 The regulatory processes

A major feature of the privatization process has been the accompanying divestment of regulation. Independent regulators have been set up in many countries. In Britain there is OFTEL for telecommunications, OFGAS for gas, OFWAT for water, OFFER for electricity, and OFRAIL for the railways. In Australia a centralized agency—the Australian Consumer and Competition Commission (ACCC)—is the national watchdog for all sectors (although there are signs that specialized watchdogs are being supported, such as the decision in March 1998 by the Federal government to transfer the regulatory role for the finance sector to the Australian Securities Commission). Each state in Australia has its own watchdog such as the Independent Pricing and Regulatory Tribunal (IPART) in New South Wales. The selection of a single centralized 'umpire' in contrast to a set of specialized umpires is in itself an interesting issue. Kolsen (1996) argues that a single regulatory agency is unlikely to have the detailed expertise necessary to work closely with a specific industry sector and to secure some sense of confidence from that industry.

These offices are responsible for two essential regulatory tasks—price control for (natural) monopoly and promotion of competition in situations where there is a typically high starting market share for the incumbent. They also provide a sharp focus for the first time for consumer complaints.

The enterprises that display a more-or-less permanent natural monopoly must be subject to price controls involving price caps (or rate-capping), popularly referred to as CPI − x, where CPI is the consumer price index. This formulation enables the regulator to exact reasonably tough conditions in terms of future financial performance and productivity. Prices are allowed to move with the general level of inflation (as measured by the consumer price index) less a fixed amount x which reflects productivity improvements. An enterprise can make any changes it wishes provided that the average price of a specified basket of goods and/or services does not increase faster than CPI − x. The value of x has to be negotiated up front based on how a business or industry could perform, and then the agreement is in place for a fixed period. In many countries, a period of five years has been selected. Performance benchmarking is a crucial input into the determination of x. Best-practice operators will achieve the lowest possible x value.

This form of price control has in general met with strong support. To ensure its effectiveness however, the independent regulator depends on three sources of information:

- Cross-sectional comparisons (local or worldwide) to assist in the review and negotiation of monopoly prices under a price control. This establishes best practice. Performance monitoring and benchmarking (see Sect. 5.6.6.2) has flourished under this regulatory regime.

- Cash-flow oriented predictions based on required rates of return. This information is critical. It requires a gradual move away from slavishly adhering to accounts as evidence of what the *ex ante* cash flow is going to be in the next five years or whatever period is agreed upon.

- Evidence of the required rate of return on assets. This is especially important for establishing the set of regime prices for accessing infrastructure.

These data requirements are deeply embedded within legislation in many countries. For example, the Water Act in Britain requires cross-sectional comparisons. It has consequently recognized explicitly the regulator's need to have comparisons by making very difficult any horizontal mergers in the English water industry. To preserve any challenges to incumbent managers, takeover is allowed provided there is no horizontal merger. The basis of any future change to the number of incumbents is conditioned on the need for the regulator to make comparisons. The possible disappearance of evidence is a strong counter merger requirement.

Furthermore, there has been a willingness to learn from stock market dealings about the required rate of return on capital. The challenge is to identify existing listed businesses that have a similar risk profile to the entity to be privatized. A capital asset pricing model is an important tool in this debate.

For industries without natural monopoly characteristics, the regulator has to ensure that competition is promoted and that fair play ensues. Rail operations, airlines, shipping, trucking, and buses are examples of competitive industries. The regulator is charged with the task of creating opportunities to enter the market, using a managed competitive policy. Before the 1980s the UK's general competition law was weak in dealing with incumbent large firm power. Subsequently regulators had to be given power to stop predation and other forms of undue discrimination. The antitrust law in the USA was not so weak because of the compensation possibilities which were absent in the UK (see the discussion in Ch. 3). In the USA, for example, an incumbent proven to be damaging a competitor can be open to suits for damages at 300% of the cost of the damage. Under the competitive policy promoted by the independent regulator, there is a broad non-discriminatory clause so that a firm can be in breach of its licence if it discriminates unduly. The burden of proof of good behaviour is on the incumbent. This allows for the possibility that the incumbent might cost-justify any discrimination as might arise where she is trying to combat an entrant. For example, this feature of the process has prevented British Telecom from providing any effective counter to Mercury's capture of its big accounts. The cost to British Telecom of trying to eliminate a small competitor is too high. The regulator's response would require British Telecom to discount to all customers rather than just the large customers (the latter being the set where competition from Mercury is most directed). The same situation is occurring in Australia between Telstra and the new entrants Optus and One-Tel.

The strength of this approach comes from the regulator being pro-active with an ongoing monopoly or antitrust policy. The actual opportunities to enter the market are themselves a function of regulatory change. This makes for a very dynamic and market-responsive regulatory process. Indeed an efficient market will always have movements in the incumbents and entrants.

The regulatory task involves two idea sets in economics, commonly referred to as the Austrian view and the neoclassical view. The neoclassical view starts from a paradigm of competitive equilibrium and considers shocks to the system and perturbations of cost and demand. The Austrian view regards market processes as signalling information with profits motivating a response. There is no equilibrium. Profit as the capitalist's engine comes from innovation, watered down eventually by competition, but with profits extracted along the way. Whereas the neoclassical view starts from the position of entry conditions being the same for all players, the Austrian view starts from the position of there necessarily being differences due, for example, to asymmetry of information. The Austrian view is centred on disclosure, profit-seeking, information, and disequilibrium. The neoclassical view emphasizes regulated prices, resource allocation, and productivity.

The Austrian view is central to a regulator managing competition, where the sources and disappearance of profits are the question—do they really exist or not. In contrast the neoclassical emphasis centring on long-run efficiencies and performance does not address the reality of making money against different changing opportunities. Kirzner (1997) provides a rich review of the essential differences between the Austrian and neoclassical approach to entrepreneurial discovery and the competitive market process. Essentially Austrians take exception to the way in which neoclassical theory has portrayed the individual decision as a mechanical exercise in constrained maximization. This robs human choice of its open-ended nature in which imagination and boldness play central roles. The process of discovery is a mainstay of the Austrian approach in which competitive processes always move markets towards equilibrium but reject the idea that the world is at all times in the attained state of equilibrium.

The regulatory task embraces both views in conducting a cost-benefit analysis on behalf of society, where some arguments are approached by the neoclassical response including welfare implications in line with a commitment to the consumer interest. A paradox for the regulatory process is that if regulators become highly skilled in the areas necessary to run a competitively efficient business, there is a high probability of defection from the regulatory profession, with regulators entering the industry they previously regulated and making money as a consequence of the acquired skills. This is the reverse of regulatory capture.

2.2.5 Some lessons for government

Privatization highlights the extent to which public enterprises may have 'conned' ministers over many years in respect of service and cost. The need to 'turn stones' arises because of the focus on a prospectus. Disclosure processes often reveal the lack of price control and hence the relative state of inefficiency. The experience with independent regulatory authorities highlights the benefit of constructing a regulatory framework that minimizes the costs of differences in information and objectives between the principal (government) and the managers of public enterprises (agents). Privatization is particularly concerned with the role of ownership and management in this regulatory framework (Beesley and Hensher 1992).

The focus thus far has been on privatization through the sale of assets. Experience has demonstrated that the scope for privatization via competitive tendering (in contrast to sale of assets) may be preferred in situations where the product specification is relatively uncomplicated and the technology is well known, so that the difficulties of prescribing contracts and of differences in the information

available to the independent regulator and the regulated are relatively small. We now turn to ways of involving competitive forces in the privatization process.

2.3 Opening up markets to competition

The role of competition has been highlighted in the discussion of privatization through the sale of assets. In many transport sub-sectors it may be argued that even with economic deregulation, it is unlikely that there will be more than one supplier. With the possibility of such a natural monopoly outcome, the need for competitive forces to 'select' the incumbent still remains. This can be achieved by economic deregulation wherein any incumbent is always subject to potential competition (or competition for the market); or by competitive regulation wherein the incumbent is the 'winner' of a controlled tendering process, that protects the successful tenderer for the duration of the contract provided compliance with the contract occurs. Failure to comply should result in re-tendering. After the agreed contract period, re-tendering should occur if the true spirit of competitive tendering is to be adhered to. This is often not the case with renewal clauses subject to performance (see Sect. 2.5).

In this section, we introduce a number of technical concepts that are essential in the debate on the role of competition; namely yardstick competition, contestability, and natural monopoly. Once these ideas are understood then one is in a better position to advance the debate on the merits of alternative market models.

2.3.1 Contestability, competition, natural monopoly, and yardstick regulation

There is a growing interest by regulators in identifying what role head-on and/or potential competition among transport operators plays in servicing a mar-

ket. This has led to questions being asked by government officials and others about the extent to which contractual arrangements in non-deregulated markets actually engender a sufficient threat of potential competition from operators not currently competing with an incumbent in order for the current contracting procedures to be truly *contestable* contracts. It has also led to an interest in establishing the extent to which specific transport operations are a natural monopoly as might be implied where contractual arrangements, negotiated or competitively tendered, limit supply from one operator.

To answer these questions we must have clear definitions of contestability and natural monopoly. Clear definitions may suggest that contestability is not the valued objective it is so often assumed to be. The loose use of strictly economic concepts creates misleading impressions about the purposes of particular policies. What we are really seeking to achieve is 'competition for the market' which is not a phrase interchangeable with 'contestability', as we will show below. Before presenting formal definitions we need to be clear about the underlying objective of government policy which motivates government involvement.

2.3.2 The objective: constrained maximization of social welfare

The underlying objective usually driving government intervention in the transport sector is to ensure that the (social) welfare of the community is maximized. This objective can be translated into a pricing strategy (see Ch. 6) which will, if implemented properly, ensure that services are provided at costs and prices that *maximize social welfare.* Underlying this objective in an assumption that a business is operating cost efficiently in that a given level of service is being provided at the lowest cost, given the price of all inputs.

There are two social welfare pricing strategies (i) unconstrained social welfare maximization and (ii) constrained social welfare maximization. The latter is of particular interest. Constrained social welfare maximization says that prices should be set at a level at which demand for services is determined subject to the operator covering their average costs including an acceptable return on investment (the latter an alternative notation for normal profits). There would be no subsidy to the operator. In contrast unconstrained social welfare maximization tends to lead to lower prices than those covering average costs and hence the possibility of subsidy is very real.

Many transport businesses in the public sector or those under contract to deliver a government-determined service level (e.g. ports, passenger rail, local scheduled route buses, and school buses), have what are called community service obligations (CSOs). They are derived from the gap between constrained and unconstrained social welfare maximization, placing the onus on the government to decide if a non-commercial service should continue as a CSO. Two common CSOs are the pricing CSO and the service level CSO. A pricing CSO is based on the difference between prices charged and agreed benchmark prices. For example, in Sydney, the benchmark for the setting of government bus fares is the maximum fare scale approved by government for private bus operators less a discount of 1.5% in relation to multiple tickets (TravelTen and Travel-Pass). A service CSO is often based on efficient costs and revenues associated with the provision of non-commercial services agreed with government in excess of a set of agreed minimum level of services standards. The full details of these pricing objectives are left to Chapter 6.

The alternative to social welfare maximization in its various guises is profit maximization. Economic deregulation is typically attuned to this pricing objective, although any shortfall in service delivery to the market due to the absence of commercial incentives which may have disappeared as a result of unfettered competition, can be accommodated by what are known as gap-filling competitively tendered contracts, open to any pre-qualifying bidder. Under economic deregulation, an operator earning above-normal profits (i.e. more than covering their average costs and an acceptable return on investment) will attract potential competition *into* the actual market. If a natural monopoly exists then only one operator (not necessarily the incumbent) will survive in the market.

A nagging question is the extent to which the market outcome under economic deregulation is reproduced by restricted competition through competitive tendering. Since there is no real market test under competitive regulation, we might never know. Even benchmarking against best practice (itself derived from competitively regulated competition) may not guarantee the most efficient outcome.

2.3.3 A brief definition of contestability in its strict economic interpretation

Definition: A contestable market in its strict definition is a market in which there are potential entrants whose costs of entry and exit are zero (i.e. free entry and free exit), and where the market responds to entry *by keeping prices constant.*

Free entry and exit enables a potential entrant to adopt hit-and-run behaviour whenever the incumbent shows any signs of making above-normal profits. This pure definition has also been referred to as ultra-free entry. If the market is *strictly* contestable then the current arrangements ensure that a monopolist acts in the way it would act if faced with effective potential competition.

Restrictions placed on prices and minimum service levels, for example, that are beyond the control of a particular transport operator, would have to be equivalent to the outcome of an ultra-free entry model of market behaviour if one is to refer to the conditions as strictly replicating the outcomes of competitive forces. If we might expect lower prices than the maximum in the presence of potential competition, the upper limit on prices is not anti-competitive in a contestable market *unless* operators opt for the maximum price without any consideration of potential competition. The deviation between maximum prices and prices consistent with constrained social welfare maximization is one indicator of violation of pure contestability. The extent to which individual operators set prices below the maximum is clearly important in the discussion.

The assumption that the market responds to entry by keeping prices constant was overlooked at the time of initial discussions on contestability (when Baumol and his colleagues first introduced the idea; Baumol *et al.* 1982). It is now recognized as the Achilles' heel of contestability. It supposes distinctly improbable behaviour on the part of the incumbent. Unless an incumbent is very stupid or constrained, it will reduce prices when under attack by an entrant. The entrant will presume this, and thus will not enter. In other words, to be contestable, a market must be dominated by incumbents that are, in effect, willing to destroy themselves when entrants appear. The results of (pure) contestability theory are strong, but they are based on very implausible assumptions (Shepherd 1984).

Rigorous tests of contestability have yet to come up with any market that is *strictly* contestable. The US airline market was suggested as being contestable, though it is clear that the price constancy assumption is a stumbling block. These days, incumbents on a route respond within three hours to the price initiative of an entrant. This is hardly consistent with contestability. Empirical tests suggest that price-marginal (or average) cost ratios are an inverse function of the number of firms in the market. This is directly inconsistent with contestability, which maintains that as long as the conditions are satisfied, the number of firms in the market does not affect prices (even recognizing that potential competition keeps them at a minimum). There is some evidence that potential competitors for a market have a very weak negative effect on price (in contrast to actual competitors in a market). In other words, potential competition may have a weak effect on monopoly pricing, even where entry and exit are free.

The important message from this discussion is that competition for the market is a worthy challenge but that its interpretation as market contestability is not likely to be valid under the strict economic definition. Rather we should concentrate on the interpretation of 'competition for the market' in the Demsetz (1968) sense. With many transport services, there could be strong competition for the market, and competitive tendering could yield constrained optimal prices in a Chadwick–Demsetz auction. The latter results in a contract awarded to an operator who undertakes to provide a specified service at the lowest price or alternatively at the price-quality combination which is judged superior to all others (Chadwick 1859; Demsetz 1968). This approach is detailed in Section 2.5. However the market is not necessarily contestable. The difficulty with the tendering option arises when measuring which competitor offers the lowest 'prices' in a multi-service context, in which quality is a variable as well. Measuring quality is extremely difficult.

Prioni and Hensher (1999) and Hensher and Prioni (1999) have developed a service quality index (SQI) derived from the preferences of transport users and proposed a regulatory benchmark regime based on SQI + z to effect target-matching for the renewal of natural monopoly contracts, where z is the predesignated improvement over a period of time. This enables the regulator to take into account both cost efficiency and service effectiveness when determining the value of x in a price-capping review. SQI + z is analogous to the CPI – x productivity formula used to regulate public utilities discussed above. The SQI + z formula provides a target in line with a predesignated increase in the service quality level. In the case of the service previously provided by an incumbent operator, authorities can impose an SQI target at the midpoint of a contract and a final SQI target at the end of the contract.

We must recognize that best-practice service quality will change over time and hence the target will be revised. Such a revision should be used to reset the value of z for the next contract period and should not be backdated. In practice all potential entrants must be provided with the computational formula for SQI. According to their managerial and operational capability, they will decide on how to decompose such an index into the individual attribute components to achieve the targeted SQI. The required service quality level will then be evaluated by bidders and added into the cost of providing the higher level of service to determine the bid price. The contract will be awarded to the lowest price offer (with the cost of service quality internalized). Once successful in winning the contract the operator has a strong incentive to meet the new levels of service. Compared to a traditional tender contract specification (see below), the inclusion of SQI in the contract secures improvements in cost efficiency while meeting the new levels of service effectiveness as prescribed by a user-defined service index.

2.3.4 A definition and interpretation of a natural monopoly

Definition: A natural monopoly exists where one or more of the following effects exist: *economies of scale, economies of scope,* and *economies of network integrity.*

Economies of scale in its very strict definition exist where the average cost of production falls as output expands (often called increasing returns to scale or decreasing costs—see Ch. 5). Output under the definition of scale is assumed to be homogeneous (e.g. there is one category of vehicle kilometres or passengers carried on only permanent school contracts *or* local scheduled route services, or a single class of rail freight tonne kilometres). When one starts looking at the implications of a diversified portfolio of services, as is the case for most transport operators, we talk of *economies of scope.* One can demonstrate positive economies of scope by reducing total costs through supplying a diversified set of services (e.g. vehicle kilometres of permanent school contract, charter/tours, and local scheduled route services; first, business, and economy class air travel) while holding total service levels fixed compared to supplying the same level of vehicle kilometres with one type of service (e.g. only local scheduled route services, only single class air travel, a dedicated bulk freight activity).

Positive *economies of network integrity* arise because of the opportunity, within a natural monopoly context, to provide a more integrated service within an area than that provided by more than one operator. Both economies of network integrity and scope are also linked to the ability to share some costs between different services, which is lost when such services are provided by separate operators. The issue of shared costs often gets confused with internal cross-subsidy (see below). When one broadens the definition of economies of scale and network integrity to include the benefits to users in the form of lower *user costs* (i.e. waiting times, service uncertainty) with increasing patronage or freight (which is more likely with a single operator), we see an additional benefit of a natural monopoly. What we have here is a benefit derived from the demand side of the market, in contrast to the more commonly promoted supply-side arguments centred on economies of scale. Economies of scale can thus be due to increased benefits to users as measured by reduced user cost, even if the costs to the transport operator of providing the service do not fall. In transport sectors where constant returns to scale are observed, it is the benefit to users (through lower generalised cost—see Ch. 4) which supports the idea of a natural monopoly. The possible operating environments are summarized in Figure 2.2.

Thus the case for a transport supplier displaying the attributes of natural monopoly relies completely on the argument that one firm can supply a more convenient service (i.e. less expensive in a generalized sense) than two or more can. To develop the discussion of natural monopoly and contestability, it is important to introduce three additional economic concepts: internal cross-subsidy, avoidable costs, and shared costs.

2.3.5 Avoidable and shared costs defined

Definition: Economic costs are usefully divided into avoidable and shared costs. The *avoidable costs* of a service are those costs which could be saved if the services were to be reduced to some specified level or

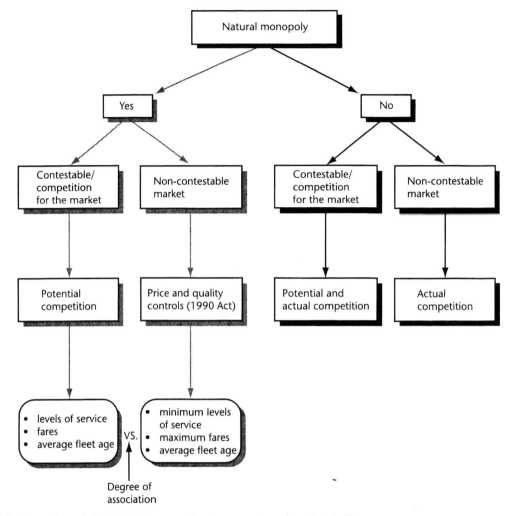

Fig. 2.2 Alternative relationships between natural monopoly and contestability

withdrawn entirely. Conversely the avoidable costs are the additional cost outlays incurred if a service were expanded or introduced from scratch.

Each service, no matter what its nature (e.g. a specific freight consignment contract, all permanent school contracts, a particular scheduled air service, a cruise ship activity, a rail branch line), will have its own avoidable costs. However there may be extra costs shared between two or more services that can only be eliminated if both services are withdrawn. These are defined as *shared costs*. This distinction is important when discussing internal cross-subsidy. It is also important when identifying the costs associ-

ated with any change in a particular service. Section 5.2 provides more details on avoidable and shared costs.

2.3.6 Internal cross-subsidy

Definition: Internal cross-subsidy in its simplest definition is assumed to occur where the revenue from one activity is used to fund another activity whose costs would not otherwise be covered.

Where shared costs exist, as is common in many transport contexts, the simple definition is potentially quite ambiguous. There may be confusion in the literature between internal cross-subsidy and shared costs. The former can unambiguously be associated with a particular service not covering its avoidable costs and being cross-subsidized by a service which more than covers its avoidable costs. A non-zero internal cross-subsidy can be argued and justified as consistent with rules of overall constrained social welfare maximization where there are substantial *shared* costs between types of services offered (e.g. passenger and freight rail, container and roll-on shipping, school runs and scheduled services), since there is no widely accepted rule on how shared costs should be assigned to each activity. Network integrity linked to shared costs is a major user benefit (e.g. allowing easy transfer and the ability of schoolchildren to move from say permanent school contract bus services to scheduled route bus services). Since the allocation of shared costs is ambiguous, the determination of the presence of real internal cross-subsidy is itself ambiguous except to the extent that *avoidable* costs of particular services are not being covered. Chapter 5 discusses the important role of 'what the market will bear' (often called the inverse elasticity rule) in 'allocating' shared costs.

2.3.7 The importance of this armoury of definitions

With the important definitions now set out, the interest is in establishing the extent to which effective competition requires competition *in* the transport market in contrast to competition *for* the transport market. A market is deemed potentially competitive where there are sufficient potential entrants willing to enter a market, but they are holding back for various reasons including the natural monopoly argument—namely that the market is such that there are economies of scale and/or scope and/or network service integrity to support the presence of only one operator in the market charging efficient prices which reflect the lowest average (generalized) cost of service provision.

2.4 Yardstick competition, actual competition and regulation?

We would like to think that the set of prices and level of service actually provided by transport operators is the most efficient in an allocative sense regardless of whether the pricing strategy is (constrained) social welfare maximization or profit maximization. The major options open to achieve this ideal are economic deregulation (competition *in* the market) and various strategies to deliver it through competition *for* the market. We will now take a closer look at the latter, deferring further discussion of economic deregulation until Chapter 3.

There are various ways of interpreting competition for the market:

1. the traditional interpretation of potential competition for the same service, which might be described as the original strict economic definition of 'competition for the market' in the Demsetz sense;

2. the threat to survival and resulting competitive tendering attributed to industry benchmarks changing as a consequence of 'better local performers' changing the yardsticks so that some incumbents can no longer provide a service complying with any revised minimum levels of service and/or maximum prices; and

3. (less importantly) acquired evidence from non-local contexts of achievable service improvements influencing the revision of price and quality controls—what might be referred to as the (*inter*)*national bandwagon effect*.

Implicit in the earlier discussion of competition for the market is the concept of *yardstick regulation*. It is introduced here as an appropriate interpretation of a way that innovative practices of incumbent operators under a natural (territorial) monopoly will work to improve the efficiency of the industry as a whole, operating *as if* they are competing in the market. Although referred to as *yardstick competition* in some literature, it is understood, incorrectly, by many transport businesses as *competition among operators*. This terminology is suitably vague, disguising the important distinction between competition in and competition for the market. This idea is not contestability at all—there is nothing about potential competition having an impact on pricing in it. It is really yardstick regulation. In the longer term this form of industry self-regulation (i.e. yardstick self-regulation) may demonstrate an ability to establish optimal prices within a cost-efficiency regime with due allowance for quality, and hence replicate the spirit of 'competition for the market'. It is unlikely to comply with the somewhat theoretical ideals of contestability. Hence the preferred use of the phrase 'competition for the market' rather than contestability from here on.

The essence of yardstick (self-)regulation is the use of best-practice markers and performance indicators to provide a credible threat to all operators via the revision that occurs to price and quality controls as a consequence of improved practices in the industry. Competition is potential in that an operator who cannot adjust performance to conform with any revision of price and quality levels will encourage competitive entry via competitive tendering. The minimum levels of service are likely to be revised upwards as a consequence of innovative practices and improvements in cost efficiency.

An alternative mechanism for adjusting maximum prices is to link them over time to CPI − x. As discussed in a previous section, CPI − x is a formula for price regulation that allows a franchised operator to raise its prices over an agreed period of time in line with the general level of inflation (as measured by the consumer price index) less a fixed amount x which reflects productivity improvements. Yardstick regulation provides a way of avoiding the manipulation problems of revising x in CPI − x price regulation. Under a yardstick regulation rule, the x would not depend on a particular operator's own performance but rather on the performance of a *similar* operator in a *different* territorial market. Yardstick regulation would select an x based on productivity improvements achievable by best-practice operators after making reasonable adjustment to control for any particular factors that may be difficult to transfer to the industry as a whole which could discriminate in a way that might lead to bankruptcy rather than efficiency.

As an example of yardstick regulation in practice, it appears to exist in the following sense only under the 1990 New South Wales Passenger Transport Act. The government together with the bus and coach industry initially developed a set of minimum levels of service quality (quality controls) and a maximum fare level (price control) using *historical* practice as the yardstick. It was subsequently recognized that a historical yardstick may not be indicative of a potential competition yardstick level. That is, there was a need to allow the historical benchmarks to evolve (some would say become a *moving target*) in a way which moves the industry closer towards a set of price and quality controls which replicates the outcomes consistent with constrained social welfare maximization. The evolution under yardstick regulation occurs through *improved practices* of operators. The government regulator monitors the changing profile of industry performance in order to identify the nature and extent of productivity gain over time, so that this is a mechanism for reviewing and changing the minimum levels of service and maximum fares. The regulator as custodian of competition policy is charged with ensuring that the number of operators through takeover/merger does not diminish to a level that threatens the viability of benchmarking. The importance of monitoring of overall productivity becomes critical to this process.

2.5 Competitive tendering and outsourcing

2.5.1 Introduction

Tendering by negotiation for the supply of facilities and/or services has been a common activity in the transportation sector for many decades. The high level of current interest in the topic stems from the growing tide of economic reform in those transport sub-sectors where the level of subsidy from consolidated revenue has become unacceptable. The 'new' emphasis on cost recovery, productive efficiency, and the increasing interest in the participation of the private sector in areas of service provision, commonly the domain of the public sector, has spawned a healthy debate on the merits of competitive tendering of services in order to reduce the financial burden of escalating deficits on the State.

The debate on competitive tendering (or competitive bidding) recognizes that markets and firms are alternative instruments for completing a related set of transactions and that whether a set of transactions ought to be executed between firms (across markets) or within a firm depends on the relative efficiency of each approach. The costs of writing and executing contracts across a market vary with the characteristics of the decision-makers who are involved with the competitive tendering process on the one hand and the objective properties of the market on the other (such as the number of potential competitors).

In this section we outline the role that tendering as a competitively defined procedure can play in the provision of transportation and logistics services. Contracts and franchises, and alternative ways of defining a competitive tender are distinguished. Competitive tendering in the transport context is being applied to services in which the levels of demand are uncertain. Competitive tendering as an alternative to *negotiated contracts* has been shown in a number of contexts to yield cost savings (for a given level of service) before administrative charges are netted out of 20% on average.

2.5.2 Clarifying the notion of competitive tendering

Definition: A competitive tender (CT) is a bid for a contractual promise to supply a pre-defined service during a pre-determined period of time, in exchange for a contract fee, which allows for the level of anticipated cost or revenue generated by the service.

We distinguish between competitive tendering and competitive franchising (CF). Within the transport sector, the difference is inherent in the specification of the end-service to be supplied. In the case of CT, the end-service is predetermined. All potential bidders compete for the right to supply a common service. A competitive franchise, by comparison, requires each potential competitor to design their own end-service supply. There has been a tendency to opt for CT in the transportation sector because it is viewed as an administratively easier alternative. The ability to evaluate the bids and to arrive at a minimum cost supplier for the given level of service removes the complexities associated with evaluating a heterogeneous set of proposals, which may be based on different service levels.

There are two major categories of CT: a cost-only contract and a minimum-subsidy contract. The former involves the tendering authority paying the operator for supplying a specified service, with receipts in part or full remitted to the tendering authority or netted off against costs. In submitting a bid for a London bus route service, for example, the applicant is supplied with a service specification for days of operation, timetable, route, type of vehicle, and inter-working requirements with other services. The risks associated with service supply are largely carried by the tendering authority. The minimum-subsidy contract, after an agreed support bid, requires the contractor to satisfy a service need in return for an obligation from the tendering authority to provide a subsidy in line with the level of receipts collected. Cost-only contracts and minimum-subsidy contracts can be either sealed-bid tenders or bids open to public scrutiny. In the latter situation, the prices and the range of tenders received and the successful tenderer are usually published. There are many variations on each type of contract; however there are some broad specifications that we now focus on.

2.5.3 The appeal of competitive tendering

For both direct transport services (DTSs) or non-transport support services (NTSSs) competitive tendering offers businesses a mechanism for looking beyond the inside so that the competitive benefits of a non-introspective approach to decision-making can be maximized. The extent of any gain is dependent on the amount of competition, the packaging of the offer, the existing internal efficiency of the incumbent's commitment, and the negotiating skills of the tendering authority.

Importantly, the CT process is established to offer opportunities for increased productive efficiency for both incumbent and potential entrant, regardless of ownership profile. For example, some NTSSs previously supplied by London Underground have been secured by an internal contractor unit based on a new unit cost, eliminating unnecessary work practice constraints by negotiation with the trade union. A bid at the old unit costs would have resulted in a contract with an external supplier. CT seeks to break the nexus of culture and loyalty to internal service functions where neglect of the impact on the overall performance of the organization is at risk. It, however, does not suggest that there is any inherent efficiency benefit in external supply; it merely argues the need for a market environment that imposes appropriate conditions for better performance. In the context of London Buses, for example, nearly 50% of all route-level contracts in the first 10 years of CT were awarded to London Bus Limited (LBL) at cost levels approximately 20% (net) lower than the public monopoly levels existing prior to CT (Hensher and Beesley 1989).

The challenge of CT is to identify the contexts in which competitive tendering is an appealing approach, and to establish some guidelines on the appropriate processes needed for successful implementation and administration. It is essential that there is a clear set of responsibilities between the contractor and the client (or tendering authority), and that the criteria for evaluating the bids are both simple and unambiguous to all parties. The experiences in a number of countries serve to highlight some of the more important issues, which are briefly summarized below:

1. The client has the responsibility for determining the appropriate areas for competitive tendering, designing appropriate contracts, pre-screening the contractors, undertaking the tendering process, evaluating and selecting the successful tenderer, monitoring performance, and controlling the contractor. An internal tendering unit has the task of determining the competitive range for unit costs and preparing a programme for reducing internal unit costs to the competitive range. This is often exacerbated by the presence of significant shared costs, especially for DTSs, which must put the onus on the tendering authority to consider the ability and desire to separate out the supply of particular services in situations where there are major gains from joint production. The potentially limiting effect of joint production makes NTSSs a more attractive source of CT contracts (at least in the early period of a CT programme).

2. Since work practices condoned/supported by an employee union influence the productive efficiency of service supply, it is critical to time the CT process on the client side to the contractor schedule for negotiating reduced costs with the union(s). This is a major source of cost reduction, and is essential where the threat of competition could result in a loss of activity to a non-unionized (or different union-based) supplier. There are a growing number of instances where unions have been increasingly willing to renegotiate in the interests of preserving jobs for the majority of the incumbent workforce (e.g. London Underground, the ports in New Zealand, bus services in the UK, railways in Australia). Union negotiations are assisted when the internal contractor management can demonstrate that the internal contractor unit could win the tender based

on new unit costs but would not be awarded the contract based on unit costs existing under current union conditions. This temporal consideration should not, however, become a means to deferring any tendered award.

3. Quality gains often accompany competitive tendering due to the increased emphasis on performance standards, as well as job requirements by both management and staff. The quality gain is highly dependent on the quality of implementation of CT. The ability to terminate contracts and to monitor performance not only reduces costs, but also increases the quality of performance. In London Underground, for example, the competitive tendering of support services such as rolling stock maintenance, cleaning services and permanent way maintenance has resulted in increased attention to overhead cost reduction, a key area of competitive advantage.

4. The growing popularity of contract hire and rental to cover specific requirements, and the move to operating leases for across-the-board financing of vehicles (e.g. trucks, buses, coaches, train sets for Virgin's lines in the UK, ships) is giving incumbents and potential entrants a competitive advantage as well as demonstrating the virtual absence of sunk costs in the transport sector.

5. A detailed specification may be very costly to prepare and may discourage the less articulate. The size of irrecoverable costs, the length of the contract, and the perceived probability of success will be critical factors in determining how many bidders come forward. That is, the selection process could be anti-competitive if made too complex. The large incumbents are likely to do everything legal to reduce the competitiveness of the selection process. This latter situation has encouraged a view that incumbent dismemberment is often a desirable pre-condition to successful CT. For example, the development of independent public bus operations at the depot level or the breaking up of a rail network or airports and ports is likely to be necessary if some competitive threat is to be achieved from a range of potential sources (existing industry operators, worker and/or management group buy-outs) without any actual ownership profile necessarily arising as the service providers become productively more efficient.

6. In contexts where public or privately regulated monopolies have existed for some period of time, it is likely that the tendering authority will have a symbolic relationship with the main tenderer. This relationship, real or perceived, will take time to eliminate through staff changes. This can create some major obstacles for a transparent tender bidding system that at the very least will be viewed suspiciously by potential new entrants. For example, London Regional Transport (LRT) and the Rail Access Corporation (RAC) of NSW have worked very hard to minimize this effect. History now shows that there was a definite distancing problem while the management of the publicly owned London Bus Limited were previous employees of LRT. Dismemberment and privatization of LBL assisted in the distancing task. The experience of British Rail suggests this will be effective only when much of the management of the newly privatized smaller units is replaced. RAC has appointed a large number of senior staff from outside the organization previously responsible for rail infrastructure, the State Rail Authority of NSW.

7. A less desirable but alternative approach could follow a modification of the French Gerance contract in which management teams bid for the right to run a private company to supply services in which the financial risk is taken largely by the public authority.

2.5.4 The bidding process: some considerations

Experience with competitive tendering suggests a grouping of the key issues under cost-side tendering, the rigidity of tendering, and information asymmetry.

2.5.4.1 Cost-side tendering

Cost-side tendering is an appealing approach where restrictions are imposed by the tendering authority on prices and/or service levels. Under these circumstances it is difficult to pass the real risk for revenue to the contractor. The successful incumbent has no incentive to increase revenue and to serve the travelling public beyond the maintenance of the revenue target. The desire to establish a centrally determined prices/service policy is incentive-incompatible; it may give the operator inadequate incentive to collect revenue. However, this can be overcome by appropriate revenue-enhancing incentive conditions in the contract and the incurrence of monitoring and enforcement costs.

The arguments in favour of cost-side tendering are heavily linked to the use of tendering for the supply of service to parts of an integrated network. Targeting supply to a part of an existing network can be achieved precisely by a cost-only contract. If a minimum-subsidy (or *bottom-line*) tendering process were adopted for the supply of service to routes or sub-area networks, the tendering authority could face the situation of one service increasing its revenue while operating in a way that reduces the overall effectiveness and value of the entire network. This problem is compounded when an integrated pricing policy is in place. Arguments over the allocation of revenues back to particular services will become a major feature of the contracting process (or the operator refuses to carry users of integrated price facilities such as a multi-modal travel pass). The question of price adjustment in the light of unexpected drops in patronage or freight could also be a problem, since the essence of a bottom-line contract is that after an agreed support bid, the contractor has responsibility for, and is financially affected by, the level of receipts collected.

If competitive tendering for a spatially independent network of services were introduced, then the arguments for a revenue support (minimum-subsidy) contract or a cost-only contract are much more positive, especially for the former type of contract where the opportunity for entrepreneurial flair is combined with the *ex ante* advice of the tendering authority to produce a minimum-subsidy area-wide service. An example of such a scheme could involve the services currently supplied by a truck depot, a bus depot, or rail line. This effectively gives a competitive franchise unless the tendering authority imposes limits on the nature of the service (tariffs, frequencies, vehicle types, carriages, etc.). The bid-

ding is not an auction, but an authority to supply a service of any kind. The major limitation, however, is in establishing criteria for evaluating a potentially disparate set of offers, which is one of the reasons for the popularity of cost-only contracts. The idea of supplying a given level of service at minimum cost also becomes meaningless; however, this is not all bad provided the basis of social cost-benefit analysis is accepted for selecting a contractor. Increasingly, regulators are calling on the establishment of not only commercial criteria but also social criteria in evaluating the benefits and costs of market reforms (see Sect. 3.4).

One of the most successful reform programmes has been the competitive tendering of London bus services (Kennedy 1996). The London assessment of bus service suppliers was simple: the bid price was defined in terms of pounds per bus mile, and the contracts written in terms of points to be served at specified minimum frequencies and minimum capacities at the various times of day and week. The bidder is permitted to suggest how the specification will be met and can propose vehicle types and sizes. As of early 1998, London Transport had competitively tendered 80% of its bus services, with 100% conversion completed in 1999. A total of 150 competitive contracts were awarded to almost 40 companies. Between 1985 and 1996, services were expanded by 28.7%, and real operating expenses reduced by 30% (Cox *et al.* 1997). Cost per vehicle kilometre fell by 46%, an annual reduction of 5.4%, with patronage up by 3% (compared to a 30% reduction outside of London under economic deregulation). Passenger fares now covered 94% of operating and capital costs compared to 60% in the regulated era. Cox *et al.* (1997; Cox and Van de Velde 1998) review progress in tendering of bus services throughout the world, where we see unit cost reductions varying from 18% (Denver, USA) to 46% (London).

The message is clear: cost-only contracts are the essence of simplicity in monitoring, evaluating, and operating; they are heavily linked to the productive efficiency criterion. They imply a fixed (not necessarily maximum) net social benefit (NSB). Competitive franchise and to a lesser extent bottom-line (including zero-support) contracts are more complex requiring broader evaluation criteria and complex assessment, but can maximize NSB. The main advantages and disadvantages of (strictly) cost-only and (strictly) bottom-line (net-subsidy) contracts in the context of service supply (as typically implemented around the world) are summarized in Table 2.1.

A number of the disadvantages can be overcome. For example, a bonus component can be introduced into a cost-only contract that is paid when revenue reaches an agreed level; alternatively, operators can retain revenue in excess of an agreed figure in relation to cost. Another approach might involve submission of both a cost-only contract and a minimum-subsidy contract. The offer representing the best value for money after allowing for revenue forecasts and any other extra costs such as administration, auditing, and so on is selected.

2.5.4.2 Rigidity of tendering

The desire for legitimacy in a legal and evaluative sense is very important, especially in circumstances when the tendering authority and an incumbent bidder have strong historical associations. Historical links will be strong in the transportation sector because of the likelihood that the tendering authority will be the planning branch of a government agency previously supplying transport services.

The benefits of legitimacy can often come at the expense of excessive rigidity in the tendering process. For example, it is common to exclude second bids or negotiation after submission of a bid; or to publish the results of the bids and supply feedback to unsuccessful bidders. This absence of a competitive learning process can limit the offer of bids in subsequent tenders, as well as raise suspicions about the tendering authority's capacity to be fair, especially

Table 2.1 Summary of advantages and disadvantages of cost-only contracts and bottom-line contracts

	Cost-only contracts	Bottom-line (net *subsidy*) contracts
Advantages	Reduced costs to the Authority.	Incentive to operate to maximize revenue.
	Authority takes full benefit of revenue.	Marketing/attention to service performance.
	Revenue risks spread over a number of contracts.	Known financial commitment to the Authority.
	Encourages competition in tendering.	Reduced level of audit/on-mode ticket inspection.
	Authority can have total control over prices and price conditions.	
	No problems with ticket inter-availability.	
Disadvantages	No incentives to attract revenue sources.	Need for revenue audits on-board.
		Little incentive to operator to promote the service and/or maximize use unless a share of revenue is retained.
		Whole risk on the operator leading to higher prices.
		Prices can only be subject to general control by the Authority.
		Authority has a fixed financial commitment irrespective of service performance/revenue generated.
		Authority will not know revenue forecast if re-tendering is required.
		Fewer operators likely to tender because of the risk factor.
		Uncertainty: if forecast of revenue is not achieved, the operator may pull out of the contract.
		Problems of resolving inter-availability of ticketing.

Note: The cost-only contract column assumes no revenue incentive.

where the contract is awarded to the incumbent or a dominant firm. The lack of knowledge on how close one's bid was to the awarded bid can erode the sources of accumulating competition. This is a potentially crucial concern where bid prices are inversely related to the number of bidders and the uncertainty of the offered service, and especially in the context of cost-only contracts where the opportunity to observe the incumbent sales on a service (as an information-gathering strategy) is less relevant in contrast to access to the accounts.

As an example of practice, in London one private bus operator in the late 1980s came within + 0.6% of the cost of the LBL bid. For an extra £3,867, in a bid of £6.6 m., an award could have been made to the private operator as a demonstrated means of encouraging competition (since prior to this the success rate for private bidders was very low compared to that for LBL) as well as demonstrating the success of independent operators. LRT selected LBL. Such information is currently not revealed to the bidding set. In Auckland, New Zealand, the local bus service bids are released as a spread (i.e. the lowest and highest), but not the number of bids. The reason for not publishing the number of bids is to preserve the bidding threat in the interests of securing the lowest possible bid price. This may be eroded where the number of bidders is low.

2.5.4.3 Information asymmetry

Individual firms can, in a second-best situation, take advantage of information asymmetry to achieve operating advantage and/or strategic advantage in the tendering process. The issue of relevance is the extent to which these advantages are efficiency-enhancing. Operating advantages give a firm lower costs and/or more favourable demand conditions than any potential entrant. Strategic advantages may arise simply because a firm is already established in the market as the incumbent, such that a potential entrant can acquire the same tangible and intangible assets on less favourable terms.

The issue of strategic advantage is played out in the pre-entry competitive stage of the bidding process. An incumbent-dominant firm may rationally exploit its strategic advantage by using information on costs and demand conditions, as well as greater expertise in bluffing the tendering authority.

Information asymmetry as a possible source of dominance need not favour the incumbent. Indeed, as an example, in many contexts it could be argued that a non-incumbent private operator may have an operating advantage over the public operator in that there is a strong base of evidence that they are more cost-efficient. As a source of potential competition, if competitive tendering were introduced on particular routes or sub-area networks this could act as a compensating effect to the local knowledge of the incumbent who may be obliged to make quite radical changes to the cost structure of supply in order to compete effectively with a private operator bid. On strict economic efficiency criteria, it can be argued that the private operators have operating advantages that may or may not outweigh the strategic advantages of the public incumbent when and if the market were liberalized. The potential threat of competition prior to the bidding stage can, however, work to improve the competitive advantage of the current loser. Already we can see efforts being made throughout the world to improve the productive efficiency of public operators in most areas of transport endeavour, designed to narrow the operating advantages. In a sense the private operators are supplying a yardstick for potential improvement in the public area.

2.5.5 A brief comment on the theoretical emphasis

The discussion up to this point has identified the salient features of competitive tendering and documented some of the points of principle and practice that the transport sector has tried to accommodate in a number of applications of CT. These experiences can be used to assist in identifying the strands of a theoretical framework that may help us to better understand the process of a CT, If for no other reason, theoretical insight may eventually provide guidance on the relationships which need to be identified between the actors in the process and the process itself. The success or failure of competitive tendering is strongly linked to the behavioural motivations and abilities of human beings. The opportunity for strategic game-playing, incentives, rivalry, and opportunism behaviour may very easily make a mockery of traditional interpretations of the way markets operate. This is the Austrian school of thought on markets at work.

Transaction cost theory, developed many years ago, has long recognized that a transaction (e.g. a deal, a contract, etc.) can be accomplished through either market or internal procurement. The choice of source of supply is tied in with the relative transaction costs. These costs are an important component of the assessment procedure and must enter into the calculation of the net efficiency benefit of alternative approaches. The renewed interest in transaction cost economics coincides with the growing interest in determining the role of competition and ownership in the supply of many services which have traditionally been the domain of the public sector. Transaction cost economics is nothing more than a comparative institutional assessment of alternative means of contracting (Williamson, 1987) including the real possibility of internal contracting.   -

2.5.6 **Conclusion and summary of key points**

Competitive tendering (and franchising) provide an opportunity to introduce competition into contract negotiation, and in so doing should contribute to improving the overall efficiency of service provision. The success of any form of competitive tendering will be very dependent on the existing levels of potential competition and the ability of the tendering process to encourage the emergence of competition through time. We anticipate a growing commitment to competitive outsourcing in transport markets as a way of reinforcing the conservative nature of the transportation industry, where complete reliance on the market through economic deregulation is still viewed with great suspicion.

It is thus essential that any proposal to consider the introduction of competitive tendering pay special attention to the following items:

1. Contracting out the supply of goods and services involves a two-step decision process. The first is whether to 'make or buy'; the second is how to structure the contract so that performance will be sustained over its lifetime. The former decision involves a straightforward comparison of costs; the latter is more subtle and requires consideration of four essential elements. First, specifications of the service or product will need to be determined, together with the design of the competitive tendering mechanism that will be used to identify potential operators. The theoretical implications of using different bidding schemes are comprehensively surveyed in McAfee and McMillan (1987) and discussed also by Waterson (1988).

2. The selection of the winning bid. This turns out to be a more complicated decision than would appear at first sight. For example, selecting the lowest bidder in a sealed tender auction can sometimes result in serious performance problems after the contract is awarded. Domberger *et al.* (1987) discuss some of the evidence when a very detailed pre-registration process is not in place to ensure that the lowest price is reflective of a cost-efficient operation and not one which will struggle to survive because of poor costing in arriving at a bid price.

3. To ensure contract compliance the supplier will have to be monitored during the contract term. This involves collecting and interpreting information that can be used to determine whether the specified goods/services are being delivered. Finally to correct deviations of actual from desired performance the contract will have to be enforced. Enforcement will be based on incentives and penalties that will be applied when such deviations are observed.

4. The uncertainty associated with contractor selection arises from two sources. The contract specifications will need to be precise, but it may nevertheless be difficult if not impossible to encompass all the required performance characteristics in them. Hence the contracting authority will need to ascertain that the selected operator can meet those implicit requirements. The other source of

uncertainty, which is potentially more troublesome, is that the output or service contracted for is not observable at the time of 'purchase'. Hence the 'quality' of the prospective contractor is essentially unknown and the contracting authority has to rely on past performance as a proxy, that is, on reputation. The use of reputation proxies for goods and services whose characteristics are difficult to ascertain at the time of purchase is a widespread phenomenon. Its importance has been recognized and explored in the theoretical contributions of Klein and Leffler (1981) and Shapiro (1983), among others

5. In these circumstances contracting authorities resort to screening devices, the most important and ubiquitous of which are pre-qualification restrictions—a preliminary vetting process of potential contractors. Pre-qualification allows the contracting authority to sort potential operators into those of high and low expected quality before the tendering actually takes place. Such separation is important because if low and high quality contractors bid simultaneously, difficulties will arise in distinguishing low bids that are due to cost efficiency from those that involve reduced quality of service. Moreover the trade-off between price and expected quality is not one that can easily be made explicit. It is therefore preferable to establish the minimum level of quality expected from the contractor, identify those contractors that are deemed to satisfy those requirements, and only then invite this group to submit a tender. This two stage process ensures that tendered prices are strictly comparable and do not reflect unwarranted variations in likely performance. The competitive element that is retained will also ensure that the cost of provision does not stray far from the minimum consistent with the required quality standard. Where tendering occurs frequently because contracts are short lived, there will be economies in using an existing pre-qualification list. It is also worth noting that the costs of bidding incurred by potential contractors are sunk—they cannot be recovered if the bid is unsuccessful. Hence by screening out contractors who are unlikely to be selected irrespective of their bid price, total sunk costs can be significantly reduced.

6. Another potential problem to be addressed at the pre-qualification stage is known as the 'winner's curse'. This occurs in 'common-value' auctions where bidders have to estimate the value of the object that is bid for. In the context of publicly contracted services, a serious underestimate of the costs of provision could lead to serious deterioration in performance after the contract is let. Pre-tender screening allows the contracting authority to select those contractors whose previous performance record makes such outcomes unlikely.

7. The problems faced by a public sector organization in its efforts to secure contract compliance fall into the classic principal–agent mould. The principal is the contracting authority (the contractee) and the agent is the contractor hired to perform a predetermined level of service. The agent can have an incentive to reduce the degree of input/effort, particularly where a highly competitive bid has resulted in slim profits. This in turn jeopardizes the quality of service provided by the contractor. Asymmetric information—the principal's difficulty in observing the agent's actual activities—serves to exacerbate the incentive problem. Some variations in the agent's contractual performance may be beyond its control due to random factors. As a result the principal will not always be able to disentangle the effect of the agent's efforts from the consequences of random factors. Rewarding or penalizing contractors according to service performance under these circumstances becomes a serious issue of effective contract enforcement.

8. To mitigate information asymmetries and adverse incentives, specific monitoring mechanisms should be written into contracts. The most common are regular inspections, the use of performance indicators, and certification of contract compliance prior to payment. To further align incentives with respect to specifications, contracts might include renewal clauses that are conditional on satisfactory performance over the contract term.

9. The structure of the existing supply which is planned for CT needs to be well understood. Will effective competition require dismemberment to a size that is attractive to potential entrants? What are the consequent trade-offs if economies of scale, net-

work density, and scope exist? An implication of these questions is that reasonable time is required to enable effective negotiation with the incumbent so that suitable preparation and compromise can be achieved to maximize the efficient implementation of competitive offers from internal units. What responsibilities should the tendering authority and the contractor have? For direct transport services it is essential to consider the trade-off between the size of the tendered entity (for example, a route, a network, a line, etc.) and the objectives that the tendering authority wishes to accommodate (e.g. maintenance of an integrated pricing policy, subsidization of certain non-commercial services). The size of the irrecoverable costs, the length of the contract, and the perceived probability of success will also be critical factors in determining how many bidders come forward as well as the type of contract.

10. Innovation in contracts is always encouraged but it must be balanced against increased barriers to entry. For example, an opportunity via the specification of contracts to broaden the specification condition to include environmental and social obligations (ESOs) has been implemented in Sweden (Finnveden 1997). Green contracts in Sweden are intended to improve the environmental performance of public transport vehicles (see below). Local authorities can opt for a green competitive tender for bus services whereby a percentage of the bus fleet must comply with environmental targets, achieved by the use of biogas vehicles. This idea can be generalized to any social and/or environmental conditions in any transport sector so long as they have operational meaning for all parties involved in bidding and monitoring. ESOs are potentially a barrier to entry in the specification of tendered services (and deregulated services). In order to balance the benefits of ESO conditions against loss of efficiency through reduced competition in bidding or in the market, careful determination of actual ESO conditions is essential. The biogas condition in Sweden may be seen as a major entry barrier in many countries, with an ESO target such as 'x% growth in rail or bus passenger kilometres' much more realistic and blunt in terms of creation of a serious barrier to entry.

11. It is desirable that the tender evaluation committee comprise members from within the industry as a whole, and that each member should make an independent assessment according to a small number of well-defined common criteria. Competitive learning is essential and can be achieved by a further set of well-defined feedback rules so that the committee is not overburdened.

The serious interest in competitive tendering in the transport sector is emerging slowly. The scope for CT is limited only by one's imagination. It opens up an extensive number of opportunities for improved performance, and can include such applications as maintenance of equipment, cleaning, catering, developing and operating timetables, operating the reservation booking system, managing particular transit/rail stations, public relations, painting, the accounts system, and even the tendering process itself. The current practice of internal supply or external (non-competitive) negotiation may not be the most efficient way of supplying the service.

Discussion issues for Chapter 2

1 Where the market is unable to act efficiently and effectively as the watchdog, governments use regulatory instruments. Discuss.

2 You cannot sell anything to the capital market without selling something. Discuss.

3 Opening up markets to competition tends to require more rather than less economic regulation. Discuss.

4 The loose use of strictly economic concepts creates misleading impressions about the purposes of particular policies. Give some examples where this can occur in the debate over competition and ownership. Discuss.

5 A nagging question is the extent to which the market outcome under economic deregulation is reproduced by restricted competition through competitive tendering. Discuss.

6 What are the relative advantages of cost-only contracts and bottom-line contracts?

7 Contestability is a much misused and misunderstood notion. Why do you think this is so?

8 Why might you prefer competitive tendering over economic deregulation as a way of encouraging efficient competition?

9 If transport services were directly competitive, less intervention would be required because (natural) monopoly incumbents would always be effectively threatened by potential entrants. In this situation what economic safeguards should be introduced to prevent the operators from exploiting their monopolies?

10 In the absence of direct competition from potential entrants, public intervention is likely to be required to prevent (natural) monopoly operators from exploiting users. Minimum levels of service and maximum fares are strategies consistent with this position. Discuss.

11 *Yardstick self-regulation* combined with competitive tendering provides a way of encouraging efficient practices and ongoing improvements in performance with the ultimate sanction of competitive tendering when an operator fails to comply with the ever-moving price and quality controls. Discuss.

12 Consider the comparison of combining loss-making and profit-making activities in a privatization that may reduce value of entity and hence share values at sale time versus separating loss-making activities and having them put out to tender and minimum subsidy. On balance what is likely to be the net revenue to government from higher share price plus net subsidy (i.e. subsidy after rather than before) versus lower share price and no additional subsidy?

13 Will a wise institutional investor in a privatization deal support inclusion of a loss-making component in order to buy cheap and convert the loss-making part into a commercial activity (clearly they would have to know whether it is possible to convert to a commercial activity)?

Appendix 2A **Efficiency concepts**

It is useful to review a few basic concepts and terminology in measuring economic performance. Economists refer to *technical efficiency*. This refers to whether or not inputs are being used efficiently in the production process; that is, for a given level of production, reducing use of one input must be offset by some minimum increase in some other input reflecting currently available technology. Economists illustrate this with an isoquant as in Figure A2.1a. It shows the technical requirements for two inputs x_1 and x_2 to produce a given level of output $\hat{y}$. If enterprises use more inputs than indicated by the isoquant (called an efficiency frontier), they are using resources unnecessarily. The excess of resource use (i.e. the difference between points A and B and the isoquant) is often referred to as *X-inefficiency*, a waste of resources from a social point of view (regardless of the cause of the inefficiency, hence the X). A ray from the origin to points A and B in Figure A2.1a would provide a proportional measure of the degree of technical inefficiency of points A and B.

There is a further dimension to efficient performance. In Figure A2.1a, all firms operating on the isoquant are technically efficient. But given that inputs have prices associated with them, the economically efficient combination of inputs is the least-cost combination. This is found by focusing on the combinations of inputs that can be purchased by different outlays. The well-known solution is shown in Figure A2.1b. The *isocost* or budget lines show the amounts of inputs purchased for different expenditures. The straight line reflects the given relative input prices. In Figure A2.1b, point C represents the optimal input combination to produce output level $\hat{y}$. Point C is not only technically efficient, it is also *cost efficient* or *allocatively* efficient in respect of input prices. Economists often use the phrase *productive efficiency* in this context. Note that point D, although technically efficient, is inefficient if cost efficiency is the criterion. Further, note that point B which is technically inefficient, is also cost inefficient although less so than point D which itself is a technically efficient use of inputs.

The implication is that measures of technical efficiency of production are not necessarily a guide to efficiency in a general economic sense. It will be important to understand which concept of efficiency is implied by alternate performance measures.

Figure A2.1 illustrates efficient input use. For multiple output enterprises, there are analogous efficiency con-

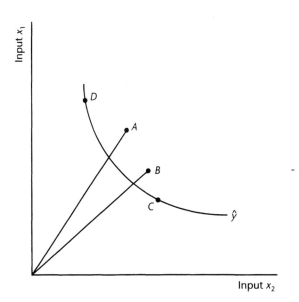

Fig. A2.1a Illustration of technical efficiency: location of production points relative to isoquant

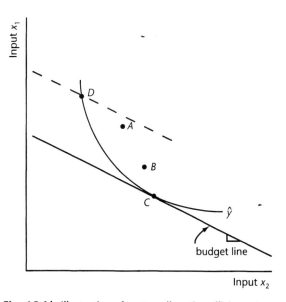

Fig. A2.1b Illustration of cost or allocative efficiency in contrast to technical efficiency

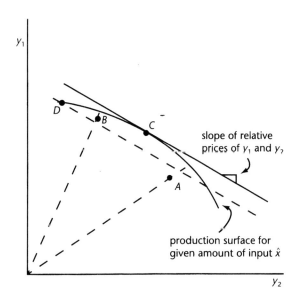

Fig. A2.2 Illustration of multiple outputs

(or composite) input $\hat{x}$. The curvature reflects an assumption that there are some complementarities in the production of the outputs together. As before, firms using $\hat{x}$ amount of inputs but unable to produce on the frontier are technically inefficient, although this time measured by a shortfall of their production levels relative to the output transformation surface or frontier. Output combinations on the frontier are all *technically efficient*. However, from an economic perspective, some output combinations are more desirable, that is, we can realize greater economic value from some combinations than others. For given output prices, Figure A2.1*b* shows that the highest value is realized for point *C*. Using input $\hat{x}$ to produce some other combination such as point *D*, while still efficient in the sense that it is on the production frontier, is less efficient economically than point *C*. And as constructed, note that point *B* is less inefficient economically than point *D*, despite the fact that point *B* was technically inefficient whereas point *D* was not.

It is possible to combine both output and input allocative efficiency in measures of performance, although very often only the input side is examined explicitly. *Profit functions* must be formulated rather than just cost or production functions, that is, functions which optimize efficiency in both outputs *and* inputs.

cerns about output combinations. The simplest illustration is Figure A2.2. It shows different outputs y_1 and y_2 that can be produced by a given amount of some single

3 Institutional and market environment: economic deregulation, competition policy, and case studies

3.1 Introduction

Economic deregulation is considered the ultimate release of a transport activity to the market. When we talk of economic deregulation we are referring to the relaxation of price and quantity controls, leaving it to the market to establish allocatively efficient prices and levels of service. It is assumed that an efficient market is one in which competitive forces can produce allocative efficiency in the sense of ensuring that prices delivered to the market reflect the efficient costs of providing services. The mapping of costs into prices is determined by the pricing objective of a business. These include profit maximization and social welfare maximization, both discussed in detail in Chapter 6.

Economic deregulation does not mean that non-economic issues such as safety are jeopardized. Standards such as those related to safety remain the responsibility of a regulatory authority and must not be confused with the arguments surrounding economic deregulation. Furthermore, economic deregulation implies that we are exposing transport activity to the ideals of a truly competitive market in the interest of achieving optimal allocative efficiency. Where the market fails to deliver such a competitive outcome, we have market failure, and the government, preferably via an independent regulator (as discussed in Ch. 2), has the responsibility of intervening to assist in reinstating the market to its competitive status. The neglect of responsibility by government to do this is an example of government failure.

Effective economic deregulation will require a new set of regulators and a regulatory umpire to secure the benefits of market reform. Often, the supposed failure of economic deregulation is blamed on the failure of the market when it is the failure of the regulatory regime to do its job to protect the efficiency opportunities of the market that is the problem. How often has unfettered or wasteful competition been blamed solely on the failure of markets? If governments via their regulators were doing their job of preventing such activity as predatory pricing, prices well below avoidable costs, and blatant violations of safety standards, many of the benefits of competitive markets might emerge.

In contrast to the ideals of an efficient market, supported by an independent regulator charged with promoting these ideals, it is argued by some that competitive regulation through tendering is unlikely to replicate the efficiency gains from real markets. The economic information that regulators/tendering authorities need in order to intervene beneficially is likely to be quite beyond the practical reach of a regulator. Economic deregulation as an alternative to economic regulation will in theory encourage much needed innovation (Hensher and Beesley 1997; Porter and Van der Linde 1995). Competitive tendering is at best a restricted interpretation of economic deregulation. It might be described as competition allied with planners' wisdom. Supporters claim it preserves the possibility of an efficiently planned transport system. However since tendering depends on promoting effective competition, it might be argued that an essential step is economic deregulation and planners are unable to make good any revealed deficiencies in competition by their wise use of centralized purchasing power. In practice, however, the opportunity to identify the efficiency delivered by economic deregulation, as a benchmark on how close tendering comes to delivering the same level of efficiency, is extremely difficult if not impossible to achieve. Thus we have come to rely on performance benchmarking (see Ch. 5) as the basis of measuring best practice and hoping that it approximates the ideals of market outcomes.

Economic deregulation, with an appropriate watchdog regulatory regime, and the lifting of statutory controls on entry, is designed to create competitive markets. If access to inputs such as labour and capital at competitive prices is not denied by other property rights such as patents, and a unique location for operations owned, contestability will be governed by the existence of sunk costs. Sunk costs are costs that are not recoverable when a business exits a market, and are a major barrier to the existence of contestability (as defined in Ch. 2). So by removing control on entry attributed to economic regulation, we have to ask if there are any substantial substitute controls a potential incumbent can rely on, and what is the impact on sunk costs? The proponents of economic deregulation argue that there are no important rights that would substitute for economic regulation.

One very interesting conspicuous by-product of economic regulation is the existing firm-size distribution. Since regulation gives a pay-off to firm scale, the latter will, on strict competitive grounds, fall. Over the range of services offered, constant returns to scale seem to exist in transport sectors such as urban bus services, railways, and airports. Any evidence of fewer and larger operators may hint at some element of inefficient markets for inputs and outputs.

In the transport sector many costs are highly divisible and flexible under deregulated conditions, so sunk costs consist mainly of the supply of capital; however these can and currently often are removed by pooled risks (e.g. leasing). The extent to which it is possible to have many variations in contract terms (ownership, leasing, part-time operation, etc.) without economic deregulation is a case that argues for the effect of deregulation occurring in other market environments, especially markets for inputs.

Without economic deregulation, it can be argued that competition in a regime of tendering or franchising will be less effective because:

- It is likely to be combined with the preservation of existing regulatory constraints. It is likely to be good for existing operators, with competition likely between existing operators.

- Existing authorities will prefer a gradual approach. While this may create 'learning by doing', it could be a recipe for delaying improvement/innovation, and aiding collusion.

Bidding systems, because of their complexity, are likely to require competition among operators on one or, at most, two competitive variables—most likely price and frequency. This is the difficult one—and involves defining, evaluating, and monitoring contracts. The deregulated market has more degrees of freedom in its 'contract'—price, discounts, and size.

Practical problems of operating a franchise over time include exploitation of the successful bidder, exploitation by the successful bidder, competition for monopoly, and with an auction among bidders, promises for future conduct. A real risk of subsidy entitlement with competitive bidding is that over time more services get earmarked for this treatment, with the real likelihood of bringing us back to where we tried to leave!

This belief in the role of competition in markets as a pre-condition for efficient delivery of transport performance is the kernel of a competition policy which many countries are now embellishing through a mixture of institutional and legal structures. We now outline the range of approaches operating in Europe, the USA, Australia, and New Zealand.

3.2 Competition policy and law: the key issues

3.2.1 Background

Competition law has its antecedents in the USA in the form of antitrust laws, through the Sherman Act 1890, the Clayton Act 1914 and the Federal Trade Commission Act 1914. All OECD member countries have progressively introduced competition laws since the early 1950s. The most important body of competition law in Europe is the European Union with Articles 85 and 86 of the Treaty of Rome the core of competition policy. Australia and New Zealand came late to the process, introducing trade practices laws in 1974 and 1986 respectively. In recent years competition laws have been adopted in Eastern Europe and the former Soviet Union as part of a transition to a market economy. In newly industrialized countries such as Korea and Taiwan, competition laws have been adopted and slowly other South-East Asian nations are adopting such laws.

'Competition policy' refers to all forms of policy that affect the state of competition and the economy, domestically and internationally. It can include elements of law associated with tax, trade, intellectual property, and foreign investment, and associated policies. Antitrust laws are only one element of competition policy, designed to prohibit anti-competitive agreements, practices such as price-fixing agreements between competitors, resale price maintenance, and exclusive dealings; and misuses of market power such as predatory pricing. Much of this section draws on information presented in Fels (1995).

3.2.2 Why a competition policy?

The importance of market processes in achieving an efficient allocation of resources has been recognized for over 200 years. The pursuit in markets by individuals of their own interest generally served to maximize the interests of the public as a whole provided there was competition.

Most economists consider that competition policies can make an important contribution to the achievement of efficient outcomes in a productive (i.e. cost-efficient) and allocative sense. With national borders being liberalized to encourage open trading, pressure is mounting to establish effective domestic competition policy to secure the full benefits of competition in the supply chain.

3.2.3 The nature of antitrust law

Antitrust law in the USA is almost exclusively concerned with the objective of competition. The most important feature of the law prohibits various kinds of anti-competitive conduct with provisions for divestiture of incumbent monopolies. Adherence is extremely rigid. It is enforced by the Department of Justice, the Federal Trade Commission, and the courts. Any defensible economic evidence that anti-competitive behaviour brings benefits to the public is irrelevant, with minor exceptions in special circumstances such as a case where some mergers may bring considerable gains in allocative efficiency.

The European approach is quite different. Many European countries have a form of competition law based on a prescription of neutrality to monopoly. The emphasis was placed upon the need to prevent monopolies from abusing their power (i.e. they are not necessarily harmful) rather than achieving competitive outcomes. The ideals of economic efficiency and broad public interest often overrode the objective of competitive resolution. Restrictive practices such as price-fixing agreements between competitors were often permitted providing they were not shown to be against the public interest.

Competition policy of the European Union has focused upon the abuse of market power and a range of restrictive practices, with the main focus being restrictions on competition that may limit trade between member countries. Over time this has led to some differences between competition policy in the European Union and in the USA. For example, the European Union has exhibited a far higher concern with vertical trade restrictions such as exclusive dealing and parallel import restrictions as these are seen as limiting trade between member countries. The USA has placed greater emphasis on horizontal restrictions on competition and a lesser emphasis on vertical restrictive practices (Fels 1995).

European antitrust law has shown higher faith in administrators making decisions than has the USA where the rule of law applies more rigidly. The USA approach is highly litigious with breaches of the law being prosecuted in Court both by the enforcement agencies and by private individuals. Litigation in Europe is much less frequent with private litigation rarely promulgated. Criminal and civil penalties including jail sentences apply in the USA, in contrast civil penalties only apply in Europe.

Australia, Canada, and New Zealand steer something of a middle path between the USA and Europe. They have generally sought to adopt stronger forms of competition policy than in Europe by having a higher degree of court enforcement of the law while allowing exceptions to competition law by enabling anti-competitive behaviour to be authorized in certain circumstances if its benefits outweigh the detriment to competition. In Australia and New Zealand, private litigation is generally allowable to enforce the law. The prohibitions in the laws of Australia are much the same as in the USA except for public interest authorization; while many of the same prohibitions apply in the European Union but with public interest exemptions. Part IV of the Australian Trade Practices Act 1974 contains the typical prohibitions of an antitrust law.

3.2.4 Taking a closer look at prohibitions in Australia

The essential feature of the Australian position on competition can be paraphrased as:

- Any business behaviour which has the purpose or effect of substantially lessening competition in a market is prohibited. However, any such behaviour may be authorized by an independent commission following a public process if the public benefit from the behaviour is found to outweigh the detriment to competition.

The approach taken in some countries varies, but the differences are not large. Some prefer to have a broad prohibition of the kind above enacted in their law, leaving it to courts or regulators to rule on whether specific behaviour breaches the law, while others prefer to specify in statute the exact forms of behaviour which are prohibited, thereby narrowing the scope of the judgements which courts and regulators have to make.

Horizontal anti-competitive agreements (e.g. between two competing rail operators using the same track) are prohibited. If competitors agree on prices this is prohibited outright (or *'per se'*). Law enforcement agencies do not have to prove that the agreements affect competition. Other agreements between competitors (e.g. territorial demarcations, which it might be argued are quite explicit in bus contracts in Australia) are prohibited where they substantially lessen competition. Another example would be an agreement not to supply a particular customer for whatever reason (for example, a specialist electronic toll company refusing to provide technology and advice to a tollroad company which competes with the former company's own tollroad). Evidence of some form of communication between parties is essential to argue the case for an impact of competition.

The misuse of market power, prohibited under the Act, occurs when a transport business with substantial market power takes advantage of its position to deter or prevent new entry or in some other way to limit competition. An example would be a monopolist's refusal to supply a potential upstream or downstream competitor whose role in such markets depends upon the supply of the monopolist's product (King 1997). Specifically this could be a rail company that owns and controls access to the only railway serving a particular pair of cities, and denies access to the use of the track to a potential competing freight train operator. Another example (of predatory pricing) is a vehicle manufacturer which might provide coach chassis at below average variable cost to drive out a competitor prior to raising prices to above-normal profit levels.

Vertical trade restraints such as exclusive dealing and resale price maintenance are not allowed if they are likely to exhibit anti-competitive behaviour which substantially lessens competition. An example of the former is the practice of supplying an airline or shipping company on condition that the airline or shipping company does not obtain any services from the competitors of the supplier that lessen competition.

An important element of competition law is its treatment of mergers or acquisitions which are likely to lessen competition substantially. Competition law covers horizontal mergers between competitors and to a lesser extent vertical mergers, since the latter tend only to lessen competition in particular circumstances such as where two businesses compete at more than one level in an integrated system. An example would be two coach companies which both compete for passengers and which both own two of the three coach body-building businesses.

Most of these practices can be authorized by the Australian Consumer and Competition Commission (ACCC) if, following a public process of inquiry, the ACCC is satisfied that the benefits to the public would outweigh the detriment of reduced competition. There is a right of appeal to the Australian Competition Tribunal. Action to enforce the Act can be taken either by ACCC or by private parties that can establish a relevant interest in the matter.

Individual parties may take their own action to secure injunctive relief, secure damages, and other court orders. In most jurisdictions private actions constitute over 60% of court actions. The availability of private actions keeps the enforcement of antitrust law alive at times when governments reduce the budgets of enforcement agencies. The availability of private actions means that agencies do not devote their resources to resolving disputes between major businesses who are able to look after their own economic interests. This enables agencies to focus on public interest questions and on the protection of consumers and businesses. In the USA where there is a treble damages regime, where representative actions are more customary, and lawyers are paid on the basis of contingency fees, and with unsuccessful plaintiffs not having to bear the costs of the losing party, there has been some misuse of private action from time to time.

The major ways of handling complaints and evidence of non-compliance include (Fels 1992):

1. the court issuing an injunction ordering the parties breaching the Act that their behaviour must cease,

2. the imposition of penalties, which in Australia are up to $10 million per offence, with penalties against individual executives up to $500,000,

3. damages actions,

4. other court orders including divestiture for anti-competitive mergers. There is not however a power to require divestiture for firms with market power even if they abuse it,

5. limited administrative powers for regulators, for example, to obtain and accept consent orders.

The significance of remedies cannot be overstated. It is one thing to determine that behaviour is anti-competitive but it is crucial that there be adequate and appropriate legal remedies if the law is to have an effect.

There often exist a number of exceptions to the application of competition law that are the result of policy decisions, for example, labour markets, intellectual property, and exports. There are also political concessions associated with agriculture, the professions, and government-owned businesses.

3.2.5 Putting antitrust law in context

Antitrust law is only one component of the broader picture of competition policy. The restrictions imposed on competition by other policies such as international trade restrictions and regulations imposed by governments that have anti-competitive effects exist and have to be taken into account under the umbrella of public interest benefits.

Many economists argue that the most important factor influencing competitive behaviour in a market is the structure of the market. In many countries there is no power to seek divestiture to split up established business enterprises. The USA has been the most successful with major divestiture action in markets such as oil, tobacco, and telecommunications, but this has not been a feature of other coun-

tries. In many OECD countries major divestitures have occurred in recent times with respect to publicly owned enterprises. Divestiture policy in Australia, however, has been based on the views of government ministers and their departments rather then embodied in antitrust law. In Eastern Europe this role has been complemented by an advisory role played by the competition authorities.

In Eastern Europe limitations do not mean that antitrust policy is unimportant. On the contrary it has had large beneficial effects on conduct. However, its role needs to be seen in the wider context of competition policy of which it is part. The most important priorities for competition policy are the removal of restrictions on international trade, the removal of government laws and regulations that limit competition, and the adoption of comprehensive antitrust laws.

3.3 A sectoral case study: rail's long haul back to the world of business and service

3.3.1 Introduction

Railways are possibly the most complex of all transport systems, with interrelated networks and historical obligations for both infrastructure (i.e. access) and operations (i.e. use). In contrast to other competing land modes, the railways face the challenge of allocating capacity (train paths, station platforms, etc.) to train operators; of allocating costs to these users in line with a pricing regime for access to the infrastructure, mindful of the joint infrastructure costs in handling both freight and passenger traffics on the same network; determining the overall level of costs, and of deciding whether users should pay the full costs of rail infrastructure.

Railways have also been the most hampered by a historical legacy of market dominance in the absence of the car and the truck and heavily protected work practices and conditions, and have suffered greatly in many countries since the car and

truck took away most of their passenger and freight activity. Competing modes were also less constrained by labour institutions and a desire to preserve the old culture of rail management. In the railways you *were* (and in many situations still *are*) first and foremost a rail person; secondarily you were responsible for delivering a service to the market. Times are changing but very slowly. The country comparisons given here are the exceptions rather than the rule in the turnaround of rail business with a dominating customer focus, in contrast to the supply-driven perspective, where the principles of service and cost effectiveness ('doing the right things') and productive efficiency (i.e. doing these right things right) prevail. We discuss the British and Japanese experiences in detail, while also recognizing that major change has been occurring in other countries such as New Zealand (King 1996), Sweden, Germany, and Australia (Nash and Dodgson 1996).

Efforts to retain a role and expand into new

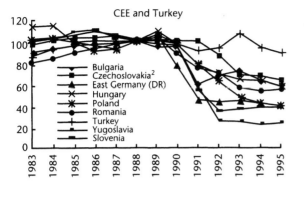

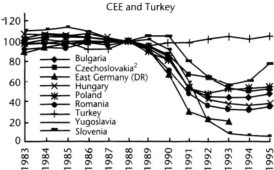

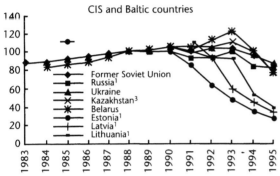

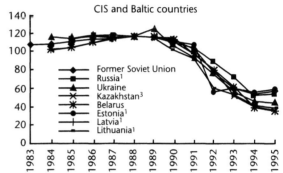

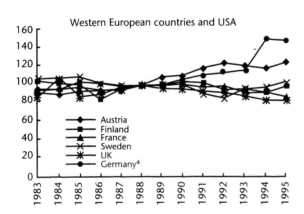

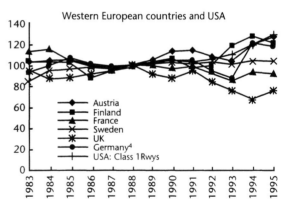

Fig. 3.1*a* Passenger trends 1983–1995 in selected countries and regions

Notes: 1. 1988 baseline data estimated. Some data not available before 1990.
2. 1993 data aggregate of Slovakia and Czech Republic as provided by UIC.
3. 1994 data as of 30 Sept. 1994.
4. Germany as W. Germany only before 1994.
Source: Thompson (1997).

Fig. 3.1*b* Freight trends 1983–1995 in selected countries and regions

Notes: 1. 1988 baseline data estimated. Some data not available before 1991.
2. 1993 data aggregate of Slovakia and Czech Republic as provided by UIC.
3. 1994 data as of 30 Sept. 1994.
4. Germany as W. Germany only before 1994.
Source: Thompson (1997).

opportunities have been tough, and continue to be so; not only in countries where the impact of the automobile hit hard early, but also in nations which are evolving into economic giants (e.g. China, Russia). Increasing individual wealth and the desire for flexible mobility remain as very powerful forces in all nations shaping the profile of the modal composition of the passenger *and* freight transport sector, as vividly shown in Figure 3.1 (Thompson 1997).

The winds of (non-technological) change have blown slowly over the rail sector although some noticeable progress is evident. The experiences in Japan, New Zealand, and the UK provide important examples of the role of privatization, competitive franchising, and subsidy in facilitating the reorientation of the rail system to a more efficient, effective, and competitive sector, recognizing its niche role in the overall transport task. New regulatory responsibility often accompanies market reform. For example, the UK regulator who heads the Office of Rail Regulation is responsible for ensuring that access to the network and track charges are fair, that competition is promoted, and that consumer interests—including those related to network benefits—are protected. With the change of government in Britain in 1997, the regulator is now obliged to pay more attention to franchisee compliance with social and environmental obligations.

3.3.2 The diversity of change in rail systems: the UK approach

The privatization of British Rail, under the 1993 Railways Act, involved a mixture of franchising and deregulated sale of assets and operations. The previously unified and nationalized railway was restructured into over 100 separate companies, including 25 passenger Train Operating Companies (TOCs), the infrastructure company Railtrack which is responsible for earthworks, track, signalling, and stations; six rail freight companies, three rolling stock leasing companies, plus other companies covering maintenance, engineering, and other support services. During 1995–7 all passenger services were franchised to private sector operators, while all other companies were sold outright to the private sector. Railtrack is required to cover all its costs, primarily through charging train operators for the use of the network (Nash and Dodgson 1996) and is expected to fund renewals out of the access charges; if it does not do so and as a result the reliability of services declines, then it will be liable for penalty payments to operators. Operators are expected to procure new rolling stock as a result of the incentive of lower operating costs or higher revenue, with the investment being funded by rolling stock leasing companies. Infrastructure enhancements are as a result of negotiated deals between Railtrack and operators.

The privatization process is essentially complete (Table 3.1). Thirteen franchisees make up the successful suppliers of rail services, with National Express winning five of the 25 contracts, Prism two contracts, and five other 'consortia' holding two contracts each (Table 3.1). Of the 25 organizations with contracts, three are management buy-outs, and 15 are bus operators such as Stagecoach, National Express, and First Bus.

A rail regulator licenses rail operators, regulates charging and access to the network, and sets the basis of competition. Passenger rail services are under the control of the Office of Passenger Rail Franchising (OPRAF) which issues contracts via competitive tendering to the private sector to provide passenger rail services. These franchises run for between seven and 15 years. Overall the level of regulation is fairly minimal for the rolling stock and engineering companies and for freight, but is relatively comprehensive in the case of passenger services.

This regulation has been designed essentially to safeguard existing rail services and customers. Although the privatization took place once transport policy had shifted towards a demand management approach, the 1993 Act was conceived under the old 'predict and provide' regime (Nash and Dodgson 1996). The suitability of this industry and regulatory structure for implementing demand management policies was thus not part of its basic design. Since early 1997, the newly elected Labour government in Britain has, however, within the limitations of the

Table 3.1 Rail franchises in the UK

Franchise	Franchisee	Years	Subsidy Yr. 1 (£ m.)	Subsidy Yr. 2
Great Western	MBO	10	59.9	31.6
South West Trains	Stagecoach	7	60.1	40.3
InterCity East Coast	Sea Containers	7	64.6	0
Midland Main Line	National Express	10	16.5	−10.0
Gatwick Express	National Express	15	−4.6	−22.6
LTS Rail	Prism	15	29.5	11.2
South Central	Connex	7	85.3	34.6
Chiltern Railways	MBO	7	16.5	2.9
South East Trains	Connex	15	125.4	−2.8
South Wales and West	Prism	7½	70.9	38.1
Cardiff Railways	Prism	7½	19.9	13.3
Thames Train	MBO	7½	33.2	0
Island Railways	Stagecoach	5	2.0	1.75
Regional Railways North West	GandW Holdings	10	191.9	125.5
Regional Railways North East	MTL	7	223.2	145.6
North London Railways	NEG	7½	54.8	16.9
Thameslink	GOVIA	7 yrs 1 mth	−2.5	−28.4
ICWC	Virgin	15	76.8	−220.3
Scotrail	NEG	7	280.1	202.5
Central	NEG	7	198.1	132.6
Cross Country	Virgin	15	112.9	−10
Anglia	GB Railways	7 yrs 3 mths	35.9	6.3
Great Eastern	First Bus	7 yrs 3 mths	29	−9.5
West Anglia Great Northern	Prism	7 yrs 3 mths	52.9	−24.8
Merseyrail	MTL -	7	80.7	60.0

Note: Negative subsidies indicate payment of a premium.

Source: *Local Transport Today*, 13 Mar. 1997 and Nash (1997).

existing legislation, introduced new objectives, instructions, and guidance for the franchising director to make explicit the charge to increase the number of passengers travelling by rail, to manage existing franchise agreements so as to promote the interests of passengers, and to secure a progressive improvement in the quality of passenger and station services available to rail users. These new guidelines for OPRAF obscure the boundaries between the Office of Rail Regulation (ORR) and OPRAF, limiting the powers of the regulator as the independent champion with powers to protect the public interest.

Track charges are designed to cover Railtrack's total costs and give correct signals for utilization of the existing network and for investment (or re-investment) in the system (Fig. 3.2). The charges devised have been divided into 'negotiated' charges for commercial traffics, and 'administered' charges

for subsidized passenger services. Although economic principles have been followed in ensuring that, for example, charges at least cover avoidable costs, the initial charges appear to vary too little with use to ensure efficient use of existing capacity (Nash 1996).

The UK model involves a high degree of vertical and horizontal segregation to provide competition both in functions (rolling stock leasing, maintenance, etc.) and services. While the already completed process of sale and concessioning confounded some of those who had doubted the practical feasibility of this model, it is considered to be too early to make any judgement on this approach. In particular, the allocation of responsibility and hence relationship between Railtrack and the service operators has already given rise to some conflicts, and the great optimism of some of the winning bidders seemed to foreshadow some form of winner's curse. If that

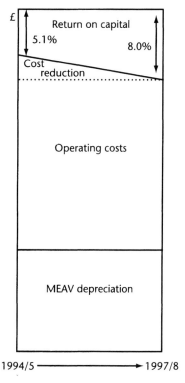
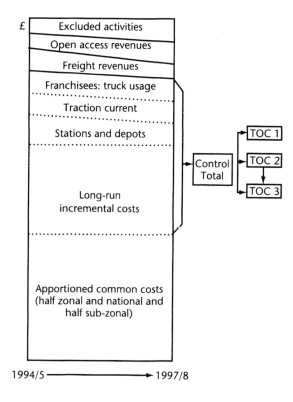

Fig. 3.2 Railtrack revenues and costs

Source: Office of the Rail Regulator, *Framework for the Approval of Railtrack Access Charges for Franchised Passenger Services*, July 1994 and Beesley (1997).

phenomenon did occur the whole process of failure and/or renegotiation might still be costly and damaging. The Labour government is reviewing the entire institutional framework with a view to rationalizing the number of regulatory components.

One concern for the future is the risk of under-investment. Since the current franchise periods are seven to fifteen years, it may be that investors will want investments to be profitable over that time-scale, while the life of assets is actually longer. In addition, Railtrack uses a discount rate of 8%, while the social rate is lower (6%). Another problem arises if enhanced services on additional capacity will not be profitable, but would yield social benefits. OPRAF thus has to estimate the benefits and pay the operator accordingly. It may also have to give commitments to employ the new rolling stock or infrastructure beyond the end of the life of the existing franchise. Moreover, the benefits of any par-

ticular infrastructure may be split between a number of operators, which may reduce the incentive for anyone to take the lead in pursuing proposals.

Somewhat paradoxically, social cost-benefit analysis appears to experience enhanced use under privatization, with OPRAF given a crucial role in investment as well as subsidy decisions. Even though the privatized companies use financial criteria, as a public sector body OPRAF uses cost-benefit analysis. A key component of the evaluation process is the value for money argument used to defend the level of agreed subsidy, which was necessary to attract bids. Beesley (1997) has investigated this matter in great detail. The government's platform of preserving and even increasing output to the market meant that subsidy 'would be concentrated at the stage of the franchise auctions' (Beesley 1997: 238). Subsidy has been used to buy commitments to improving efficiency and effectiveness in advance by setting up

Table 3.2 Estimated subsidy (£ m.)

Franchise	1st yr.	7th yr.	Final yr. if >7 yrs.	7 yr. subsidy reduction	Current turnover
Great Western	59.9	40.09	31.6	19.81	156.0
South West Trains	60.1	40.3		19.8	221.0
InterCity East Coach	64.6	0	0	64.6	217.0
Midland Main Line	16.5	−2.05	−10	18.55	58.0
Gatwick Express	−4.6	−13	−22.6	8.4	27.0
LTS Rail	29.5	20.96	11.2	8.54	53.0
South Central	85.3	34.6		50.7	158.0
Chiltern Railways	16.5	2.9		13.6	22.0
South East Trains	125.4	65.57	−2.8	59.8	215.0
South Wales and West	70.9	38.1		32.8	40.0
Cardiff Railways	19.9	13.3		6.6	5.7
Thames Trains	33.2	0		33.2	46.0
Island Railways	2	1.75		0.25	0.7
Regional Railways North West	191.9		125.5	46.48	47.8
Regional Railways North East	223.2	145.6		77.6	68.0
North London Railways	54.8	16.9		37.9	54.0
Thameslink	−2.5	−28.4		25.9	76.0
ICWC	77	−61.6	−220	138.6	219.0
Scotrail	280.1	202.5		77.6	104.9
Central	198.1	132.6		65.5	65.6
Cross Country	112.9	55.55	−10	57.35	106.0
Anglia	35.9	6.3		29.6	38.0
Great Eastern	29	−9.5		38.5	120.0
West Anglia Great	52.9	−24.8		77.7	119.8
Merseyrail	80.7	60.0		20.7	18.7
Total	**1913.2**	**883.09**		**1030.11**	**2257.2**

Note: Franchises of 7 years 1 month or 7 years 3 months have been treated as 7 years in this table.

Source: *Local Transport Today*, Mar. 1997 and Nash (1997).

the inducements via long-term contracts and taking a risk on the eventual size of the subsidy bill (see Tables 3.1 and 3.2). To ensure an opportunity for savings in subsidy, a lot of *ex ante* effort by OPRAF had to be devoted to establishing the terms of access charges to Railtrack for train operating companies and the master lease for rolling stock terms, leaving the balance of costs as the essential negotiated instruments of the bidders. Minimum output levels were specified as were maximum prices. Rates of return and cost of capital risk remained unknown, however. Despite all this symmetrical information, limited bids were executed; partly because of the esoteric skills thought to be needed to run a railway. Some element of longer-term conversion of monopoly franchises to open competition was thought to be a mechanism for moderating competition (Beesley 1997).

What is the potential saving in subsidy from pri-vatization via long-term franchised contracts? Beesley (1997) made estimates in September 1996 based on the first 14 franchises, which prior to franchising accounted for 34% of the total subsidy to British Rail, while Nash (1997) made estimates in April 1997 based on all 25 contracts. Table 3.2 suggests a saving of over £1,000 m. Nash, however, warns that this 'saving' is being compared to a British Rail subsidy bill in 1994/5 of close to £2 bn., which in 1993/4 was only £1.1 bn. The escalation of British Rail subsidy was due to a new charging basis for the use of infrastructure and operations. Thus the long-term trend in subsidy (distorted by changes in charging regimes in 1994/5) reveals a negligible saving in subsidy from franchising. When one includes the administrative costs of servicing OPRAF and ORR (net of other earlier regulatory obligations) the gap is small indeed. With the one-off sale of the rolling stock companies, Railtrack, and other parts of British Rail which netted £4.3 bn. and a privatization process costing £0.25 bn., the long-term savings in subsidy (assuming no significant reduction if privatization had not occurred) are argued by Nash (1997) to be notable although '... not nearly as much so as implied by a simple examination of the trends [Table 3.2] in support of the franchise agreements'. Beesley concludes that there will be substantial benefits in subsidy reduction. He predicts a continued reduction in public expenditure, 'far more certainly than in the last 40 years'. But he cautions us that this rate of reduction cannot be expected to be repeated with sustained outputs. Both Nash and Beesley see a major challenge for the regulator who under revised price control will have an uncertain and significant question of future subsidy levels to contend with. As Nash says 'This also presupposes that these reductions in support are actually achieved'.

3.3.3 The struggle for change in the Japanese rail system

Japan's first railway opened for business between Tokyo and Yokohama 127 years ago. The initial 27 km. has grown to over 20,000 km. in 1997. In 1964 Japan heralded the beginning of high speed rail with the Shinkansen services of over 552 km. between Tokyo and Osaka. Although the Shinkansen services generated substantial profits, they were unable to offset the growing deficits in the rest of the rail system (Table 3.3). The response to this situation was both political and economic—to adopt the processes of privatization as a way of reducing the financial burden on the state.

Despite the intent, full privatization has yet to take place. The more appropriate terminology is corporatization and commercialization. Structurally, this process, leading ultimately to privatization, proposed the privatization of JNR Freight Division as one nationwide company, JR Freight; and the creation of six regional JR passenger operations, geographically denoted to relate to the regional distribution of demand to ensure a sound managerial base. The seven Japan railways were to be incorpor-

ated as joint stock companies and their stock sold to private investors as soon as possible after the establishment of a sound financial basis for their management. This condition provided an unfortunate open-ended time-line for full privatization. However, to encourage a private interest, government involvement was to be increasingly distanced from the management of each business except where there was a felt need for intervention.

Under the privatization banner, issues of management, debt, and labour became primary issues of transition. In particular, the number of staff was to be adjusted to levels appropriate for efficient running of the business; the disposal of JNR debt was to be secured through the sale of unused land and by the listing of JR's stocks; and management was to be assisted in settling in through the adjustment of profits between the new JRs. The JNR Settlement Corporation (JNRSC) was set up as a residue for JR debt burden and as a central institutional mechanism for achievement of declared profits and avoidance of losses by the seven JRs.

All of these explicit commitments by government were essentially a way of committing itself to long-term improvements in the level of service offered to the public, a flow of sufficient long-term capital investment in the rail network, and the opportunity to improve labour–management relations and hence increase labour productivity. Table 3.4 confirms the turnaround of financial results; however, while these were laudable for each of the seven JR companies, the debt was not eliminated but simply transferred to JNRSC. Cosmetically it looked good and at least gave the operators a second opportunity to get on with the job without carrying what might be regarded as the debt burden from substantial historical government interference. JR Freight was supported financially by a requirement that only the avoidable cost of use of the rail network be charged, with the track owned by the JR passenger companies. Thus by paying track access fees at avoidable cost, profits flowed. The Management Stabilization Fund (MSF), introduced to stabilize profits between the JRs, provided public subsidies that enabled the three island JRs (Hokkaido, Kyushu, and Shikoku) to move from being very unprofitable to profitable entities.

Table 3.3 Profits/losses and interest payments of the seven JRs, SHC, and NRSC (billion yen)

Company	Fiscal Year									
	1987	1988	1989	1990	1991	1992	1993	1994	1995	1996
Profits/Losses										
Six passenger JRs and JR Freight	156.0	220.9	289.9	303.7	307.1	236.2	224.4	142.1	219.6	236.3
Shinkansen Holding Corporation	1.8	9.5	15.6	14.9	150.1 1041.5	–	–	–	–	–
JNR Settlement Corporation	2315.2	1780.7	740.1	322.9	561.8	182.2	173.6	956.8	993.3	n/a
Total	2157.3	1550.0	434.5	641.5	404.8 786.5	246	398.0	814.7	773.7	n/a

Note:
1. The 1991 total includes the figures for SHC for 6 months until its dissolution on 30 September 1991.
2. In 1990, JNRSC earned 882.2 billion yen from the sale of Teito Rapid Transit Authority shares.
3. In 1993, JNRSC earned 1,075.9 billion yen from the sale of JR East shares.

Source: Official Gazette.

Table 3.4 Disposition of JNR debt (trillion yen)

Company	1987	1988	1989	1990	1991	1992	1993	1994	1995	1996
Seven JRs	5.9	5.5	5.0	4.8	4.6	4.5	4.5	4.3	4.3	4.3
SHC	5.7	5.6	5.5	6.2	6.2	6.1	6.0	5.9	5.8	5.6
Railway Development Fund JNRSC	25.5	26.1	26.9	27.1	26.2	26.4	26.6	26.0	26.9	27.6
Total	37.2	37.3	37.5	38.0	37.0	37.1	37.1	36.3	37.0	37.5

Notes:
1. JR East, JR Central, and JR West assumed a further liability of +9.1 trillion yen for the purchase of the four existing Shinkansen from the SHC on 1 October 1991.
2. The SHC assumed a long-term debt to the JNRSC of +2.9 trillion yen on 1 April 1987. This figure is shown here as part of the liabilities of the JNRSC.

Source: Smith (1997).

3.3.4 North America

The Canadian and US railways are very similar in operations and commercial orientation, although there are some important structural differences to note. Historically, a preference for competition and distrust of monopoly in the USA made it difficult for railroads to extend their territory. The US Class I rail industry was a patchwork of rail lines across the country. In contrast, the Canadian Pacific and Canadian National Railways were nation-wide systems, including extensions into the USA. The government-owned CN (privatized in 1996) operated with substantial independence. Both countries had regulatory bodies that regulated rates. Noting the rising competition facing railways, Canada granted substantial pricing freedom to railways in 1967, which led to an even stronger commercial orientation than before.

The US rail industry was stagnating by the 1970s.

Although still efficient by world standards, productivity growth was low, and the financial picture was gloomy. Starting in the mid-1970s, a series of regulatory reforms culminated in the Staggers Rail Act of 1980. Although some residual regulatory provision persists, for the most part the US railroads have been free to restructure and compete. The restructuring has been substantial, and paradoxical. The Class I rail industry has simultaneously both downsized and merged. Large railroads became larger as they extended their reach to serve wider networks. At the same time, a substantial number of 'feeder lines' were closed or sold off to 'short line' operators. These developments were partly 'union busting' to gain greater flexibility by rail workers, but also reflected modern management strategies to concentrate on core business (large volume, long haul) and rely on more nimble smaller carriers to provide feeder services. For the most part, the US rail industry has done well since 1980. Productivity growth is substantial, and finances have improved.

The USA has taken few steps regarding facilitating access to track. The merger movement has given rise to concerns about the foreclosure of running rights formerly granted to other railways following the merger of 'end to end' railroads. The USA also retains residual regulation concerning captive shippers. The maximum rate is limited to the 'standalone costs': in principle, this is the amount it would cost a shipper to move the goods him or herself, allowing them to combine their movements with other traffic available in calculating the full costs of carrying their traffic. This is regulation and not a means of fostering competition in these captive markets. In contrast, Canada no longer has regulatory protection for 'captive' shippers, but does provide for the right of such shippers to invite other railways to bid for their traffic and carry it over the serving railway's track at prescribed (regulated) rates (CLRs or competitive line rates). The Canadian legislation effectively undermines some property rights of the incumbent or serving carrier in an attempt to promote competition. However, thus far there have been very few CLRs as railways seem reluctant to encroach on others' territory.

3.3.5 Developments in Australia and New Zealand

In contrast to the British and European systems, New Zealand has gone for fully fledged privatization of a vertically integrated rail system, without open access. New Zealand Railways are predominantly freight, although there are some long-distance and commuter passenger services. The latter are provided under contract in Auckland and Wellington, but the long-distance passenger services are not supported by government. After initially being restructured as an arm's-length company, New Zealand Rail was offered for sale in 1992 and sold to a consortium which included the (US) Wisconsin Central, the US Berkshire Partners, and Fay, Richwhite of New Zealand (King 1996).

One of the most innovative recent development in Australasia is in New South Wales. The Transport Administration Act 1996 restructured the New South Wales (Australia) State Rail Authority (SRA) into four corporatized entities, each with two shareholders neither of whom is the portfolio minister. The four agencies are: Freight Rail Corporation of NSW operating as FreightCorp which is a rail-based freight transportation business; State Rail which provides commuter transport under CityRail (Sydney metropolitan) and CountryLink (non-metropolitan); the Rail Access Corporation with responsibility to own, operate, maintain, and enhance rail infrastructure and to actively market access to those facilities by existing and potential rail operators; and the Railway Services Authority which is the railway engineering and maintenance group with a mandate after two years to be totally commercial.

Rail services are affected directly by the new competition policy in Australia (as set out above). In 1995 each Australian state government agreed with the Federal government to implement a national competition policy under the Council of Australian Governments (COAG) National Competition Policy Agreement. One aspect requires access to essential infrastructure facilities which are important to competition in other markets (i.e. are intermediate inputs), that would be difficult to replicate, and

ECONOMIC DEREGULATION, COMPETITION POLICY 53

which are of national significance. New South Wales is developing its own rail access regime to comply with this.

Users of the infrastructure should not be at a disadvantage in relation to the infrastructure provider, in other words there should be competitive neutrality. This is seen to require a clear accounting separation for rail infrastructure, but not structural separation on the British and Swedish lines.

The RAC is responsible for negotiating access to the infrastructure. This has required the SRA to improve its cost and revenue data allocation, and its negotiation and contract documentation. The National Rail Corporation, which has taken over loss-making inter-state freight traffics, requires access to SRA tracks and hence an access-pricing regime, while SRA's own Rail Freight requires access to track and yards in the Sydney area. Other, private, companies have entered the inter-state freight market.

A fixed-formula approach to access charges has been rejected in favour of a cost-based system with negotiation of access prices with users or potential users. This raises similar issues of cost allocation and asset valuation as in Britain. The individual states in Australia have different views on track-access pricing. Views range from equal pricing to Ramsey pricing (see Ch. 6) and price equal to the opportunity cost of the marginal revenue forgone.

An interesting issue concerns the charges for transporting Hunter Valley export coal. This has been a very profitable traffic for the SRA, and the profits have in the past been regarded as a kind of mineral exploitation royalty. Now with open access, the mining companies wish to handle the traffics themselves, or contract with third parties. However the potential loss of cross-subsidy is a serious political consideration.

Pricing rail access is also complicated by very different market segments. In the east–west corridor, rail has a market share approaching 80%, and this is the only corridor that recovers fully distributed costs. The eastern rail corridors attract only 20 to 30% of the general freight market. In long-distance passenger transport the rail share is less than 6%. In urban public transport the share of the railway is around 30%.

There are worries that, in a country of long low density transport corridors such as Australia, a combination of open access and privatization could lead to monopoly services combined with inadequate investment and a heavy burden of subsidies on the state for loss-making activities. That is, many question how effectively competition can work in such a system.

3.3.6 European approaches

In contrast to the British approach of privatizing and franchising various components in a competitive framework, what might be termed the European model concentrates on the separation of infrastructure from operations, with emphasis on the development of free and non-discriminatory access for competition in service supply. While this model is widely accepted at the conceptual level, it is not yet fully operational. One obstacle still remaining is fostering infrastructure access across national boundaries.

Restrictions on the free movement across boundaries by road have been almost totally eliminated, but there is far to go for rail operations. This will be indispensable for promoting intermodality and rail-truck competition.

In Sweden the rail infrastructure authority, Bahnverket, was established in 1988. A major rationale was to place road and rail transport on a comparable basis. Both types of operators now pay charges based on marginal costs. There is an annual charge per vehicle and a charge per vehicle kilometre varying with the type of vehicle. These do not cover total costs. Bahnverket also uses social cost-benefit analysis investment criteria like that used in the road sector. There has been a substantial increase in rail infrastructure investment. For the time being, the state-owned company (ST) remains the monopoly train operator on the main lines, although secondary routes are put out to competitive tender. A greater degree of open access is under discussion, but there is no intention at present to privatize Bahnverket or ST (Bruzelius *et al.*, 1996).

The German experiment is complicated by the

merger of two systems. In January 1994 the two state-owned German railways, DB (former West German) and DR (former East German), were merged into the German Rail Corporation, Deutsche Bahn AG. (Traffic loss has been particularly rapid on the former Eastern system since reunification, and the Federal government has taken over responsibility for much previous debt and for excessive staff costs on both former systems.)

Track and signalling have been separated from operations. DB AG has been divided into three parts: Track Network PLC, passenger traffic, and freight traffic. There is to be open access to the infrastructure for third parties, and there are published access prices. These prices distinguish between 10 categories of line, and seven types of passenger trains and five types of freight trains. There are price variations for track wear and tear related to the weight of trains, and for the operator's requirements in terms of punctuality. There are also discounts related to volume and advance purchase which have led to criticisms that the established operator will be at an advantage in relation to entrants. Another controversial feature has been the high level of charges because of a desire to recover total costs. High charges for track discourage frequent services, particularly regional and local services. This caused charges for such services to be revised. (It appears that even before this revision charges were not recovering total costs.)

3.3.7 Challenging the view that network industries such as railways are a natural monopoly: the open access debate

A number of countries have vertically separated infrastructure from operations in transport sectors where networks and economies of coordination are a major focus. Examples are gas pipelines and rail track. It is most often suggested that this vertical disintegration recognizes the natural monopoly profile of infrastructure supply and the competitive profile of operations above the track. A burgeoning litera-

ture is emerging which questions the extent to which this division of administrative and regulatory convenience is defensible. Notions of open access throughout network industries suggest that the notion of railways as a natural monopoly is questionable and open to challenge.

Open access in its broadest interpretation exists where anyone wishing to move goods and/or passengers has access to rail track. Where this has occurred in practice or is being considered, the precursor is a separation (or vertical disintegration in the words of Bruzelius *et al.* 1996) of rail track and right of way as well as control structures from rail movements, the latter now called access. This split affords opportunities for a large number of configurations of railways, interconnections, and networks. In particular, currently spatially independent railways can grant rail track rights to one another and extend their networks across borders currently restricted by archaic regulation. European Union Directive 91/440, for example, requires that all railways of the European Union member states provide track rights for international passenger services. Open access to rail track is emerging fast in Europe (including Britain), Australasia, and the USA. But what is its attraction?

Dodgson (1996) documents proposed levels of access charges for the passenger business sectors in the UK for the intercity network southeast and regional railways. These charges include electric traction current and station-leasing charges. The charge per route kilometre per annum (£1994/5) varies from £80,360 for the intercity network, to £84,750 for the regional railways to £215,600 for the network southeast. This translates into an access charge per train kilometre (and passenger kilometre) for the respective networks of £8.79 (£5.65), £5.02, (£12.05), and £6.10 (£6.36).

The fundamental issue is access rights to rail track infrastructure. Open access to rail track requires a right to move trains over a track segment in some well-defined way. The allocation process is essentially an allocation of the *capacity* of track to carry train movements. Such movements can range from a complete train movement through to space allocated on a specific wagon over a specified time period. Importantly capacity is subdivisible, even when indivisibilities in track exist. What this suggests is that the indivisibility problem disappears once rail access rights are defined as a right to some movements per some agreed unit of time such as a quarter, over a pre-defined rail segment. This is called an undivided interest in the natural gas pipeline industry (DeVany and Walls 1997).

This open access interpretation of the rail infrastructure company obligates the rail access company to supply movement 'slots' over its right of way and rail track. It may retain some of its capacity to move its own trains, contract out some amount of movements, and possibly place the remainder in a spot (or auction) market. When the access company is itself a user of the track as well as a competitor with open access entrants, there is the potential for anti-competitive practices against third-party access; this is when a set of established pricing regimes (and an effective regulator) are required to ensure that there is no discrimination in favour of the access company. In establishing appropriate prices, it has been suggested (e.g. King 1997) that rate-of-return procedures be implemented which take into account the value of infrastructure assets, such that an allowable return to owners of track is consistent with competitive structures with due allowance for upstream and downstream competition. We return to this important issue later since the pricing regime, given the cost structures and upstream-downstream competition, will have a major impact on the acceptability of an in-house competitor in the open access market.

Placing a ceiling on the amount of contracts negotiated outside the spot market is desirable as a way of taking market power away from a few major access players and decentralizing price making to the market. The market as defined will include these major players but will also involve in time the many shippers and forwarders who as part of the supply chain will not be directly involved in actually accessing the rail network *per se* and running trains. This is a way of extending the definition of rail customers. Such customers can purchase transport rights from many sources, including the track owners, contractors with capacity rights, brokers, and so on. Customer's requirements can be met in any movement dimen-

sion as appropriate, such as a wagon load, tonne kilometres carried, and so on. The 'creation of a market' becomes an essential step.

The concept of natural monopoly ceases to be relevant when the rail infrastructure is organized according to open access with market pricing of rail track rights (DeVany and Walls 1997). The essential component of this diversified access portfolio is capacity rights to a fixed and indivisible facility. That is, the rail track is indivisible but its capacity can be divided among several owners by creating a property right in transportation. A right to move trains over track segments could then be used to avoid the problem of natural monopoly (on the supply side). The issue that will need careful scrutiny is the existence of empirical evidence that there exist economies of network integrity (the demand-side argument for natural monopoly), even when the supply-side case for economies of scale inherent in natural monopoly is not substantiated. The extent to which multiple owners of property rights can coordinate their operations will be the real market test of economies of network integrity being unsatisfied, if indeed they are present.

DeVany and Walls (1997) suggest that a manager be hired to coordinate the use of individual rights, realizing economies of scale with decentralized output. This is an interesting and controversial issue potentially adding another layer of (in)efficiency, and a regulatory headache in ensuring maintenance of competitive practices between the owners of individual rights. The regulator's role moves from controlling the prices of a 'natural' monopolist to preservation of competitive prices emanating from the operations of a competitive market. One might hope that this freeing up of supply will open up opportunities for efficiency-enhancing entrepreneurial activity. If we believe that economic deregulation benefits the end users, provided the regulatory processes in place are there solely to protect the competitive process and hence consumers, then this open access approach must be applauded.

The Swedish model, which is one of the first applications of vertical separation of rail infrastructure and access, recognizes the opportunities promoted above, yet the bounds imposed on it through

Swedish regulation have to date failed to deliver the real benefits which such decentralization might offer. The rail infrastructure authority, Bahnverket, was established in 1988 with the aim to achieve a fair balance with road. Users of both road and rail infrastructure would pay an annual charge per vehicle and a charge per vehicle kilometre, varying with the type of vehicle. The revenue from this source falls a long way short of covering total cost. The state-owned company (ST) remains the monopoly train operator on the main lines, although secondary routes are put out to competitive tender. A greater degree of open access is under discussion, but there is no intention at present to privatize Bahnverket or ST.

Bruzelius *et al.* (1996) have reviewed the Swedish experience and are critical of its outcomes to date. They ask the question: 'Will competition between several enterprises on the same track lead to more effective railway service for the country as a whole?' They raise the supplementary question as to why, if the competitive model can offer the advantages propounded by its supporters, the new organizational structure has not emerged before given the very long history of rail transportation; even in past times when public regulation was not a constraint. Bruzelius *et al.* (1996) suggest that the historical vertical integration is the result of driving forces pertaining to the production of activities.

Indeed the debate on vertical separation or integration is at the heart of the literature on transaction costs, which refers to the costs of maintaining and running a market. Such costs are associated with the vertical separation of infrastructure and operations as well as the additional regulatory activity. They include the development of prices, purchasing, and contracting. Indeed a careful review of Bruzelius *et al.* (1996) suggests that their main opposition to 'vertical disintegration' is the considerably higher level of transactions costs (compared to air, sea, and road), and the claim that infrastructure costs amount to almost 50% of total rail costs compared to 5 to 10% for other kinds of traffic such as road, rail, and sea. Bruzelius *et al.* (1996) promote a vertically integrated commercial approach with cooperative activity between a number of possible users of the right of way. Whether this will be shown to be a preferred model to the vertically separated model applied in the UK remains controversial.

The broad literature provides some guidelines for further consideration:

- regulating the access provider's profits is an appealing mechanism for solving the concerns which accompany natural monopoly;

- establishing a set of efficient access prices in the context of a rate-of-return regulatory constraint requires industry-specific information in respect of the nature of downstream (i.e. individual track users') competition and the relationship between the track 'owner' (the upstream agent) and the downstream competitors;

- efficient access prices will be determined by either a downstream market exhibiting *open entry* (essentially driving super-normal profits to zero), or a downstream market with a *fixed number* of competitors. The latter will require a role for the access company (or companies) and the regulator in setting prices to reflect marginal costs (which is equivalent to drawing super-normal profits down to zero in an open market). In practice it is unlikely that the downstream market will exhibit open entry characteristics;

- if the upstream access company is also a competitor in a downstream market defined by a fixed number of competitors, then there will be conflict between the access provider and the regulator (King 1996). The socially optimal access prices will differ substantially from the prices preferred by the access provider since the upstream owner has no incentive to establish an access pricing regime which will optimize the number of downstream competitors;

- issues of the 'allocation' of shared costs will play a major role here, since the opportunity to pass on contributions to the infrastructure must be dealt with in such a way that we ensure efficient use of the track as well as an equitable contribution from each potential downstream operator. The application of Ramsey pricing (see Ch. 6) and the inverse elasticity rule may mean that commercial fortitude argues in favour of a constrained social welfare maximization pricing regime (price marginal cost subject to covering average total cost) rather than social welfare maximization (price=marginal cost). This trade-off may be necessary in order to establish a rate of return in upstream operations that does not deter investment. The challenge is to identify a rate of return that is generous enough to encourage (non-excessive) investment while at the same time not undermining economic welfare;

- a 'third-best' compromise in the absence of appropriate data for the regulator to determine a single set of efficient prices downstream is to set the per unit access price equal to short-run marginal cost accompanied by a pre-set fixed access fee to ensure that all costs are covered under the rate-of-return constraint.

3.4 Green and socially responsible contracts for bus service provision: the way of the future?

Interest in alternative forms of service delivery such as economic deregulation and competitive tendering emphasizes comparative cost savings and, to a lesser extent, levels of service, with minimal focus on the broader social and environmental implications of the market reform process. At the same time transport services are expected to contribute towards economic management issues, in particular playing a part in reducing general traffic congestion, as part of an air quality strategy and to help reduce emissions of gases contributing to global warming.

This section reviews ways in which the wider transport policy agenda can be integrated into the market reform process to ensure the achievement of broad strategic goals of efficiency, equity, and environmental sustainability. There is a desire, especially in Europe (including the UK) to include incentives in competitively tendered contracts and registration procedures for deregulated service provision which achieve network coherence, strategically specified environmental goals, and quality partnerships. In so doing, the challenge remains to ensure that these contract specifications can be achieved without creating significant barriers to entry and monitoring costs.

3.4.1 Introduction

There is a noticeable return in Europe to a recognition that while cost efficiency is important, success in market reform must not neglect the interfaces

between cost efficiency and the broader strategic goals of social and environmental sustainability. For example, public transport as an instrument of transport policy should be *Accessible*, *Affordable*, and *Available* (Viegas and Macário 1997; Potter and Enoch 1997; Mathieu 1997). The triple-A banner has become the symbolism for a new order (or might we say a return to an old order from the 1960s). The major difference in the 1990s was the desire to achieve triple-A status while still ensuring cost efficiency and minimum (if not zero) subsidy.

This section emphasizes three themes consistent with the triple-A philosophy:

- the linkages between objectives at the strategic, tactical, and operational levels;
- a framework within which we can support the integration of hierarchical objectives;
- specific details of incentives necessary to achieve outcomes consistent with the broader goals of transport policy.

3.4.2 Objectives for effective delivery of transport services

Transport policy, planning, and operations exist within a hierarchy of objectives functionally split into three layers—strategic, tactical, and operational (see Fig. 3.3 in the context of public transport).

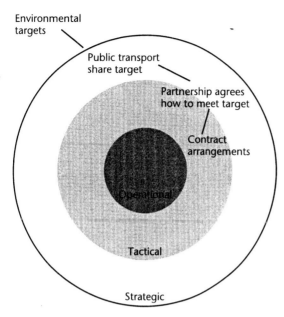

Fig. 3.3 'Layers' of public transport objectives and an illustratory path linking them

3.4.2.1 The strategic level

At the strategic level we have three goals—efficiency, equity, and environmental sustainability. These goals set reference points against which more practical objectives can be assessed, such as the three As associated with the achievement of networks of transport systems—*Accessibility* to vehicles and infrastructure, *Affordability* in terms of tariff levels, and *Availability* in terms of coverage of services. The three As suggest a greater emphasis on efficiency and equity; however, there is tacit recognition of the importance of environmental quality.

Although the three goals are admirable, to be operational they need translation into a set of performance measures. An example of a strategic objective (Fig. 3.3) is an environmental target defined very specifically as an increase in public transport share, such that public transport operators and regulators can have an unambiguous interpretation of their obligations.

3.4.2.2 The tactical level

At the tactical level, where there is an emphasis on planning, actions should be driven by a set of pol-icies emanating from a strategic focus that have definition, interpretation, and specification. An example of a planning task linked to the environmental target of an increase in public transport share is the establishment of a partnership agreement between the tendering authority, the infrastructure supplier, and the service operator on measures to attain the public transport target. Clear definitions of the allocation of such measures to all involved parties are essential. This involves not only specifications of service enhancements but also all support measures such as infrastructure and information systems.

3.4.2.3 The operational level

At the operational level, the tendering authority (for competitive bids), the independent regulator (for deregulated operations), the support services suppliers, and the service suppliers should work together, with incentives and non-compliance penalty clauses imposed on all parties to achieve an agreed quality of service. Importantly, the tendering or regulatory authority should be subject to the same set of incentives and penalties as the end-suppliers in recognition that all parties are responsible for the specified outcomes. For example, if there is an agreed package between local authorities and operators to enhance services involving the provision of specific transport priority measures (e.g. bus priority, pedestrian access, and increased rail service frequencies), not only should the operator incur a penalty if they fail to deliver the service frequency, but the public authority would also have to pay the operator if they fail to deliver the priority measures.

3.4.3 The planning framework

The development of strategic policies to address transport's equity and environmental impacts would yield great benefits to transport operators. Yet in practice this synergy is seldom realized; instead of a culture of mutual benefit there is typically a tension and adversarial relationship between private operators and planners with strategic responsibilities. This problem appears to relate to a weakness in the tactical link between strategic planning (the remit of the state) and transport operations (the remit of the operators). It is here that the interface between strategic planning and operational regulatory frameworks is weakest and often contradictory. Potter and Enoch (1997) explore this issue for bus and rail.

The end-result of what should be a complementary relationship between strategic policy and transport operators fails to develop. Operators perceive policy makers to be 'interfering in their business' and policy-makers are frustrated at operators' 'lack of vision' and feel they 'have to do much of their work for them'. This results in mutual disbenefit to all concerned; progress is limited, slow, and falls well short of what is achievable.

3.4.3.1 The idea of a Citizens' Network for public transport

The *Citizens' Network* concept indicates the challenge faced in turning a strategic concept into operational reality. The Citizens' Network is the European Commission-led proposal that the thousands of separate public transport networks in the European Union be coordinated in order to provide the same standards of service and style of delivery to the user. For the road system we already have a coordinated system, even though it is provided by thousands of separate agencies by different methods. Only one driving licence is needed for all of Europe and the same logic should apply to other transport services. Information (road signs, etc.) is standardized, ways of obtaining fuel are basically the same, and there are only minor variations in driving regulations. But for public transport there are a vast number of different ticketing systems, information is provided in different ways (if at all), and the whole logic of the systems is often vastly different. Travelling by each individual network involves a whole new learning process. Were the general style and logic of the services to follow a common format and conform to a minimum quality and service standard, this would be likely to enhance the use and role of public transport. As with roads, although the standard of service and style of delivery would be understandable

throughout Europe, the methods by which public transport services are delivered can differ.

This is not an unreasonable vision, and one that has been achieved at the national level (for example in the Netherlands, where even ticketing is integrated—a local ticket is valid anywhere in the country). But however desirable, combining the development of the Citizens' Network with a deregulating, competitively tendered, and privatized public transport operating industry represents a challenge. Such an approach has only previously been delivered by a very centralized, state-dominated structure, which is clearly now out of the question.

The question of translating strategic objectives (such as the aims behind the Citizens' Network concept) into agreed tactical aims and operational practices is explored in Potter and Enoch (1997) and Viegas and Macário (1997). Both indicated that at the tactical level of planning there needs to be a fundamentally different approach, involving a partnership agreement by stakeholders on strategic goals, how these can be translated into operational practices, who is responsible for the various elements needed, together with a clarity in financial arrangements. *Such an approach requires a cultural change by both planners and operators alike.* It was also emphasized that no 'best' universal model planning and regulation exists and a preoccupation in seeking such a model is distracting. A more useful approach is to establish how a partnership process can be applied under different organizational and planning forms. Key issues will include:

- clear identification of objectives and allocation of responsibilities,
- contractual incentives,
- competitive pressure (direct or indirect) over the system.

Strategic goals relate to developing public transport services to particularly address environmental issues such as congestion, air quality, and global warming gas emissions. These lead on to targets for market share which inevitably require a coordinated mix of factors regarding service quality, cost, integration of networks, stability of provision, and good public information.

3.4.4 The tactical interface

Several key issues make up the tactical interface between the strategic and operational levels. The most important are incentives, quality partnerships, preserving network interdependence and integrity, and extending contract or regulatory conditions to accommodate environmental and social objectives.

3.4.4.1 Incentives

Incentives are an essential feature in achieving the tactical link between policy-maker-led strategic planning and transport operations, the latter usually led by the operators. This relates to a number of key issues at the tactical level, including achieving network coherence, addressing specified environmental and social goals, and innovation in performance, systems, and hardware. Incentives can include tax credits, tradable rebates, image enhancement, and supportive infrastructure with commercial benefits. Bus priority is a good example of the latter that might involve a deal whereby the bus operator invests in service enhancement in return for the provision of support mechanisms. This is also a good example of a quality partnership between a bus operator and a local authority or road supplier.

3.4.5 Quality Partnerships

Quality Partnerships are a method emerging in a number of countries under a deregulated public transport provision system. Quality Partnerships are local agreements between the city authorities and the public transport companies for each to provide their elements in a quality package as part of an agreed enhancement to public transport services. To some extent these local agreements are putting in place things that normally occur as part of a tendered system, but which are difficult to guarantee in a deregulated system. These include, for example, agreed quality standards of vehicles, minimum service levels, information systems, good quality interchange facilities and infrastructure improvements

(e.g. bus lanes, busways, or other priority measures). In a number of cases, Quality Partnerships have reversed the decline in public transport use so characteristic of many deregulated systems.

Although Quality Partnerships may not deliver much more than a tendered or state-owned system does as a matter of course, they are important regarding the *process* involved. This, at a local level, is the partnership agreement between independent actors who recognize that by cooperating they can achieve mutual benefits. The Quality Partnership approach involves agreeing on how strategic goals can be translated into operational practices, who is responsible for the various elements needed, and a clarity in financial arrangements.

3.4.5.1 Preserving network interdependence and integrity

A somewhat institutionalized approach to developing partnerships between stakeholders is Austria's proposed *new alliance company* system, detailed in Heschtera (1997). This lays particular emphasis on maintaining and enhancing network interdependence and integrity in the context of deregulated on-the-road competition between operators. The partnership is between transport operators in setting up an *alliance company* with a revenue distribution agreement. Income from fares and other sources goes to the alliance company which allocates it to operators. Under this system, when an operator introduces a new route that increases overall public transport use, but decreases another operator's revenues, a balancing mechanism in fares revenues comes into play.

The aim of this institutional arrangement is to overcome a major disadvantage of economically deregulated public transport systems in that network benefits, although real, are not captured by individual operators. The *new alliance company* system captures and allocates network benefits and thus provides an incentive to individual public transport operators to enhance the network and reduces the risk to individual operators of market development.

This creates a structure of cooperation within which competition takes place and represents an alternative to the state-led tendered system which aims to do much the same. Whether this industry-led alternative can, in practice, provide such benefits was the subject of pilot schemes in Austria in the late 1990s.

3.4.5.2 Extending contract or regulatory conditions

An opportunity exists via the specification of contracts (or via the regulatory conditions for entry into a deregulated market) to broaden the contract specification condition(s) to include environmental and social obligations (ESOs). Finnveden (1997) illustrates this idea through green contracts in Sweden that are intended to improve the environmental performance of public transport vehicles. Local authorities can opt for a green competitive tender for bus services whereby a percentage of the bus fleet must comply with environmental targets, which are achieved by the use of biogas vehicles. This idea can be generalized to any social and/or environmental conditions so long as they have operational meaning to all parties involved in bidding and monitoring.

Despite the broad appeal of ESOs, they are potentially a barrier to entry in the specification of tendered services and deregulated services. To balance the benefits of ESO conditions against loss of efficiency through reduced competition in bidding or in the market, careful determination of actual ESO conditions is essential. The biogas condition in Sweden may be seen as a major entry barrier in many countries, with an ESO target such as 'x% growth in bus passenger kilometers' much more realistic and blunt in terms of creation of a serious barrier to entry.

3.4.6 Conclusions on broadening the institutional reform process

There are a number of options that could form part of a partnership to tactically link strategic objectives to operational practices. This is a key pioneering area

and one that is of increasing importance given the growing awareness of the social and environmental impacts of transport and the central role public transport has in resolving these.

In establishing effective linkages between broader strategic goals and operational objectives, it is suggested that:

1. local planning authorities, transport operators and other key stakeholders establish a partnership to agree how strategic objectives can be translated into operational practices;

2. as part of the partnership approach, passenger transport be repositioned to place greater emphasis on the user and the citizen and less on the means of delivery. This implies that more flexibility in contracts is required to allow improved services where there are real market needs and to 'fine-tune' policy as needed;

3. 'Quality Partnership' agreements be established between the various service suppliers such as transport operators, suppliers of infrastructure, information, and on-road/on-track services. These should clearly indicate who is responsible for the various elements needed and have a clarity in financial arrangements;

4. competitive tendering extend beyond the end-use services (such as bus and rail operations) to include planning, timetabling, and information systems for an integrated public transport system. This is an inevitable consequence of a partnership approach;

5. the tendering/licensing process and the regulatory responsibilities associated with economic deregulation include specific environmental and social obligations in the conditions of service delivery;

6. incentives be improved to partly compensate for the more demanding contract conditions. Such incentives for compliance might include extended contract periods, greater share of the revenue (where applicable), and Quality Partnership support to market-integrated services.

3.5 Case study: emissions trading as an example of efficient allocation of an environmental externality: greenhouse gas emissions

3.5.1 Background to global warming

Global climate change and its consequences for global warming, whether naturally evolutionary or enhanced by human habitation, is recognized by many governments as a matter of significant concern to the future of the planet. National governments in particular have recognized an obligation to improve their understanding of the agents which contribute to climate change in both positive and negative ways and to introduce policies through various instruments (e.g. pricing, regulation, prohibition, incentive schemes) designed to reduce the accumulation of harmful agents of global warming.

At the centre of the debate on climate change is the phenomenon called the *enhanced greenhouse effect*, which warms the earth's atmosphere and its surface beyond the temperature associated with the natural greenhouse gas effect. The mean temperature of the earth's surface is about 33°C warmer than it would be in the absence of natural greenhouse gases such as water vapour, carbon dioxide, methane, nitrous oxide, and ozone. In the absence of this natural greenhouse effect, the earth would be uninhabitable. Within the bounds of the long-term balance maintained between the solar energy entering the atmosphere and energy leaving it, interactions among the earth's atmosphere, snow and ice, oceans, biota, and land cause variations in global and local climate change (US Congress 1991; Fig. 3.4).

Although there is a substantial amount of scientific uncertainty about the climatic system's eventual response to greenhouse warming, associated with the accumulation of human activities which have generated substantial increases in the atmospheric concentrations of carbon dioxide, methane, and nitrous oxides in particular, the balance of current opinion is that global warming will occur. There is strong disagreement, however, as to the timing, magnitude, and regional patterns of climate change. The limited scientific 'evidence' from modelling, observation, and sensitivity analyses suggests that the sensitivity of global mean surface temperature to a doubling of the atmospheric concentration of carbon dioxide is in the range of 1.5 to 4.5°C (Houghton *et al.* 1992).

Despite the uncertainy and disagreement in the scientific community, the greenhouse effect and its *potential* consequences for global warming and global climate change have captured the attention of the public, the media, and governments of many nations. It is with this background of uncertainty and perceived importance that the Climate Conference series has arisen. There have been nine significant meetings:

February 1979 (Washington)
First World Climate Conference that established the world climate programme

October 1985 (Villach, Austria)
Assessment Conference on the Role of Carbon Dioxide and Radiatively Active Constituents in Climate Variation and Associated Impacts

September 1987 (Villach, Austria)
The Effects of Future Climate Changes on the World's Bio Climatic Regions and their Management Implications

November 1987 (Bellagio, Italy)
Priorities for Future Management—A New Policy Agenda

June 1988 (Toronto, Canada)
The Changing Atmosphere: Implications for Global Security

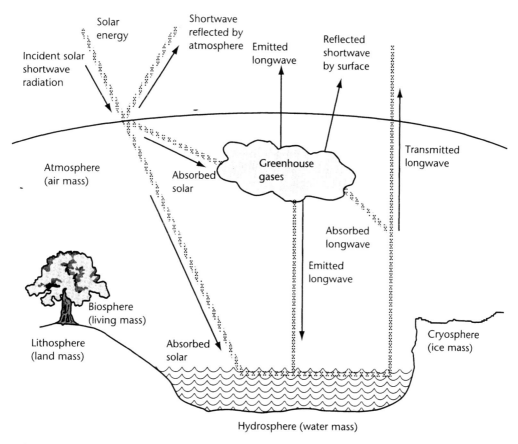

Fig. 3.4 The essential components of the greenhouse effect

November 1989 (Noordwijk, The Netherlands)
Ministerial Conference on Atmospheric Pollution
and Climate Change

June 1992 (Rio de Janeiro, Brazil)
A Framework Convention on Climate Change
(FCCC)

1995 (Berlin, Germany)
First Conference of the Parties (COP1) to the
Convention

1996 (Geneva, Switzerland)
Geneva Conference (COP2)

December 1997 (Kyoto, Japan)
The Kyoto Protocol (COP3)

The November 1987 meeting in Italy led to
recommendations that greenhouse gas emissions be
limited and adaptation measures be adopted. The
Toronto meeting, attended by 48 nations, was the
major political watershed. It called for a comprehensive international framework convention and a 20%
reduction in carbon dioxide releases from fossil fuels
by 2005. The Intergovernmental Panel on Climate
Change (IPCC) was created in November 1988 by the
World Meteorological Organization (WMO) and the
United Nations Environment Programme (UNEP).
The Noordwijk Conference in 1989 produced a ministerial declaration which recognized the need to
stabilize the emissions of carbon dioxide and some
other greenhouse gases, while ensuring sustainable
development of the world economy. A caveat was
included that developing countries would need to be
assisted financially and technically.

These resolutions were the key to securing the
cooperation of developing countries and in

establishing an obligation by industrialized nations to take the lead in reducing emissions and to compensate the developing countries for any diminished economic growth that might ensue from actions which might stabilize or reduce emissions. The United Nations Conference on Environment and Development convened in Rio de Janeiro (Brazil) in June 1992. The *First Assessment Report* prepared by the IPCC obtained a United Nations General Assembly-approved Resolution 45/212 establishing the Intergovernmental Negotiating Committee for a framework convention on climate change, to be supported by WMO and UNEP. Resolution 45/212 directed the Intergovernmental Negotiating Committee to prepare an effective framework convention on climate change for the Rio Conference.

The Rio Climate Change Convention, signed by 154 nations in June 1992, is a framework document, containing a process of adopting future amendments and protocols (which may in the future be legally binding).

The ultimate objective of the Convention (Article 2)

is to achieve . . . stabilisation of greenhouse gas concentrations in the atmosphere at a level that would prevent dangerous anthropogenic interference with the climate system . . . within a time-frame sufficient to allow ecosystems to adapt naturally to climate change, to ensure that food production is not threatened and to enable economic development to proceed in a sustainable manner. (United Nations 1992)

At the heart of the Convention is Article 4 on commitments. The most important provisions under the commitments include the preparation of national inventories of greenhouse gas sources and sinks and national programmes to address climate change, and to cooperate in preparing for adaptation to the impacts of climate change.

Many countries have committed themselves (under subparagraph 4.2(*a*)) to '. . . adopt national policies and take corresponding measures, by limiting anthropogenic emissions of greenhouse gases and protecting and enhancing its greenhouse gas sinks and reservoirs'. Under subparagraph 4.2(*b*) countries have committed themselves to provide detailed information on its policies and measures,

including the projected effect on its net emissions of such policies and measures for the period up to the end of the decade 'with the aim of returning individually or jointly to their 1990 levels of these anthropogenic emissions of carbon dioxide and other greenhouse gases not controlled by the Montreal Protocol'.

In supporting the Rio Convention, many governments have embarked on a major assessment of alternative strategies to achieve stabilization of carbon dioxide emissions to 1990 levels by the year 2000, and to establish policies which would carry them well beyond the year 2000 in their commitment to improve atmospheric quality. The First Conference of the Parties (COP1) to the Convention in Berlin in 1995 mandated negotiation of a new set of post-2000 (up to 2020) commitments from Annex 1 Parties but no new commitments for developing countries. The 1996 Geneva Conference (COP2) called for accelerated negotiations on the text of a new legal instrument, to be adopted at COP3 in Kyoto in December 1997. Agreement at Kyoto on the so-called Kyoto Protocol was open to signature for 12 months up to 15 March 1999 with ratification of 55 parties required to have the Protocol in force. The Protocol sets out quantified emission limitation or reduction commitment as a percentage of the base year output. Each country is expected to reduce emissions, relative to the 1990 base-year output, by the commitment period 2008–12. In aggregate signatory countries are to reduce greenhouse gas emissions by at least 5% below 1990 levels. The major gases (set out in Annex A of the Kyoto Protocol) are carbon dioxide (CO_2), methane (CH_4), nitrous oxide (N_2O), hydrofluorocarbons (HFCs), perfluorocarbons (PFCs), and sulphur hexafluoride (SF_6). These gases are radiatively active, absorbing the infra-red radiation emitted by the Earth as a result of warming from solar radiation. The infra-red radiation absorbed by direct greenhouse gases is re-emitted upwards (and away from the Earth's atmosphere) and downwards keeping the atmosphere warmer that it otherwise would be. CO_2 is the major greenhouse gas emission in the transport sector, typically about 90% of the total tonnes of emissions produced annually by passenger cars.

3.5.2 The appeal of emissions trading

The Kyoto Protocol allows for various mechanisms to meet agreed targets to control the increase in greenhouse gas emissions. Many countries are seeking out ways of providing positive incentives for industry and individuals to reduce their production of greenhouse gas emissions. Emissions trading has been singled out as an environmental strategy that uses markets to produce a cleaner environment.

The philosophy behind emissions trading is that it is a way of achieving environmental goals at minimum cost. It is assumed that it is less expensive for some organizations to reduce their greenhouse gas emissions than others and hence it is more cost efficient to allow the market to decide where emission reductions will be made than for governments to require uniform reductions across an industry. Businesses that find it expensive to reduce emissions could purchase emission rights instead. The real challenge is in identifying the best way of creating a market for emission debits and credits. Like any new programme, one has to establish the 'value' of the stock of emissions in the base year as well as the incidence of this stock within and between all sectors that contribute to greenhouse gas emissions. A major aspect of the determination of obligation is the extent to which the historical evolution of activity that emits such gases is the sole product of private self-interest or was also an outcome of the failure of regulatory authorities to impose appropriate regulations to prevent such outcomes. One solution is to suggest that the past was the product of a shared self-interest of all parties and that a good starting-point is to measure existing levels of emissions by source and allocate shares to each emitter.

Under a share specification, an emitter would get a permit to emit a certain volume of gas per period of time. The share would be owned forever but the volume of gases it permitted could vary if a country's allocation varied, for example, because of new international agreements. The permits could be bought and sold within a country and/or internationally. Two methods have been proposed to allocate shares or permits—grandfathering and auctioning. Grand-

fathering is recognition of incumbency and involves allocating shares on the basis of past emissions. Organizations would buy extra permits if they increased their emissions or would be able to sell those they did not need as a result of emission reductions. Auctioning involves selling permits off to the highest bidder (the method used by the USA to allocate SO_2 permits to power-stations). Auctioning is the equivalent of competitive tendering and hence can be structured to achieve the same cost-efficiency targets of tendering in the supply of transport services (see Ch. 2).

The choice between grandfathering and auctioning is at the heart of the determination of an appropriate and administratively feasible framework. The arguments for and against grandfathering and auctioning include:

1. grandfathering involves a free allocation at the outset in recognition of an historical presence and avoids the increase in costs of doing business with the pre-existing levels of emissions (which would have to be purchased under auctioning);

2. the free allocation of shares preserves the status quo of the competitive situation with organizations in other countries;

3. if the initial allocation is based on current emissions there is unlikely to be enough incentive to make the reductions required to achieve the Kyoto Protocol;

4. grandfathering advantages incumbents over new entrants, potentially stifling domestic competition and innovation and hence delaying abatement action. This suggests incentive non-compliance and possible violation of rules of competition policy. One possible way of accommodating these concerns would be to allocate the sector average levels of shares to new entrants;

5. specifying how the auctioning bid process would work is complex and possibly politically unacceptable compared to the administratively easier grandfathering approach.

A number of other issues that need careful consideration are:

1. the timing of introduction of emissions trading in one nation compared to another nation. Early introduction could disadvantage a sector that is in competition with overseas businesses. In contrast, early introduction can permit national trials to accumulate experience with the trading process;

2. the extent to which the trading market should be limited to a domestic market or opened up to international entrants. During early trials there would be much to gain by a closed domestic market to avoid leaving local markets short (through international buying) when and if international trading of permits occurs;

3. international emissions trading may result in substantial transfers of income between countries. An alternative might be to limit trading to national boundaries but to allow existing emitters to acquire permits for free and new emitters to buy permits at an internationally agreed fixed price (e.g. $US10 a ton of carbon). How one established internationally negotiated prices without market trading may be controversial. The market would be limited to deciding where emissions reductions would take place and how much reduction would occur. This contrasts with other price methods where a cap is placed on the amount of emissions allowed and the market sets the price of permits;

4. international trading has appeal however. It facilitates emission reductions in countries where it could be achieved at a much lower cost, such as in Russia. Western countries such as the USA and Australia and New Zealand are more costly as are Japan and the European Union which are the most costly. It has been suggested that international trading can reduce the costs of meeting the Kyoto commitments for countries like Australia by 20% compared to limiting trading to a domestic market (provided that there are no transactions costs, no cartels affecting prices, and perfect compliance).

An alternative to reducing greenhouse gas emissions is to increase the number of carbon sinks. These are known as carbon offsets through carbon sequestration. The best example is forest growth— trees, while growing, absorb CO_2 and emit it after the tree is lopped and processed. The Kyoto Protocol enables countries to take account of increasing carbon sinks in their calculation of emissions. Afforestation, reforestation, and deforestation are important inputs into greenhouse accounting. While sequestration may contribute a small proportion of overall global targets, it can be significant for countries with substantial forest activity such as Australia and New Zealand. Businesses can buy up carbon rights associated with growing forests to offset their gas emissions. For example, Tokyo Electric Power has committed itself to an investment programme in 10,000 hectares to 40,000 hectares of NSW State Forests over the period 2000 to 2010. An unknown in these green accounts is the amount of carbon an area of forest is worth, currently limiting trading to bilateral swaps between forestry organizations and electricity generators. Once the forest product on offer is standardized, the way will be open for auctions of carbon rights and possibly continuous trading with the market setting the price.

A new twist in establishing a framework for emissions trading is to recognize that some of the costs of emitting greenhouse gases might be described as avoidable costs for a specific firm but shared costs for an industry sector as a whole. That is, some of the improvements in practice to reduce emissions can be achieved more efficiently and effectively by the development of technology that benefits an entire industry. To encourage this to happen, there is an argument that the allocation of shares to an organization should be limited to those emission activities that cannot be reduced in impact through an industry-wide 'solution'. Each business will receive a quantity of shares in accordance with the avoidable costs of emission activity with a quantity of shares determined by the contribution of the industry sector as a whole (i.e. shared costs) to emitting such gases. This approach provides a very strong incentive for industry-wide cooperation and spreads the costs of emission reduction in recognition that whatever solution is possible for one organization is available for another organization.

While emissions trading and carbon sequestration

can make an important contribution they are unlikely to remove the need for other instruments to contain and reduce greenhouse gas emissions.

Emissions trading can, however, complement the introduction of other policy instruments, increasing their chances of success.

3.6 Conclusions

This chapter and the previous one have introduced a broad spectrum of market and institutional reforms designed to increase the efficiency of transport businesses in serving all stakeholders. The main message has been the search for ways of using inputs to provide a given level of service at the lowest possible cost (i.e. cost efficiency). We have investigated the role of competition, markets, and ownership in the delivery of transport services. It should be clear that the reform of the transport sector through privatization and exposure to competition (by tendering and economic deregulation) requires a very strong and effective pro-active regulator that works in cooperation with (but independently of) industry. The days

when the regulator 'interfered' in ways that not only distorted the efficient operations of markets rather than providing the context in which market failures are removed are hopefully long gone.

The following chapters introduce many of the important analytical tools needed to advance the debate on institutional and market reform. Knowing your markets, knowing your costs, and knowing your prices are essential inputs into the determination of efficient transport activity. Both markets and government have major roles to play in cooperative partnership; designed, it is hoped, to eliminate both market failure and government failure.

Discussion issues for Chapter 3

1 Identify transport sectors which it might be argued have the essential characteristics of a natural monopoly.

2 Consider the proposition that there are two ways of representing competition for the market: (i) direct potential competition either through economic deregulation or competitive tendering and (ii) yardstick self-regulation.

3 Direct potential competition is the ability (and willingness) of potential entrants to enter a market where the incumbent makes above-normal profits through high prices and/or low levels of service which create above-normal profits, and through competing with the incumbent in a natural monopoly setting, to cause either the exit of the incumbent or the exit of the new entrant. The latter is described as hit-and-run entry in the contestability literature. Zero sunk costs are assumed. Discuss.

4 Yardstick self-regulation involves the use of industry best-practice as a mechanism for adjusting levels of service and maximum fares. Any changes to price controls are linked to productivity improvements after allowing for the general level of inflation. Is yardstick self-regulation likely to be as effective as economic deregulation in achieving allocative efficiency?

5 Consider the following view: all transport organizations should have a business strategy, regardless of whether they are a public authority, a privatized business, a private company

operating as a public monopoly, a private monopoly competitively regulated through competitive tendering, or operating in an economic deregulated market.

6   When thinking about strategy, the most discerning feature is differentiation—seeking out a set of activities (known as an activity system) that makes you 'different' in such a way that potential competitors cannot imitate your entire activity system and take market share. Unlike performance measurement through benchmarking designed to identify and implement effective performance, which actually works to eliminate differences, strategic advantage promotes the creation of differences. The success of South West Airlines' 'no-frills' activity system illustrates how niche differentiation is a recipe for strategic advantage. Discuss.

7   Traditionally we strove for technical excellence but not market or business excellence. Historically lots of people were employed whose job was to hinder progress. Comment.

8   Sale of NZ Rail—there were six bidders with Bankers Trust responsible for coordinating the sale as an independent agent. All bidders were treated equally in terms of access to information—(due diligence). The railway does not own the alignment but they do own track, etc. There are public policy issues to do with alignment preservation, indigenous rights. What might they be?

9   Comment on the following: 'I work in the inter-state transport industry and one thing that has bugged me for years is not being able to deliver to post office boxes. There is an airfreight company called Pseudo Air Express which is half owned by an airline called Superfast and half by the government post. Because they have this relationship with Govt post, Pseudo Air Express can offer a service of delivering to post office boxes. I was just wondering that even though PAE (Pseudo Air Express) is half owned by government post wouldn't this be thought of as a government institution giving the one company which we are in direct competition to an unfair advantage and hence creating a monopoly by not allowing other companies which are in the same business access to delivering to these P.O. boxes'.

10   In promoting sustainable land passenger transport systems:

- should a government policy be established to promote the stability of transport service from the perspective of the user;
- should a government policy be established to promote cost efficiency in the provision of transport service as well as investment in monetary and human transport capital;
- should antitrust legislation be enacted to address market concentration and anti-competitive practices in the provision of transport service;
- should coordination between transport providers and government decision-makers be promoted;
- should cooperative planning and delivery of integrated transport services be promoted?

Part 2

The cornerstones of transport economics

4 Knowing your market: what influences choice and demand

4.1 Introduction

The success of any business will ultimately be decided by its relevance to the market. No matter how well run a transport operation is, its long-term justification is premised on a demand for its services, regardless of whether the purpose of being in business is to make profits and/or satisfy social objectives. Doing things right in business through being cost efficient (as promoted in Ch. 3) is no guarantee to a secure future if one neglects to keep track of the demands in the market for services, which evolve and change constantly.

Knowing what the market wants and being in a position to service these wants are the fundamental cornerstones of a successful marketing and advertising strategy. However to be in a well-informed position to predict the total size of a market as well as the share one might secure, requires some understanding of individuals' preferences and how they are transformed into actual choices when subject to constraints such as the ability to pay, the set of alternatives on offer, and their associated characteristics such as price, quality, reliability, availability, and convenience.

The objective of this chapter is to introduce the essential principles and practice required to explain and predict travel choice and demand. The literature is very extensive and highly analytical; however, there are some very simple and powerful principles which can guide the specification of analytical models capable of studying the phenomenon of choice and demand. We concentrate on the essential entry-level toolkit necessary to appreciate the very precise meaning of travel demand appropriate in determining market opportunities in all transport sectors, be they passenger or freight.

The key themes which capture the 'essential toolkit' include the derivation of a travel demand function based on the preferences of individuals, their budget constraint, the available alternatives in the choice set, and their associated prices and quality. This derivation is critical to an appreciation of what assumptions underlie the interpretation of 'demand for a service'. Ancillary outputs such as own and cross-price and quality demand elasticities (which provide an indicator of the responsiveness of individuals to changes in product prices and other attributes of service), and marginal rates of substitution (which represent trade-offs between attributes of alternative services), provide insights into how individuals process information in arriving at a choice of travel opportunity, be it a mode of transport, the timing of travel, the destination, and the frequency of travel. To operationalize the 'essential toolkit', we introduce the main statistical methods and data sources used in establishing empirical estimates of total travel demand and demand shares. These are the linear regression model for studying total demand at a point in time; the discrete choice model for studying market share typically as a single cross-section of market observations; and the time series processor for explaining influences on demand over time.

Whereas the majority of travel demand models rely on data captured from actual markets, there is a burgeoning interest in capturing a knowledge of preferences through evaluating individuals' choice responses to offers of alternative bundles of services that contain combinations of service levels and product opportunities that are not observed in actual markets. These stated choice methods extend our ability to source an understanding of demand as future markets provide opportunities that are not available in today's markets. Examples would include alternative-fuelled automobiles, high-speed rail, new tollroads with tolls much different to those on existing toll roads, major changes in levels of service of existing forms of transport, new light rail initiatives, and supply chain offerings with substantially different transaction and delivery times. Throughout this chapter we provide examples to illustrate how these statistical and data methods provide assistance in explaining and predicting total demand and market share.

4.2 Back to basics: deriving travel demand from a knowledge of preferences, choice sets, and budgets

The most important piece of information that we all own is the knowledge of why we make specific decisions. By definition, each and every individual has far more information than any observer can ever provide to influence the way in which they make choices. This information is captured in the notion of an 'individual's preferences' which describe tastes for one outcome over other outcomes. A logical starting position in a study of travel choice and demand is the recognition of the individual's preferences. We recognize that each individual has a unique set of preferences, although many individuals may be described as having similar preferences; and hence we might reasonably classify individuals into preference or market segments. We can conveniently start with one individual whose preferences are representative of a population of consumers. You can see immediately that this assumption if applied to a total population is assuming one market segment. Later as we understand more about how markets work, we can define many market segments of consumers based on their different preferences. Market segmentation is nothing more than differentiating consumers in terms of their diversity or heterogeneity of preferences for a particular travel activity under study.

4.2.1 Understanding preference rules

To advance the basic role of preferences, let us assume a homogeneous preference function. This is another way of saying that if, for example, we were to offer a sample of individuals' combinations of travel times and prices for a trip between the same two locations, each individual would have identical preferences for each combination. If this can be quantified on some scale such as a 0–100 satisfaction or utility scale, then we would observe the same numerical level of satisfaction or utility.

Once we know the representative consumer's preferences we can define the preference function. This is a mapping of the relationship between alternative goods or services designed to deliver the same level of utility. The alternatives can be thought of as nothing more than bundles of underlying attributes such as travel time, cost, comfort, reliability, and convenience, which together with an image associated with the bundling (often called a product brand such as a truck, a car, a destination, a train) represent the sources of utility. Individuals choose to travel to work or to the shops by car rather than train, and shippers choose truck over rail because, in the main, it offers a preferred bundle of levels of attributes which are important in making the choice between available alternatives. Available alternatives are traditionally referred to in demand theory as the available set of technologies.

In implementing their preference rules, individuals implicitly attach weights to a set of attributes that influence their choice, and choose an alternative from the available set. The challenge facing the market analyst is to identify these weights and in so doing obtain knowledge of what attributes drive an individual's choice. An attribute with a very low weight would be unimportant. Unfortunately the analyst has to limit the set of attributes under study, possibly to the major set that are identified from a survey of consumers. This is where the preference function of the consumer and the analyst's attempts to reveal it exactly part company. Whereas all of these attributes are known with certainty by the individual chooser, the analyst has less-than-full information. Consequently, as shown later, we can only explain choice and demand up to a probability of it occurring.

4.2.2 **An individual's budget constraint**

Thus far we have introduced the idea of an individual's preferences, the underlying sources of utility which define a preference function, the attributes of available alternatives such as price and service level, and the limiting effect on preference maximization due to the available set of technologies. To complete the set of items needed to derive a demand function, we have to introduce the individual's budget constraint. This constraint can be generalized to include not only an individual's purchasing power (i.e. income) but also a time budget. The latter is especially important in transport demand because of the amount of time that one has to commit to travel, in competition with the time that has to be committed to other non-travel activities.

4.2.3 **Deriving travel demand**

Since the ideas of choice and demand are inherently economic concepts, we will use an economic framework to assist in the derivation of a travel demand function. To simplify the presentation, without diminishing the general result, we will assume that an individual is evaluating one good (X) against the alternative good (Y) that we will later simply call money not spent on good X, or savings. We will also simplify the derivation by assuming one attribute, price, which is money outlay. In a later discussion we will replace this with the notion of *generalized price* where all attributes are combined after conversion to a single measurement unit.

Our representative consumer's preferences are revealed through a trace of the levels of utility associated with a large number of combinations of good X and a numeraire commodity Y. If we plot these utility levels in a two-way diagram (Fig. 4.1) where all points in the graph represent a level of utility, we will find that there are many coordinates with the same level of utility. By drawing a line through the points of equal levels of utility, we have created an indifference (or I) curve. As the name implies, an individual is indifferent as to which combination of X and the numeraire good Y are chosen along the indifferent line. There will be many such I-curves, each one representing a different level of constant utility along its surface.

In Figure 4.1, we have plotted four I-curves, with increasing utility as we move away from the origin. The slope of an I-curve has rich information on an individual's preferences. There are two important concepts related to indifference curves:

1. marginal rate of substitution (MRS_{XY}) defined as the amount of Y a consumer is just willing to give up to get an additional unit of X, and maintain the same level of satisfaction;

2. marginal utility (MU_X) is the change in total utility (TU) that would result from a one unit increase in consumption of X, when all other things (including the quantity of Y) are held constant ($A \rightarrow C$), that is:

$$MU_X = \frac{\Delta U}{\Delta X} \mid Y = \bar{Y}$$

Similarly

$$MU_Y = \frac{\Delta U}{\Delta Y} \mid X = \bar{X}$$

The concept of marginal utility is not used in indifference curve analysis because it involves movement *between* curves even though it is central to demand modelling. However, it is possible to show the relationship between all these concepts. Let us demonstrate this. Assume a single indifference curve. It has a slope, such as that in Figure 4.1 between A and B. Remember we are talking about marginal changes and hence AB is really very small. The slope of I_0 is $-(\Delta Y/\Delta X)$ where Δ represents the size of the change in Y or X. When the size of the change is very small (often called marginal) Δ is replaced by d as a recognition of partial derivatives in calculus used to evaluate small changes. We can see that ΔY and ΔX are part of the definition of MU_Y and MU_X. Hence by rearrangement,

$$\frac{\Delta Y}{\Delta X} = \frac{\Delta U/\Delta X}{\Delta U/\Delta Y} = \frac{MU_X}{MU_Y} \text{ or } -\left[\frac{\Delta Y}{\Delta X}\right] = -\left[\frac{MU_X}{MU_Y}\right]$$

Also if a given change in utility occurs, that is, $\Delta U_X = \Delta U_Y$, then we are effectively looking at the relationship between X and Y for a given level of utility or satisfaction. Hence we are moving along a single indifference curve. Thus $\frac{MU_X}{MU_Y} = MRS_{XY}$. The MRS_{XY} is very important in travel demand studies. We will show later that the marginal rate of substitution between the money price of a trip and the travel time involved represents the value of travel time savings or the amount of money that an individual is willing to outlay to save a unit of travel time, holding income, tastes, and technology fixed. The trade-off between the price of travel and any other attribute influencing choice which is not in dollar units reveals the value (i.e. what someone is willing to pay), at the margin, of a unit of the non-dollar attribute.

By imposing the behavioural assumption that all individuals act as if they are maximizing utility, we

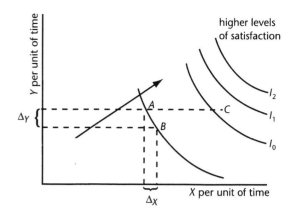

Fig. 4.1 A preference map

are able to identify the utility-maximizing solution to the trade between the two goods by seeking out the indifference surface with the highest level of constant utility. This solution is of limited interest without allowing for the individual's budget constraint. The budget constraint is typically a linear curve defined by knowledge of the prices of the alternative goods, assumed to be given to the consumer, and the individual's total income. We ignore the possibility than an individual is sufficiently powerful in the market to influence prices, and thus acts as a price *taker* (in contrast to a price *maker*). Given these prices and income, we can draw the budget constraint as shown in Figure 4.2.

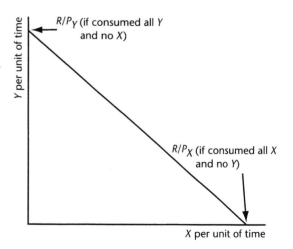

Fig. 4.2 The budget constraint

The slope of the budget constraint defines the relative prices, often called the market rate of exchange between X and Y. Its location defines the available resources to spend. Total resources (R) (i.e. income) available to spend on X and Y is given by $R = P_Y \cdot Y + P_X \cdot X$. This states that we will spend all resources on X and Y, and the amount of X and Y we can have is influenced by, among other things, their prices. To show the slope, we can rearrange the budget constraint,

$$R/PY = Y + \frac{P_X}{P_Y} \cdot X$$

$$Y = R/P_Y - \frac{P_X}{P_Y} \cdot X$$

Given the analogy to the simple algebraic relationship $Y = a + \beta X$, where β is the slope of the line, then $-P_X/P_Y$ is the slope of the budget line, likewise R/P_Y is the location of the line. Importantly from the discussion above, the ratio of the prices is an indication of what an individual 'can do', whereas the MRS is an indication of what the individual is 'willing to do'.

When we overlay Figure 4.2 onto Figure 4.1 (as shown in Fig. 4.3), we will see that the budget constraint will be tangential to some I-curves and cut across other I-curves. A utility-maximizing consumer will seek out that combination of X and all the other goods (usually called the composite or numeraire good) which enables achievement of the highest level of utility subject to the budget constraint. In Figure 4.3 this occurs where X_1 and Y_1 are consumed. If the numeraire is the balance of income not spent on good X, then we can call it 'savings'. Formally then, utility is maximized at the point where the budget line is tangential to an indifference curve (i.e. at the highest point attainable). Since

$$MRS_{XY} = -\frac{\Delta Y}{\Delta X} \text{ and } \frac{P_X}{P_Y} = -\frac{\Delta Y}{\Delta X}$$

Then

$$MRS_{XY} = P_X/P_Y$$

at tangency or optimal level of consumption for a given budget.

The consumer is in a position where she can *just do* what she is *willing to do*. As the individual moves down an indifference curve, she or he will experience *diminishing MRS$_{XY}$*. That is, the more a consumer receives of X, the less Y he is *willing to give up* to get one more unit of X and still preserve the same amount of satisfaction (Fig. 4.4). The MRS_{XY} is found by computing the slope and removing the sign.

The utility-maximizing combination of good X and the numeraire 'good' Y is the solution to a

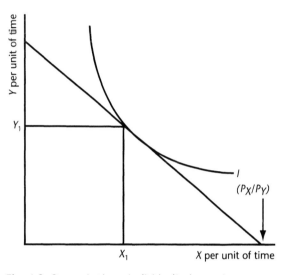

Fig. 4.3 One point in an individual's demand curve

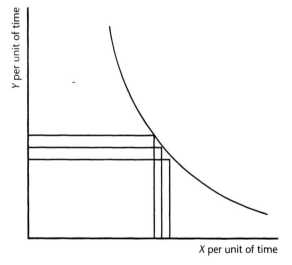

Fig. 4.4 Diminishing marginal rate of substitution

choice problem which is conditional on the given prices of the two goods and the individual's income level. This is an important point since it tells us that there will be a number of utility-maximizing solutions, each dependent on the relative prices of the two goods and the available budget. We can trace out the distribution of solutions in many ways. A particularly useful way is to vary the price of good X while holding the prices of all other goods and income constant (Fig. 4.5). When we hold particular components of a solution constant we say 'all other things being equal' or 'ceteris paribus'. The trace of the price of X (Fig. 4.5), given tastes (i.e. the shapes of the preference or I-curves), prices of other goods and income, provides a distribution of utility-maximizing amounts of good X consumed. It is now useful to think of good Y as being money (M) available to spend on goods other than X, including saving the money (Fig. 4.5). If we were to plot the price of X on the vertical axis and the amount of X consumed on the horizontal axis (Fig. 4.6), we will be moving from utility space in Figures 4.1 to 4.5 to goods or demand space. By joining the points of intersection between price and amount of X consumed at that price, we trace out a demand curve. This demand curve defines the relationship between the *price of* X and the *quantity of* X *demanded, ceteris paribus*. This solution is only valid for given prices of other goods and services, the individual's income, tastes, and the available technology. Movements along a given demand curve report changes in the quantity demanded as the price of the good changes.

4.2.4 Distinguishing changes in quantity demanded and changes in demand

The phrase 'quantity demanded' is specific to a *given* demand curve. Movements between demand curves can occur when one element of 'ceteris paribus' is changed. For example, if we were to return to Figure 4.3 and increase the amount of income, then we would trace out a different set of utility-maximizing

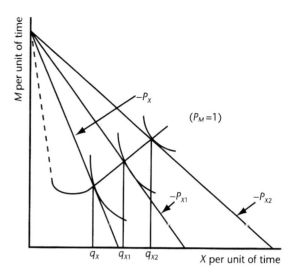

Fig. 4.5 The price consumption curve in a money economy

quantities of X consumed at each price of X. This would translate into Figure 4.7 as another demand curve. For a higher income, given the shape of the individual's preference curves, the individual demands more of X at a given price than before. Thus the new demand curve is further to the right for each price. When we compare two demand curves and allow for a movement between them, this is referred to as a *change in demand*. The word 'quantity' is now dropped since it only applies to movements along a given demand curve. This distinction is very important. For example, the great majority of empirical studies of travel demand restrict policy responses to reactions that permit movements along a given demand curve. Thus we might increase the price of travel, and observe the change in the quantity demanded, and infer the role of price in influencing this change in quantity demanded. But the inference is based on *ceteris paribus*. In reality, other factors may be changing such as an improvement in service quality associated with a price increase. Failure to allow for other sources of change can result in misleading inferences about the role of price. Thus we must recognize that if we were to change the level of the attribute on the vertical axis in Figure 4.5, which is the sole source of variation in quantity demanded

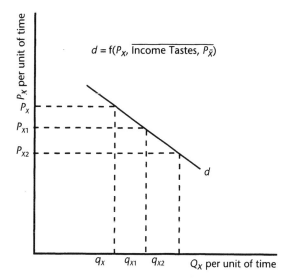

Fig. 4.6 The individual's demand curve

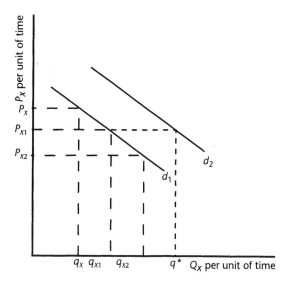

Fig. 4.7 Changes in demand

along a given demand curve, and other attributes also change which are not represented on the vertical axis, then there should also be a change in demand.

Transport analysts often prefer to work with movements along a given demand curve and attempt to accommodate this by replacing a single price attribute on the vertical axis with a multi-attribute variable, called generalized price. This is feasible provided that all attributes can be measured in the same units. It is common in transport studies to include travel time after converting it into dollar amounts via a conversion indicator called the behavioural value of travel time savings (BVTTS). The sum of money price plus time price is the generalized price of travel. In a later section we show you how to derive this important valuation indicator.

We have spent a lot of time deriving the travel demand function because this knowledge is essential in an appreciation of any empirical evidence in the literature. One should always want to establish the realism of 'all other things being equal' and hence the appropriateness of applying empirical methods (see below) that trace out movements along a given demand curve in contrast to movements between the demand curves. When one is looking at travel modal switching behaviour where each alternative mode has its own demand curve, we are interested in capturing both movements along and movements between mode-specific demand curves. Indeed in a multi-modal setting one can expect multiple demand curves within and between modes (see Ch. 7 where we illustrate this phenomenon). In a later section we use this knowledge of travel demand to specify empirical models that capture the wider set of influences on demand, allowing for attributes of alternative transport technologies such as price, travel time, comfort, reliability; characteristics of individuals such as income, gender, and age; and the general state of the economy. With such a rich array of variability in influences on choice and hence demand, the need for market segmentation is clear. We will show you how we do this through the inclusion of additional variables that capture the heterogeneity of a population.

4.3 Visiting the behavioural engine of travel choice and demand functions: identifying behavioural response

Transport analysts use information from demand studies in two main ways. First, they develop a travel demand model and assess changes in attributes influencing choice or demand by manipulating the levels of the attributes. Secondly, they also derive from such models or from before and after studies, indicators of the behavioural response of the market segment to a change in the level of an attribute, known as elasticities. In both instances, *ceteris paribus* is assumed; however, the application of a model system opens up the possibility of allowing for changes in other attributes (this being dependent on how the travel demand models are specified); whereas the elasticity approach imposes *ceteris paribus*.

Formally, the elasticity of demand is a unitless index that describes the relationship between a percentage change in the level of an attribute of a travel alternative (or a characteristic of an individual or a firm) and the percentage change in the *quantity* demanded, *ceteris paribus*. Because the index is unitless, the shape and slope of a demand curve cannot be used strictly as a way of determining elasticity. To be specific, one can produce a different slope simply by changing the units of price from dollars to cents. In practice a steep slope does provide some indication that an individual is less sensitive to a change in the level of an attribute than would a slight sloping demand curve. The behavioural information associated with the idea of elasticity is summarized in Table 4.1 in the context of price changes for a single travel good. There are five categories of elasticity, which impact on demand and revenue according to whether price is increased or decreased. The demand and revenue implications generalize to markets for more than one travel good.

The two extreme categories of perfect inelasticity and perfect elasticity are generally of no empirical interest, but usefully bound the value of an elasticity. An elasticity can take on any sign; although for the

Table 4.1 Relationship between elasticity of demand, price change, and revenue

Price ↑	Revenue ↑	Revenue ↑	Revenue unchanged	Revenue ↓	Revenue ↓
Price ↓	Revenue ↓	Revenue ↓	Revenue unchanged	Revenue ↑	Revenue ↑
Name	Perfectly inelastic $\varepsilon_D = 0$	relatively inelastic $0 < \varepsilon_D < 1$	unit elastic $\varepsilon_D = 1$	relatively elastic $1 < \varepsilon_D < \infty$	perfectly elastic $\varepsilon_D = \infty$
Diagram					

Hint: I for inelastic.

relationship between a good's own price and the quantity of that good demanded, we expect it to be negative since a price increase (decrease), will, *ceteris paribus* lead to a decrease (increase) in the quantity demanded. An increase (decrease) in the price of a competing good will however, *ceteris paribus*, lead to an increase (decrease) in the demand for the good, yielding a positive sign. The sign for some attributes, such as the individual's characteristics, can be ambiguous. For example, if an individual's income increases, we cannot suggest a positive sign; it all depends on the status of the good in relation to other ways of spending the increased income. For example, if the good is 'first class travel by air', we might expect a positive income elasticity; if the good is discount economy travel by air, we might expect a negative income elasticity (assuming that the decision to consume air travel has already been taken).

4.3.1 The range of elasticity measures

A number of elasticity concepts have been mentioned in the previous paragraph. It is useful to formally summarize the set of measures. We can classify elasticities in terms of 'relationships', magnitude of change, applicable time period, and travel-specific versus commodity demand. There are two relationships—direct (or own) and cross. A direct (*cross*) elasticity measures the relationship between a percentage change in the level of an attribute of a travel alternative X (*travel alternative Z*) and the percentage change in the quantity demanded of X, *ceteris paribus*. The general definition can be formally written as a mathematical expression, once we have decided whether the size of the change in the attribute is 'small' or 'large'. The determination of size is essentially decided in terms of whether the change produces the same elasticity value by using the 'before' attribute level or the 'after' attribute level. If the answers are different then it is assumed that the change is non-marginal and a formulation is required which takes into account both the before and after levels of an attribute. This distinction pro-duces a point (or marginal) elasticity and a non-marginal elasticity often called an arc, mid-point, or shrinkage ratio elasticity. A point elasticity can be derived by using limit theory in calculus and taking the partial derivative of quantity demanded with respect to price, and multiplying the result by the ratio of the before price (P_b) and before quantity demanded (Q_b). The non-marginal elasticity involves measurement of the price and quantity demanded before and after the change. When the change in price is non-marginal, there are a number of alternative ways of incorporating the information along the continuum of the range of the price change. A point elasticity is always a special case of the more general non-marginal elasticity. Thus if one were to apply a non-marginal elasticity formula (see below) to a very small change, one might expect the answer to be (almost) identical to the point elasticity estimate.

The point elasticity is mathematically $\varepsilon_p = (\partial Q_d / \partial P) * (P_b / Q_b)$. Where do we obtain $\partial Q_d / \partial P$ from? The most common source is a statistical model. For example, if we define a very simple linear travel demand model of the form: number of public transport trips demanded (Q_d) = $\beta_0 + \beta_1 * P$, then $\partial Q_d / \partial P = \beta_1$. β_1 is the taste weight (commonly called a parameter or coefficient) which defines the impact of a one-unit change in public transport fares on the change in the quantity demanded. For example, if β_1 is -0.35, Q_d is three trips per week, and P_b is \$2 per trip, the direct (own) point price elasticity of demand for public transport travel is -0.233. Thus a one percentage increase (decrease) in fares will, *ceteris paribus*, lead to a 0.233 percentage decrease (increase) in the number of public transport trips demanded. For a small change, typically up to 10% in some markets such as the commuting market, a 10% increase (decrease) in fares will, *ceteris paribus*, produce a 2.33% reduction (increase) in the number of public transport trips. More complex statistical models can be specified to account for the presence of competing alternatives as well as non-linearity in the relationship between demand and price. Some examples of such functional forms are given in Table 4.2 together with their elasticity formula. Models M2 and M3 are the most interesting. M2 recognizes that the price

Table 4.2 A selection of elasticity formulae derived from alternative functional forms for the travel demand model

Model	Definition	Functional form	Direct elasticity
M1	Double logarithmic	$\ln Q_d = \beta_0 + \beta_1 * \ln P$	β_1
M2	Non-linear price effect	$Q_d = \beta_0 + \beta_1 * P + \beta_2 P^2$	$(\beta_1 + 2\beta_2 P) * (P_b/Q_b)$
M3	Interactive alternatives	$Q_{dx} = \beta_0 + \beta_1 * P_x + \beta_2 P_x P_z$	$(\beta_1 + \beta_2 P_z) * (P_b/Q_b)$
M4	Strictly linear	$Q_{dx} = \beta_0 + \beta_1 * P_x$	$\beta_1 * (P_b/Q_b)$

elasticity of demand is itself a function of the level of own price. Depending on the sign and magnitude of β_3 the elasticity of demand could change at a decreasing or increasing rate as prices increase or decrease. Model M3 by contrast allows for the possibility that the price of one alternative, P_x, is not independent of the price of a competing alternative, P_z.

When the change is non-marginal, we have a choice of at least two specifications as a replacement for $\partial Q_d/\partial P$ and P_b/Q_b. The shrinkage ratio (sometimes called the line elasticity or loss ratio) evaluates the percentage change around the 'before' price and quantity demanded. It is mathematically defined as $\varepsilon_{sr} = \{(Q_a - Q_b)/Q_b\}/\{(P_b - P_a)/P_b\}$, equivalent to $\{(Q_a - Q_b)/(P_b - P_a)\} * (P_b/Q_b)$. In this formula, a change from P_b to P_a is not equivalent to a change from P_a to P_b. This specification assumes a linear curve over the price and quantity changes, and hence takes the alternative descriptor 'line elasticity'.

The arc or mid-point elasticity eliminates differences between elasticities in the two directions. This is a convex curve at a constant value of the price elasticity. It is mathematically defined as $\varepsilon_{sr} = \{(Q_a - Q_b)/[0.5*(Q_b + Q_a)]\}/\{[0.5*(P_b + P_a)]/\{(P_a - P_b)\}$, equivalent to $\{(Q_a - Q_b)/(P_b - P_a)\} * \{(P_b + P_a/(Q_b + Q_a)\}$. The arc elasticity can be calculated from a statistical model by knowing the before and after price, and the before and after quantity demanded. The 'after' quantity demanded is predicted directly from the parameterized demand model by substituting the after price into the model. If there are other attributes in the demand model then they can be held at their current level or changed as well. If they are changed then one has to be very careful in interpreting the arc elasticity since it is now confounded with an external change that is no longer part of *ceteris paribus*.

To distinguish between impacts that are due to a change in the one (primary) attribute and changes associated with multiple influences, it is common to differentiate between short-run and long-run impacts. We are, however, making the assumption that all additional influences take time to impact on the initial change in quantity demanded associated with the primary attribute. This may not be true, and requires careful judgement by the analyst in determining what sources of influence occur in the short run and which occur in the long run. The distinction is very important since short-run elasticities are often significantly lower than long-run elasticities. This is due in part to the amount of time required for the full impact of an attribute change to take effect. The differences are well illustrated in Figure 4.8, derived from a summary of the literature by Goodwin (1992) showing price elasticity becoming more elastic as travellers have more time to adjust. For

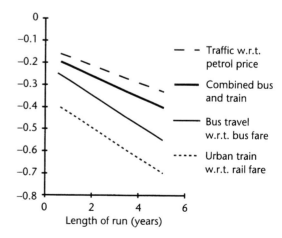

Fig. 4.8 Length of time and urban travel demand elasticities

example, for peak commuters, any response to travel price in the short run is likely to lead to a fairly quick switch between modes or public transport ticket types. In the longer run, there may be more durable responses, such as changing residential location or work pattern, resulting in a change in the total amount of peak commuter travel. Such changes are reflected in the long-run generation elasticity in addition to modal switching elasticity.

Given the range of elasticity specifications, it is useful to comment on the relationship between each of them. For very small changes in price, all measures produce similar values. For non marginal price changes, the shrinkage ratio differs considerably from the arc elasticity. For large price increases, the arc elasticity is numerically larger than the shrinkage ratio. For large price decreases, the opposite applies. Arc elasticities are generally more stable than the shrinkage ratio. In practice the shrinkage ratio is most widely used due to its simplicity, but arc elasticities are clearly more realistic for the many nonmarginal price changes.

4.3.2 The extended consideration for freight activity

In the freight sector, the selection of an appropriate elasticity measure is complicated by the distinction between travel demand and commodity demand. Travel is a derived demand, and as such is dependent on the demand for commodities. That is, the demand for freight services is derived from the demand for commodities being transported. To appreciate this important difference, we need to determine the relationship between the elasticity of travel demand and the elasticity of commodity demand in the freight sector. We will develop two scenarios—the situation where there is only one modal supplier and the situation where there are competitive alternatives.

Situation A: one supplier (eg. rail or air only): Let us define the transport price elasticity of demand as $\varepsilon_T =$ (percentage change in Q_D/percentage change in P_T), where $P_T =$ freight rate per unit of commodity shipped, $Q_D =$ number of units of commodity shipped. The percentage change in the quantity demanded depends on the relative importance of the freight rate to delivered price of commodity (i.e. $P_T/(P_T + P_C = a)$, where P_C is the free-on-board (f.o.b.) delivered price of the commodity, and the elasticity of demand for a commodity in its market (ε_D) (i.e. percentage change in delivered price = $a*$(percentage change in P_T)). If freight rates change by $S\%$, the impact on the price of commodity being shipped is aS in percentage terms. Since $\varepsilon_D =$ (percentage change in Q_D/percentage change in P_C), which also equals (percentage change in Q_D/aS), then the percentage change in quantity shipped = $\varepsilon_D\, aS$. But given that ε_T (transport demand) = (percentage change in Q_D/percentage change in P_T), then $\varepsilon_T = \varepsilon_D a$; a is typically less than 10% in practice (but this clearly varies between situations).

Situation B: existence of other suppliers (road vs. rail, road vs. air): Define the elasticity of transport (rail) demand as $\varepsilon_{RT} = 1/\Gamma(\varepsilon_{Da} - (1 - \Gamma)\,{}^*\varepsilon_{cross}$ where: $\Gamma =$ rail market share, $\varepsilon_D =$ elasticity of commodity demand, and $\varepsilon_{cross} =$ cross-elasticity of demand between rail and truck or rail and air. The total change in rail traffic due to rail rate decreases (assuming no truck retaliation) depends on the *ceteris paribus* conditions: (i) the increase in total traffic due to the rail rate decrease and (ii) the amount of traffic shifted from truck to rail.

To account for the elasticity of supply ε_S of a commodity, define $\varepsilon_D = a\{\varepsilon_S\varepsilon_D/(\varepsilon_S - \varepsilon_D\,(1 - a))\}$. The elasticity of demand for transport varies directly with the product of ε_D and ε_S, directly with a, and inversely with the sum of elasticities since $\varepsilon_D \leq 0$ and $\varepsilon_S \geq 0$. Unfortunately poor data in practice often inhibit the use of such useful formulae. We usually end up assuming (without realizing it) that ε_S approaches infinity (i.e. perfectly elastic supply) and that ε_T is independent of ε_D. If $\varepsilon_D > \varepsilon_T$ and $\varepsilon_S < a$ then ε_S tends to reduce the elasticity of demand for transport. That is, existing estimates are upward biased.

4.3.3 Deriving elasticities from other elasticities and supplementary data

The direct and cross-elasticities are important behavioural measures. For the many analysts who do not estimate their own travel demand models and who rely on published elasticities, suitable cross-elasticities are often difficult to find. The published studies tend to report direct elasticities. A simple formula enables us to identify the cross-elasticities from a knowledge of direct elasticity and other data items. The mapping is given below in the context of modal demand, but can be generalized to any demand setting such as number of trips to a destination.

$$\varepsilon_{pj} = -\varepsilon_{di} * p_i * (m_i/m_j)$$

where ε_{pj} = the cross-elasticity of demand between mode i price and mode j demand, ε_{di} is the direct price elasticity of demand for mode i, p_i is the proportion of the increase in mode i trips as a result of a price change that are diverted from mode j; m_i is the modal share for mode i, and m_j is the modal share for mode j. Determining p_i may be difficult and hence may limit the value of this approach to reconstructing missing cross-elasticities.

There is an extensive literature on empirical elasticities, summarized in great detail by Oum et al. (1992) and Goodwin (1992). Typical direct elasticities for a number of applications are summarized in Table 4.3. You will see that the range for many of the direct price elasticities is very large, and is a warning about carefully sourcing published elasticities. The differences, due to the particular context such as existing market share, attractiveness of competing modes, the discretionary versus mandatory nature of travel, the quality of data, and method of modelling, all contribute to explaining differences in the values. Nijkamp and Pepping (1998) have investigated sources of differences in public transport demand elasticities in

Table 4.3 Illustrative direct price elasticities

Setting	Low estimates	High estimates
Car use—USA short run	−0.23	−0.27
Car use—Australia short run	−0.08	−0.24
Car use—UK short run	−0.28	−0.28
Car use—USA long run	−0.28	−0.71
Car use—Australia long run	−0.22	−0.80
Car use—UK long run	−0.24	−0.71
Urban public transport—time series	−0.17	−1.32
Urban public transport—cross-section	−0.05	−0.34
Urban public transport—before/after	−0.10	−0.70
Air passenger—leisure time series	−0.65	−1.95
Air passenger—business time series	−0.4	−0.67
Air passenger—leisure cross-section	−1.52	−1.52
Air passenger—business cross-section	−1.15	−1.15
Intercity rail—business time series	−0.67	−1.0
Intercity rail—non-business time series	−0.37	−1.54
Intercity rail—business cross-section	−0.70	−0.70
Intercity rail—non-business cross-section	−1.40	−1.40
Rail freight—all commodity classes	−0.09	−1.06
Rail freight—food products	−1.04	−2.58
Rail freight—iron and steel products	−1.20	−2.54
Rail freight—machinery	−0.16	−3.50
Truck freight—all commodity classes	−0.69	−1.34
Truck freight—machinery	−0.78	−1.23
Truck freight—food products	−0.52	−1.54

the Netherlands, Finland, Norway, and the UK, and conclude that country, number of competitive modes, and type of data collected have the strongest explanatory power on the magnitude of elasticities. Thus care should be taken in comparing elasticities from different countries even when the estimation methods are the same. Cultural differences do affect sensitivity to prices and service levels. Increasingly, site-specific travel demand studies are being undertaken to gain more confidence in how the local market will respond to changes in prices and other attributes influencing travel choice and demand.

To illustrate the magnitudes of cross-elasticities, Table 4.4 summarizes the available evidence on traveller responses to changes in urban public transport fares. The findings are rather limited. Indeed authors such as Glaister and Lewis (1978) have stated that the evidence on elasticities for the impact of public transport fares on car traffic for the off-peak are largely guesswork. The cross-elasticities for rail and bus with respect to bus and rail fares are very similar, with an unweighted average value of 0.24 ± 0.06. The car-to-public transport and public transport-to-car cross-elasticities, however, are quite different.

Table 4.4 A synthesis of the empirical evidence on the cross-elasticity of urban public transport fares

Elasticity context	Result	Data type	Reference
Car use with respect to bus fares for peak work trips:			
London (1970–5)	0.06	Time series	Glaister and Lewis (1978)
Boston (1965)	0.14	Cross-section	Kraft and Domencich (1972)
Cook Country, Illinois (1961)	0.21	Cross-section	Warner (1962)
San Francisco (1973)	0.12	Cross-section	McFadden (1974)
Melbourne (1964)	0.19	Cross-section	Shepherd (1972)
Car use with respect to train fares for peak work trips:			
Sydney (1976)	0.09	Before and after	Hensher and Bullock (1979)
Car use with respect to bus and train fares for peak work trips:			
Sydney (1981)	0.06	Cross-section	Madan and Groenhout (1987)
Rail use with respect to bus fares for peak work trips:			
San Francisco (1973)	0.28	Cross-section	McFadden (1974)
London (1970–5)	0.14	Time series	Glaister and Lewis (1978)
Rail use with respect to bus fares for off-peak travel:			
San Francisco	0.28	Cross-section	McFadden (1974)
Rail use with respect to bus fares for all hours:			
London (1970–3)	0.25	Weekly time series	Fairhust and Morris (1975)
Bus use with respect to rail fare for peak work trips:			
San Francisco (1973)	0.25	Cross-section	McFadden (1974)
London (1970–5)	0.14	Time series	Glaister and Lewis (1978)
Bus use with respect to rail fares for off-peak work trips:			
London (1970–5)	0.28	Time series	Glaister and Lewis (1978)
Car use with respect to rail fares for off-peak work trips:			
San Francisco (1973)	0.13	Cross-section	McFadden (1974)
London (1970–5)	0.06	Time series	Glaister and Lewis (1978)
Bus use with respect to rail fares for all hours:			
London (1970–3)	0.25	Time series	Fairhurst and Morris (1975)

The average cross-elasticity of car demand with respect to bus fares is 0.09 ± 0.07; and with respect to train fares it is 0.08 ± 0.03. These values are significantly higher for travel to central city destinations where the propensity to use public transport is greater (i.e. higher initial modal share).

This evidence is based on studies using data collected primarily in the 1970s. The studies from which the reported cross-elasticities are drawn do not consider the variations in cross-elasticities with respect to ticket type, trip length, or time of day. Table 4.5 provides recent evidence on direct and cross-price elasticities by ticket type for Sydney. The direct elasticities are given as the bold diagonal numbers and the off-diagonal estimates are cross-elasticities. The latter are read by column; for example, if we can reasonably assume a fixed total demand for commuting trips, a 10% increase in bus TravelTen will lead to a 1.31% reduction in the share of trips by bus TravelTen, and a 0.19% increase in the share of trips using a bus single ticket, *ceteris paribus*. The estimates in Table 4.4 that distinguish time of day refer to modal substitution within that period, not substitution of travel by a given mode between times of the day. Using unpublished data from a number of US consultant cross-section studies, Ecosometrics (Mayworm *et al.* (1980) have made estimates of peak/off-peak fare cross-elasticities ranging between 0.03 and 0.38 for peak demand elasticity with respect to off-peak fares, and 0.02 and 0.03 for off-peak demand elasticity with respect to peak fares. The wide range for peak demand elasticities with respect to off-peak fares compared to the off-peak elasticity suggests that there is greater flexibility in switching from the peak to the off-peak than vice versa. This appears counter-intuitive and begs further empirical investigation.

4.3.4 Valuing the trade-offs between attributes influencing demand

An important output of travel choice and demand studies is the determination of the marginal rate of substitution (or trade-off) between any pair of attributes influencing demand. Knowing the taste weights attached to each attribute enables the analyst to quantify this trade-off. If one of the attributes is price then it is possible to establish the value of one unit of the non-price attribute in dollars. Examples of such valuations include the value of travel time savings (in vehicle, walk, wait, and transfer), the value of noise reduction, the value of transaction time savings, the value of improvements in vehicle fuel efficiency, and the value of service reliability (measured by the variability in delivery time).

The great majority of research in transportation on valuation has focused on travel time savings. This is

Table 4.5 A full matrix of direct and cross-elasticities for urban commuting, Sydney 1996

Travel	Elasticity of demand with respect to fare or travel cost by:						
	TRAIN			BUS			CAR
By mode and fare type	Single	Weekly	TravelPass (BFT)	Single	TravelTen	TravelPass (BFT)	
Train single	−0.228	0.000	0.000	0.066	0.010	0.000	0.217
Weekly	0.000	−0.167	0.000	0.000	0.000	0.003	0.141
TravelPass (BFT)	0.000	0.000	−0.212	0.000	0.004	0.000	0.344
Bus single	0.037	0.000	0.000	−0.340	0.019	0.008	0.212
TravelTen	0.007	0.000	0.001	0.024	−0.131	0.011	0.193
TravelPass (BFT)	0.000	0.009	0.000	0.011	0.012	−0.097	0.066
Car	0.010	0.030	0.006	0.018	0.013	0.004	−0.094

in large measure due to the importance of time savings in many transport investments, which typically represent over 70% of the direct benefits to users of transport facilities. We draw on the literature on the valuation of travel time savings (VTTS) to introduce the way in which attributes are valued; but the approach is generalizable to all attributes influencing the transport context being studied.

4.3.4.1 Travel time as a commodity

The realization that time is a scarce resource which affects the demand for market goods and services, just like the allocation of scarce money resources, suggests that time is an important input in consumption activities. It is also a factor in production activity (i.e. work). The use of time in 'nonproductive' activities thus involves an opportunity cost that must be valued. Theories of time allocation form a natural framework within which to derive a theoretical measure of VTTS. Key ideas are presented below. More detail may be found in many sources such as Hensher (1997) and Jara Diaz (1998).

Time can be viewed as a commodity because it can generate utility directly for the individual when 'consumed' in specific activities. But at the same time, it also acts as a *means for the consumption* of market goods and services, just as money is a means for the purchasing (and hence consumption) of these goods and services. In its role as a commodity, time in a specific activity i is not the same commodity as time in another activity j. The individual's utility function can be expressed as:

$$U = U(x_1, T_1, x_2, T_2, \ldots, x_n, T_n) \qquad (4.1)$$

where $\{T_1, \ldots, T_n\}$ is the time spent in activities 1 to n, and $\{x_1, \ldots, x_n\}$ are market goods and services consumed jointly with time in the activities. 'Commodities' denote market goods and/or services and/or time inputs into activities, the latter defined in terms of inputs rather than 'output'. In its role as a means for the consumption of goods and services, x_i, time is subjected to a resource constraint:

$$\sum_{i=1}^{n} T_i \leq T_0 \qquad (4.2)$$

Similarly, the means for purchasing the x_i's are also subjected to a resource constraint:

$$\sum_{i=1}^{n} p_i x_i \leq M \qquad (4.3)$$

Time consumption in many activities is not entirely a matter of an individual's own free will. So in addition to the time-resource constraint (4.3), there are time consumption constraints:

$$T_i \geq a_i x_i; \; i = 1, \ldots, n \qquad (4.4)$$

These constraints include technological and institutional constraints. Examples of technological constraints are the available set of transport modes that have limits on the combinations of travel times and costs that can be offered. An example of an institutional constraint is the legal speed limit. The application of microeconomic theory recognizes these limits imposed on a solution to the value of transferring time.

To establish the trade-off between time and price, we have to define the consumer's optimization problem as that of maximizing utility subject to the time and money resource constraints and the time consumption limit, as follows (using a standard technique referred to as Lagrange Multiplier which specifies the objective function and the set of three budget and time consumption constraints):

$$L = U(\underline{x}, T) + \mu(T^\circ - \sum_i T_i) + \lambda(M - \sum_i p_i x_i) + \sum_i \kappa_i(T_i - a_i x_i) \qquad (4.5)$$

The first-order conditions for maximum utility are required to establish the marginal rate of substitution between time and money, noting that $\partial U/\partial z$ is the marginal utility of attribute z:

$$\frac{\partial U}{\partial x_i} = \lambda p_i + \kappa_i a_i \qquad (4.6)$$

$$\frac{\partial U}{\partial T_i} = \mu - \kappa_i \qquad (4.7)$$

$$\frac{\partial U}{\partial M} = \lambda \qquad (4.8)$$

$$\kappa_i(T_i - a_i x_i) = 0 \qquad (4.9)$$

To derive the value of travel time savings we divide (4.7) by (4.8).

$$\frac{\partial U/\partial T_i}{\partial U/\partial M} = \frac{\mu - \kappa_i}{\lambda} \qquad (4.10)$$

This identifies the marginal rate of substitution between commodity-time T_i and the numeraire good at constant (maximum) utility level. It is referred to as *value of time as a commodity in activity i*. The difference between $\frac{\mu}{\lambda}$ and $\frac{\mu - \kappa_i}{\lambda}$ is binding if $T_i = a_i x_i$, and hence $\kappa_i \neq 0$. This difference is referred to as the *value of saving time consuming x_i* or value of time-saving in activity i (DeSerpa 1971). This gives us the *shortfall in value* that can be obtained from a unit of time spent in activity i. If an individual is completely free to spend time in activity i, then he will only spend the amount T_i such that at the margin its value is equal to its shadow price (μ/λ). The shadow price is the marginal price of time as a resource if it is homogeneous such that its value is the same in all activities, in which case maximum utility can be obtained from this activity. If one is constrained to spend at least a minimum amount of time ($a_i x_i$) in this activity, and *assuming* that this minimum level *exceeds* the level at which the individual derives the optimal value from time consumption, then the marginal value obtained from time is less than its shadow price (optimal value). The difference is the *loss* in value (utility) of time spent in this activity. This is the value of time *savings*. If the individual could save this marginal unit of time, she could *potentially* save this value from being lost. The *actual* value of the saving, however, depends on where the unit of saved time is spent. If it is spent in a leisure activity (defined as one that has a non-binding time consumption constraint), then actual saving equals potential saving. If it is spent in an 'intermediate activity', of which travel is a good example (defined as one which has a binding time consumption constraint), then the actual saving in value would be less than the potential saving (κ_i/μ). Armed with this theoretical framework, we can now seek out ways to quantify the value of travel time savings (VTTS).

4.3.5 Identifying the empirical elements of the value of travel time savings

The value of travel time savings has been shown to have two components: an opportunity cost component reflecting the economic value of the resources associated with the 'consumption' of time (referred to as the shadow price of time), and a relative (dis)utility component reflecting the alternative circumstances under which a unit of time is 'consumed'. For example, 10 minutes spent waiting for public transport engenders greater disutility to a traveller than 10 minutes travelling in public transport or a car. A two-hour freight delivery time every day over a month for the same trip engenders lower disutility than a daily average of two hours with a monthly variation of 90 minutes to three hours. The amount of time resource is the same and hence the opportunity cost is equivalent. This important distinction, linked back to the theoretical model, has been translated into an appropriate empirical model of consumer (or traveller) behaviour choice by Truong and Hensher (1985) and Bates (1987) of the form:

$$V_i = a_i - \lambda C_i - \kappa_i T_i \qquad (4.11)$$

where V_i represents the (indirect) utility expression associated with mode i, a_i is a constant measuring the average influence of the unobserved influences on choice of mode i, C_i is the monetary cost of using mode i, and T_i is the travel time associated with mode i. Importantly the parameter λ associated with money cost is independent of mode i; in contrast the parameter estimate κ_i associated with travel time is dependent on the particular mode. The latter reflects the different circumstances under which travel time is consumed in the use of each mode (e.g. train vs. bus vs. car; truck vs. rail). The value of travel time savings is given by κ_i/λ. If the shadow price of time (time being a scarce resource) and its actual value in a specific activity are the same, then κ_i/λ equals μ/λ. That is, the relative disutility of travel time is zero.

The important implication of this derivation of an empirical indirect utility expression (4.11) from economic theory as applied in a mode choice context above is that it is not possible to identify the resource value of travel time unless we can assume that the relative disutility associated with spending time on alternative modes of transport is zero. What we can measure is the value of transferring time from activity i to some non travel activity. To be able to separate out the resource price of time from the value of saving time, we would need to know a priori the resource price of time. Treating the differences in mode-specific values of transferring time (due to different parameter estimates for each mode) as zero (i.e. by constraining the parameters to be identical across the modes) is not a mechanism for obtaining a resource value, without imposing the strong assumption that the marginal (dis)utility of time spent travelling is zero, in contrast to it being constant for all modal alternatives.

The value of travel time savings presented above is strictly a behavioural value, derived from a trade-off of the relative importance of time and money to a representative individual in a pre-defined market segment (e.g. commuters, shoppers, intercity business travellers, freight shippers). We can quantify λ and κ_i by collecting data from a sample of passenger or freight activities of the components of travel time and cost associated with competing modes for a specific trip. By observing the mode that is chosen, which reveals a preference for a particular mode, we can estimate a travel choice model (see Sect. 4.4) and hence derive the behavioural VTTS.

To obtain appropriate values of the cost to society of time resources consumed in travel we have to adjust these behavioural values. Assuming that the opportunity cost associated with the time resource is suitably measured by the (competitive) market price, and that market prices are often distorted true resource (shadow) prices due to the presence of a number of externalities, practice has involved some limited adjustments to allow for distortions created by taxation (see Sect. 4.3.7). Other distortions have not been considered (such as regulations, price capping, etc.), with the consequence that best estimates of the *social* value of travel time savings derived from utility-maximizing behaviour is often assumed to approximate the behavioural values of travel time savings. Before discussing resource corrections, we

introduce another paradigm for valuation that is appealing in the context of trade-offs between travel and work.

4.3.6 **The production cost approach**

Hensher (1977) suggested an alternative approach to deriving the value of travel time savings for work-related travel. The approach recognizes a number of components of opportunity cost and relative disutility. Traditionally, an alternative to the behavioural approach to travel time savings valuation in the work-travel context was the adoption of marginal productivity theory which states that an employer can be expected to employ labour up to the point at which the total costs of employment equate with the value of production. The value of working travel time savings is then estimated as equal to the gross wage rate (including on-costs, i.e. those costs incurred by an employer in addition to the gross wage) plus a marginal wage increment to allow for any savings in overheads associated with a worker travelling in contrast to spending the equivalent time in the office. This approach makes questionable assumptions about the transfer of travel time to other purposes, it neglects possible productive use of in-travel time (particularly at the marginal rate), and ignores the utility to the worker of time spent at work compared to travelling.

A revised interpretation of the productivity approach to the valuation of savings in travel time associated with work-related travel (or more specifically any travel which is related to the generation of income) was developed by Hensher (1977) in the context of business air travel. The approach has been applied since in the context of commercial car travel in Sweden, the Netherlands, and the UK. There are four main elements of the formula—a productivity effect, a relative disutility cost, a loss of leisure time, and any compensation transfer between employer and worker. These components are combined into the following formula:

$$VTTS = (1 - r - pq) * MP + \frac{1-r}{1-t} * VW + \frac{r}{1-t} * VL + MPF \tag{4.12}$$

where r = proportion of travel time saved which is used for leisure; p = proportion of travel time saved at the expense of work done while travelling; q = relative productivity of work done while travelling compared with the equivalent time in the office; MP = the marginal product of labour; VL = the value to the worker of leisure relative to travel time; VW = the value to the worker of work time while in the office relative to travel time; MPF = the value of extra output generated due to reduced fatigue; and t = worker's personal tax rate, the inflation of rVL and $(1-r)VW$ reflecting compensation. An employer has to compensate a worker for travel, in terms of travel time savings rather than increased income, to allow for the fact that increases in the worker's utility are not subject to tax.

VL is the traditional behavioural value of travel time savings associated with trading travel time with leisure (i.e. non-work) time, obtained from equation (4.11). The traditional category of business/commercial car travel is usually reserved for 'travel as part of work'. However, a significant amount of work-related travel involves activities such as driving to the airport or a client's office. Since a high percentage of the travel time associated with the latter activity occurs outside *normal* working hours (i.e. the person would not be travelling at this time during the normal period of work expected by the employer), there is a leisure time trade-off being made. The value of travel time savings in some work-related circumstances thus can be expected to be lower than the average gross wage rate, reflecting the mix of both employer time and non-work time.

In applying this formula to business air travel, Hensher (1997) concluded that the value to the employer of saving an hour of travelling time is less than the full wage rate, and typically around 70% of the average gross wage rate. Unpublished studies undertaken by The Hague Consulting Group in 1994 in the Netherlands, the UK and Sweden, using Hensher's model (Hensher 1977) provide supporting evidence for business values of travel time savings being significantly less than the gross wage rate. Overall, the value to the employer of savings in car travel times in the UK is approximately 50% of the average gross wage rate, 61% in the Netherlands, and

32% in Sweden. The lower Swedish value is attributable to greater productivity in the car (especially due to high growth in mobile phones).

4.3.7 Adjusting behavioural values for non-resource elements and equity considerations

In deciding on a practical resource value we have to establish the nature of the alternative use activity. Rather than assume that all travel time saved is associated with one particular activity (e.g. work or leisure), a lot of time saved in travel involves a mixture of trading off leisure-travel and work-travel. For example, an individual travelling between Los Angeles and San Francisco by air on business is likely to travel during a period in which the alternative time use would be partly leisure and partly work time.

There is a continual need to identify typical circumstances in which various trips involve time that is a mix of leisure and work time. One way of helping the process is to focus on elasticities such as of hours worked with respect to the gross wage rate and the response of hours worked and that taken in leisure as a result of savings in travel time. Forsyth (1980) discusses this issue. The extent to which time savings are associated with changes in leisure time, work time, and wage rates is critical to the selection of the final resource values for *working time* values. The possibility of time savings for a work-related trip being associated with a mix of leisure and work time makes the use of the phrase 'value of *working* time savings' somewhat ambiguous. Current practice is adopted in part for convenience and in part due to the paucity of empirical evidence on the mix of alternative use time between leisure and work time.

For all work-related activities (i.e. travel taking place during time that is contributing to the productive output of a business), marginal productivity theory suggests that the value of output to an employer is its return net of any indirect tax, and the cost of labour to the employer is its price (including on-costs) inclusive of income tax. If the resource cost of labour is its price in employment before the removal of income tax, then it is traditionally valued before indirect taxation is added. When work-related travel time, such as a business trip to the airport or to a client's location, occurs during a period commonly thought of as leisure time, a weighted average of the appropriate work and non-work values should be used.

The weights represent the proportions of time in and out of *normal* working hours. In the majority of studies, all such time has been assumed to occur during normal working hours. Defining normal working hours in respect of alternative time use is quite difficult for some groups in the community. The criteria for determining whether a traveller in saving time is actually trading with leisure time (non-work time) or work time should be determined according to whether the transferred time is converted to an income-generating activity which is subject to tax or not. The use of elasticities is the correct way of determining the substitution mix.

For non-working or 'leisure' time, the willingness to trade time for money approach assumes that the traded money would have been spent on goods that carry indirect taxation. The resources associated with the time trade are thus equal to the expenditure less the indirect taxation. Therefore, non-working time savings should be valued at the behavioural value adjusted by the inverse of (1 + the average rate of indirect taxation). The taxation adjustment is normally applied to an equity value of time savings; that is, a behavioural value which treats everyone as if they had the same mean income, although this is not an approach which should necessarily be recommended. Where the rate of indirect taxation differs widely between alternative use activities, then the application of an average rate will be grossly misleading. Some attention is required to be paid to the distribution of actual rates of indirect taxation to establish if this really matters empirically.

The empirical challenge is in establishing the extent of leisure–travel and work–travel substitution. If we had appropriate elasticities, we could use them to 'weight' the respective leisure and work time values to obtain a weighted average VTTS for the particular application context. Since there is likely to be a distribution of combinations of leisure and work

trading situations, from a practical point of view we could select an *average from the distribution*.

There is a view that for non-working time the behavioural value of time savings should be the same for all modes/routes and trip purposes. The resulting equity value is consistent with the position that the scarce investment dollar should not be directed towards projects that are more likely to benefit individual travellers with a higher willingness to pay simply because they have a greater ability to pay. This argument rests on the proposition that the value of travel time savings is a function of personal income. Although the empirical evidence on the relationship between VTTS and personal income is controversial, despite its theoretical appeal, equity 'behavioural' values of travel time savings can be derived from the behavioural values for non-working time. If equity values are used, then the resource value for non-working time should be derived from this equity value.

4.3.8 Updating time values over time

Updates of time savings values are typically based on kilometre-weighted average gross personal income for the relevant trip purposes and modes. Hours travelling are preferred to kilometres travelled, to allow for the differential influence of traffic congestion. For working time, the marginal wage increment has to be updated to allow for changes in the cost of employment-related 'add-ons'. If the pattern of trip-lengths for different income groups is likely to change through time; for example, the low income trips become longer and the high income trips become shorter, then it is possible that the real value of time savings could decline. This appropriate updating procedure is an added burden because of the general absence of reliable data on kilometres travelled, particularly when it has to be income-related.

Table 4.6 summarizes indicative Australian values of travel time savings. They are not recommended for general application; instead we would encourage location-specific studies to reveal appropriate

Table 4.6 Indicative values of travel time savings per person: an Australian summary (1999 dollars)

I. Non-work Urban/local non-urban	Behavioural		Resource	
	in vehicle	out of vehicle	in vehicle	out of vehicle
Commuter by private car	4.65	12.50	4.08	10.96
Commuter by company car	7.87	21.20	6.90	18.60
Social/recreation as driver or passenger	3.40	8.50	3.00	7.40
Commuter by private car as passenger	3.25	9.40	2.85	8.25
Commuter train	3.36	10.08	2.95	8.77
Commuter bus	4.45	8.50	3.87	7.40
Long distance city pairs: non-business	7.45	16.00	6.53	13.91

II. Work (i.e. trips made in the course of work)	Employer behavioural value	Resource value
Urban (car) travel as part of work long distance	12.25	20.8
city pairs [air, car]	28	47.6

III. Non-work equity values [1]		
In-vehicle time	4.54	
Out-of-vehicle time	13.42	

Note: [1] Assuming average annual gross income of $35,000 with 2,000 annual hours worked.

behavioural values. The effective average rate of indirect tax is assumed to be 14%. It is calculated from the ratio of indirect taxes less subsidies to gross domestic product at market prices. Company taxes are based on (a flat rate of) 36 cents in the dollar.

A number of studies have investigated the influence of travel time reliability and traffic congestion on VTTS (e.g. Hensher *et al.* 1989; Senna 1994; Calfee and Winston 1998). To illustrate the heterogeneity of VTTS, we designed a stated choice experiment and implemented it in New Zealand in 1999 as a computer-based survey instrument to capture the influence of the composition of travel time as variations around the levels observed in real car driving markets (i.e. revealed preference (RP) data). We focus on travel time defined by the time under free-flow conditions (i.e. not slowed by other traffic), time that is slowed up by other traffic (but faster than stop/start/crawling), and time associated with stop/start/crawling conditions. In addition we identify the extra time (i.e. contingency) that needs to be allo-

cated to be reasonably sure of arriving at a destination by a set time (i.e. the measure of destination arrival time reliability). The time composition is traded in the choice experiment against car running costs and toll charges. Stated choice experiments are discussed in detail in Louviere *et al.* (2000), but an example of a survey screen is provided in Figure 4.9.

The values of travel time savings (VTTS) obtained from a multinominal logit model (as discussed in a later section) are summarized in Tables 4.7 and 4.8 and refer respectively to local (i.e. urban) travel and long-distance travel. There are three model specifications: model 1 in which time and cost are each treated as homogeneous, model 2 in which time is disaggregated but cost is not, and model 3 in which both time and cost are disaggregated into their heterogeneous components. The following comments will assist the reader in an assessment of the evidence:

1. The door-to-door VTTS in which we treat all time as homogeneous (essentially an

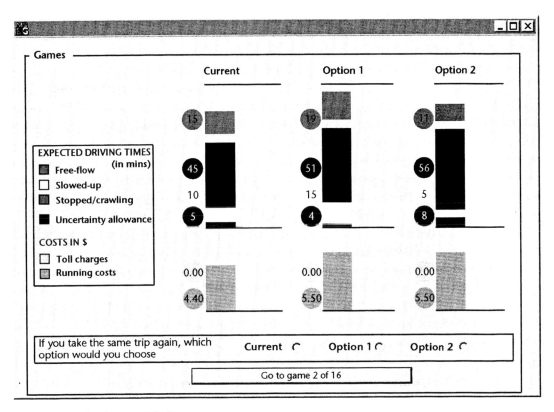

Fig. 4.9 An example of a stated choice screen

unweighted average across all components of time) varies from a high of $NZ10.96 per person hour for local commuters to $NZ5.06 for long-distance (over 3 hours) social-recreation trips.

2. This study has excluded business trips; the closest trip purpose we have to business travel is the journey to work. We might expect it to have the highest value. If we limit the comparison to the four main segments, we find values of $NZ10.96 (local commuter), $NZ5.99 (local non-commuter), $NZ9.12 for long distance (less than 3 hours), and $NZ6.97 for long distance (over 3 hours).

3. We expect local commuting values to be greater than local non-commuting values. The ratio of the two values is 1.83, within the range of a priori expectations and previous experience. The long-distance values are interesting and suggest that the value of travel time savings decreases as trip length increases. When we look at the values

for each trip-purpose segment for long-distance travel we find systematically higher estimates for the shorter distances across all trip purposes. That is, for the shorter distances we have $NZ7.28 for visiting friends and relatives (VFR), $NZ9.50 for social-recreation trips, $NZ8.69 for shopping; for the longer distances we have $NZ6.27 for VFR, and $NZ5.06 for social-recreation trips.

4. When we include two cost attributes we introduce the challenging issue of which one to use to identify values of travel time savings. There are sound theoretical arguments for distinguishing types of costs that are differential in the way they are perceived and processed. In particular, a toll is expected to be associated with a benefit in travel time, whereas an increase in running costs is not. Furthermore, a toll is lumpy and quite noticeable in contrast to running costs,

although as we introduce electronic tolling with EFTPOS, this differential breaks down.

5. The values of travel time savings are systematically greater for local travel when using the toll in contrast to running cost parameter estimates and inversely for long-distance trips. This makes good sense, reflecting the fact that the toll is a higher proportion of costs in local trips and the inverse in long-distance trips. Importantly though, when we compare the ratio of each time attribute to free-flow time (e.g. slowed-down time to free-flow time), they are identical for both the toll-based and running cost-based values.

6. In all circumstances, there is an intuitively plausible relativity between the values of time savings for free-flow time, slowed-down time, and stop/start time. We expect the values to increase from free-flow time through to stop/start time and this is exactly what happens. The ratios of each time value component relative to free flow supports the a priori theory that the value of travel time savings increases as the quality of travel time deteriorates away from free-flow time.

7. The ratios of 'slowed-down time to free-flow time' and 'stop/start to free-flow time' for local commuters are respectively (subject to rounding) 1.0 and 2.25. The equivalent ratios for local non-commuting, long distance (up to 3 hours) and long distance (over 3 hours) are respectively 2.7/4.5, 3.5/7, and 2/2.4.

8. These ratios are intuitively plausible and suggest a number of implications. First, although local non-commuters have lower values of time savings than local commuters for all categories of time, they place a much higher *relative* value on delays compared to free-flow travel than do commuters. This is due principally to the people visiting friends and relatives in contrast to those undertaking a social-recreation trip (where the ratios for the latter are very similar to local commuters). The highest ratios are for long-distance travel up to 3 hours where we also note the highest absolute values of travel time savings for slowed-down time ($NZ13.68–22.31 depend-

ing on cost source) and stop/start time ($NZ25.64–41.86).

9. Slowed-down time is valued more on long-distance trips compared to local trips except for local VFR. The same applies for stop/start time. The argument seems to be that for long-distance trips, much of which are free flow and which are also undertaken relatively less frequently, any delays are more likely to be *unexpected*, and so the relative disutility is higher compared to local trips. Local commuter trips in particular experience a higher amount of expected delay for which there appears to be greater tolerance and thus lower time savings values for the lower quality time.

10. Uncertainty is defined as the extra time one would need to allow for a trip to be reasonably confident about arriving at the destination at a particular time. The value of contingency time savings as a measure of uncertainty varies from a low of $NZ3.70 per person hour for local non-commuter to $NZ8.76 per person hour for long-distance trips over 3 hours.

11. It is common practice to express values of time savings as a percentage of average personal income expressed in terms of the average wage rate, using 2,000 hours per annum as the typical working year. We have presented the values as a percentage of a relevant sub-sample's average wage rate. We see that the values, all non-business related, are within a range that is normally accepted. In particular, the local commuter value is 68.9% of the average wage rate, the local non-commuter value is just under 50% of the average wage rate, the two long-distance values (up to 3 hours and over 3 hours) are respectively 63.6% and 43.5% of the average wage rate. These are all very plausible.

12. The long-distance values of time savings up to 3 hours are higher than the values for over 3 hours primarily because of social-recreation trips and the presence of shopping trips in the former segment. There are no shopping trips in the models over 3 hours.

Table 4.7 Values of travel time savings for urban travel ($ per person hour, 1999 NZ$)

Attributes	Local commuter	Local non-commuter	Local non-commuter: social-recreation	Local non-commuter: visiting friends and relatives	Local non-commuter shopping
Model 1					
Total time	10.96	5.99	6.52	6.62	5.28
As % ave. wage rate	*68.9*	*49.6*	*48.5*	*57.5*	*41.1*
Model 2					
Free-flow time	7.92	2.75	4.52	2.59	2.10[1]
Slowed-down time	8.86	7.46	5.86	10.52	6.17
Stop/start time	17.75	12.07	13.0	14.77	13.08
Uncertainty	4.92	3.70	6.31	1.28[1]	3.41
Model 3 for running cost					
Free-flow time	6.55	1.69	3.09	2.00	0.75[1]
Slowed-down time	7.17	4.69	3.90	7.54	2.44
Stop/start time	14.6	7.95	9.39	10.8	6.27
Uncertainty	4.06	2.29	4.38	0.9[1]	1.44
Model 3 tolls					
Free-flow time	7.99	2.78	4.53	2.93	1.84[1]
Slowed-down time	8.75	7.71	5.71	11.1	5.97
Stop/start time	17.9	13.07	13.74	15.8	15.3
Uncertainty	4.96	3.77	6.41	1.3[1]	3.52

Note: [1] Not statistically significant.

Table 4.8 Values of travel time savings for long-distance travel ($ per person hour, 1999 NZ$)

Attributes	Long distance (LD) > 3 hrs	LD < 3 hrs: visiting friends and relatives	LD < 3 hrs: social-recreation	LD < 3 hrs: shopping	Long distance > 3 hrs	LD > 3 hrs: visiting friends and relatives	LD > 3 hrs: social-recreation
Model 1							
Total time	9.12	7.28	9.50	8.69	6.97	6.27	5.06
As % ave. wage rate	*63.6*	*52.9*	*59.2*	*69.5*	*43.5*	*37.9*	*32.8*
Model 2							
Free-flow time	3.98	0.32[1]	5.88	7.54	3.84	4.38	1.52[1]
Slowed-down time	13.9	13.39	11.4	15.65	10.09	9.25	6.33
Start/stop time	28.49	29.44	28.33	17.97	25.95	15.51	40.9
Uncertainty	4.97	0.98[1]	9.16	7.99	8.76	9.74	7.98
Model 3 for running cost							
Free-flow time	6.18	0.62[1]	8.38	7.98	5.44	6.03	1.65[1]
Slowed-down time	22.31	22.7	16.90	16.47	15.16	13.57	6.95
Stop/start time	41.86	45.6	38.70	19.14	33.4	17.97	43.2
Uncertainty	7.69	1.42[1]	12.64	8.52	12.59	13.73	8.64
Model 3 tolls							
Free-flow time	3.78	0.36[1]	5.59	7.47	3.43	3.93	1.51[1]
Slowed-down time	13.68	13.37	11.27	15.42	9.57	8.84	6.35
Stop/start time	25.64	26.77	25.82	17.91	21.09	11.71	39.13
Uncertainty	4.7	0.83[1]	8.42	7.97	7.94	8.94	7.87

Note: [1] Not statistically significant.

4.4 Analytical tools to assist in explaining and forecasting travel demand

The ability to improve our understanding of how decisions are made in the freight and passenger markets is very dependent on the quality of data available and the methods used to analyse such data, both to explain travel behaviour today and to forecast likely behaviour in the future. This section discusses the types of data required to study travel demand and the statistical methods available to identify the important influences on travel choice and demand. Since the literature is extensive and highly analytical, the challenge is to distil the most useful elements of this material that will be beneficial to practitioners whose primary interest is in estimating models to derive policy outputs such as elasticities and marginal rates of substitution between attributes and in applying such models to provide a forecast of the future profile of travel demand. We will discuss the types of data that can be useful in explaining travel behaviour at a point in time (i.e. a single cross-section) and across time (i.e. longitudinal data such as a panel and a time series).

The most common data available are usually a single cross-section or a time series. The former is typically a compilation of data items associated with a sample of agents such as individuals, households, or organizations that have been collected at a single point in time. The latter is usually data of a more aggregate nature provided by a national agency such as a government census or statistics bureau and reported quarterly or annually for a population of individuals, households, or businesses. Both types of data have strengths and weaknesses relative to the other. In particular, a single cross-section often has richer behavioural information than a time series, enabling detailed comparisons of behaviour between the sampled agents; however the behavioural relationships are static in nature and imply some sense of established equilibrium that is portable into the future once the role of potential influences on travel demand has been determined through some statistical analysis (such as cross-tabulation and/or estimation of a travel demand model).

In contrast, a time series approach accommodates changes through time, but is by its highly aggregate nature devoid of the rich cross-sectional variations in behaviour. This potentially limits the usefulness of time series data to broad-based projection analysis at a macro level. This may be adequate for forecasts of population growth, aggregate economic indicators such as gross domestic product, and even aggregate demand for air travel out of a particular country; but it is likely to fall short when the interest is in explaining and predicting the demand shares for specific modes of transport as a consequence of a changing set of opportunities in the market as represented by the introduction of new forms of transport (e.g. high speed rail, tollroads, B-doubles, i.e. double articulated trucks) and changing levels of the attributes influencing demand. A third type of data are a panel of agents followed through time, which gives the richness of the behavioural diversity of a single cross-section and accommodates the temporal variations inherent in time series data. Such data are rare unfortunately, although a lot of good information of this type is often hidden away in organizations and never collated in a way to make it useful for travel demand analysis. As a compromise that falls short of a fully fledged panel, a series of single cross-sections linked via their commonality with a closed population (e.g. all businesses in a capital city, or all households in the same locality), known as a repeated cross-section, can provide some richness of cross-sectional and temporal variation provided one can accept some aggregation of the data into groups or cohorts in order to recognize the absence of a temporal linkage for specific sample units.

This discussion of a taxonomy of data forms reveals that the key to the usefulness of data is the richness of the representation of the true behavioural variability which exists in real markets within and between time periods, and the opportunity that specific types of data provide in being able to explain the variations in travel choice and demand by identifying systematic variations in attributes of alternatives (modes, destinations, routes, etc.) and characteristics of the decision agents.

Before discussing specific modelling strategies that draw on the available data to identify the influences on market behaviour and changes in market behaviour, it is worth reminding readers that much can be learned from simply immersing oneself in the descriptive information in a data set. Simple cross-tabulations, histograms, scatterplots, and partial correlations between the behavioural variable under study (e.g. number of kilometers travelled by a mode) and the attributes of alternatives (e.g. door-to-door travel time and cost) can reveal a large amount of useful information on what is happening in the market and what might happen if there was a change in some aspect of service or price. This is useful information in itself as a basis for formulating a set of hypotheses on cause and effect to investigate more formally in a multivariate statistical model.

We now turn to an overview of the most useful statistical tools in the case of a single cross-section and a time series. We refer the reader to Hensher et al. (1992) and Golob et al. (1997) for details on models using panels and repeated cross-sections. The two most useful analytical tools for a single cross-section are the linear regression model where the dependent variable is continuous (e.g. number of trips, kilometers travelled, expenditure on a consignment), and the multinomial logit model where the dependent variable is discrete (choice of mode, choice of freight forwarder, choice of port, choice of airline, choice of technology). Linear regression is also a suitable method for time series modelling.

4.4.1 Linear regression models

The method of linear regression is concerned with seeking out statistically significant systematic variations between one or more attributes of a good or service and/or characteristics of the sampled agent, and the travel issue under study (e.g. number of trips

per capita to a shopping centre). Underlying the regression specification is a method for revealing the taste weights (or coefficients) to be attached to each of these attributes and characteristics as the means of signalling their relevance in explaining variations in the travel issue being studied. The method commonly associated with a linear regression model is called *ordinary least squares* (OLS) regression. To illustrate the OLS approach, consider the data in Table 4.9 on the number of trips to the shops, collected from a single cross-section survey of a sample of shoppers.

The number of household shopping trips under taken on a Saturday is the dependent variable (Y_i). The prediction of Y_i is hypothesized to be a function of the number of people in household i (z_i). This is the explanatory or independent variable. A simple linear relationship between Y_i and z_i is given as equation (4.13)

$$Y_i = b_0 + b_1 z_i \qquad (4.13)$$

where the b's are taste weights (or coefficients) to be identified. Ideally, we want to determine the b's in equation (4.13) that will give predictions of the number of shopping trips (Y_i's) that are as close as possible to the actual observed number of shopping trips (Y_i's, as shown in Table 4.9). The difference or deviation between the observed and predicted number of shopping trips can be expressed mathematically as

$$\text{deviation} = Y_i - (b_0 + b_1 z_i) \qquad (4.14)$$

We need some procedure to determine the values of b_0 and b_1 that produce the smallest possible deviations relative to observed data. Such a method can be solved by a mathematical program whose objective is to minimize the sum of the square of deviations, or

$$\min y(b_0, b_1) = \sum_i (Y_i - b_0 - b_1 z_i)^2 \qquad (4.15)$$

The minimization is accomplished by setting partial derivatives equal to zero; that is:

$$\frac{\partial y}{\partial b_0} = -2 \sum_i (Y_i - b_0 - b_1 z_i) = 0 \qquad (4.16)$$

Table 4.9 Number of trips undertaken to the shops on a typical Saturday

Household number i	Number of shopping trips on Saturday Y_i	Size of household i z_i
1	3	4
2	1	2
3	1	3
4	5	4
5	3	2
6	2	4
7	6	8
8	4	6
9	5	6
10	2	2

$$\frac{\partial y}{\partial b_i} = -2\sum_i z_i(Y_i - b_0 - b_1 z_i) = 0 \qquad (4.17)$$

giving

$$\sum_i (Y_i - b_0 - b_1 z_i) = 0 \qquad (4.18)$$

$$\sum_i z_i(Y_i - b_0 - b_1 z_i) = 0 \qquad (4.19)$$

or

$$\sum_i Y_i - nb_0 - b_i \sum_i z_i = 0 \qquad (4.20)$$

$$\sum_i z_i Y_i - b_0 \sum_i z_i - b_1 \sum_i z_i^2 = 0 \qquad (4.21)$$

where n is the total number of households. Solving these equations simultaneously for b_0 and b_1 gives

$$b_1 = \frac{\sum_i (z_i - \bar{z})(Y_i - \bar{Y})}{\sum_i (z_i - \bar{z})^2} \qquad (4.22)$$

$$b_0 = \bar{Y} - b_1 \bar{z} \qquad (4.23)$$

This approach to determining the values of estimable taste weights (b's) is referred to as OLS regression. It can be shown that for the data values given in Table 4.9, the smallest deviations between the number of predicted and actual shopping trips will be given by the equation (4.23). As an exercise, the reader should substitute the relevant information from Table 4.9 into equations (4.22) and (4.23) to produce equation (4.24).

$$Y_i = 0.33 + 0.7 z_i \qquad (4.24)$$

Manual calculations using simple algebra are relatively easy when there is only one explanatory variable. When many possible influences on demand are present, as is usually the situation, taste weight values (b's) are best estimated by a computer program. The generalized formulation for establishing the vector of taste weights for an OLS model is given in matrix notation as (4.25).

$$\mathbf{B} = (\mathbf{z'z})^{-1}\mathbf{z'Y} \qquad (4.25)$$

where $\mathbf{B}$ is a vector of b_n's, $\mathbf{z}$ is a matrix of attributes and characteristics, and $\mathbf{Y}$ is the vector of dependent variables; $\mathbf{z'}$ is the transpose (in matrix algebra) of $\mathbf{z}$. Although we have identified the taste weight for household size, we cannot assume that this characteristic is a statistically significant influence on the number of Saturday shopping trips. After all, we now have identified a single taste weight that is an average for the sample. To determine if it is a good representation of the taste weights applicable to each member of the sample, we need to determine how well the range of taste weights cluster around the mean estimate of 0.7. Where the distribution of the taste weights around the mean is tight (i.e. a small variation) in contrast to loose (i.e. a high variation) we would expect that the 0.7 estimate is a more representative estimate for the sample as a whole. Tests have been developed to be able to decide this and are available in numerous statistics texts. For the practitioner they will need to be able to interpret the meaning of a t-statistic, which is the ratio of the mean estimate of a taste weight to its standard error (the latter being defined as the square root of the estimate of variance). By assuming a particular distribution for this variation around the mean, typically a normal distribution which is bell shaped and having a mean of 0 and a standard deviation of 1, we are able to compare the t-value from the model with a critical value associated with a normal distribution at the level of confidence we wish to attach to our acceptability of the estimated mean of 0.7. It is standard practice to adopt a level of confidence of 95%, which means that if the t-value is equal to or greater than 1.96 we can be 95% confident that a t-test of the null and alternative hypothesis of $b_i = 0$ instead of 0.7 is false. That is, the correct answer will be provided by using 0.7 in repeated samples. Standard statistical packages automatically calculate the standard error of the estimate for each taste weight and report the t-value.

The implied elasticity of demand for shopping trips with respect to household size can be calculated by the formula $\varepsilon = (\partial Y_d/\partial z)*(z/Y_d)$. Since equation (4.24) is linear, we can use the average value of Y and z across the sample (noting that for a non-linear model one should do the calculation for each household and then calculate a weighted aggregate mean using the number of shopping trips as the weight for each household). A non-linear model is one in which the relationship between Y and z is strictly additive and does not involve a transformation such as taking logarithms, exponentials, or even defining an explanatory variable as a quadratic (e.g. z^2). You may wish to prove that the non-linear and linear calculation are identical for this example given the form of equation (4.24). There are 32 shopping trips, or 3.2 per household, and 4.1 persons per household. $\partial Y_d/\partial z$ is equal to + 0.7 (from equation (4.24)). Thus the implied elasticity of demand for shopping trips with respect to household size is, *ceteris paribus*, (+ 0.7*4.1/3.2) or + 0.897. Hence, a 1.0% increase in household size (say from 4.1 to 4.14) will, *ceteris paribus*, increase the number of trips per household by 0.897, from 3.2 to 4.097. To identify the predicted number of trips by a household of seven members, we would simply feed 7.0

into equation (4.24) and obtain the best estimate, which is 0.33 + 0.7*7 = 5.23 trips per Saturday.

As a word of warning, equation (4.24) was estimated on a sample with household sizes varying from two to eight. In applying the model to predict shopping trips for a household, one should never go outside the range of the explanatory variables used to derive the taste weights. Such a practice is very risky and liable to lead to nonsense predictions, simply because the model is being forced to represent a type of household which was not present in the initial data. If one wants to undertake such an extrapolation, then it is necessary to collect data from a more representative sample that captures this prediction context. Where the explanatory variable of interest is an attribute of a good or service (as distinct from a characteristic of an agent) it is advisable to enrich the data on real markets with data designed into the survey through a stated choice experiment (as outlined in a later section).

4.4.1.1 The demand for automobile travel as an example of OLS

Another example is the demand for automobile use in six capital cities in Australia (Sydney, Melbourne, Brisbane, Adelaide, Perth, and Canberra) estimated using OLS regression. There are three equations in the model system for annual vehicle kilometers associated with (i) travel as part of work plus travel to/from work, (ii) other travel, and (iii) non-urban travel. Separate regression equations were estimated for each of one, two, and three-plus vehicle households. The results are summarized in Table 4.10.

Annual vehicle use is a function of the cost of operating an automobile. This attribute embodies the fuel performance of an automobile as well as the mix of city and highway driving cycle (different fuel efficiency situations). Other influences on vehicle use include the extent to which public transport is used for commuting, and the socio-economic characteristics of a household. Vehicle operating cost (OPCOST) is fully decomposed to contain information on fuel efficiency, fuel prices, and excise duties for petrol, diesel, compressed natural gas, and electric vehicles. Applications such as the imposition of a carbon tax and a congestion charge impact on the individual traveller via the operating cost of the vehicle:

OPCOST = [{cityFuel*propCityF + hwyFuel*
(1 − propCityF)}*0.01]*
[tPricePetrol*(1 − propnDiesel) +
tPriceDiesel*propnDiesel +
carbonTax*{carbLitD* propnDiesel
+ carbLitP*(1 − propnDiesel)}] +
(cTank + carbonTax*carbTAlt)/
rangealf + (cCharge +
carbonTax*carbTElc)/rangeelc

where:

cityFuel	=	city cycle fuel efficiency (litres/ 100 km.)
hwyFuel	=	highway cycle fuel efficiency (litres/100 km.)
propCityF	=	proportion of use which is in the city fuel cycle (default = 0.7)
propnDiesel	=	proportion of conventional-fuelled vehicles using diesel
tPricePetrol	=	wpricepetrol + expricepetrol (cents per litre)
wpricepetrol	=	wholesale price of petrol (cents per litre)
expricepetrol	=	excise component of price of petrol (cents per litre)
tPriceDiesel	=	wpricediesel + expricediesel (cents per litre)
wpricediesel	=	wholesale price of diesel (cents per litre)
expricediesel	=	excise component of price of diesel (cents per litre)
carbonTax	=	carbon tax (cents per kg.)
carbLitD	=	carbon per litre of diesel (kg./litre)
carbLitP	=	carbon per litre of petrol (kg/litre)
carbTElc	=	carbon per full electric recharge (kg)
carbTAlt	=	carbon per tank of alternative fuel (kg.)
cTank	=	wctank + extank (cents)
wctank	=	wholesale cost of a tank of alternative fuel (cents)
extank	=	excise component of cost of a tank of alternative fuel (cents)

cCharge	=	wccharge + excharge (cents)
wccharge	=	wholesale cost of a full electric recharge (cents)
excharge	=	excise component of cost of a full electric recharge (cents)
rangeelc	=	range of electric vehicle on a fully charged battery (km.)
rangealf	=	range of alternative-fuelled vehicle on a full tank (km.)

The equations in Table 4.10 are driven by vehicle operating cost, use of public transport for commuting, the city-specific dummy variables, and socio-economic characteristics such as household income, number of workers in a household, and the household's stage in the life cycle. Operating costs have the expected negative relationship with vehicle use with implied elasticities of vehicle use ranging from −0.04 to −0.28. In Table 4.2 we indicated that the implied elasticity in a double logarithmic model is the taste weight, and since operating cost is defined as its natural logarithm and the dependent variable as the natural logarithm of vehicle use, we can read the elasticity directly from Table 4.10. These are short-run elasticities, holding location and vehicle ownership decisions fixed. One-vehicle households appear to be the least sensitive to operating costs for commuting but the most sensitive for non-urban vehicle use. There is very little difference in sensitivity to operating costs across all three fleet sizes for other urban vehicle use. One-vehicle households which use a car for commuting appear to be constrained in terms of the opportunities for modal switching or use adjustment after allowing for the household income effect. In contrast, multi-vehicle households appear to have more opportunities including automobile switching as well as modal and time of day switching.

There are some interesting influences of life cycle on annual vehicle use. Households with no children tend to have lower vehicle kilometres for non-work related urban travel for all fleet sizes, although the influence is greater in three-plus vehicle households. Single parent families tend to have fewer non-work related urban kilometres in one-vehicle households, but do more kilometres in multi-vehicle households.

Table 4.10 Vehicle use and composition results

Variable	Units	1-vehicle Hhld	2-vehicle Hhld	3-vehicle Hhld
Sample Size		271	770	292
LVKMW Model				
Constant		9.0300 (29.26)	9.1369 (12.03)	9.0886 (22.32)
Ln (fuel cost)	c/km.	−0.08844 (1.75)	−0.2017 (−1.56)	−0.28224 (−1.87)
Household income	income in $000	0.03828 (1.75)		0.002011 (1.58)
Household income/no. of workers	$000/worker		0.0021231 (5.27)	
Probability of using public transport	0 to 1	−0.1838 (−2.01)	−0.62963 (−1.59)	−0.02478 (−1.54)
Adelaide City	1, 0	−0.2695 (3.25)		
Single-person family	1, 0		0.66966 (2.76)	
Two parent family	1, 0		0.37943 (2.12)	
No. of children	1, 0			0.22241 (1.64)
Single person	1, 0			0.53802 (2.37)
R-squared		0.10	0.10	0.11
LVKMEL				
Constant		8.5486 (24.92)	9.1156 (37.7)	8.1498 (19.32)
Household income	income in $000	−0.005235 (2.75)		
Household income/no. of workers	$000/worker		0.000396 9 (1.6)	
Ln (household income)	log of income in $000			0.074312 (1.78)
Ln (fuel cost)	c/km	−0.16499 (−2.21)	−0.16052 (-1.55)	−0.15264 (−2.01)
Single-person family	1, 0	−0.45680 (−3.23)	0.16777 (1.45)	0.28983 (1.93)
No. of children	1, 0	−0.12454 (−1.63)	0.11945 (−2.34)	−0.38300 (−2.63)
Single person	1, 0	−0.135191 (−1.6)	0.34217 (1.54)	
R-squared		0.12	0.23	0.21
LVKMCO				
Constant		7.0951 (5.31)	8.7013 (36.5)	7.0715 (18.08)
Ln (fuel cost)	log of c/km	−0.12757 (−1.78)	−0.056266 (−1.89)	−0.044317 (1.99)
Household income	income in $000	0.010919 (1.92)		
Household income/no. of workers			0.00335 (2.51)	0.00335 (2.63)
Single-person family	1, 0		−0.14893 (−1.43)	−0.14893 (−1.76)
Single person	1, 0	−0.58612 (−1.61)		
Other household life cycle			0.18614 (1.86)	0.19245 (1.65)
Adelaide City	1, 0	−0.99708 (−2.36)		
Canberra City	1, 0		0.14879 (2.13)	0.12876 (2.10)
Perth City	1, 0	−0.91783 (−1.98)	−0.06918 (−1.43)	−0.06523 (−1.57)
R-squared		0.15	0.14	0.15

Notes: t-statistics in parentheses. LVKMW = natural log of kms to and from work and urban travel as part of work, LVKMEL = natural log of kms. which are urban non-work-related, and LVKMCO = natural log of kms. which are non-urban.

The fleet size effect may be telling us a lot about lifestyle and possibly limited opportunities for such travel in the single parent household.

We evaluated the implications of modelling each city separately but found that a pooled model with city-specific dummy variables for Perth, Adelaide, and Canberra was appropriate. A city-specific (1,0) dummy attribute is called a shift effect in that it moves the relationship between vehicle use and city up or down relative to other cities. Thus a negative sign implies that vehicle use is lower in that city after accounting for all the other influences in the model. Adelaide commuters with one vehicle generally travel fewer kilometres to and from work and as part of work and out of Adelaide than do those in the other five cities. In multi-vehicle households, we see a lower average annual use for Perth households of vehicles for non-urban travel, possibly reflecting the very long distance to major inter-state locations, better served by air travel.

Finally, each model has an index of its overall explanatory power, called *R*-squared. It tells us how much of the overall variability in the dependent variable is explained by the variability in the explanatory variables. For example in Table 4.10, 23% of the variability in the natural log of urban non-work kilometres for two-vehicle households is accounted for by systematic variation in the five explanatory variables. *R*-squared varies between 0 and 1, and is an appropriate measure of overall explanatory power as long as we have a linear model. It is often used as an approximation in non-linear models.

An important warning to analysts—be careful about how much importance you might place on the magnitude of *R*-squared. The overall explanatory power in Table 4.10 varies from 0.10 (10%) to 0.23 (23%). This may not appear to be very high; yet the data is provided at the most disaggregated level possible—namely the individual's travel. At this level there is a large amount of variability in vehicle kilometres to explain across the sample. Often studies get higher *R*-squareds by using aggregate data such as the average annual kilometres per household per local government area. At such a spatial level of aggregation, there is clearly less variability in the dependent variable across a sample, and also the accompanying explanatory variables (such as average income per household in the local government area (LGA)). Across the total sample of LGAs there is consequently less variability to explain and typically the remaining variability is accounted for to a far greater degree by the aggregated explanatory variables, producing a higher *R*-squared. The comparison with the more disaggregated model is quite spurious and should be avoided. The disaggregated model is likely to be more useful in policy applications because it will be more sensitive to changes in the real levels of the explanatory variables facing each sampled member of the population. In sum-

mary, whereas the aggregated specification may reproduce existing market demand in total better than the disaggregated model, it is less useful in applications involving *changes* in the levels of explanatory variables, which is the basis of forecasting.

4.4.2 Discrete choices and multinomial logit model

Many transport decisions involve making a choice between alternative ways of travelling and moving freight. For example, the individual shopper chooses whether to go to the shops by car as a driver, by car as a passenger, by train, or by bus. The freight forwarder chooses whether to ship a consignment by road, by rail, or by sea. Not only do agents make decisions on what mode to select for a specific activity, they also make decisions on when to undertake the activity (time of day), where to go (destination), how often to undertake an activity (frequency), and what route to use. They also consider the class of travel in some circumstances—for air travel we have a choice of first, business, full economy, discount economy, off-peak, and standby; choice of single, return, weekly, and off-peak discount seasonal ticket for urban public transport; for freight movements we have express priority (over night), the next day, in five days' time, and so on. Households and businesses also make decisions on what types of vehicles they might acquire and the size of their fleet. Transport businesses decide where to locate their activities to take advantage of the efficiencies offered by alternative ports, airports, and road infrastructure, given the location of markets for their services.

All of these travel and travel-related decisions involve making a choice from among a set of available alternative ways of achieving the desired outcome. This set of alternatives is referred to as a set of mutually exclusive discrete alternatives. To explain the choices made by agents in various settings requires us to seek out an explanation for why one alternative was chosen and the other alternatives were not chosen. The literature that embodies this problem is known as discrete choice modelling.

In this section, we introduce the most commonly used statistical methods for investigating travel choices. Specialized texts provide more detail (Hensher and Johnson 1981; Ben-Akiva and Lerman 1985; Louviere *et al.* 2000). A general model of travel choice behaviour requires three key factors to be taken into account:

1. objects of choice and sets of alternatives available to decision-makers known as choice set definition,

2. the observed attributes of decision-makers and a rule for combining them, and

3. a model of individual choice specifying the distribution of behaviour patterns in the population.

4.4.2.1 A random utility model of discrete choice

It is assumed that agents compare alternatives and choose the one that provides the greatest level of satisfaction or utility. Formally, let U_{iq} be an index of utility associated with the ith alternative and the qth agent. Further assume the utility index can be partitioned into two components: a systematic component or 'representative utility', V_{iq}, which describes the role of the set of observed (or measured) attributes influencing a choice, and a random component, ε_{iq}, reflecting the agent-specific idiosyncrasies of tastes which are not observed. If we assume that these two components of utility are independent, then we can add them up to give equation (4.26).

$$U_{iq} = V_{iq} + \varepsilon_{iq} \qquad (4.26)$$

V_{iq}, subscripted q, is an index of all the observed attributes associated with alternative i which influence the choice. We have to decide on how these attributes might be represented. The simplest assumption (which can be changed in more complex models) is to define them as linear in the taste weights and additive in the attributes (often shortened to *linear additive*) as shown in equation (4.27)

$$V_{iq} \left(= \sum_{k=1}^{K} \beta_{ik}\, x_{ikq} \right) \qquad (4.27)$$

The explanatory variables, denoted by X_{ikq} vary across alternative i, and agent q. There are $k = 1, \ldots, K$ attributes. The βs are taste weights (or parameters) assumed initially to be constant across individuals (but these can vary across alternatives). That is, only taste weights and not attribute levels are independent of q. Taste weights can be allowed to vary across the sampled observations (as random rather than fixed parameters) but this adds further complexity.

The systematic component is assumed to be that part of utility contributed by attributes that can be observed by the analyst, while the random component is the utility contributed by attributes unobserved by the analyst. This does not mean that individuals maximize utility in a random manner; on the contrary individuals can be deterministic utility maximizers. Randomness arises because the analyst cannot 'peep into the head' of each individual and fully observe the set of influencing factors and the complete decision calculus; which, in turn, implies that the analyst can only explain choice up to a probability of event selection. The systematic utility maximization function can be thought of as a 'perceived maximization' function, because imperfect markets should encourage individuals to try to maximize utility to levels they perceive as maxima. This raises the interesting question of how one introduces actual levels of attribute changes in application and adjusts them for perceptual differences, given that a behavioural model should ideally be estimated on the perceived levels of attributes describing alternatives.

The above discussion provides most of the basic concepts necessary for us to formulate a travel choice model. In particular, we assume that individuals will try to choose an alternative that yields them the highest utility. Hence, the empirical structure of the utility function is critical to modelling individual choice, and represents the process by which the attributes of alternatives and individual's socio-economic environments combine to influence choice probabilities, and in turn, the predictive capability of the choice model.

The key assumption is that individual q will choose alternative i if and only if (iff)

$$U_{iq} > U_{jq} \qquad j \neq i \in A \qquad (4.28)$$

From equation (4.26) alternative i is chosen iff

$$(V_{iq} + \varepsilon_{iq}) > (V_{jq} + \varepsilon_{jq}) \qquad (4.29)$$

We can rearrange (4.29) to place the observables and unobservables together to give (4.30)

$$(V_{iq} - V_{jq}) > (\varepsilon_{jq} - \varepsilon_{iq}) \qquad (4.30)$$

The analyst does not observe $(\varepsilon_{jq} - \varepsilon_{iq})$, hence cannot determine exactly if $(V_{iq} - V_{jq}) > (\varepsilon_{jq} - \varepsilon_{iq})$. One can only make statements of choice outcomes up to a probability of it occurring. Thus the analyst has to calculate the probability that $(\varepsilon_{jq} - \varepsilon_{iq})$ will be less than $(V_{iq} - V_{jq})$. This leads to the following equation (4.31)

$$P(y_{iq} | x_q, J) = P_{iq} = P[\{\varepsilon(x_j) - \varepsilon(x_i)\} < \{V(x_{iq}) - V(x_{jq})\}]$$
$$\text{for all} \quad j \neq i, j = 1, \dots, J \qquad (4.31)$$

Equation (4.31) can be interpreted as follows. The probability that a randomly drawn individual from the sampled population, who can be described by attributes x and choice set J, will choose y_i equals the probability that the difference between the random utility of alternatives j and i is less than the difference between the systematic utility levels of alternatives i and j for all alternatives in the choice set. The analyst does not know the actual distribution of $\varepsilon(x_j) - \varepsilon(x_i)$ across the population, but assumes that it is related to the choice probability according to a distribution yet to be defined.

4.4.2.2 Imposing some structure on the random component

To be able to apply some statistical procedures to accommodate the role of $\varepsilon(x_j)$ we have to decide on how it is distributed in the sampled population of agents and across the alternatives in the choice set. We impose a very strong assumption in the first instance, which can be relaxed in more advanced specifications of discrete choice models. The assumption we will work with is that these unobserved influences are independently and identically distributed (IID) in the sampled population. To explain what we mean intuitively, imagine a sample of 100 individuals choosing between car and

train for a vacation trip. We know that there are some influences on each person's choice which we, as analysts, cannot measure and include in the model via the V index. We do not know, however, what role these unobserved influences might play for each person (indeed we might not even know what they are). So to be able to incorporate such loosely specified information we will assume that this information is randomly distributed across the 100 people according to some distribution. This distribution has a mean and a variance to define its 'shape'. Furthermore, we will simplify the task of including this information by assuming that the distribution (still to be determined) will take the same shape for each alternative—car and train (i.e. will be identically distributed), and that these distributions are independent of each other such that there is no information in the car index that is correlated with information in the train index.

This IID assumption is very strong (but testable) and has underpinned the great majority of practitioner studies incorporating a discrete choice model. Fortunately enough empirical experience has been accumulated over time to suggest that this strong assumption is very robust to violations provided the analyst includes the set of really important attributes in the index of the observed influences, and uses highly disaggregated data which is not confounded by aggregation. On the latter point we are referring to the need to measure the attributes of the alternatives (e.g. travel time and cost) such that they are the values that each agent faces and not some average across market segments of agents. Failure to include the relevant set of attributes measured at a disaggregated level increases the possibilities of violation of the IID condition. Much of the research in discrete choice modelling focuses on ways of replacing the IID condition with behaviourally more realistic assumptions. However, the gains in behavioural realism can come at the expense of increased complexity of travel choice modelling. See Louviere et al. (2000) for an overview of efforts to relax the IID assumption.

The model of equation (4.31) is called a random utility model (RUM). Unlike the traditional economic model of consumer demand, we have introduced a more complex but more realistic assumption about agent behaviour to account for the analyst's inability fully to represent all variables that explain preferences in the utility function. Now we can specify the structure of the choice model in more detail, but first we briefly recap the goal of choice modelling. Specifically, the goal of a choice model is to estimate the significance of the determinants of V_{iq} in equation (4.31). For each agent q the analyst observes an ordering of the alternatives, and from these data infers the influence of various attributes in the utility expression V_{jq}. Specification of the functional form of V_{iq} in terms of attributes (i.e. the relationship between decision attributes and observed choices) must be determined in so far as this will influence the significance of attributes. However, there is little loss of generality in assuming a linear, additive form.

The procedure developed thus far for the basic choice model only requires the analyst to observe the agent's choice and the defined choice set, not the rank order of all alternatives. Alternatively, one could observe a complete or partial ranking of alternatives, but the reliability of such information is questionable if alternatives are not frequently used. The next step is to specify a probability model for the observed data as a function of the parameters associated with each attribute, and apply probabilistic assumptions that permit adequate statistical tests. A statistical estimation technique is required to obtain estimates of the parameters associated with attributes. The approach we use to estimate the parameters of the basic choice model is called 'maximum-likelihood estimation' (MLE). Briefly, the maximum-likelihood estimates are obtained by maximizing a probabilistic function with respect to the parameters or taste weights to reveal the best set of taste weights that can explain the role of each attribute in influencing travel choice. For further details on estimation methods see Hensher and Johnson (1981) and Ben-Akiva and Lerman (1985) or any statistical text on probability theory.

In summary, choice model development proceeds in a series of logical steps:
- First, we assume that an agent q will select alternative i iff U_{iq} is greater than the level of utility

associated with any other alternative in the choice set (equation (4.29)).
- Then we calculate the probability that the individual would rank alternative i higher than any other alternative j in the choice set, conditional on knowing V_{jq} for all j alternatives in the individual's choice set. Assuming that the known value of V_{jq} is v_j, then equation (4.29) can be expressed as

$$P_{iq} = P(U_{iq} > U_{jq} | V_{jq} = v_j, j \in A_q) \, \forall \, j \neq i \quad (4.32)$$

Equation (4.32) is a statement about the probability that the unobserved random elements (ε_{iq}'s) take on a specific relationship with respect to the quantities of interest, the V_{jq}'s.
- Once an assumption is made about the joint distribution of the ε_{iq}'s, namely IID, and the V_{jq}'s are specified in terms of their taste weights and attributes, we can apply the method of maximum-likelihood estimation to estimate the empirical magnitude of the taste weights. The model form for estimation is given in (4.33)

$$P_i = \frac{\exp V_i}{\sum_{j=1}^{J} \exp V_j} \quad (4.33)$$

Equation (4.33) is the basic choice model consistent with the assumptions outlined above, and is called the multinomial logit (MNL) model.

4.4.2.3 A simple illustration of the basic model

The example focuses on the choice of means of transport to work. The data consist of $Q = 1000$ commuters, in which the choice set ($J = 4$) available to each commuter includes drive-alone car driver (*da*), ride share (*rs*), train (*tn*), and bus (*bs*). Five alternative-specific attributes (asvs) were used to specify the utility of each mode, together with personal income which is included in the utility expression for car drive alone to test whether individuals on higher incomes are more likely to choose to drive to work by themselves. In-vehicle cost was defined to be generic which means that the taste weight of X_{invc} is the same in each utility expression (i.e. $\beta_{jk} = \beta_k$ for all $j = 1, 2$). The other attributes are defined as alternative specific so that the taste weights are different for each mode. The attributes of the four modes are:

wlk = total walk time (minutes)

wt = total wait time (minutes)

$invt$ = total in-vehicle time (minutes)

$invc$ = total in-vehicle cost (cents)

pkc = parking cost (cents)

In addition, an alternative (or mode) specific constant (MSC) is included for $J-1$ alternatives. It is arbitrary which alternative the constant is excluded from. The observed components of the four utility expressions are:

$$V_{da} = \text{MSC}_{da} + \beta_{da1} * invt_{da} + \beta_1 * invc_{da} + \beta_{da3} * pkc_{da} + \beta_{da} * persinc_{da}$$

$$V_{rs} = \text{MSC}_{rs} + \beta_{rs1} * invt_{rs} + \beta_1 * invc_{rs} + \beta_{rs3} * pkc_{rs}$$

$$V_{tn} = \text{MSC}_{tn} + \beta_{tn1} * invt_{tn} + \beta_1 * invc_{tn} + \beta_{tn3} * wlk_{tn} + \beta_{tn4} * wt_{tn}$$

$$V_{bs} = \qquad + \beta_{bs1} * invt_{bs} + \beta_1 * invc_{bs} + \beta_{bs3} * wlk_{bs} + \beta_{bs4} * wt_{bs}$$

The results of maximum-likelihood estimation of the model are summarized in Table 4.11. The same interpretation of the taste weights and t-statistics applies as for the linear regression. The measure of overall goodness of fit is different to OLS because the MNL model is non-linear. The non-linearity arises because the relationship between the attributes and the probability of choosing an alternative is calculated via an exponential formula as given in equation (4.33). To determine how well the basic MNL model fits a given set of data, we would like to compare the predicted dependent variable with the observed dependent variable relative to some useful criterion. Unfortunately, this is a virtually meaningless exercise in the case of discrete choice models because we observe the actual discrete choices but the estimated model produces probabilities P_{iq}.

The log-likelihood function evaluated at the mean of the estimated taste weights is a useful criterion for assessing overall goodness-of-fit when the maximum-likelihood estimation method is used to estimate the taste weights of the MNL model. This function is used to test the contribution of particular (sub)sets of attributes. The procedure is known as the likelihood ratio test. The null hypothesis is that the probability, P_i of an individual choosing alternative i is independent of the value of the parameters in the MNL function (Table 4.11). If this hypothesis is retained, we infer that the taste weights are zero; that is, the null is that all βs in Table 4.11 are zero (except mode-specific constants). Similar to the case of testing the significance of R^2 in OLS regression, the hypothesis of independence is almost always rejected for a specific model. Thus, the usefulness of the likelihood-ratio test is its ability to test whether subsets of the βs are significant. The generalized likelihood-ratio criterion has the following form:

$$\Im = \max L\,(\omega)\,/\,\max L\,(\Omega) \qquad (4.34)$$

where $\Im$ is the likelihood ratio, $\max L\,(\omega)$ is the maximum of the likelihood function in which M elements of the parameter space are constrained by the null hypothesis. For example, in testing the significance of a set of βs in the MNL model, $L\,(\omega)$ is the maximum with these βs set equal to zero (constrained) and $\max L\,(\omega)$ is the unconstrained maximum of the likelihood function. It is well known that $-2 \ln\Im$ is approximately chi-square distributed with M degrees of freedom for large samples if the null hypothesis is true. Therefore, one maximizes L for the full MNL model, and subsequently for the model with some βs set to zero (i.e. some x's are removed). The next step is to calculate $\Im$ and see if the quantity $-2 \ln\Im$ is greater than the critical value of χ^2_M from some preselected significance level (e.g. $a = 0.05$). $\ln\Im$ is the difference between two log-likelihoods. If the calculated value of chi-square exceeds the critical value for the specified level of confidence, one rejects the null hypothesis that the particular set of βs being tested is equal to zero.

The likelihood-ratio test can be used to compare a set of nested models. A common comparison is between a model in which an attribute has a generic taste weight across all alternatives and a model in which alternative-specific taste weights are imposed. If we have four alternatives then we are comparing the overall influence of one generic taste weight and four mode-specific taste weights. After estimating two models with the same data, we can compare the log-likelihood (at convergence) for each model and calculate the likelihood ratio as $-2 \ln\Im$. This can be compared to the critical value for three degrees of freedom (i.e. three extra degrees of freedom for the

Table 4.11 Parameter estimates for the illustrative example

Attribute	Alternative	Taste weight	t-statistic
drive alone constant	drive alone	0.5879	2.32
ride share constant	ride share	0.3249	1.23
train constant	train	0.2987	1.86
in-vehicle cost (cents)	all modes	-0.002548	-2.58
in-vehicle time (mins.)	drive alone	-0.05251	-4.32
in-vehicle time (mins.)	ride share	-0.04389	-3.21
in-vehicle time (mins.)	train	-0.03427	-2.67
in-vehicle time (mins.)	bus	-0.03523	-2.75
walk time (mins.)	train	-0.07386	-3.57
walk time (mins.)	bus	-0.06392	-3.25
wait time (mins.)	train	-0.11451	-2.18
wait time (mins.)	bus	-0.15473	-4.37
parking cost (cents)	drive alone	-0.07245	-2.59
parking cost (cents)	ride share	-0.00235	-1.24
personal income ($000)	drive alone	0.03487	5.87
log-likelihood at zero	-2 345.8		
log-likelihood at constants	-2 023.7		
log-likelihood at convergence	-1 534.6		
likelihood ratio (pseudo R²)	0.346		

alternative specific variable model compared to the generic model) using a chi-squared test at say 0.05% significance. If the calculated value is greater than the critical value we can reject the null hypothesis of no statistically significant difference at 5% significance. If the calculated value is less than the critical value then we cannot reject the null hypothesis.

A *likelihood-ratio index* that can be used to measure the goodness-of-fit of the MNL model, analogous to R^2 in ordinary regression is given in (4.35)

$$\rho^2 = 1 - (L * (\hat{\beta})/L * (0)) \qquad (4.35)$$

We note from Table 4.11 that $L * (\hat{\beta})$ will be larger than $L * (0)$, but in the case of the MNL model this implies a smaller negative number, such that $L * (\hat{\beta})/L * (0)$ must lie between zero and one. The smaller this ratio, the better the statistical fit of the model (i.e. the greater the explanatory power of the x's relative to an aggregate, constant-share prediction); and hence, the larger is the quantity '1 minus this ratio'. Thus, we use ρ^2 (rho squared) as a type of pseudo-R^2 to measure the goodness-of-fit of the MNL model. Values of ρ^2 between 0.2 and 0.4 are considered to be indicative of extremely good model fits (based on extensive simulations by Domencich and McFadden

(1975) that equivalenced this range to the range 0.7 to 0.9 for a linear function). Hence, analysts should not expect to obtain ρ^2 values as high as the R^2s commonly obtained in many ordinary least squares regression applications.

The attributes in the model all have t-statistics greater than 1.96 (95% confidence) except for the parking cost associated with ride share and two mode-specific constants. Overall the model has a pseudo-R^2 of 0.346 when comparing the log-likelihood at zero and log-likelihood at convergence. The constants alone contribute 0.13 of the 0.34 suggesting the attributes in the utility expressions do have an important role to play in explaining mode choice. A simple MNL model will always reproduce the aggregate market shares even though the predicted choice for an individual (as a probability) is unlikely to equal the actual choice. This is not a major concern since the model has external validity at the sample level and not for a specific individual unless the analyst has sufficiently rich data to be able to estimate a model for each individual. This is sometimes possible with stated choice data (see below) with many replications or a large and long panel of repeated observations on the same individuals. Thus even an MNL estimated with only the $J-1$ mode-specific constants will reproduce the aggregate sample market shares.

The signs of all taste weights in Table 4.11 are correct and unambiguous—we would expect that a negative sign would be associated with time and cost since an individual's relative utility will increase when time or cost decreases (and vice versa). The sign on personal income might be positive or negative; although we would reasonably expect it to be positive in the utility expression for drive alone. That is, all other things being equal, we would expect an individual to have a higher probability of choosing to drive alone as their income increases. In contrast, if we had placed the income variable in the public transport alternative's utility expression we might have expected a negative sign. A characteristic of an individual or any other variable that is not an attribute of an alternative in a choice set cannot be included in all utility expressions in a stand-alone specification since it does not vary across the alternatives. That is, a person's income does not vary by mode unless it is defined as net of modal costs. To enable a non-modal attribute to be included in all utility expressions, it must be interacted with an alternative-specific attribute. For example, we could include income in all utility expressions by dividing cost by income; or we could interact travel time with income by multiplication. There are many ways of doing this, but a sensible behavioural hypothesis is required to justify this additional complexity.

The taste weights for in-vehicle time for bus and train are almost identical which suggests that we could save one degree of freedom by imposing an equality restriction on these two taste weights, treating them as generic. The parking cost attributes could be eliminated from the ride share alternative given its statistical non-significance, saving an additional degree of freedom. All the other specifications should be retained for the derivation of elasticities and for policy analysis. The behavioural value of travel time savings for in-vehicle time, walk time, and wait time can be derived from Table 4.11 for each mode (see equation (4.11)). The value of in-vehicle time savings varies from $12.24 per person hour for car drive alone to $8.09 per person hour for

train. You can confirm this by dividing the taste weight for in-vehicle time by the taste weight for in-vehicle cost and multiplying by 60 (to convert from cents per minute to cents per hour). The reader might wish to calculate the value of walk time savings and wait time savings for public transport modes and confirm that for train the ratio of VTTS for walk time compared to in-vehicle time is 2.15:1, and the ratio of VTTS for wait time compared to in-vehicle time is 3.34:1. This latter ratio tells us that an individual is willing to pay up to 3.34 times more to save a minute of time waiting for a train compared to a minute of time in a train, *ceteris paribus*. This highlights the importance of service frequency.

4.4.2.4 Identifying direct and cross-elasticities

The appropriateness of various policies can be evaluated using the measures of responsiveness of demand to changes in each attribute that influences the demand. Direct and cross-elasticities can be estimated. Direct elasticities are percentage changes in the probability of choosing particular alternatives in the choice set with respect to given percentage changes in attributes of those alternatives. Cross-elasticities are percentage changes in the probability of choosing particular alternatives in the choise set with respect to given percentage changes in attributes of competing alternatives. The size of the change in the level of an attribute has an important bearing on whether the elasticity measure should be point or arc (see below). Software packages automatically generate point elasticities, which is fine for small changes in the level of an attribute.

Direct point elasticities in the MNL model can be written as follows:

$$E\frac{P_{iq}}{X_{ikq}} = \frac{\partial P_{iq}}{\partial X_{ikq}} \cdot \frac{X_{ikq}}{P_{iq}} \qquad (4.36)$$

that can be interpreted as the elasticity of the probability of choosing alternative i for individual q with respect to a marginal (or 'small') change in the kth variable which describes the utility of the ith alternative for individual q. The equivalent cross-elasticity formula replaces the ith alternative index on x with the jth alternative.

Applying equation (4.36) to equation (4.33) produces a single point elasticity formula for the basic MNL model, summarized as equation (4.37).

$$E\frac{P_{iq}}{X_{jkq}} = \beta_{jk}X_{jkq}(\delta_{ij} - P_{jq})$$ (4.37)

$$\text{where } \delta_{ij} = \begin{bmatrix} 1 \text{ if } i = j \text{ (a direct point elasticity)} \\ 0 \text{ if } i \neq j \text{ (a cross point elasticity)} \end{bmatrix}$$

The direct elasticity approaches zero as P_{jq} approaches unity, and approaches $\beta_{jk}X_{jkq}$ as P_{jq} approaches zero. The converse applies for the cross-elasticity. The IID condition underlying the MNL model carries with it a major limitation on the cross-elasticities. It forces all of them for a particular attribute associated with a particular alternative to be the same for all other alternatives. Thus the drive-alone in-vehicle time cross-elasticity is the same in terms of its impact on the probability of choosing ride share, train, and bus.

Equation (4.37) yields elasticities for each individual. For aggregate elasticities applicable to the total population, one might be tempted to evaluate equation (4.37) at the sample average x_{jk} and $\hat{P}_j$ (average estimated P_j). However, this is not generally correct because the MNL model is non-linear, hence, the estimated logit function need not pass through the point defined by these sample averages. Indeed, this mistake commonly produces errors as large as 20% (usually over-estimates) in estimating the responsiveness of choice probabilities with respect to some variable X_{jk}. Thus, a better approach is to evaluate equation (4.37) for each individual q and then aggregate, weighting each individual elasticity by the individual's estimated probability of choice. This technique is known as the 'method of sample enumeration', the formula for which is:

$$E\frac{\bar{P}_i}{X_{jkq}} = \left(\sum_{q=1}^{Q} \hat{P}_{iq} E\frac{P_{iq}}{X_{jkq}}\right) \bigg/ \sum_{q=1}^{Q} \hat{P}_{iq}$$ (4.38)

where $\hat{P}_{iq}$ in an estimated choice probability and $\bar{P}_i$ refers to the aggregate probability of choice of alternative i. It should be noted here that the weighted aggregate cross-elasticities calculated from an MNL model are likely to differ across alternatives. This

may seem odd given the limiting condition of constant cross-elasticities in a model derived from the IID property. The calculations and software are likely to be correct because the IID condition guarantees identical cross-elasticities at the individual level *before* probability weighting is undertaken. Some software packages give the user the option to select an unweighted aggregation based on a summation across the sample and a simple division by sample size. This naïve aggregation will produce identical aggregate cross-elasticities, but it is not correct since it fails to recognize the contribution of each observation to the choice outcome of each alternative. Unfortunately, MNL models are of limited use in providing behaviourally useful cross-elasticities. To be able to get meaningful cross-elasticities we need to relax the IID condition, which is achievable by additional complexity. Discrete choice models such as nested logit, heteroscedastic extreme value, and mixed logit allow us to obtain behaviourally plausible cross-elasticities (see Sect. 4.5 and Louviere *et al.* 2000; Bhat 1995, 1998; Hensher and Greene 2000).

The elasticity formulation above is derived from partial differentiation of the choice function, assuming any changes in X are marginal. If changes are non-marginal, as frequently happens in practice, an arc elasticity formula is appropriate if the change in the level of the independent variable does not result in a level of X outside of the distribution of values used in estimation. This elasticity is calculated using differences ($X^1, X; P^1, P$) rather than differentials:

$$E\frac{P_{iq}}{X_{ikq}} = [(P^1_{iq} - P_{iq})/(X^1_{ikq} - X_{ikq})]/[0.5(P^1_{iq} + P_{iq})/$$
$$0.5(X_{ikq} + X_{ikq})]$$ (4.39)

$$E\frac{P_{iq}}{X_{jkq}} = [(P^1_{iq} - P_{iq})/(X^1_{jkq} - X_{jkq})]/[0.5(P^1_{iq} + P_{iq})/$$
$$0.5(X_{ikq} + X_{ikq})]$$ (4.40)

Weighted aggregate point elasticities for all variables and choices were calculated by applying the method of sample enumeration discussed in the last section. The results, presented in Table 4.12, are for direct elasticities only. They are all negative since we expect an increase in a travel time component or cost, *ceteris paribus*, to reduce the probability of

Table 4.12 Direct point elasticities for choice of mode of travel to work

Attributes	Direct elasticities Drive alone	Ride share	Train	Bus
Walk time	—	—	−0.587	−0.682
Wait time	− −		−0.765	−0.798
In-vehicle time	−0.362	−0.324	−0.426	−0.437
In-vehicle cost	−0.114	−0.102	−0.246	−0.279
Parking cost	−0.141	—	—	—

choosing a particular mode and hence results in a reduced market share.

Interpreting the estimated elasticities is straight-forward. For example, the value of – 0.362 for in-vehicle time associated with drive alone implies that a 1 per cent increase in the time travelling by car as a sole driver will, all else equal, cause a 0.362% decrease in the overall probability of drive-alone choice of commuter mode. Other elasticities may be interpreted similarly. The empirical evidence in this example suggests that commuters are more sensitive to travel time changes than to cost changes, and are most sensitive to changes in time waiting for a public transport mode.

The more dispersed the distribution of attribute values, the lower the weighted aggregate elasticity relative to the aggregate elasticity, the latter calculated at the sample average (X_{jk} and $\hat{P}_j$). This is because as the differential in the relative levels of an attribute increases, the response of aggregate demand to changes in that variable decreases (Westin 1974). For example, Gillen (1977) illustrates this effect by calculating weighted and unweighted aggregate elasticities for four variables, and obtains (– 0.29, – 0.34), (– 0.59, – 0.68), (– 0.31, – 0.38) and (– 0.19 and – 0.25).

The elasticities can be combined in many ways, which can be very convenient and useful if one wants the average level of responsiveness across a number of market segments. For example McFadden (1979) summarized some aggregation rules:

1. Aggregate elasticity over *market segments*, which is the sum of segment elasticities weighted by segment market shares. This rule assumes that the percentage change in the policy variables is the same in each segment.

2. Aggregate elasticities over *alternatives*, which is the sum of component alternative elasticities weighted by the component share of the compared alternative (e.g. all public transport). This rule assumes an equal percentage change in each component alternative as the result of a policy.

3. Elasticity with respect to a *component of an attribute*, which is the elasticity with respect to the attribute times the component's share in the attribute. For example, the elasticity with respect to bus fare when we only have the estimated elasticity with respect to total trip cost.

4. Elasticity with respect to a policy that causes an equal percentage change in several attributes equals the sum of elasticities with respect to each attribute.

The estimated utility expressions can be processed in a spreadsheet to identify the impact of a change in one or more attributes on market shares. This gives the MNL model a very strong policy role in assisting analysts in evaluating the impact of many policies (as defined by specific mixes of attributes modelled in the utility expressions).

4.5 Accounting for behavioural variability over time

4.5.1 The basis of forecasting

There are many transport applications where the interest centres on understanding how a particular travel response varies between different points in time. If the relationship between explanatory variables and a dependent variable is likely to be different at each point in time, then we need to know this and investigate whether there are any observed patterns that we can identify and use in forecasting into the future. The essence of forecasting involves answering two questions: on the basis of limited data, what can be inferred about the past? and on the basis of inferences made about the past, what can I predict (forecast) about the future? This section provides an overview of methods suitable for helping us to answer these two questions.

All prediction rests on the belief that the phenomena under study possess regularity and stability over time. Regularity means that there are relationships that occur in some systematic way over time; for example, that there are high seasons for air travel in school holidays. Stability means that the rules for making the appropriate transformation are stable; for example, the underlying trend of traffic volume is linear with respect to time. That is, we want to assume that the functional form is stable. However, all prediction is subject to error, due to the selection of variables, the selection of appropriate functional forms (e.g. double logarithmic), and the estimation of the 'correct' values of the predictor variables. These concerns are as relevant to a cross-section as they are to the study of behaviour over time.

Forecasts may be made for ascertaining the possibility of change in the course of an action currently being pursued. If the desirability of change is indicated, a search for new courses of action may be required. Forecasts are then made to determine the likelihood that each course of action under evaluation will attain specific objectives. That is, forecasts are typically used in the process of choosing among alternative courses of action. Courses of action under evaluation may be largely *responsive* (e.g. changing some services in response to reduced travel demand); largely *initiated* (e.g. launching a new marketing campaign for the purpose of increasing demand for the organization's products and services), or a combination of responsive and initiated (e.g. responding to a competitor's price reduction by reducing one's own prices and at the same time improving service levels).

Forecasts are made to cover a variety of decision situations. The forecasting-choice problem can be considered under two subclasses: those related to highly programmed, repetitive, responsive, and largely internally controlled (and usually lower-level) decisions; and those related to unprogrammed, sporadic, responsive-initiated (and usually higher-level) decisions. Programmed decisions exist when a more or less definite well-structured set of ground rules is available for choice. For example, add another level of service (an extra bus run, an extra truck delivery, extend port operating hours, add another container shipment) when demand is forecast to reach or exceed some given level up to another threshold where even more capacity is required. Decisions can be made more or less automatically once the rules are set up. Unprogrammed decisions involve a much more diverse set of courses of action. Problems are typically non-routine, and the effects of various courses of action may extend over a long future time period. For example: a five-year forecast indicates a likely inability to meet a goal level for revenue. This may then set in motion a search for other courses of action (e.g. new product introduction, change in price policy, acquisition of a competitor, etc.). Once the new alternatives are formulated, a new set of forecasts must be prepared to advise on the likelihood that each candidate course of action will meet the said goals.

The consequences of poor forecasts between programmed and unprogrammed decisions are likely to differ greatly. A wrong decision on the second bus run may carry a relatively small cost, with immediate feedback enabling some compensating action. A wrong decision on the introduction of a new product or acquisition of a competitor's service may carry a sizeable economic consequence. The opportunity to restore balance may be non-existent—no second chance is possible. These consequences are tied up with the nature of forecasting uncertainty.

The future can be viewed in a number of ways. It depends on how sensitive the decision is to the unknown events of interest and how willing those involved in making decisions on forecasts are to 'absorb uncertainty'. If a particular action is assumed to be superior to all other possible actions, irrespective of the course of future events, no forecast of these events is required. If the consequences of a wrong decision may be quite sensitive to the unknown event(s) of interest, the effort spent on reducing the uncertainty is warranted. The treatment of uncertainty is an important consideration.

Let us view the future in *certainty equivalent terms*. Some forecasters are limited by their client's willingness to assume only one possible outcome associated with a particular course of action. That is, replace a whole distribution of possible events by a single number: 'don't confuse me with ranges and probabilities; all I want is your best single guess of what traffic volume will be next year'. Alternatively, a more professional and scientific approach would require the analyst to express a forecast in terms of a range of possibilities. This includes some statement about the likelihood that the 'true' value will fall somewhere within the range and an expression of the chances that some outcome, say traffic volume, will exceed a specified value. Importantly, however, all forecasts are in a sense, *acts of faith* that perceived past regularities will persist into the future. One thing we know for sure about forecasts is that they will be wrong—what interests us primarily is minimizing the amount of 'wrongness'. This will be aided by creativity in model building, seen essentially in the level of rules at which stability is assumed. The comment 'our business is changing too fast to model it' is naïve. The challenge is to up-scale the level of abstraction at which stability must necessarily be assumed. There are a large number of forecasting techniques available to assist this process, with varying degrees of complexity.

4.5.2 Forecasting tools

Forecasting problems can be classified into three classes: projecting a single data series based on its own historical pattern; projecting a single data series based on its historical relationship to other data series; and finding patterns in the relationship of two or more variables as measured over administrative (i.e. cross-sectional) units rather than over time. It is important often to project simultaneously more than one related data series and their total; for example, the breakdown of air travel by destination and fare class and in total. For all three classes of problems, forecasting will benefit by using a combination of statistical and judgemental forecasting procedures. The ability to read behind the numbers is a necessary skill to enhance the value of specific forecasts.

The key analytical approaches available can be described as either extrapolative or correlational. Extrapolative techniques use past changes in only the variable of interest as a basis for future projection of the variable. The only explanatory variable is 'time'. Such techniques include naïve models, time series decomposition, and exponential smoothing. Correlation techniques utilize past relationships between the variable to be forecast and other variables that are thought to be related to the variable being forecast. The key steps in correlational analysis are quantifying the past relationship between dependent and explanatory variables (e.g. by regression) and forecasting values of the explanatory variables. This has already been discussed in the OLS examples, except that we have yet to allow for the possibility that the level of a dependent variable or explanatory variable in past time periods may have an important influence on current and future levels of a dependent variable. For example, the amount of aviation turbine fuel and gasoline in time period t may be a function of the fuel prices in period $t-1$ and fuel burnt in $t-1$ and $t-2$. The demand for annual new car registrations is a function of the number of new car registrations in the previous year.

4.5.2.1 Extrapolative techniques—forecasting with a trend

The simplest form of extrapolation is trend analysis, in which typically an application such as traffic volumes per unit of time is some linear function of Time, where Time is defined by the number of time periods: $Volume_t = \beta_0 + \beta_1 {}^*Time_t$. A timeplot (or linegraph) is a useful way of looking graphically at successive values of a variable against time and should always be undertaken for any data series you want to forecast. This visual method provides the single best picture of your data and suggests the proper choice of forecasting technique (Fig. 4.10). Features to look for in a timeplot include upward or downward trend, repetitive seasonal variations, abrupt jumps in level (e.g. a pilot's dispute which reduced air traffic substantially), and missing values.

Seasonality, defined as a regular, repetitive pattern of demand in a data series is common to many transport services and products. Depending on your task, you may want to exploit seasonality or eliminate it. You should exploit seasonality if you are making month-to-month forecasts of a data series that has a stable pattern of highs and lows. For example, if December traffic volumes are usually higher than November volumes, you should incorporate that fact into any traffic forecasts for those two months. You should eliminate the seasonal pattern if your job is to

uncover and project the underlying trend beneath the seasonality. For example, predictable Christmas peaks and summer lows obscure the underlying trend. That traffic is higher in December matters less than whether it is higher to the usual degree.

The classical time series decomposition, or the ratio-to-moving average method, decomposes a data series into three constituent parts: an *underlying trend* reflecting long-term changes in the data; *seasonal multipliers*, one for each period in the seasonal cycle; and an *irregular or noise component*, representing the influences of short-term and random factors, such as weather and strikes (Fig. 4.11). The seasonal multipliers quantify the average relationship between the actual data and the underlying trend during each phase of the seasonal cycle. Some analysts also refer to *cyclical* data patterns. These are similar to seasonal patterns, but the length of a single cycle is generally longer than one year. It is the most difficult pattern to predict because it does not repeat itself at constant intervals of time. Timeplots may help to identify such phenomena.

Each component has its own uses. Trend shows the big picture in the data with short-term fluctuations smoothed away and predictable seasonality eliminated. Seasonal multipliers capture the size of the repetitive patterns. The irregular component isolates the effect of 'one-time' events like a power failure, a strike, a war. The original data from a time series is constructed (or reconstructed) from Data = Trend × Seasonal × Irregular. Thus a seasonally-adjusted series is derived from the original data (i.e.

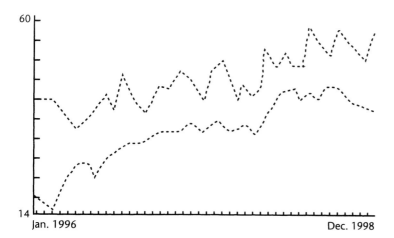

Fig. 4.10 Two data series with a trend

Note: Use double exponential smoothing or simple moving average on such data.

60

14
Jan. 1996   Dec. 1998

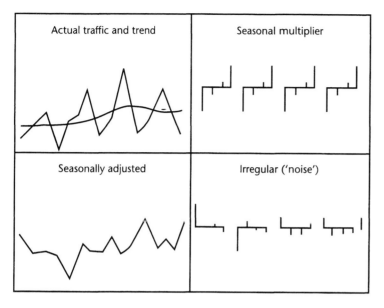

Fig. 4.11 Decomposition of a time series

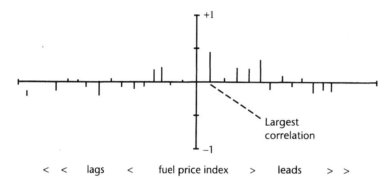

Fig. 4.12 Searching for leading indicators: approach 1

Note: Fuel price leads truck kms. by one quarter.

Data/Seasonal) as the product of Trend and Irregular. The seasonally adjusted data reflect both long-term (trend) and short-term (irregular) influences.

To assist in forecasting, analysts are always on the lookout for 'leading indicators'. A leading indicator is a variable whose changes anticipate changes in some variable of importance to you. For example, knowing current new car sales lets you better predict next quarter's sales in the automotive after-market for accessories. A cross-correlation plot (see Fig. 4.12) enables the analyst to identify the extent to which the value of one variable predicts values of the other variable at past and future times, and hence suggests graphically what may be a suitable lagged dependent variable to include as a determinant of a future level.

4.5.2.2 Forecasting a series without a trend

If a timeplot shows that data fluctuate around a level that does not change much with time (see Fig. 4.13), neither rising nor falling, then a series has little or no trend. In this case the forecasting problem amounts to smoothing out the fluctuations to uncover the basic level of data. Two techniques suitable for this are: single exponential smoothing and simple moving average.

Single exponential smoothing uses all the data in

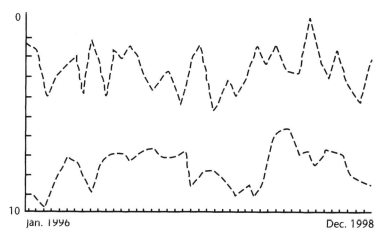

Fig. 4.13 Searching for leading indicators: approach 2

Note: Two data series without trend: use single exponential smoothing or simple moving average on such data.

the series but gives successively less weight to older data. By giving more weight to more recent data, such smoothing adjusts to abrupt shifts in the underlying level of a data series, such as a sudden jump up to a new, higher level (Fig. 4.15). A simple moving average uses only a selected number of recent data values, weighting them all equally (Fig. 4.13). In choosing how many data values to average, a trade-off is involved. If you average only a few recent values, the approach reacts better to abrupt changes in the underlying level of the data. It is, however, less able to home in on a fairly steady underlying level.

4.5.2.3 Forecasting a series with a trend

If a data series has a steady upward or downward trend, then single exponential smoothing and simple moving average consistently lag behind the trend. Thus these methods consistently under-predict or over-predict. Double exponential smoothing tracks not only the level of data but also changes in the level so is well suited to data with a trend. Double exponential smoothing is also referred to as second-order exponential smoothing or Brown's linear-exponential smoothing. Linear moving average works better with trending than the simple moving average.

4.5.2.4 Forecasting a series without a seasonal variation

A data series with a seasonal component has predictable highs and lows recurring over time (see Fig. 4.15). Exponential smoothing and moving average methods tend to average out these seasonal cycles and remove them from the forecast. However, you might want to predict the seasonal variation along with the underlying level and trend of the data series. For example, you may want to know not only next year's total demand for a product, but also how that demand is distributed from month to month.

Winter's exponential smoothing method tracks seasonality and builds it into forecasts. Two kinds of seasonal pattern characterize data: additive seasonality and multiplicative seasonality. For additive seasonality, the absolute size of the seasonal variations stays the same even if the level of the series changes. For multiplicative seasonality, the seasonal pattern keeps the same percentage relationship to the underlying trend, even though the absolute size of the seasonal highs and lows changes with the level of the series. Once again, a timeplot can assist in deciding which seasonality pattern is likely to apply to a particular data series.

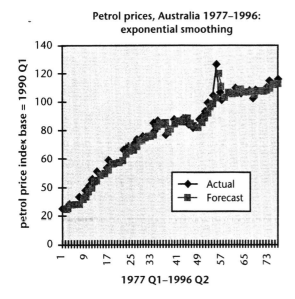

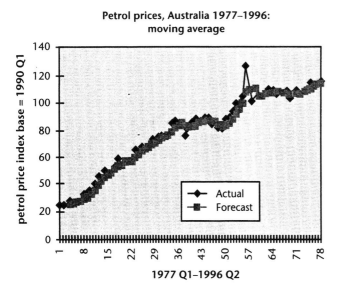

Fig. 4.14 Examples of exponential smoothing and moving average

4.5.2.4 Forecasting a series using regression analysis

This method imposes some causal structure on the forecasting task and moves away from essentially extrapolative techniques. The opportunity to relate a variable to be forecast to other variables either con-temporaneously or by lags (e.g. Fig. 4.16) and leads exists with causal models. The standard OLS regression technique is used, with the well-known measures of goodness-of-fit and statistical significance of individual explanatory variables as presented previously.

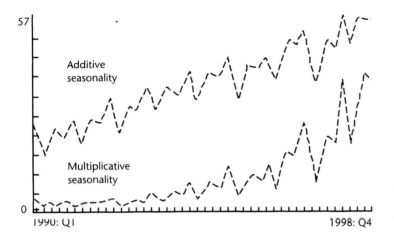

Fig. 4.15 Accommodating seasonal variation in a series

Note: Use either additive or multiplicative Winter's method on such seasonal data.

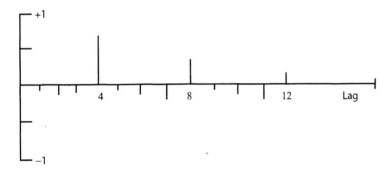

Fig. 4.16 Searching for the appropriate number of lags

Note: The largest autocorrelations arise at lags 4, 8, and 12. This shows a seasonal pattern repeating every 4 quarters.

4.6 Concluding comments

Identifying the demand for transportation facilities and services is a complex but important element of the practice of transport management. This chapter has introduced the key tools that a transport analyst should be familiar with (or at least know what the 'expert' in demand analysis should be capable of providing).

Discussion issues for Chapter 4

1   It is not sufficient to be able to establish the statistical fit of a travel choice or demand model. One needs to ensure that the outputs are behaviourally plausible. Discuss this warning.

2   Elasticities are important tools for investigating the role of policy instruments. Why do we have such a large array of alternative specifications?

3 The valuation of travel time savings has an important influence on travel choice. Why is this and what are some of the challenging empirical issues in establishing suitable values?

4 To be in a well-informed position to predict the total size of a market, as well as the share one might secure, requires some understanding of individual's preferences. Discuss.

5 The quantity of train trips demanded by level of fare is given in Table 4.13 for two income groups. Plot the two demand curves and comment on the implications of varying income. What assumptions have you made in interpreting the relationship between changes in fares and changes in the number of trips demanded? Why is a knowledge of preferences important?

6 Using the data shown Table 4.13 on fares and travel demand, calculate the direct point and arc fare elasticities for each adjacent fare level. If you obtain differences in the answers, explain why you think they are different.

Table 4.13 Identifying the demand for travel

Number of one-way daily train trips, income $30,000	Number of one-way daily train trips, income $50,000	Average fare ($)
100	75	3
150	95	2.60
200	130	2.20
250	150	1.80
300	195	1.65
350	245	1.40
400	300	1.30

7 What are the key steps in the specification and implementation of a study of travel choice?

8 You are given the task of identifying the major influences on international air travel over the last 20 years. How do you plan to approach this topic and what methods are most likely to reveal the major influences?

9 The Minister for Transport yesterday attacked a Treasury submission to the Independent Pricing and Regulatory Tribunal seeking fare rises up to 30 per cent for the 'affluent few' who used public transport. The bureaucrats argued for the fare rises because revenue had fallen since 1994–5 and the bulk of taxpayer-funded subsidies went to 'upper middle to very high income range' households.

'I was not consulted about it,' the Minister said. 'Basically, it's a couple of Treasury bureaucrats putting their two cents in, who have drawn conclusions which are offensive, wrong and I don't agree with them . . . I've chucked it in the bin. I think these couple of bureaucrats probably don't get let out much. I don't think they travel on public transport too often.' Treasury officials were unavailable for comment yesterday.

But the Minister reiterated his support for 12.5 per cent to 15 per cent fare rises sought by RailCorp and the State Transit Authority, because commuters were not 'paying a high enough contribution given the improvements we're making'. He said the fare proposals, to be put to the tribunal from Monday, would help pay for 80 new trains, 100 buses, 14 ferries, 33 railway station upgrades and security guards on trains.

But the Opposition and welfare groups said the Government had claimed during the election campaign that its transport infrastructure plans were fully funded and contained in Budget forward estimates. 'It's one of the big lies of the campaign,' the Opposition transport spokesman said. 'Two months after the election and the Government needs more money.' The Minister said 'not all' of the transport improvements had been budgeted for.

The Oppositional Leader said fare increases were unacceptable when commuters constantly complained about dirty, late and overcrowded trains. 'I wouldn't have thought when we're getting the level of complaint that we are about the public transport system . . . that this is the time to be talking about fare increases,' she said.

Last March, when RailCorp sought a 10 per cent fare increase, the Minister said 'any claim that is not broadly in line with inflation will not be approved by the Government'. The pricing tribunal later approved a 3.2 per cent rise. Yesterday the Minister said: 'In previous years I did not support anything beyond (what was) broadly in line with inflation, because we had not embarked on these huge improvements.'

Fare rises up to 15 per cent and a 10 per cent goods and service tax (GST), which is expected to be levied from July 1 next year, would see the cheapest RailCorp train ticket rise from $1.60 to $2 and the cheapest weekly pass increase from $12 to $15.

The Minister said the Government wanted a public transport system that was 'reasonably affordable and greatly improved' and was concerned about the impact of the GST. 'Look at the Prime Minister, already going to whack a GST on public transport . . . This year I believe it's appropriate [for a] between 12.5 per cent and 15 per cent increase', he said. (*Sydney Morning Herald*, 5 June 1999.)

Discuss this newspaper article in terms of the positions of Treasury officials and the Minister. Who has got it right? What role can a knowledge of travel demand play?

5 Knowing your costs

5.1 Introduction

Knowing the costs of running a transport business is one of the essential elements of effective business practice. Whether the environment in which you operate is one of competition or monopoly, the case for making decisions with a knowledge of costs is indisputable. Strategic thinking, in particular benefits from an awareness of the costs of doing business and how one might 'allocate' these costs to the range of activities undertaken. Some costs have a very clear mandate in the delivery of service (often called separable or avoidable costs); other costs, however, are quite ambiguous in the way we treat them in the determination of who might pay for them (often described as non-separable or shared costs).

This chapter takes a close look at the costs of operating a transport business at the level of the individual firm and for an industry sector as a whole. The great majority of transport firms are interested in how they can be more cost efficient in the delivery of services (see App. 2A for a discussion of efficiency concepts). However, transport firms do not exist in a vacuum; their future is very much influenced by the performance of their industry as a whole and its interfaces with the rest of the economy. Regulators require information on the health of a transport sector (e.g. ports, rail, shipping, airports, and roads) in making judgements of the performance and obliga-

tions of that sector. This information includes knowledge of the extent of economies of scale, density, scope, and network. With such information, arguments are advanced as to the legitimacy of specific market practices, especially in respect of the impact on consumers and the community and the cost to government where subsidy and/or direct ownership are entailed. The tools used by industry watchers to monitor structure, conduct, and performance are presented in a way that highlights their practical value, avoiding the complexities which economic theory has imposed on many such useful empirical constructs.

The chapter begins with the individual transport business, introducing the way in which costs should be viewed if managers think strategically. A case study for the bus sector illustrates how the ideas are translated into good practice. This case study is selected because of its generic relevance to all transport modal sectors and logistics. We then introduce the industry-level perspective, and draw on examples in coastal shipping, urban car use, long-distance trucking, the airlines, and local bus services to illustrate how costs are assessed sectorally. Further details on the operating costs of cars and trucks are given in Chapter 7 in the context of evaluation of transport subsidy.

5.2 Costing in a transport business

A study of the costs of an individual transport business must begin with a clear understanding of the reasons underlying a need to know about costs. All transport firms have tax obligations and need to keep accurate records for the purpose of legitimately minimizing taxation. A good tax accountant has this sole interest in mind when specifying the record-keeping task. While important to efficient and effective practice, this is not the only financial activity of a transport business. Everyday decisions must be taken on resources required to participate in market activities, be they in a (natural or protected) monopoly market or a market with varying degrees of competition.

What we might describe in broad terms as the planning process requires an understanding of costs in a way that is often quite different to the way in which cost data are compiled for taxation planning. It is one thing to be able to identify all sources of cost (called attribution); how these attributed costs are allocated to specific activities, however, is quite a different planning task. It is one, as we shall see, that is quite complex and certainly contains strong elements of ambiguity or what has been described as a somewhat arbitrary 'allocation'. This latter idea arises from the presence of cost items, many of which are lumpy, which have no unique mapping to a specific service, and which are not meaningfully allocated through a simple pro-rata rule such as vehicle hours of operation. The best example is capital costs, although the principles set out below apply to all inputs. For example, if we have a coach operation servicing two markets—a monopoly market and a highly competitive market—how might we decide on the contribution of each market to the recoupment of the annualized cost of capital? The answer is not unambiguous. The answer is—'it depends' (see later discussion for the range of solutions).

The ideas promoted so heavily by the accounting profession of fixed and variable costs are of limited value in a setting where the primary objective is to identify and apportion costs to activities in such a way that one maximizes either profits or (constrained) social welfare. The name of the game for a transport business is to deliver to their chosen or competed-for markets at a level of service which is cost efficient and allocatively efficient, the latter reserved for the mapping of all costs in accordance with the pricing strategy of the business (see Ch. 6). An essential ingredient to the final decision is a knowledge of the markets in which services are to be delivered, because different markets can bear costs at varying levels of absorption. In total, however, a transport firm wants to cover all of its costs and make an acceptable return on investment (i.e. profits). The principles promoted in the chapter provide the framework within which strategically thinking transport operators should attribute and 'allocate' costs. Operators who reject this view on costing are, we would argue, non-strategic thinkers and are missing out on market opportunities, regardless of what their pricing objectives are. In summary, transport costing at the individual business level is necessary in order to:

- establish the basis for setting prices for the provision of goods and services;
- monitor performance by route, area, or market sector and to assess claims on subsidy, merger, deregulation, privatization, etc.;
- evaluate specific changes in service levels, networks operated, and traffic levels.

A costing study is concerned with identification of the resources required to provide a service and the unit costs of such resources

5.2.1 What is a cost?

There are two broad categories of costs: economic costs and accounting costs. *Economic costs* are the opportunity costs of the resources (inputs) used by a transport firm in the provision of transport services.

The *opportunity cost* of a resource employed by a transport firm is what the resource could earn in its most profitable alternative use. If a competitive market for resource inputs exists, its opportunity (or economic) cost would be measured by its market price.

The *accounting cost* for this resource is not its opportunity cost if the wage rate paid for labour (for example) is not a market-determined rate. The union constraint in transport firms suggests that accounting costs are not opportunity costs. Many self-employed people undervalue their worth by paying themselves an income that is less than they could receive in a competitive market from another employer. Even allowing for the division between an owner's salary and dividends as a way of minimizing tax in countries where the marginal tax rate is higher for personal income than for company income, the rewards are often less than the opportunity cost of labour. Since economic costs based on opportunity cost in a competitive input market are *efficiency-linked* costs, deviations in accounting costs from economic costs represent distortions or deviations from efficiency costing. *Examples* of distortions are monopoly rents, hidden subsidies, artificially determined floors and ceilings on input prices. Feather-bedding is a common phrase to describe inflated costs associated with inefficiency in the input market.

In practice, it is often difficult to know how to adjust the costs outlaid to correct for distortions associated with deviations from competitively delivered resource inputs. Where such corrections are made, the resulting cost levels are often called 'shadow costs' in recognition of their non-visibility in practice. Indeed from a transport business's perspective, the costs that matter at the time of identifying activity costs (e.g. when putting in a competitive tender, negotiating a job, or simply working out the cost of undertaking an existing activity) are those which the firm will have to outlay, regardless of the degree of distortion. The regulator, however, is interested in the nature of distortion and what impact it has on deviations from competitive practice and the costs of servicing the community. The regulator's interest applies to both commercial and non-commercial services, where the latter are being internally cross-subsidized and/or are receiving external subsidy from government. Where we can identify the magnitude of distortion, then action might be taken to promote strategies to move closer to efficient costs of inputs. It is in the interests of both transport operators and the regulator to eliminate such distortions; however, the lack of reliable information often denies both parties the opportunity to reveal such distortions.

Many transport businesses have very poor information on the costs associated with running their own businesses. This is frequently revealed when firms employ consultants to assist them in identifying the costs of specific activities—the ideal of finding the necessary base data on a management information system is a rare occurrence. Many transport businesses are small (e.g. up to 20 workers) and heavily operations focused, and spend little if any time keeping records of their activity costs. Broad aggregates are about the best available, compiled solely for the tax accountant and broad-ranging quotes. Consequently, when pricing a specific service, the estimates are often ball-parkish at best and wild guesses at worst. A coach operator recently indicated that he uses the rule of 'four times the wages level' in quoting on coach contracts. When asked why this rule was chosen, the reply was 'my father has always used this rule'. The challenge in this chapter is to provide convincing arguments for an improved approach to knowing one's costs.

5.2.2 Attribution and allocation

A typical costing exercise involves four activities:

1. identification of all potential sources of cost;
2. analysis and attribution of each cost item at the maximal practical level of disaggregation of activity (e.g. the route by time of day, then route, then branch/depot, then division, etc.). The definition of specific activities can be quite complex; for example, a railway may classify by line and then commodity types (passengers, bulk freight, non-bulk freight). An airport may classify by aeronautical and non-aeronautical activities, and

within aeronautical activity by landside (e.g. customs, maintenance) and runway (e.g. gates, apron), and then by aircraft type, time of day, and airline. A trucking business may classify activities by market (e.g. London–Glasgow/Edinburgh, Sydney–Melbourne), by direction of travel, by vehicle type, and commodity carried;

3. development of a procedure to allocate costs to these traffics. This may involve a simple or complex statistical model whose validity can be verified against aggregate cost sources. A major distinction is between avoidable and shared costs (see below), where the division is based on a set of principles and not a set of pro-rata rules;

4. together with revenues derived from these traffics, identify commercial and non-commercial traffics.

This process is complicated by the quality of information, the definition of activities, the presence of shared costs, and the challenge to establish an accepted rule for determining how the shared costs are to be recouped from the market.

5.2.3 The essential principle of costing

The basic concept used in establishing the costs associated with a particular service is that of *avoidability*. Some literatures use the jargon of escapability, separability, or non-shared costs, but these are all equivalent concepts.

Definition: the costs which can be properly attributed to a service are those outlays which could be avoided if the firm were to withdraw entirely from carrying that particular traffic or engaging in that activity. Costs are assessed in turn for each service on this basis.

This is a simple rule, but a complex one to apply in practice. Some costs are avoidable in the long run but not in the short run. Some costs are shared and only avoidable in that sense. Some costs are avoidable for small but not large changes in output. Some costs are avoidable in all senses. The spectrum of

avoidability varies with the time period (temporal) and the range of output (technical). It has nothing to do with fixed and variable costs *per se*. For example, a specific cost item such as a leased truck or a leased aircraft can be avoided immediately in a circumstance where it is dedicated to a specific route and closure of that route service enables the asset to be returned immediately to the leasing company without penalty. If the leasing contract requires a 'penalty' clause for early return prior to full lease period, then there is some element of cost that is not avoided immediately, but will be avoided if one kept the asset for the duration of the lease and worked it on another service.

The sum of avoidable costs associated with various services will be less than the total system costs because of the likely presence of shared costs between different services/activities. Such shared costs, while not discoverable for any specific services, have to be met for system/division operation, either by receipts from customers or external support.

5.2.4 The avoidable cost concept in detail

Avoidable cost is the sum of those outlays which could be saved if provision of the service were to be reduced to some specified level or conversely, the additional outlays entailed if output of the service were to be expanded. This cost is the difference between the total outlays for operating the transport system at the present and contemplated scales of service provision.

With a reduction in output, the potential savings are those which could be realized from appropriate management action to cater for lower levels of traffic contemplated: for example, reductions in assets such as rolling stock, buses, planes, station/depot/terminal operations, technical support services, and so on. All other transport services in the firm are assumed constant in quantity and quality. In determining a service's avoidable cost, the relevant outlays embrace all those affected by the assumed change in output, including both capital and working expenditures.

Avoidable costs must relate to alterations to traffic levels that are capable of being realized through actual business decisions. The output changes considered may be relatively large (to begin or to cease carrying a substantial commodity or passenger class) or small (as when variations for a type of traffic are being considered, given a general commitment to its carriage).

The relevant time period for the calculations may vary. It is largely governed by business options under consideration:

1. the time period affects the extent to which prospective outlays can be saved,

2. One normally expects the time period for a change in output to be correlated with size—the bigger the change, the longer it will take for the effects to work through;

3. the longer the time period, the more it is possible to shed labour, equipment and other assets;

4. eventually all resources can be dispensed with— through sale, finding alternative uses, or natural wastage.

Because of the requirement to aggregate across the whole of a business, the time horizons for establishing cost avoidability must, when defined, be adhered to for all services and activities. Avoidable costs should be measured for at least two potential kinds of change in the scale of service: total withdrawal or commencement of an existing or new service and a variation around the existing level of provision.

Avoidable costs should be estimated for classes of commodity or passenger most relevant to the firm's market decisions. For example:

1. the likely long-term savings to the railways for getting out of the grain business altogether (including the option on competitive tendering for external provision of capacity above the off-peak requirements during the peak period);

2. eliminating the peak in grain carryings during the harvest period while allowing for a continuation of the base-level movement in that period.

In principle, the avoidable costs associated with less than total output reductions should also be estimated to enable the optimum set of adjustments to be more closely specified. If all existing services are in turn subject to an avoidable cost test, some portion of total costs are likely to remain unaccounted for. These *residual costs* cannot on any meaningful basis be attributed to particular traffics. These residual costs are *shared costs*. They have two main characteristics—*commonness* and *jointness*. In practice, it is usual to refer to all shared costs as joint costs, although the distinctions still apply, especially in respect of rules for allocating such costs. The rules are somewhat arbitrary from an economic-theoretic perspective, and controversial. Before discussing issues of allocation of shared costs we need to set out some definitions.

5.2.5 Shared costs: common and joint

Definition: shared costs are said to be *common* costs if transport services that share these costs are not jointly determined, that is, if one service does not unavoidably create another.

Clarification: although incurred if a certain range of output is to be entered at all, no individual unit of output within this range necessarily entails the production of any other unit. A common cost can be avoided but only for a given range of output. Within the range it is unavoidable and common to all units using it. For example, a given shipment or passenger transported from Amsterdam to London does not necessarily result in another shipment or passenger being transported from London to Amsterdam, and thus the shared costs are common.

Definition: a shared cost is *joint* when one transport service does not unavoidably result in the creation of another transport service.

Clarification: joint costs occur where the provision of a certain service necessarily entails output of some other service. For example, if a vehicle that travels from Amsterdam to London must return to Amsterdam (a bus, a train, a truck, a plane, a ship), the trip from Amsterdam to London is the fronthaul (or outward leg) and the trip from London to Amsterdam is the backhaul (or return leg) of the round trip.

The fronthaul trip has unavoidably created the backhaul trip.

A useful procedure for identifying shared costs involves notionally withdrawing each service in turn and comparing the sum of their avoidable costs with those entailed in maintaining the whole system. Assume two sectors—passenger (p) and freight (f). The combined service costs $80m. To consider the avoidable costs of passengers and freight separately, we have to specify an output change for each. Assume a complete withdrawal of respective services. Withdraw p—total costs are $30m. Withdraw f—total costs are $70m. Costs specifically attributed to p are $50m. (80 – 30). Costs specifically attributed to f are $10m. (80 – 70). Joint costs are $20m. (80 – 60), which cannot be traced to either p or f, and are therefore only assignable to the system as a whole, not to any smaller part of it. How one assigns them is the essence of strategic thinking (see below).

On financial criteria, p should be required to make at least $50m. to be deemed commercial on avoidable cost criteria (here we have established one basis of defining a commercial service). If all dollars earned were not contributed in part from tax payers' sources (i.e. government subsidy in all its definitional guises (CSO etc.)), then any internal cross-subsidy to cover losses in respect of not covering avoidable costs is quite acceptable other than from an internal efficiency perspective. It does signal, however, that some review of such a service is warranted.

If p can more than meet its avoidable costs, by however small a margin (i.e. it is a commercial service), then financial results would be somewhat worse if it were not carried. Similar arguments apply to f. There are also the $20m. shared costs to be covered, if the system is to be viable; that is, not lose money. We are beginning to see a distinction between commercial and non-commercial services and commercial/non-commercial systems/businesses as a whole. There are also the intermediate groupings such as the cluster of services/routes, depots, and divisions.

How this sum is to be raised has nothing logically to do with the relative scale of the two service types and supposed 'shares' in the $20m. which cannot be allocated between them. The critical issue is that the services together must raise at least sufficient *extra* revenue (over their attributable costs) to do this between them. That is, the respective *markets* must be able to yield the required revenue. It is hoped the markets may raise more to establish a profit. It is this philosophy on shared costs which is demand-based (in contrast to arbitrary supply-based rules) which places a major obligation on an operator to put a lot of effort into the revenue-side of the equation in the context of developing a cost model. Ignoring the revenue side is essentially failing to recognize the role of the market in 'allocating' shared costs.

Central to this philosophy on shared costs is 'what the respective markets will bear', which in turn will largely depend on customers' alternatives (i.e. modal competition). A knowledge of direct and cross-elasticities of quantity demanded with respect to prices and levels of service becomes very important (see Ch. 4).

Since the markets for different freight items and passenger classes differ widely, it is to be expected that, as a result of this search to cover costs and make profits, there will be substantial differences in the relation of charges to avoidable costs in each. This discussion supports the notion of a bottom-up strategy to the establishment and application of costing and revenue determination in contrast to a top-down strategy.

The arguments apply to all forms of transport, and to all levels of multi-product supply of service within a single firm. It is clearly desirable to have a common set of principles throughout the transport sector, especially if efficient resource allocation is dependent on the outcomes of competition between the modes.

5.2.6 Further comments

The avoidable cost exercise establishes the minimum revenues which particular traffics must generate to survive. This sets lower limits to their respective prices (both net and gross of subsidy depending on the social need status of a service). Simply identifying that a currently provided service is a loss-making service does not automatically establish a right to call it a community service obligation. We have to prove that the community actually needs the service and that this is the best way of providing such a needed service.

If the avoidable costs of *all* services are assessed, the results will show, by deduction from total system costs, the scale of shared costs to be met. Only then is it possible to consider the overall scale of contributions required from the various traffics, and whether sufficient revenue is being recovered from the different service activities taken together. That is, having comprehensively costed all outputs in the manner described, and discarded those failing to meet their avoidable costs, one can then address the question of how to raise the necessary total contribution to shared costs, by examining what the different markets will bear.

So long as this sum is raised, the relative contributions made by different traffics will not matter. All traffics making some contribution, however small, may be regarded as acceptable. The approach outlined above differs in a number of ways from the traditional treatment of shared costs (in particular, the way common costs are handled—see below). We take a specific decision-oriented view. We do not start with categories of long-term or short-term costs, or fixed and variable costs. The issue is: what consequences flow from a specific type of decision involving options? The particular calculations involve a prospectively permanent change in output, and so relate to costs avoided in the long run, that is, to the situation in which all necessary adjustments have been worked out, new contracts struck, labour levels changed, and so on.

Costs are not 'allocated' in the usual way. For example, costing the movement of a commodity would normally involve defining costs directly associated with its movement, and then apportioning or allocating other costs according to some rule. Instead, the approach outlined above looks to the change in total costs occasioned by the decision contemplated. For example, track maintenance and repair costs are not assigned over the sectors using a measure of relative sector output. Instead, the change in track costs associated with a specified con-

traction of total rail output and the resulting change in gross tonne kms. are identified.

There are some elements in common with the more usual approaches (especially in respect of joint costs). The preferred approach is the one most consistent with answering questions concerning alternative effects on transport finances, notably in respect of matters of pricing, investment, and disinvestment:

Measures to improve transport financial performance require the driving force of a strategy looking far enough ahead—2 to 10 years depending on the modal context—to permit major changes in the range of products the transport firm supplies, operating strategies, pricing methods and so on. Such a plan should start by examining the avoidable costs and revenues of the main sectors of the transport firm's business at the present time, recognising that the relevant data for this exercise is neither that given by traditional cost allocation procedures, nor that given by marginal cost studies of small changes in output. Opportunities for future growth, improved operating methods and more remunerative pricing are then examined for each sector. The plan itself consists of putting together the sectors in a way which ensures that each sector, and combination of sectors, recovers its avoidable costs (with specific subsidies being included where social considerations justify retention of unprofitable sectors) and the contribution to truly joint costs of each sector is maximised as market conditions allow. Any remaining deficit would then clearly need to be borne by the subsidised sectors if the firm is to continue. (Beesley and Kettle 1986)

5.2.7 The debate about rules for 'allocating' shared costs

There are three basic issues in the allocation of shared costs: identification of the shared cost, identification of the transport movements that incur (and thus are to share) the shared cost, and the selection of a rule for allocating the shared cost among the transport movements that incur it. Our preferred approach is market-oriented, as presented above. An alternative approach, often described as the supply-side approach, uses simple pro-rata rules regardless of 'what the market will bear'. This traditional treatment of shared costs adopts supply-side allocation rules for common costs and an essentially demand-side rule for joint costs. Before developing a detailed case study, some examples are set out below for allocating common and joint costs.

5.2.7.1 Pro-rata rules for allocating common costs

Three classes of pro-rata rules are given below with specific examples. All of these rules are known as *single capacity rules*. For multi-product or activity settings, they do not consider the cost of capacity that is used exclusively by the amount of a given type of movement in order to determine the movement's cost allocation of the shared capacity. They only look at the aggregate cost for all movements. If this exclusive capacity cost were known, management of the transport firm could compare this cost with the movement's cost allocation of the corresponding shared capacity and establish any possible cost inefficiency in the use of its present capacity.

Rule a: the ratio rule: Fixed common costs such as overhead costs are allocated among specific movements in proportion to revenue generated by these movements.

Rule b: the tonne/tonne-km. rule: Terminal/depot fixed costs are allocated to specific movements in proportion to tonnes/passengers originated and terminated. Line-haul fixed costs are allocated to specific movements in proportion to tonne-kms.

Rule c: percentage markup: Fixed costs are divided by total operating expenses to obtain the fixed-cost markup percentage. This percentage is multiplied by the operating expense (avoidable cost) incurred by a particular movement to obtain this movement's share of the fixed cost. Talley (1988: 180–6) discusses other rules.

5.2.7.2 Rules for allocating joint costs

The generally accepted rule is known as the Walters rule, which says that a joint cost is allocated between fronthaul and backhaul trips in proportion to the marginal expected joint costs of the trips. This is similar to the philosophy of the preferred approach in that the formula used to obtain the marginal expected joint costs requires a knowledge of demands for each type of trip. Thus we need say no more about this demand-side 'allocation' rule.

5.3 Knowing your costs in a bus and coach business: a case study

All bus and coach operators from time to time may want to be considered for a contract to run regular services as well as to bid for the provision of buses and coaches for major events such as an Easter show or an international sports meeting. They may also want to have an appreciation of the true costs to them of providing regular services such as permanent school contracts and individual route services.

In identifying the relevant set of costs, an operator should know what question to ask. The question is: what costs would be incurred if I were to introduce or change a service or what costs would be avoided if I were to eliminate a service?

The answer to this question will form the basis of calculating the relevant set of costs. The distinction between fixed and variable costs commonly used by accountants is quite irrelevant. The only issue which is relevant is which costs would not have been incurred (i.e. would have been avoided) if we were not to provide a particular service? These are the minimum costs you would incur if you provided the service.

In answering this question an operator also has to determine how each item of cost varies as the level of service varies. In particular:

- which costs vary by vehicle kilometres?
- which costs vary by bus hours provided?
- which costs vary by driver paid hours? and
- which costs vary by the number of buses and/or coaches used?

To calculate the contribution of each type of cost to the overall cost, an operator has to apply unit cost rates together with the resource requirements in order to work out the total cost. A unit rate is required which reflects the manner in which costs vary and helps in knowing how to spread a cost across a number of services.

For example, if fuel costs are 25 cents per km., then a contract involving 200 kms. per day will have to cover its fuel costs of $50. However, the additional cost of employing a mechanic may be zero because he is already employed and there is spare capacity. That is, there is no need to have him work extra hours. There will, however, be additional maintenance materials. As discussed below, an operator may want to allocate some of this mechanic's time as a cost to this service, but it is up to the business how it allocates a cost that is shared among a number of services. Fuel and non-labour materials in this example are avoidable; maintenance labour is not necessarily avoidable.

5.3.1 The basic structure of operating costs

The costs of running a bus and/or coach fleet are best categorized under five broad headings:

1. direct operating costs,
2. driver costs,
3. repair and maintenance costs,
4. vehicle fleet overheads,
5. vehicle capital-related costs.

Taking each cost category one at a time, we will make sure that you understand which cost items are associated with each category before we worry about how they vary. The list of attributed costs is not exhaustive, but is indicative of the classes of costs that any bus and/or coach operator incurs.

1. *Direct operating costs*: Direct operating costs include fuel, oil, lubricants, tyres, and tubes.

2. *Driver costs*: Driver costs include the driver's gross wage and all on-costs. An important distinction must be made between the set of costs applicable to full-time drivers and those relevant to casual drivers. The full set of driver-related cost items is summarized in Table 5.1 drawn from a typical Motor Bus Drivers Award (the award that applies to all drivers employed by bus operators in NSW). The specific on-costs vary in content and value across the world, but the principles are the same. On-costs are all the additional costs that the employer has to pay to employ a worker over and above the actual wage paid. These include payments for benefits such as holiday and long-service leave pay, superannuation, workers compensation, and government charges such as payroll tax.

3. *Repair and maintenance costs*: Repair and maintenance costs include labour and non-labour items. The labour costs are mechanics' gross wages plus all relevant on-costs. The same rules for driver on-costs apply to mechanics. Non-labour items include spare parts.

4. *Vehicle fleet overheads*: Included within this category are vehicle cleaning costs, rent and rates for depots, administrative staff costs (including on-costs), comprehensive insurance, registration and third-party insurance, and depot and administration overheads.

5. *Vehicle-related capital costs*: Each operator needs to have an annual estimate of the cost of their capital. Depreciation and interest (if applicable) have to be calculated as well as an identification of the actual and an acceptable return on investment. Return on investment is included under the heading of 'capital cost' because it is useful to think of it as an additional capital expense which has to be recovered if an operator is to replace his

Table 5.1 Itemized driver-related cost items with current rates

Item	Percentage on-cost		Current rates	
	Full-time %	Casual %	Full-time $	Casual $
Base hourly wage			11.57	13.31
% of base wages				
Holiday pay	8.333	8.333	0.9471	1.0892
Long-service leave	0.000 44	pro rata	0.0005	
Occupational superannuation	4.238	pro rata	0.4906	
Workers' compensation	2.0–3.0	2.0–3.0	0.23–0.34	0.23–0.34
Sick pay:				
<12 mths	(5 days)	—	431.90 pa	—
>12 mths	(8 days)	—	691.04 pa	—
Public holidays	(2 weeks)	—	795.61 pa	—
Casual loading	—	15.000	—	1.704 8
% of base wage plus on-costs				
Payroll tax	7.0–8.0	7.0–8.0	0.79–0.91	0.79–0.91
Other items				
Uniforms			200	200
Driver				

Permanent worker—38 hours per week $431.90		
Ordinary time		$11.57 per hour
1.50 time		$17.36 per hour
1.75 time		$20.25 per hour
2.00 time		$20.35 per hour
2.50 time		$28.94 per hour
Casual worker		
Ordinary time		$13.31 per hour
15% casual loading		$1.99 per hour
1/12th holiday pay		$1.10 per hour
Total pay		$16.41 per hour
Allowances per day, where applicable		
Dual capacity (no fares)		$2.50
Dual capacity (collect fares)		$4.23
Driver—articulated bus		$3.91
Broken shift finishing after 10 p.m.		$1.87
Early start/late finish		$1.38
Amenities allowance		$1.38
Meal allowance		$6.60
Permanent conductors		$386.70

buses and/or coaches and remain in business in the longer term. Some vehicles are leased and some are purchased outright or on hire purchase. These costs have to be identified. Given the complexities of calculating an annualized cost of vehicle capital, we need to discuss the calculation of capital charges separately in a later section.

5.3.2 The variability of cost items

When an operator needs to calculate the cost of providing so many driver hours, vehicle hours, and vehicle kilometres of service under either a contract or some other arrangement, it is necessary to decide on which costs are related to each of these three ways of calculating unit rates. In addition, some costs will vary according to the number of vehicles required regardless of distance or hours.

Our task now is to decide on how best to describe the variation in each cost item. Cost items assigned to the same class vary by a common source of variation as summarized in Table 5.2. Direct operating costs and non-labour repairs and maintenance costs are directly related to the work performed by buses and coaches. They vary directly with the number of kilometres travelled. Driver costs vary in part with the amount of time involved in working. Some of the on-costs are determined independently of the duration of work. Casual drivers have costs that do vary more directly with the work performed, although minimum time payments apply. It is common practice to relate driver costs to the number of paid (as distinct from actually worked) hours. Repair and maintenance labour costs (i.e. mechanics) are usually assumed to vary by the number of vehicle hours, although there are thresholds due to minimum hours of employment for a permanent worker and the differences in possible costs due to the extent to which an excessive amount of repair and maintenance may result in higher amounts of overtime. Vehicle fleet overheads are primarily determined by the size of the fleet. Some cost items will differ for different vehicle types, notably comprehensive insurance, but in the main it is reasonable to use fleet size. Vehicle-related capital costs tend primarily to vary with the age and mix of the fleet, and with the method of financing. A separate unit cost for each type of vehicle and method of financing may be useful.

5.3.3 Avoidable and shared costs

Now that we have identified the types of costs and how they vary, we have to decide on which costs have to be included in the calculation of the cost of providing (or withdrawing) a particular service. The golden rule is:

To cover your avoidable costs and make some contribution to your shared costs. Your avoidable costs should include an acceptable return on your investment.

The magnitudes of avoidable and shared costs will vary from operator to operator and from cost category to cost category. To illustrate the distinction between avoidable and shared costs, let us assume that an operator has two types of services; say either scheduled route services plus permanent school contracts, or scheduled route services and charter/tours. Taking each cost category, we find that:

1. *Direct operating costs and non-labour maintenance and repairs* vary directly with the number of kilometres or bus hours performed. These costs are therefore readily avoidable in that they are uniquely associated with each service on the basis of vehicle kilometres, and thus there are no shared costs. Thus if you adjust the vehicle kilometres, the direct operating costs and non-labour maintenance and repairs are fully avoided.

2. *Driver costs*: may be considered as falling into three categories:

- those which are avoidable for permanent school

Table 5.2 The nature of variation of costs

Cost category	Unit of variation	Unit rate
1. Direct operating costs	Vehicle kilometres	$/vkm
2. Driver costs	Driver paid hours	$/dhrs
3. Repair and maintenance costs	Vehicle kms. for non-labour	$/vkm
4. Vehicle fleet overheads	Vehicle hrs. for labour	$/vhrs
5. Vehicle-related capital costs	No. of vehicles by type	$/veh

Note: vkm = vehicle kilometres; dhrs = driver paid hours; vhrs = vehicle hours; veh = vehicles.

contracts, such that they would not be incurred if all permanent school contracts were eliminated;

- those which are avoidable for scheduled route services;
- those which are shared between permanent school contracts and scheduled route services, being driver costs which would not be avoided if either permanent school contracts or scheduled route services were withdrawn. Full-time drivers who are paid to operate scheduled route services but who also provide labour for some permanent school contracts are an example of a shared cost. If an operator currently providing scheduled route services, permanent school contracts, and charter services were to withdraw from the charter market and lay off three drivers (two of whom previously also did some permanent school contracts) without affecting the number of drivers required to service the scheduled route service and permanent school contract markets, then the avoidable cost is three drivers. Likewise if the operator were to bid for a contract for charter work which required the hiring of three additional drivers who would be dedicated to charter work, then the driver cost is three drivers.

3. *Vehicle fleet overheads and capital costs* also have an element of avoidable and shared costs, depending on the circumstance. This is the classic 'it depends' response. You have to ask the fundamental question: 'what additional costs would be incurred (or avoided) if a service were to be introduced or withdrawn?' in order to decide on the incidence of avoidable and shared costs.

The distinction between shared and avoidable costs is crucial for any bidding for contracts of any sort, as discussed in Chapter 2. Why do you think this is so important? The answer is: being able to identify the avoidable costs lets you know what is the minimum cost that you have to charge (quote) to at least recover the additional costs incurred as a result of changing the service level. An operator can then decide if it is possible to get away with a contract cost above this minimum cost in order to help cover the shared costs. However, at least knowing the avoidable costs gives you a base from which to

decide to what extent you can get away with a mark-up above the avoidable cost without running the risk of not getting the contract.

'Allocating' shared costs is not based on any simple or agreed rules. You should really decide on this in the context of the market in which you are operating. The common method of allocating shared costs according to the percentage of vehicle hours or vehicle kilometres involved in particular services is a supply-side approach usually devoid of any knowledge of what the market will bear. Such pro-rata rules signal a lack of strategic thinking in business planning.

5.3.4 Strategic and non-strategic bids

Deciding on how to allocate your shared costs is part of the process of determining the extent to which one is operating in an environment where there are varying degrees of competitiveness. Where competition exists, one has to recognize this and determine how to handle shared costs strategically. Where there is no competition one can operate non-strategically, although good practice should dictate that non-strategic costing should not misuse the monopoly power because some day it may disappear.

A non-strategic bid is one designed to cover what the operator considers their costs to be without taking into account the actions of competitors. On the other hand a strategic bid would first take into account the operator's costs, which may, however, be altered in the light of the anticipated action of competitors. If an operator is particularly keen to win the contract he or she may lower the bid price. This is done by allocating none or only part of the shared costs to that service but allocating them instead to other services. In doing this, however, one must be aware of the shared costs which have to be covered by the other services. One should also not lower a bid below the avoidable costs for that service. It is a dangerous long-term strategy to run services that cannot cover at least the avoidable costs and make some contribution to profits.

Bus and coach operators have to spend time learning about the markets they are in and markets they may wish to enter so that they can make informed judgements about the sensitivity of each market to price and hence the ability to allocate shared costs to each market. This approach to 'allocating' shared costs is known as 'what each market can bear'. Markets that are more price (or cost sensitive) should be allocated less of the shared costs than markets that are less price sensitive. Operators who reject this rule for shared costs in preference to a pro-rata rule such as proportion of vehicle kilometres associated with each service are missing out on opportunities to increase profits and/or to deliver a service at a more attractive cost while still ensuring overall profits (expected to be higher than those associated with the pro-rata view of the world).

5.3.5 **The capital cost of buses and coaches**

The appropriate cost of an asset to be charged against operations during any given period is the cost of using it during that period. When evaluating the capital cost of a bus or coach, the relevant cost to be considered is the entire capital cost, to be regarded as an outlay in the period the vehicle is acquired minus its residual value on sale (scrapping), to be regarded as a cash receipt at the time when the vehicle is disposed of. The cost of the capital has to be spread over the life of the asset. The capital cost of a vehicle can be determined in one of two ways: as the sum of depreciation and interest, the former usually calculated on a straight-line basis, or using capital recovery factors to determine the annual outlay which would be equivalent to future cash outlays resulting from an investment decision.

The second approach tells the operator what the cash value in a year is of the money which was invested in a bus or coach rather than invested elsewhere and which now has been spent as a result of one year of vehicle use. All operators must aim to cover both depreciation of the asset and a reasonable interest rate if their businesses are to be viable in the longer term or alternatively to recover costs to a level which gives an acceptable return on the investment

in buses or coaches. It is assumed that the economic life of a vehicle is influenced primarily by elapsed time. Differential utilization rates for a specific vehicle model and vintage have a negligible influence on the market price. The capital recovery formula used to calculate the average annualized cost of capital (denoted as C) has three elements defined as: $C = (A - B) \times$ amortization factor (AF) where $A =$ the vehicle real purchase cash price (regardless of whether leased, hire purchased, or paid cash, we are interested in what the vehicle is worth, not how it is financed) in constant dollars, and $B =$ the residual value of the coach after 15 years.

It is important to appreciate why the vehicle purchase cash price is used instead of the price actually paid under the chosen financing strategy. By using the market value of the vehicle at the time of purchase regardless of how the vehicle is financed, we are protecting the operator from any risks in the future associated with a very good finance deal today which cannot be guaranteed to apply in say 15 years, time. We recognize that this approach can work in favour of the operator if the future deal is actually better than that secured today (there will be a financial gain); in contrast if the financial deal in the future is worse, then the use of a market price protects the operator against such risk and the need to incur additional debt. There will always be risk, but the intent is to minimize it where possible.

All dollar items are also calculated net of inflation—known as real dollars. This approach is also designed to protect against the high level of uncertainty of inflation rates in the future period over which the annualized cost of use of the vehicle has to be recovered through charging the passengers. We can confidently say that predicting inflation each year over the next 15 years is extremely difficult—even the Treasury experts get it wrong. By working out the annualized cost in inflation-free dollars, we can convert the cost to actual dollars of the day in the previous year (closer to when we need to know for costing and setting prices) or over the next two to three years if a contract is being made. This time period is a lot more predictable, given the advice from Treasury and other forecasting agencies, than a 15-year annual forecast.

The amortization factor is calculated by knowing the long-term real interest or discount rate, and the years of useful coach life. The formula for calculating the amortization (or cost recovery) factor is:

$$AF = \frac{r}{1 + \dfrac{1}{(1+r)^n}} \qquad (5.1)$$

where r = real interest rate and n = number of years. For example, at a real rate of interest of 8% (r = 0.08) and an economic life of 15 years, the amortization factor is 0.1168. This figure can also be obtained by looking up a table of amortization factors. The amortization factors over the range of useful life of a bus or coach from one to 25 years at a real rate of interest of 8% have been calculated using the above formula and are shown in Table 5.3.

To obtain an estimate of the residual value of a bus or coach, one has to either know this or take a sample of a number of market prices obtained for vehicles disposed of in a particular year. The prices have to be averaged to ensure a uniform change in relative prices between years. The prices are then converted to constant dollars by calculating the compound rate of increase of a new vehicle over a 15-year period (approximately 13%) and applying this to the nominal vehicle prices. The decline in value per annum is then calculated, and the value projected to a constant 15-year life (the average life

assumed by the private bus and coach sector). The ratio of the value projected in constant dollars to a constant 15-year life over the historical cost can be expressed as the average percentage residual or scrap value of a 15-year-old coach. Typical working percentages for the residual value (as a percentage of the new purchase price) vary from 5% to 15%.

To calculate the average capital cost of a bus per annum, let us assume a purchase price in 1995 (A) equal to $200,000, with a 15-year useful (i.e. economic) life for the business, and a residual value after 15 years (B) of $65,000. The rate of return on investment is assumed to be 15% comprising a rate of inflation (CPI) of 7%. The real rate of interest is thus 8% per annum. The amortization factor over 15 years and for an 8% real rate of interest is 0.1168. Given the formula for average capital cost per bus per annum: $C = (A - B)$ *amortization factor, we substitute the data above as $C = ($200,000 - $65,000)$ *0.1168. This produces an annualized cost of capital of $15,768 in 1995 dollars. Column 2 in Table 5.4 lists the annualized cost of capital each year in constant 1995 dollars.

When it comes to applying the result each year, we have to convert the $1995 figure into dollars of the day (i.e. nominal or current levels). For example, the 1996 estimate assuming inflation of 7% is: $ nominal (1996) = $15,768*(1 + 7/100) = $16,872. We can calculate the estimated capital cost in 1997 by either

Table 5.3 Amortization factors for annualizing investment cost (based on an assumed 8% real interest rate)

Useful life	Amortization factor	Useful life	Amortization factor
1	1.0800	14	0.1213
2	0.5608	15	0.1168
3	0.3880	16	0.1130
4	0.3019	17	0.1096
5	0.2505	18	0.1067
6	0.2163	19	0.1041
7	0.1921	20	0.1019
8	0.1740	21	0.0998
9	0.1601	22	0.0980
10	0.1490	23	0.0964
11	1.1401	24	0.0950
12	0.1327	25	0.0937
13	0.1265		

adding the rate of inflation to the 1996 nominal estimate or by applying a compounding formula to the initial 1995 figure. If we do the calculation using the previous year's nominal estimate then we simply multiply the estimate by (1 + rate of inflation) such as 1.07 if the inflation rate is 7% in 1997. The compounding approach would take the 1995 estimate and multiply it by (1.07)*(1.07). The answer of $18,053 is the same using both approaches. An important message from this example is: would you be able to estimate inflation in the year 2004 in 1997? We very much doubt it; hence the reason for making the inflation adjustment for identifying the annualized cost of capital in a particular year at a time much closer to the year in which costs have to be recovered.

5.3.6 Applying the costing principles to a competitively tendered contract

Let us assume that the Department of Transport wishes to tender and re-tender for contracts on late-night passenger services from 11 p.m. until 6 p.m. to replace trains with buses. Any operator is free to submit a bid for the advertised routes. The tender documents supplied to each inquiring operator include:

1. a draft agreement;

2. service specifications;

3. a tender form, a tender form cover sheet, and service detail schedules for each tender that an operator has expressed an interest in; and

4. the conditions of tender.

For our case study we are interested in seeing how an appropriate set of costs is calculated. It is important that costs are identified and calculated very carefully, because the bids can often be very close. This is illustrated in Table 5.5 which shows the total cost, in 1990 dollars, for the whole contract, made in bids submitted for one route.

The tendering authority describes the service in sufficient detail for an operator to be able to under-

Table 5.4 Calculating average capital cost per bus per annum: an example (real and nominal rates of interest and constant dollars)

| Years | Average capital cost per annum | |
	$ 1995	$ Nominal
1995	$15,768	$15,768
1996	$15,768	$16,872
1997	$15,768	$18,053
1998	$15,768	$19,316
1999	$15,768	$20,669
2000	$15,768	$22,115
2001	$15,768	$23,664
2002	$15,768	$25,320
2003	$15,768	$27,092
2004	$15,768	$28,989
2005	$15,768	$31,018
2006	$15,768	$33,189
2007	$15,768	$35,513
2008	$15,768	$37,998
2009	$15,768	$40,658

Notes:
- A real rate of interest is a rate after eliminating the rate of inflation.
- The nominal rate of interest is the sum of the real rate of interest and the rate of inflation.
- The expression 'constant dollars' is often used to refer to a situation where all dollar items are converted to equivalent dollars of a particular year.

take appropriate cost calculations. The service is described in terms of:

- a very specific route,

- the total distance in kilometres,

- the number of buses required to operate the basic service,

- additional buses required to provide back-up for particular services,

- the detailed timetable,

- the section fares and the location of section points,

- concession fare instructions.

In addition to service specifications, information is provided on:

- vehicle requirements (capacity, quality, heating, security, communications, etc.)

Table 5.5 Bids for nightride contracts

Bidder 1	$2,139,886	$2.20 per bus km.
Bidder 2	$1,948,341	$2.01 per bus km.
Bidder 3	$1,813,605	$1.87 per bus km.
Bidder 4	$1,951,524	$2.01 per bus km.
Bidder 5	$2,300,475	$2.37 per bus km.
Bidder 6	$2,209,539	$2.28 per bus km.
Bidder 7	$2,128,539	$2.20 per bus km.

- on-board taxi booking facility requirement,
- details of driver qualifications (licence, attire, experience with fares, communications, etc.),
- performance bond requirements.

The remuneration is an agreed sum representing the annual cost of providing the service. The agreed amount is indexed and adjusted in accordance with details set out on how indexation is applied. Indexation is applied by the Department of Transport to the following items:

1. *Drivers' wages*: reviewed annually on the anniversary of the commencement date, based on movements in the base rates of the Motor Bus Drivers Award;

2. *Fuel (Distillate)*: based on movement in the purchase price for bulk distillate obtained from Shell Company. Contract rates are reviewed annually on the anniversary of the commencement date.

All other costs are *not* indexed. It is therefore important that an operator apply indexation to these items, or increase them by whatever factor they think is appropriate, for the second and subsequent years of the contract. Some variations to contract payments are allowed for:

1. Where additional vehicles are required to undertake the service, the Director-General of Transport (DGT) seeks the first quote for supplying such vehicles from the contractor, but he is also entitled to approach and/or make other arrangements to contract other operators where he is of the opinion that it is in the best interest of the public. The subsequent remuneration is negotiated at the appropriate time.

2. Where, in the day-to-day operation of the contracted service, the DGT requires the vehicle to travel additional kilometres in excess of the scheduled kilometres, the driver costs per hour or a quarter thereof as specified in the schedule, *plus* an operating cost per kilometre, are remunerated. The operating cost per kilometre for this service is the annual cost for fuel plus all other annual operating costs as given by the contractor, divided by the estimated service kilometres.

3. Where the DGT cancels any additional vehicles which he has requested one day or less prior to the service, the contractor is entitled to charge a cancellation fee of an agreed amount.

4. Where the vehicle undertaking the service is unable to meet any connecting service and the fault cannot be attributed to the DGT, except where a failure is a consequence of an act of God, fire, and so on, or other matter over which the contractor has no control, the contractor shall be held responsible for providing a replacement service.

From the tender documentation an operator is able to work out the resource requirements. For example, we will assume a contract for two routes that we will call No. 1 and No. 2. For these routes the service requirements are as summarized in Table 5.6. From the tender documents let us assume that a bidder has calculated the following resource requirements:

Drivers' hours	19,000 per annum
Vehicle kilometres	255,736 per annum
Total seat kilometres (56 seaters)	1,4321,216 per annum
Vehicle hours	22,000 per annum
Fuel efficiency of each bus on average	15 litres/100 km.
Additional call-out hours per annum	5,680
Cost per extra kilometre	40 cents/km.

and made the following assumptions:

1. no additional buses are required to the ones the business already has in the fleet;

2. on-board radio communication equipment has to be installed.

Table 5.6 Resource requirements for nightride contract for routes no. 1 and no. 2

Route no.	Kms.	One-way services per night	Additional service per week	Total services per week	Total kms. per yr.
No. 1	38	10	4	74	146,224
No. 2	26	11	4	81	109,512
Total	64	21	8	155	255,736

Notes: Estimated call-outs per year: weekdays = 10, Saturday = 2, Sunday = 1, public holiday = 7. Average hours per call-out = 3.

The questions to ask are:

- how much of this cost should be included in the current tender proposal?
- does this equipment have other uses? and
- can it be shared with other services?

These should all be asked in order to try and enhance the chance of winning the contract. A bidder thinking strategically must ensure that he or she at least covers avoidable costs and handles the shared costs appropriately.

Using the information in the tender documents and the resource requirements calculated above, the cost of providing the contract services may be calculated using a format such as that shown in Table 5.7. This will give us some help in deciding what costs need to be taken into account when asking and answering the question about avoidable costs. Each cost item will be an avoidable cost, a shared cost, or an 'it depends' cost. Any cost that is determined to

be shared will have to be recouped from somewhere in the full set of services supplied by a transport operator. Whether the operator should recoup part or all of any shared costs from this competitive tender must depend on any intelligence about how competing bids might treat shared costs. Applying a pro-rata allocation rule to shared costs (e.g. the proportion of each bus's annual vehicle kilometres associated with this contract service) will almost certainly ensure an unsuccessful bid. We invite the reader to contemplate which costs they would include in their bid offer.

From these cost figures an operator may be interested in calculating some commonly used performance measures which would allow a comparison of the cost of providing these services with the cost of some of the other services or with industry averages. For example, the unit cost per bus operating kilometre is $3.33. The unit cost per seat kilometre is $0.06.

5.4 Maritime coastal vessel costing

The principles outlined above together with the case study in the bus sector apply with equal strength to all modal sectors (see discussion issue 9). In this section and the next sections, we provide an outline of the types of costs which exist in the maritime and private vehicle use sectors.

The costs associated with a shipping business can

be classified into capital costs, operating costs, voyage costs, and cargo-handling costs. In presenting the main features of each cost category, we recognize that there will always be differences between countries in the treatment of items such as taxation; however, the fundamentals of costing are sufficiently generic to be applicable internationally. There are

Table 5.7 Calculation of nightride tender contract costs

Year	1999		
Cost item	Quantity	Unit cost $	Total cost $
Costs which vary by person hours			
Driver hours: penalty	25,000	18	450,000
Drivers' on-costs (36%)			162,000
Inspector hours: penalty	400	18	7,200
Inspectors' on-costs (36%)			2,592
Costs which vary by vehicle kms.			
Fuel	255,736	0.23	58,819.3
Non-labour maintenance	255,736	0.20	51,147.2
Tyres and tubes	255,736	0.10	25,573.6
Costs which vary by vehicle hours			
Administration labour hours: normal	300	15	4,500
Administration labour hours: penalty	300	24	7,200
Admin. labour hours on-costs (36%)			4,212
Administration materials	22,000	0.2	4,400
Capital costs			
Registration			3,000
Insurances			2,000
Annualized capital cost of vehicles[1]			70,097.7
Total cost			**852,741.8**

Notes: 1. The following assumptions are made in calculating the annualized cost of vehicles:

Rate of return on investment	15%
Rate of inflation (CPI)	7%
Real rate of interest	8%
Amortization factor	0.1168
Initial purchase price of *all* buses	600,000
Years of useful bus life	15

2. For the subsequent years of the contract (2000 and 2001 in the case of this two-year contract), for those items which are not automatically indexed by the Department of Transport, you need to determine by how much you expect them to increase and adjust them accordingly.

eight major determinants of capital costs: vessel acquisition costs, a drawdown schedule, the effective working life of a vessel, residual (or scrap) value, financing arrangements, taxation measures, exchange rates, and the method of establishing the annualized cost of capital (such as the cost recovery method outlined for buses).

With rare exceptions (e.g. the USA), vessels can be acquired from any country under a variety of ownership and registration arrangements. The major classes of vessel acquisition costs are the yard cost (the largest component of cost); placement, administration and project costs; cargo equipment costs (applicable primarily to roll-on/roll-off vessels), and other expenses such as upgrading outlays to comply with flag of convenience vessels to meet accommodation standards under the International Maritime Organization (IMO) conventions. Applebaum Consulting Group (1995) established indicative estimates of such costs for the three classes of vessels—dry bulk (35,000 dead-weight tonnage (d.w.t.) defined as the difference between the displacement of the vessel loaded to its summer load-line and the light displacement), product carrier (30,000 d.w.t.) and Ro/Ro (5,000 d.w.t.) (Table 5.8). Payment profiles defined by drawdown schedules identify how the vessel acquisition costs are paid for over time up to the date of commissioning. Typical six-monthly drawdown percentages are 5, 10, 25, 20, and 40.

Table 5.8 Annual vessel acquisition costs, 1994 ($US m.)
(based on a 10-year repayment)

	Ro/Ro	Product carrier	Dry bulk
Yard cost	35.0	36.0	24.0
Placement, administration, and project	0.7	1.5	1.8
Cargo equipment	2.4	n/a	n/a
Other expenses	0.6	0.5	0.4
Total	38.7	38.0	26.2

The effective working life of a coastal vessel is linked to an acceptable rate of return on capital, as required by the vessel owner and any organization with a financial interest (e.g. banks). Fifteen years is commonly accepted as the economic life of the asset, with a residual value determined by the health of the international maritime market for sales of vessels. Typical sale values for scrap in South-East Asia are between 0.5 and 2% of the new vessel cost. These are clearly very low residual values.

Although we note that most coastal vessels are financed on a 60–40 debt-to-equity funding ratio with a 10-year loan repayment at fixed interest rates (close to a real rate of interest of 6% in Australia in 1994), we have suggested in the previous case study that the minimum risk strategy for establishing the annualized cost of capital should be based on market value independent of the strategy for financing the asset. In some countries such as Japan, shipowners have access to interest rate subsidies from the Japanese Development Bank typically lowering such real rates by as much as 20% compared to international levels. Using the cost-recovery method as a way of identifying discounted cash flows, we can then determine how much revenue must be raised each year that can enable the shipowner to replace the vessel at the end of its economic life with a vessel of equivalent quality without having to acquire debt beyond that obtained with the existing investment. Exchange rates have to be taken into account in arriving at the final real rate of interest.

Operating costs include manning, repairs and maintenance, stores, hull and machinery insurance, administration, overheads, protection and indemnity insurance, annual provision for dry docking, victualling (the provision of consumables to the crew such as food), and a range of industry charges.

Manning costs are the largest element of operating costs. After capital costs that represent 60 to 75% of total costs, manning accounts for 7 to 26% of all costs or over 50% of operating costs for product carriers (BIE 1995, table A5.3; Stopford 1988, table 3.5). The manning cost incidence varies from a low of 7% for Germany to a high of 26% for Japan, with Australia having 21%, the USA 18%, Korea 10%, and the UK 12%. The proportional breakdown is similar for Ro/Ro and dry bulk vessels. Manning costs include direct gross wages and on-costs (just like the bus case study, except that some items are not included and there are additional on-costs such as joining and leaving costs, employer-funded training, and industry calls).

Annual repairs and maintenance of vessels include voyage repairs and spare gear, annual survey fees, and hull and machinery insurance excess. To maintain class for insurance purposes, all merchant vessels must undergo regular surveys. The ship must be dry docked every two years and every four years must have a special survey by one of the classification societies, approving the seaworthiness of the vessel (Stopford 1988). Maintenance costs increase with age and can dominate operating costs in older tonnage.

Hull and machinery insurance involves coverage of the ship's hull and machinery for total loss and damage. The loss component is based on the vessel's insured value adjusted for its condition, its flag, management, crew type, the operator's record and experience. Stores include engine room stores, marine and deck stores, stewards' store excluding victualling. Administration and overhead costs include internal administration, overheads, and management fees to external agencies. Protection and indemnity insurance protects against third parties and environmental damage. It varies according to the owner's maritime performance, trading patterns, cargo type, flag/crew composition, and experience of owners and managers as well as the cost structure of the insurer. Other industry-related expenses include light dues, marine navigation levies and conservancy, and oil pollution levies.

The operating cost structure tends to be linked to the size and nationality of the crew, maintenance policy, age and insured value of vessels, and the administrative efficiency of the shipowners and management. A summary of operating costs for selected countries is given in Table 5.9, compiled from various sources. Bunker or fuel costs are included in operating costs although they are often separated out under voyage costs together with port and agency costs. Fuel costs are typically 7% of total

vessel costs, which is identical to the contribution to total bus costs.

Shore-based shipping costs are primarily port charges, stevedoring, customs brokers' fees, and road/rail transport. In 1995, such charges for handling containers in dollars per TUE for a 35,000 gross registered tonnage (GRT) vessel varied from A$103 GRT for the port of Johor to A$404 per GRT for the port of Oakland (USA). Australian ports ranged from A$326 for the port of Sydney to A$296 for the port of Adelaide (BIE 1995). TUE is a 20-foot equivalent unit (20 by 8.5 by 8.5 feet).

A shipowner and/or operator should include all of the cost items presented here in establishing the costs of doing all maritime business, and apply the principles of avoidable and shared costs when determining how the costs of each activity are to be recovered, including an acceptable return on investment. Mindful of the differential nature of competition in each market currently being served or potentially available to enter, a strategically thinking operator will carefully assess how best to apportion the shared costs when determining what shipping rates to charge.

5.5 Determining the marginal vehicle operating costs for each road section

An important cost item in studies of transport user charges (see Ch. 6) is the determination of the costs to users of operating their vehicles (cars, trucks, etc.) on the road network. For example, in addition to travel time savings benefits (as discussed in Ch. 4), the promotion of a tollroad often depends on a marketing campaign which highlights the savings in vehicle operating costs if one were to opt for a toll road rather than continue to use a lower standard road with many at-grade intersections, and traffic lights. Many countries have vehicle operating cost (VEHOP) models designed to calculate vehicle operating costs for individual vehicle types under operating conditions which can allow for differences due to

vehicle speed, vertical and horizontal alignment of the road (i.e. grade and curvature), the volume/capacity ratio, the road surface type, and the road surface condition. Due allowance for all of these characteristics of a road system is important in obtaining estimates of the unit cost per kilometre of vehicle use.

We can use the relevant set of use-related vehicle operating costs to obtain cents per km. estimates of fuel cost, oil cost, tyres cost, and vehicle repair and maintenance. We have excluded the set of vehicle operating costs that are a function of the age of a vehicle. It should be noted that a primary use of vehicle operating cost models is in generating unit

Table 5.9 Illustrative operating costs of coastal vessels, 1994 (as % of operating costs)

Cost item	Australia	Japan	Germany	Norway	Korea	USA	NZ	UK
Manning	36	56	23	36	26	58	38	28
Voyage bunker costs	23	14	27	25	26	10	20	20
Repairs and maintenance	25	16	20	17	26	10	18	28
Stores	2	2	3	3	3	3	2	2
Administration	3	2	6	3	5	3	7	7
Hull and machinery insurance	2	2	3	3	3	3	2	2
Protection and indemnity insurance	2	2	3	3	0	3	2	2
Other insurance	0	0	0	0	0	0	2	0
Victualling	2	2	3	0	3	3	2	2
Provision for dry docking	5	6	12	10	8	10	7	9
Industry specific fees	0	0	0	0	0	0	0	0

resource costs for inclusion in an economic evaluation. We are also interested in the behavioural costs actually faced by users and hence have added in non-resource components of cost such as taxation and excise. For example, in 1992, the average price of a litre of petrol at the pump in Sydney was 69 cents, comprising 38.9 cents of resource value and a balance of non-resource cost items. The assumptions we have adopted to accommodate the range of non-resource items are given in Table 5.10.

Table 5.11 summarizes the range of information that we can input into the calculation of the marginal vehicle operating costs using the car as an illustration. This information has been compiled for each section of road we have designated as a section for

the purposes of a user calculating their own vehicle operating costs for a tolled and a non-tolled route. Together with differences in travel time and the overall relative stress, a user will have sufficient information to make a rational choice.

5.5.1 Fuel consumption

Determination of fuel consumption (in litres per 100 km.) is important in the calculation of unit vehicle operating costs. Time trials with vehicles fitted with fuel-monitoring equipment provide a very good way of securing the necessary data. Data obtained from time trial on-board computers which

Table 5.10 Non-resource cost mark-ups applicable to marginal vehicle operating costs (%)

Non-resource cost items	Fuel	Oil	Tyres	Repairs and maintenance
State franchise fee	9.5			
Product excise	37.1			
Royalties	0.4			
Resource rent tax	6.8	6.8		
Sales tax			20.0	20.0
Total mark-ups	53.8	6.8	20.0	20.0

Notes: Product excise is an impost levied by the Commonwealth Government on the sale of motor spirit.
Royalties (ad valorem) and resources rent royalty are paid to the Commonwealth and State governments as payments averaged over the total monthly domestic indigenous crude/condensate sales.
Resource rent tax on crude oil/condensate is a secondary tax levied by the Commonwealth Government on the taxable profits of most offshore petroleum projects, ascertained by reference to the excess of assessable receipts over deductible expenditure. The estimated tax is weight-averaged over the total monthly domestic sales of indigenous crude oil/condensate.

Table 5.11 Vehicle operating costs for a tollroad and the alternative non-tolled roads: illustrative output for cars and light commercials

	Peak		Off-peak	
	Tollroad	Free route	Tollroad	Free route
Route characteristics				
Speek (km./hr.)	80	50	90	60
Grade (1–5)	2%	2%	2%	2%
Curve class (0–4)	0	0	0	0
Volume/capacity ratio (0.0–1.0)	0	6	0	6
Road surface type	S[1]	S[1]	S[1]	S[1]
Surface condition (1–5)	5	3	5	3
Material consumption	8.3	10.0	9.0	10.1
Fuel (litres/100 km.)	27.3	23.6	28.0	24.7
Oil (litres/10,000 km.)	0.5	1.0	0.6	1.2
Tyres (per 10,000 km.)				
Costs	5.70	6.91	6.19	6.99
Fuel cost (cents/km.)	0.88	0.71	0.90	0.74
Oil cost (cents/km.)	0.60	1.20	0.72	1.47
Tyres (cents/km.)	8.05	9.24	8.05	9.24
Repair and maintenance (cents/km.)				
Total unit cost (cents/km.)	15.23	18.05	15.86	18.44
Saving by using toll road (cents/km.)	2.82		2.58	
Total stop cost ($)	0.00	1.32	0.00	1.32

Note: The results in this table are based on an assumption that the entire trip is either along a tollroad or the alternative route and that the VEHOP fuel consumption formula for cars is adopted which cannot distinguish cars in terms of their characteristics such as number of cylinders. Average route characteristics are assumed which are misleading for particular sections, as well as giving a misleading answer for highly non-linear cost items.

[1] Smooth.

supplied data on fuel consumption, average speed, and vehicle cylinders, can be used to run a regression equation where the dependent variable is fuel consumption (litres per 100 km.) and the explanatory variables are speed and number of cylinders. The parameterized model can then be used to obtain predictions of road section fuel consumption, given average section speed and vehicle cylinders.

Where such data are not available, there are alternative ways of securing suitable information. Another way to obtain an estimate of the unit fuel cost (in cents per km.) for cars is to apply a series of formulae and simulate an average estimate for type of car and light commercial vehicle.

The steps are as follows:

1. Obtain the highway (i.e. tollroad) and city (i.e. alternative free route) recommended manufacturer fuel consumption cycles from an available vehicle attribute database, and use this to calculate an average for each of the three categories of 4, 6, and 8 cylinder cars and light commercials.

2. To convert to more reliable on-road estimates, apply the adjustment formula developed by Hensher *et al.* (1992):

On-Road Fuel Consumption
(*ORFC*) =
0.988462 + 0.871080 * Handbook
(laboratory testing) estimate

3. Given the average price of a litre of fuel (e.g 69 cents for leaded or unleaded petrol and 60 cents for diesel, building in an average discount of 4 cents per litre for diesel), we can apply the formula:

Table 5.12 Average unit fuel costs for road and vehicle settings

Fuel indicators	4 Cylinder		6 Cylinder		8 Cylinder	
	Highway	City	Highway	City	Highway	City
Litres/100 kms.	7.84	10.35	9.91	13.71	12.46	18.12
Cents/km.	5.41	7.14	6.84	9.46	8.60	12.50
Fuel price (cents/litre)	69.0	69.0	69.0	69.0	69.0	69.0
Kms./litre	12.76	9.66	10.09	7.29	8.03	5.52

Notes: Light commercial vehicles include vehicles such as Mitsubishi Express and Toyota Hi-Ace, and are treated exactly like cars in respect of fuel consumption and fuel cost. The car figures allow for the mix of manual and automatic vehicles. Automatic vehicles are less fuel efficient than manual vehicles.

Source: Institute of Transport Studies database on vehicles under 3 tonnes, 1991.

(*ORFC* * unit fuel cost per litre)/100 * no. of kilometres travelled

For example: if *ORFC* = 8 litres per 100 km. and fuel is 69 cents per litre, it costs 552 cents per 100 km. If the trip is 10 kms. then the fuel cost is 55.2 cents.

The data in Table 5.12 are our best estimate of differences in the average fuel cost per kilometre (independent of speed) for categories of vehicles using a tollroad and the alternative routes, assuming that the tollroad typifies the *highway cycle* and the alternative routes typify the *city cycle*.

5.5.2 Impact of stops on operating costs

Each section of a non-tolled road has a number of traffic lights, which affect the fuel consumption of each vehicle. To allow for this source of operating cost difference between the tollroad and alternative routes, we have calculated the cost per stop for different categories of vehicle. The time trials collected data on the average number of stops per section, which have been combined with the unit cost to obtain our best estimates of section stop costs. These costs are summarized in Table 5.13.

5.6 Transport costs at the industry level

An individual transport business will always see its number one priority in its quest for a knowledge of costs directed towards its own operations. However, strategically focused operators will also see a high priority in understanding the nature of costs for the industry sector to which they belong. A knowledge of industry costs and performance will provide valuable information to strategically position oneself against current and future competitors. It will also provide early warning signals about the overall health of the industry sector and what possible actions regulators and competitors may be planning to circumvent one's competitive position and opportunities for restructuring and growth. To practise in a vacuum from the realities of competition, regulation, and other possible interventionist activities in the broader community (e.g. the environmental lobbies) is a long-term recipe for being marginalized and even becoming defunct.

Table 5.13 Section stopping costs on a typical tollroad and a major arterial road

Section	Route	Ave. no. of stops		Total stop cost ($)		
		Car	Truck	Car	Light truck	Heavy truck
1–2	Toll	0	0	0.00	0.00	0.00
2–3	Toll	0	0	0.00	0.00	0.00
3–4	Toll	0	0	0.00	0.00	0.00
4–5	Toll	0	0	0.00	0.00	0.00
5–6	Toll	0	0	0.00	0.00	0.00
6–7	Toll	0	0	0.00	0.00	0.00
6–15–9	Toll/free	11.13	10.02	0.70	1.15	3.57
7–15–9	Toll/free	7.13	5.33	0.45	0.61	1.90
7–8–9	Toll/free	4.63	4.00	0.29	0.46	1.42
7–9	Toll	0	0	0.00	0.00	0.00
9–10	Toll	0	0	0.00	0.00	0.00
10–11	Toll	0	0	0.00	0.00	0.00
12–13	Free	0.24	0.46	0.02	0.05	0.16
13–14	Free	4.09	5.40	0.26	0.62	1.92
14–6	Free	9.17	11.35	0.57	1.31	4.04
6–15–16	Free	4.00	4.07	0.25	0.47	1.45
16–17	Free	1.88	2.15	0.12	0.25	0.77
17–11	Free	1.71	2.38	0.11	0.27	0.85

Note: Stop costs for car = 6.25 cents/stop.
Stop costs for light truck = 11.50 cents/stop.
Stop costs for heavy truck = 35.60 cents/stop.

Example: 11.5 cents/stop = (0.05 litres/stop * 69 cents/litre) + 8.1 cents/stop, where 8.1 is non-fuel operating cost per stop.

Source: Roads and Traffic Authority (1992).

This section of the costing chapter introduces a number of important concepts which define the framework within which the cost structure of a transport sector is revealed, and input into the wider debate on pricing, service, and investment decisions in the industry as a whole. The feasibility of competition between transport businesses of different sizes and service mixtures is an important regulatory issue. The presence of scale economies raises important debates about (natural) monopoly, efficiency, and financial viability where efficient pricing at marginal cost is promoted, since the presence of financial deficits becomes a real possibility. Through an industry-level understanding of the cost structure of its members, opportunities exist for an assessment of comparative performance. After identifying sources of difference within and beyond an individual business's control, valuable feedback is available to assist individual businesses in working to improve their competitive advantage.

5.6.1 The multi-output nature of transport businesses

When studying the aggregate structure of any transport sector, it is very clear that most businesses deliver more than one product to the market. Bus operators deliver scheduled route services, charters and tours, and school services; railways deliver freight and passenger services to metropolitan, intra-state and inter-state markets, for bulk and non-bulk freight and for various classes of passenger service; airlines deliver national and international services to a range of classes of passengers (first, business, full economy, discount economy); trucking/logistics companies service local and long-distance routes using a myriad of types of vehicles; all forms of infrastructure—roads, airports, maritime ports, railways—perform multiple services; and shipping delivers container, dry bulk, liquid bulk, cruising services internationally and domestically (coastal).

Many of the costs of running a business are shared by the range of outputs, and hence complicate the identification of the efficiency of an industry in delivering specific services. For example, the determination of the productivity of business-class air services cannot be established without making some assumptions about the 'allocation' of shared costs.

This section discusses a number of important ideas in economics associated with the cost structure of a multi-product or multi-service transport firm and industry. The main concepts are economies of scale, economies of scope, product-specific scale economies, and multi-product scale economies. We highlight the importance of product differentiation and that treating output as homogeneous, as is implied by economies of scale, tells only part of the story of how transport firms can supply a given level of output at the lowest cost, given the prices of inputs.

To motivate the importance of a knowledge of the structure of costs across transport businesses in the same or a closely related sector, we present a number of examples. The central most discerning feature of these examples is the recognition made, not of the potential gains in reducing average costs by increasing the size of a business where there are a lot of fixed costs, but also that many of the financial gains can be achieved by a single firm producing a given level of output of each product or service more cheaply than a combination of separate firms, each producing a single product at the given output level. This latter phenomenon is called 'economies of scope' and complements the older concept of 'economies of scale' which assumes a single or homogeneous product or service. Positive economies of scope exist when they arise from *sharing* or the joint use of inputs.

The usual characterization of the single-output production function is inadequate to explain the way economies of scope arise. It is necessary to examine the component parts and stages of production to see how inputs may be used by different processes of production. For example, the shared factor *station master* confers an economy of scope on the joint production of rail passenger and freight services. Importantly, this economy of scope exists even when there are constant unit costs in all stages of production so that scale economies are lacking.

Robotics is an example of a recognition of economies of scope. By varying the order in which parts are transferred between different machine tools, the robot production line has the flexibility to handle a variety of separate products, and thus use *economies of scope* to achieve the large quantities necessary to take advantage of economies of automation. Thus robotics is an example of a way of linking economies of scale and scope to current technology and methods of production. Assembly-line production with human labour is most economical for single-product runs of large scale.

Indivisibility is another phenomenon where economies of scope can contribute to reducing average costs. A *fixed* input (over most levels of output) such as rail-track infrastructure leads to economies of scale (cost spreading over higher outputs). Suppose, however, that we have excess capacity of this fixed infrastructure input at the current level of demand. Then the sharing of the infrastructure between rail freight as well as passenger services will confer an economy of scope.

Transport networks are an important feature of delivering seamless transport across a supply chain. The recognition of movements between parts of a network suggests some gains to users from preservation of the integrity of a network. In aviation, the ability to hub between city pairs and collect higher levels of patronage from regional networks and transfer them onto larger aircraft means that the cost per seat kilometre is much lower on the main city pair routes. This scale economy provides an incentive for airlines to organize provision of services by offering a networking arrangement involving one-stop (hub) service. Thus by *hubbing*, economies of scale of a specialized input, airplanes, can be reaped. This also opens the potential for greater scope of operations in that an airline can coordinate the scheduling of services to a variety of city-pair markets. In trucking, terminals are located to consolidate shipments dispersed over a network (Wang and Friedlaender 1984).

Another example of a class of scope economies is economies of transacting. A multi-product firm may emerge when several industries require similar knowledge but there are transacting difficulties affecting the transfer of that knowledge. The marrying of a trucking company with a high-tech computer-dispatching business is a good example.

When we move beyond the simple idea of a single product or service business, it creates a boundary problem in defining firms and products. Is the combined trucking and computer-dispatching business part of the trucking industry and/or the information industry? In order to identify any separate industries or joint industries, we need clear statements on the interrelationships of production costs of the separate outputs. To identify the component elements of cost structures and of functional components of production and distribution it is necessary to introduce the relevant set of cost concepts for the multi-product firm, treating the traditional single-product firm as a special case.

5.6.2 Economies of scale in a single product/service business

Formally, economies of scale are defined as the relationship between levels of cost and levels of a single class of output. There are three outcomes for economies of scale—where average total cost increases as output increases, we have increasing costs or decreasing returns to scale; where average total cost decreases as output increases, we have decreasing costs or increasing returns to scale; and where average total cost does not change as output increases, we have constant costs or constant returns to scale. The notion of 'scale' refers very precisely to a comparison of the lowest achievable average total cost for each level of a fixed input. At any point in time, it is assumed that certain inputs cannot be varied as the level of service is varied.

For example, at this given point in time, referred to as the short run (which can be an hour, a day, a week, a month), a period within which certain inputs are fixed, we are able to vary the level of output within bounds. We may be able to vary the amount of throughput at a port by varying levels of labour, but not capital, and can only vary capital over a longer period of time (the long run) when we have enough time to expand capital capacity. Of course, some capital is sufficiently readily available in the short run, such as extra containers for example, that one must not assume that no classes of capital are capable of being varied in the short run. Another example is where a trucking company has the ability to immediately hire extra truck capacity for certain tasks on a given contract (as in the Chilean case study below), but is unable to establish new contracts to extend the service network without more time to invest in promotion, negotiation, and establishment of a new depot at a spatially appropriate location. Figure 5.1 summarizes the relationship between short-run average total cost for each given level of fixed inputs, output, and the trace of all minimum average total costs for a given fixed input. Since the trace of the minimum short-run average total costs against a single class of output is accounting for change in the level of the inputs that are fixed in the short run, it represents the long-run average total (variable) cost curve.

The graphical relationships in Figure 5.1 can be expressed mathematically as equation (5.2). When $S > 1$ we have increasing returns to scale; when $S < 1$ we have decreasing returns to scale, and when $S = 1$ we have constant returns to scale. Most usefully, we can see that economies of scale are measured by the ratio of the average cost of a service to the marginal cost of a service. To help in understanding this ratio, we define marginal cost (MC) as the change in total cost (dc) associated with a one-unit change in output (dY) (i.e. $MC = dc/dy$). Output, defined by Y, is homogeneous and hence represents all *aggregate* 'output'. Average cost is the ratio of total cost to total output. (i.e. $AC = C(Y)/Y$). When the ratio of total cost to total outputs is the same at two levels of output, the change in total cost resulting from a one-unit change in output (the definition of MC) is exactly equal to AC because average cost has not changed. Thus the ratio of AC/MC is 1.0. This is called constant costs or returns to scale because the average cost of producing each additional unit of output is the same as it was for the previous level of output. Only when MC is greater than AC do we see that the average cost of producing all output is increasing, and vice versa.

There is a drop in the *AC* when *MC* is less than *AC*. The link with scale economies should now be very clear. A closer look at equation (5.2) will suggest that the last term is the reciprocal of the elasticity of cost with respect to output. Thus if we can develop a simple regression model of total cost against total output we should be able to measure the nature of scale economies empirically. We look at this later.

Economies of scale function

$$S = \frac{AC}{MC} = \frac{C(Y)}{Y(dC/dY)} \quad (5.2)$$

Regulators in particular need to know if a transport business displays increasing, decreasing, or (approximately) constant returns to scale over a particular output range in order to be able to form a view on the extent to which there is a case for larger and fewer transport businesses, given the importance of the number of players in the determination of effective competition. If there is strong evidence to support constant returns to scale (typified by many transport sectors: Oum and Waters 1996, see table 1), then there is no argument on cost-efficiency grounds to promote larger and fewer suppliers in the market. The interpretation of economies of scale herein has been limited to the 'supply side' of the equation of business profiles: traditionally seen as the strict relationship between the cost of delivering a given level of service. The regulator, however, does not ignore the demand side of the business profile, where certain size organizations can confer an economy of demand-side benefit, often referred to as economies of network integrity. Where there is evi-

Scale economies misleading when transport business providing more than one class of output

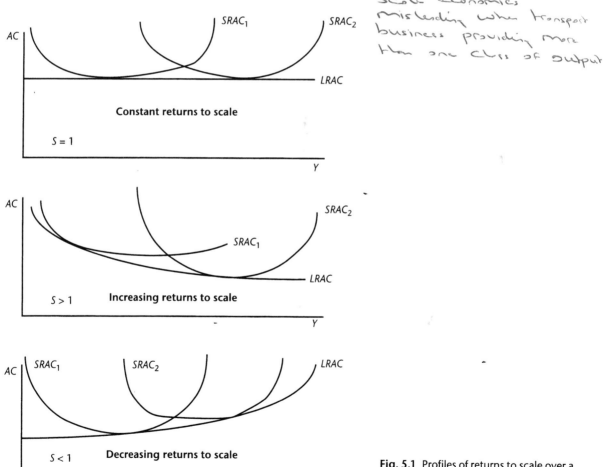

Fig. 5.1 Profiles of returns to scale over a given output range

dence to support the idea of having one operator providing services in an integrated supply chain (e.g. regional and city-pair air travel, local bus operations between specific origins and destinations which must be connected and able to be used on a single integrated fare system), then even the presence of constant returns to scale on the supply side can be overridden in supporting a natural monopoly outcome. Historically, natural monopoly (see Ch. 2) has been justified on the basis of the presence of increasing returns to scale over the range of (homogeneous) output required to service a market.

[The use of scale economies to justify natural monopoly is premised on a single class of output.]Once we allow for the real possibility of transport businesses providing more than one class of output (as noted above), the criteria to support the presence of natural monopoly are no longer unambiguous; and indeed concepts such as scale economies are potentially misleading and maybe irrelevant. We need now to find a way of recognizing the heterogeneity or diversity of products and services supplied by transport businesses in the definition of 'industry-wide' measures of cost efficiency.

The example of freight and passenger services illustrates the fallacy of aggregating all output (if it can be defined in common units) so that it can be treated as 'homogeneous'. Such a process of aggregation into a *single* output is equivalent to assuming identical MCs (i.e. variable costs) so we can aggregate. That is, two services with constant MCs. This is clearly questionable and requires a new treatment of business producing multiple outputs. Aggregation into a single (homogeneous) output is wrong.

5.6.3 Accommodating the composition of output as well as economies of scale

Recognizing the heterogeneity of output can be achieved by a simple redefinition of the cost function, replacing $C(Y)$ in equation (5.2) with equation (5.3) and the marginal cost of a single output by the output-specific equations (5.3a and 5.3b). We now have two outputs, each of which can display different cost profiles in their delivery to the market. We now need to see if it is possible to preserve the notion of economies of scale in a multi-product business.

$$C = C(Y_1, Y_2) \qquad (5.3)$$

and

$$MC_1 = \partial C(Y_1, Y_2)/\partial Y_1 \qquad (5.3a)$$

$$MC_2 = \partial C(Y_1, Y_2)/\partial Y_2 \qquad (5.3b)$$

There are a number of ways of investigating this matter. We will begin with the most obvious approach—treat the two outputs as having a fixed proportionality between them such that the composition of output remains fixed when we vary the scale of output. Another way of saying this is that we package the two outputs into a bundle such that we can map costs as the aggregate output varies while holding the mix of the two outputs fixed. This is quite restrictive since in practice the composition is likely to change as the level of each product/service changes. However, it enables us to start to appreciate the challenge which lies ahead when we try to relax this assumption in the search for a multi-product specific notion of scale economies. This fixed composition version of economies of scale is referred to as ray economies of scale. Formally we can develop this idea by redefining average cost as equation (5.4), to represent movements of costs as output changes along a fixed ray of proportionality of outputs. This is called ray average cost (RAC).

$$RAC(Y) = \frac{C(tY^0)}{t} \qquad (5.4)$$

where Y^0 is the composite output vector indicating amount of each output, and t is the output scalar indicating the proportionality of the two (or more) outputs. This is shown diagrammatically in Figure 5.2. We now have an equivalent construct to average cost in a single-output firm/industry, albeit under very restrictive conditions.

Ray scale economies (RSE) are defined as

$$RSE = \frac{dY/Y}{dC/C} \qquad (5.5)$$

where

$$Y = tY^0 \qquad (5.6)$$

Given the definition of economies of scale in equation (5.2) as the ratio of AC to MC, we can replace AC with tY^0 (simplified in (5.6) as Y), and replace MC with the summation of the MC of each output, weighted by the contribution of each output to the overall cost of producing the two outputs. This results in equation (5.7).

$$RSE = \frac{C(Y)}{\Sigma Y_i MC_i} \qquad (5.7)$$

RSE is greater than one if $C(Y) > \Sigma Y_i MC_i$, and less than one if $C(Y) < \Sigma Y_i MC_i$. Since product mixes rarely are constant as output changes, changes in ray average cost will typically not be observed. Since in reality output bundles themselves change, ray scale economies do not adequately describe the full behaviour of costs.

An additional scale economy construct can be introduced to show how costs change as the output of one product/service changes, holding the output of the other product/service fixed. In Figure 5.3, if we hold the output of one activity at a fixed level (e.g. at F), then we can measure costs as we vary the other product to the right of FB. We need to introduce another average cost construct that allows output of one product to vary with the other remaining constant. It is called average incremental cost (AIC) of output 1, and defined in equation (5.8).

$$AIC_1(Y) = \frac{C(Y_1, Y_2) - C(0, Y_2)}{Y_1} \qquad (5.8)$$

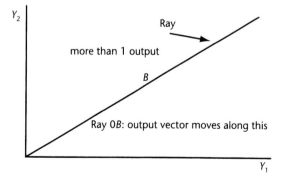

Fig. 5.2 Proportionality of outputs along a ray

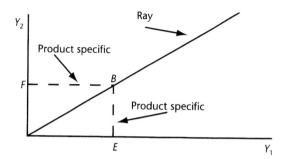

Fig. 5.3 Varying one output only

Equation (5.8) defines the average incremental cost of output activity Y_1 for a given level of output of activity Y_2. It follows logically from equation (5.7) where we replace the ray average cost with AIC, that product-specific scale economies for output 1 is given as equation (5.9). The same interpretation of returns to scale (with respect to output 1 for a given level of output 2) applies for values of $S_1 > 1, = 1$, and < 1.

$$S_1 = \frac{AIC_1(Y)}{MC_1} \qquad (5.9)$$

This is also a limiting interpretation of scale economies, since the average cost of specific services alone cannot be unambiguously defined since the fixed (sunk) costs are shared. There remains a major problem of cost 'allocation' between the two services, despite the fact that the incremental cost of either service can be defined readily as $C(Y_1, Y_2) - C(0, Y_2)$. In many transport businesses there often exist no product-specific returns to scale (i.e. constant marginal (variable) cost) even though there are returns to joint production. A product-specific economy could be achieved if say one class of rail variable facility is not fully used over some range of output, and we decided to increase output over this range; so we have economies of joint production *and* product-specific scale economies.

5.6.4 Economies of scope

The problem remains that S_1 reflects the effect of output mix upon costs in a partial manner since it measures the effect on costs 'all other things remaining unchanged' in one output type. A global measure to reflect fully the effect of changes in composition of output on costs is *economies of scope* (S_c). Such an economy exists if the cost of producing both outputs by the one business is less than the cost of having them supplied by two different organizations (equation (5.10)). In Figure 5.4, scope economies at output point B exist where $Y_1 = E$ and $Y_2 = F$ if $C(B) < C(E) + C(F)$. The formula for economies of scope is given in equation (5.11).

$$S_c \quad \text{exist if} \quad (Y_1, Y_2) < C(Y_1, 0) + C(0, Y_2) \quad (5.10)$$

Economics of Scope Function $$S_c = \frac{C(Y_1, 0) + C(0, Y_2) - C(Y_1, Y_2)}{C(Y_1, Y_2)} \quad (5.11)$$

$C(Y_1, 0)$ indicates that product Y_1 is produced and not product Y_2. In the presence of scope economies, firms with diversified product mixes will tend to have total costs lower than total costs of firms with specialized product mixes for comparable levels of output. We have now introduced all the necessary constructs to be able to combine economies of scale and scope to produce a single indicator of variation in costs when more than one product/service is provided by a single transport business. The most important concept is called *multi-product scale economies* (MPSE).

Given the definition of ray scale economies $S = \dfrac{C(Y)}{\Sigma Y_i MC_i}$ for a two-product case, we have

$$S = \frac{C(Y_1 Y_2)}{Y_1 MC_1 + Y_2 MC_2} = \frac{C(Y_1 Y_2)}{Y_1 \partial C_1 / \partial Y_1 + Y_2 \partial C_2 / \partial Y_2} \quad (5.12)$$

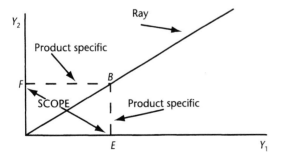

Fig. 5.4 Economies of scope

The degree of multi-product economies of scale is defined by the ratio of total costs to the weighted sum of product-specific marginal costs, where the weights represent the different levels of output. If $MC_1 = MC_2$ then we have a single-output measure of scale economies. From equations (5.12), (5.11), and (5.10) we can obtain a formulation of multi-product scale economies in terms of product-specific and scope economies:

$$MPSE = S_{1,2} = \frac{WS_1 + (1 - W)S_2}{1 - S_c} \quad (5.13)$$

where

$$W = \frac{Y_1 \partial C / \partial Y_1}{Y_1 \partial C / \partial Y_1 + Y_2 \partial C / \partial Y_2} \quad (5.14)$$

Equation (5.14) represents the share of variable costs of production incurred for product 1. The overall degree of scale economies for both products is a weighted average of the degree of scale economies pertinent to products 1 and 2, magnified by economies of scope through the factor $1/(1 - S_c)$. Sufficiently strong scope economies can confer scale economies on the entire product set (MPSE > 1) even with product-specific constant returns or some degree of negative returns in the separate products. For example, *uncongested track* may infer positive scope economies since separate production would require duplicate track. With uncongested track, we have ray scale economies as fixed costs associated with the track that will spread over higher output levels. So if $S_1 = 1$, $S_2 = 1$, $S_c > 0$, it implies that $S_{12} > 1$. Changes in output composition in the presence of product-specific decreasing returns to scale, *ceteris paribus*, will lead an increase in output Y_i to cause incremental costs to rise more than proportionately, but in the presence of economies of scope, costs may be spread over more products.

The implications of this result are very important in practice. It provides guidance to organizations and regulators in respect of the opportunities to become more cost efficient and cost effective through the selection of mixtures of products and services provided by a single business or by more than one business. It also provides essential information in the determination of the impact of the structure of transport forms on the promotion of competition. ⌉

5.6.5 Operationalizing the industry-level costing approach: the trucking sector

To illustrate the usefulness of the industry-level perspective, we draw on the empirical contributions of Jara Diaz (1988) who is one of the few researchers to identify both scale and scope effects in a multi-product transport business. Using data on truck flows between different origins and destinations in Chile, Jara Diaz applies the formulae presented above to obtain OD-specific economies of scale and scope. The empirical study is one of a very few which have recognized that transport costs cannot be studied adequately without a specific recognition of spatial or network effects. Unlike other studies in trucking (and indeed in all modal sectors), the contributions of Jara Diaz explicitly define the movements of output between origins and destinations, avoiding the aggregation of OD (origin–destination) specific flows over all OD pairs. It is rare indeed to find empirical evidence on economies of scope; yet it is crucial to know this. The vast majority of transport studies have aggregated output into a single measure, 'avoiding' the need to determine multi-product scale economies and economies of scope, and raising serious questions about the value of such studies. ⌉

The data set defines the movement of general freight from Santiago to destinations throughout Chile by one major carrier, giving us a useful case study for one firm, which could be generalized to all trucking businesses if such data were available. It is worth noting that the industry-wide constructs can be applied to a single transport firm if the data are sufficiently rich. The truck movements of this single Chilean operator stretch the full north–south distance of Chile—4,274 km.—and the east–west distance of 180 km. The trucking company has 90 vehicles (ranging from 9 to 27 tons), rents additional vehicles when extra capacity is needed, has four

warehouses in Santiago for goods in transit, and serves 14 destination zones throughout Chile. The most distant destination is Punt Arenas, 3,110 kilometres to the south; the closest destination is Valparaiso, 152 km. directly west of Santiago on the coast. Data were collected over a 24-month period on monthly flows to each destination zone together with the operating costs per item and input prices. The operating costs include vehicle renting, maintenance, administration, agencies' fees, fuel, lubricants, spare parts, tolls, and other incidental expenses. The only input prices that are available as explicit items are fuel and lubricants, even though all inputs are included in the cost of trucking.

The OD flows are spatially aggregated by Jara Diaz to make the analysis manageable in a statistical sense, reducing the 14 destinations to four ($i = 1, 2, 3, 4$), called north (five destinations), centre (three destinations), south (four destinations), and austral (two destinations). The criteria for spatial aggregation were similar distances to Santiago, similar numbers of actual destinations within each destination zone, and similar geographic context (i.e. climate and topography). The north is desert and dry with the major pan-American highway straight and with a low gradient; the centre has a mild and pleasant climate with higher gradient roads; the south is rainy with low vertical curvatures of roads; and the austral zone, accessed via Argentina, is rainy and cold with difficult internal communications. The aggregation of output was both distance weighted and unweighted, although the former was shown to be more realistic and is used to develop the results presented below.

To be able to determine empirically the nature of scale and scope economies, an empirical cost model has to be estimated in which costs are some function of the level of output, input prices, and other contextual influences (e.g. topography). There are a number of alternative ways in which we might define the cost model; however, a popular form is called the quadratic system, where output and input prices for the same destination are expressed both as a linear influence and a squared (or quadratic) influence. This specification has the advantage of producing empirical measures of scale, scope, and marginal cost which are a function of the levels of output and input prices for movements to a specific destination as well as possible complementary effects of linkages to other destinations. A strictly linear specification would produce a single result for scale, scope, and marginal cost for all destinations, which would fail to isolate any differences if they exist. The ability to reveal possible variations in scale, scope, and marginal cost between each destination is important for understanding the sources of costs associated with running a trucking business and the extent to which particular parts of the spatial network should continue to be served or activity increased.

The total cost model can be defined as equation (5.15). The literature on cost models is technically complex, but it is sufficient here to recognize the functional form of a cost model and to use it to derive the important behavioural outputs—marginal costs, economies of scale and scope, and cost complementarity.

$$C = A_0 + \sum_{i=1}^{4} A_i \bar{Y}_i + \sum_{j \geq i}^{4} \sum_{i=1}^{4} A_{ij} \bar{Y}_i \bar{Y}_j + \sum_{i=1}^{2} B_i \bar{w}_i +$$

$$\sum_{i=1}^{4} \sum_{j=1}^{2} D_{ji} \bar{Y}_i \bar{w}_j + \varepsilon \qquad (5.15)$$

where $(\bar{Y}, \bar{w})$ represents deviation from a base level of outputs and input prices defined as at October 1981, w are input prices for fuel and lubricants ($j = 1, 2$), Y is distance-weighted output in tons per month; A, B, and D are parameters to be estimated and ε is the random disturbance term in a statistical model. You can see that if we expand out the terms associated with $\sum_{j \geq i}^{4} \sum_{i=1}^{4} A_{ij} \bar{Y}_i \bar{Y}_j$ that we have quadratic terms (e.g. $\bar{Y}_i^2$) where destination $i = j$ and interactions where destination $i \neq j$ (e.g. $\bar{Y}_i \bar{Y}_j$). The formulae for deriving marginal cost, economies of scale, and economies of scope at the *point of approximation* (i.e. values of outputs and inputs in October 1981) are:

Marginal cost $(C_i) = A_i d_i$

Cost complementarity $(C_{ij}) = A_j d_i d_j$

Degree of economies of scale $(S) = A_0 / \left(\sum_{i=1}^{4} A_i Y_i^0 d_i \right)$

Degree of economies of scope $(SC_T) =$

$$\left(A_0 - \sum_{i=1}^{4} A_i Y_i^0 d_i + \sum_{j \leq i}^{4} \sum_{i=1}^{4} A_{ij} Y_i^0 d_i Y_j^0 d_j \right) / A_0$$

Equation (5.15), estimated on monthly data for each of four destinations, produced the results shown in Table 5.15. Cost complementarity exists when equation (5.16) is satisfied. It reflects the convenience of serving both flows since the marginal cost of moving Y_i decreases as Y_j increases. This is similar to but not the same as economies of scope; since the latter refers to the entire bundle of outputs whereas cost complementarity emphasizes flow pairs. The scope economies results in Table 5.14 involve comparison on one destination against other destinations. For example, SC_1 is equivalent to $SC_{\neq 1}$; $SC_{12} = SC_{34}$. Thus SC_1 defines the degree of economies of scope relative to a subset $T = 1$ of flows.

$$C_{ij} = \frac{\partial^2 C(w, Y)}{\partial Y_i \partial Y_j} < 0 \qquad (5.16)$$

We see strong evidence that constant or slightly increasing returns to scale are present in the operation of the trucking system for this one business in Chile. However, marginal costs vary between the four destinations with unreliable marginal costs associated with movements towards the centre (destination 2) and the southern locations (destination 3 with a t-value of 0.91). Jara Diaz also reports an estimate of 2.18 when all output is aggregated across all OD pairs, supporting evidence from other studies that the treatment of output as a single total measure of tonne-kilometres (or whatever other output measure is used) is problematic and over-estimates the true relationships between changes in costs and changes in output.

Economies of scope vary from -0.28 to 3.62. A positive value of economies of scope indicates that servicing all flows by one trucking business would be less costly than servicing the flow by two geographically specialized businesses. A negative value would favour specialization. In Table 5.14 only three scope estimates are statistically significant, and all

Table 5.14 Empirical estimates of marginal cost, cost complementarity, scale, and scope economies

Behavioural output	Estimate	t-value
C	14,100,000	43.6
Marginal costs (Chilean $/kg.)		
C_1	10.09	3.41
C_2	—	—
C_3	2.84	0.91
C_4	49.74	3.74
Cost complementarity (Chilean $/kg.)		
C_{11}	−0.000 008 6	1.77
C_{22}	−0.000 011	1.31
C_{33}	0.000 024	2.30
C_{44}	0.000 55	2.55
C_{12}	−0.000 032	1.23
C_{13}	0.000 087	4.20
C_{14}	−0.000 12	2.06
C_{23}	−0.000 047	2.26
C_{24}	−0.000 027	0.18
C_{34}	−0.000 094	1.23
Scale economies		
S	1.18	5.44
Scope economies		
SC_1	−0.26	0.6
SC_2	2.98	4.20
SC_3	−0.06	0.08
SC_4	2.46	2.78
SC_{12}	0.04	0.11
SC_{13}	3.62	4.53
SC_{14}	−0.28	0.54

are positive. Thus there are notable gains from a single trucking business operating throughout the entire network. When we contrast the economies of scope of each destination zone relative to the rest with the scope effects for pairs of zones relative to the other pairs (given only four destinations in total), we observe some interesting results. For example, SC_1 and SC_{14} have (statistically non-significant) diseconomies of scope, whereas SC_4 has significant economies of scope. Thus we would conclude that the movement of freight to destination 1 (i.e. Y_1) is the reason for diseconomies of scope in system operations and not movements to destination 4.

Assuming symmetry between each pair, there are ten cost complementarity results. Given the condition in equation (5.16), cost complementarity exists between all pairs of freight flows except for (Y_1, Y_3), which is positive. Jara Diaz (1988) points out that cost complementarity exists where there are noticeable imbalances of freight flows, in contrast to destinations 1 and 3 where the monthly average is almost the same (i.e. 698 and 650 tons per month respectively, in contrast to 316 and 67 tons per month for destinations 2 and 4 respectively). Another way of expressing this is that the marginal cost of transporting freight to destination i decreases as the marginal cost of transporting freight to destination j increases, if the magnitudes of Y_i and Y_j are substantially different. $C_{14} < 0$ indicates the attraction of producing long-haul flows jointly; by contrast $C_{13} > 0$ suggests regional specialization. Overall, when the economies of scope findings and all cost-complementarity indicators are considered, there is strong empirical support for servicing an entire network.

5.6.5.1 Considering service quality

The Chilean case study has suggested that when allowance is made for the spatial disaggregation of freight flows, the estimate of scale economies approaches constant returns, in contrast to the high degree of scale economies when output is spatially aggregated to a single 'aspatial' flow.

There is another body of literature, however, which even questions the empirical validity of constant returns to scale. It draws on accumulating evidence from very aggregate studies of a sample of trucking companies, primarily in the USA. Spatial networks are invariably ignored with output treated as single homogeneous measures such as ton-miles. Rather paradoxically, when we spatially disaggregate the freight flows as Jara Diaz has done, it seems that constant returns to scale better represent the industry than increasing returns to scale; however when, as shown below (based on Allen and Liu 1995), we introduce service quality to distinguish the quality of a given movement of freight, there is strong evidence to support reinstating increasing returns to scale. The explanation for this reversal is tied up with the quality benefits associated with differences in demand-side influences of choice of a particular trucking operator such as transit time and reliability over the network. Some studies have referred to this as the economies of network integrity and supply chain fulfilment. Thus when the demand side of the definition of output is introduced through some measure of service quality, we begin to see a more complete picture of the relationship between costs and service levels (defined by both physical output and output quality). Allen and Liu (1995) provide very convincing evidence to support the importance of economies of network integrity through improved service quality. Thus the evidence on constant returns to scale from Jara Diaz is not rejected; rather it is incomplete. The reason why most empirical studies do not find large trucking companies to have significant cost advantages over smaller businesses is:

not because the industry has a constant returns to scale structure, but rather because large carriers have exhausted their cost advantages to provide higher quality service than small carriers. Because the existing studies did not control for carriers' service quality levels, they thus could not discover large carriers' cost advantages. This suspicion has long been raised in the literature but has never been tested. (Allen and Liu 1995: 500)

In contrast to Jara Diaz (1988), Allen and Liu (1995) spatially aggregate their data on output but introduce a service quality index, the latter measuring a carrier's performance in transit time, routing, and equipment; and a convenience index indicating billing, tracing, electronic data interchange capability, and claims settlement. These rating indices are relative to all competitors in the market, so an improvement over time does not necessarily mean that a particular transport business rating increases—it could decrease due to better performance of a competitor. The ratings scale is 0 (unacceptable) to 5 (outstanding). Allen and Liu used a sample of less-than-truckload (LTL) motor carriers over a period of five years (1985–9) to estimate a long-run total cost model as a function of output level, service quality, and convenience, carrier-operating characteristics (such as average length of haul), input prices, and a time trend. The full details of the cost model, a second-order translog function, are given in Allen and Liu (1995); however, the method is now quite standard in industry-wide studies of transport costs. We introduce the translog model below in a case study on local bus services.

The policy implications which regulators in particular need to recognize are that the important arguments for the existence of fewer and larger trucking companies (and by implication transport businesses across all modal sectors) are related to the servicing of demand. High service quality along with competitive or even lower costs give large and high quality carriers significant competitive advantages. This evidence supports the occurrence of a large number of LTL bankruptcies in the USA since economic deregulation and the increasing dominance by a few large and high quality carriers. A similar finding exists in Australia for intercity coach operations since economic deregulation, with only three major players in the market in 1998. The argument that the presence of constant returns to scale and economic deregulation permits a large number of competing carriers to exist is questionable, due principally to the gains from improved service quality and network integrity with scale. This suggests that only a small number of large network LTL carriers can coexist in equilibrium, supplemented by many small carriers serving mostly linear markets. This is very akin to what is happening in deregulated airline and coach markets. Additional discussion on service quality is provided in Chapter 2.

5.6.5.2 General comments

When we combine the evidence from Jara Diaz and from Allen and Liu, two of the better empirical studies of trucking industry cost structures, we are tempted to conclude that, when allowance is made for spatial disaggregation and service quality, the long-distance trucking industry displays (slight to high) positive economies of scale. These findings are particularly important for the economic regulator who has to decide on the role of firm size in impacting on cost efficiency and competition. What is missing in such studies, however, is the adjustment for economies of scope, whereby an operator may be able to reduce unit costs through diversifying the product set. One suspects that when this occurs the network integrity argument is so strong as to support positive multi-product scale economies. The evidence in the airline sector is quite revealing, supporting the importance of network effects. Caves *et al.* (1984) have shown that differences in scale have no role to play in explaining higher costs for small US regional airlines compared to US truck airlines—that is, constant returns to scale exist. The differences in costs are the result of *returns to density*, defined as the proportional increase in output made possible by a proportional increase in all inputs, with 'points served, average stage length, average load factor, and input prices held fixed' (Caves *et al.* 1984: 474). Thus economies of density exist if unit costs decline as airlines add flights or seats on existing flights (through larger aircraft) with no change in

load factor, stage length, or the number of airports served. This is equivalent to holding the network fixed. In contrast, returns to scale are defined as the proportional increase in output and points served made possible by a proportional increase in all inputs, with average stage length, average load factor, and input prices held fixed. Oum and Waters's (1996) review of transport cost function research is critical of most empirical studies, especially in trucking, for failing to control for network coverage, which denies empirical separation of economies of scale and density. Ideally, we would like to see a study along the lines of Jara Diaz (1988) which incorporates multiple outputs (defined in Jara Diaz (1988) by four OD flows), service quality, and specific measures of the characterization of the network serviced by the trucking company. Since most of the studies on economies of scale do a poor empirical job of accommodating multiple outputs and network effects, it may be suggested that we still have a lot to learn about the true magnitude of scale, scope, and density in all transport sectors. The need for richer data is clear.

The case for spatial natural monopoly appears to be moving to the role of demand-side factors in determining the nature of transport operations. The economics of network integrity are increasingly coming to the defence of larger and fewer transport suppliers in a market, as shown for trucking (Allen and Liu 1995), local bus services (Evans 1990*a*), and city pair airlines (Caves *et al.* 1984).

5.6.6 Using a cost function to measure productivity: the case of local bus operations

To complete this chapter on costs, we present a case study of local government bus services in Australia over the period 1980/81 to 1986/7, which uses a cost function to measure the relative productivity of transport operators. This section is more advanced and can be skipped by those not wishing to understand the derivation and application of a flexible cost model for determining the productivity of a transport firm.

The most important new construct is total factor productivity (*TFP*), defined as the ratio of total output to total inputs, or the growth in total output minus the growth in total inputs. The simple definition is complicated by the presence of more than one type of output (Q), such as passenger kilometres from scheduled route services and from permanent school contracts, and a number of input (x) categories such as labour, fuel, non-labour maintenance, and capital. Output can be measured on the supply side (Q_s) in terms of the provision of annual vehicle kilometres, and on the demand side (Q_d) in terms of passenger kilometres. A preferred specification involves the functional specification of a relationship between passenger kilometres and vehicle kilometres: $Q_d = f(F, Q_s, Z)$, where F is the exogenously determined fare per passenger and Z is a vector of other influences on bus use.

The total factor productivity index is commonly derived from a parametric specification of a transformation function $G(Q_s, x, t) = 0$ which represents the underlying technology facing a bus operation. The time (t) variable captures the shifts in technology which represent changes in technical efficiency. A bus operator is assumed to operate under a regime that is equivalent to the rule in equation (5.17)

$$\max\{FQ_d - px: G(Q_s, x, t) = 0, \quad Q_d = f(F, Q_s, Z)\} \quad (5.17)$$

where p is a vector of input prices. The cost function of a bus operator can be defined as

$$C(p, Q_s, t) = \min_x \{px: G(Q_s, x, t) = 0\} \quad (5.18)$$

where C is total cost. Equation (5.18) can be substituted into (5.17) to give

$$\max\{FQ_d - C(p, Q_s, t), Q_d = f(F, Q_s, Z)\} \quad (5.19)$$

Totally differentiating (5.18) with respect to time, we have

$$(dC/dt) = \sum_i \left(\frac{\partial g}{\partial p_i} \cdot \frac{\partial p_i}{\partial t} + \frac{\partial g}{\partial Q} \cdot \frac{\partial Q}{\partial t}\right) + \frac{\partial g}{\partial t} \quad (5.20)$$

Given the well-known result from Shepherd's lemma, i.e. $\partial g/\partial p_i = X_i$ and the definition of the elasticity of cost with respect to output ε^{cq} of $\partial g/\partial Q \cdot Q/C$ equation (5.20) is equivalent to:

$$\frac{\partial C}{\partial t} \cdot \frac{1}{C} = \dot{C} = \sum_i (p_i X_i/C)\dot{p} + \varepsilon_{cq} \dot{Q} + C^{-1}\left(\frac{\partial g}{\partial t}\right) \quad (5.21)$$

where $\dot{C}$ is the proportionate change in total cost, $\dot{P}_i$ is the proportionate change in the price of input i, and $\dot{Q}$ is the proportionate change in output. In discrete time the proportionate change can be approximated by $\Delta \log Q = \log Q_t - \log Q_{t-1}$. The end term in equation (5.21) is the proportionate shift over time in the cost function ($\dot{B}$) equal to the change in cost minus the change in aggregate inputs minus the change in aggregate output. Equation (5.21) establishes that if there are multiple inputs the weight for aggregating such inputs is the share (S_i) of cost due to each input in each time period. If there are multiple outputs, the weights are the contribution of each output to cost in each time period, measured by the cost elasticity of output. The derivation above has assumed a single output. The term $\varepsilon_{cq}\dot{Q}$ is the scale effect. If the cost elasticity of output is not available, revenue is typically used which is an appropriate weight only if the firm prices at marginal cost and exhibits constant returns to scale.

Define *TFP* as the proportionate rate of growth of output minus the proportionate rate of growth of inputs. The proportionate shift in the cost function is not strictly equivalent to the rate of growth of *TFP*. Denny *et al.* (1981) have shown that only when the production function exhibits constant returns to scale is *TFP* equal to $\dot{B}$. To derive *TFP* from equation (5.21) when $\varepsilon_{cq} \neq 1$ we have to adjust *TFP* by $(1 - \varepsilon_{cq})\dot{Q}$. Thus

$$\dot{TFP}_g = -\dot{B} + (1 - \varepsilon_{cq})\dot{Q}. \quad (5.22)$$

Equation (5.22) defines *TFP* in terms of intertemporal shifts or technical change and scale effects. In the empirical study we define returns to scale in terms of annual vehicle kilometres. $\dot{B}$ can be derived directly from the cost function as a fully parametric derivation in which cost is then an estimate ($\tilde{C}$), or from a measured calculation given ε_{cq} in which it is the residual from the change in *actual* costs minus the change in aggregate input, where factor shares are the *actual shares*, minus the scale effect. In the empirical analysis we have selected the fully parametric approach, so that

$$T\dot{F}P_g = -\partial \log \tilde{C}/\partial t + (1 - \varepsilon_{cq})\dot{Q} \qquad (5.23)$$

5.6.6.1 The modelling approach

The necessary inputs into $T\dot{F}P_g$ are derived from a cost model of the translog functional form. The data for seven financial periods from 1980/1 to 1986/7 were compiled from a questionnaire sent to each of the eight urban public bus operators in Australia. Given the available data we assume that each bus firm uses four competitively priced inputs—labour, fuel, maintenance materials, and capital—to produce annual vehicle kilometres. The cost function is given in equation (5.24).

$$\mathrm{Ln}(C/p_k) = a_0 + \beta_1 \ln Q_s + \frac{1}{2}\beta_2 (\ln Q_s)^2 + \Sigma \delta_i \ln(p_i/p_k) +$$

$$\frac{1}{2}\Sigma\Sigma\delta_{ij}\ln(p_i/p_k)\ln(p_j/p_k) + \Sigma\Sigma\sigma_i\ln(p_i/ \qquad (5.24)$$

$$p_k)\ln Q_s + \Omega_t t + \Sigma\delta_{it}\ln(p_i/p_k)t + \beta_t \ln Q_s t$$

The translog form provides a second-order approximation of the true cost function at a point. We have selected the sample means for all explanatory variables at the point of approximation. The financial data are expressed in 1980/1 dollars. To satisfy symmetry and linear homogeneity in input prices we impose the following restrictions and divide each of the price variables and total cost by the unit price of one of the inputs selected as capital:

$$\delta_{ij} = \delta_{ji}, \ \Sigma\delta_i = 1, \ \Sigma\delta_{ij} = 0, \ \Sigma\sigma_i = 0, \ \Sigma\delta_{it} = 0$$

Time is interacted with the prices of each input and output so that the relationship through time between cost, input prices, and output is relatively unrestricted. From equation (5.24) the input share equations are:

$$S_i = \delta_i + \sum_j \delta_{ij}\ln(p_j/p_k) + \sum_i \sigma_i \ln Q_s + \delta_{it}t, \qquad (5.25)$$
$$i = L, F, M$$

The inclusion of the share equations aids in reducing the high correlation between many of the cross-products terms, and the dropping of one share equation, any one when maximum-likelihood esti-

mation (MLE) is used, ensures non-singularity in the error variance-covariance matrix (Greene 1997).

The demand equation is assumed to be log-linear with exogenous variables representing fares, level of service, income, and the cost of alternative forms of transport:

$$\ln Q_d = \kappa_0 + \kappa_f \ln(\text{fare}) + \kappa_{\text{los}}\ln(vkm) + \\ \kappa_y \ln(income) + \kappa_a \ln(auto \ cost) \qquad (5.26)$$

Iterative MLE for seemingly unrelated regression is used to obtain parameter estimates for the system of demand and cost equations. The estimated cost model is used to derive the cost elasticity with respect to output and the estimate of intertemporal shifts in the cost function. Fixed effects are introduced to allow for the mean effect of unobserved operator-specific effects.

The input prices are defined as follows. Labour is expressed in terms of dollars per hour, fuel in dollars per litre, non-labour maintenance in dollars per vehicle kilometre, and the economic cost of capital in dollars per vehicle kilometre. The treatment of capital assets, in particular bus capital, has traditionally been a very superficial exercise in nearly all public bus operations in Australia. The average capital cost per annum (AKC) for a bus is calculated using the cost recovery formula in Section 5.3.5. The riskless cost of borrowing in Australia stood at 17.03% at the end of 1989. A corporate borrowing premium of 1% brings this to 18%. The riskless rate plus the general risk premium of 7% is the cost of equity. If we were to equate the rate of return on a bus firm's stock to the rate of return on the market portfolio (i.e. a beta coefficient of 1.0), then the risk-adjusted nominal cost of borrowing would be 25.03%. If a bus firm has government protection as do all public bus operators in Australia and we treat it as a riskless entity, then the nominal rate of return would be 10.03%, approximately equivalent to an 8% real rate of interest.

To obtain an estimate of the residual value, we sampled a number of market prices obtained from vehicles disposed of in 1988 in the private bus sector. The prices have been averaged to ensure uniform change in relative prices between years. The prices are then converted to constant dollars by calculating the compound rate of increase of a new bus over a

Table 5.15 The translog cost system (Model 1: Output = annual passenger kilometres; Model 2: Output = annual vehicle kilometres with endogenous annual passenger kilometres)

Variable		Model 1		Model 2	
		Parameter estimates	t-ratio	Parameter estimates	t-ratio
Constant	α_0	15.103	12.07	12.076	13.62
Output	β_Q	2.721	5.71	1.171 4	3.12
(Output)^2	δ_{QQ}	−0.143	−0.69	−0.276 17	−1.08
Price of labour	δ_L	0.752	54.92	0.747 07	150.71
(Price of labour)^2	δ_{LL}	0.141	12.23	0.132 01	9.81
Price of fuel	δ_F	0.017 7	17.29	0.078 08	47.34
(Price of fuel)^2	δ_{FF}	0.039 9	7.37	0.034 85	7.13
Price of maintenance	δ_M	0.061 1	15.25	0.059 79	41.61
(Price of maintenance)^2	δ_{MM}	0.054 4	19.87	0.057 12	17.93
$P_L * P_F$	δ_{LF}	−0.026 5	−4.20	0.019 11	−3.07
$P_L * P_M$	δ_{LM}	−0.032 9	−7.37	−0.032 12	−6.41
$P_M * P_F$	δ_{MF}	−0.016 7	−5.52	−0.015 40	−5.39
$P_L *$ output	σ_{LQ}	0.017 6	4.28	0.016 97	3.81
$P_F *$ output	σ_{FQ}	−0.005	−3.55	−0.004 456 5	−2.96
$P_M *$ output	σ_{MQ}	−0.005	−4.23	−0.004 435	−3.23
Time	Ω_t	−0.075	−0.52	0.048 58	1.48
Time * output	δ_{tQ}	−0.019	−0.43	0.073 68	2.07
New South Wales		5.971	3.94	1.525 8	−1.41
South Australia		4.777	3.54	1.265 9	−1.33
Queensland		3.898	3.36	1.656 8	−1.97
Victoria		3.341	3.42	1.484 1	−2.00
Western Australia		4.222	3.11	1.499 9	−1.54
Australian Capital Territory		3.167	3.31	0.652 77	−0.86
Tasmania		2.660	3.10	1.294 5	−1.98
	K_F			−0.102 77	−1.49
	K_O			−0.036 059	−1.08
	K_{LOS}			1.135 0	36.5
Log-likelihood at convergence		−32.6		−36.3	

15-year period (approximately 13%) and applying it to the nominal bus prices. The decline in value per annum is then calculated, and the value projected to a constant 15-year life. We have selected 15 years in order to be consistent with the mean life assumed by the private bus sector. The ratio of the value projected in constant dollars to a constant 15-year life over the historical cost can be expressed as the average percentage residual or scrap value of a 15-year-old bus. The suggested working percentage is 15%.

5.6.6.2 The empirical measure of total factor productivity growth

Equations (5.24) to (5.26) were jointly estimated with the linear homogeneity and symmetry restric-tions imposed. In addition we estimated equations (5.25) and (5.26) with a demand-side measure of output to investigate the empirical implications of exogenizing demand. The results are given in Table 5.15. Using Model 2, we tested the joint hypothesis that the parameter estimates associated with the interactions between inputs and output, between inputs and time, and between output and time were all equal to zero. The only condition that was satisfied on a likelihood-ratio test was the interaction between inputs and time. We excluded this set of three interactions from the final models.

A comparison of the two models is very revealing. The implied scale economy at the mean of the sample is close to zero (− 0.1714) when annual vehicle kilometres is the output measure, and the demand for passenger kilometres is itself a function of annual vehicle kilometres. This evidence supports the widespread view that the urban bus industry exhibits constant returns to scale. By contrast, the treatment of output as the exogenous level of annual passenger kilometres suggests that the scale economy at the sample mean is – 1.72, significant diseconomies of scale.

The demand equation contains only two significant variables, the average fare and level of service. Fares are set by governments, with the operators relying heavily on changes in the overall level of service (as measured by frequency and vehicle kilometres) to increase revenue. Data on service frequency is not available and so annual vehicle kilometres are used as the measure of the overall level of service. The vehicle kilometre variable is statistically very significant, in contrast to the mean level of fare that is significant at the 93% level of confidence given the degrees of freedom. The parameter estimate for fare (– 0.103) is the direct-price elasticity of demand for passenger kilometres. Likewise the direct-vehicle kilometre elasticity of demand for passenger kilometres of 1.14 suggests that Australian urban bus user demand is elastic with respect to level of service. A 1% increase in vehicle kilometres leads to a 1.14% increase in passenger kilometres, *ceteris paribus*. It is important to note that the dimension of passenger demand is passenger kilometres, which is more likely to be elastic with respect to vehicle kilometres than is total passengers. Likewise the change in passenger kilometres with respect to fares is likely to be less responsive than would be passengers.

To account for unobserved operator-specific effects we have included firm-specific dummy variables in the cost model. The Northern Territory operator is set to zero as the base. Since nearly 98% of the variability occurs between operators rather than within operators, the time-invariant firm effects are appropriate indicators of additional differences between firms which are not accounted for by inputs, demand and supply-side measures of output, time, and fares. The mean estimates of the firm effects are much smaller in the model system that includes endogenous demand. This suggests that differences in the profile of passenger demand have an

important role in explaining the overall levels of costs of operation. A failure to recognize the correlation between the unobserved influences on both passenger kilometre demand and total costs of service provisions is a potential source of specification error.

The application of equation (5.23) generates a matrix of indices of total factor productivity growth. The results are summarized in Table 5.16. The decomposition of TFP_g due to technical change and the scale effect is given in Table 5.17a and 5.17b. The mean annual TFP_g derived from the market equilibrium model varies from 8.3% (New South Wales (NSW)) to – 13.9% (Northern Territory (NT)). The variation over time is also reasonably uniform within each firm. Two operators with negative TFP_g (Northern Territory and Tasmania) have had little success in reversing the trend downwards; however, Victoria (VIC) and the Australian Capital Territory (ACT) began to show improvements in the last three periods.

When TFP_g is decomposed into the contributions due to the shift in the cost function and movement along the cost function, we can establish the source of growth. For example, South Australia's TFP_g is due almost entirely to shifts in the cost function; the mean scale effect of – 0.0006 is negligible in the downward direction. In contrast, however, for the ACT, the small but positive contribution of technical change (except in the first year) is discounted quite substantially by the small but negative scale effect. With the exception of the ACT, the scale effect contributes very little to the overall growth in TFP.

The partial equilibrium model with exogenous demand gives quite different results, except at the overall firm mean through time for SA (South Australia) and NSW (Tables 5.17a and b). The mean TFP_g ranges from 9.8% (NSW) to 17.6% (NT), but with wide variations within each firm. The rank orderings at the mean also change with VIC and NT the only operators with the same ranking (sixth and eighth respectively). The different treatments of output highlight the dependence of the findings on the treatment of output in general and the role of demand in particular. Without the inclusion of the demand equation, it is not possible to allow for the possibility that negative TFP_g may reflect a decline in patronage rather than a decline in productivity *per*

Table 5.16 Total factor productivity growth

(i)	SA	NSW	WA	ACT	TAS	QLD	VIC	NT
80/81–81/82	0.048	0.101	0.094	0.279	0.299	0.030	0.014	−0.221
81/82–82/83	−0.297	0.118	0.187	−0.230	0.041	−0.022	0.219	−0.084
82/83–83/84	−0.022	0.099	0.111	−0.133	−0.043	0.148	0.002	−0.343
83/84–84/85	0.152	0.052	0.134	−0.039	0.047	0.118	−0.179	−0.136
84/85–85/86	0.073	0.078	0.012	0.114	−0.005	0.074	−0.177	0.115
85/86–86/87	0.273	0.048	0.049	−0.006	0.119	0.105	0.095	−0.152
Overall mean	0.038	0.083	0.098	−0.002 5	0.076	0.076	−0.004	0.176
(ii)								
80/81–81/82	0.044	0.081	0.057	−0.006	−0.031	−0.007	−0.022	−0.139
81/82 82/83	0.044	0.085	0.058	−0.002	−0.032	−0.011	−0.020	−0.136
82/83–83/84	0.044	0.084	0.060	−0.001	−0.032	−0.016	−0.021	−0.136
83/84–84/85	0.044	0.083	0.060	0.009	−0.032	−0.018	−0.017	−0.136
84/85–85/86	0.043	0.082	0.061	0.003	−0.034	−0.020	−0.018	−0.133
85/86–86/87	0.043	0.083	0.061	0.005	−0.035	−0.022	−0.005	−0.127
Overall mean	0.044	0.083	0.060	0.001	−0.033	−0.016	−0.017	−0.139

Notes: (i) Output = annual passenger kilometres; (ii) Output = annual vehicle kilometres, with endogenous passenger kilometres

Table 5.17*a* Decomposition of total factor productivity growth

(i)	SA A	NSW A	WA A	ACT A	TAS A	QLD A	VIC A	NT A
80/81–81/82	0.076	0.092	0.086	0.054	0.055	0.077	0.060	0.017
81/82–82/83	0.079	0.093	0.086	0.058	0.055	0.078	0.058	0.018
82/83–83/84	0.080	0.093	0.085	0.058	0.056	0.076	0.057	0.018
83/84–84/85	0.079	0.093	0.084	0.063	0.056	0.076	0.063	0.019
84/85–85/86	0.078	0.093	0.085	0.059	0.055	0.076	0.062	0.017
85/86–86/87	0.075	0.094	0.084	0.060	0.053	0.075	0.066	0.019
Overall mean	0.078	0.093	0.085	0.059	0.055	0.076	0.061	0.018
(ii)								
80/81–81/82	0.046	0.083	0.057	−0.004	−0.033	0.012	−0.02	−0.136
81/82–82/83	0.044	0.084	0.060	0.001	−0.032	0.017	−0.020	−0.129
82/83–83/84	0.045	0.083	0.060	0.003	−0.032	0.018	−0.022	−0.132
83/84–84/85	0.044	0.083	0.060	0.011	−0.032	0.019	−0.017	−0.132
84/85–85/86	0.043	0.083	0.062	0.001	−0.034	0.021	−0.014	−0.132
85/86–86/87	0.043	0.083	0.061	0.006	−0.035	0.023	−0.005	−0.123
Overall mean	0.044	0.083	0.06	0.003	−0.033	0.018	−0.016	−0.131

Notes: Contributions due to: A. shift in the cost function (technical change). (i) Output = annual passenger kilometres; (ii) Output = annual vehicle kilometres, with endogenous passenger kilometres

se. The intuitive technical relationship between vehicle kilometres and factor inputs together with the role of vehicle kilometres as a service proxy in influencing passenger demand provides a more appealing framework in which to establish the annual changes in total factor productivity. It also recognizes the importance of the integrity of service levels across a network.

Table 5.17b Decomposition of total factor productivity growth

(i)	SA B	NSW B	WA B	ACT B	TAS B	QLD B	VIC B	NT B
80/81–81/82	−0.027	0.009	0.009	0.225	0.244	−0.047	−0.046	−0.238
81/82–82/83	−0.376	0.026	0.101	−0.288	−0.015	−0.100	0.161	0.066
82/83–83/84	−0.103	0.006	0.026	−0.192	−0.013	0.071	−0.055	−0.362
83/84–84/85	0.072	−0.041	0.050	−0.102	−0.009	0.042	−0.242	−0.155
84/85–85/86	−0.006	−0.015	−0.073	0.055	−0.060	−0.004	−0.239	0.018
85/86–86/87	0.197	−0.045	−0.034	−0.067	0.066	0.030	0.029	−0.171
Overall mean	−0.065	−0.01	0.013	−0.062	0.045	−0.001	−0.06	−0.101
(ii)								
80/81–81/82	−0.002	−0.001	0.0001	−0.002	0.002	−0.004	−0.002	−0.002
81/82–82/83	−0.0006	0.0007	−0.002	−0.003	0.0007	−0.006	−0.0005	−0.007
82/83–83/84	−0.0002	0.0001	−0.0009	−0.004	0.0006	−0.002	−0.0003	−0.005
83/84–84/85	−0.0001	0.003	0.0002	−0.002	−0.0006	−0.001	0.0	0.003
84/85–85/86	−0.0002	−0.0003	−0.0008	0.002	−0.0003	−0.001	−0.004	−0.001
85/86–86/87	−0.0002	−0.0001	−0.0001	−0.009	−0.0001	−0.0004	−0.004	−0.003
Overall mean	−0.0006	0.0007	−0.0006	−0.001	−0.0004	−0.002	−0.002	−0.003

Notes: Contributions due to: B. movement along the cost function (scale effect). (i) Output = annual passenger kilometres; (ii) Output = annual vehicle kilometres, with endogenous passenger kilometres

5.7 Conclusions

This chapter has introduced a large number of cost-based concepts that are crucial to an understanding of costs for an individual business and for an industry sector. We have also shown how a knowledge of costs is important to the measurement of the performance as represented by cost efficiency and cost effectiveness. In addition, the economic regulator must be well informed about cost profiles and performance to ensure that an individual business is delivering services to the market that are deemed consistent with principles of good competitive practice. In the absence of direct competition, the regulator will rely heavily on benchmarking of cost efficiency and effectiveness against best practice.

Furthermore, an industry assessment to reveal the extent of economies of scale and scope will help establish the case for natural monopoly or the encouragement of increasing the number of firms in a market as the way of establishing competitively efficient practices.

Knowing your costs (Ch. 5) together with knowing your market (Ch. 4) provides necessary information inputs into the determination of efficient prices. We are now well prepared to move to Chapter 6 where we use knowledge of costs and demand to establish rules for efficient pricing under alternative pricing strategies.

Discussion issues for Chapter 5

1   The spectrum of avoidability varies with the time period (temporal) and the range of output (technical). What do we mean by this?

2   When we talk about strategic and non-strategic thinking in the context of knowing your costs, what do we mean?

3   In a multi-product sector such as transport, does the traditional notion of an industry make sense?

4   Discuss the challenges that an empirical study faces in terms of the quality of data usually available.

5   Why is the notion of economies of scale of limited value in the transport sector?

6   The distinction between fixed and variable costs commonly used by accountants is quite irrelevant. Discuss.

7   Accounting for service quality has raised new concerns about the role of scale in cost efficiency. Discuss.

8   Why are economies of density and scope of interest to a regulator?

9   The case study in the text focuses on a bus business. The ideas have broad relevance across many sectors. To test your understanding of the approach presented, describe how you might prepare a procurement tender for a logistics contract. The background to the logistics bid offer is presented below.

The Bowral Retail Chain has decided to outsource its entire logistics activity and has issued an invitation to a number of pre-registered logistics specialists to submit competitive bids leading to a three-year contract. The tender documents supplied to each pre-registered logistics specialist included:

1. a draft agreement;

2. the service specifications;

3. a tender form, a tender form coversheet, and service detail schedules;

4. the conditions of tender.

For our case study we are interested in seeing how an appropriate set of costs are calculated. It is important that costs are identified and calculated very carefully, because the bids on previous occasions for other retail outlets have been very close. This is illustrated in Table 5.18 which shows the total cost, in 1999 dollars, for the whole contract, made in bids submitted for the supply of the logistics services for Smithton and Jones Yummy Foods Chain.

Bowral Retail Chain has hired the Bid Brothers Pty Ltd. to organize the tender. They have described the logistics activities in sufficient detail for you to be able to undertake appropriate cost calculations. The service is described in terms of:

• the number of orders to receive and process each week,

• the nature of goods and services to be delivered,

• the typical origin–destination pattern of customers,

In addition to logistics service specifications, information is provided on the following requirements:

Table 5.18 Bids for logistics outsourcing for Smithton and Jones Yummy Foods Chain, 1999 (1999 dollars per annum)

Bidder 1	$2,139,886
Bidder 2	$1,948,341
Bidder 3	$1,813,605
Bidder 4	$1,951,524
Bidder 5	$2,300,475
Bidder 6	$2,209,539
Bidder 7	$2,128,539

1. the experience of the tendering logistic specialist,

2. the history of other current contracts in the same area,

3. performance bond requirements.

The remuneration is an agreed sum representing the annual cost of providing the logistics support services. The agreed amount is indexed and adjusted in accordance with details set out on how indexation is applied. Indexation will be provided by the Bid Brothers to the following items:

1. all labour inputs: reviewed annually on the anniversary of the commencement date, based on movements in the base rates of the relevant award;

2. fuel: based on movement in the purchase price for bulk distillate obtained from Shell Co. Contract rates are reviewed annually on the anniversary of the commencement date.

All other costs are *NOT* indexed. It is therefore important that you apply indexation to these items, or increase them by whatever factor you think is appropriate, for the second and subsequent years of the contract.

Some variations to contract payments are allowed for:

- where additional logistics services are required beyond the agreement of the contract, the Bid Brothers on behalf of Bowral Retail Chain will seek the first quote for supplying such additional services from the contractor, but they are also entitled to approach and/ or make other arrangements to contract other logistics specialists where the Bid Brothers are of the opinion that it is in the best interest of Bowral Retail Chain. The subsequent remuneration is negotiated at the appropriate time;

- where the Bid Brothers on advice from Bowral Retail Chain cancels any additional logistics services which have been requested one week or less prior to the service, the contractor is entitled to charge a cancellation fee of an agreed amount;

- where the logistics service provided is delayed for reasons unrelated to the activities undertaken by Bowral Retail, and hence they are unable to meet their contractual obligations, except where a failure is a consequence of an act of God, fire, etc. or other matter over which the contractor has no control, the contractor shall be held responsible for providing a replacement service;

- from the tender documentation a logistic specialist placing a bid is able to work out the resource requirements.

Table 5.19 Weekly resource requirements

Orders placed and processed	80 hrs. @ $30 per hr. labour	$2,400
Material in order process		120
Phone calls	600 @ 25 cents per call	150
Phone rental		420
Office energy bill		120
Packaging materials		240
Drivers' wages	300 hours @ $30 per hr.	9,000
Drivers' on-costs	40% of base gross wage	3,600
Truck insurance	3 trucks fully insured	1,300
Truck registration	includes third-party insurance	750
Fuel	1,200 litres @ 30 cents per litre diesel	360
Truck maintenance	4 cents per km. for 2,500 km.	100
Truck annualized capital cost	3 trucks	36,000

Notes: 1. The following assumptions are made in calculating the annualized cost of vehicles:

Rate of return on investment	15%
Rate of inflation (CPI)	7%
Real rate of interest	8%
Amortization factor	0.1168
Initial purchase price of *all* trucks	$600,000
Years of useful truck life	15

2. For the subsequent years of the contract (2000 and 2001 in the case of this three-year contract), for those items which are not automatically indexed by Bowral Retail Chain, you need to determine by how much you expect them to increase and adjust them accordingly.

Let us assume that the service requirements have been costed as summarized in Table 5.19. In evaluating these costs in order to establish which ones are avoidable, which ones are shared, and how much of the shared costs might be paid for through this logistics offer, we need to note the following:

- there are three other companies placing an offer;
- one of these competing companies already has a contract with Bowral Retail Chain;
- we have through market intelligence found out that one of the competing companies has spare capacity in its trucks and only needs to purchase two more trucks;
- we have no spare trucking capacity (we are a very lean logistics organization);
- we do however have spare capacity in the office with our full-time staff estimated to have the capability of performing the equivalent of an extra 20 hours of order processing per week;
- the hourly rate below is based on full-time labour working extra hours but we might consider casual rates instead;
- the truck maintenance costs are based on an in-house servicing but outsourcing of such maintenance may be a possibility (will it reduce costs?);
- the energy bill relates to all electricity expenses for the central office where the orders are placed and processed. Order processing for other clients would represent 95% of the labour time if the contract were awarded.

Using the information in the tender documents and the resource requirements shown in Table 5.19, the cost of providing the logistics bid offer can now be calculated. The calculations can be done using a calculator, but if you are familiar with a computer spreadsheet package this is ideal for such an exercise.

The challenge is to decide:

1. which costs are avoidable?

2. which costs are shared? and

3. who might contribute towards the cost of the shared costs?

On the latter issue, a knowledge of the market and competitors is essential. Someone, however, has to pay for these shared costs so that at the end of the day a business recovers all of its costs and makes an acceptable return on its investment.

Performance measures: From these cost figures you may be interested in calculating some commonly used performance measures which would allow you to compare the cost of providing these services with some of your other services or with industry averages. For example:

1. the unit cost per truck operating kilometre,

2. the unit cost per labour hour.

6 Knowing your prices

6.1 Introduction

Previous chapters have presented the institutional and market environments in which transport businesses operate. They have also introduced the role of knowledge of travel demand and costs in the delivery of transport services. In this chapter we bring together information on demand and costs to establish a pricing regime for transport services. Fundamentally, the prices to be charged in a transport market should have strong links with the costs of delivering services and the responsiveness of the market to such prices. This includes recognition of the role of subsidy under conditions of community service obligation (CSO). The precise functional relationship between prices, costs, and demand will be influenced by the pricing strategy of a particular transport business in either the public or private sector, for both access to infrastructure (e.g. airports, roads, railways, ports) and operations (e.g. travel on airlines, buses, trains, ships).

We begin by setting out the main alternative pricing strategies—profit maximization, social-welfare maximization, and constrained social-welfare maximization (often referred to as Ramsey pricing). A knowledge of average and marginal cost (Ch. 5), and the direct and cross-price elasticities of demand (Ch. 4) for a particular service is essential to determine an allocatively efficient price. The development of an appropriate set of prices will be influenced by the nature of competition; for example, if there are demand-interdependent services in a competitive market in contrast to demand independence under monopoly. The role of both substitute and complementary services is taken into account, since the opportunity for a transport operator to increase the prices in one market (e.g. first-class air travel) without losing traffic to a competitor (because some travellers switch to business class) needs to be identified. Once we have an understanding of the relationship between costs, demand, and prices we take a closer look at the sensitivities of prices to assumptions on cost and price elasticity of demand. We show that the determination of prices is particularly sensitive to the empirical estimate of price elasticity. This is a worrying result since it suggests that we are unlikely to be able to identify truly allocatively efficient prices but rather quasi or approximately efficient 'banded' prices. However, the links between prices, costs, and demand remain strong and should always be sought out under the specific pricing strategy.

Armed with an appreciation of basic rules of pricing, we introduce the topic of transport user charges, distinguishing between efficiency objectives and other broader considerations of equity and financing. Alternative models of user charges are presented, which to varying degrees support short-run and long-run marginal cost pricing. The important issue is the distinction between the costs imposed on the transport system by users, which should be recouped through an efficient user charge, and the role of user charges in contributing to the cost of replacing the infrastructure which is not a direct function of use. The arguments are complex and controversial, including the view that the community as a whole benefits from transport infrastructure (and not just users) and thus infrastructure replacement policy should be funded in part (at least) by general taxation rather than charges on users only. In addition, if users made a direct financial contribution to the cost of infrastructure replacement (and even high-level maintenance) above the marginal social cost of use, then the infrastructure may be underutilized—the excess capacity argument. This debate is applicable to all transport sectors, although the veracity of debate has been particularly strong for roads, airports, and maritime

ports. We use examples from all three sectors to illustrate the major issues in establishing and implementing efficient transport user charges. Traffic congestion is a major concern directly related to the debate on efficient prices. For completeness we extend the set of costs to include both intra-sectoral (e.g. accidents) and inter-sectoral (e.g. air pollution, global warming) externalities.

6.2 Alternative pricing strategies

The three pricing strategies—profit maximization, social-welfare maximization, and constrained social-welfare maximization—can be summarized as special cases of the more general relationship between price (P), marginal cost (MC), and price elasticity of demand (η). The functional relationship between these three items is given as equation (6.1), assuming initially a demand-independent service. Lambda (λ) is called the Ramsey number, taking values from zero to one depending on the pricing strategy. When $\lambda = 1$ we promote profit maximization, when $\lambda = 0$ we promote social welfare maximization, and when λ lies between 0 and 1, we support constrained social-welfare maximization. We now look at each Ramsey condition.

$$\left(\frac{P - MC}{P}\right)\eta = -\lambda \qquad (6.1)$$

When $\lambda = 1$, substitution into equation (6.1) and rearranging terms produces equation (6.2). Under conditions of price-taking behaviour, where a particular transport business has no influence on prices, it can be shown that the right-hand side of equation (6.2) is equivalent to marginal revenue (MR). Marginal revenue is defined as the change in total revenue associated with a one unit change in output. With price-taking behaviour, this is equivalent to the price of the additional unit of output (the reader can show this once they recognize that $\partial P/\partial Q = 0$, given the definition of $\eta = \partial P/\partial Q * Q/P$). The rule for short-run profit maximization, assuming prices are given, becomes $MC = MR$. The determination of price under

these conditions is shown diagrammatically in Figure 6.1. We have drawn Figure 6.1 as representing the range of competitive and monopolistic practices in the transport sector. They vary from a strictly monopolistic market typified by one airport, port, bus company, or railway servicing a given geographical catchment area, through to some degree of (imperfect) competition where there are a few or a lot of operators in the market, often competing between modes (e.g. truck vs. rail, car vs. bus vs. rail, car vs. plane, airline 1 vs. airlines 2–10), in contrast to within a mode. The fact that the demand curve is downward sloping indicates that consumers are sensitive to prices offered by any one competing or monopoly operator.

$$MC = P(1 + 1/\eta) \qquad (6.2)$$

Marginal cost (MC) equals marginal revenue (MR) at point E; producing at Q_m and setting price equal to P_m. This is point C on the demand curve. Profits (π) represented by the area P_mBDC are revenue in excess of normal profits, where the latter is the profits a firm would accept in competitive equilibrium. For a particular transport sector, normal profits vary a lot, being anything from 2% to 8%, adjusted for inflation. Supernormal profits P_mBDC arise where a monopolist restricts output and raises prices above competitive levels giving an element of monopoly power. Governments sometimes respond in the presence of the potential for monopoly pricing by price regulation ('price capping') as discussed in Chapter 2.

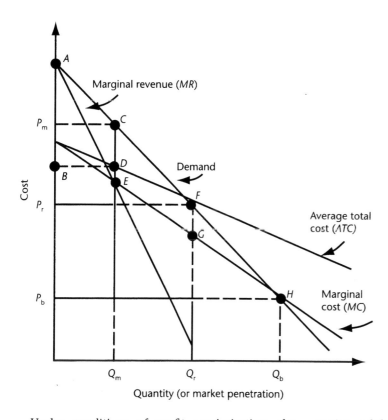

Fig. 6.1 Alternative pricing strategies

Notes: P_m = the monopoly price ($MR = MC$)
P_r = the Ramsey price ($P = ATC$)
P_b = the 'best' price ($P = MC$)

Under conditions of profit maximization, the emphasis is on establishing prices given the equality between MC and MR. When we contemplate a pricing strategy that is focused on delivering maximum benefit to consumers and producers, we have to redefine the rules for establishing prices. The real possibility of financial losses exists and hence the need for subsidy in line with community service obligations (if a non-commercial service can be shown to be consistent with social obligations—see Ch. 3). Underlying the determination of social prices are the ideas of consumer and producer surplus, which represent the benefits to consumers and producers. The concept of consumer surplus is presented in Chapter 7. Consumer surplus measures the difference between the amount consumers would be willing to pay for a service and what they actually have to pay for it (assuming that the price difference has a negligible effect on income left over for other consumption and investment activities). Producer surplus is the difference between the price a transport supplier would be prepared to accept to supply a

service and the market price for that service. It is not an economic cost of supplying the service but the rent that is transferred from the consumers to suppliers. Producer surplus will exist if the supply curve for transport services is upward sloping and the cost of such services increases as more of it is demanded. Where demand increases raise the market price for transport services, the market price will include an element of rent (called producer surplus) for those transport suppliers who were prepared to supply at the lower price. In situations where the change in demand is not sufficiently large to lead to an increase in the price of transport services and/or where the supply of transport services is perfectly elastic (i.e. a horizontal supply curve—see Chapter 4), there will be no producer surplus. In practice, most analysts make this assumption and concentrate on the changes in consumer surplus.

Under the pricing rule of constrained social-welfare maximization, aggregate social welfare is defined as the sum of consumer and producer surplus (equation (6.3)).

$$W(P) = CS(P) + PS(P) \qquad (6.3)$$

where $W(P)$ is aggregate social welfare at price P, $CS(P)$ is consumer's surplus, and $PS(P)$ is producer's surplus. $CS(P)$ is the triangle ACP_m when a monopolist's price prevails. The competitive market is the benchmark for pricing efficiency. Firms in competitive markets maximize the social-welfare criterion by choosing to produce at levels described by equation (6.4). Under competitive pricing, $\lambda = 0$. It is assumed, as for all pricing strategies, that a necessary condition for allocatively efficient prices is that a business is cost efficient (i.e. delivering a given level of service at the lowest cost). In practice, this latter condition often does not hold (except for operators described as 'best practice') and so the determination of efficient prices may be distorted when relating them to inefficient costs. Recognition of the link between efficient costs and efficient prices nevertheless is a good discipline to aspire to.

$$((P - MC)/P)\eta = 0 \qquad (6.4)$$

After some rearrangement it can be shown that this sets price equal to marginal cost. Transport businesses just earn in competitive equilibrium normal profits and provide service to everyone who is willing to pay the MC of production. For a natural monopoly, MC is less than average cost AC (see Fig. 6.1). That is, each additional unit of output adds less to cost than does the previous unit of output, so the firm operates at a loss when $P = MC$ ($= P_b$ in Fig. 6.1), at output Q_b. Thus, although the firm would maximize social welfare at P_b, each unit sold at P_b does not cover AC. A regulated natural monopoly in this circumstance must be subsidized if operations are to continue.

The final pricing strategy involves recognition of the social-welfare objective but a desire to avoid subsidy. This translates into a constraint that prices charged should cover average total cost (ATC), with this break-even price including an acceptable return on investment, alternatively referred to as a normal level of profit. Corporatization of public sector agencies grew out of this ideal. Imposing the cost coverage constraint on social-welfare maximization is represented by a value of λ lying between 0 and 1.

Ramsey pricing originates from the objective of cost recovery under the social-welfare objective. In Figure 6.1, P_r associated with Q_r allows a firm to break even, earning only normal profits. For a single-product natural monopoly, the break-even price is the second-best solution to the social-welfare problem because it results in a lower value for the social-welfare criterion than the first best price (when $P = MC$). The break-even price is known as the Ramsey price. This leads to a formal definition of the Ramsey price as the price that results in the lowest value for the Ramsey number (i.e. λ) which fulfils in equation (6.1) the constraint of allowing a firm to earn a normal profit (i.e. cover its ATC).

In general, the value of the social-welfare criterion increases as the Ramsey number decrease from 1 to 0. This is a popular strategy for a regulator with economic goals, who does not want to subsidize the operation of a transport business. It is often applied in the context of rate-of-return regulation. An interesting question can now be raised: 'which is less expensive to society—the cost of regulation or monopoly pricing?' An alternative is to award contracts by competitive bidding which is intended to provide monopoly services at competitive prices without extensive government regulation and its associated costs (as discussed in Ch. 2). Firms bidding competitively may be expected to choose the lowest possible price that allows normal profits. Will the contract-winning firm maintain the competitive price for the duration of the contract agreement? Often the firm or the tendering authority specifies future price changes as part of the contractual arrangements. This has its drawbacks: given the uncertainties of inflation and service innovation, it could be difficult to establish what constitutes competitive prices for a contract that extends into the future. The alternative may be contestable markets, as discussed in Chapter 2. Even monopolies may then maintain competitive prices. This raises some interesting issues. Exclusive contracts with generous time limits are clearly undesirable. Non-exclusive contracts allowing for the possibility of competitive entry is more desirable. Thus if a transport business in the market which currently has a contract (a monopoly contract) does not provide services at competitive prices, entry is allowed. Entry can occur by re-bidding or allowing someone to commence operations at competitive prices and see who survives. The onus is then on the incumbent monopolist to ensure that supernormal profits are never earned.

6.3 Pricing for multiple services

The discussion so far on Ramsey pricing has assumed a single service or output. What is the rule if there are multiple outputs as is common in transport? In general, prices should be set so that the percentage deviation from $MC^*\eta$ is constant among all services. In the presence of declining ATC, Ramsey prices are achieved when λ is the same for all services and takes the lowest value that allows a normal profit. Such Ramsey prices are efficient from the perspective of both society and of a competitive firm. We will look at two cases: two demand – *independent* services and two demand-*interdependent* services.

Two demand-independent services are represented by equation (6.5).

$$\left(\frac{P_1 - MC_1}{P_1}\right)\eta_1 = \left(\frac{P_2 - MC_2}{P_2}\right)\eta_2 = -\lambda \qquad (6.5)$$

A transport firm already operating as a monopoly supplier in a market, but fearing competitive entry from other firms offering related services may also find that Ramsey prices represent the best long-run pricing strategy for discouraging competitive entry (i.e. it keeps profits at their normal level). $(P_1 - MC_1)/P_1$ is the percentage by which price is marked up over MC. The service with the more inelastic demand (i.e. lower absolute η) must have the higher mark-up in order to preserve the equality of λ between the two markets. This has also become known as the inverse elasticity rule (IER). To see why, consider the two situations in Figure 6.2. If we think of service 1 as rail commuters and service 2 as rail non-commuters, we expect that commuters after a fare increase are less likely to switch out of rail compared to non-commuters who are far more price sensitive.

The recognition of the higher price increase in the price-inelastic commuter market and the lower price increase in the higher price-elastic non-commuter market represents the allocation of shared costs according to 'what the market will bear', as discussed in Chapter 5. Indeed the historical arguments in many cities for keeping commuting fares low in order to attract patrons away from the car has proved to be unsuccessful since this market is very price insensitive.

When translating this differential pricing policy into practice, we see that raising the price of commuter travel involves reducing consumer surplus by less than an equivalent increase in the price of the demand-elastic non-commuting. Note that fewer consumers are excluded from the market when price is increased for inelastic service demand than when it is increased for elastic service demand. For a multi-service transport operator, many different combinations of prices may yield a normal profit (the challenge of optimal mix of services using principles of yield management). Figure 6.3 is a useful alternative way of looking at this issue since it traces out combinations of prices for the two markets which yield the same levels of consumer surplus or profits. Such traces are called isocontours. Maximum profits occur at point A where $MR = MC$. After we have identified profits, we also have to consider social welfare. The formula for social welfare includes both producer and consumer surplus. For a natural monopoly, producer surplus is fixed by the requirement of zero excess profits, so we can concentrate on consumer surplus. The Ramsey pricing problem is solved by finding prices that maximize consumer surplus and also yield normal profits. A given level of consumer surplus (CS) may be achieved by many combinations of prices: for example, the two isocontours each representing different levels of surplus for CS in Figure 6.3. As price decreases, CS increases. So the leftmost iso-contour line is the highest level of CS. The tangency of the CS's isocontour closest to the origin and the zero-excess profit isocontour identifies the Ramsey prices. At a tangency, CS is the highest for any set of prices that allows the firm to earn a normal profit. This is point B in Figure 6.3.

ZZ is the trace of all tangencies between CSs and profit isocontours; thus all points along this line are solutions to the Ramsey pricing rule of equation (6.5), for $0 \leq \lambda \leq 1$. In particular, at point A, marginal cost equals marginal revenue, $MC = MR$ and hence $\lambda = 1$. At point C, price equals marginal cost and hence $\lambda = 0$. Somewhere between A and C is the Ramsey optimal price, namely B.

When two services are not independent it means that the change in the price of one service has a direct influence on the demand for another service (e.g. switching between classes of air travel or between modes of travel for passenger and freight movements). A knowledge of both direct and cross-price elasticities is required, adding a considerable burden to the empirical determination of efficient prices in each market. Two demand-interdependent services are represented by equation (6.6).

$$\left[\frac{P_1 - MC_1}{P_1}\right]\eta_{1,1} + \frac{P_2 - MC_2}{P_1}\frac{x_2}{x_1}\eta_{2,1} =$$

$$\left[\frac{P_2 - MC_2}{P_2}\right]\eta_{2,2} + \frac{P_1 - MC_1}{P_2}\frac{x_1}{x_2}\eta_{1,2} = -\lambda \qquad (6.6)$$

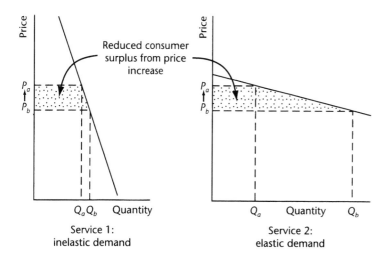

Service 1:
inelastic demand

Service 2:
elastic demand

Fig. 6.2 The change in consumer surplus resulting from an increase in the price

Notes: P_b and P_a are the price of travel before (P_b) and after (P_a) the price increase. Q_a and Q_b are the number of travellers before (Q_a) and after (Q_b), the price increase.

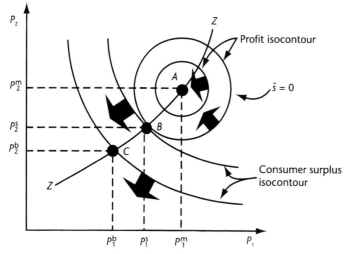

Fig. 6.3 Ramsey pricing for two demand-independent services

Notes: P_1^m is the profit-maximizing price for service 1. P_2^m is the social-welfare-maximizing price for service 2. P_1^b is the social-welfare-maximizing price for service 1 —the 'best' price. P_2^b is the social-welfare-maximizing price for service 2 —the 'best' price. P_1^s is the Ramsey, or constrained social-welfare-maximizing price for service 1. P_2^s is the Ramsey, or constrained social-welfare-maximizing price for service 2. A is the profit-maximizing set of prices. B is the Ramsey, or constrained social-welfare-maximizing set of prices. C is the social-welfare-maximizing set of prices.

The direct (or own) elasticities are given by $\eta_{1,1}$ and $\eta_{2,2}$; and the cross-elasticities are defined by $\eta_{1,2}$ and $\eta_{2,1}$.

When two (or more) services are interdependent they can be either substitutes or complements. This distinction is important since it has an important role in the determination of prices. To illustrate the differences between substitutes and complements we redraw Figure 6.3 as Figure 6.4. We will simplify the analysis by assuming identical marginal costs and direct and cross-price elasticities.

For substitutes, the consumer surplus isocontours are more convex than in the demand-independent case, and profit isocontours are elliptical instead of circular. Why? The shapes indicate that if either profits or CS is to be held constant, a price decrease for one service must be offset by a larger price increase for another service than when services are independent. For complements, profits and CS isocontours are less convex in the area of point B than is the case for demand-independent or substitute services. The more complementary the services (i.e.

the larger are the negative cross-elasticities of demand), the less convex are profit and CS contours.

For substitute services, the potential for pricing inefficiency is most severe. For example an all-class airline responds to other airline competition by lowering price of business-class travel. To maintain profits, the price of first-class travel must be increased, but the required price increase is higher when first and business-class travel are substitutes than when they are demand independent. When they are substitutes, a price drop for business class also reduces demand for first-class travel. For complementary services, a loss of consumer surplus resulting from a price change is not large because the slope of CS and profit isocontours is nearly the same. Depending on the nature of complementarity, an efficient pricing strategy may seem counterproductive. For example, D and E in Figure 6.4 identify Ramsey prices when one good is priced above the monopoly price P_m that would prevail for independent services.

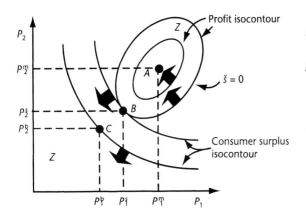

Ramsey pricing for two substitute services

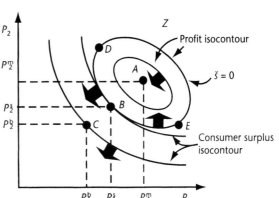

Ramsey pricing for two complementary services

Fig. 6.4 Examples of substitute and complement services

Notes: P_1^m is the profit-maximizing price for service 1. P_2^m is the social-welfare-maximizing price for service 2. P_1^b is the social-welfare-maximizing price for service 1—the 'best' price. P_2^b is the social-welfare-maximizing price for service 2—the 'best' price. P_1^s is the Ramsey, or constrained social-welfare-maximizing price for service 1. P_2^s is the Ramsey, or constrained social-welfare-maximizing price for service 2. A is the profit-maximizing set of prices. B is the Ramsey, or constrained social-welfare-maximizing set of prices. C is the social-welfare-maximizing set of prices. D is a feasible set of Ramsey prices when service 1 is a strong complement. E is a feasible set of Ramsey prices when service 2 is a strong complement.

6.4 Problems in practice with Ramsey pricing

The theoretical framework presented above is appealing in setting benchmarks for establishing allocatively efficient prices in markets with various degrees of competition and interdependencies between services. A major concern centres on the reliability of measures of demand elasticities and marginal cost which define the empirical foundations of the approach. Translating this into practice to identify (at best) indicative prices is a real challenge. The quality of data on costs and market sensitivity to prices is always a problem, but transport operators, regulators, and policy agencies do their best in using approximations (and sometimes guesstimates) of these inputs into the determination of prices.

To illustrate the challenges in taking a theoretically popular pricing strategy and applying it in practice, we draw on an empirical inquiry undertaken by Tye (1984) where the demand for each postal service is independent. He applied Ramsey pricing to the determination of charges for the delivery of letters, recognizing that the prices necessary to achieve the revenue requirements are determined by maximizing consumers' and producers' surplus. Pursuit of this solution results in prices set so that the percentage deviation from marginal costs for each service is inversely proportional to the price elasticity of demand. λ has been referred to as the factor of proportionality in the rearranged equation (6.1), as given in (6.7):

$$\frac{P_1 - MC_1}{P_1} = \frac{\lambda}{\eta_1} \qquad (6.7)$$

Vickrey (1974) has shown that λ is the fractional leakage of revenue from a rate increase lost from the resulting drop in demand, and $1/(1 - \lambda)$ is the marginal cost of net revenue, the latter defined as the loss of consumer surplus resulting from a rate increase producing a \$1 increase in net revenue.

Numerical examples show some serious problems with the application of the inverse elasticity rule (IER); linked specifically to the quality of empirical information on marginal costs and elasticities of demand. Tye (1984) found that if rates are set by the inverse elasticity rule, small changes in the elasticity of demand estimates lead to substantial changes in the prices for the respective classes of service. Estimated consumer surplus was not significantly different for a broad range of price structures involving shifts of hundreds of millions of dollars in the burden of shared costs. He concluded that such small changes in elasticity have a trivial effect on the intended objective of maximization of consumer surplus, even though they lead to large leverage in *assignment* of shared costs. Consequently, there is no evidence that any of the rate proposals (as summarized in Table 6.1) is superior to others in regard to this principle.

Table 6.1 indicates substantial discrepancies in elasticities. The econometric analysis (R76–1) did not lend credence to the IER. While it eliminated much of the vagueness in R74–1, it only sharpened the perceived shortcomings of IER by explicitly showing the weakness of the underlying assumptions. The fourth-class zone rated parcels and first-class mail have virtually identical historical elasticities (– 0.224, – 0.238). This is contrary to the rationale for substantial differences in cost coverage (i.e. revenue/variable cost) offered in earlier rate cases. This illustrates that substantially different rate increases and cost coverages in R74–1 were justified on grounds of purported differences in 'prospective' elasticities; but retrospective evidence in the next case (R76–1) never demonstrated the 'purported' elasticity differences in the last case. Credibility of IER as an objective rate-making device was harmed when it was observed that the R76–1 rate structure and proposed rate increases were very similar to R74–1 despite the great discrepancy in elasticity of demand in each case. In the determination of rates, the courts questioned whether ratepayers who paid higher rates would benefit in the light of demand inelasticity for every class of mail.

Table 6.1 Alternative ranking of mail classes by demand elasticity (in ascending order of demand elasticity)

Docket No. R74–1: 'Historical'	Docket No. R74–1: 'Prospective'	Docket No. R74–1: 'Implicit' in revenue forecasts	Docket No. R76–1: At 1974 rates
First class	First class (–0.10)	Second class regular rate (–0.058)	Second class regular rate (–0.12)
Second class regular rate	Third class bulk regular (–0.15–0.20)	First class (–0.076)	Fourth class zone rate (–0.224)
Special rate fourth	Parcel post (–0.25)	Air mail (–0.187)	First class (–0.238)
Third class bulk regular	Special rate fourth (–0.25–0.30)	Special rate fourth (–0.246)	Fourth class special (–0.289)
Parcel post	Second class regular rate (–0.40–0.50)	Third class bulk regular (–0.331)	Fourth class catalogues (–0.300)
Past rate increases	Proposed rate increases	Third class single piece (–0.371)	Third class regular (–0.551)
		Fourth class catalogues (–0.427) Parcel post (–0.645) (For all other subclasses, elasticity is zero)	

Note: R47–1: 'Historical'—Arthur Eden Testimony, pp 36–7. (No elasticity estimates were present—only the rankings of relative inelasticity to determine mark-ups over costs).

R74–1: 'Prospective'—Arthur Eden Direct Testimony, p. 40. (Elasticity coefficients are those submitted to William Vickrey for his answer to the Interrogatory by the Chief Administrative Law Judge (Tr. 2410).)

R74–1: 'Implicit'—OOC Interrogatory 2(a) addressed to Beckler (Tr. 1193) (implicit in before and after rate change volume projections).

R76–1: 'at FY rates'—Testimony of USPS Witness Bernard Sobin, Docket No. R76–1. These were estimates selected from a variety of econometric estimates that were often highly sensitive to the selected functional form. They were introduced to correct for subjectivity and discrepancies in demand elasticities in R74–1.

Although IER rates do not improve consumers' surplus over other proposed alternatives, they are extremely sensitive to relatively small errors in estimated demand elasticity within the range of costs and demand under consideration. If we define $r = \lambda/\eta$ where $r = (P - MC)/P = 1 - 1/(P/MC)$, and define $P/MC = S$ ('cost coverage'); then we can see that cost coverage equals $\eta/(\eta - \lambda)$.

Let us take one class of mail, and consider the effects of a change in η on the mark-up ratios and plot this in Figure 6.5. Small errors in the estimation of demand where it is inelastic make substantial differences in the cost coverage. As η approaches λ, the required cost coverage explodes upwards. A change in η has major consequences for the IER rates. Suppose η (first-class mail) = – 0.20 instead of – 0.10, a large relative error but a small error in terms of measurement error in econometric demand studies of postal services. The leakage ratio (η) is doubled to 0.1070 at the cost coverage initially assumed ($P = MC$

to cover ATC). The prescription according to IER would be to cut first-class rates slightly and raise all others since the leakage ratio for first-class mail is now the greatest. So the application of the rule requires a very precise estimation of *very inelastic* demands to prevent shifts of millions of dollars of revenue requirements that actually cause a reduction in CS when the deviation in η among classes is small. This will apply to all pricing strategies that require knowledge of η, not just Ramsey pricing. As controversial and disturbing as this evidence may be, it should encourage much more detailed acquisition of quality data on costs and demand, and in application be qualified by the nature of the information available to make professional comment on the likely benefits of a specific pricing profile. The Ramsey pricing framework *per se* remains very attractive despite this empirical challenge. Extensions to the pricing of externalities in recognition of the wider set of costs of transport services is an important direction for continuing research. To gain an appreciation of the wider set of costs and prices we now move to a consideration of transport user charges.

6.5 Transport infrastructure user charges

It is widely recognized by transport economists and planners that users of transport infrastructure in congested traffic environments are not paying the full social and environmental costs associated with their use of transport facilities. This under pricing is well summarized by the following statement in the context of roads: 'our roads are no more "doomed" to hopeless congestion than our meat counters would be if we sold steak for the price of dog food. The "shortages" in every case would be man-made and man-fixable by rational pricing, not hopeless, irremediable acts of God' (Elliott 1992: 527).

The rationale for charging for the use of transport infrastructure such as roads, airports, maritime ports, and rail track is typically linked to the four key objectives of economic efficiency, financial balance, equity, and environmental sustainability. These objectives recognize the diversity of obligations of stakeholders—users, government, and the community at large. Economists would argue that economic efficiency should be the primary basis of an initial set of user charges, covering both internal and external costs to the user. External costs can be subdivided into *intra-sectoral externalities*, which transport users impose upon one another (notably congestion and, to some extent, accidents) and *environmental externalities*, which are shifted to society at large (air pollution, noise, view/blight, and

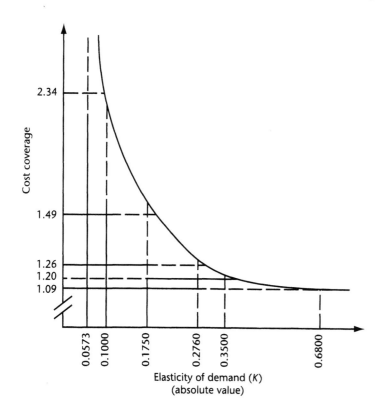

Fig. 6.5 Effect of changes in elasticity on cost coverage

Note: For simplification, this example assumes the class to be small enough so that changes in cost coverage do not affect the revenue requirements of other classes.

also accidents). Because of these external costs, there is typically overconsumption of transport infrastructure.

A pricing policy attempts to meet the objectives by the following procedures:

- it measures aggregate demand for transport, and hence determines the profitability and/or social efficiency of transport investments. It thus helps to decide what proportion of national resources should be allocated to the transport sector;

- in the short run it determines effective demand (i.e. demand compared to supply) for competing transport services by allocating traffic between them;

- in the long run it not only determines whether effective demand warrants the continuation of existing services—rationalization and dis-investment—or the provision of new or improved ones—by innovation and investment—but also affects the type and pattern of social and industrial location. These long-run effects are particularly important since they involve decisions that cannot easily be reversed.

6.5.1 Broadening the interpretation of marginal cost

In order to understand the rationale for specific user charges in both the short run and the long run, it is important to understand the role of marginal costs (*MC*). Although *MC*s have been prominent in the determination of prices under alternative pricing strategies (see Sect. 6.2), it is necessary to return to some basics and build up the toolkit of economic concepts in more detail than we have done thus far. We will develop the ideas in the context of roads (and later for ports), but recognize that the approach is applicable to all transport infrastructure. We begin with a single road trip and, following Walters (1968), define the cost of a vehicle trip in terms of the resources (i.e. the goods and services) forgone in order to undertake that journey. Walters identifies three elements of trip cost:

1. vehicle operating cost—fuel, vehicle wear-and-

tear, and wages of the driver—borne by the motorist;

2. variable maintenance cost which is primarily wear-and-tear on the road, and the cost of traffic control—borne by the road authority. These costs are *variable* in the sense of varying with use of the road for one additional trip; and

3. congestion cost—the cost an additional vehicle imposes on the rest of the traffic stream—borne by all other users of the road.

These three elements of cost are those arising out of use of the road. The costs of providing the highway such as rent for the use of the land, construction, and invariant maintenance costs, are disregarded because 'no fraction of these resources [the resources invested in the highway] can be saved if the [individual] motorist forbears to take his journey' (Walters, 1968: 10). This enumeration of cost components excludes costs imposed on the general community (which are external to road users as a group) such as air and noise pollution. Assuming one could measure these costs accurately, they could be included in the marginal social cost function without altering its basic shape. However, these community costs will be omitted until the next section, so as to focus on one major intra-sectoral externality—congestion costs.

Operating cost is regarded as a private cost because the user incurs it and presumably weighs this cost against the benefits derived from the journey. One could argue, however, that many users fail to recognize the total magnitude of operating costs arising out of an individual journey when deciding whether or not to make the journey. This discrepancy between actual and perceived costs is due to such factors as payment for fuel by credit cards (on a monthly, rather than per trip, basis), undervaluation of time spent travelling, and the reckoning of depreciation on a lump-sum as opposed to a per trip basis. In the following theoretical presentation we ignore the differences between perceived and actual costs, and comment on these differences in Section 6.5.5.

The variable maintenance and congestion costs of a journey are considered social costs because they are not assumed directly by the marginal user. It is these social costs, in particular congestion costs, that marginal cost pricing schemes are aimed at capturing. If these costs are not properly exacted from the motorist, she will be induced to undertake too many trips, to add unduly to the congestion. If, on the other hand, user charges exceed the sum of the variable maintenance cost and the congestion cost, then the vehicle user will be dissuaded from undertaking certain vehicle trips although the true cost is less than the returns. Taking into account the user charge, she may find that the sum of the operating cost and user charge exceeds the returns she expects from the trip. The journey is actually worthwhile but the unduly high charge prevents her from making it. Consequently, potentially valuable services of the road are wasted.

Congestion is a negative externality. As additional people use a facility or service, the quality of service received by all users declines. One extra consumer after a certain point is reached will dilute the quality of service provided to other consumers. When drivers use a highway, they do not pay the costs that they may be imposing on other drivers. Ideally, traffic should flow smoothly at the speed limit. But as traffic increases, eventually the addition of one more vehicle will slow the flow and increase the travel time of other vehicles. At this point congestion (the negative externality) begins. Thus the user (social) charges must be set exactly equal to the sum of the variable maintenance cost per vehicle kilometre and the congestion cost per vehicle kilometre so that 'the private cost of the vehicle owner—including the user charge per vehicle-kilometre—will reflect all the consequences of his decision to use the road' (Walters 1968: 12).

With a user charge reflecting the social cost, road users can decide whether their interests are best served by 'buying' the road trip or by purchasing some other commodity; and the resources will be devoted to the use that gives greatest satisfaction. When prices reflect efficient costs, resources will be efficiently distributed between road trips and other things, and between one sort of road and another, and between one agency and another.

Figure 6.6 introduces many of the concepts which economists use to describe the basis for establishing user charges consistent with allocative efficiency. The horizontal axis represents traffic volume on a given road in vehicle journeys per day (or, if one prefers, vehicles or vehicle journeys per hour), and the vertical axis represents cost per vehicle journey (or vehicle kilometre). It is assumed that all vehicles and drivers are homogeneous so that at a given level of traffic all vehicle journeys cost the same and all vehicles impose the same costs on all other vehicles. This assumption can be relaxed. It can be seen that variable maintenance costs (the line AB) are constant for each vehicle and for each volume of traffic. This assumes that each car does as much damage to the surface of the road whether it is in a dense or sparse traffic stream. The sum of operating and variable maintenance costs (constituting short-run average cost—$SRAC$) is shown by the backward-bending curve, CE, and the short-run marginal cost ($SRMC$) function is represented by the continuously rising curve CF, which is independent of traffic flow up to Q_0 trips per day.

At relatively low traffic volumes, vehicles do not interfere with each other very much, and there are no spillover costs as additional vehicles enter the facility—in other words, private operating costs are constant at the level AC and the short-run average and marginal cost curves are identical. However, beyond a certain traffic volume (in this case Q_0) operating costs begin to increase as vehicles get in one another's way. Each increase in volume leads to lower average speed and a higher incidence of stop-and-start driving which in turn leads to increased fuel, vehicle wear-and-tear, and travel time costs. The short-run average and marginal cost curves begin to diverge, since the contribution to total travel costs of additional drivers (represented by the $SRMC$ curve) will exceed their own personal costs (represented by the $SRAC$ curve). Beyond Q_0, the short-run marginal cost function is the slope, or first derivative, of the short-run average cost function. It can in a sense be termed a congestion cost function, because it measures the increase in short-run average cost, dy, with respect to an increase in traffic volume (i.e., congestion dx). At traffic levels below Q_0, the congestion cost due to the nth vehicle (defined as the total of vehicles minus the *SRAC* of the *n*th vehicle) is zero, so that the marginal cost of an additional vehicle journey is simply that vehicle's cost (*OA* plus *AC*). At traffic volumes greater than Q_0, the congestion cost due to the *n*th vehicle is positive, causing the marginal cost curve to lie above the average cost curve.

As the density of vehicles on the road further increases, speed declines so much that the flow of vehicles reaches a maximum of Q_{max}, meaning that if any more vehicles attempted to enter the traffic stream, the reduction in speed would be so large that the flow would actually decrease.

The equilibrium volume of traffic is determined by the intersection of the demand function *DD'* (which may be interpreted as the marginal social benefit (*MSB*) function) and some cost function. If the road authority decided to charge *OA* per vehicle journey to cover variable maintenance expenses, the relevant cost function would be the short-run average cost curve, which would intersect with the demand curve to yield a volume of traffic *Q* at price *K*. However, at this level of traffic, the true cost of a journey (which includes the extra costs of congestion that an additional vehicle imposes on others) is *N*, whereas the cost perceived by the motorist is *M*: 'To make the marginal valuation of a vehicle journey equal to its true cost we must raise a congestion levy equal to the difference between the true cost and the private cost (including the OA paid to the road authority)' (Walters 1968).

Thus, if the authority imposes a charge of *MN*, the interaction of supply and demand will bring volume slightly below *Q*, and the charge can be slightly lowered; this process of simultaneous adjustment of traffic volume and the congestion charge will continue until the volume falls to Q_{opt}, which remains a stable equilibrium point so long as the authority imposes a congestion charge of *PT*. The adjustment in traffic volume under a particular congestion pricing regime will be influenced by the price elasticity of demand, which represents the 'shape' of the demand curve. At this point the price *P* which users pay for the journey will be equal to the additional true cost of the journey, that is, the sum of variable maintenance costs, private vehicle operating costs, and congestion costs. The above explanation can be further clarified as follows: at any level of traffic between Q_{opt} and *Q*, some drivers are making trips with net benefits to them less than the additional costs these trips impose on other drivers (*OA* is less than *AC*); only at Q_{opt} is there an equality between net benefits and congestion costs (the amount *PT*), meaning that those who find it least worthwhile to use the road receive net benefits equal to the costs they impose on other drivers. In order to achieve and maintain this optimum traffic flow, the road authority must charge an additional amount (over and above the amount *OA*) equal to *PT*. Note that the individual driver is already paying *AS* at Q_{opt}; thus the three components of the cost of a trip is *AS* plus the two components of an efficient user charge—*OA* and *PT*.

The marginal cost pricing alternative is therefore

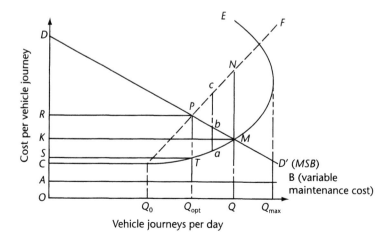

Fig. 6.6 Essential relationships between costs, demand, and user charges

efficient because only those who value a particular journey (namely, the route, direction, and timing of the journey) by an amount equal to or greater than the additional costs to other users will undertake it. This alternative is also efficient because it yields the greatest net benefits: at a level of traffic Q (which occurs in the absence of a congestion charge), net benefits are equal to DKM (total benefits $ODMQ$, equivalent to total consumer surplus, minus total costs $OKMQ$); however, at Q_{opt} net benefits are $DSTP$, which is clearly larger than the area DKM. An important point of interpretation is that the congestion charge revenue $RSTP$ is not included in the net benefits because it is merely a transfer payment from users to the rest of society. The public authority that collects the charge can use the revenue to finance additional roads or other public works projects that in turn will benefit other members of society. Moreover, to argue that the efficient solution improves the welfare of society as a whole requires further assumptions and value judgements, the most important of which are (i) that benefits as revealed by willingness to pay are an adequate representation of individual utilities and (ii) that society is better off following a change in resource allocation if the increases in net benefits to some exceed the decreases in net benefits to others. The first assumption is controversial because of imperfect income distribution.

It should be pointed out that some degree of demand elasticity is necessary in order for the congestion charge to bring traffic flow to the optimum level, and that the more inelastic the demand for vehicle journeys is with respect to price, the higher the congestion levy will have to be. Empirical evidence (as cited in Ch. 4) indicates that of all trip purposes, the commuter trip (the prime contributor to urban congestion) is the most inelastic; it is especially inelastic with regard to timing and destination, and slightly less so with respect to route and mode.

6.5.2 Adding in extra environmental externalities

We are now better equipped to generalize the user charge analysis to include a larger set of externalities. A number of studies throughout Europe, Canada, and the USA have consistently shown that transport users generally do not pay enough user taxes and charges to cover their external costs. In a review of five major studies, Gomez-Ibanez (1997) concludes that public transport users do not pay their way largely because the fares they pay are not sufficient to cover the capital and operating costs, not because they generate significant amounts of pollution and other social costs. For automobile users, by contrast, government capital and operating expenses constitute only about 20% of total external costs. Among the external costs, parking accounts for about 20%, air pollution for about 20%, accidents for about 20%, and energy security for about 20%. These figures are approximations, but they do highlight where the externalities exist. Some of the international evidence is summarized in Table 6.2, with a very detailed analysis for the UK by Peirson and Vickerman (1997) summarized in Table 6.3. It should be interpreted with great caution since our knowledge of costing many of the items is both immature and often subject to huge variations caused by the context in which transport services are provided. The higher estimates in the range for the USA are for urban peak trips. The Australian evidence for the automobile suggests that there is overpayment for automobile use, which might be queried for urban congestion contexts. The message is simple—there is much scope for correcting the (under) pricing of externalities via a mix of pricing and technological change to eliminate/reduce such external impacts. There is also a need for much more research into identifying the variation and sources of variation in each of the unit cost items.

The Peirson and Vickerman (1997) study is particularly interesting because they report 'efficient' prices (assuming constant returns to scale) based on long-run marginal cost pricing and current prices charged for a range of passenger transport modes.

Table 6.2 Estimates of external costs and subsidies for typical urban passenger trips

Cents/passenger km. (US cents, 1994)	Germany Car	Germany Train	Australia Car	Australia Bus	Australia Train	USA Car	USA Bus	USA Train
Government								
Capital			1.64*	10.5*	13.9*	0.25–1.4	0.18–4.4	8.75
Operating and maintenance						0.0–2.2	27–33	19.0
Other govt. (police, fire, etc.)						0.18–1.1	0.07–0.16	0.06
Subtotal			1.64	10.5	13.9	0.4–4.7	27.1–37.2	27.6
Societal								
Congestion			2.8	0.01	0.0	0.25–9.7	2.3	0.0
Air pollution	2.4	0.38	2.0	2.4	2.2	0.6–4.7	1–2.8	0.9–3.2
Noise pollution	0.24	0.06	0.9	0.2	1.0	0.06–0.5	0.03–0.3	0.13
Water pollution			0.1	0	0	0.06–7.5	0.06	
Solid waste						0.13	0.0	
Accidents	1.7	0.18	1.7	0.1	0	0.88–2.1	0.43–1.4	0.38
Energy			0.8	0.1	0	0.44–3.2	0.56–1.8	0.25–0.8
Parking			0.5	0	0	0.5–6.8		
Other						0.008–5.2	0.25	
Subtotal	4.25	0.59	8.8	2.81	3.2	2.8–12	4.66–8.88	1.69–4.4
User payments			16**	8**	7**			
Fares, tolls						0.0	8.8–11.9	8.8
Taxes and charges	2.1		-			0.4	0.0	0.0
Subtotal	2.2		16	8	7	0.44–1.3	8.8–11.9	8.8
Net subsidy	2.13		−5.56	4.81	10.1	2.8–14.5	23–34.1	21–23

Source: Gomez-Ibanez (1997). Germany and Spain data are from the European Federation for Transport and the Environment; the US data are from the World Resources Institute, the National Defence Council, and Todd Litman (an independent consultant), Australian data are sourced from Austroads (1994).

Notes: * sum of capital operating and maintenance costs.
   ** includes operations, ownership, and fares.

On average, current prices for interurban travel in the UK are similar to the full external cost. Car external costs are slightly lower than estimates of current costs including current taxes. Although car has higher external costs than rail (almost three times in Table 6.3), determined mainly by congestion costs, the high internal costs of rail, especially in the provision of capacity, outweigh the external car costs. If one were to emphasize short-run marginal (user) costs then car is clearly inferior on most scores.

This fuller range of environmental externalities can be represented diagrammatically in Figure 6.7 which is a variation on Figure 6.6. The horizontal axis defines output in appropriate units that we might call mobility. For road transport this would be vehicle kilometres, for public transport it could be passenger kilometres, for airports it might be passenger throughput, and for the waterfront it might be throughput of cargo in tonnes. The vertical axis measures costs and benefits in monetary values, with each source of externality converted to a dollar value. The market equilibrium N^0 is at the intersection of the demand (or average revenue) curve, which is equal to the marginal private and social benefits ($D = MPB = MSB$), and the marginal private cost curve (MPC). With identical transport users, MPC may be equated to average social cost (ASC); it is positively sloped because of intra-sectoral externalities. The ASC curve is drawn in the range of mobility before the backward-bending effect in Figure 6.6 sets in.

Taking account of intra-sectoral externalities, MSC

Table 6.3 Marginal external costs of passenger transport in the UK (pence per passenger km.)

Transport mode	Global warming	Air pollution	Noise pollution	Congestion	Accidents	Total MEC	LRMC	Efficient price	Current price
Interurban									
Rail	0.01	0.12	0.02	0.04	0.03	0.22	9.67	9.89	7.11
Car	0.02	0.35	0.08	0.85	0.15	1.45	5.15	6.60	7.78
Coach	0.01	0.39	0.01	0.15	0.01	0.57	3.00	3.57	3.09
London									
Underground peak	0.01	0.13	0.09	0.72	0.03	0.98	45.18	46.16	10.12
Underground off-peak	0.01	0.13	0.09	0.00	0.03	0.26	15.80	16.06	8.94
Rail peak	0.01	0.13	0.09	0.80	0.03	1.06	20.11	21.17	6.88
Rail off-peak	0.01	0.13	0.09	0.07	0.03	0.32	12.56	12.87	6.88
Car peak	0.03	1.67	0.39	15.08	1.50	18.43	7.12	25.55	11.28
Car off-peak	0.02	1.25	0.39	1.65	1.50	4.81	6.54	11.35	10.04
Bus peak	0.01	2.42	0.09	3.79	0.88	7.19	15.27	22.46	10.63
Bus off-peak	0.01	1.82	0.09	1.83	0.88	4.62	13.00	17.62	10.63

Source: Peirson and Vickerman (1997, table 1: 281).

then represents marginal social costs; when we also account for the marginal environmental external costs MEC, TMSC gives the 'total marginal social costs' (Verhoef *et al.* 1996). Optimal road use is then found at N^*, where net social benefit (the area between the curves MPB and TMSC) is maximized, and the shaded welfare loss, *hel*, is avoided.

The identification of N^* as 'optimal' is contingent on the welfare criterion applied. The principle of considering total welfare as the sum of individuals' welfare classifies any change in mobility as an improvement as long as the winners could compensate the losers in such a way that eventually everyone is better off (or at least nobody is worse off). This is called the potential Pareto principle. The question of whether such compensations actually take place is a political matter, not relevant for the evaluation of change. This commonly accepted potential Pareto criterion to a considerable extent bypasses issues of the 'social feasibility' of government policies, that is not so much dependent on the question of whether society at large benefits, but rather on the distribution of such a (net) welfare improvement—expressed, for instance, in the number of winners and losers, combined with the intensities of individual welfare changes.

To illustrate this, we consider two environmental instruments proposed by Verhoef *et al.* (1996) for

achieving the optimal solution N^* in Figure 6.7—optimal physical regulation (such as a prohibition on mobility between N^* and N^0) and the optimal effluent fee r^*. Table 6.3 summarizes the welfare effects of both policies for each group as the size of corresponding areas in Figure 6.7. With optimal physical regulation, the road users generating the optimal mobility N^* will enjoy a welfare gain due to reduced congestion costs, represented by the area *abdc*. The mobility forgone, between N^* and N^0, implies a loss of benefits equal to area N^*N^0eh and a reduction in private costs of N^*N^0eb, producing a negative net total of *beh*. In addition, external congestion costs within this group will disappear, equal to the total reduction of external congestion costs, *beif*, minus the fraction *abdc* enjoyed by the remaining road users. Thus the total welfare effect given in the second column in Table 6.4 results. Finally, the reduction in the environmental externality implies a welfare gain to its 'victims' equal to *filh*. Summing over the three groups, a social welfare gain equal to *hel* can then indeed be derived.

Optimal regulatory taxation yields identical welfare effects for the mobility forgone, for the 'losers' from the recovery of the environmental externality, and for society at large. However, the remaining road users are now worse off, as total tax revenues, *abhg*, (necessarily) exceed the reduction in congestion

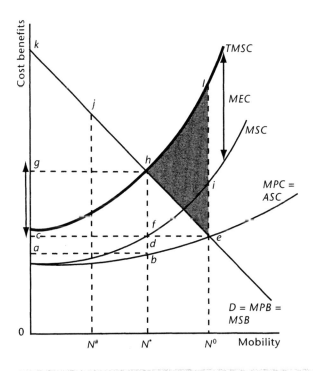

Fig. 6.7 Welfare implications of regulation

Source: Verhoef *et al.* (1996).

Table 6.4 The welfare effects of optimal physical regulation and optimal effluent fees

Optimality policies	Road users: $O - N^*$	Road users: $N^* - N^o$	Victims of the environmental externality	Regulator	Social (total)
Optimal physical regulation	+ abdc	− beh + beif −abdc	+ filh	0	+ hel
Optimal regulatory fees	− cdhg = abdc − abhg	− beh + beif − abdc	+ filh	+ abhg	+ hel

Source: Verhoef *et al.* 1996.

costs, *abdc*. These tax revenues accrue to the government. Therefore, in this stylized setting, where the two instruments are equally efficient in terms of accomplishing N^*, they are certainly not equivalent in terms of social feasibility:

The road users generating optimal mobility enjoy a welfare gain with physical regulation, whereas they are worse off with regulatory fees. Since the other groups are likely to be indifferent between both policies, physical regulation will be more socially feasible than regulatory taxation. If, in the case sketched above, we assume the ratio of mobility of road users to be constant along the horizontal axis, a majority of road users would even be in favour of physical measures, while all road users would be opposed to the effluent fee (an important assumption here is that internal (time) costs do not differ among road users). (Verhoef *et al.* 1996)

The different regulatory instruments will usually also differ in terms of allocative efficiency. The assumption of both instruments achieving optimality is quite unrealistic, especially for physical regulation. A regulator is unlikely to apply 'optimal' physical regulation by identifying and prohibiting the socially excessive mobility between N^* and N^o.

With physical regulation, the regulator runs the risk of also affecting mobility with relatively high economic benefits. In contrast to fees, which will make the road users give up mobility between N^* and N^0 (where benefits fall short of the sum of the internal costs and the fee), a physical measure might even affect mobility between O and $N\#$ (with $N\# = N^0 - N^*$). Regulation may then even be inferior to non-intervention, as in the case where the benefits forgone, $ON\#jk$, exceed the savings in social costs, N^*N^0lh. With physical regulation, there is no guarantee that the remaining mobility represents the highest benefits.

6.5.3 Alternative views on the appropriate user charge

6.5.3.1 The Walters approach

The approach developed above is associated with Walters (1968). The Walters model emphasizes efficient economic charges to be faced by the individual traveller when deciding on a journey. The charges for the use of a road should cover variable maintenance costs, equal to the infrastructure resources used up in making the trip; congestion costs equal to the delay costs to other vehicles imposed by the vehicle trip; and operating costs of the vehicle which are borne by the user of the infrastructure and are internal to the decision regarding use. The cost of *new investment* is not part of the costs of the vehicle trip: the solitary vehicle does not 'cause' the investment. Decisions made regarding investment are independent of decisions whether or not to use existing roads.

Because of the 'lumpiness' (indivisibility) in infrastructure investment, in practice it serves many uses, complicating the single-user exposition. There is the issue of shared costs, both common and joint, as presented in Chapter 5. Thus additional rules must be devised in order to 'finance' the cost of extension. Walters separates pricing and investment decisions in the sense that investment in roads does not arise directly from pricing signals. Thus short-run marginal costing (*SRMC*) rather than *LRMC* is the

appropriate pricing strategy. Walters would presumably support short-run social (and constrained social) welfare maximization. *SRMC* equals *LRMC* only when capacity is optimally adjusted to the volume of output. This requires no indivisibilities or joint production (i.e. capacity and road service quality) in the supply of roads, neither of which holds in practice. Road capacity is highly indivisible, and is thus over- or under-used. In summary, the Walters approach is a rigid short-run approach, with user prices set equal to *SRMC*.

6.5.3.2 The Kolsen approach

An alternative view has been proposed by Kolsen *et al.* (1975). The emphasis is on the joint product nature of outputs from the transport industry. They distinguish common plant, non-separable capacity, and maintenance costs. Common plant such as a road or a railway is assumed to supply a number of outputs (e.g. freight and passenger). Some production costs can be assigned by the nature of their occurrence to the direct use made of roads by individual vehicles. This is the same as in Walters. Some other costs can be attributed not to the individual vehicle but to *groups* of vehicles, distinguished in various ways. There is a class of user of roads.

An example of a 'group'-linked cost is the cost of providing crawler lanes for heavy vehicles. These costs are called long-run separable costs, defined as costs that can be avoided in the planning stages by not providing the capacity for the user classes for which they would be incurred. Because such costs can be attributed to a particular user class, these long-run and short-run separable costs are not joint costs as defined in Chapter 5. Separable costs in the Kolsen model can only be attributed to classes of vehicles, not individual vehicles. So there still remains some element (unavoidable) of jointness at the individual vehicle level.

Non-separable capacity and maintenance costs are incurred in providing services to users as a whole. Examples are directional signs, road lining, culverts, and planned commitment of resources involved in providing the basic track bed. These costs cannot be allocated to particular users or groups of users.

Kolsen *et al.* (1975) favour the 'what the public will bear' approach. Prices should be set at greater than or equal to long-run marginal separable cost for each product. The sum of prices of all products equals *LR* separable *MC* plus *LR* non-separable *MCs*. In summary, the Kolsen approach promotes covering *LRMC* in the sense that some capacity costs are allocatable to particular user classes.

This system of user charges based on short-run costs (the Walters approach) or the enhanced Walters approach of Kolsen *et al.* where long-run separable costs are also covered, while efficient from the viewpoint of allocating traffic throughout an existing road network, does not provide built-in guidelines for long-term investment decision. This has to be based on cost-benefit analysis. Thus typically,

these transport user charges recognize the component costs in Figure 6.8 but not the investment related costs in Figure 6.9.

6.5.4 Equity considerations in transport user charges

Congestion charges will be regressive in the equity sense of charging the lower income person a greater percentage of their income than the higher income earner for the same level of benefit. Elliott (1992) has argued that congestion charges would be much less regressive than the existing road use financing instruments, which charge lower income earners disproportionately to subsidize the richer indi-

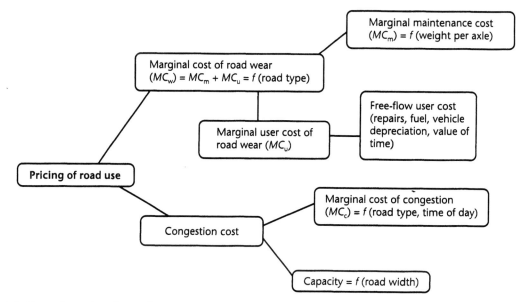

Fig. 6.8 Dimensions of road user charges

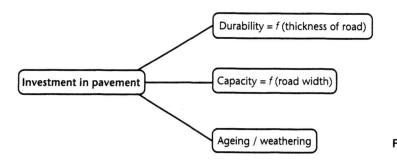

Fig. 6.9 Dimensions of road investment

viduals. For example, non-car owning taxpayers on low incomes support car users by paying for courts, fire stations, hospitals, and especially the police to protect automobile users.

A congestion toll may involve a redistribution of income from low income to high income travellers. A toll is regressive in that, among those who pay, it would be larger relative to total income for the relatively poor than the relatively rich. For the vehicle users who continue to pay the toll, it is not easy to predict the effect of congestion pricing. In the standard demand and cost diagram shown in Figure 6.10*a* we have a predicted reduction in consumer surplus (*CS*) of the tolled group. Before the toll consumer surplus is area *ACFE* and after a toll, it is *ABE*. However, the conclusion that the 'tolled' users will be worse off than previously may be reversed if a simplifying assumption is discarded. In the case of most transport infrastructure, cost and demand are interdependent. In presenting a single demand curve (Fig. 6.10*a*) we fail to recognize this. The quality of the road when carrying a vehicle flow of *OL* is less than when it carries only *OH*. So two separate demand curves must be drawn to represent the willingness of consumers to pay for the two different qualities of road service—as shown in Figure 6.10*b*.

Before the toll, the road transport price to each consumer equals *OA*. Demand at this price equals *OS*, given the relevant demand curve D_1. After the toll, vehicle flow decreases and road *quality* increases. A new higher demand curve is relevant. If the new demand curve is D_2 (parallel to D_1), price equals *OB* and traffic volume equals *OH*. The consumer surplus for the group is larger without a congestion toll (= *AEKJ*) than with it (= *BFL*). If the new demand curve is more inelastic as in D_3, the opposite is the conclusion. Consumer surplus is smaller without the toll (= *AEPN*) than with a toll (= *CGQ*). Thus it is not possible to determine by logic alone whether the tolled group will be better or worse off under congestion pricing. This reinforces once again the importance of a knowledge of the influences on demand for travel (as presented in Ch. 4).

6.5.5 Is congestion pricing feasible?

Traffic congestion is not a new phenomenon. Julius Caesar in 45 BC declared the centre of Rome off limits between 6 am and 4 pm to all vehicles except those of officials, priests, high-ranking citizens and visitors.

(Dobes 1995: 1)

Traffic congestion, more than any other single item, provides a daily reminder to all of the inefficiencies in the current transport system. Traffic congestion adds almost billions of dollars to travel costs in all sectors. For example, in the USA in 1994, congestion costs defined by the value of travel time delay as perceived by motorists and the cost of fuel wasted in traffic was estimated by the Texas Transportation Institute (1997) to be $US53 bn. per annum, and growing at about 2% per annum. $US8.6 bn. occurs in Los Angeles, the worst aggregate congestion cost of all US cities. On a per capita basis, however, Washington DC has the higher cost of $860 per person. In the urban passenger sector, calls for improved public transport are a common response. Calls for congestion pricing are rare (although increasingly being heard), and calls for discouraging road construction as a contribution to reducing traffic congestion through encouraging the use of public transport and assisting the move towards a more compact urban area are on the increase. It is true that urban mobility in many cities throughout the world is being 'strangled' by the large amounts of time unnecessarily wasted in traffic jams, draining the urban economy. It has also been said that 'congestion is the sign of a healthy urban economy—what is lacking however is the presence of organised congestion'.

Congestion pricing does not eliminate congestion—rather it ensures that the level is the outcome of efficient prices. The supply-side response of more roads is not an efficient or sensible 'solution' in the presence of distortionary pricing which is way out of line with the full set of environmental externalities that arise from the effects of such pricing. This does not preclude the development of strategic road links built for reasons other than congestion mitigation, such as links to major transport hubs like seaports and airports.

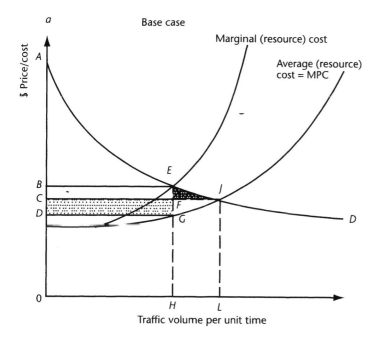

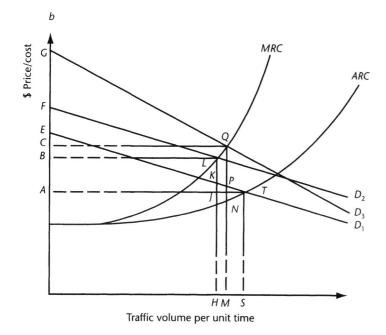

Fig. 6.10 The implications of changing demand on the net benefits of congestion charges

We must continue to make the case for appropriate charges (as distinct from taxes) which reflect the real cost of resources consumed in travel. Congestion pricing is arguably the only policy that will make a noticeable difference in peak congestion levels in the world's most congested cities. Other policies can create real and substantial benefits, but cannot do much to reduce the most severe congestion. There is so much latent demand for car travel at peak periods and during the shoulder periods that whatever capacity we can feasibly expect to build, or that can be freed up by enticing a few drivers off the road, will quickly become filled by people who are now being deterred only by congestion itself. This is a well-documented empirical reality known as the 'fundamental law of traffic congestion' (Downs 1962, 1992).

Neutze (1995) in commenting on the relationship between roads and urban patterns says:

I believe that if you correctly price roads, you will increase the extent to which the investment will cause movement of employment to the outer parts of cities. If you price them correctly, the areas where the price will be high will be in the inner urban areas because that is where the road costs and land costs are high. Land is scarce, therefore it is expensive to provide roads just as to provide buildings in those areas. That will discourage the use of roads in urban areas and that is one of the reasons why, even with optimal investment, you will have and should have high levels of congestion in places where land prices are high.

Implementation of congestion pricing involves recognition of the following issues:

- congestion pricing would cause some motorists to change their behaviour;
- congestion pricing would result in a net benefit to society;
- congestion pricing is technically feasible;
- institutional issues are complex but can be resolved;
- all income groups can benefit given an appropriate distribution of revenues;
- some motorists will lose;
- congestion pricing would reduce air pollution and save energy;
- the political feasibility of congestion pricing is uncertain;
- evaluation of early projects is crucial (see Luk and Chung 1997a);
- an incremental approach is appropriate.

Efficient pricing however is a necessary but not sufficient condition for a socially desirable outcome. There must be a role for other policy instruments such as physical planning. The limits to pricing as a planning tool are vividly illustrated in a UK House of Commons Transport Committee hearing in which the expert witness, Goodwin, said:

there is the intriguing test of intuitive common sense. It is noticeable that there are some transport policies that nobody suggests should be determined by 'willingness-to-pay'. An example is the division of road space between vehicles and pedestrians. It would be possible to say that the relative width of sidewalk and carriageway should be determined by the amounts that pedestrians and vehicles are willing to contribute, or even more specifically that pedestrian-actuated traffic signals should require the insertion of a coin. The logic in one sense is similar to that of road pricing, but it does not command serious consideration. Nor does there exist (as far as I know) an underground of hard-line road prices biding their time until the moment is right to implement pedestrian charging with push-chair supplements and a penalty for elderly slow walkers. (Goodwin 1995)

Efficient pricing signals and physical planning ordinances should be viewed as being as much potential complements as they are potential substitutes. The 'dark green' end of the environmental spectrum has tended to treat physical planning (constraints) as an alternative, at least partially, to 'failed' pricing. Pricing, however, differs from physical planning in one important aspect—it provides money. The revenue raised from road pricing of cars will be large:

for Sydney alone, with nearly 2 million cars and station wagons, averaging 15,000 km per annum, with 12,000 kms in Sydney, if we assume that 6,000 kms will be on the roads subject to a congestion charge (after allowing for the price elasticity) and the charge is 5 cents/km, the revenue raised is of the order of $600m. per annum, 150% of the State Rail annual deficit. (ibid.)

Under the new realism banner, eloquently documented by Goodwin et al. (1991), it is argued that the huge revenue sums raised from any change in road user prices should in part at least be allocated in a way which is consistent with the preferences of both society and transport users.

Allowing for both economic reasoning and political reality, the 'rule of three' is actively promoted in a number of countries. The road space initially released by congestion pricing can be used as follows: one-third reclaimed for environmental improvement, including pedestrian and non-transport uses, one-third used for extra traffic for which the reduction in congestion would be important: for example, use the revenue to favour buses, delivery trucks, emergency vehicles, and disabled travellers. A final third would have the effect of reducing congestion delays for all remaining traffic. To maintain this benefit will require a combination of pricing and non-pricing instruments to offset the tendency for traffic growth to eliminate the achieved speed increase.

6.5.5.1 Tollroads, toll collection technology, and attitudes towards tolls

While the preceding examples sketch out the case for how social cost pricing can reduce highway congestion and potentially make all drivers better off, will it work in practice? For about the last three decades economists have advocated congestion pricing to control road use, but toll collection was an impediment. Stopping traffic to collect tolls is self-defeating. Recent electronic toll collection devices, however, make congestion pricing feasible (see Hau 1992). Cars can now be equipped with electronic devices that emit signals relayed to highway monitors, and car owners are billed for their highway usage. Highway and bridge tolls are now collected electronically in, for example, Australia, California, Florida, Oklahoma, Texas, France, Italy, and Norway.

Even after clearing the practical hurdles to implementing congestion pricing, other obstacles hamper its acceptance. Some critics suggest that charging for highway use discriminates against low income people (e.g. Litman 1997), who spend a greater percentage of their income on transportation than high income people, and often need to commute during rush hours when tolls would be imposed. Tax credits or other measures affecting the distribution of income could alleviate this hardship and still allow congestion pricing to improve the efficiency of

highway use. A review of public acceptance of congestion pricing by Luk and Chung (1997a) concluded that support is greater in cities where congestion is more severe such as Hong Kong in the 1990s; that there is a not insignificant proportion of the community who prefer traffic restrictions to pricing (citing Japanese and British studies); that support will increase where there is tangible evidence of significant benefits especially in the form of travel time savings; and support is higher where the collection method is simple and the charge is known in advance.

On the specific issue of tollroads as an indication of attitudes towards user charging, respondents in a series of opinion surveys in Sydney, Melbourne, and Brisbane see the need to have private sector involvement if no other funding is available, but there is still considerable wariness about the idea, as demonstrated in Table 6.5. What is evident is that the majority of the community are not opposed to toll roads *per se*, as might have been judged from publicized events such as protests against the M2 tollroad in Sydney and the South East Tollway in Queensland. These protests may be more a function of lack of consultation, current environmental impact assessment processes, and heightened environmental consciousness, rather than opposition to the concept of privately funded tollroads. Loveday (1993) found that 56% of respondents supported the concept of electronic road pricing. In general, surveys have found that most people are comfortable with the concept of 'user pays' in the cities which already have tollroads, though their experience with tollroads may influence their response. It is likely that cities without tollroads would face greater community concern over the concept.

People dislike tolls, and some argue that technology, instead of pricing, could relieve congestion. Technology can improve highway use, but a phenomenon called latent demand will frustrate efforts to relieve congestion. A reduction in congestion resulting from technological innovation or from new capacity encourages others to drive during hours or on highways they normally avoid. In other words, adding more highway lanes, for example, will

Table 6.5 NSW community attitudes to tollroads

Statement	% who chose statements		
	1992	1993	1994
Agree that user should pay for roads	17	20	19
Agree that users should pay only if a free alternative is available	37	45	41
Agree that users should pay if there is no other way of funding road development	30	23	30
Disagree that users should pay	15	11	10
Don't know	1	1	—

Sources: Frank Small and Associates (1994); RAMIS (1992, 1993).

also add more drivers. Thus, even travel on congested highways does not represent the full, potential demand to use them. Therefore, asking people to pay the cost that their use imposes on others not only provides for rational use, but also eases the dilemma between those who want to expand facilities and those opposed to expansion.

An important issue in the debate on road pricing is the way in which a traveller perceives the cost imposed on them via various possible mechanisms of payment such as cordon pricing using manual tollbooths, supplementary licensing, off-vehicle recording systems such as automatic vehicle identification (AVI), and on-vehicle charging systems such as smart card technology.

The visible nature of a toll and the inability to pay in advance by a stored value card or to defer payment, options now available with electronic toll collection, makes private car travellers in particular quite sensitive to tolls. There will need to be significant quantitative and qualitative savings in travel time to justify a toll for private car users. The extent of this will depend on the available route alternatives, especially the mix of delay and free-moving time for a total time saving. An empirical study undertaken for the entire Sydney Metropolitan Area as part of an inquiry into tollroads (Hensher *et al.* 1989) highlighted the importance of the total saving in time, with the mix of delay and free moving time being of limited benefit if total time savings are small.

In considering the sensitivity of the travelling public to tolls, it is important to link this exercise in with the specific context in which a road-priced facility will be supplied. The value of time savings is likely to be a function of the magnitude and composition of the time savings. Maximum return will not be achieved by uniform pricing. Consideration should be given to tolls that can vary by distance travelled, time of day, direction of travel, and type of vehicle. Current practice tends to emphasize only vehicle-type differentiation, primarily for administrative ease in toll collection via tollbooths. The opportunity to improve both social and financial return by differential pricing by time of day should be considered, given the differences in toll elasticity of demand between the peak and off-peak periods.

The potential gains in time savings from tollroads introduced into an overall system of mixed tolled/untolled roads can be eroded by limitations on entering and leaving the tollroad. Not only can this erode the potential time benefits, in the early days of tollroads it can result in a bad reputation. When combined with the time saving loss due to manual tollbooth collection, there is a very real problem of effective time savings. Once again it becomes essential to look at the particular context in some detail. The same principles can be applied to both long and short tollroads, although short tollroads (e.g. up to 5 kilometres) should be assessed with the possibility of having the toll imposed on a longer section than a current 'missing link'. This serves the purpose of giving the user a greater time benefit for the same toll determined in relation to the costs of supplying only the 'missing link'.

The toll collection procedure can itself have a very

important impact on the net time savings, especially in contexts where there are relatively good non-tolled alternative routes. Electronic toll collection (ETC) is a feasible approach (Hensher 1989a; Luk and Chung 1997a) in place in a number of locations such as Alesund (Norway—Larsen 1988; Philips 1988a), the Dulles Toll Road (Virginia, USA—Davies *et al.* 1989), Toronto highway 407 (Luk and Chung 1997a), the M2 in Sydney, and the CityLink project in Melbourne. ETC should be given consideration where the anticipated time savings could be seriously eroded by manual toll collection. The availability of a number of non-tolled alternatives makes the loss of any gained time savings critical in the overall impact of the toll facility. The toll study reported in Hensher *et al.* (1989) indicated that a maximum time saving of 15 minutes on a current 45 minute trip could be eroded by as much as 6 minutes if cash-only tollbooths were introduced. Indirect means of revenue collection such as automatic vehicle identification (AVI—Philips 1988a) will lower the toll elasticity of demand, although the reduction in sensitivity is not known.

Although an electronic toll collection system is the most efficient way of collecting tolls on *all* lanes, most commentators believe that in the foreseeable future it is unlikely that such a complete scheme could be implemented. They suggest that, for some considerable time, there will be a need for some non-electronic tollbooths to cater for the irregular users of the road and those regular users who do not in the first instance wish to participate in ETC. The Norwegian evidence is that it is essential that the toll set for ETC should be heavily discounted relative to the toll paid by those drivers opting for the non-ETC lanes so as to encourage adaptation to ETC. The level of discount could be established in advance by a small stated preference survey (as outlined in Ch. 5) where potential users of the tollway would choose between up-front purchase of stored value accompanied by varying discounts and time savings, and pay-as-you-travel accompanied by a full toll and delays in payment at the tollbooth. The CityLink project in Melbourne, for example, plans no tollbooths, however. This 25 km., A$1.8 bn. road project opened in 2000 is the first large-scale free-flow multi-lane system collecting tolls from an estimated 600,000 vehicles per day with up to 2,500 cars a lane-hour.

6.5.5.2 Issues to consider in road pricing schemes

Some of the issues to consider in road pricing schemes are:

1. 'Bounded rationality' exists on the part of the driver's cognitive limitations. This suggests a case for avoiding complex and continuous pricing gradation.

2. Perception and response to prices varies for a whole host of reasons. The important ones include (i) who is paying (the driver, the company), which has tax-deductibility implications, (ii) when are you paying—*ex ante* or *ex post*, (iii) how are you paying (direct and indirect mechanisms), (iv) past and current experience with various pricing regimes (i.e. learning and adaptation), especially what the user receives in return for the charge, and (v) the size of the payment. The administrative cost to the *user* needs to be minimized, since this is part of the perception of the cost of paying the congestion charge.

3. Although we might be in a better position to list potential sources of differences in the way charges are perceived, of particular interest is the extent to which the perceived cost differs from the actual cost. Some definitional clarification is required. A four-level classification has been suggested in the literature:

Perceived	The measure on which decisions are made by the individual which may not be measured by the individual in terms of a recognizable scale.
Reported (perceived)	The answers obtained to questions. This is subject to reporting biases (e.g. rounding, post-purchase bias) and is assumed to be the closest empirical measure of perception.
Synthesized	The physical measure obtained by the researcher through the use of a statistical model subject to measurement and averaging errors.

Table 6.6 Perceptions of a congestion charge

Class	Description	Sensitivity
C1	User pays, cash transaction	highest
C2	User pays, *ex post* (deferred) commitment	
C3	User pays, *ex ante* (advanced) commitment	
C4	Non-user pays	lowest

Actual   The actual characteristics of a journey.

It is generally accepted that an individual's perception of an event or attribute is the appropriate dimension for explaining behaviour, in contrast to the actual consumption level of attributes, the latter being appropriate for resource allocation assessment. It is not possible to measure directly how people perceive a situation, instead we proxy this by the reporting process. Reporting is assumed to reflect how individuals consciously perceive reality, but is not necessarily a reliable indicator of how this perception influences behaviour. In the absence of any strong evidence, reported-perceived estimates are assumed to be the best proxy for true perceived values.

4. What is the evidence? This is a complex area, with rather limited study undertaken on how the perceived congestion charge relates to the actual charge under various contexts. Importantly we are dealing with a charge that is much more lumpy and visible than the usual set of marginal operating costs of automobile travel. Tolls are the only form of 'out-of-pocket' expense that we currently have which are similar in lumpiness to congestion charges, which would be imposed on the user. A number of points can be made:

(a) The difference between the reported-perceived and actual charge significantly diminishes as the user gains more experience with the payment. There is evidence to support this from a study of the Trondheim toll ring in Norway (Tretvik 1992). The study suggests that learning closes the gap between perceived and actual levels, that users of a congestion-priced facility (compared to users of free but relatively more congested routes) post-rationalize the value of the charge by over-estimating the time benefits and more so where payment is by a tag rather than cash and/or where someone else is paying.

(b) The perceived cost would tend to be closer to the actual cost where the user outlays payment at the time of the trip (i.e. a tollbooth collection), in contrast to where the method of payment is *ex ante* (e.g. purchase of stored value card or where the road authority extracts a certain amount of money via a credit card facility). The *perceived cost per trip* will still be noted where it is a fixed price (e.g. $1.50 per car regardless of time of day), but the traveller is less sensitive to the toll.

(c) The important message is that there will always be a number of categories of travellers in the early years of road pricing who will have different perceptions of the congestion charge. They can be categorized as shown in Table 6.6:

(d) Users tend to over-estimate the benefits compared to non-users (i.e. the cost per minute of saved time, which ultimately determines the decision to use a road-priced facility). They perceive the gains in travel time to be greater than the actual gains in travel time. This is not a misperception of the congestion charge but a misperception of the real benefit of the charge. Unlike automobile operating costs which are predominantly petrol costs and which are difficult to attribute to each kilometre travelled (hence the significant misperception of unit cost), road pricing by its nature is much more visible where it is limited to a few discrete levels. If we ever have marginal cost charging by the second, we would be back to the same dimension of deviation of perceived from actual unit cost as we face with fuel. Thus assuming a few levels of congestion charges (regardless of the mode of collection), the level of the road price per trip will be much more transparent. This means a greater likelihood of being more sensitive to such a charge than to fuel prices, but at the same time there is a potentially greater benefit flowing from this lumpy charge. As one moves to remote collection of the charge (either *ex post* or *ex ante*), the 'lumpiness' will diminish only in the sense that the user discounts the pain of payment, but it is unlikely to equate to the gap between the actual and perceived fuel cost per trip. Rather the user becomes less sensitive to a well-defined actual cost of use, the cost being communicated by information boards or electronically every time a user passes a collection point.

(e) There is an argument for slowly increasing the congestion charge over a period of time rather than a one-off large price imposition, to give individuals sufficient time to experience the benefits of an efficient pricing regime. As they come to see the real (time) benefits for a given financial outlay, it becomes easier to gain acceptance for a further small increase in the price. There is greater sensitivity to large once-off price changes than to a number of smaller cumulative price increases.

5. Finally, how sensitive are individuals to tolls? For empirical application, we should assume reasonably that the elasticity of demand for travel with respect to a congestion charge is more elastic than that for petrol (the dominant out-of-pocket cost), but that it is at its highest in the user pays/cash transaction market segment and at its lowest in the non-user pays/*ex ante* remote collection market segment. The important linkage with time savings is

what really matters. To give some pointer in respect of sensitivity to fixed cash-based tolls under various time savings regimes in Sydney in 1994, we offer the following empirical model parameters as a basis of calculating the appropriate toll elasticity using the formula for a multinomial logit route choice model (see Ch. 4):

direct toll elasticity = (1 − prob of using toll road) * toll * coefficient of toll variable

The coefficients for the linear functions are − 2.1095 (private commuter), − 2.073 (business commuter, i.e. using a company car), − 1.9025 (travel as part of work), and − 2.0905 (social-recreational travel). The analyst has to define a travel time saving, since each toll elasticity is conditioned on a time saving. This makes good sense given the link between road pricing and time benefits. For example, for private commuting, with a $1 toll, and a time saving of 10 minutes, the direct toll elasticity is approximately (1 − 0.59)*1* − 2.1095 = − 0.865. For a business commuter this equivalent scenario gives an elasticity of − 0.332.

Figures 6.11 to 6.14 provide a series of diversion curves for each of the four trip purpose segments. Each point on a diversion curve gives a probability of choosing the tolled route for a given toll and time saving. The equivalent to a route share can be read off the appropriate figure. For example, for the private commute trip (Fig. 6.11), with a toll of $1 and a time saving of 6 minutes, the proportion of private commuters predicted to use the tolled tunnel route is 36%. This increases to 62% if the toll is reduced to 50 cents, and decreases to 16% if the toll is increased to $1.50. These graphs can be used to establish the switching behaviour of motorists given knowledge of total traffic levels in the area and potential time savings.

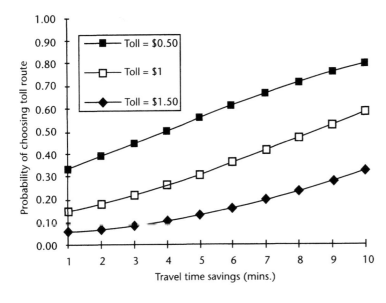

Fig. 6.11 Probabilistic diversion curves for private commuting, 1994

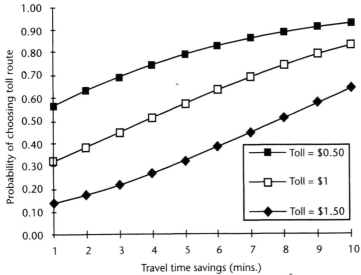

Fig. 6.12 Probabilistic diversion curves for business commuting, 1994

6.6 Case study: the benefits of waterfront reform

Figure 6.15, based on BTCE (1993a), illustrates the effect of stevedoring industry reform, a topic of immense interest internationally as well as domestically. In Australia, Patrick Stevedores, on 8 April 1998, terminated the contracts of 2,100 members of the Maritime Union in Australia, and hired non-union contract labour, as part of their commit-ment to remain internationally competitive. Although contractual arrangements are normally between stevedores and ship operators/owners for the supply of stevedoring services, stevedoring demand is best measured in terms of cargo volume than numbers of ships serviced. In bulk shipping, where a shipper contracts for the use of the entire

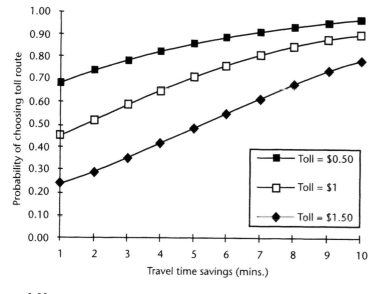

Fig. 6.13 Probabilistic diversion curves for travel as part of work, 1994

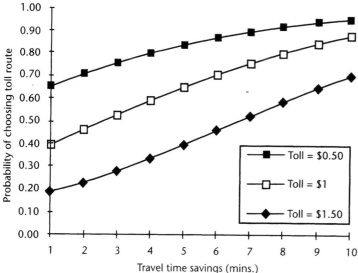

Fig. 6.14 Probabilistic diversion curves for social-recreation travel, 1994

vessel, there is often a direct transaction between shipper and terminal operator. The volume of cargo will, with all other things held constant, depend on the quality of service provided by the stevedore and on stevedoring prices assumed to be passed through in full to freight rates and cif prices.

The demand for waterfront services prior to waterfront reform can be represented by *DD*. The supply of waterfront services is represented by *SS* and the equilibrium price is *P*, with quantity Q traded. After waterfront reform, for example, we might expect improvements in waterfront quality of service to reduce the cost of exports and imports. This induces an increase in the flow of goods into and out of a country. The demand for stevedoring services is now greater than previously at any given price. The demand curve shifts out to *D*D**. At the pre-reform price of *P*, the volume of cargo and demand for stevedoring services increases to *Q**. However, with lower production costs following waterfront reform, the supply curve shifts down to *S**S***.

The supply curves in Figure 6.15 are representative

of container terminals characterized by high fixed costs. Prior to reform, labour costs also had a large fixed component. The average cost and marginal cost curves both fall with increased output until congestion occurs. Performance monitoring of the waterfront in Australia has generally shown spare capacity rather than congestion. Under these conditions, prices must at least equal average costs to sustain continued operation. Stevedoring price monitoring in Australia indicates that, over the period monitored, stevedoring prices have generally been close to average costs. The supply curves in Figure 6.15 can then be interpreted as average cost curves.

This results in a further potential increase in quantity to Q^{**} provided at price P^{**}. The extent of the increase from Q^* to Q^{**} depends on the extent to which the reduction in stevedoring prices is passed through to freight rates and eventually to the price of cargo. Prior to waterfront reform, the consumer's surplus of shippers is represented by area a (after extending DD to the price axis) in Figure 6.15.

After waterfront reform, the shippers of the previous amount, Q, gain from the increased quality of service by an increase in their consumer surplus represented by area b. Area c is a transfer from the producers of waterfront services, initially to ship operators. Part of this transfer is recouped by the stevedores through increased productivity of existing resources. The productivity improvement is a welfare gain to the economy. The balance of the transfer is made up of a loss of profits to the stevedoring companies and a loss of input rents to labour through more stringent working conditions, although there is no evidence in Australia that stevedoring costs and revenues suggest that there were any economic rents prior to the reforms (BTCE 1993a).

The shippers of the increased amounts of exports and imports $(Q^{**} - Q)$ following waterfront reform realize a consumer surplus equal to area d plus area e. Area e represents net consumer surplus to shippers who have been successful in increasing exports or imports because of the reduction in waterfront costs. Area d represents net consumer surplus to shippers who have been successful in increasing exports or imports because of the improvement in waterfront quality of service.

The net welfare gain of the reforms can be considered in two parts. The first part is the reduction in stevedoring prices and is represented by c plus e. Because the demand for stevedoring services is a derived demand, the elasticity of demand is small. Consequently the area e will be small relative to area c. The second part, equal to areas b plus d, is due to improved quality of service. Again the area d is likely to be small relative to area b. If vessel operators were to capture a proportion of the stevedoring cost reductions due to waterfront reform, this would be equivalent to a smaller downward shift in the stevedores' supply curve having occurred. The effective price to shippers, although lower than P, would be higher than P^{**}, and the quantity traded would be less than Q^{**}, although still higher than Q^*.

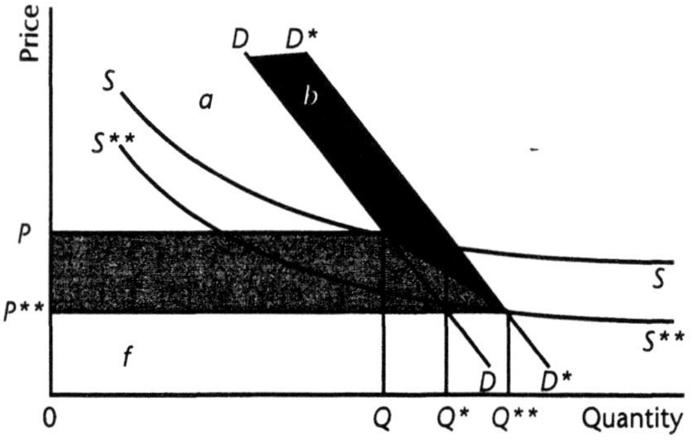

Fig. 6.15 The effect of reform on stevedoring prices and demand
Source: BTCE (1995)

6.6.1 Broadening the port reform to establish a preferred port pricing regime

Central to the reform of the waterfront is the determination of an efficient pricing regime. For example, what role do wharfage charges (i.e. a charge on cargo) play as the basis of port pricing in contrast to charges on facilities actually used and services provided? A central tenet of the debate on port pricing is that wharfage charges are allocatively inefficient (as defined in Ch. 2 App. 2A) because they fail to provide any incentive to maximize throughput. Rather charges should be imposed that more closely approximate the cost of providing the berth or terminal. In particular cross-subsidization between areas of activity and even between ports is a major issue in establishing an efficient port access pricing regime. Objectives such as 'total revenues recovering total costs' adopted by a number of port authorities, provide grounds for widespread cross-subsidization. The arguments developed in earlier sections of this chapter as well as in Chapter 2 on access regimes (where the mixture of a fixed fee and a user charge is a practical compromise under rate-of-return regulation) deserve consideration in the port context.

An alternative to a cargo charge is a tonnage charge based on ship size and berth hire for the time the vessel is in port. This two-part pricing regime matches revenue components with the manner in which costs are incurred (Bennathan and Walters 1979). A berth-hire charge linked to financial information on all costs and revenues, including overhead costs, is designed explicitly to place pressure on the port to be cost efficient and cost effective. In contrast, a wharfage-dominated charge associated with revenue earned from every tonne that crossed its berth creates a spending pattern unrelated to the costs of service delivery and capital input—the classical cross-subsidy outcome. An important fiscal attraction of the berth-hire charge is the closer scrutiny on capital needs of the port, in particular because users will have a strong incentive to minimize their berth requirements (Joy 1991).

Tonnage charges are promoted as a way of recognizing the cost of providing channels for ships serving a port, to be collected from the ships regardless of who ultimately bears the cost (e.g. cargo owners). Such a charge is based on a vessel's gross registered tonnage (GRT) as a practical approximation to recover the costs associated with delivered benefits. GRT, while less open to abuse than net registered tonnage (NRT), is itself not highly correlated with cost or cargo-carrying capacity. Bennathan and Walters (1979: 199) suggest that length of ship might be a better basis for entry fees, related to the cost of providing quay length and manoeuvring basins, but it is rarely used by ports. Haifa and Ecuador however charge berth hire by ship length. A ship's draft is also another reasonably efficient basis for port dues but there are measurement problems since a ship's actual draft may vary widely from its maximum. Rotterdam's policy of charging by actual draft or depth of water in the dock has the disadvantage that the port may be tempted to direct a small draft ship into a deepwater dock.

There is a contrasting view to the rather straightforward and appealing two-part tariff of a berth-hire charge and a tonnage charge. Kolsen (1991) also argues that the port authority should attempt to maximize throughput subject to recovering total costs from revenue (or some other positive net revenue constraint). However, since all costs cannot uniquely or unambiguously be assigned to particular cargoes (the shared or non-separable cost issue—see Ch. 5), Kolsen suggests a different two-stage pricing strategy—the establishment of avoidable costs as a lower limit on prices and the 'allocation' of shared costs according to the inverse elasticity rule.

This is equivalent to Kolsen's approach in Section 6.5.3.2 where long-run separable costs are tied to specific types of traffic according to the demand elasticities for the cargo *plus* the characteristics of ships, which he says can sit comfortably with short-run marginal (avoidable) costs in the determination of efficient prices, with the remaining cost items being treated under an investment plan (conditional on the efficient pricing regime). Demand elasticities reflect a range of price responses, with prices going from high to low respectively for containerized imports, imported cars, containerized exports, coastal container traffic, containerized primary products, and empty containers. This two-part pricing strategy is not the same as the channel and berth-hire charging discussed above, since this latter two-part charging regime is based on two activities rather than notions of avoidability and group-wise separability.

Kolsen proposes a cargo exchange ratio (CER) as a way of assessing the effects of different types of port charges for the recovery of the shared (i.e. long-run separable) costs. The CER is defined as the weight or volume of cargo unloaded plus the weight or volume of cargo loaded at a port, divided by the GRT of the ship. Kolsen argues that selecting a charge reflecting non-separable costs on a ship or a charge on cargo would be decided as a matter of convenience only when ships are loaded or unloaded at the full capacity of their GRT and they carried cargoes with identical demand characteristics. Since in practice there are noticeable differences in demand elasticities and amount of capacity utilized, then the distinction between a ship charge and a cargo charge is important. The CER takes this into account and is an appealing way of recognizing the ship/cargo composition.

6.7 Conclusions

This chapter has presented a number of alternative pricing strategies and shown how they lead to different pricing outcomes given a knowledge of costs and demand. The development of the theoretical conditions is relatively straightforward. A real challenge is the identification of appropriate cost and demand inputs to arrive at efficient prices. We have placed a lot of emphasis on the way in which charges should be established for use of the transport network, emphasizing the sets of costs directly incurred by users and the broader set of externality costs that are imposed on the transport system and society as a whole.

Congestion has been highlighted as a major environmental externality and used as a basis for establishing an efficient economic charging regime to recover from users the costs that they impose on others through their actions. The discussion of congestion serves to highlight the range of charging regimes that are available for recouping the true costs of transport activity. We illustrate this in the contexts of roads and the waterfront.

This chapter completes the development of the set of economic skills that are essential to enable one to study the large number of transport policy and planning issues that face the public and private sectors.

Discussion issues for Chapter 6

1 Which is less expensive to society—the cost of regulation or monopoly pricing?

2 In the presence of multiple services, prices should be set so that the percentage deviation from $MC^* \eta$ is constant among all services. Discuss.

3 Numerical examples show some serious problems with the application of the inverse elasticity rule. What are these concerns?

4 Why is consumer surplus a more useful indicator of benefit under a social-welfare pricing rule than under profit maximization?

5 Efficient pricing is a necessary but not sufficient condition for a socially desirable outcome. Discuss.

6 What are some of the practical challenges involved in introducing road pricing?

7 Pricing is a necessary but not sufficient condition for establishing an optimal investment programme. Discuss.

7 Evaluating the role of subsidy in supporting public transport services in urban areas: theory and application

7.1 Introduction

Developments in the reform of urban public transport in the 1980s and 1990s have highlighted the extent to which it is possible to deliver public transport without subsidy. Corporatization, commercialization, privatization, and economic deregulation have to varying degrees added to an organization's ability to operate cost efficiently and to set prices which ensure allocative efficiency on the output side (see Chs 2 and 3). However, even in countries where market reforms have been most active, such as the UK and New Zealand, local urban bus and rail services continue to attract subsidy, albeit to a lesser extent than previously. In most other developed and developing economies, subsidy is a 'way of life' for public transport. The justification for subsidy must rest with obligations to deliver a specific level of service deemed to have community value that would not be guaranteed through the forces of commercial activity in a competitive market. Consequently, we see the need for minimum subsidy (or net) competitive tenders where there is a commitment to use the market to its limit, and direct negotiated subsidy where a

service is delivered in a protected public or private monopoly setting.

This chapter presents a method for establishing the justification for subsidy to all forms of public transport. The approach developed and applied herein has as its centrepiece the notion of net social benefit and its relationship to a dollar of committed subsidy. It draws on the earlier contributions of Glaister (1984, 1987), Beesley *et al.* (1983), Dodgson (1983), and unpublished research by Hensher and Milthorpe (1989). We begin with a discussion on the theoretical justification for subsidy, and the economic model of surpluses which provides the framework within which changes in net social benefit and subsidy level are determined. We then introduce the components of an operational model—demand, supply, and equilibration; followed by an application of the impact of fare increases for bus and ferry services to illustrate how one identifies changes in net social benefit per dollar of subsidy. Optimal subsidy would be established through maximization of net social benefit per dollar of subsidy.

7.2 Some theoretical issues in justifying subsidy in the presence of externalities

The justification for subsidy can be linked to the presence of externalities and the need to ensure that public transport services are delivered in line with the ideals of competitive neutrality, and community (i.e. social) and environmental service obligations. We would like to think that the delivery of public transport services can be achieved in the most cost-efficient manner (see Ch. 5), and that price setting should be based on a mapping of prices with costs given the adopted pricing policy. In this chapter we assume that a public transport operator is acting as if they are a social welfare maximizer (see Ch. 6) and sets fares to reflect marginal social costs. In addition we assume that the costs of delivering services are established under principles of cost efficiency such that the community is receiving a given level of transport service at the lowest achievable cost given the price of inputs. The idea of competitive efficiency also enters into the argument for subsidy under the banner of levelling the playing-field. It is argued by public transport providers that the cost of car use in an urban area is under-priced and, for public transport to compete with the car, there is a need to set fares at a level that necessitates some subsidy support.

The identification of an optimal public transport subsidy can be presented as follows. Let us define road congestion costs (RC) as those costs imposed on all road users by the presence of a class of users, such as car or bus users. Other externalities such as accident and environmental costs (i.e. noise, visual, chemical pollution), both of which are highly correlated with the volume of traffic, might also be included as additional negative externalities associated with traffic congestion. Thus RC is defined to include external costs imposed by the operation of public transport (PT) on other road users, such that:

$$RC = f(PKM, VKM) \qquad (7.1)$$

where PKM is the total passenger kilometres by bus public transport and VKM is the total vehicle kilometres of service offered by bus public transport. Typically, $\partial RC/\partial PKM \leq 0$ (i.e. a greater use of buses means a reduced use of other vehicles); and $\partial RC/\partial VKM \geq 0$ (i.e. an increase in PT kilometres, given PKM, increases total traffic per unit of time). These traffic congestion costs add to the conditions for net benefit maximization. The contribution of (7.1) can be included in the generalized optimal fare formula (7.2):

$$F = PKM * \partial P/\partial PKM + C * \partial C/\partial PKM + \partial RC/\partial PKM \qquad (7.2)$$

where F is the average fare per passenger kilometre, P is the passenger congestion cost (within the PT mode it includes waiting and boarding time) per passenger kilometre (an increasing function of PKM and a declining function of VKM), and C is the operator's cost function ($C = C(PKM, VKM)$). Equation (7.2) implies pricing at marginal social cost, the pricing policy for social-welfare maximization. Where $\partial RC/\partial PKM < 0$, the optimal fare is reduced by an amount reflecting the effects of increasing PKM on the level of traffic congestion. It follows that:

$$F*PKM - C = \{\partial RC/\partial PKM * PKM + \partial RC/\partial VKM * VKM\} + VKM * PKM * \mathrm{d}T/\mathrm{d}(VKM) \qquad (7.3)$$

where T as a function of VKM is the non-fare component of the generalized cost of PT. The net effect of road congestion on the level of subsidy depends on the effects of PT on road congestion at the margin. If attracting passengers to rail services through lower fares reduces road congestion (i.e. $\partial RC/\partial PKM < 0$), all other things being unchanged, then the optimal subsidy exceeds – $VKM*PKM*\mathrm{d}T/\mathrm{d}(VKM)$. If the effect of lower fares on road congestion is zero (i.e. $\partial RC/\partial PKM = 0$), other things remaining unchanged, the optimal subsidy (or 'value-for-money' level of subsidy) will be less than – $VKM*PKM*\mathrm{d}T/\mathrm{d}(VKM)$.

7.3 The benefit-cost evaluation theoretical framework

The value for money notion of subsidy is formally quantified in terms of the net social benefit (NSB) associated with a given level of subsidy. NSB is the sum of two economic constructs: producer surplus and consumer surplus. The former represents changes in revenue (net of costs) to the supplier of public transport consequent on fare and service-level changes (and possibly improvements in cost efficiency); the latter represents the changes in the money and time outlays of users of each of the transport modes consequent on the same policy changes (see Ch. 6 for further commentary).

To illustrate the effect of a pricing policy on producer and consumer surplus, we examine the effects of an increase in a rail fare in a market of three alternative modes—rail, bus, and car. The consumer surplus changes are shown in Figure 7.1 (based on Beesley *et al.* 1983). The vertical axis defines the generalized price of travel, which includes the time cost as well as the fare. An increase in the rail fare raises the generalized price paid for rail services from P_1 to P_2 in Figure 7.1*a*, and reduces rail demand, measured in passenger kilometres, from Q_1 to Q_2. Because the rail price has increased, the demand schedules for bus and car use shift to the right, as in Figures 7.1*b* and 7.1*c*. Losses of consumer surplus are shown as cross-hatched areas. For each of the three sets of consumers, the total loss of consumer surplus comprises two components: losses to those consumers priced off that mode altogether, and losses experienced by those who remain and bear the relevant generalized price increase. Losses to those priced off the rail system, that is, $Q_1 - Q_2$, are measured as the triangle *ABC*. Losses to the remaining rail users Q_2 are measured as the rectangle P_1P_2BA. Losses experienced by bus and car and other road users are calculated with similar reasoning. Although bus fares are assumed to remain unchanged in this example, the effective price increases because of increased crowding and the likelihood that the waiting time will be increased. For other road users, increased vehicle flows reduce

speeds and hence increase the price paid by increasing journey time. Changes in resource cost are represented by the areas bounded with broken lines. In the case of buses and other road users, these resource cost changes are offset to the extent that income is transferred from the rail users. However, increases in resources used remain at net cost. This is approximately the area *RSTU*.

An example will assist in motivating the discussion on criteria for evaluating subsidy change. Assume a fare increase for public bus services, and that we have six interdependent transport modes, each being affected by fare and service changes to varying degrees. The fare increase will (via the bus fare direct elasticity of demand) switch some users out of buses. The cross-elasticities of demand for ferry, car, rail, and private bus with respect to bus fares will determine how many of the bus switchers convert to other modes (the remaining switchers ceasing to travel). Adjustments in passenger kilometres on each public mode will affect boarding times that together with changes in car traffic will affect speeds of buses and cars. The change in speed will affect operating costs and travel time and hence user money and time costs which are the basis of changes in consumer surplus. The change in public operator revenue net of any change in costs is the source of producer surplus.

The sources of surplus from a fare and/or service-level change are identified from the relationship between the travel demand and (marginal) cost functions associated with each mode of transport. The implications of a change in fare and/or service level can be evaluated in terms of eight sources of benefits and costs. Let us define A = consumer surplus, B = operating profit, C = total costs of supplying a bus service, and D = benefit to new users which is not extracted in the form of profits to the operator. A decrease in fare, for example, has the following impact on A,B,C, and D (Fig. 7.2): the willingness to pay of the new users increases by $D' + B'' + C'$, they

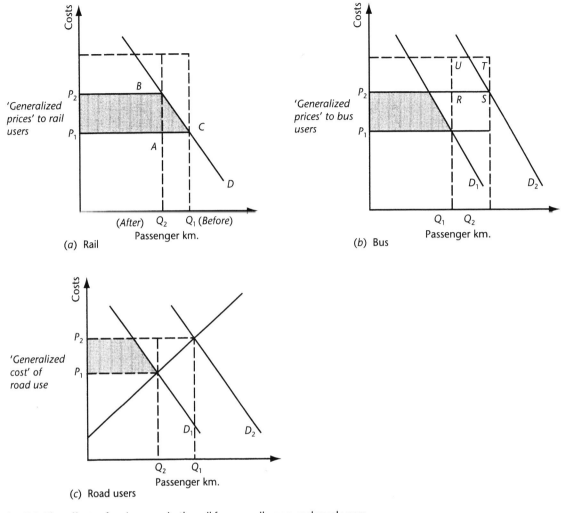

Fig. 7.1 The effects of an increase in the rail fare on rail users and road users

Source: Beesley *et al.* (1983).

pay $B'' + C'$, and receive net benefits of D'. B' is the transfer to the existing users of what was previously revenue. The change in subsidy (or change in profits/losses) is equal to $B' - (B'' + C') + C' = B' - B''$. Total net social benefit, defined as benefits to existing users plus benefits to new users minus increased subsidies, is thus $B' + D' - (B' - B'')$ or $D' + B''$. These sources of benefit have to be calculated for each mode in the interdependent transport system, enabling us to establish the external effects of public transport policies. To distinguish consumer surplus from producer surplus, we can redefine $D' + B''$ as follows:

$$D' + B'' = (B' + D') + \{[(B + B'' + C + C') - (7.4)$$
$$(C + C')] - [(B' + B + C) - C]\}$$

where $B' + D'$ is the extra consumer surplus generated, and the other element on the right-hand side is the change in revenue net of costs (i.e. extra producer surplus).

The calculation of NSB in the context of six interdependent modal demands can be represented by a series of mathematical expressions that allow for the sources of surplus identified in the single-mode example above. It is assumed that users in choosing

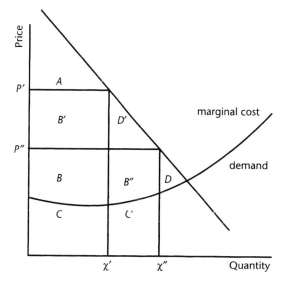

Fig. 7.2 The sources of change in surplus

transport services maximize utility subject to an overall expenditure constraint. An equivalent assumption (Glaister 1981) is that an individual chooses transport services so as to minimize expenditure associated with the achievement of a predetermined level of utility. Any standard textbook on consumer theory shows that the solution to this expenditure minimization problem is an expenditure function of the form:

$$E(p, t, u) = n(p, t, u) + \sum_{i=m}^{M} p_i x_i(p, t, u) \qquad (7.5)$$

where $E(\cdot)$ is the total expenditure on transport and non-transport goods and services, $n(\cdot)$ is expenditure on the composite non-transport goods, p_i is the unit (generalized) price of modal travel, x_i is the quantity of modal travel (in passenger km.), p is the money price of travel, t is the time price of travel, and u is total utility.

When a money price and/or travel time for a passenger kilometre changes, the change in the expenditure function is the quantity of money which is forgone or received by the individual in order for him to be no better or worse off after the change than before the change. This definition of surplus is referred to as compensating variation (CV). It allows for the possibility of an income effect in addition to a price (or

substitution) effect from a policy change. The CV can be defined in terms of a large number of possible changes in money prices and travel times across all the interdependent modes; and is typically the sum of the effect of each mode-specific item of change, holding the other items constant. Given that changes in money prices and times can occur along the full continuum of the demand function, we can use integration to calculate the areas under the demand function which are used to calculate the CV. If we assume that the income effect of a change in public transport fares and/or service changes is a negligible proportion of an individual's expenditure on all goods and services, an assumption commonly used in transport project evaluation (at least in mature economies), then CV is equivalent to our definition of consumer surplus. The distinction between consumer surplus and compensating variation is shown diagrammatically in Figures 7.3 and 7.4.

Assume an initial utility-maximizing level of consumption associated with price p_1. We then reduce the fare to p_2. For a given budget, the individual can now purchase more travel and other goods; hence the budget line moves from $M_0 P_1$ to $M_0 P_2$. The individual can now reach a higher indifference curve at point B which is tangential to the new budget line. To decide how much better off this person is at B than at A, we need to measure how much better off an individual is in buying $0X_2$ of X at p_2 than compared to p_1. The answer is BC. The Hicksian CV is designed to measure how much better off an individual is now that they can purchase X at p_2 than compared to p_1. A consumer could pay $M_0 M_1$ for the right to purchase X at a new lower price and still be as well off as he was at A, *since payment of this amount would move him to D* (on the same indifference curve as A). Note that $M_0 M_1 > BC$; $M_0 M_1$ is associated with an unconstrained privilege of buying X at P_2, whereas BC is associated with a constraint that $0X_2$ units be purchased. The two measures will be identical if indifference curves are parallel at X_2 with units of X, that is, where the income effect of a change in price, DP, = 0. If the income effect with respect to X is zero, $D = C$, lying on I_0 directly beneath B for CS and CV to coincide. A zero income effect implies that an

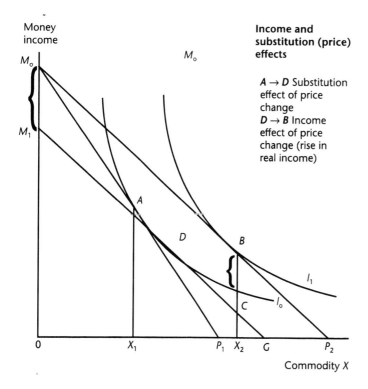

Fig. 7.3 Price and income effects

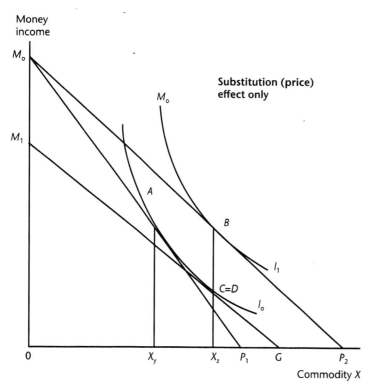

Fig. 7.4 Price effect only

individual will purchase the same quantity of X both before and after an income change (Fig. 7.4).

Using as an example a proposal to evaluate a change in price and travel time from $(p_{i1}, p_{j1}, t_{i1}, t_{j1})$ to $(p_{i2}, p_{j2}, t_{i2}, t_{j2})$, where both price and time are simultaneously changed in two interdependent markets (i.e. bus and ferry markets), the CV is given by:

$$CV = E\,(p_2, t_2, u) - E\,(p_1, t_1, u) \qquad (7.6)$$

$$CV = \{E\,(p_2, t_2, u) - E\,(p_1, t_2, u)\} + \{E\,(p_1, t_2, u) \quad (7.6a)$$
$$- E\,(p_1, t_1, u)\}$$

The first pair of terms in (7.6a) is the CV as the price changes, holding times at their new values; the second pair is the CV as time changes, holding prices at their old values. The CV construct is a derivative of a compensated demand function (which is derived directly from an expenditure function). It is well established in the transport economics literature (e.g. Glaister 1981) that any path of integration (i.e. evaluation of a particular effect holding the others constant at any level, new or old) can be selected without influencing the net social benefit (NSB) result. This property of path independence enables the integration of the evaluation expression used to calculate changes in CV or consumer surplus to be greatly simplified without any loss of information. Thus one integration path that will represent the

process of evaluation to establish the change in CV is:

$$\int_{P_{i1}}^{P_{j1}} x_1\,[k, P_{i1}, t_{j1}, t_{i2}, u]\mathrm{d}k + \int_{P_{i2}}^{P_{j2}} x_2\,[P_{j1}, k, t_{j1}, t_{j2}, u]\mathrm{d}k \qquad (7.7)$$
$$+ \int_{t_{i1}}^{t_{j1}} \tau x_1\,[P_{i1}, P_{i2}, k, t_{i2}, u]\mathrm{d}k + \int_{t_{i2}}^{t_{j2}} \tau x_2\,[P_{i1}, P_{i2}, t_{j1}, k, u]\mathrm{d}k.$$

Equation (7.7) is an important expression in evaluating consumer surplus benefits. Each of the terms in the version of equation (7.7) which is generalized to six interdependent modes of transport corresponds to a change in the area under a demand curve as a respective fare or service-level change, holding other fares (prices) and service levels constant. The net social benefit is obtained by removing the change in subsidy (equivalent to a change in producer surplus net of costs) from the CV calculation. Given that the market for public transport offers a range of fares (full, half, excursion etc., and free travel, together with a set of reimbursements), the implementation of this model' must make allowance for this in calculating NSB. We are now ready to develop a set of procedures to implement the evaluation framework outlined above. We draw on Sydney data in the empirical formulation of the application system; however, the approach is readily generalized to any urban setting.

7.4 The important components of a model to study the impact of public transport subsidy on net social benefit

7.4.1 Demand (passenger kilometres)

The demand for each mode is assumed to depend on the money and time costs per passenger kilometre and those of competing modes. A knowledge of time values and elasticities is required in order to determine the influence of changes in fares and/or service

levels and hence the implications for subsidy to each PT mode. The demand model takes the following form:

$$PK_m = PK_m^b \exp\left\{\sum_{k=0}^{m} \lambda_{km} g_k\right\} k = 0, 1, \ldots, \text{M modes} \quad (7.8)$$

where λ_{km} is the elasticity of PKM_m with respect to the money cost of using mode $k(p_k)$, divided by p_k;

and $g_k = (p_k - p_k^b) + (t_k - t_k^b)$, the change in the generalized cost of using mode k. The demand elasticities are all proportional to their respective prices rather than constant. Prices for public transport are defined as a fare per passenger kilometre, taking into account the mix of full adult fare, concession fare, and excursion fare passengers. Price for cars and commercial vehicles is the operating cost at the current speed divided by vehicle occupancy; 'b' refers to the base value of a variable, and t is a vector of time components expressed in money units. Typically, t_k has two components:

$$t_k = (z * w_k) + \left(\frac{1}{v_k}\right) * \tau_k \qquad (7.9)$$

where z is the ratio of the value of wait time savings to in-vehicle time savings (typically 2.0—see Hensher 1986, 1997; Madan and Groenhout 1987), w_k is the waiting time for mode k (itself a complex function of a load factor), v_k is the average in-vehicle speed on mode k (itself a derivative of suitable speed-flow equations parameterized to reflect the application context), and τ_k is the value of in-vehicle travel time savings.

7.4.1.1 The value of travel time savings

The value of in-vehicle travel time savings is an important parameter, since it controls the conversion of travel time in time units to a time cost in money units. There is an extensive literature on the value of travel time savings, reviewed by Hensher (1988a, 1997) and Chapter 4.3. To obtain an appropriate set of values for each mode, we have to recognize that the evaluation of public transport fares and subsidies requires us to use a time value which represents travel during both the peak and off-peak periods for all trip purposes. We have weighted the appropriate trip-purpose values by the incidence of such travel by each mode in the peak and off-peak for work and non-work related travel. Work-related travel is defined to include travel to/from work and travel as part of work. We distinguish car travel to work by private and company car to recognize the higher behavioural value for users of company cars.

The peak period accounts for 50% of all government bus and rail passengers, but only 25% of car passenger trips. Weighted average time values for each mode are derived as follows.

Car travel: private commuter = $4.08 per person hour; company car commuter = $6.90 per person hour; non-work related travel = $2.54 per person hour (Hensher 1988a); 90% of commuter car travel is private; 14.37% of car trips are work/peak; 10.62% are non-work/peak; 24.07% are work/off-peak; and

Table 7.1 The composition of Sydney's traffic

Mode	Peak %		Off-peak %		Passengers (no.)	
	Work	Non-work	Work	Non-work	Peak	Off-peak
Public						
bus	45.5	54.5	19.4	80.6	105,056,752	83,996,248
rail	70.3	29.7	32.5	67.5	103,522,388	124,707,951
ferry	74.6	25.4	18.8	81.2	10,509,253	10,634,747
car driver	57.5	42.5	32.1	67.9	1,765,000,000[1]	5,343,000,000[1]
car passenger	26.4	73.6	8.1	91.9		
Private						
bus	13.1	86.9	6.3	93.7	1,392,840,000	5,986,000,000
other	17.3	82.7	19.1	80.9	361,350,000	527,790,000,000

Note: [1] Includes drivers plus passengers.
Source: From the 1981 Sydney travel survey.

50.92% are non-work/offpeak. Thus the weighted average value of time savings for car trips is $4.362*0.3845 plus $2.54*0.6155, equal to $3.241 per person hour, or $5.83 per car.

Public transport travel: data on commuter values for train and bus trips are available, but typically information on non-commuter public transport time values is unavailable. Non-commuter values are typically lower than commuter values, with the difference being based upon the car values (i.e. 58% of the commuter values). Unlike car travel, which is door to door for a substantial amount of travel, the public transport trip involves an element of walking to and from the mode. Current public transport travellers switching away from bus and ferry are going to change their in-vehicle and walk time (plus wait time). Walk time in Sydney averages 10.5 minutes for a train trip and 7.47 minutes for a bus trip (Hensher 1986), which is respectively 19.3% and 16.3% of train and bus travel time. An adjustment in bus and ferry travel due to a fare adjustment affects both in-vehicle and walk time. Thus the correct value of time savings to use (which is distinct from wait time) is a weighted average of in-vehicle and walk time. This value is calculated using data in Hensher (1988*a*) to give a value for bus travel of $3.51 per person hour, and for rail, $2.45 per person hour. Data on ferry values is not available; however, we assume that ferries are more akin to rail services than bus services, and so we adopt the rail value.

An equity value of time savings has been selected for all passenger modes. This is based on the premises that the scarce investment dollar should not be directed towards projects which are more likely to benefit individual travellers with a higher willingness to pay simply because they have a greater ability to pay. The selected equity value is $3.93 per person hour.

7.4.1.2 Composition of passenger kilometres in terms of fare type

Not all public transport travellers are sensitive to fare changes. For example, for CityRail in Sydney, the travellers can be divided into at least six categories: full-adult fare travellers, concession (or half-fare) reimbursed travellers, half-fare non-reimbursed trav-

ellers, excursion travellers, schoolchildren on school passes, and free travellers. The last two categories are not responsive to fare changes, whereas the other categories are. The demand analysis accommodates this situation by separating out the annual passenger kilometres of travel associated with each of the six categories and weighting the base fare to allow for the composition of fare-paying passenger kilometres of travel. A proper allocation of revenue between categories of travel is critical in the evaluation of subsidy. Practices in Sydney appear to involve an element of notional allocation of Treasury funds as reimbursement, with the balance of the shortfall of revenue if the full fare were paid being included in the revenue supplement. Thus the revenue supplement is not necessarily an appropriate measure of subsidy as an operating loss. In the current application, the revenue we are interested in eliminating is the difference between total costs and total revenue, where the latter is defined to include traveller revenue and non-traveller revenue. The fare elasticities, however, reflect only the component of revenue which is paid out directly by the travelling public.

7.4.2 Speed-flow relationships

The operating costs of cars, commercial vehicles, and buses are influenced by the traffic speed, which is itself determined by the traffic flow. These costs define the money price (per passenger kilometre) for cars and commercial vehicles. A number of speed-flow relationships are considered although any functional form is permissible.

Speed-flow relationships are obtained for four road types, grouped in terms of the Austroads functional classification. The speed-flow equations were derived from the NAASRA (1984) Technical report T-8 (pp. 43–53) with adjustments to allow for the speed ranges used in Sydney. These equations can easily be modified as more current parameter estimates are identified. The four road types are given below together with the proposed speed-flow equations:

FWY   freeway (functional classes 9, 10, 11)

DIV.MA   divided major arterial (functional classes 5, 7, 13)

UNDIV.MA   undivided major arterial (functional classes 4, 6)

MIN.UA   minor undivided arterial (functional classes 1, 2, 3)

FWY   speed = $71.80 - 0.00304F - 0.0000015$ (FSQ),

DIV.MA   speed = $64.50 - 0.0072F - 0.0000015$ (FSQ),

UNDIV.MA   speed = $44.84 - 0.0094F - 0.0000018$ (FSQ)

MIN.UA   speed = $52.96 - 0.01248F - 0.0000018$ (FSQ).

where F = flow in passenger car units (pcu) per hour, and FSQ is the square of F. The speed-flow relationships are a critical input into a study of the road congestion effects of subsidy adjustment.

7.4.3 The bus, ferry, and rail waiting time formulae

$$w_{bus} = \{[w^b_{bus} vkm^b_{bus}]/[1 + z^b_{bus}/ \quad (7.11)$$
$$(1 - z^b_{bus})]\} * vkm^{-1}_{bus} * [1 + z_{bus}/(1 - z_{bus})]$$

where:

$$z_{bus} = \beta L^5_{bus} - \gamma L^4_{bus} + \omega L^3_{bus} - \theta L^2_{bus} \quad (7.11a)$$

L_{bus} is the bus load factor, and vkm is vehicle kilometres; w_{bus} is inversely proportional to vehicle kilometres. As the average load factor increases, the probability that the first bus to arrive will be full increases, implying an increasing wait time. In the absence of data for Australia, the parameter estimates in equation (7.11a) are obtained from a study in the UK in the London context (Dodgson 1983). As loading factors increase, so does the level of passenger discomfort, expressed in terms of increased waiting time equivalent units.

For rail services, waiting time is assumed to be inversely proportional to vehicle kilometres of service (equation 7.12); for ferry services the same assumption as rail applies for the effect on waiting time of headway changes, but the effect of changes in waiting time due to load changes is calculated using equation (7.12a):

$$w_{rail} = [w^b_{rail} vkm^b_{rail}] * (1/vkm_{rail}) \quad (7.12)$$

$$w_{ferry} = [w^b_{ferry} z^b_{ferry}] * (1/z_{ferry}) \quad (7.12a)$$

The sum of the results from the application of equations (7.12) and (7.12a) gives the new waiting time for ferry services.

In summary, vehicle speeds (i.e. in-vehicle times and hence congestion) are affected through the speed-flow curves; and waiting times are affected by demand levels through the public transport load factors and/or vehicle kilometres of service. The impact on road congestion of changes in government bus and ferry fares and/or service levels is determined on the demand side by adjustments through the set of equations given above.

This discussion of the demand system has introduced the important issues of user costs, waiting times for public transport, vehicle operating costs, and speed-flow relationships. Defining the functional forms for each of the equations representing each item as well as assumptions on elasticities and time values for each temporal and spatial context is a most important task of the implementation process.

7.4.4 The supply-side module

There is an extensive literature on operating costs (see Abelson 1987 for a review or Hepburn 1994). The unit cost of operating a car or a commercial vehicle in dollars per vkm is given by the standard formula:

$$C = a + b/v + cv^2 \quad (7.13)$$

where C is cost per vehicle kilometre, v is road speed in k.p.h., and a, b, and c are parameter constants. The quadratic terms allows for the non-linearity of the function between very low and very high mean speeds. Since we are including the entire road network in Sydney in our model, the non-linear effect must be allowed for. This model is calibrated on data contained in Abelson (1987, table 4.10: 83), updated to 1987/8 prices:

$$C = 12.4863 + 60.2810/v \quad (R^2 = 0.90) \quad (7.14a)$$

$$C = 11.2860 + 76.1987/v + 0.000190653\, v^2 \quad (7.14b)$$
$$(R^2 = 0.98)$$

The empirical formula for commercial vehicles is an update of the NAASRA (1984) equations for vans, rigid trucks, and articulated trucks. An assumed split of the three commercial vehicle types (on the advice of NSW Department of Transport's Transport Data Centre) of 90%, 7%, and 3% is used to obtain the commercial vehicle operating cost equation in 1987/8 prices:

$$C = 0.142182 + 4.0264557/v \qquad (7.14c)$$

The overall statistical fit of the three equations used to derive (7.14c) is not reported in the NAASRA publication.

The operating cost formula for buses is based on an assumption that some costs are a function of the amount of service supplied (as measured by vkm and the speed of the buses); and other costs are independent of service levels. The latter are typically about 40 to 60% of total costs. The higher the bus kilometres, the more buses and drivers required; the slower the speed in the traffic stream, the lower the productivity of factor inputs (i.e. labour, fuel, capital) (Hensher 1987, 1988a, 1989a).

$$C_{bus} = \text{fixed costs} + \text{variable costs } \{(v_b/v) * (vkm/vkm_b)\} \qquad (7.15)$$

where $v^{-1} = 1.538/v^{all} + passkms*boarding\ time\ penalty/vkm$ after the change; and v^{all} is the road speed of a bus before any adjustment downwards to allow for slower b speeds (by 35%) than the general traffic.

The rail and ferry operating costs are also divided into variable and fixed costs, with variable costs assumed to change in direct proportion to the number of train or ferry kilometres operated:

$$C_{rail} = b + q\ [(vkm)/(vkm^b) * v^b/v] \qquad (7.16)$$

where b are fixed costs and q are variable costs.

7.4.5 Equilibration of demand and supply

The method presented here enables a public transport operator, or any planning agency or regulator, to evaluate a wide range of fare and/or service changes, and to identify their impact on existing public transport users, public transport resource costs, and the external travelling population. The subsidy implication in the context of changes in NSB is automatically established by the procedure. The approach has value beyond simply assessing the value for money of a subsidy. Like any modelling exercise, it is essential that the approach is able to reproduce the current or base situation before one embarks upon evaluation of change. Some aspects of the current profile are supplied externally in the data input set up and can be assured of reproduction, subject to the reliability of the data source. Other aspects of the current profile must be determined within the model system, by an initial equilibrating procedure. In particular, we must ensure that the unit operating costs of cars and commercial vehicles are acceptable, which means that both the speed-flow and speed-cost equations for each road type must be acceptable. Furthermore the allocation of passenger kilometres between the six fare groupings must reproduce the reported levels of revenue and reimbursements, so that the correct revenue supplement, after removing non-travel revenue, can be defined in the base situation.

A computer model, applied below, commences by the application of the sets of demand-side and supply-side equations to the base input data, and seeks an equilibrium which displays the necessary base data to be used in the evaluation of changes in fares and/or service levels. The user will have to devote a lot of time to establishing the correct base, and so initial runs of the model should be devoted to a study of no change in fares and/or service levels. In a model system that is seeking to study the direct and external impacts of change within a transport system which has complex modal interdependencies, there are many potential sources contributing to error in the base equilibrium (e.g. behavioural values of time savings, passenger kilometre allocation to fare types, wrong speed-flow equation parameters, incorrect allocation of variable and fixed costs, elasticities too high or low, etc.). There could also be a concern with the formulation of the demand and supply equations.

Once the base equilibrium is accepted, the analyst can commence searching for scenarios of fares and/

or service levels which result in elimination of the revenue supplement. The aim is to establish the change in NSB which accompanies the elimination of the subsidy as well as the best ratio of NSB per dollar of subsidy; and to decompose the change in NSB into producer and consumer surplus for each of the modes in the total transport system, distinguishing continuing and switching traffic. By this procedure we are able to identify the nature and extent of externalities in the make-up of NSB. We standardize the NSB by setting it equal to zero for the base situation, so that we can readily identify the change in NSB as the social impact of elimination of the subsidy. In searching for a zero subsidy solution, we have to allow for the possibility that a feasible equilibrium may not be achievable solely through changes in fares and/or service levels. If this were the

case, then changes to costs will have to be contemplated. This is a reasonable strategy given that removal of subsidy typically leads to improvements in cost efficiency (Frankena 1983; Hensher 1987*a*).

In establishing a base equilibrium and in applying the model to fare and/or service-level changes, we have to decide whether the interest is in the short run or long run. We have adopted the very reasonable assumption that subsidy elimination is a long-run strategy (i.e. five years) and that for all the parameter estimates where a short-run/long-run distinction is possible (e.g. elasticities), we have selected the long-run values. The modelling approach, however, is sufficiently flexible to handle applications where short-run impacts are also of interest. Long-run elasticities are typically higher than short-run elasticities (Goodwin, 1988; Oum *et al.* 1992).

7.5 Application of the model

In this section, we use the example of a 100% fare increase to illustrate the workings of the model and how the outputs are interpreted. In the following section, we then present the final results of the grid-search for a zero-subsidy fare/level of service mix, and establish the change in NSB that is an externality. The output file contains the following information:

1. passenger kilometres (pkm) per annum by mode (base, new, and % change)

2. vehicle kilometres (vkm) per annum by mode (base, new, % change)

3. passengers per vehicle (base, new, % change)

4. average fare per passenger kilometre by mode (base, new, % change)

5. annual revenue by PT mode (base, new, % change)

6. Annual costs by mode (base, new, % change)

7. Total bus flows in pcu per hour and speeds on each road type (base, new, % change)

8. PT journey times for headway, in-vehicle, and boarding times (base, new, % change)

9. changes in consumer surplus (money and time components) and NSB for each mode and in total

10. average NSB per extra dollar of subsidy

11. marginal indicators of a 1% change in fares and service levels: NSB per extra dollar of subsidy, by mode, and direct and cross-service elasticities implied by the changes.

7.5.1 An example: a 100% fare increase for both bus and ferry services

The first page of the output (reproduced in Appendix 7A) indicates the change in fare and/or service level being investigated for each public mode. There is a request for whether you wish to optimize on net social benefit, by searching for changes in fare and service levels that produce the highest positive NSB. Since we are currently interested in minimizing the subsidy by selecting the combination of fare and service-level changes which minimizes the reduction in NSB, the answer to this question is no. We use a separate grid-search procedure for subsidy elimination. If you say yes, you have to request some starting values for the marginal NSB. These would typically lie between 0 and -0.002.

The substantive part of the output begins with a summary of the physical indicators associated with each of the modes. The table of annual passenger kilometres enables us to identify the absolute and percentage changes in traffic levels for each mode. There is a substantial switch away from bus (18.15%) and ferry (15.78%). The percentage increase in rail patronage (SRA pkm) is higher than car (1.14% compared to 0.71%). The absolute switch to car is over 143 million pkm per year, and to rail it is 159 million pkm. These diversion results are heavily influenced by the direct and cross-elasticities, with the new numbers being the result of equilibration as the program oscillates throughout until the pkm allocations settle down. That is, a 100% increase in bus fares switches pkm out of bus, with some going to rail according to the cross-elasticity for rail demand with respect to bus fares. The build-up of rail patronage can lead to increases in rail waiting times, which via further changes in generalized cost could affect the demand for rail pkm, and from an implied service elasticity calculated by the model, will result in some reswitching back to bus or to another mode or no travel.

Since it is most important to establish the composition of the total pkm by fare type (for purposes of establishing which subset of travellers are sensitive to fare changes, as well as for calculating the reimbursements for each eligible category), we also report the effect that the fare increase has on each of the fare-type markets. We use a single fare elasticity in the current specification of the model, hence the percentage switch will be a constant within the fare-paying categories (-23.88% for bus) and zero for non-fare-paying travellers. Note that although there is a 1.31% increase in rail pkm within the fare-paying subset of pkm, this translates into 1.14% of total rail pkm.

The total annual vehicle kilometres for each mode before and after the fare change are reported in Table 7A.2. There is no change in the vkm for public modes since we have only changed the fare level; however, the increase in car pkm is reflected in an increase of vkm. The software assumes that all new car pkm switch to car contexts with the previous mean car occupancy of 1.8. If we had a model for choice between car driver and passenger (using the multinomial logit model in Ch. 4), it would be possible to establish the impact of pkm change on vkm. The mean level of occupancy would not, however, be expected to change significantly. As expected, there is no change in total vkm for commercial vehicles. Table 7A.3 summarizes the effect of the fare change on the loading levels for each mode. We note that the average number of passengers per bus has declined from 14.771 to 12.090; for ferry it has changed from 184.878 to 155.698 per vessel; but for rail it has increased from 173.949 to 175.938 per train set.

The next block of output is a set of financial indicators (Table A7.4). The base and new fare per passenger kilometre for each public mode (and unit operating cost for car and commercial vehicles) are summarized together with the percentage and absolute changes. This is the first time that the user will identify the cost per pkm for car and commercial vehicle that is implied by the model system. It is important to check the base operating costs for car and commercial vehicle as a way of establishing confidence in the speed-flow and speed-cost equations. These unit costs are resource costs, which in the current application are 7.8055 cents per km for car and 23.1177 cents per km. for commercial vehicle.

The operating costs of cars and commercial vehicles are then given in Table A7.5 to enable identification of the percentage and absolute changes in total annual operating costs. A doubling of bus fares has (via changes in total road traffic) increased annual car costs by $13.153 m., and commercial vehicle costs by $0.959 m. The public transport cost changes are summarized in Table A7.6 together with the levels of revenue before and after the fare change, for each category of traveller. For bus services, total annual costs have declined marginally (by 0.967%) to yield an absolute cost saving of

$2.060 m. per annum. If we were to allow for changes in cost efficiency in response to the reduction of the subsidy level, then one would anticipate substantial cost savings. The latter has not been allowed for in this example run.

The detail in the revenue and cost table enables the analyst to identify the sources of revenue change for bus services. It is important to be able to establish the extent to which the increased revenue comes from fares, concession reimbursement, excursion reimbursement, and school travel reimbursements. The total revenue change of $77.824 m. comprises $41.484 m. of fares, $8.065 m. of concession reimbursements $12.119 m. of excursion reimbursements (which we believe contain a component of hidden subsidy), and $14.095 m. of school travel reimbursements. It is important to recognize that fare strategies also affect reimbursements. The change in ferry revenue is considerably smaller, $10.722 m., with $9.583 m. coming from fares. The doubling of fares has eliminated the bus subsidy and reduced the ferry subsidy by $10.722 m. to $2.617 m. The sum of the bus profit and the ferry loss yields a profit of $6.977 m. Given that the ferry subsidy is 44% of total income (compared to 32.0% for bus), and that fares are a much higher percentage of passenger-related revenue for ferry than bus, it is not surprising that the elimination of the ferry subsidy will be harder to achieve by a fares policy alone. The lumpiness of capital also makes the cost-efficiency opportunity less likely than for the buses. Finally, rail benefits from the bus fare increase by a $4.386 m. increase in revenue (or equivalent reduction in subsidy). As a percentage of the current rail subsidy, however, it is a 1.9% improvement.

Traffic statistics for the road network are given for each road type. Table A7.7 summarizes the total vehicle flows in pcu hours before and after the fare change, with the bus flows supplied in parentheses. This table gives the mean hourly traffic flows in the base situation for each road type, and is thus an important source of confirmation for the reasonableness of the input data. Since the flow data are used to predict mean speeds, it is crucial to establish confidence in the input data. The 100% fare increase has increased total road traffic by a small amount,

ranging from 0.59% to 0.60%. Together with the speed change given in Table A7.8 we are able to establish a major externality effect of bus subsidy reduction. When converted to a change in net social benefits, the speed/flow effect gives us a dollar value for the loss of surplus to the community associated with road traffic externalities. The bus speeds improve marginally by 1.751%, supporting the widespread view that fare increases have little impact on the equilibrium traffic speed, because the majority of the road traffic is cars and commercial vehicles. Only 3.34% of total annual road pkm are by bus. The slight improvement in bus speed is linked to an improvement in waiting and boarding times.

We present the changes in the journey times for bus and ferry in Table A7.9. Fare changes affect waiting, in-vehicle, and boarding times via the changes in passengers and traffic flows. The new waiting time is derived from changes in the loading factor and headway (with the latter being affected by service-level changes). We see that a 100% fare increase has reduced bus waiting time by 12.09%, from 1.296 minutes per pkm to 1.139 minutes per pkm. All of the change has come from the change in the loading factor. In-vehicle time has also changed slightly by 0.464%, from 2.530 mins. per pkm to 2.542 mins. per pkm. Bus boarding time has improved substantially, by 18.14%, from 0.336 mins. per pkm to 0.275 mins. per pkm. The overall journey time effect of a doubling of fares is a reduction in total time of 0.206 mins. per pkm, a 4.95% improvement. These figures can be used, if desired, to convert the travel time to an average per passenger trip. The impact on ferry travel time is negligible, primarily because the boarding time and journey time are unaffected by total passenger numbers.

The benefit appraisal table (Table A7.10) gives the important dollar values for consumer and producer surplus before and after the change. Together with the change in subsidy, the change in NSB enables us to identify the social implications of subsidy change. The change in producer surplus is the change in fare revenue net of changes in costs. It is effectively the change in operating loss/profit to the bus business (and the railway). The change in consumer surplus is decomposed into the change associated with the direct monetary cost of travel to the traveller, and the change associated with the travel time, converted via the value of travel time savings, to dollars. To enable a distinction to be made between the change in benefits and costs to continuing and switching bus and ferry users, we report the results separately. The sum of the producer and consumer surplus change associated with each mode gives the change in net social benefit (NSB) of a fare change. Since the NSB is set to zero in the base, we have established in dollar terms the loss of surplus to society associated with a particular policy change.

It is important to note that public transport fares are a transfer payment and that although the change in revenue from fares is included in the consumer surplus, it is cancelled out of the NSB because it is included also in the producer surplus. Since we cannot cancel out the change in reimbursement revenue by the same process (since it is not included in the change in consumer surplus, but could be included in the producer surplus), we include the financial benefit of a change in reimbursement revenue as a separate item. This additional source of revenue to the bus company ($36.243 m.) clearly plays a role in reducing the subsidy level.

The 100% fare increase has resulted in a total reduction in NSB of $35.237 m. per annum. This comprises a reduction of $22.386 m. for car users, $7.115 m. for commercial vehicle users, and a $3.560 m. increase for rail users. There is a substantial increase in producer surplus for the buses from bus services ($43.545 m.), and a positive travel time benefit to continuing users of the buses ($17.023 m.). The NSB for bus has decreased by $6.2 m. The major loss of consumer surplus is felt by continuing bus users who pay an additional $60.445 in fares. The switchers from bus incur a loss of $10.534 m., the difference between what they were willing to pay to use the bus and what they now have to pay.

The 100% fare increase on buses and ferries has eliminated the total bus and ferry subsidy giving $6.977 profit (i.e. − 9.594 + 2.617). This has resulted in a reduction in total NSB of $35.237 m. That is, in order to reduce the subsidy from $81.568 m. to a profit of $6.977 m., society as a whole has incurred $35.237 m. of lost net benefit.

The ratio of net social benefit change to the change in subsidy is a measure of the incremental benefit/subsidy ratio. It is 0.379 (i.e. − 35.237/ − 92.932). This tells us that every additional dollar of subsidy will increase gross social benefit by $1.379. Alternatively, the average net effect of $1 of additional subsidy is an increase of $0.379 of benefit to society. The results in Appendix 7A report the NSB per $1 of subsidy. Gross social benefit = (1 + NSB). The externality component can be separated out from the direct effect on continuing bus and ferry users. In this example of a 100% fare increase, $29.501 m. of NSB is a negative externality (imposed on original car and commercial vehicle users due to the presence of more car traffic), and $3.560 m. is a positive externality (imposed on the railway). The ex-bus users (i.e. switchers) are worse off by $6.323 m. Thus of the 37.9 cents of additional net benefit associated with a dollar increase in subsidy, the greater percentage of the benefit assists in eliminating the negative externality, since the original car and commercial vehicle traffic is most affected by the elimination of the bus subsidy (after the continuing bus users).

The last part of the output presents the implied vkm elasticities (direct and cross) which underlie the final results. In addition we present the marginal net social benefit per dollar of subsidy. The incremental benefit/subsidy ratio is an indicator of the average effect of subsidy change due to fare and/or service changes, and provides a suitable measure for choosing between different ways of spending a given amount of extra subsidy or different ways of reducing a given amount of lost subsidy. So if the amount of subsidy change is to remain unchanged (which is the assumption herein) then the average NSB per extra dollar of subsidy is the appropriate measure of performance. If, however, different quantities of subsidy are to be evaluated in some consistent way (such as increasing bus and ferry fares while holding all other fares and all service levels constant) one would expect the average NSB per dollar of subsidy to change. In particular, as subsidy levels fell one would expect average NSB per dollar of subsidy to increase. Thus the average measure of NSB per dollar of subsidy could be a misleading measure of the NSB from a marginal dollar of subsidy. The results in the last table of the output provide an empirical measure of the marginal index. The magnitude of this index, although not of great importance *per se* in the zero subsidy application, does serve an ancillary role. It indicates the extent to which there is potential for improvements in the policy mix; when the values for fares and vkm are the same, then at the margin there are no further gains to be made by varying the mix of

fare and vkm changes. That is, it guides the running of the model to find the point at which a dollar of subsidy gives the same marginal NSB whether it is spent or saved on fare changes or service changes. As a guide to establishing a policy equilibrium (only a guide given the relevance of other issues in the final development of policy), it is very valuable. It is this indicator which is linked to the request in the runstream for optimization of net benefit.

7.6 Concluding comments

The approach presented in this chapter enables a public transport agency and other affected organizations to identify each of the sources of influence on the determination of optimal subsidy. The applica-

tion is a useful case study to highlight the complex interrelationships between all modes of transportation and infrastructure in the search for efficient mode-specific strategies and policies.

Discussion issues for Chapter 7

1 Why must an assessment of a value for money public transport subsidy involve a consideration of all competing modes of transport?

2 Sourcing data for developing an integrated assessment of the impact of a public transport fares policy is demanding. Discuss what you see as the most difficult data items to source.

3 The implications of a change in fare and/or service level can be evaluated in terms of eight sources of benefits and costs. What are these sources?

4 What role does the full matrix of direct and cross-elasticities play in the determination of levels of subsidy?

5 Why might we be interested in including commercial vehicles in a study of the performance of the public transport sector?

Appendix 7A Output of a 100% bus and ferry fare increase

Title of Dataset: State Transit Authority Region Current Operation, Year Modelled: 1987/1988

Input Data File: Sydney.dat

Policy Variables	Percentage changes from base data
Bus fare	100.000
Ferry fare	100.000
Bus km	0.000
Ferry km	0.000

Table A7.1 Physical indicators

Mode		Passenger km. per annum (millions)		
		Base value	New value	% change
Car pkm		20,224.80	20,367.92	0.71
Bus pkm		875.10	716.29	−18.15
Ferry pkm		172.60	145.36	−15.78
Rail pkm		3,575.00	3,615.87	1.14
Commercial vehicle pkm		1,111.20	1,111.20	0.00
Including:				
Bus	Full fare	378.48	288.11	−23.88
	Concessionary non-reimbursed	26.25	19.98	−23.88
	Concessionary reimbursed	201.27	153.21	−23.88
	Excursion	59.07	44.96	−23.88
	School	183.77	183.77	0.00
	Free travel	26.25	26.25	0.00
Ferry	Full fare	138.51	114.75	−17.16
	Concessionary non-reimbursed	3.45	2.86	−17.16
	Concessionary reimbursed	15.53	12.87	−17.16
	Excursion	1.29	1.07	−17.16
	School	8.63	8.63	0.00
	Free travel	5.18	5.18	0.00
Rail	Full fare	2,377.38	2,408.62	1.31
	Concessionary non-reimbursed	53.63	54.33	1.31
	Concessionary reimbursed	536.25	543.30	1.31
	Excursion	143.00	144.88	1.31
	School	286.00	286.00	0.00
	Free travel	178.75	178.75	0.00

Table A7.2 Vehicle km. per annum (millions)

Mode	Base value	New value	% change
Car km.	11,236.00	11,315.51	0.71
Bus km.	59.25	59.25	0.00
Ferry km.	0.93	0.93	0.00
Rail km.	20.55	20.55	0.00
Commercial vehicle km.	926.00	926.00	0.00

Table A7.3 Passengers per vehicle (no.)

Mode	Base value	New value	% change
Car occupancy	1.800	1.800	0.000
Bus occupancy	14.771	12.090	−18.148
Ferry occupancy	184.878	155.698	−15.784
Rail occupancy	173.949	175.938	1.143
Commercial vehicle occupancy	1.200	1.200	0.000

Table A7.4 Financial indicators

Mode	Average full fare per passenger km. (cents)			
	Base value	New value	% change	Absolute change
Car	7.8055	7.8152	0.1246	0.0097
Bus	15.3400	30.6800	100.0000	15.3400
Ferry	9.8200	19.6400	100.0000	9.8200
Rail	9.9100	9.9100	0.0000	0.0000
Commercial vehicle	23.1177	23.2040	0.3734	0.0863

Table A7.5 Operating costs of cars and commercial vehicles ($ m.)

Mode	Base value	New value	% change	Absolute change
Car	1,578.649	1,591.802	0.833	13.153
Commercial vehicle	256.883	257.843	0.373	0.959

Table A7.6 Public transport revenues and costs ($ m.)

Mode		Base value	New value	% change	Absolute change
Bus	Fares	79.407	120.891	52.243	41.484
	Concessionary reimbursed	15.438	23.503	52.243	8.065
	Excursion reimbursed	23.197	35.315	52.243	12.119
	School reimbursed	14.095	28.190	100.000	14.095
	Passenger revenue	132.136	207.900	57.337	75.763
	Other revenue	12.627	12.627	0.000	0.000
	Costs	212.993	210.933	-0.967	-2.060
	Subsidy	68.230	-9.594	-114.061	-77.824
Ferry	Fares	14.589	24.172	65.688	9.583
	Concessionary reimbursed	0.763	1.264	65.688	0.501
	Excursion reimbursed	0.325	0.539	65.688	0.214
	School reimbursed	0.424	0.847	100.000	0.424
	Passenger revenue	16.101	26.822	66.591	10.722
	Other revenue	0.959	0.959	0.000	0.000
	Costs	30.398	30.398	0.000	0.000
	Subsidy	13.338	2.617	-80.381	-10.722
Rail	Fares	270.920	274.480	1.314	3.560
	Concessionary reimbursed	26.571	26.920	1.314	0.349
	Excursion reimbursed	36.279	36.755	1.314	0.477
	School reimbursed	14.171	14.171	0.000	0.000
	Passenger revenue	347.941	352.327	1.261	4.386
	Other revenue	63.560	63.560	0.000	0.000
	Costs	642.300	642.300	0.000	0.000
	Subsidy	230.799	226.413	-1.900	-4.386
Total	Fares	364.915	419.543	14.970	54.628
	Concessionary reimbursed	42.772	51.687	20.844	8.915
	Excursion reimbursed	59.801	72.610	21.420	12.809
	School reimbursed	28.690	43.209	50.606	14.519
	Passenger revenue	496.178	587.049	18.314	90.871
	Other revenue	77.146	77.146	0.000	0.000
	Costs	885.691	883.631	-0.233	-2.060
	Subsidy	312.367	219.436	-29.751	-92.932

Table A7.7 Traffic statistics

Total vehicle flows (bus flows) (pcu per hour)			
Network	Base	New	% change
Freeway	3,100.39 (15.235)	3,119.13 (15.235)	0.60
Divided major arterial	3.317.33 (32.471)	3,337.28 (32.471)	0.60
Undivided major arterial	1,623.44 (12.500)	1,633.22 (12.500)	0.60
Minor undivided arterial	1,007.75 (22.040)	1,013.74 (22.040)	0.59

Table A7.8 Speeds (kph)

Network	Base	New	% change	Absolute change
Freeway	47.956	47.724	−0.483	−0.232
Divided major arterial	24.108	23.765	−1.422	−0.343
Undivided major arterial	24.836	24.686	−0.601	−0.149
Minor undivided arterial	38.555	38.459	−0.250	−0.097
Average bus speed	20.927	21.293	1.751	0.367

Table A7.9 Journey time components (mins. per passenger km.)

Component	Base	New	Absolute change	% change	% total journey change
Bus					
Headway			0.0000		0.0000
Waiting	1.2960	1.1393		−12.0942	
Load factor			−0.1567		76.0535
In-vehicle	2.5304	2.5422	0.0118	0.4649	−5.7080
Boarding	0.3368	0.2757	−0.0611	−18.1476	29.6546
Total journey time	4.1632	3.9571	−0.2061	−4.9504	100.0000
Ferry					
Headway			0.0000		0.0000
Waiting	0.7380	0.7171		−2.8327	
Load factor			−0.0209		100.0000

Table A7.10 Benefit appraisal ($ m.)

Mode	Changes in producer surplus	Consumer surplus			Net social benefit
		Money	Time	Total	
Car original	0.000	−1.963	−20.423	−22.386	−22.386
Bus continue		−60.445	17.023	−43.422	
switch		−10.534	4.21	−6.323	
total	43.545	−70.979	21.234	−49.745	−6.200
Ferry continue		−12.086	0.597	−11.489	
switch		−1.305	0.11	−1.190	
total	9.583	−13.391	0.712	−12.679	−3.096
Rail original	3.560	0.000	0.000	0.000	3.560
Commercial vehicle original	0.000	−0.960	−6.155	−7.115	−7.115
Total	56.688	−87.294	−4.632	−91.925	−35.237

Table A7.11 Summary of changes

Mode	Reimbursed revenue	Subsidy	Net social benefit	Average net social benefit per $ of subsidy
Car	0.000	0.000	−22.386	0.000
Bus	34.279	−77.824	−6.200	0.080
Ferry	1.139	−10.722	−3.096	0.289
Rail	0.826	−4.386	3.560	−0.812
Commercial vehicle	0.000	0.000	−7.115	0.000
Total	36.243	−92.932	−35.237	0.379

Table A7.12 Marginal indicators (at new subsidy level)

Policy option +1%	Net social benefit per extra $ of finance	Elasticities of					
		Demand (% change in pkm)			Cost (% change in trip cost)		
		Bus	Ferry	Railway	Bus	Ferry	Railway
Bus fares	−0.0028	−0.422	0.006	0.023	−0.019	0.000	0.000
Ferry fares	−0.0003	0.018	−0.347	0.000	0.002	0.000	0.000
Rail fares	−0.0037	0.003	0.000	−0.260	0.007	0.000	0.000
Bus km.	0.0013	0.325	−0.005	−0.018	0.521	0.000	0.000
Ferry km.	0.0000	−0.006	0.120	−0.000	−0.000	0.508	0.000
Rail km.	−0.0011	−0.002	−0.000	−0.131	−0.003	0.000	0.530

The cornerstones of organizational management

8 Knowing your organization from a supply chain perspective

8.1 Introduction

All transport and logistics businesses today exist in a supply chain context consisting of networks of suppliers, buyers, customers, and consumers. Working in a supply chain context is changing the way managers think strategically. What this means is that management has to think globally even if not involved directly in doing business internationally. With the globalization of the economy and markets, increased strain on the costs of production coupled with expanding knowledge and information technology, it is only too apparent that the transportation and logistics sectors have become increasingly complex and dynamic. This is true whether an organization sees itself as a global enterprise or not. The scope of the economic change includes fewer goods being produced for local markets, and conversely, more goods targeted for regional, national, and international distribution. Consequently, the effectiveness of transportation and logistics is vital to globalization.

The global supply chain is also changing the way organizations are responding to customers and consumers. The question is how can business leverage all of its resources to improve customer service, operate more efficiently and cost effectively, and ensure competitive success? As businesses move towards a globalization strategy, suppliers of transportation and logistics services are faced with *assumed* competitive pressures from actors within the supply chain as well as from customers seeking service improvements and shrinking resources, leading to the realization that they are not efficient enough.

'The traditional view of strategy focuses on the "fit" between existing resources and emerging opportunities, strategic intent creates, by design, a substantial "misfit" between resources and aspirations' (Prahalad and Hamel 1993). Today this is less straightforward. The issues associated with 'strategic fit' in the supply chain encompass a broad spectrum of concerns including: size of the actors within the supply chain, structural differences among the partners, market positioning, enterprise culture and resulting orientation to business strategy, customer perceptions as well as future strategies for competing in their industry (e.g. cost leadership).

While the particular fusion of change forces may be somewhat unique to any one business, there are a number of generic dimensions of strategic change, including globalization, market deregulation, changing consumer demand, accelerating technological and information innovation, and service life cycles, that shape the responses and perception of future challenges for the transport and logistics sector. Like so many things, defining supply chain management is simpler than implementing it. High levels of cooperation and coordination are required among all stakeholders, with management having to address change management and alignment issues, key themes of this chapter.

8.2 Supply chain management

Supply chain management (SCM) involves a total set of business and management activities used to convert resource inputs into products and services. Both distributed production and markets require appropriate transport and logistics services to match their diversity in degrees of time-lines, pricing, and quality. The supply of existing transport options does not meet the demands of businesses competing in a context that is made less dependent on physical location. Purchasing is moving away from bulk-order point decisions and warehousing of inventory and more towards continuous smaller orders that shift inventory either upstream onto producers or downstream onto third-party logistics operators, formerly the freight transport sector. More and more customers have pruned their businesses of inefficiences and expect that others in the supply chain have also streamlined their operations to lead to cost savings and adding value.

SCM is an important tool for all transport and logistics business as it creates a mindset to secure success through knowing when, how, and where to develop and leverage value. For example, a transport service provides time and place value since it transports customers according to pre-arranged times as well as places of departure and arrival. Similarly, a third-party logistics provider supplies time, place, and possession value through transporting freight or products. Logistics management is critical to service demand in terms of deciding where to locate business facilities, for example, head office, warehouse, depot; the design of facilities, for example, where, when, and how to accumulate inventory; purchasing arrangements; size and capacity of operations. All of these factors influence transport and logistics business outcomes in terms of productivity, performance, quality, reliability, innovation, speed, and flexibility.

In some way, each and every enterprise is linked to another. This linkage characterizes the supply chain relationship among enterprises. Linkages can be internal, for example, the activities of a supplier can have an impact on the way a manufacturer structures its operations; staff of one company are employed in another or change in inventory management can restructure a manufacturing process, or external, for example, one enterprise is the marketing arm for another. These linkages can be central or peripheral. Central relationships are critical to core business processes while peripheral ones are more likely to provide resources in areas that support core business (Porter 1985). One of the important tasks of management is to understand the various networks of which they are a member and to identify the nature of the relationship that they hold with other members. This process is referred to as supply chain mapping (Christopher 1998) and is important for understanding how to structure the enterprise, integrate logistics processes internally and externally, and manage change.

8.2.1 The strategic context of SCM

The objective of SCM is twofold: efficiency (making best use of resources) and effectiveness (addressing customer and consumer demands) (see also Ch. 5). To address these goals, a number of key decisions need to be taken into account including service design such as the nature of service, quality, cost, and capacity decisions in relation to demand, variation, and scheduling.

SCM has to be addressed at all levels and processes of the transport and logistics business. Managers confront a complex array of decision-making that needs to be linked to transportation and logistics strategies. For example, strategically management needs to decide whether to emphasize high quality regardless of cost, lowest conceivable cost regardless of quality, or some other mix. Depending on what decision is made, this will determine factors such as use of technology, service design and specification, quality control, and price. Conversely, management needs to understand that decisions at the strategic level influence logistic strategies in regard to transport, technology, work design and processes, resources, planning, space, and layout.

8.2.2 **The marketing context of SCM**

Porter (1985) suggests that any business strategy is essentially a choice of where to draw the line between competitors and substitute products and services, between existing businesses and potential entrants, and between current business and suppliers and buyers. In practice, the strategic mindset of management is often influenced by the definition of the competitive field. According to Porter, too restricted a definition may result in competitive sources being neglected, whereas too extensive a definition may result in confusion and 'no practical direction-setting value'. This position leaves management with a dilemma when seeking to define the competitive context. How broad or narrow should the strategy be? If the competitive context is determined by the satisfaction of customer demands, there may be a need for multiple strategies for each transport and logistics business. Perhaps the appropriate response is not to have just one business strategy, but many. These definitions need to be driven by different views of customer demands and disassociated from how the business perceives its current market boundaries. The upshot of this is that management has to be innovative and take intellectual risks, particularly in regard to how they see their relationships with competitors. Implicit in any market-driven definition of a transport and logistics business is that those that address customer demands optimize competitive advantage. The following six dimensions are useful in shedding some light on the meaning of competitive advantage:

1. focusing your business by capturing the opportunity (quality, price, competency, service, innovation) ahead of rivalries;

2. having a view to cross-border (national, regional, industry, function) flows of goods, services, know-how, and capital;

3. leveraging competence, technology, products, services, brand names, or capital;

4. developing innovative practices, products, and services;

5. management that is market and learning orientated;

6. expanding revenue or asset base through taking advantage of any or all of the above.

8.2.3 **The operational context of SCM**

The management of the operational context involves a decision-making process focused on investment in business capacity which determines not only the quantity of value output but also the quality of value output that management seeks. Specifically, this type of decision involves the quantity and quality of investment in resources to meet customer and consumer demand right along the supply chain. For example, a provider of passenger transport services needs to determine the size of its fleet and workforce to serve its consumers. Capacity decisions are high-risk ones due to the trade-off between uncertainties of future service demand and investment in fleet, facilities, and people. Estimating consumer demand is an important component of processes of investment capacity decision-making.

Facilities decisions such as location and design plan, and technology utilization are key components of SCM. Facilities refer to workplaces, depots, warehouses, and offices where various processes of the transport and logistics business are conducted. Location to transportation is a major part of facilities decisions for distribution purposes. Designing these facilities is related to flow of product and services and has important implications for work organization and design (see Ch. 10). It is important to provide a brief overview of the core components of the operating context of transport and logistics businesses, which include

1. physical distribution management;

2. technology management;

3. inventory management;

4. shipping and transportation;

5. productivity management.

Physical distribution management: The significance of physical distribution management (PDM) is more evident today as management appreciates how it can develop and leverage time, facilities, reliability, and cost management coupled with the growth in electronic commerce worldwide.

Technology management: Most organizations today are service organizations, which rely on people delivering a service to customers. Technological design and utilization influence the nature of the output, quality, cost, workforce utilization, and work design. Technology decisions concern the set of procedures for transforming inputs into services or products. With the rapid enhancements to telecommunications and information technology, many labour-intensive operations have been converted to capital-intensive ones for delivering services. The growth of electronic commerce is evident in almost every aspect of business, but for manufacturers, third-party logistics providers, freight forwarders, and other transport providers, its greatest impact can be found in the supply chain. Not only does electronic commerce affect the way supply chains function and interact, but it also has opened up new avenues of opportunity for enterprises to gain market share, increase profits, and provide better customer service.

Electronic commerce is the trading of information, products, and services through information and telecommunications networks, gradually replacing traditional transactions. It facilitates the coordination of the supply chain, which has a significant, potential impact on reducing costs in delivering the required service. Transport and logistics products and services contain many features conducive to an electronic commerce environment. Deregulation in many parts of the transportation industry and restructuring of the logistics industry aid a shift towards more electronic means of conducting transactions. In freight terms, more intelligence has been put into the package, either as bar codes that trigger access to records in an information network scanning the packages or in the form of on-board information storage that provides key inputs to the control system regarding routing, contingencies, and so on. Further, the development of electronic data interchange (EDI) standards to facilitate intra-

enterprise and inter-enterprise communications in regard to bills of lading, credit, customs, invoices, and the creation and reconciliation of shipment documentation will have a significant impact on the current users of the transport infrastructure.

In regard to electronic commerce, a number of responses can be identified based on a study conducted by the Cranfield Centre for Logistics and Transportation (Hammant 1995) which seems five years later to be somewhat dated:

- growth in time-based performance: achieved by speeding up movement within existing supply chain structures. These accelerated movements need to be mirrored in the transport infrastructure but are being achieved by taking advantage of all the information technology trends to transform existing supply chains. Electronic Commerce will certainly speed up this process;

- supply chain efficiency improvement: EDI is one of the main enablers of SC efficiency improvements. Most, if not all, key logistics documents will be transmitted electronically by 2001;

- reduction in number of warehouses: the number of warehouse tiers will be reduced, leading to a reduction in the number of warehouses. Achieved by greater investment in IT to enable greater supply chain integration and hence support a reduction in total supply chain inventory;

- increase in number of transshipment warehouses: warehouses will continue to develop away from the traditional storage function to a transshipment role. Achieved by investment in advanced warehouse technologies such as fork-lift truck mounted Radio Data terminals and bar-code technology, together with EDI links between the warehouse and other parts of the supply chain;

- growing importance of retailers: experts predict that with growing concentration of ownership in the retailing sector worldwide, retailers are likely to become an increasingly important force in shaping the design and operation of supply chains. This will inevitably lead to increasing supply chain integration and EDI links between retailers and their suppliers;

more evident today as management appreciates how it can develop and leverage time, facilities, reliability, and cost management coupled with the growth in electronic commerce worldwide.

Technology management: Most organizations today are service organizations, which rely on people delivering a service to customers. Technological design and utilization influence the nature of the output, quality, cost, workforce utilization, and work design. Technology decisions concern the set of procedures for transforming inputs into services or products. With the rapid enhancements to telecommunications and information technology, many labour-intensive operations have been converted to capital-intensive ones for delivering services. The growth of electronic commerce is evident in almost every aspect of business, but for manufacturers, third-party logistics providers, freight forwarders, and other transport providers, its greatest impact can be found in the supply chain. Not only does electronic commerce affect the way supply chains function and interact, but it also has opened up new avenues of opportunity for enterprises to gain market share, increase profits, and provide better customer service.

Electronic commerce is the trading of information, products, and services through information and telecommunications networks, gradually replacing traditional transactions. It facilitates the coordination of the supply chain, which has a significant, potential impact on reducing costs in delivering the required service. Transport and logistics products and services contain many features conducive to an electronic commerce environment. Deregulation in many parts of the transportation industry and restructuring of the logistics industry aid a shift towards more electronic means of conducting transactions. In freight terms, more intelligence has been put into the package, either as bar codes that trigger access to records in an information network scanning the packages or in the form of on-board information storage that provides key inputs to the control system regarding routing, contingencies, and so on. Further, the development of electronic data interchange (EDI) standards to facilitate intra-

enterprise and inter-enterprise communications in regard to bills of lading, credit, customs, invoices, and the creation and reconciliation of shipment documentation will have a significant impact on the current users of the transport infrastructure.

In regard to electronic commerce, a number of responses can be identified based on a study conducted by the Cranfield Centre for Logistics and Transportation (Hammant 1995) which seems five years later to be somewhat dated:

- growth in time-based performance: achieved by speeding up movement within existing supply chain structures. These accelerated movements need to be mirrored in the transport infrastructure but are being achieved by taking advantage of all the information technology trends to transform existing supply chains. Electronic Commerce will certainly speed up this process;

- supply chain efficiency improvement: EDI is one of the main enablers of SC efficiency improvements. Most, if not all, key logistics documents will be transmitted electronically by 2001;

- reduction in number of warehouses: the number of warehouse tiers will be reduced, leading to a reduction in the number of warehouses. Achieved by greater investment in IT to enable greater supply chain integration and hence support a reduction in total supply chain inventory;

- increase in number of transshipment warehouses: warehouses will continue to develop away from the traditional storage function to a transshipment role. Achieved by investment in advanced warehouse technologies such as fork-lift truck mounted Radio Data terminals and bar-code technology, together with EDI links between the warehouse and other parts of the supply chain;

- growing importance of retailers: experts predict that with growing concentration of ownership in the retailing sector worldwide, retailers are likely to become an increasingly important force in shaping the design and operation of supply chains. This will inevitably lead to increasing supply chain integration and EDI links between retailers and their suppliers;

- rise in prices of road transport: road prices are forecast to rise significantly more than for other modes of transport. In order to offset these price rises, investment in in-cab technology will continue to increase;

- increase in cross-border transport: significant increase in cross-border transport likely to lead to increased in-cab technology and also in IT to support cross-border supply chain integration.

Although shippers' demands for time-definite delivery, both on a domestic and global basis, are pushing transport providers into redesigning their operations and service offerings, the advent of electronic commerce (e-commerce) still needs to address distribution and transport issues. These issues are a major impediment in streamlining the supply chain further.

Inventory management: Most industries find it difficult to predict inventory turnover precisely, taking into account the results of seasonal and promotional downturns and upturns. To manage the periods of uncertainty in the past, management often felt compelled to carry high levels of inventory or to require a third party to do so. This period preceded the arrival of just-in-time (JIT), postponement, and vendor-managed inventory (VMI), all of which result in lower inventory requirements and more rapid replenishment of stock.

Inventory management is an important part of PDM, particularly for purchasing and handling inputs and managing in-transit inventories that are central to transport and logistics businesses today. In particular, materials requirement planning (MRP) is a system that assists management to monitor inventory and replenish as stock levels approach minimum requirements. JIT delivery systems are the most important types of systems used to minimize the need for maintaining high levels of inventory. A benefit of both MRP and JIT is that they modify the need for large warehousing facilities and capital investment in inventory waiting to be used, or at least, provide management with greater choice over warehousing and distribution capacity. In-transit inventories are controlled by the transportation and distribution systems. Management has to monitor

these inventories to ensure that it is in the right place at the appropriate time as well as to ensure delivery to customers.

Postponement: The way inventory is managed creates more efficient supply chains particularly for manufacturing and retailers and at the same time reduces costs. Reducing costs needs to be viewed as a minor consideration relative to customer service and on-time delivery. This is where the principle of postponement is useful. Postponement is an important part of inventory management today. It is a process whereby a supplier or third party configures product—either through component assembly, testing, cleaning, and/or special packaging—for a particular market just before it is needed.

Vendor-managed inventory: VMI occurs where the supplier coordinates the replenishment of stock on behalf of the customer who determines inventory threshold levels. The flow of information is central to VMI. Specifically, electronic data interchange (EDI) and e-commerce provide an electronic flow of information that collates and integrates real-time information for actors on the supply chain as well as giving them some indication of logistics services and capacity in the global chains. There are some obvious benefits from this including those summarized in Table 8.1.

In principle through electronic means much of the guesswork in inventory management is eliminated, notwithstanding changing consumption patterns and geographical limitations. EDI provides management with the capacity to forecast and implement a single plan for inventory and shipment levels. Electronic commerce will eventually lead to innovations in inventory management.

Shipping and transportation: Distribution is about the transporting of products and delivery of services from the place of production or design through to the consumer. Distribution relies on transactions among multiple customers. All parties along the supply chain have a common objective of ensuring that the distribution process does not hamper the level of customer service through the

Table 8.1 Inventory management implications

Reduced inventory	Increased inventory
• Labour and labour costs • Stockholding and accounts receivable • Routinization and superfluous administration • Customer contact due to on-line transactions	• Consumer response • Customer service (both actual and perceived) • Cash flow due to the effective management of trade creditors • Need for training staff in the use of information and telecommunications technology

cost, quantity, nature, and timing of the products or services. Management needs to select the appropriate channel structure (i.e. collection of organizations and organization units), the third-party operators, who can enhance efficiency by creating time, place, and possession, to be used, and ensure that information and control systems reinforce performance objectives such as speed of delivery, communications, and costs. This process is referred to as transaction channels. It is important to have a good understanding of distribution channels in terms of the flow of products and services as well as information from producer to customer.

Productivity management: Increasing productivity is important in contributing to the profitability and ultimately, the survival of the business. Productivity is considered in a number of ways: *organization-wide* view such as total factor productivity (TFP) which looks at the relationship between outputs and all inputs such as labour, capital, investment in materials and technology, as well as energy costs. Productivity is also considered in terms of the sub-unit as well as the performance of individual workers. The previous chapters are devoted to looking at a number of approaches that transport and logistics businesses can use to enhance their TFP as well as the performance of individual workers. Perhaps the two most significant strategies that transport and logistics businesses can use are one based on SCM and the other on managing worker commitment.

So far this discussion has focused on operational decisions that impact the efficiency of SCM. However, all of these operations influence output in terms of quality, price, and availability that impact customer demand. SCM allows management to coordinate and integrate a number of organizational functions, specifically human resources, operations, marketing, information, and outputs. The integration of these functions brings together a detailed analysis of the nature of customer demands (needs and wants) and how these are satisfied when purchasing a service or product. SCM decisions based on markets are more effective than those based solely on operations or technologies. To illustrate this point, a business has to consider itself in its supply chain (i.e. market) context rather than focus solely on its operational context, a problem of the past. The operational context (e.g. physical distribution) is quickly modified by the market (i.e. adding value to the core service). By using an SCM approach, management is better equipped to identify appropriate strategic objectives that will guide the best use of the business's resources.

Consequently supply chain mapping is increasingly difficult, as transport and logistics businesses are more boundaryless with their activities becoming increasingly integrated. One of the factors which is usually not taken into account in the TFP equation, at least in a quantitative sense, is organizational design which is vital if the transport and logistics business is to achieve high levels of coordination and integration across the supply chain. Table 8.2 identifies the linkages between business strategy, organizational structure and design, technology, marketing and operations, and workforce performance.

The purpose of Table 8.2 is twofold: first, to outline the key components of strategy, structure, operations, and performance and, secondly, to demon-

Table 8.2 Integration of strategy within the enterprise

Strategic focus	Structure and design	Facilitators	Performance measures
Strategic relationship	• Integration • Decentralization • Coordination	• Control of integrated performance • Vertical and horizontal supply chain management	Qualitative • Shared values concerning stakeholder value delivery Quantitative • TFP • Profitability • Cash flow *(see Chs. 3–5 for discussion of these)*
Structural relationship management	• Culture • Work design	• Supply chain roles and tasks	• KPIs (subunit) • Competence • Learning
Operational processes	• Resources allocation and management of physical, human, information	Aplication of logistics processes technologies: • EDI/E commerce	• as above

strate the linkages between the organizational components and how change in one component has ramifications for other parts of the organization. For example, an expanding transport and logistics business might decide to drop its functional design and adopt a matrix (e.g. project team) to better cope with environmental uncertainty. Introducing a team approach will lead to a cultural change and management has to decide whether to make this a strategic change or allow it to evolve. Moving to a team culture will modify the human resource strategy in terms of selection criteria, performance review, and benefits.

Further linkages outlined in Table 8.2 suggest that a change in a work sequence may arise from a new technology and most certainly lead to changes in work processes and work practices. Modifying work sequence may lead to a relocation of input and output points, work stations, facilities planning, order fulfilment, control and quality management processes. In terms of the latter processes, new and more efficient methods of monitoring inventory and assessing quality may reduce the time required in the supply chain.

The last column in Table 8.2 focuses on performance, the most important component in the organization. Prompted by technological changes, management will need to invest more in the upgrading of workforce skills, knowledge, and abilities. Subsequently, management will need to introduce new training programmes and selection criteria. Technological change will also modify performance and attitudes. An organization wanting to improve performance might develop a new incentive scheme, for example, performance-based pay for workers, or introduce performance-based training. Many of these changes lead to new perceptions, expectations, and values, which are addressed in Chapter 9.

8.3 Organizational design

It is important to understand the logic of each organization form (structure) as each gives rise to key variances in performance and outcomes. The structural profile of an enterprise differentiates two types of organization: static hierarchies and dynamic networks (Kvande and Rasmussen 1995) (see Fig. 8.1). Static hierarchies are described as outmoded forms in which management maintains patriarchal power relations, and where 'thinking is done at the top and people lower down in the organisation are not expected to think about what they do'. Static hierarchies produce expressly 'masculine' cultures, which affect both men and women, located in peripheral functions and roles of the organization. Static hierarchies do not lend themselves easily to distributed work processes. A transport and logistics business in a dynamic service market, requiring flexibility and high customer responsiveness, cannot sustain a static hierarchy. If it does sustain one, the enterprise will not survive simply because it cannot be customer-responsive. More importantly, it will be less capable of being a flexible member of a supply chain network.

8.3.1 The structure of organizations

Organisations can be characterized in various ways ranging from functional, divisional, process, matrix, network, or a combination of these (defined below), often referred to as 'hybrid' or 'global' as shown in Figure 8.1. Global or hybrid organizations are modified forms of functional, divisional, process, or matrix to suit a particular business's unique needs. Channon (1982) shows a clear trend away from single and dominant businesses between 1950 and 1980 and an increase in the proportion of related businesses and partnerships over the same period. With increasing globalization, strategic partnerships are being formed among organizations as management change their view of their competitors from foe to potential ally amidst the rivalry of global supply chains. Ensuring a rapid response to customer demands is critical to what adds value to the supply chain today. Partnerships can form in various ways including:

- vertical upstream towards suppliers;
- vertical downstream towards customers based on market channel transactions;
- horizontal towards competitors based on partnershipping, sharing technology, and even information, marketing, transportation, and so on;
- diagonal towards organizations, for example joint venturing between a private enterprise and a government agency.

Partnerships can be based on a long-standing or transitory relationship depending on whether it is the sharing of resources, costs, and/or access to one another's markets, and the amount of trust that exists among the stakeholders.

Functional organization: Workers performing similar functions are grouped together into work units or departments. Centralized control and coordination are the key organizing dimensions, whereby supervisors are able to manage more people since they perform a similar function. Work is controlled at least one layer higher than where it is conducted. Functional organization relies on compliant workers who defer to higher levels of management for decision-making. Decision-making within this structure is slow if it incorporates two-way communication. However, in reality, communications tend to be more linear—moving up and down a single channel in the organization. It is unlikely that workers in this structure are involved in strategic decision-making. Influence extends top down in the form of official instructions, authorizations, and so on.

Divisional organization: This is similar in most respects to functional organizations with the exception that those working together are grouped according to specific markets that the corporation is

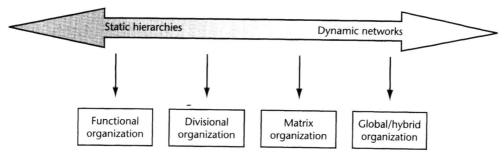

Fig. 8.1 Typology of organizational designs

engaged in. For example, in an airline corporation there may be a number of divisions including rental cars and a hotel chain. Each division acts as a business within an enterprise, competing directly with each other, although sharing some centralized functions.

Matrix organization: people work in a project structure, which is a mix of product/service and functions. Groupings tend to be smaller than functional departments with dual supervision by project leader and functional manager, with each supervisor having dual reporting responsibilities. The matrix structure tends to be more temporary than in functional or divisionalized forms, as workers group and re-group according to the dictates of projects, some of which are highly transient.

In contrast, dynamic networks move from independent competitive strategies to competitive-collaborative strategies, and from integrated hierarchies to loosely coupled network organizations, with an accent on participative teamwork and a culture of collaboration. Dynamic networks tend to operate with a gender balance where all workers supplant dominant male values by a high work orientation and motivation. According to Kvande and Rasmussen (1995), both women and men get on better in these organizations than they do in static hierarchies because work is organized in teams and across functions and tasks, where all members contribute knowledge and effort on an equal basis. As they work together people get to know each other's capacity. In this structure, women, and in particular their contribution, become visible to their co-workers and management.

8.3.2 Towards an integrated structure

As previously stated, organizations around the world respond to an increasingly competitive global business environment by moving away from centrally coordinated, multi-level hierarchies and towards a variety of flexible structures that more closely represent networks rather than traditional pyramids. Established organizations downsize to their core competence, de-layering management hierarchies, and outsourcing a wide range of activities. Global and hybrid organizations may be more efficient and appropriate in responding to contingencies created by changing markets, technology, and other facets of a dynamic business environment.

Global organizations operate as a hybrid between a market and a hierarchy (chain of command). Management seek partnerships with independent suppliers, producers, and/or distributors. Sometimes these are enduring and long term and at other times short term. Some organizations desire the capacity to associate and dissociate at relatively short notice. Examples of hybrid organizations include joint ventures and consortia that maximize resources, particularly information exchange between organizations. Where trading information was once seen as a threat, this is less so today as enterprises appreciate the need to share information and resources to maximize their competitive position. These organizations require 'global' leadership, an approach that is quite different to a single-business focus. The social processes (e.g. communication and influence) that structure the network organization are directed by a management core, or 'hub' (still top down in a sense), but there is more opportunity for workers to influence their supervisors depending on their leadership style.

With the trend towards disaggregation and loose coupling, management needs to trial various organizational arrangements. Instead of using plans, schedules, and transfer prices to coordinate subunits, they need to use contracts and other cooperative agreements to link together external components into various network structures. Dynamic linkages rely on performance-based equity, full information disclosure, and the freedom for partners to withdraw from the partnership. The key is to create a structure that coordinates and captures organizational capacity while simultaneously maintaining flexibility and autonomy for the associated membership.

Most organizations are a hybrid of the forms outlined above. While there is no one best organizational form, whether it is functional, divisional, matrix, or hybrid, each structure has something to offer. The most appropriate organizational form is contingent upon the nature of the business and potential markets, the strategy being pursued, organizational strengths and weaknesses, leadership and culture, technology, size, and business life cycle. Nevertheless there is one way to resolve the structural dilemma by attempting to address the conditions of centralization and decentralization for both the internal structure (internal reporting relationships and work design—see Ch. 10) and the external structure of the business (external relationships up and down the supply chain channels).

8.4 Centralization versus decentralization

Centralization is the systematic retention of control by executive management. An example of external centralization is that the business acquires and subsequently controls as much of the supply chain from serving its own inputs through to customers and consumers as is practicable. An example of internal centralization is the systematic retention of power and responsibility by senior management. Decentralization is the systematic delegation of power and responsibility to the middle levels and lower reaches of the organization and is usually achieved through work design (see Ch. 10). A typical organization today embraces both types of control. Head office centralizes business policy, strategic planning and change, business investment and acquisition, and decentralizes operational responsibility to subunits, often including profit-making.

The decision to centralize, decentralize, or balance these forces within a business has to serve a purpose that is centred around *strategic control*. Strategic control is conceived in terms of: (i) locus of control: the domain(s) of corporate action; (ii) the process of control: markets, finance, operations, and transporta-

tion; (iii) degree of control: quality and performance; and (iv) extent of control: accountability and responsibilities at the level of work groups, workers, and contract workers.

The issue of strategic control for most businesses is wider than the enterprise itself. As stated above, this depends on what domains or business arenas senior management wish to operate in. Domain control also has to take into account supply chain relationships, that is, how to coordinate all the key actors in the supply chain (i.e. buyers, suppliers, customers) so as to be able to respond to end-user customers efficiently and effectively. Businesses have to find a way to integrate the efforts of all functions across the supply channels, minimizing conflict wherever possible. The process of *integration* is the extent to which the business can achieve both corporate, business, and functional control vertically and horizontally throughout the supply chain. The higher the degree of integration, the greater the need to emphasize coordination and find a responsive organizational form to maximize coordination. There are two types of integration processes: vertical and horizontal.

8.5 Vertical integration

Enterprises may become more competitive through cooperation with others rather than through contest for the purpose of becoming entrants in the global supply chain (SC). Under these conditions, the 'logic' of competition may be fallacious (Moore 1996). The total supply chain has a profound influence on the way managers should think about future challenges.

Vertical integration is achieved when a business forms a dynamic network, either through acquisition, merger, or partnership, with distribution centres and freight-forwarders to maximize the physical flow through from wholesale level to retailers. This process is termed 'forward vertical integration'. Alternatively, a business could rely on commercial freight carriers (as opposed to the company's truck fleet) to transport to distribution centres and then onto retailers. If this is the case, the logistics function has not been vertically integrated. However, if a retail company owns its own warehouse, it is vertically integrating backwards. The direction of vertical integration, that is, forwards or backwards, depends on where the business is positioned in the supply chain. Vertical integration is not only about functional control but also about the degree of strategic and performance control (as previously described) in relation to the customer in the supply chain. Vertical integration has implications for the way work is designed and performed; that is, the responsibilities of each enterprise and their workforce (see Ch. 11).

When businesses are not vertically integrated, they have to rely on negotiating trade agreements with others in the supply chain (backwards and forwards) for supply, storage, distribution, transport, and meeting delivery deadlines to consumers. Porter (1985) outlines the advantages and disadvantages of vertical integration in Table 8.3.

Vertical integration introduces additional complexities into the business enterprise such as differentiation and conflict. Differentiation is the extent to which an enterprise is divided into discernible businesses and, hence, specializations. The assumption is that the more unstable and dynamic the competitive context, the more differentiation the business needs to establish. If the competitive environment is relatively stable and predictable, less differentiation is needed. Once a business engages in differentiation, particularly across the supply chain, it has gone beyond its core business and hence core competencies. This situation often leads to functional outsourcing, for example, inventory management.

8.5.1 Outsourcing

Welch and Nayak (1992: 23) maintain that the reason for outsourcing is the antithesis of vertical integration. The advantages of outsourcing include:

- the conversion of fixed costs to variable costs;

Table 8.3 Advantages and disadvantages of vertical integration

Advantages	Disadvantages
Secure economies of scale and/or scope	Cost of overcoming mobility barriers
Tap into technology	Increased operating leverage
Ensure supply and/or demand	Reduced flexibility to change partners
Enhance ability to add value to business processes	Higher overall exit barriers
Heighten market channel entry and exit barriers	Capital investment requirements
Enter a higher-return business	Differing managerial requirements
Defend against foreclosure	Greater need for coordinating techniques

Source: Porter (1988)

- the opportunity to reduce capital investment requirements;
- the potential to reduce all total costs (through partners' economies of scale/scope and lower wage structures);
- a redefined and balanced workforce in terms of worker type, gender, and experience;

- the acceleration of new product/service developments;
- gains in access to invention and innovation from partners, and
- a focus on high value-added activities

8.6 Horizontal integration

Horizontal integration is achieved when management focuses inwardly by comparing operational and functional processes and, in particular, the responsibilities of work groups and workers. When a business enterprise becomes vertically integrated along the supply chain, the internal organization has to undergo *restructuring horizontally*. An example of this is business process re-engineering discussed below.

Taking a step back for a moment, a vertically integrated business sees itself quite differently to a functional or divisionalized organization. A vertically integrated business is a dynamic network and its key functional areas are reorganized in terms of the supply chain and tend to resemble processes such as inbound logistics, operations, outbound logistics, marketing and sales and service. According to Porter (1985), this is how value is created. The primary functional areas include (Porter 1985):

- *inbound logistics*: relationships with suppliers including all activities required to receive, store and disseminate inputs, for example, materials handling, warehousing, inventory control, and transport scheduling;
- *operations*: the set of organizational activities required to process resources into products and services. Each business establishes operating systems which control transformation processes, including everything from receiving and handling inventory, for example, just-in-time (JIT), to performing the steps in service provisions such as scheduling, planning services, and itineraries.

When a customer purchases a service, they are paying the service provider to do something for them, for example, pay a freight forwarder to transport documents or products. Operations are a central function to any business in terms of quality, cost, design, demand, flexibility, and location;

- *outbound logistics* are activities required to collect, store, and distribute products and/or deliver services;
- *marketing and sales* are processes to communicate with all customers along the supply chain about products and services;
- *services* are activities needed to maintain the product or service once delivered to customers with a particular focus on end-user, for example, addressing transport needs, training, consulting, supplying parts, and repairs.

The horizontally structured business enterprise attempts to integrate across inbound operations, and outbound logistics in particular ways. It may achieve this with the assistance of strategic networks, discussed below. *Horizontal integration*, as it is termed, is aimed at developing and leveraging value, which is ultimately passed onto customers. The essential question is 'how does the business create and manage value in the supply chain?' The process of horizontal integration is not unlike the *matrix* form described above. Porter (1985) identified four generic processes that assist in the transformation to horizontal integration:

- *human resource management*: activities associated

with the acquisition, motivation, development, and deployment of the workforce, which shape performance, competence, and overall productivity and business capacity;

• *infrastructure*: just as the transport system relies on infrastructure such as roads, rail, and shipping channels; cities depend on water, electricity, sewage, and government; businesses are dependent on business processes including distribution channels, warehousing, financial, legal, planning and enterprise structures, and not least, flow of information;

• *acquisition* involves acquisition of all resources to the business including the supply, purchasing, ordering, and transactions;

• *technology* involves equipment, hardware, software, and technical expertise brought to bear on the business.

Most businesses are involved in countless activities, and the manner in which these are conducted and managed ultimately affects business survival. The main focus of management is finding the 'best fit' between supply chain relationships and internal organizational processes (see Fig. 8.2).

Further, achieving the 'best fit' is aimed at developing and building value as depicted in Figure 8.3. Figure 8.3 shows that when organizational members view their organization in supply chain terms, it turns the organization 'on its side'—hence the traditional organizational pyramid is rotated to the right.

Seeing the organization as the backbone to the supply chain leads to horizontal integration of functional units into a matrix of interlinked activities for the purpose of serving customers (internal and external) all the way along the supply chain to consumers. This is what developing and leveraging value in the supply chain means.

A further need for enterprise analysis is the requirement to address heightened internal differentiation between process functions, occupational and skill groupings in terms of values, skills, attitudes, and performance. The achievement of horizontal integration depends on essential unification of primary function areas. This integration starts at the point of *inbound logistics*. For example, this might include identifying customer needs through market research, introducing an on-line ordering system as well as a proficient procurement process. At the point of *operations*, the organizational matrix includes highly trained operational staff and information/process technology to support this. At the point of *outbound logistics*, the organizational matrix integrates distribution workers, fleet management, or freight contracts, and an appropriate loading system. At the point of *sales*, the matrix comprised a highly skilled sales force, a distribution network, appropriate advertising, and on-line customer ordering. At the point of *service delivery*, the organizational matrix includes customer-focused staff and appropriate processes to handle customer grievances and so on.

Develops, builds, adjusts

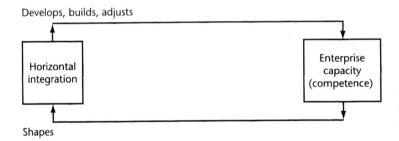

Shapes

Fig. 8.2 The relationship between horizontal integration and enterprise capacity across the supply chain

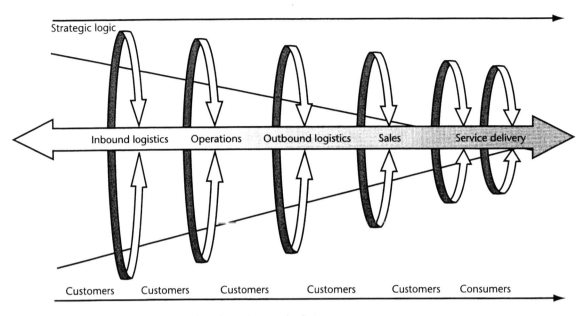

Fig. 8.3 Developing and leveraging value along the supply chain

8.7 Strategic change management

As traditional, multi-level hierarchies move towards a variety of more flexible structures that more closely represent linked supply chains (often *synergistic*) rather than isolated, traditional pyramids, management needs to find ways to manage this change. Even in a less dynamic context, change management efforts have often been unsuccessful (Kotter 1995). In part this is due to increasing instability in the enterprise's context, with an unfolding of unique conditions that have only a limited historical background or precedent. It is also due to management focusing on certain problems in isolation—to the exclusion of other, possibly more important, problems. Is management choosing appropriate routes to organizational change? This question is crucial in a supply chain context.

Broadly speaking, organizational change is any substantive modification to the enterprise, such as business process re-engineering (Hammer and Champy 1994) or some part of the business, such as continuous improvement. Most businesses are undergoing modification continuously, usually in an ad hoc way. Organization change is most often a response to an intended, unintended, anticipated, or unanticipated change in the competitive context. Table 8.4 shows the external sources of organizational change.

Businesses seek to maintain an efficient and effective adjustment by managing these factors in a supply chain context. Strategic supply chain management seeks to align an enterprise's corporate and business strategies, structure (i.e. relationships), information, operations and technology, and culture to establish a 'best fit' with the aim of developing and leveraging value. Another way of expressing this is to say that any change made to macro aspects of the organization, for example, corporate strategy and structure, will have (or should be planned to have) micro implications, for example, work design (see Ch. 10). In the past, management has often overlooked this important process of aligning strategic processes with tactical ones (i.e. at the operational core of the business). Strategic alignment is contingent on numerous factors and is based on the premise that

Table 8.4 External demands of organizational-change

Global demands	Physical Government policies and regulations Economic e.g. deregulation Socio-cultural e.g. values Technological e.g. information, communications, transportation
Industry demands	Suppliers Human and material resources Size and growth Structure Distribution channels Costs Critical success factors
Customer demands	Market segments Consumer motivations Purchasing patterns
Competitors	Identifying competitors Size, growth, and profitability Objectives and ownership Cost/revenue structure Entry/exit barriers

there is no 'best way' to manage change. Achieving strategic change depends on the external and internal contingencies in a specific organization to attain a 'best fit'. The contingencies include not only the human and technical aspects of the organization as in the socio-technical approach, but also the cultural and political aspects of organizational life (Tichy 1983).

The contingency view of strategic change assumes that the organization is composed of various spheres of interest which need to be in balance for the organization to survive. The main spheres are strategic, structural, cultural, systems, and leadership. Each sphere has its own focus: strategic on the core business of the organization such as its main services or products; allocation of resource including influence and rewards within the organization. A further sphere is cultural which focuses on the interpretations of historical and current events in the organization, and making sense of the shift between the two. Systems focus on technical aspects, for example, product and service design, and leadership focus which reinforces the management style of the enterprise.

Strategic change is managed along the lines of identifying these key strategic contingencies, which provides management with a choice of strategies for managing change in different circumstances. Based on a force-field model, it is important to examine typologies of drivers of competition as well as to investigate organizational responses and future challenges towards a more integrated approach to the management of change. Almost instinctively, managers consider their enterprise as competing for success and survival in an adversarial arena. Management's task is to match the business's capabilities with the forces imposed by the competitive context such as expanded markets and the proliferation of services and products, to provide an advantage in the marketplace.

8.7.1 Field theory

The contingency model is based on a series of driving and restraining forces (Lewin 1951) as well as the notion of 'strategic fit' (Miles and Snow 1984). A forerunner of the rational approach is Lewin's (1951) 'field theory' which categorizes the forces of change as either 'regulatory' or 'non-regulatory'. Regulatory forces are factors that maintain the existing status quo while non-regulatory forces revise the status quo in some way. When the pressure emanating from each set of opposing forces is approximately equal, there is a state of 'quasi-stationary equilibrium', as demonstrated in Figure 8.4.

Force-field analysis proposes that while driving forces are more easily influenced by change, modifying them increases opposition, creating tension, and ultimately resistance.

Lewin's model assumes the presence of resistance in the change process. When the driving and restraining forces are identified and analysed, it is possible for them to determine change direction. Each set of driving and restraining forces is experienced at a different level of intensity and quantified accordingly as depicted by the varying arrows in Figure 8.4.

The spider model (Fig 8.5) is similar to Lewin's force-field analysis. All four fields (each represented by two axes) have important impacts on:

- level of transport demand;
- transport price;
- modes used,

which are regarded as the main force fields for the development of policy and planning of transport systems. The order of items on each of the eight axes is such that the:

- interior points are more associated with non-intervention strategies (e.g. market forces, liberal attitudes),
- exterior points reflect the result of policy interventions (e.g. land use planning, control strategies, regulatory measures) (Nijkamp *et al.* 1997).

8.7.2 Internal change management

Various pressures inside the organization may also lead to change intentionally or unintentionally (see Table 8.5). Many of these internal pressures are imposed by the competitive context and so the two sets of change sources should not be seen as distinct but rather, interrelated. However, most internal sources of change are externally induced, and therefore tend to be reactive. A reactive mode tends to be

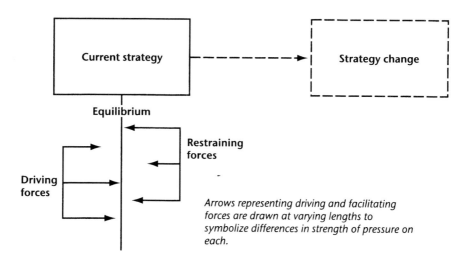

Arrows representing driving and facilitating forces are drawn at varying lengths to symbolize differences in strength of pressure on each.

Driving forces of strategy change
- Changing markets
- New technologies
- Changing workforce attributes and attitudes

Restraining forces of strategy change
- Fear of loss of control
- Rigid operational policies and procedures
- Existing norms and practices
- Lack of resources

Fig. 8.4 The driving and restraining forces of organizational change

Source: Based on Lewin (1951).

less than strategically focused and results in a fragmentary and ad hoc approach.

Planned change is always preferable to ad hoc change. Total quality management (TQM) is one example of planned change that, if applied in a holistic way, will lead to a successful integration of all the factors that have to be taken into account in a change management programme. More often than not, management are not implementing TQM in a holistic way. When change, such as TQM, is inadequately applied, it becomes fragmented and falls short of an integrated approach, which is the reason why so many change programmes fail in organizations. It is only when change programmes address both external and internal pressures for change that businesses gain the capacity to address customer demands, shorten process cycles and response times, reduce cost, and strengthen innovation and quality.

8.7.3 Business process re-engineering (BPR)

The re-engineering approach to change management gained momentum in the 1980s. While the rise in significance of BPR is reflected in the increasing interest in it in the popular business media as well as the information technology literature, there has been little empirical testing of its validity and effectiveness in organizations.

Various terms are used for 'business re-engineering'; most relate to the version put forward by Hammer and Champy (1994; also Hammer and Stanton 1995). Hammer is acknowledged as the 'father of re-engineering', having published his original manifesto in 1983. He defines BPR as 'the fundamental rethinking and *radical redesign* of business *processes* to bring about *dramatic* improvements in performance' (Hammer and Stanton 1995: 3;

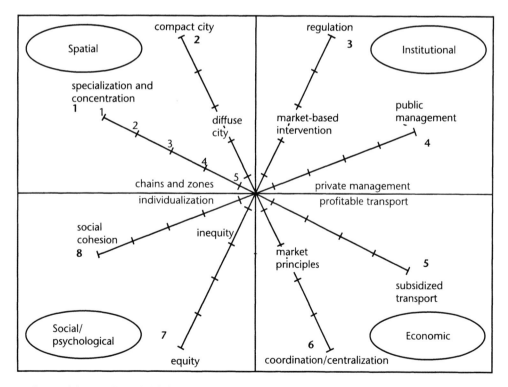

Fig. 8.5 Spider model: main force fields for policy and planning of transport systems

Source: Nijkamp *et al.* (1997). Reproduced with permission.

Table 8.5 Internal sources of organizational change

Internal sources	
People	Management capabilities
	Workers' competence
–	Industrial relations environment
	Motivation
	Turnover and absenteeism
	Work practices
Organizational	Leadership
	Strategy, structure, and decision-making
	Work processes
	Communication
	Culture
	Planning
	Relationships
	Partnerships
Operational	Cost and availability
	Inventory management
	Economies of scale
	Operational efficiency and utilization of capacity
	Research and development
	Innovation
Financial	Ability to raise capital
	Relationship with stakeholders
	Price-earnings ratio
	Flexibility of capital structure
	Cost control
	Accounting system
Marketing	Diversity of service procedure
	Market segmentation
	Channels of distribution
	Pricing strategy and flexibility
	After sales service

emphasis in the original). A process is defined as any series of interconnected activities organized together for a purpose. A process comprises steps that have a natural order. A core process is one that delivers a product or service to the customer. Radical redesign relates to reconceptualizing processes in the organization such as strategic focus, culture, and perceptions.

Applying this concept to SCM, it is aimed at an integration of logistic activities into key supply chain processes. The elements involved in BPR are important to understand: problem, rule, and assumption. A problem is a specific aspect of performance that management wants to address; for example, to increase throughput. A rule is a specific element of process design that leads to the problem;

for example, a given set of procedures on how to perform the work. An assumption is something that is taken for granted in the organization and leads to the rule; for example, that people in operational/tactical positions cannot be entrusted with responsibility (Hammer and Stanton 1995).

In practice, BPR tends to rest on a structural-system model of change management. The objective is seen as being to compile and appraise information on factors in the 'environment', followed by a rational use of that information to redesign processes in order to produce ultimately the desired customer response in line with strategic objectives.

The BPR approach also tends to hold that processes, not people, can be re-engineered and, further, that organizational analysis is a waste of time and may inhibit organizational change (Hammer and Stanton 1995). In cases where BPR has failed, its proponents mostly blame the transition from redesign of the process to implementation of the change. But this area of vulnerability is intrinsic to most change management efforts and points to the need for understanding enterprise culture and learning (see Ch. 9).

8.7.4 Designing a change intervention

Figure 8.6 shows that identifying forces, understanding which part(s) of the organization will be affected, methods used, and designing appropriate change strategies is important in terms of achieving the intended (i.e. desirable) outcome.

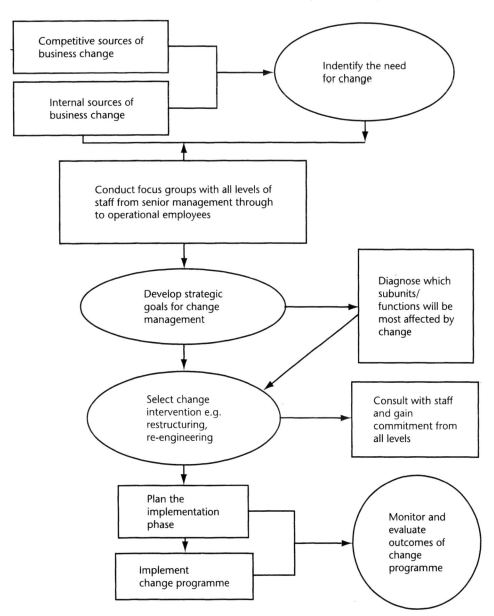

Fig. 8.6 Framework for designing a change intervention

Plans for change need to be evaluated through reference to an internal as well as an external standard of performance and accountability. Too many managers seek solutions elsewhere characterized by the rise in benchmarking, re-engineering, and continuous improvement programmes. The outcome of this approach is that solutions are being sought which are largely external to the business. This is essential, providing enough internal reflection and learning is taking place to ascertain how new ideas will be received. For *real* change to occur in the organization, people will need to address a number of questions:

- Are people willing to challenge assumptions held by key stakeholder groups and investigate evidence to substantiate these?

- Are the architects of change and the implementors engaged in joint action?

- Are both management and workers willing to reflect on successes and failures?

- Is the change intervention selected likely to lead to expected outcomes?

- Are stakeholder groups involved in underlying or overt conflict?

- Are people's careers tied to a specific organization, which leads them into enthusiastically safeguarding their interests?

- Are people prepared to let go of the past?

Most labels describing organizational change and improvement efforts have become meaningless. For example, when management talks about building a team-based organization, they could mean infusing team spirit in a generalized way throughout the organization, introducing temporary task forces to solve problems, redesigning work along group lines such as quality circles, developing self-directed work teams, or all of these. 'Re-engineering' is a similar case in point. Re-engineering sometimes describes layoffs or traditional slash-and-burn cost-cutting exercises. Sometimes, it means a change in the organization's structure; in other cases, it means installing new information technology systems. In its broadest definition, re-engineering can refer to a radical revamping of the macro, strategic processes that establish how most work and customer interactions flow across the organization.

A planned approach to change management suggests that efforts to implement it in any setting will be successful as long as the people involved in the change process learn and apply the given principles underlying the programme. The aim of planned change is directed towards the improvement of the current performance setting, and relies on participants in the change process 'playing by the rules of the game', usually dictated by principal stakeholders (e.g. chief executive officers, directors, senior executive, board members).

8.7.5 Resistance to change

Attempts to introduce change often prove futile simply because the planned approach is aimed at changing routine actions and strategies rather than fundamental thinking (Argyris 1990), and in doing so, is little more than ad hoc and adaptive. Again re-engineering is an example of this. Why is this the case? First, in some situations, modifying routine action is all that is needed, but in many others, changing thinking (usually management thinking) is essentially required. Secondly when a change programme proves to be successful in one business, similar principles are applied in different businesses over and over again with little analysis of the context.

Principles underlying planned change programmes reinforce existing business practices and block any changes that are likely to modify conventional and entrenched patterns of thinking in the organization. One reason for this is that change threatens the existing power bases that people hold in the business. Clearly, some forms of control are more significant in some contexts than others. When one form of control is eliminated at the expense of another, change is perceived by people as imposed and threatening.

A second reason is that the interaction between the principles of the change programme, people, and the organization context are overlooked. Implementing change without knowledge of the context, or without taking it into account, is self-defeating, because it introduces and reinforces organizational rigidities such as inappropriate communication, decision-making, and belief patterns on the human side, as well as operational and technological rigidities, thus creating problems rather than minimizing them.

A third reason is that the principles of the change programme itself become the major focus, and its champions are eager to defend it. This approach suggests that a certain amount of agreement or defensiveness is imperative for organizational change to occur. When change is supported by consensus or is championed by change agents, it will be pushed through but whether or not it succeeds is another question. In this situation, outcomes are characterized by the discouragement of questions and fears that workers wish to express about change, especially when it is imposed on them. When the underlying reasons for change remain implicit, people feel out of control and less supportive of the change itself.

8.8 Strategic partnerships networks as the new concept of organizing the supply chain

Strategic networks are an aggregation of autonomous organizations that retain their own identity and governance while recognizing a synergistic relationship for mutual value management. The purpose of forming strategic networks focuses on commercial objectives, strategic vision, and leadership, and ways of gaining a competitive advantage in volatile markets. More specifically, strategic partnerships seek to acquire a form of organizational flexibility to adjust to change, to develop the organizational capacity (skills and resources) to develop successful products and services, and to achieve operating economies and efficiencies (Powell 1987).

In understanding this new concept of organization, Quinn (1992) referred to strategic networks as 'intelligent enterprises' that comprise complex, global information and decision support systems superseding many of the control and operational functions of their conventional counterparts. These issues in turn lead to a new concept of organizing in terms of recreating a 'flatter' hierarchy with a membership-oriented culture concentrating on shared values, new learning and knowledge, and integration (Webster 1992). The manner in which this is achieved varies from one organizational context to another (Ring and Van de Ven 1992) and will be elaborated below.

Transformational leadership is an important aspect in forming strategic networks and managing change within them. The pressure to align enterprises brought about by new market structures and the extension of market boundaries beyond national ones is redefining the future organizational form, particularly in the airline industry. There is increased pressure for enterprise leaders to understand the organizational prerequisites for successful networks such as a well-developed infrastructure of culture, process of organizational learning, and rewarding ways to achieve integration among network partners.

8.8.1 Partnership culture

In a strategic network, each enterprise represents a culture that has a varying degree of influence over its members' beliefs and behaviour. Enterprises 'like persons, have values and these values are integrated into some coherent value system ... In any [enterprise], the members generally have a set of beliefs about what is appropriate and inappropriate organisational behaviour' (Goodstein 1983: 203–4). In the same way that personality is not a direct explanation for a person's actions, enterprise culture is only one factor contributing to the performance of an network. Culture is related to the concept of 'strategic fit' (see Ch. 9) as well as the extent of similarity and diversity that exists between potential enterprise members in a strategic network. One assumption is that the greater the similarity between the value systems of potential members, the more likely they will find accord. Enterprises whose cultures are more similar to each other will develop networks more successfully and at a more appropriate time (Harrison 1972; Malekzadeh and Nahavandi 1988), and will have greater financial success (Porter 1985).

8.8.2 New learning and knowledge

An important aspect of developing membership culture is the process of organizational learning that network members engage in, jointly and separately (Argyris 1977). Increasing competitive pressures are fuelling concern over the extent to which networks can 'learn' jointly. One perspective is that strategic networks are less likely to foster learning when exposed to competition, instead leveraging their market position to obtain competitive advantage (Barnett and Burgelman 1996). The fundamental dilemma for any strategic network is how to maintain its enterprise identity while simultaneously developing the network. Network development calls for substantial shifts in maintenance strategies to effect the active support and contribution of network members.

Strategic networks require that members convey their learning to one another, develop shared understandings, and externalize what they have learnt (Lyles and Schwenk 1992). Organizational learning occurs when the actions of one party, in this case an enterprise member, contest the values of another and there is pressure to replace 'their' ideas with 'different' ones. A high level of cultural synergy may inhibit organizational learning where enterprise members 'think' in a similar way. In other words, too

much similarity may constrain the potential benefits of the network because too little in terms of added value and innovation is being contributed by enterprise members to the network. Others have argued, for example Parkhe (1991), that inter-enterprise cultural diversity adversely affects performance. However, there is another perspective in which cultural synergy may not equal cultural similarity. Two dissimilar cultures may reach synergy through the process of 'double-loop' learning (Argyris 1977).

Members do not agree upon clear boundaries, cannot identify shared solutions and do not reconcile beliefs and multiple identities. Yet, these members contend they belong to a culture. They share a common orientation and overarching purpose, face similar problems, and comparable experiences. However, these shared orientations and purposes accommodate different beliefs and incommensurable technologies, these problems imply different solutions, and these experiences have multiple meanings . . . Thus, for at least some cultures to dismiss the ambiguities in favour of what is clear and shared is to exclude some of the most central aspects of members' cultural experience and to ignore the essence of their cultural community. (Meyerson *et al.* 1991: 131–2)

In other words, learning jointly allows 'culture' to be 'unbundled' into its important components in a way that might not occur within a single enterprise. Yet, learning is often a slow process simply because, as enterprises are currently structured, they retard the transferring of information, ideas, and expertise among partners. Organizational learning is instrumental to collective efficacy, defined as the belief of enterprise members about whether they can perform successfully or not within a strategic network (Bandura 1977). Networks that have a low sense of efficacy are more inclined to respond negatively to organizational change than those with high efficacy (Beehr and Newman 1978). How is high efficacy achieved?

Consensus-building with interactions among members plays a significant part in developing collective efficacy (see also Ch. 11). Strategic networks provide 'blurred boundaries' for learning to occur. The process of developing collective efficacy in networks is assisted by 'skilled organizers' who span the enterprise boundaries of each member and transfer learning (Brown and Hosking 1986). Innovations by one member need to translate into network-wide innovation. The network needs to be structured in a way that facilitates the emergence and action of these types of liaison role for organizational success.

8.9 Organizational prerequisites for successful partnerships in the supply chain network

In practice, partnerships have had a high failure rate (Flanagan and Marcus 1993), which has led to a focus on the factors that contributed to the formation of the partnership, but these may have little to do with a failed outcome. Success of a strategic partnership is predicated on organizational performance (OP) and organizational outcomes (OC). OP is a function of actions congruent to organizational goals. Action takes the form of establishing a shared vision, communicating clearly, building inter-member trust, collaborating and sharing knowledge, and decision-making. These processes grounded in an impelling business strategy are essential from the outset of partnership formation (Kanter 1989).

Performing successfully in a strategic partnership not only involves capability but also choices, for example, the choice to expend effort and invest and the extent of this as well as the choice to commit resources including knowledge and trust. Organizational outcomes include the degree to which enterprise members have met the goals and the extent to which they are satisfied with the strategic partnership. If one of the members perceives the partnership to be unfair, the choice about their potential investment will be modified. The relationship between OP and OC is best understood in terms of the concept of organizational integration.

A strategic partnership rests on the premise that each member brings unique commitments to the partnership, requiring a process of integration. To integrate member commitments, each constituency in the partnership needs to understand and share in a collective mission. Success has to be grounded in the integration of culture and people which leads to a greater probability of strategic and operational attainment. However, if the interrelationship between the partners is based largely on self-interest, competition, and overt conflict, the members' attachment to the partnership is loose. Conversely, when the relationship between the constituencies is collaborative, partners become engaged in a partnership characterized by collective interest and equality. One of the difficulties in integrating the separate goals of various members in a partnership is the fundamental conflict over their individual control of scarce resources. Sources of conflict include information (technical expertise, quality); capital, physical resources, time (to learn), and intangible assets such as industry reputation (Barney 1986; Hill 1990). The relative control of these resources is reflected in each transaction within the partnership. Conflict over resources also mirrors the degree of trust among members.

8.9.1 Partnerships based on exchange

To explain this point fully, a relationship of exchange is compared to that based on integration. Strategic partnerships are firmly established on a relationship of exchange, highlighting the interdependence between the enterprise members. A partnership based on 'exchange' is founded on a reciprocal relationship, with the members' contributions each linked to the other, based on fair exchange of contributions, and outcomes proportional to investment. Trust is also an important part of an exchange relationship in terms of the extent to which each member believes that the other(s) will meet their commitments to the partnership. Exchange sets up a competitive context, the nature of which is characterized by each member in the partnership declaring 'If I give you something, I want something in return'. The outcome subsequently leads to 'winners' and 'losers', depending on which member is best able to maximize their control over scarce resources. 'Losers' are more likely to resort to threat as a form of reprisal. Strong competition and fear of reprisal can be minimized through structuring the partnership along equitable lines. This is achieved by, for example, ensuring that each party has equal access to resources and opportunity to control them. In a partnership based on exchange, there is an element of uncertainty that is reduced with each transaction. Under these conditions, the culture of the partnership is at best 'cooperative' but remains a 'hollow' network as is often witnessed among carriers.

8.9.2 Partnerships based on integration

Partnerships that go beyond exchange and strive for an integration of interests, goals, resources, and values take on a different 'rationality' from those based purely on self-interest. A number of researchers (Johanson and Mattsson 1988; Malekzadeh and Nahavandi 1988) have stressed the significance of integration as an ideal process for strategic partnerships. Booz et al. (1985) report that cultural integration was the most important factor, ahead of financial and strategic factors, in the success of acquisitions.

A strategy of integration establishes common interests among members through a process of ongoing negotiation. With the understanding that not all partnerships are founded totally on conflict or calculative action, integration is the approach most likely to lead to the initiation, development, and maintenance of a strategic partnership. An integrative strategy therefore encourages a 'negotiated order' within the partnership (Strauss 1978). Negotiation is aimed at the maximization of equitable outcomes for all members. Negotiation allows each con-

stituency not only to preserve a cohesive social relationship but also to dissent without fear of reprisal about contribution and outcomes in the partnership. Members experience a sense of working towards a 'commonality' characterized by 'what is good for us is good for the partnership'. Integration is associated with enhanced efficacy and ultimately organizational capacity of the partnership. Strategic partnerships based on integration are genuinely adding value for customers and shareholders.

Walter (1985) found culture a significant factor in the performance of hybrid organizations. A strategy of integration involves a major 'gelling' of distinct cultures, workforces, and orientations. Integration requires a collective orientation to strategic purpose, implying a mutual understanding and acceptance of the goals and strategies by various members. An integrative strategy addresses four main factors that affect the performance outcomes of partnerships: breadth of purpose, boundary determination, value creation process, and stability mechanisms (Borys and Jemison 1989). The purpose of the partnership is dynamic and varies over time as markets fluctuate, technologies change, legislation is modified, and work structures are redesigned.

So what do successful strategic partnerships require? If the means to the end have changed (as evidenced by partnerships, mergers, and acquisitions), new strategies are called for, requiring a renewed 'responsiveness' from enterprise members who are located either at the 'centre' or its boundaries. Strategic partnerships often mean that people essentially have 'divided' loyalties and ambiguous commitment. Partnerships will be less 'hollow' and successful when:

- new ways of thinking and doing emerge, and blockages are 'unfrozen';

- there is an emphasis on the interactive processes among stakeholders;

- underlying conflicts among stakeholders are identified and addressed;

- stakeholders engage in genuine problem-solving;

- tensions between dominant and weak logics and between old and new ones are overcome;

- stakeholders who possess the most appropriate organizational knowledge are sourced;

- it is pre-determined under what conditions it is

appropriate for the dominant member to possess information without sharing it;

- psychological contracts support and reinforce innovative behaviour among stakeholders.

8.10 Integrating stakeholders in the supply chain

Despite how the word stakeholder is interpreted in a supply chain context, its use has legitimate implications for effective SCM. Stakeholder theory, popularized by Freeman (1984), provides an answer to the question 'to whom should business owners and management be responsible?' In addressing this question, the following list provides examples of generic groups of stakeholders:

- shareholders,
- customers,
- management,
- employees,
- suppliers and consultants,
- government,
- professional and industrial associations, and
- the community at large.

8.10.1 Defining the term stakehold

Any dictionary defines stakehold as an interest (an advantage, benefit, gain, profit) in which a person or persons wish to invest and subsequently feel they have rights to and which is aggressively defended when potentially eroded. For example, customers as stakeholders will defend their rights vigorously when a service or product either declines in quality and/or is no longer offered. It is important to acknowledge the expertise, influence, and action of stakeholders by understanding the:

- value of the stakehold in terms of people's livelihood, career, effort, and commitment;

- contributing factors leading to a change in stakeholders' 'territories';

- perceived outcomes for stakeholders;

- meaning of change in regard to power, rewards, career;

- value of the ongoing working relationship among stakeholders;

- investment of stakeholders in the organization: past and potential.

8.10.2 Creating stakeholder value

There are very important practical reasons why stakeholders need to be considered. Managements who perceive stakeholders (other than shareholders) as negligible, face greater financial risks than those who act responsibly (McGuire *et al.* 1988). First, stakeholders play a significant role in directing change. Both from within and outside the organization, various constituents and coalitions pursue interests that might not reflect the interests of business. Secondly, individual stakeholders and coalitions frequently construct crises in order to introduce change (Neilson and Rao 1987).

It is important that all stakeholders can enjoy a bigger, better cake which is the basis of managing value in the supply chain, and depends on:

- motivated employees and customers,

- loyal consumers,

- strong reputations within industry including competitors, and

- good relations with the community.

Stakeholder involvement is vital to the management of the business and its supply chain. Management has to find a way to address the needs, interests, and competencies of all stakeholders. Clearly, 'no matter how impressive the performance characteristics of an innovation may be, its adoption and implementation will conflict with some interests and jeopardise some partnerships' (Kimberly 1981: 93). For example, a plan for change, such as to outsource a function, is clearly threatening for some stakeholders and not for others. Regardless of the threat, everyone will experience uncertainty. Managers need to seek ways to address the interests and goals of stakeholders to avoid adverse actions. To do this it is important to understand that there is likely to be some correspondence between the pattern of stakeholding and empowerment since those with little power or influence can expect to gain little and have little incentive to broaden their input into the company.

Stakeholders exercise primary or secondary influence over the business (Ansoff 1965). People with primary influence usually hold an official position or are contracted to the organization involved in its core business. Examples of primary stakeholders include board members, the executive, management, suppliers, customers, consumers, and workers. People with secondary influence are indirectly involved in the organization. Examples of secondary stakeholders include community groups, professional and industrial associations. Today, the distinction between primary and secondary stakeholders is arbitrary as there is considerable overlap between the two groups as the issues vary. In a given context, one group of stakeholders will be of primary interest but in another, the same group will be of secondary concern. In many situations today, there will be multiple stakeholders with primary influence.

The stakeholder relationship is understood by viewing it in context; the strategies employed and the interaction among all stakeholders. There are three dimensions to assist in this analysis:

1. *context*: institutional including markets, political arena, position of the stakeholders in the supply chain, member organizations, status, authority and influence, skills, information, knowledge;
2. *strategy*: interests, objectives, and actions used;
3. *interaction*: strategic and interpersonal aspects of relating with other stakeholders.

Consumers and workers are among the most important groups of primary stakeholders for an enterprise and in that sense their stakehold is a right rather than a favour. It is important to strengthen the stakehold of workers who are vital in service and product delivery. Four stakeholder groups are identified:

- *mixed-blessing*: highly significant because these types of stakeholders are potentially both threatening and cooperative. Examples include specialist skill groups who are in short supply as well as customers who use a highly competitive product or service;
- *supportive*: highly committed to managerial strategy and style and are highly cooperative. Interests are wide-ranging and cover a number of aspects of the organization.
- *marginal*: not particularly threatening or cooperative and usually include groups looking after the interests of customers, workers, and shareholders. Interests are very specific.
- *non-supportive*: highly threatening and least likely to be cooperative, for example, a business adversary, resistant workers. Interests are diverse and fluctuate from one context to the next. Non-supportive stakeholders can become mixed-blessing types if their interests are addressed appropriately (Savage *et al.* 1991).

8.10.3 Working out the stakes

The stakes in an organization are related to the direct influence of stakeholders over decision-making processes. Stakes are multi-faceted and involve various types of influence and include, for example, share of equity capital or control over supply chain and organizational resources. Stakeholders use different sources of power ranging from cooperative through

Table 8.6 Framework for working out the stakes

1. Value image	Basic priciples that guide action (beliefs, ideals, and perceptions that are associated with the stakeholder making the decision)
2. Trajectory image	Future directions (goals that stakeholders wish to achieve in the future)
3. Strategic image	Desired actions for achieving future goals (proposed actions of stakeholders)

to coercive tactics. Working out the stakes is vital in interpreting and influencing stakeholders. The opportunity and incidence of conflict is high because the stakes are important to each of the constituents involved. It is important to separate the objectives and strategies of each of the stakeholders. A useful framework outlined in Table 8.6 is used here to identify the stakes.

8.10.4 Stakeholder analysis

The term stakeholder analysis is associated with the notion of 'prisoner's dilemma'. Prisoner's dilemma applies to the relationship where stakeholders are organized and active and the viability of each depends on the survival and success of the other. Axelrod (1976) found that 'tit for tat' is a strategy aimed at modifying the actions of stakeholders. The strategy is aimed at maximizing mutual gain and minimizing self-interest. The four principles are:

1. avoid being the first to exit from a relationship or take advantage of a dissenting stakeholder; always demonstrate openness and commitment;

2. ensure that stakeholders appreciate that others will reciprocate their actions by reward, cooperation, or revenge competitive actions;

3. avoid making stakeholders feel remorseful for non-cooperation;

4. ensure that stakeholders know the other party's objectives and interests, and they understand theirs.

You should attempt to move from a 'tit for tat' position to one of the positions outlined below (based on Walton and McKersie 1965):

1. Distributive bargaining (win-lose): each stakeholder attempts to maximize its share of fixed-sum payoffs. It is important to understand the structure of the bargain over any issue:

   What do stakeholders really want on this issue?

   What are stakeholders aiming for?

   What is the point at which stakeholders will not be co-opted?

2. Integrative bargaining (collaborative): each stakeholder is willing to explore options to increase the magnitude of mutual advantage overlooking which party gains more at this time.

3. Attitudinal restructuring (trust): each stakeholder attempts to modify the other's perceptions, attitudes, and to downplay the conflict between themselves.

The following is a checklist that can be used to prepare a bargaining session with stakeholders:

- bargaining power: high or low,
- balance of power: favourable to unfavourable,
- length of stakeholder relationship which influences commitment,
- value placed on trust,
- distributive or integrative approach.

The expectations, interests, values, and objectives of each group of stakeholders is likely to be different, although overlapping aims and interests are highly probable. In addition to the above stakeholder analysis, it is important to gauge the impact of their influence on organizational change. Three issues are important:

1. the legitimacy of coopting stakeholders;

2. the feasibility of coopting stakeholders;

3. the development of active stakeholders.

1. *The legitimacy of coopting stakeholders*: Coopting stakeholders is a successful strategy only when a significant number of people are persuaded that their involvement in the change process is relevant and essential. The best results are achieved from a collaborative process which is representative of all stakeholder interests. Through this process, people realize that they can exercise some degree of choice over issues concerning their interests, objectives, and outcomes. Informed debate and communication programmes increase the number of people engaging in the official change process, because they are better informed about complex issues and prepared to make appropriate choices.

2. *The feasibility of coopting stakeholders*: Too many managers believe that stakeholders are uninterested in decision-making about business directions or changes; that it is too difficult to get the various stakeholders together, or that they are too diverse a group to have discussions with. Managers avoid the feasibility of appealing to stakeholders because of not knowing how to overcome apathetic stakeholders or fear their potential hostility to change.

3. *The development of active stakeholders*: Active stakeholders emerge because their stake in the business or business process is strengthened. Business and supply chain communications need to be designed to introduce the relevant strategic issues to stakeholders and provide them with a thorough analysis of each issue and its implications for them. Discussion of key issues, details of proposed changes, and how each organizational constituency perceives this needs to take place. Feedback from stakeholders is important and official channels need to be provided so that this occurs.

8.10.5 The power of management as a key stakeholder

Management's role centres upon 'surveillance' which includes observers, correcting inappropriate action and rewarding appropriate action, and evaluation:

Whenever a [change] arises, [management] are likely to seek a solution that will avert threats to important values in a way that will not adversely affect their relationships with any 'important people' within the organisation, especially to those to whom they are accountable, and that will not be opposed by subordinates who are expected to implement the new policy decision . . . They want to maintain or enhance their power, compensation, and status within the organisation and to continue to obtain social support from their personal network. (Janis 1989: 45)

Power is subjective, relative, and dynamic. The mobilization of power varies daily in an organization especially in periods of change. How strong the exercise of power is depends on competing stakeholders, how they see it, and their control of resources that fluctuate over time. Power revolves around the distribution of rewards, the integration of interests, the degree of commitment of various stakeholders to the specific change, their constituency, and the organization, as well as managerial control.

Consideration of the stakeholder relationship requires analysis of the following:

1. How important is the change event going to be for them, directly and indirectly?

2. What are the advantages and disadvantages for stakeholders?

3. What favours stakeholders?

4. What works against them?

5. What organizational or personal resources do they need?

6. How are the stakes weighted by each constituent? Will they push to win at any cost?

7. What structures the relationship among stakeholders?

8.10.6 **The politics of stakeholders**

Political activity among stakeholders is determined by the degree of dependence. The more dependent a stakeholder is on others, the less influence he or she can exercise in relation to another stakeholder. Stakeholders' ability to influence others depends on the opportunity and willingness to do so. Dependence results in stakeholders being defensive, reactive, or confronting.

Cooperation among stakeholders is also a possibility and increasingly this is the case with the increasing number of strategic partnerships being formed between organizations, managements and unions, unions and unions, and so on.

8.10.7 **Conflict perspectives**

Managers often act to avoid conflict only to have to confront it later. Conflict takes on a spiralling effect, either increasing or decreasing over time. For the purposes of this analysis, conflict is '. . . the deliberate interaction of two or more complex social units which are attempting to define or redefine the terms of their interdependence' (Walton and McKersie 1965: 3). Conflict is fundamental to an analysis of stakeholder relationships. In any relationship there is a divergence of opinion, a variety of vested interests, different beliefs and values. Managers often perceive that stakeholders are not acting or responding appropriately in the situation. It is difficult to get everyone to see the situation in the same light and, consequently, gaining agreement is never an easy process.

In organizational contexts, most people do not welcome conflict for the sake of it. In any context, the stakeholder's capacity, opportunity, and willingness to threaten or cooperate needs to be considered (Freeman 1984). Conflict ensues when one group or another withholds or withdraws consent or cooperation. Sometimes this is overt (people refuse openly to comply) and sometimes this is covert (people do not communicate their real agenda). The relationship between stakeholders has to be viewed in relation to time, either short or long term. Obviously, a long-term relationship requires a different degree of cooperation than a short-term one. It is important to address the risks or potential risks of conflict to this long-term relationship. People have to deal with each other and also deal with the aftermath of disagreement.

There are various strategies to coopt stakeholders ranging from rational, expert, negotiated, and action-orientated, depending on the context in which they are employed. Contextual factors to consider include: financial considerations, nature of the change, time-frame, nature of the people involved, social and industrial context, and organizational structure.

1. **Rational**

Source of change	legislation, regulatory, ministerial union, managerial policy
Key characteristic	imposed or declared
Decision making	interest or resource based
Evaluated	given technical or administrative criteria
Response	fear, resistance, compliance
Perceived obstacles	lack of resources, great time urgency, lack of immediate expertise
Outcome	organizational: little success; for members: learning but not in the expected direction, many unintended consequences such as apathy, conflict

2. **Expert**

Source of change	new knowledge, skill, technological change
Key characteristic	scientific and planned
Decision-making	planned
Evaluated	given technical or administrative criteria
Response	fear, resistance, compliance, or cooperation
Perceived obstacles	lack of resources, time, poor understanding of context

Outcome   technical success but poor social success; for members: learning but does little to contribute to the organization, insecurity, conflict

3. Negotiated

Source of change	people-orientated
Key characteristic	social reciprocity, emergent or planned
Decision-making	participative
Evaluated	agreed-upon criteria
Response	acceptance, defensive
Perceived obstacles	lack of resources, time
Outcome	organizational: successful; for members: some learning, conflict, potential for 'losers' to emerge later

4. Action-orientated

Impetus for change	new idea, practice
Key characteristic	emergent or planned
Decision-making	experimental and exploratory
Evaluated	satisfaction relating to social, industrial, and political criteria
Response	learning and commitment
Perceived obstacles	lack of resources, time, expertise
Outcome	organizational: success; for members: greater learning but not in the expected direction, least unintended consequences, a greater sense of collective capacity to reconstruct the organization in a desirable direction, secure change and new values

8.10.8 Coopting key stakeholders: processes of consultation

Through communication and negotiation, a continuing process is going on among stakeholders in order to reach a level of confidence where some common action is possible (Gray *et al.* 1985). Managements need to comply with the expectations that stakeholders have for the business or else they run the risk of losing credibility and support from them (DiMaggio and Powell 1983). Overcoming resistance to change may be nothing more than management's attempt to maintain the support of key stakeholders. For example:

- mixed-blessing stakeholder management needs to use collaboration;
- supportive stakeholder management needs to maintain involvement;
- non-supportive stakeholder management needs to reduce dependence;
- marginal stakeholder management needs to monitor issues, context, and progress continuously.

The conflicts generated by one or more issues by stakeholders are resolved through collaboration, consultation, negotiation, mediation, or a blend of all of these. These processes

- encourage the involvement of supportive stakeholders and are consistent with democratic principles;
- provide an opportunity for stakeholders to prepare aims and strategies;
- facilitate change and adjustment as well as the resolution of issues. While they may slow or impede the process of change, in the long run they are slower than a rational approach.

In working out the best strategy to deal with stakeholders, it is not possible for any one stakeholder to define or even guess at all the possible actions when faced with a proposal. There are simply too many avenues for action to know about, investigate, and employ. The more constrained the situation, the more risky and costly the courses of action and the more uncertain the outcomes. Often, it is difficult for stakeholders to distinguish between latent and manifest objectives. It also depends on the view of conflict (rational or action) that is held by various stakeholders.

The analysis of stakeholders is a dynamic process.

It involves strategies and counter-strategies, tactics and counter-tactics. The context never completely constrains one stakeholder or another as most comprise multi-dimensional relationships, which are the crux of relationship management in the supply chain.

8.11 A concluding case study: TranzForm

This case study provides the reader with a chance to reflect on some of the issues discussed in this chapter.

Generally, the 1990s have been a period of high uncertainty for businesses: rapidly rising interest rates, a deeply recessed economy, and over-diversification forcing a number of transport businesses to flounder and engage in major restructuring so as to improve their performance. TranzForm, operating in the third-party logistics sector, is one such business.

Operating since 1989, TranzForm is an integrated logistics business with major divisions worldwide so as to link and leverage resources in different markets and thereby supply an international coordination capability as a unique service to its global customers. TranzForm specializes in effective supply chain management for 300 customers, which involves the efficient coordination of inbound and outbound logistics systems. The organization has recently updated its information system to assist in worldwide integration of transportation, inventory, warehousing, and packaging. From 1995, TranzForm introduced the concept of key regions. The plan was to identify a key region that had developed a particular expertise due to its customer base, which could be resourced by other regions. For example, Europe specialized in retailing, Asia Pacific in packaging, the USA in warehousing, and so on. Each region consisted of a number of directors who managed customer accounts and each director was responsible for developing and supporting the customer's logistics for all the services that TranzForm could provide in that region.

In 1998, TranzForm aimed to increase its customers by 10%. TranzForm was in a much better position now than it had been five years before, when it sustained an operating deficit and was overlooked by customers in favour of its more innovative competitors. A number of factors were affecting its competitive position including lost sales, poor transportation outcomes, and high rates.

The problem for TranzForm was to renew its competitive edge to regain its position of market leadership. Its on-time reliability at the time was 96% and 92% for meeting budget. By 1999, TranzForm proposed to increase revenue in real terms by 3% or $35.5 million through a modest increase in activities and to decrease controllable costs by 5%. TranzForm was characterized as an organization with a complex strategic position. When TranzForm was first established in 1988 it was organized along traditional lines resulting in numerous layers of management. During the early 1990s, the nature of the management strategy and approach at TranzForm remained firm. By the mid-1990s, with a continuing decline in market position and decreasing share prices, TranzForm headquarters (HQ) felt it was time to address the problem.

In 1996, the first initiative of the incoming board and new management team was to develop its priorities for the future direction of TranzForm. With the focus on increasing competition, HQ set about articulating the need for:

1. improving its services in terms of quality, reliability, and customer responsiveness;

2. reducing total costs by improving operating effectiveness and efficiency through better utilization of equipment and capital;

3. increasing responsiveness to customers through consistency and reliability;

4. redefining what business or businesses to be in (or want to hold on to or acquire);

5. enhancing the company's public image and reputation through better relations with customers, suppliers, shareholders, and the general public.

Business strategies of TranzForm

These aims were translated into the following business strategies:

- creating effective business units as discrete cost and profit centres with their own business plans, accountability, and decentralized decision-making;

- providing effective management information systems through on-line networks;

- the role of account director became consultant and coordinator rather than that of line manager.

Analysis of TranzForm

It is important to understand how change emerged in TranzForm. First, several changes occurred along multiple paths, fluctuating financial markets, competition for improved efficiency and quality in the industry. Senior HQ perceived these factors as affecting the current and future performance of the organization. The way change was considered in TranzForm was: *emergent*: coming from within the organization; *imposed*: coming from markets; *imported*: mimicking international or competitor experience (Anderson and King 1991). In addition, HQ wished to ensure that the reasons for performance improvement were understood:

- most people understood the reasons behind the emergence of these issues;

- unsuccessful attempts had been made to resolve some of the issues in the past;

- the issues affected all parts of the organization and were not isolated to one subunit or division;

- restructuring TranzForm was potentially volatile due to a history of industrial disputation in the industry in some regions. Much of the change was *intended* in that HQ had established goals and strategies for improving productivity, reducing costs, and increasing flexibility. With intended change, it is assumed that the knowledge exists among organizational members concerning what structures or functions need to be changed. Even so, predicting outcomes is difficult and is always associated with a high degree of uncertainty and risk.

Before these strategies were modified, HQ had become 'stuck in the middle' by not clearly differentiating cost and quality from its competitors. Using Porter's (1985) framework, the management of TranzForm chose cost leadership as a principal strategy, which is one of the least ambiguous actions that they could employ at the time. With this strategy, HQ developed a competitive advantage. TranzForm provided services at lower operating costs than its competitors, thus making larger profits. HQ also used lower prices so as to capture a larger share of the market.

TranzForm, before its transformation, was characterized as rationally focused, which led to a number of negative outcomes for TranzForm.

Table 8.7 The interrelationship between managerial practices and outcomes

Managerial practices	Outcomes
Managed functionality	Failure to see new ideas
Overprotective of the base business at all costs	Business base eroded
Judged future solely on past experience	Inappropriate decisions about competition and markets
Rewarded uniformity rather than diversity and innovation	Loss of innovation
Promoted individuals compatible with managerial philosophy	Low commitment

Contributing factors to change

There were a number of changes influencing Tranz-Form to re-think its current strategy. In addition to change in its external context, a number of internal factors (see Table 8.5 and depicted in Figure 8.7) were perceived as affecting the current future performance of TranzForm. These factors are grouped into 'driving' and 'restraining' forces.

TranzForm needed to become more strategically focused. Most people viewed the change as 'frame breaking' or 'quantum' rather than incremental since they expected the changes to result in a definite improvement in the company's market position and new business opportunities. TranzForm HQ perceived themselves to be under immediate threat and so the *rate of change* was very rapid. Many reforms took place very quickly, in parallel rather than sequentially, sometimes in a matter of weeks, which in the past might have taken years to achieve. New ideas and techniques for project development and management and organizational restructuring emerged quickly. Given the difficult financial period the company had experienced in the late 1980s, change could not be ignored or avoided by HQ and was viewed as *strong*. The *coupling* of change was evident in that many modifications had to be dealt with simultaneously.

Adjustment to change

In the case of TranzForm, HQ reassessed their basic assumptions about strategy, style, and context and reflected this in new workplace practices. TranzForm had to re-frame itself in terms of its past in order to incorporate the new perspective. The success of the organizational change programme at TranzForm is attributed to the following factors:

- the articulation of a corporate philosophy which is now linked to the realities of the marketplace and their business strategies;

- the introduction of a collaborative rather than confronting, managerial approach;

- introduction of business units which flatten the organization and keep project teams small, facilitating feedback to individual members;

- learning and investigation of ideas cutting across traditional functional lines in the organization.

HQ and most of the workers at TranzForm appreciated the extent of organizational change retrospectively. Change did not occur as a continuous, incremental process. TranzForm people viewed the overhaul of the company as *radical*. 'Innovation radicalness can be defined in terms of existing alternatives: the more an innovation differs from the existing alternatives, the higher is its degree of radicalness' (Zaltman *et al.* 1973: 23). This points to the importance of context and an appreciation of change is always relative to historical events and people's experiences. Change is predominantly a *perceptual phenomenon*, in that individual accounts of it provide a context for what change means in particular situations.

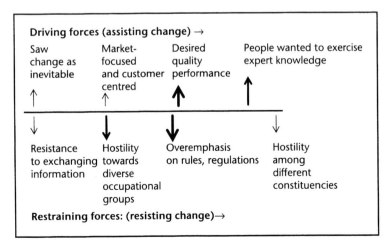

Fig. 8.7 Forces affecting change

The essence of change is the process of transformation between such modes, so that one or more forms of knowledge predominate over others at different stages in the change process. Secondly, the perception of the pace of change varies from one organization to another and one business sector to another (Grinyer and Spender 1979). What was a quantum change for TranzForm may not be for an organization in either the same industry sector or in a different one. Thirdly, the management of change is a 'process of continuing readjustment and negotiation' (Gerson 1976: 800).

What is important in managing organizational change is that constituents (managers and workers) learn to recognize a network of processes that are in a continuous state of interaction and need to be dealt with simultaneously. For purposes of convenience, these are categorized into three processes: innovation, transformation, and preservation. The extent to which each process exists in any setting depends on the organizational context.

8.11.1 Innovation

Innovation has three components: invention, adoption of change, new idea or practice independent of adoption (Zaltman *et al.* 1973). Innovation cannot exist without some aspects of the 'old order' being retained otherwise management loses credibility and there is no foundation on which to start afresh. The innovation process is aimed at ensuring that organizational members are given the opportunity to be as creative as possible. Issues concerning innovation include:

- How do new ideas emerge? Are there processes to channel these ideas to management?
- Are organizational members aware of the new ideas?
- Are organizational members provided with an opportunity to understand the advantages of changing existing processes?

Steps for encouraging innovation include:

- developing practices that stimulate new thinking from all members of the organization;

- demonstrating interest in all aspects of the business;
- investing in skill formation to ensure that workers are exposed to new ideas;
- holding regular brainstorming sessions and not referring to them as planning sessions;
- instigating an incentive scheme for new ideas that are actually implemented;
- devising an innovation audit which each supervisor completes on a quarterly basis including information about source and nature of ideas, context, and so on;
- allowing staff a period of study leave for investigating new ideas either internally or externally in the organization;
- arranging a parade of experts to visit the organization on a regular basis and allowing a cross-section of workers to meet with them.

8.11.2 Transformation

It is important that any form of organizational change has a purpose. Stakeholders need to understand the purpose of the change and gain a worthwhile stake in the process and outcomes. Resistance to change is minimized if transformation is conducted appropriately. Transformation is a process which allows managers to deal with passing from one phase to another phase in the organizational life cycle. It is important that change is as little disruptive as possible.

Steps that are important in transformation include:

- debating a vision by ensuring a representative 'voice' for various organizational constituencies;
- piloting a programme in action so that everyone can view and/or experience how it works and what the outcomes are;
- devising realistic and simple processes for providing information and eliciting opinion from organizational constituencies;
- devising an easy and direct route for feedback;
- arranging involvement strategies to promote participation.

8.11.3 **Preservation**

The organization cannot be preserved at any cost otherwise it will decline with few opportunities for new learning to emerge. Too many managers spend time changing the organization only to find that they eroded the best parts of it including the people they lost (actually and metaphorically) in the process. The problem with managing change is the uncertainty of it including its disruption and whether the organization will be any better off as a consequence.

Steps in considering preserving aspects of organization include:

- ascertaining from all organizational members what they think they do best and what they think the organization does best;

- requesting workers to identify what aspects associated with the planned change are likely to disrupt them, and how best this can be minimized.

All these factors can support the existing status quo but equally advance initiatives towards organizational change. Successful change and improvement initiatives need to be total and integrated rather than partial and fragmented. Enhancement to the business flows from the organization's basic reason for being, from its values, its vision of the future and its strategies. The effort is intertwined with the business's operating goals, systems, and measurements. These changes and improvements are not appendages to the organization, rather they are integral to it. They are tightly intertwined and connected with management systems, daily practices, and behaviour. It should be apparent that managing change is about cultural change in a business and for this reason a more detailed discussion of change management is provided in Chapter 10 with a particular focus on *resistance to change*. Readers should now for themselves seek to:

- define and interpret the problems outlined in the case;

- set goals for problem-solving;

- utilize the principles outlined in the chapter;

- draw upon their own learning (i.e. their 'theories-in-use') (Argyris 1990);

- reinterpret the problem;

- appreciate constraints;

- prescribe resolution processes and consequences of each;

- decide upon a course of action.

Discussion issues for Chapter 8

1   What is the difference between the terms *supply chain management* and *logistics management*?

2   What is the significance of the phrase 'supply chain management' for (*a*) transport organizations and (*b*) logistics organizations?

3   What structural designs are most compatible for supply chain management networks?

4   Under what conditions might you expect strategy to exert a significant influence on structure?

5   What is the conventional perspective of change in organizations?

6   What does 'planned' change mean as opposed to unplanned change? What are the implications of each approach for organizations?

7   Why is resistance to change so apparent in organizations? Review the various approaches for dealing with resistance to change in two organizations that you are familiar with.

9 Knowing your business culture

9.1 Introduction

As already suggested in Chapter 8, the development of an appropriate relationship is central to supply chain management. Relationships can be based on a long-standing or transitory relationship depending on whether it is the sharing of resources, costs, and/or access to one another's markets, as well as the amount of trust that exists among the stakeholders. Relationships are structured by how people think, feel, and act in organizations. This process does not occur by chance and is strongly influenced by 'how the organization does things'. The aim of this chapter is to consider culture, the 'conundrum' of organizations in terms of its real impact on structural and operational characteristics and, in turn, how these impact business relationships and outcomes.

9.2 Effective cultures

The culture of a business is usually considered on a continuum of effectiveness. As Senge (1990) notes, the relationship of vision (the intended direction for the organization) and the current reality generates conflict. A great deal of the conflict that surrounds organizational change occurs as a consequence of the difference between the values, norms, and artefacts that emerges among various groups and often leads to intergroup and intragroup discord. Effectiveness is often the outcome of the extent to which conflicting values shape the culture that gives rise to organizational change which is either innovative at one extreme or unstable at the other. In that sense, it is often easier to describe what an ineffective culture is rather than an effective one. An ineffective culture is characterized as:

- a function of inconsistent assumptions and values and poor group process;

- reinforcing certain values that are deeply imbedded in enterprise thinking which form a barrier to the contribution and further development of its membership;

- not utilizing process skills of organizational members to conduct meetings, solve problems, and make decisions.

An ineffective culture is a function of poorly designed systems that are an inevitable result of erroneous perceptions of causality (Senge 1990). This type of culture leads to a non-learning organization, which is full of design irrationalities by virtue of its managers not being able to overcome the limitations of cognitive biases through systems thinking. From a managerial perspective, these issues are crucial to the effective running of a business enterprise. If the culture of various groups within an enterprise, including management, prevents requisite change taking place, it is essential that management understand the nature of these conflicting values in order to correct the problems so as to unify the direction in which the business wishes to go. A number of value-sets are outlined as follows to provide some idea of the differences that can occur among stakeholders:

Strategic values: Strategic values guide the development of the business strategy for navigating markets, consumers, and customers. Strategic values are instrumental in the conception of the supply chain, organizing resources and people, structuring operations and service delivery. Business strategy and actions communicate to workers which values are significant in the organization and which are not (i.e. as appraised by senior management). Strategic values need to demonstrate consistency with the values held by members of the organization.

Business value: A business value-set is a set of coherent assumptions that underpin strategic decision-making, planning, budgeting, scheduling, and the management of people. Business philosophy is an example of an organizational value that informs the vision, mission, and goals. As described above, organizations represent multi-cultural contexts and specific values are reflected in each subculture. For example, business values represent a powerful belief system within an enterprise, indicating processes such as 'how to manage' and 'how to compete' within the work organization (Davis 1984). The belief systems are mirrored in how managers structure the authority and work relationships within the enterprise as well as external relationships. For example, compare the distinct value sets underlying logistics management including human resources, operations and marketing, and transport which are usually organized as distinct functions or functional silos (Christopher 1998). In most organizations today, the reality of integrating functional silos is self-evident. The difficulty is achieving this assimilation.

Market versus clan values: The 'market' culture is an example of a dynamic network (see Ch. 8) which emphasizes the need to respond rapidly to customer demand as opposed to the 'clan' culture, which stresses identity, trust, and support (Ouchi 1981) within the enterprise. The market-based culture assumes expertise and autonomy, and is more likely to emphasize learning and development, appraising and rewarding workers based on merit. A market-based culture emphasizes inequalities between the competing factions within the organization. On the other hand, a clan-based culture assumes collaboration and is based on identity, trust, and support, and emphasizes the importance of workers belonging to the team. A clan-based belief system de-emphasizes differences between individuals and groups within the organization, and is more conductive to active participation, consultation, and commitment. A clan culture is more significant in developing and supporting teamwork. The challenge for management is to integrate market and clan value-sets into a single business culture to exploit the benefits of each one. This cultural integration is also needed within the supply chain network so that SC partners see that they are acting in a unified direction.

Professional values: A professional culture (Mintzberg 1979) is based on a value-set that emphasizes control over knowledge or a skill domain (e.g. marketing versus logistics, human resource management versus finance). Professional values also symbolize the democratic processes that key interest groups in the enterprise expect. The implications of this is a greater requirement for worker participation, negotiation, and mediation instead of a reliance solely on authoritative command. Professional workers expect to act autonomously requiring a greater need for integrative processes to ensure that they act in unison with the organization. Most organizations contain professional subcultures. Frequently, rewards in these types of organizations are distributed equally according to criteria such as customer numbers and not according to the personal efforts of the individual worker. The conflict that emerges in this context often relates to effort-reward ratios in that some people feel that their contribution is greater than others, deserving a greater share of the rewards. While most professional workers accept or are resigned to the organizational culture in which they work, they still may differ with the business value-set and strategy. When this occurs, the 'professional worker' acts as a 'cosmopolitan' whose only real loyalty is self or occupational which detracts from the overriding business values. In other words, the expertise, autonomy, and values of the profession enable them to engage in making a choice between their professional values and those of the business (Withey and Cooper 1989).

Control values: Control values are centralized and located in a range of operational activities including the logistics strategy, performance strategy, human resource management strategy, promotional strategy, and so on. In particular, they also define the development strategy, rewards and incentives, communication patterns, work design, and business planning. All these activities are designed by management to promote the compliance of workers. When workers do not conform to the expectations of management, they are excluded or viewed as peripheral to the organization. Marginal membership of workers has a negative impact on performance.

Work design values: Work design values apply to the inherent assumptions used by management and others in the design, introduction, and implementation of tasks and technology used by workers in their workplaces. Appropriate work design bestows a degree of control on the worker without a sense of delegation, and leads to consistent action from workers. This is a form of indirect control as opposed to direct control (i.e. supervisory control)

Work values are either personally held by individual workers or collectively shared by a subgroup based on functional, gender, or other value-sets. At the personal level, work values refer to the extent to which individual workers feel that personal worth results from self-sacrificing work or occupational achievement (Blood 1969), that is, the individual work ethic. At the collective level, the work ethic

provides a framework for how members of the workforce view and approach working, and incorporate goals, standards, and beliefs that members use to preserve and justify their interests as a work and/or professional group. The work or enterprise ethic is important in understanding the manner in which the workforce responds to management and the organization overall (Aldag and Brief 1975). When the enterprise ethic is not congruent with the personal work ethic of workers, conflict is likely to occur. The outcome of conflicting values is reduced commitment from the workforce.

In designing work, managers make assumptions about workers' interests and intentions. For example, workplaces have been typically designed on the basis that workers are able-bodied, work in an environment that is relatively free of distress, have little knowledge of the technical aspects of the job, and are not interested in controlling the work processes. This approach is evident by the way work and technologies have been designed to date. Further evidence of this is found in the lack of emphasis in workplace design for workers with disabilities -or work schedules that facilitate combining work and family responsibilities for both women and men.

Rarely are work design assumptions stated explicitly. For example, an attempt to monitor workers by getting a computerized database to record work output (e.g. record the rate of picks in a warehouse) is usually couched in terms of improving work efficiency. Frequently, work is designed in a specific way because of the type of worker who is likely to perform it, such as a female word processor, a male fork-lift driver, and so on. Similarly, managers are no longer able to discriminate on the grounds of physical strength and aptitude, cognitive capacity, and age unless it is clearly demonstrated that one or more of these characteristics are an essential requirement of the work to be performed. Obviously, work design values that deny the competencies of workers have a negative impact on performance.

In summary, these value-sets have a significant impact on the way managers structure the enterprise, its business, and work. To demonstrate this, consider how organizational positions are labelled in organizations. Organizational positions are decided by external, strategic, work design, and control values. These values structure the 'internal labour market' of the organization such as the worker's job title, hierarchical position, nature and processes of the work, location, and tenure, for example, whether permanent or contract. They are a significant part of enterprise culture.

9.3 **The structure of business culture**

The culture of an enterprise shapes the behaviour, and hence performance, of its management and people, their needs and demands, and the way it understands and manages the external environment. In theory, culture encompasses the sum total of values, traditions, and priorities that characterize how the business is conducted in a particular context. In particular it specifies:

- goals and values of management, employees, and work groups;
- appropriate organizational relationships between individuals and groups;
- how performance is shaped organizationally;
- the qualities and skills of employees that are valued or not and how these are sanctioned;
- the appropriate interface between the enterprise and external environment.

As previously stated, organizations 'like persons, have values and these values are integrated into some coherent value system . . . in any organisation, the members generally have a set of beliefs about what is appropriate and inappropriate organisational behaviour' (Goodstein 1983: 203–4). These beliefs are communicated explicitly and implicitly. Culture provides a shorthand definition for how both management, workers, customers, and competitors view the relationship. Knowing your business culture provides important insights into, for example, corporate and business strategy, operational processes, the adjustment of the workforce to enterprise change performance management, and why some strategic partnerships and supply chain networks are successful while others are not. The structure of culture is outlined in Table 9.1 and provides some examples of cultural artefacts, norms, and values and demonstrates their 'observability' in a specific context.

These layers of culture need to be analysed in order to understand enterprise performance behaviour.

9.3.1 **Artefacts**

Artefacts refer to the tangible and intangible aspects that represent organizational life. Examples of 'tangible artefacts' are the architectural design of the building and its physical location, the layout of the organization including where senior management are located, the design of the office, the depot, the warehouse and distribution centre, corporate colours, emblems, and advertising slogans. Examples of 'intangible artefacts' are managerial style, communication patterns, the way performance and conflict are managed and rewarded, decision-making processes, and so on. Cultural artefacts such as the nature of operational and technological systems, internal design and layout of facilities, and management systems shape the conditions for interactions and participation within the organization.

9.3.2 **Norms**

Norms transmit past, present, and future values and behavioural codes of the organization, and its management philosophy, and are powerful ways for workers to assimilate their experiences at work. They are important but frequently overlooked aspects of culture in organizations as they form the unwritten rules of workers, work groups, and the organization. Norms are no less significant in terms of influencing

Table 9.1 The levels of culture

Observability	Cultural element	Technique used
Directly observable	Artefacts	Observation • symbols of power relationships between people and functions • language structures • stories and heroes • rituals
	Norms	Questioning • What are the unwritten rules of behaviour? • What are the meanings of the stories and symbols? • What happens to those who violate the norm?
Difficult to observe directly	Values	Inference • What values are inferred by the stories, rituals, language, symbols, and norms?

Source: Adapted from Schein (1986).

workers than the formal or official culture. In terms of organization and commitment, norms are continuously evolving and emerge out of the interaction of co-workers, managers, and workers, and include friendship networking and on-the-job experience. Unlike the formalized dimensions, which are more readily controlled by management, norms are not easily imposed, and are very much invoked by situational demands.

Organizational stories are one of the key vehicles for diffusing norms. People share stories at work and like any other form of story-telling, they are structured in time within context, intention, characters, and action. Stories do not have to be factual. Stories come complete with plot, characters, and meaning. Sometimes a story is part of an ongoing saga within the work context and subsequently may not contain a resolution to the issue or dilemma contained within it. People draw on the meanings of stories,

with a strong impact on subsequent attitudes of organizational members. Understanding the evolution of stories within a given context is insightful in terms of artefacts, norms, and values.

9.3.3 Values

Value-sets (discussed above) determine 'what is' and 'what ought to be', such as how work is and should be organized; how supervisors act and how they should act; how workers interact and how they should interact; what kinds of rewards and sanctions exist and what should exist. Even when workers hold views about 'what is' and 'what should be', these are not always consciously expressed (Schwartz 1990). Indeed, the strongest aspects of value-set are internalized and not usually expressed.

9.4 The process of enterprise culture

Enterprise culture is a process of reinforcing social relationships by giving them substance and direction, and involves several related processes such as:

• acculturation: combining or blending of existing values with new ones;

• diffusion: cultural borrowing, the spread of cultural customs or practices;

- strength and weaknesses of culture;
- innovation: adoption of a new idea, policy, practice, technique; and/or the substitute of a former practice for an innovation;
- facilitators and inhibitors of cultural change.

Each cultural element, artefact, norm, and value influences the cognitive, emotional, and behavioural status of people working together.

9.4.1 Acculturation

Perhaps the most significant element of enterprise culture is its value-sets. Acculturation, the process of blending new business values with existing ones, is significant in influencing how customers, managers, workers, new and old, come to perceive the business. In many organizations, there are preferred characteristics that shape business values (Morgan 1986). For example, some businesses place more emphasis on costs than quality, others on control, information-sharing, and yet others on operational processes. Apart from the specific emphasis, customers are foremost in management's mind when cultural innovations are planned. The success and failure of the business and its programme are defined in terms of these preferred characteristics or 'shared value' systems. For example, technological supremacy may underlie many business cultures and strategies today. Reliability translated into frequency, on-time performance, and safety is a further example of corporate values underpinning business strategy in transport and logistic organizations. These preferred characteristics are epitomized in the ease of transporting people, service-products, and freight from one destination to another; or in response time throughout the supply chain. These value systems are subsequently translated into operational strategies of innovation, reliability, and efficiency that distinguish businesses with strong market positions from weak ones.

9.4.1.1 Becoming part of the enterprise culture

The important outcome of acculturation for both new and existing workers is a sense of continuing attachment to the organization through their membership within it. Acculturation involves a personal contract being negotiated (and continuously renegotiated) that is largely psychological and is based on the expectation that individual workers not only 'play fair' but also contribute extraordinary effort in order to achieve better than usual outcomes in the workplace. Workers also translate 'correct' codes of conduct into action without a great deal of consideration.

Identification with the organization, and internalization of the organization's values and goals are central to organizational commitment (Meyer *et al.* 1989). The extent to which a worker identifies and internalizes organizational values is particularly critical to individual behaviour that is not prescribed and controlled by management. In other words, organizational value systems assist workers to appreciate what management regards as important which in turn assists the reliability of enterprise performance.

A further example where performance reliability is paramount is in aviation and air traffic control. This example shows how a shared value system is diffused over time through the actions of those who participate in it. Air traffic controllers work in a highly programmed context making judgements within it. Any highly automated system like air traffic control can fail with little forewarning. This type of system failure is termed a 'normal accident' (Perrow 1984). When it is understood how common 'normal accidents' are, it is recognized why failures in quality and safety occur. At the point of system failure, controllers are impelled to intervene by making sense of what is going on and following this up with non-routine decisions. Intervention of that kind requires skilled interpretation and a full comprehension of the complexity of the situation as well as commitment to the business values and chain of command. Deciding what to do is easy, it is making sure that the operator understands the underlying context that is difficult. The predicament of air traffic control has parallels in every type of business enterprise where systems are employed.

On the face of it and logically, performance reliability appears to be a favoured characteristic for many transport and logistics businesses. However, transport businesses that hold reliability as a shared value are complicated to manage. The reason for this is that first, transport businesses are complex, operating in dynamic contexts where rules, regulations, and performance standards are rapidly superseded by financial, technological, regulatory, and industrial changes. Secondly, businesses that value reliability are often slow to anticipate, respond, and learn from these changes with grim consequences for business performance. Often the reason for a lagged response to change is that reliability is more often than not incompatible with experimentation, feedback of information, and new learning. For example, think of a situation where the chief executive officer (CEO) of a rail corporation decides to test train schedules resulting in variability in time running followed by widespread commuter grievance, which is subsequently given unfavourable media coverage. A rail corporation will think twice before engaging in this type of experimentation again.

Consequently, culture has a powerful socializing influence on workers: 'To put it briefly, the individual ceases to be himself; he adopts entirely the kind of personality offered to him by cultural patterns; and he therefore becomes exactly as all others are and as they expect him to be' (Fromm 1941: 209).

What Fromm is describing is not an extreme form of 'cloning', rather the process of acculturation whereby individual workers come to appreciate the values, abilities, expected behaviours, and knowledge needed for assuming membership and participation in their places of work. 'I am a railway man' is the classic outcome in transportation.

Acculturation is a source of conflict for most workers as it involves not only a 'loss of self-identity' but also an assumed 'gain in security'. A complete 'loss of self-identity' results in a worker becoming a clone of the organization with diffused obligations and rights. On the whole, workers resist the organization 'cloning them' and where there is evidence of this, it is more likely to be accompanied today by a reduced loyalty to the business. The age of the 'organization person' complying with every managerial dictate is diminished. The 'loss of self' is fought against by most individuals and is contrasted with 'losing one-

self' denoting enhancement of self-identity whereby individuals are engaged in autonomous work that they enjoy and which, in turn, provides them with a sense of competence.

The discussion on acculturation points to the inner conflict felt by most workers employed in enterprises at some time in their career. Initially at least, most workers are concerned about 'fitting in' at work, without losing their self-identity, and in order to achieve this they frequently deny their self-interests. A denial of self-interests potentially results in latent conflict (Lukes 1974). Latent conflict occurs when the real interests of the least powerful groups in the workplace are not addressed. It is accompanied by workers' expectations that the existing cultural beliefs and values of the enterprise will somehow take their interests into account. The very nature of the employment relationship suggests some desire by workers for a social as well as psychological attachment to their enterprise. And if they do not find connection with the organization, they are likely to explore alternative employment options where possible, or seek contentment outside of work. Developing a culture that workers can identify with is important for attracting and maintaining competent workers.

9.4.2 Diffusion of culture

The culture of an enterprise is created and sustained through the interpersonal relationships that individuals have with each other, with work groups, other organizations, and the community. The nature of business culture is also influenced by an array of factors including:

- relationships with co-workers and supervisors,
- policies, rules, and regulations,
- behavioural norms (unwritten rules),
- leadership,
- business strategy.

Management communicates the business strategy in a way that generates commitment among workers. In organizations, some types of information are communicated easily using explicit terms such as articulating the rationale for a specific strategy, budget cuts, redundancies, and so on. Often statistics and other information can support such decisions. Workers require explicit information in times of organizational change, even though it may be misunderstood. However, due to the time involved and the expected level of immediate acceptance by organizational members, it is difficult to communicate explicitly about the:

- assumptions and values of the organization,
- preference for specific work methods over others, and
- managerial philosophy.

Explicit forms of communication are less useful when a strategy has few obvious positive benefits, and particularly when it has negative consequences. For example, when a strategy is viewed as costly in terms of time or money or both, it is frequently perceived as negative. A good example of this is worker training where the resources invested cannot always be immediately equated with outcome, except in a generalized way after a delayed period of time. In this case, the rationale for engaging in such a strategy emphasizes morale rather than financial factors such as worker welfare programmes. In these situations, managers often rely on implicit or symbolic forms of communication, because these are more charismatic in communicating strategic values and intentions.

Much of the enterprise culture is understood through the implicit information that serves to transmit what is called 'tacit knowledge' (Polanyi 1966) as opposed to rational knowledge. Harrison (1987) is often cited for the rational model, while Nonaka and Takeuchi (1995) are often cited for tacit models. Rational knowledge is the reliance on facts, data, procedures, and formulas—this type of knowledge is often termed 'expert knowledge'. While management has a prescribed decision-making protocol to be followed, more often decisions are made and problems solved on the basis of tacit knowledge. Tacit knowledge is difficult to measure and observe, but it plays a major role in most business decisions.

Today, it is more likely to be referred to as knowledge management, the kind of knowledge that is in workers' heads rather than in systems, although many intranet systems are seeking to harness and share tacit knowledge (i.e. knowledge transfer) within the enterprise. The transfer of knowledge is an essential process for global supply chain networks in terms of gaining efficiency and effectiveness enhancements (i.e. value management). In other words, knowledge transfer is a crucial dimension of value management.

How is tacit knowledge accessed? Tacit knowledge, often referred to as 'corporate memory', is powerful in terms of tapping practical knowledge and skills that have been developed by people only after spending a long time working in the business. It is this type of knowledge that makes it difficult for 'old-timers' to accept 'new blood' into the business. Tacit knowledge is vital to understand when introducing cultural change discussed below. Mostly, workers acquire culture, beliefs, managerial philosophy, and policies through implicit forms of communication, such as rituals. Ritual, ceremony, and most often, workplace humour are examples of expressive activities. Often what visibly occurs is not as meaningful as the implicit communication that underlies it. Thus, workers use expressive activities as a way of communicating ideas that are not easily articulated or quantified. Analysing expressive activities is a way of realizing tacit assumptions shared by members of the organization.

9.4.3 The strength and weakness of organizational culture

As values, norms, and artefacts are diffused throughout the organization, the culture will influence people in varying ways, strongly or weakly. Culture allows management to create a relatively comparable set of values, beliefs, and interests throughout the organization. A number of factors influence the form and strength of business culture including the:

- philosophical heritage of the organization, particularly in government, military, family-run institutions;

- personal beliefs of the 'founder' and the subsequent frequency and form of articulation;

- homogeneous set of assumptions about 'success' and 'failure';

- shared premises of policy and decision-making;

- compatibility of managerial style with the nature of the business and sector;

- psychological climate of the business.

Enterprise culture is considered 'strong' when communication coordinates and reinforces all these factors listed. A strong culture does not have to rely on a highly centralized, bureaucratic approach and can follow from a decentralized structure that facilitates rapid delegation and empowerment. The guiding principles are the shared assumptions that become central to worker performance (Deal and Kennedy 1982), particularly at times when the 'system fails'. To the extent that similar ideologies and norms are held in common throughout the business, the culture is considered a strong one (Saffold 1988) and is reflected in expressed action.

'Strong shared values provide individuals with a sense of success and fulfilment, a healthy (less cynical) assessment of the values and ethics of their colleagues, subordinates, and bosses, and a greater regard for organisational objectives and significant organisational constituents' (Posner *et al.* 1985). Market, clan-based, and professional cultures are examples of this, discussed earlier.

In contrast to a strong culture, a weak culture is one that is not widely shared by all groups of workers throughout the organization. A culture is also weakened when the dominant beliefs and structures have remained unchanged for a period of time, and the commitment to them is inconsequential for various reasons. When managing change, which is most of the time, it is useful to understand and even exploit the weakness in the organizational culture. A weakened culture presents an opportunity for new learning. How do the members of a business process new values, ideas, and knowledge?

9.4.4 Enterprise innovation

Cultural innovation concerns the adoption of a new idea, policy, practice, technique, and replaces a former practice or process. Cultural innovation is defined as the increased capacity to introduce new ideas and practices in the future within the same organization. Innovation depends on the flexibility of organizational memory and the extent of 'tacit' knowledge in the organization (Polanyi 1966). Tacit knowledge (defined earlier) is that knowledge and skill which is learnt on the job and is part of being a member of a particular organization and rarely acknowledged by management. Tacit knowledge is usually identified after it is has 'eroded'. For example, when a job is redesigned or a person leaves the organization, the knowledge or skill that the worker had is often lost. Organizations have difficulty in recovering past knowledge or skills, resulting in an impaired culture.

One of the main vehicles for cultural innovation is organizational learning. Organizational learning is a slow process simply because businesses, if they are highly centralized, retard their workers in processing new information, ideas, and knowledge. The structure of the business inhibits learning by inappropriate communication, information, and feedback channels. When businesses eventually integrate new learning, knowledge becomes institutionalized into rituals, protocols, and procedures that are difficult to transform with any degree of haste. Managers and workers tend to fixate on whatever knowledge has become institutionalized and often overlook the fact that new challenges require different knowledge and work practices. This is where a strong culture can be a liability for current members of the organization. In any situation, the role of culture is a significant tool of organizational change.

The fundamental dilemma for an organization is the maintenance versus development of its business and people. On the one hand, the continuing development of organizations depends on various changes in managerial strategies and processes that cannot be effected without the support and contribution of individual workers. Management's role is to introduce change to the organization so as to bring about a better fit between the business, its context, and customers. On the other hand, part of the management role is to restore and maintain the equilibrium of the organization and to assist workers to adjust to environmental demands such as changes in economic, financial, technological, and political arenas.

Over a period of time, the business and its workers develop an established set of relations with the context in which they operate. They learn how to deal with one another, how to perform their jobs, and what to expect next. A sense of equilibrium is reached at least for a brief period of time until unintentional sources of change emerge both externally and internally to the organization. A wide variety of forces such as competition and the pace of technological change bring about change to the business, affecting its core and sub-core parts. Many of these forces are random and clustered, increasingly rapid. Examples of this include e-commerce, systems for integrating functions, and organizations such as alliances.

9.4.5 Facilitators and inhibitors of cultural change

The emergence of conflicting values is often a signal for change. Cultural change relies on the appropriate responses of all business stakeholders in the organization. Each stakeholder or group of stakeholders needs to have their interests addressed in any change in any one of the following three modes:

- experience, experiment, reflection, and learning;
- participate actively and authentically, and in so doing enhance their competence, and
- contribute to the 'commonality', minimizing the personal risk as far as possible.

In thinking about issues which facilitate or block cultural change, it is important to consider how cultural change is introduced, implemented, and worked through in a specific context. The processes of how people think collectively need to be understood. Conflict becomes apparent among various stakeholders, that is, individuals, coalitions, or interest groups. For a variety of reasons, people feel threatened by proposed or emergent change and experience intense feelings of conflict. Of what value is an understanding of deeply ingrained feelings about change and conflict in organizations? It is often assumed that such feelings are outside anyone's personal control.

Since most of what management does today concerns managing change, which relies on the commitment of workers, planned cultural change relies on selling, persuading, and confronting workers. In viewing many experiences of organizational change, rarely is it viewed as collaborative by all stakeholders. Managers refer to it as consulting, informing, and advising. Changing the organization often results in a milieu characterized by defensiveness and feelings of insecurity. It is always difficult for people to move away from supporting what they are used to, the status quo. It is even more complex for them to say why they support the status quo, so reasons remain unconscious or unspoken, inferences are implicit or covered up, and conclusions subjected to personal and not collective evaluation. Defensiveness leads to a distortion of information, which is not necessarily intended by any one person or group. This problem is hard to diagnose and label because it involves huge personal risks in an organizational context, which is usually low on trust. Most people are aware when others are misleading them. One way of dealing with defensive thinking is through making personal accusations against another, which are denied, ignored, or challenged. In turn, threat or embarrassments are dealt with by striving to disregard realities, and by disguising the way in which these have been ignored. If no one challenges the duplicity, the defensive reasoning that people use to protect themselves now becomes acceptable and eventually entrenched in organizational practices and policies (Argyris 1990). A vicious cycle starts of which everyone is aware but which they negate. This process is unproductive and renders a particular change programme unsuccessful.

9.5 Resistance to cultural change

People desiring planned cultural change often attribute lack of success to 'resistance to change'. In this case, the instigators of change focus on resistance so as to manage it. For example, the type and amount of information provided to employees, the opportunity for employees to participate in decision-making, and the nature of the change leadership, whether directive or facilitative (Handy 1986) are ways of minimizing resistance once it has emerged. Sometimes the management of change becomes the symptomatic treatment of the negative response to the way change is introduced. All these processes are worthwhile and so there is nothing wrong in proceeding in this way, but they are akin to 'damage control' practices. In other words, it demonstrates a very hollow understanding of organizational processes, particularly of the reasons underlying the obstruction of change. People will oppose change if they are already resistant towards management. The dilemma for change agents is that, without a deeper understanding and analysis of what is going on in each business context where change is being introduced, resistance snowballs and is difficult to undo.

Individual workers and groups respond in particular ways to protect their 'own territory'. Sometimes people would like to deal with the issues more openly but feel restrained for various reasons (e.g. to protect their organizational position) and consequently avoid bringing it to a head so as not to upset others or be labelled troublemakers. When people avoid the issues long enough, their response becomes part of a repertoire of action that is repeated over and over. At this point, it becomes difficult to unravel the defensive action. Defensive routines differ from individual defensiveness in that they persist as specific organizational patterns with the coming and departing of individuals and groups due to the significance of acculturation described above.

Organizational patterns based on defensive responses lead people into feeling a double bind, which is characterized by:

- contradictory practices, communications, and strategies;

- managers and workers acting as if they are unaware of the contradiction;

- unawareness means that people find it difficult to broach since they know people will deny it and they run the risk of being made the scapegoat;

- if someone finds the courage to raise the contradiction, it is denied and so becomes further avoided;

- the outcome of the double bind is that people feel powerless;

- people fear discussing their lack of control and become cynical, helpless, or hostile;

- distrust and condemnation when one group introduces change over another, leading to observed resistance heightening these feelings.

Defensive routines form an enduring pattern of behaviour in the organization. Since cultural assumptions are acquired through acculturation, people are usually unaware of their effect on their actions. It is only when the diversity of culture is apparent in organizations that people are confronted with different assumptions and become aware of the way in which business culture influences performance. Unravelling performance problems has important implications for how information and knowledge is shared in the workplace.

Dealing with the outcomes of defensive thinking is far less manageable than preventing the cycle that contributes to organizational defensiveness. Examples of contributing factors include:

- over-tolerance for errors without resolution;

- misperceptions that others condone;

- false assumptions that are accepted without question;

- unproductive conflicts that persist over time;

- poor judgement by management and workers.

Table 9.2 Cycle of defensive thinking in organizations

Underlying culture	Projected culture	Organizational outcomes
• flawed assumptions • inadequate information • incorrect data • ambiguous information • internal conflicts	• oversimplified beliefs • relying on stereotypes • biased appraisal • impulsive action • conform to social pressures of stakeholders	• confused direction • issues ignored • disorganization • failed implementation • few zealots with too many lacking commitment to change • lack of cultural diversity • 'promotion ceiling' for both women and men

Source: Based on Argyris (1990).

In other words, if the above factors are understood and managed, there is less likely to be a second cycle of outcomes arising from them. The incidence of defensiveness in organizations is a significant explanation as to why desired outcomes do not eventuate as shown in Table 9.2.

9.6 Organizational learning

Management now appreciates that one of their most important tasks strategically is to create a learning culture, that is, whereby members can explore, even take risks, extend capabilities particularly in relation to customer service. It is important to understand how a business organization *learns* over time, and this includes *unlearning* and *relearning*. How do organizations learn? Can an organization as a whole learn or only people working within it? Organizations learn best by undoing the cycle of defensive thinking as outlined in Table 9.2. The concept of organizational learning (OL) first appeared in the academic literature in the 1970s.

it is clear that organisational learning is not the same thing as individual learning, even when the individuals who learn are members of the organisation. There are too many cases in which organisations know less than their members. There are even cases in which the organisation cannot seem to learn what every member knows. (Argyris and Schon 1978: 8)

While definitions vary by source, OL is conceptualized as a process of critical thinking about events and problems in the total organization. More specifically,

OL is defined as the enhanced capacity of organization members to innovate in the future within the same organizational context (Argyris 1986, 1990; Argyris and Schon 1978).

The philosophy of OL is that it is a frame for cultural change as a precursor to the innovation of business strategies and activities. Organizational culture becomes the pattern of basic assumptions and 'theories-in-use' that a given group has invented, preserved, or transformed in learning to adjust to new events and problems of external adaptation and internal integration (Argyris and Schon 1978; Schein 1992; Smircich 1983b). Organizational cultures are 'sites where [people] make meaning for themselves, and have their meanings shaped' (Fineman 1993: 13). OL views organizations from an anthropological perspective in that, ultimately, 'what the organisation is' dwells inside people's minds, and that consequently effective change management implies cultural change.

9.6.1 The learning process in change management

OL can take different forms. Senge (1990) distinguishes between adaptive and generative learning. Adaptive learning focuses on responding to and coping with environmental demands in an effort to solve immediate problems or make incremental improvements to the organization. A generative learning process is about continuous exploration, systemic rather than fragmented thinking, and a willingness to think beyond the immediate problem context. Others make the distinction between learning by organizations (LBO) and learning in organizations (LIO) (Popper and Lipshitz 1998). LBO refers to an *aggregated outcome* of its members' learning and is basically a metaphor used to account for the fact that organizations seem to 'learn' over time to produce quality and cost-efficient outputs. LIO refers to two notions: single-loop and double-loop learning. Single-loop learning, that is related to business process re-engineering (see Ch. 8), solves obvious problems by correcting errors, redundancies, or deficiencies through redesigning business processes. It may not solve the underlying causes that lead to the emergence of problems and is similar to Senge's adaptive learning.

Table 9.3 summarizes the main differences between organizational learning and business process re-engineering.

Double-loop learning is closer to generative learning as it addresses underlying causes by attempting to alter the logic used by organization members in situations, but usually not openly espoused (Argyris and Schon 1978). In this respect OL does not assume a time-frame for change: it can occur incrementally or radically depending on the extent of the double-loop learning.

Double-loop learning lies at the heart of OL as it requires a different mindset for organizations, principally a collective one. 'Just as individuals process information, so also do groups and units of people. In doing so they develop collective belief systems' (Quinn and McGrath 1985: 325). Collective belief systems reduce the exposure of individuals and hence the subsequent risk of scapegoating. Double-loop learning relies on 'people who over time engage in transactions with others within an institutional order' (Van de Ven 1986). The emphasis is on the interactive process among organization members and how they respond to problems requiring change. Their response is contingent on how people perceive their stake in the existing (unchanged) organization in the form of self-interest and self-identity. Changing the organization will in some cases enhance their stake and in others reduce it.

Double-loop learning provides the organization with the capacity to envisage fundamentally different possibilities compared to current opportunities by overcoming barriers to self-reinforcing solutions and striving for the less conservative option. When change is perceived as reducing the outcome for a stakeholder, it can lead to defensiveness, increased errors, and self-fulfilling predictions. This is why defensive thinking is most evident at times of

Table 9.3 Comparison of organizational learning (OL) and business process re-engineering (BPR)

OL	BPR
Emergent among members of an enterprise context	Instigated by external agent
Disseminated by a populist (leading to a bottom-up) approach	Disseminated hierarchically (leading to a top-down approach)
Processes and people are interactive	Processes and people are discrete
Detailed organizational analysis inevitable	Organizational analysis not seen as essential
Change is both incremental or radical	Change is revolutionary
Time-consuming	Dependent on rapid results
Stakeholders' interests and identity are considered	Negligible consideration of stakeholders' interests and identity
Action is viewed as non-linear and political	Action is viewed in natural steps

planned change. People find it difficult to articulate the underlying reasons for wanting to retain the status quo; their objectives remain implicit, inferences are covered up, and conclusions are subjected to personal rather than collective evaluation (Argyris 1990). When change is seen as imposed, organization members might distort information to avert the focus of attention so as to protect their stake. Conflict and resistance are likely outcomes. Another way of dealing with defensive thinking is allowing it to pass unchallenged, which condones it; and eventually it becomes entrenched in organizational processes (Argyris 1986). If resistance to change is defensive, it is important to understand defensive thinking and know how to counteract it. Understanding resistance leads to a learning organization that builds a capacity based on 'learning how to learn'. This capacity for learning leads to a high performance organization whereby people have the power to diagnose and minimize barriers to increasing effectiveness. Such members are not limited to the ranks of management; they may be located throughout the organization and will 'multiply' in a learning culture.

Organizational learning is essentially about overcoming defensive thinking by finding ways to reduce the rigidities within the organization and allowing new insights and understandings to emerge about the organization and its future directions. When this is achieved, resistance is minimized. In terms of organizational learning, these central, enduring themes or current visions need to be modified, and in some cases shattered, for new strategies, structures, and processes to emerge in the organization, in other words, for organizational change to occur. This is easier to achieve in a weak culture than in a strong one.

9.6.2 How to distinguish a learning organization from a 'non-learning' one?

Four processes of learning process are considered here labelled distrustful, fragmented, competent, and learning as shown in Figure 9.1.

The matrix in Figure 9.1 is constructed by two continuums. The vertical axis is a continuum based on thinking depicted by two characteristics: individual and collective thinking. Individual thinking is characterized by orthodox learning processes, individual rewards, and competition. Collective thinking is characterized by group processes that when complemented by high engagement are extremely effective for the learning organization as depicted in Figure 9.2. When collective thinking is associated with low engagement this produces a distrustful organization. The horizontal axis is characterized by low and high engagement as outlined in Table 9.4.

Low engagement leads to disillusionment whereby people begin to dissociate themselves from the organization because they believe that managers or

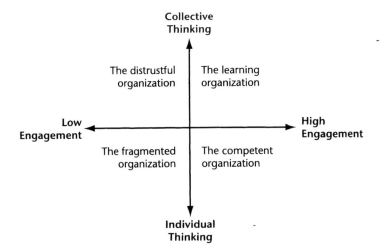

Fig. 9.1 Matrix of organizational learning

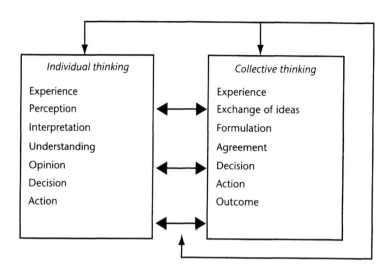

Fig. 9.2 Individual and collective thinking

Table 9.4 A comparison of low and high engagement

Low engagement	High engagement
Managerial prerogative	Shared decision-making processes
Hierarchical control	Team control based on expertise
Individual rewards	Group rewards
Top-down communication	Open, lateral communication
Personal agenda	Shared vision
External controls	Internalized control

co-workers do not support any 'extraordinary' effort from them. Disillusioned workers foster a collective thinking within the organization that is characterized by pessimism, suspicion, distrust, and lack of expectation which is transferred to others, both existing and new workers. An organization characterized by high engagement and collective thinking is creative, flexible, adjusts readily to new circumstances, and members feel a sense of autonomy.

The distrustful organization is based on formality, logic, master-servant relationship, obedience, and 'the one best way' approach to learning that is employed so often in managing people. The organization is directive, leading to contexts where people experience maladjustment, defensiveness, and are highly conservative. There are few risk-takers in this environment. The extent to which individuals engage in learning in distrustful organ-

izations is facilitated or blocked by whether or not they feel a sense of autonomy. In most organizations, it is the values of the management group that predominate in the workplace, and become the core of the learning, or in this case, non-learning culture. When individuals do not accept the values of the dominant management culture, a subculture emerges, taking precedence for them, and to which they align their interests and values.

The fragmented organization is based on a separation of thinking and action. There is a gulf between those people in the organization who are responsible for 'planning' and those who are accountable for 'implementing'. Linked to this, the organization tends to be expedient and not strategic. Training is conducted on an 'as needs' basis rather than integrated into a business strategy. People perceive training as an imposition and not a process which allows them to develop their own learning goals.

The competent organization is based on training and development, adaptability, diligence, and linking skills to business objectives. The competent organization does not subscribe to 'the one best way' approach and subscribes to a contingency approach to learning. A contingency approach attempts to match learning issues with training and development. However, the focus tends to be upon enhancements to immediate practice and pressure points such as performance problems, technological or legislative change, and customer complaints. Often improvements cease when formal training and development programmes have been completed.

The competent organization is based on learning-exchange. While managers depend on the workers for increasing the productivity and profitability of organizations, workers are dependent on managers to maximize their rewards and incentives such as opportunities for learning and skill development. Thus, the nature of the exchange is characterized by each party in the relationship assuming that: 'If I give you something, I want something in return'.

The exchange relationship focuses on competing interests in which there are always 'winners' and 'losers' depending on which party is best able to maximize their control over organizational resources. When learning-exchange is based on 'give and take', workers gain a sense of partial or semi-autonomy. In this case, the worker is more likely to experience a social relationship with managers, based on exchanging resources, trust, and support. Since group membership is still very important for each party, for example, in terms of coopting support when necessary, the worker is less likely to act independently of the main, referent group. Under these conditions, the climate of the workplace is cooperative, and the learning culture is reward-based.

The learning organization is based on continuously learning new ideas and applying them to service delivery and quality. The organization in consultation with its members develops and encourages a vision for continuous learning, which enables people to become self-directive and autonomous in their learning. Through integration, workers take on a different learning concept apart from one based purely on self-interest, and attempt to signify their learning goals through a process of ongoing negotiation. A strategy of integration therefore encourages a 'negotiated order' within the organization (Strauss 1978). After all, negotiation is part of everyday organizational life, and is a process aimed at the maximization of equitable outcomes for the various parties involved. Negotiation allows each person not only to preserve a cohesive, social relationship but also to disagree about inputs and outcomes in the organization without fear of reprisal. This process of 'negotiated order' suggests a sense of equality between managers and workers.

Workers involved in a relationship based on integration experience a sense of working towards a 'commonality' characterized by 'what is good for me is good for the organization'. Integration is similar to what Vaill (1982) referred to as 'gelled' organization which suggests a coherent but flexible enterprise. Managerial practices based on integration are likely to result in high autonomy whereby workers are encouraged to question, voice their opinion, and negotiate agreements with other organizational members. Integration works because it helps workers fulfil their need to control the work they are doing (Karasek 1979) and this is highly motivational. It is increased control that leads to the 'gelling' of worker interests. Integration is consistent with experiencing stability of purpose and action within the organization. Individual workers like to be able to affect the work they do, how they do it, and the conditions surrounding it (Conger and Kanungo 1988).

It is important to make a link between competence and integration. Workers experience autonomy within the work organization when they feel competent to act alone (Baxter 1982). The extent to which managerial strategies strengthen workers' self-determination or control needs is a form of enabling because it enhances their self-efficacy. Integration occurs when managers intentionally assist workers in becoming autonomous learners, thereby removing workplace conditions that lead to feelings of alienation and fragmentation.

The experience of autonomy for workers is felt in one of three ways. One experience is through the freedom to make choices at work in regard to quantity and quality of task output, work design, work times, and scheduling. 'Having a say' over how work is done best describes this form of autonomy. A second experience is through increased responsibility or obligation for carrying out tasks and duties in the organization. 'Feeling the buck stops here' best sums up this type of autonomy. And a third experience is through individual workers closely identifying with the organizational culture in terms of assumptions, beliefs, and values. 'Losing oneself in the organization' best informs this approach. When workers act autonomously, they make independent assessments of the organization and the work situation, and act independently. In this state, workers have little need to conform for the sake of it.

In practice, the distinction between feeling 'semi-autonomous' and 'autonomous' is the difference between workers believing that they 'have to contribute' to the work organization on the one hand, and 'wanting to contribute' on the other. A strategy of integration encourages individual workers 'to want' to contribute in their workplaces. Integration engenders the commitment of workers to organizational norms, values, and practices.

When workers feel autonomous, they believe that they are free to think critically and act independently of their referent group, especially when the situation calls for this. An autonomous response encourages a sense of responsibility and trust in the worker that leads to their commitment. The managerial strategy influences the degree of autonomy experienced by workers to the extent that the organizational structure is relatively flat, relies on expertise, and welcomes active participation. The stronger the organizational values supporting integrity, equality, and collaboration, the more likely it is that integration and commitment characterize the manager-worker relationship.

The implementation of an integration strategy leads to a climate of trust rather than fear, communicative competence rather than lack of communication, and analysis rather than complacency. Integration is based on a psychological climate whereby workers want to participate actively in their work organization, leading to consultation and collaboration with each other in order to achieve a working partnership. A working partnership ensures that workers are mutually engaged at work while retaining personal independence. The balance between mutuality and independence is important for the process of organizational citizenship to work.

A strategy of integration attempts to bring the attitudes of workers in line with those of managers. When this is not achieved, 'many situational changes such as job redesign and organisational development may not affect individuals as [managers] intended' (Ross and Staw 1986). A transport practitioner who uses an integration strategy is most likely to behave as shown in Table 9.5.

9.6.3 Creating a workplace climate for organizational learning

Transport and logistic businesses need to be designed for continuous learning that is incorporated into every aspect of their culture and processes. In designing work practices to facilitate continuous learning, the first point of focus needs to be the development of a psychological climate. One of the best ways to test for a constructive climate is to ask workers 'is this a good place to work?' Obviously, it is easier for people to work in some organizations than in others, and given the choice most workers will opt for the organization where they feel engaged, competent, rewarded, acknowledged, trusted, and happy. It is important to consider the features that lead to a positive climate. Taking into account the factors outlined in Table 9.5, a workplace climate is also characterized by issues outlined in Table 9.6.

Table 9.5 An integrative learning strategy

Support	Reinforce
• Use consultative processes • Promote participation • Build and reinforce confidence and self-esteem • Empathize with workers about difficulties, frustrations, and grievances, and address these whenever possible	• Acknowledge the expertise of workers • Ensure that responsibility is not designed out of work and that individuals and groups accept responsibility for their actions • Support workers by providing appropriate training and information
Direct	**Communicate**
• Provide direction by way of agreed aims • Promote change consistent with agreed aims • Employ appropriate decision-making processes	• Build communication networks to ensure multi-directional contact • Find ways to ensure information is communicated free of bias by reviewing how it is received by those at the operational interface for example

Table 9.6 Developing a workplace climate

Openness	Decision-making
• Open discussion which makes it easier for some issues to be canvassed compared to others • Diverse processes of communication such as informational, relational, inspirational, and political	• Appropriate involvement of individual workers in decision-making processes. The way managers facilitate worker involvement in decision-making processes is important for organizational learning. When there is little opportunity for organizational members to listen to diverse viewpoints, this leads to an inhibited organization characterized by low innovation and inappropriate work practices in the organization
Legitimacy	**Resources**
• Accepted forms of communication, such as written versus face to face • Valid processes for interpreting information • The degree of social honour and commonality expressed among individual workers and small groups	• Assign priorities for resource allocation • Communicate these priorities • Review these priorities as workplace undergoes change

9.7 Cultural implications for business restructuring

Restructuring is about modifying the culture. It is important to understand the nature of work practices that are in place to ensure at least single-loop learning and, ideally, double-loop learning (Argyris 1982). As organizations increase in size and complexity, responsibility for organizational learning becomes more diffuse. The opportunity for making errors in thinking and action increases, and at the same time, the opportunity for discovering these errors decreases. Sometimes these errors are detected and corrected and, if successfully overcome, this is referred to as 'single-loop learning' (Argyris 1982). Sometimes errors are not easily amended. One reason for this is that organizational members do not always recognize and understand errors because organizational philosophy and strategies blind them to the real issue. In this case, error correction leads to treating the problem symptomatically and so it continues. A second reason is that an error identified by a person working directly with the customer or product will not always be interpreted in the same way as by others in the organization simply because one is more directly involved than the others. This leads to various parts of the problem being interpreted differently.

The issue for managers and workers is how to modify these boundaries so as to 'unfreeze' their thinking, autonomy, and actions, which impede learning. A major way of 'unfreezing organizations' is to let workers see policies and strategies as dynamic processes rather than fixed ones. When organizational participants view organizational processes in this way, errors are treated differently and there is a greater opportunity for 'double-loop learning' (Argyris 1982).

Effective cultural change is a form of double-loop learning. Specifically, double-loop learning requires that organizational participants question the assumptions about work that they are currently using. Learning exists in action and includes the assumptions that individual workers and managers use to design and implement their work practices. These assumptions often refer to how the organization should be structured, the delegation of authority and decision-making, the acknowledgement of expertise, provision of rewards, types of training needed, and processes of communication.

Unless processes of organizational learning are identified and established, the new knowledge and information learnt by workers is lost to the organization, and may not be rediscovered for some time. A commitment to organizational learning requires additional effort in the form of people participating in decision-making processes in their workplaces.

Organizational learning requires a focus on the management matrix shown in Table 9.7.

All these process signal to organizational members that changing is a continuous and legitimate process of business. All these processes provide a greater stakehold for people involved to introduce and support desired change.

9.8 A concluding case study: Transervice

This case study provides the reader with a chance to reflect on some of the issues discussed in this chapter.

Chris Reid is a senior manager of a privately owned bus company, Transervice. The employees of Transervice have experienced a lot of change recently with many operational, administrative, and driver positions becoming redundant. The size of the workforce has been reduced by a third to about 280, with many surviving employees fearful of more cuts to labour.

Driving buses is physically and emotionally taxing, with increasing demands for customer service,

working congested routes, avoiding road rage, and dealing with schoolchildren. Most drivers work eight-hour shifts and routes within a 10-kilometre radius of the central business district. Up until 1991, most drivers had little education, with many of them leaving school by 15 years of age, serving three years as an apprentice mechanic or clerk before training as a driver. Over the last five years, the type of person recruited for driving had changed with many having experience and qualifications outside the transport industry. Supervisors directly control their work organization by establishing, for example, work schedules and practices leading to tight deadlines.

Table 9.7 Management matrix for organizational learning

Thinking	Scanning the context
• New ways of thinking and doing emerge in the organization. Blockages regarding traditional patterns are unfrozen • Organizational learning erodes the feeling that training is 'something done to a person' and replaces it with a sense of participation and control • Use of external change agents fosters continuous new thinking • Avoid rational thinking as a 'quick fix' to organizational problems	• Managements need to be very selective when deciding which environmental influences warrant a response, especially when resources are limited • Identify which stakeholders possess the most appropriate organizational knowledge • Decide under what conditions it is appropriate for the dominant coalition, e.g. management, to possess organizational knowledge without sharing it with others e.g. workforce, customers, unions • Focus attention on changing conditions in the workplace • Change needs to be monitored continuously • Survey corporate objectives among key stakeholders
Communication	**Restructuring a changeover**
• Frequent communications among people with different viewpoints • Participative work groups result in new decision outcomes • Engage in genuine problem-solving and not just pay lip service to it • Use joint problem-solving processes to overcome 'zone of indifference' (Quinn 1980) among stakeholders	• Decentralized work structures result in new work practices • Succession planning results in strategic reorientation • The efficacy of interventions needs to be evaluated against internal and external criteria • A programme of change needs to be evaluated in terms of its theoretical and practical credibility • Avoid replacing management and workforce as a way of fixing problems
Conflict management	**Innovation**
• The tensions between dominant and weak logics, old and new ones are overcome • Underlying conflicts need to be identified and addressed	• The emphasis is on the interactive process among people about new ideas in an organizational context • Psychological contracts support and reinforce spontaneous and innovative behaviour

Drivers were not encouraged to work in teams. These processes underpinned the workplace culture, which valued hierarchical management style. Despite this, there was a degree of camaraderie among the drivers.

In 1997, without consultation with the drivers, a new monitoring system was introduced at each of the depots. The monitoring system was also installed in each bus so that a central computer could track its movements. Consequently, the drivers felt change had been imposed, resulting in an erosion of personal control over their work. As the majority of drivers stated, 'it was as if "big brother" was watching them'. Chris Reid knew he had to reverse this situation and attempt to create a cultural change.

Reid decided to attend a management develop-ment workshop on cultural change. At the workshop, he learned of the potential benefits of employee participation programmes (EPP) to help develop a harmonious culture in the workplace. He also found that EPPs were infrequently used in operational settings. However, Reid was so impressed with the purported benefits of EPPs as, reported in the USA and Britain in the manufacturing and transport sectors, that he was determined to introduce one at Transervice.

When Reid suggested the idea at the next senior managers' meeting, some met it with scepticism while others thought it was a stunt. The managers, who were fairly conservative in their thinking, believed that the nature of the work as well as the type of employee working in a bus company were not appropriate for introducing EPPs. Reid felt annoyed when his colleagues referred to the personal characteristics of drivers, such as their low education, poor English language skills, assumed need for close supervision, and inability to take on responsibility. To the contrary, Reid had demonstrated over and over again that operational staff were capable of taking responsibility for their work tasks and rarely required close supervision. Other managers could not understand the benefits of EPPs, since they believed that workers had to be coerced into working effectively and that, on the whole, workers were not interested in contributing to their organization. Reid argued that workers did not know how to participate yet because they felt constrained by their supervisors, rules, and regulations. Reid believed that many workers would participate providing the opportunity was given to them. He also emphasized the necessity for the goodwill of management if worker participation was to be successful. He informed them that participating at work was like any other skill and could be developed and enhanced providing appropriate training was available.

Undaunted by the sceptical thinking, Reid discussed the idea with Sian Kohl, a colleague in a rival company whom he had known since his university days. Kohl told him that her company had produced a staff newspaper, written and edited by the employees themselves. She also informed Reid that such participation had led her employees to take on additional responsibility for scheduling work and they were now negotiating their work schedules with supervisors and each other. Reid asked Kohl whether this was time-consuming, and she told him that, while it was initially, once people got started, it became a part of their work routine. Kohl told him that the real time-savings had been made in the reduced incidence of conflict and work stoppages over unfair work practices. It seemed that now supervisors and bus drivers were prepared to talk to each other. For example, when responsibility for running on time was given to the drivers, they made sure the schedule was right. They felt it was their reputation at stake. She told Reid that all these new

activities led to increased confidence and self-esteem among the employees. Administrative staff were also interested in taking on new responsibilities now they could see the additional benefits. Kohl said that the organizational climate had improved, as new norms were starting to take over from the old, and work practices were more flexible, with benefits for everyone including an improvement in customer service.

Reid questioned Kohl about the potential obstacles in introducing EPPs. One hurdle she uncovered was the attitude of the workers in regard to their supervisors. They believed that supervisors were paid to be 'in charge' and that this was not part of their work role. This led to an 'us' and 'them' approach. The corollary of this was that while workers believed in the right of management to control them, they did not accept it and so attempted to thwart their prerogative. It had become a work game whereby workers found ways to subvert directives from supervisors. EPPs undermined this particular game since workers relied on each other and not the supervisors. The real challenge had become supervisors and middle managers who felt fearful about their loss of control over work practices and scheduling. Training was the key to unblocking this fear. Many of the tasks that supervisors should have been doing like controlling budgets, passenger surveys, liaising with local council, coordinating training and quality service had been left unattended. EPPs would free them to conduct these activities. Kohl told Reid confidentially that senior management had now embraced employee participation and wanted to extend it further, and were now finalizing a policy that would provide workers with a profit-sharing arrangement.

Reid was glad he had consulted with his old friend as he felt a sense of renewed excitement at the idea of employee participation. The only problem that he could foresee was the difficulty he would have in persuading senior management to consider the programme. His problem was how to negotiate with them so the idea would gain their commitment. Kohl suggested that he contact a management consultant group, Kari Lopez and Associates, whom she had hired in the early stages of the organizational change in her company. Reid phoned and Lopez suggested they meet over lunch.

At the initial meeting, Reid outlined his ideas and problems to Lopez. The first thing that Lopez suggested was that Reid should hold a series of lunchtime meetings and canvass the idea directly with the employees themselves before taking it any further. Lopez told Reid that the employees had to be convinced that they were important to the organization and that together they had the power to change their work organization. Indeed, the drivers had to understand that management had a lot to *learn* from them. If the workers did not like the idea, he would have to come up with an alternative approach to satisfy their interests. Reid did not want to impose cultural change on the staff. He wanted them to see the need for it for themselves. If they showed interest, a further meeting with some employee representatives could be held to outline a proposal to submit to the next senior management meeting in a month's time.

The organization and its members are one and the same. It is the imagination, effort, commitment, and sacrifice of organizational members that collaboratively make the organization what it is. It is this perspective that underlies the concept of organizational culture. In order to change the organizational culture, managers need to draw upon the imagination and effort of employees.

Readers should now for themselves seek to:

- define and interpret the problems outlined in the case;
- set goals for problem-solving;
- utilize the principles outlined in the chapter;
- draw upon their own learning (i.e. their 'theories-in-use') (Argyris 1990);
- reinterpret the problem;
- appreciate constraints;
- prescribe resolution processes and consequences of each;
- decide upon a course of action.

Discussion issues for Chapter 9

1 Define culture. How do culture and cultural variations influence work performance? Provide examples to show why knowledge of such differences is important for managers.

2 Why do cultural change programmes frequently start with downsizing?

3 Why is an integration strategy so important for organizations today?

4 Define a learning organization. What are the factors and processes conducive to organizational learning? Provide examples to show why knowledge of such differences is important for managers.

10 Knowing your work design

10.1 Introduction

Increasingly, management is playing a key role in shaping the transport and logistics industry and, indirectly, the labour market through the way it structures its business, internal organization, work design, and work practices and people. Due to the complex interplay of economic and marketing strategies and its implications on a larger industry platform, work design is no longer viewed as an isolated strategy, but is seen in the context of the market,

supply chain industry, and business strategy. Work design underpins organizational design, and it is in this way that management harnesses its core competencies, builds and leverages skills and knowledge of people, which, in turn, contribute to the strategic capability of the organization as a whole. Building strategic capability is the essence of competitive advantage.

10.2 Linking organizational design to work design

Designing work is a significant process in any business, particularly in relation to transportation and logistics since both are crucial to the efficiency and effectiveness of supply chain management (SCM). Just as organizations are becoming boundaryless through the advent of supply chain networks, so too is work. In this chapter, the term 'work' is intentionally used as a substitute for *job*. Work is essentially a process, a 'micro-supply chain' that is an internal logistics pipeline and increasingly more central and visible in the external one. A work process occurs where the worker and/or the team intervenes at significant points to meet service-level demands of various customers, both internal and external. It is important to note that it is becoming increasingly difficult to differentiate between internal and external customers. For this reason, work is no longer simply packaged as an individual job, represented by a job description and duty statement.

Thinking of work as a process, and not as a job, erodes notions such as job demarcation, which has become increasingly blurred between occupations and at a time where both SCM and, subsequently, co-relationships are a pre-requisite for performing work effectively.

Further, work competence, that is, the skills, knowledge and information required by workers today is a dynamic learning process, making the notion of 'job' incongruous with business dynamics. Just as the 'job' as we know it is disappearing, so too is the 'career' as hierarchies are flattened and downsized, and people are contracted in and out of the organization or are employed in one enterprise but perform work in another. The vertical path from a junior to a senior position is far from clear cut today, as increasingly work is designed as a seamless process aimed at specific outcomes that relate to supply chain and subunit goals. The future of work design is discussed below but first it is important to appreciate the fundamental dimensions of work design that continue to shape work organizations today.

Work is purposive, which is reflected in the way it is designed. From a managerial perspective, the way work is organized leads to specific outcomes such as productivity, coordination, cooperation, as well as forms of control. From a union perspective, it protects skill and task domains, working conditions, and levels of remuneration, and from a worker perspective, it provides rewards, discretionary control over skill and task domains, and a degree of satisfaction and well-being. The way work is organized protects all these interests to a greater or lesser extent.

10.3 Orientations to work

There are two main orientations to conventional work design: the technical and social. Both orientations are still needed for appropriate analysis of work design. While there have been many different labels to describe these, the use of the generic technical and social orientations used here serves to underline the key principles in each. Each orientation has a particular focus, which is outlined in the text boxes in Figure 10.1. The technical orientation focuses on specification, specialization, standardization, flows, and quality. The social orientation focuses on flexibility, participation, and co-relationships.

The social orientation takes into account the workplace and organizational context in which people work, as well as their psychological needs. The following issues that relate to the social organization of work need to be considered, particularly when introducing any form of change:

- nature and diversity of tasks;
- extent of specialization or integration amongst tasks and functions;
- nature of workers' skills: specialized or generalized;
- logic for grouping specific tasks together in specific functions and/or roles;
- degree of interdependency between both work functions, processes, and roles;
- extent of horizontal or vertical integration;
- relationship of competencies to tasks, functions, and/or roles;
- extent of standardization of inputs, processes, outputs, skills, training;

- degree of discretion and accountability associated with the performance of work and/or roles.

Both the social and technical orientations are important to the efficiency and effectiveness of the performance of the enterprise. It does not always follow that the higher service content requires a social orientation focus or that, as service content is reduced, the technical orientation takes precedence. In practical terms, both orientations are employed and each contributes to the nature of the service, time, place, possession utility and quality, and so on. Both orientations are discussed in turn in the following section.

10.3.1 The technical orientation

In the mid-1800s, industry was characterized by management employing the principles of Frederick Taylor (referred to as Taylorism) which assumed that there was only one best way to organize business, work, and people. These principles included the following:

- work was most efficiently done when divided up and assigned to specialists leading to fragmented work practices (i.e. division of work);
- managers and specialists planned work and workers executed it;
- processes were standardized including rate of defects/errors;
- communication was tightly controlled and hierarchical;

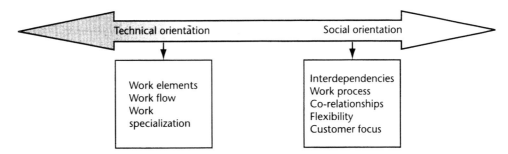

Fig. 10.1 Typology of work design

- production was organized using long runs;
- purpose-built equipment was introduced limiting skill variety and transferability;
- use of inventories was widespread;
- work was organized and conducted systematically under tight supervision (Taylor 1964).

It is well documented that Taylorism contributed to a progressive narrowing of worker skills and responsibilities (Edwards 1979; Piore and Sabel 1984). With a continuing emphasis on technical aspects of work organization, some businesses have either reinvented Taylorism or given little thought to how work performance contributes to the business strategy.

An overemphasis on technical aspects of work organization results in focusing on the *form* of work design, for example, technology, division of labour, and work scheduling. When attention is given to the *form* of work, its *substance* is usually overlooked, that is, skills, knowledge, learning processes, and more particularly, how work needs to be done in organizations today and in the future. Ultimately, it is people who make a difference to the strategic capacity of the enterprise. The outcome of a technical focus to work design is that there is little regard for the social organization of the workplace and the implicit employment contract that is so important for engendering high performance and commitment (Brewer 1993) in workers.

10.3.2 **The social orientation**

The technical perspective was seriously questioned in the 1930s with the advent of the Hawthorne Studies (Mayo 1933). While work had emphasized financial values with a focus on money, incentives, and tangible rewards, the social perspective focused more on the human ethic or an 'intrinsic' notion of work (Herzberg *et al.* 1959). The intrinsic view relates to a worker's sense of achievement and identity with work performed (Herzberg *et al.* 1959). By introducing a social perspective, work is seen as much more than a matter of simply providing workers with payment for labour. People go to work not only to earn a living but also to make friends, to gain a sense of achievement, identity, to increase their knowledge and skills, and use discretion. The design of work is so important in underpinning this process of worker motivation or commitment (Brewer 1993).

Models of work motivation describe the arousal, direction, and persistence of actions of workers that are important in leading to a performance output. The *content* models of motivation are influential in defining what motivates workers, and suggest that they perform work out of psychological and social needs primarily, and continue to do so provided they are adequately compensated. What is important in understanding these models is the notion that workers do not regard work in a purely instrumental sense, that is, as simply as a way to earn money. People work to satisfy a range of needs.

Maslow's model of motivation, referred to as the needs-hierarchy model (Maslow 1954) is one of the most widely quoted views by practitioners and academics alike. In this model, human needs are ordered hierarchically: physical, safety, social, self-esteem, and self-actualization needs. Following on from Maslow, Herzberg *et al.* (1959) proposed two categories of needs. The first category is termed 'motivators' which includes Maslow's higher-order needs. Examples of motivators included intrinsic needs, or aspects that relate to the doing of the job, such as achievement, advancement, recognition, and responsibility. The second category related to extrinsic factors, known as 'hygiene factors' which related primarily to Maslow's lower-order needs. Hygiene factors focus on work conditions that are typically considered to lie outside performance and include physical conditions, remuneration, as well as external controls such as organizational policy and managerial or supervisory strategies. Herzberg assumed that motivators and hygiene factors were independent of each other. Independency is contentious because in practice the distinction between motivators and hygiene is unclear. For example, pay is a hygiene factor as well as a motivator because it satisfies physical, status, and esteem needs for the worker. Subsequently, work factors such as pay, security, social interaction are interpreted differently by people depending on their personal needs and work situations.

A further model of worker motivation is based on three learned needs: the need for achievement (nAch), the need for affiliation (nAff), and the need for power (nPow) (McClelland 1961). The definition of these needs is apparent from the labels. This model supposes that when a person experiences a strong need, such as a high nAch, this will propel the person towards achievement of goals whether they are personal or organizational goals. In the case of a high nAch, the worker seeks tasks that are challenging and relies on relevant skills and knowledge in order to carry them out.

A later model of work motivation also categorizes needs into three classes: existence needs (E) which incorporate physiological requirements, relatedness needs (R) that are met through social interaction, and growth needs (G) which show a desire for esteem and development (Alderfer 1972). Instead of organizing needs in a hierarchy as Maslow did, the ERG

model places needs on a continuum, ranging from the more tangible, such as existence, to the less tangible growth needs. The continuum assumes that people seek more than one need at the same time. For example, a worker is motivated by multiple needs such as pay (existence need), identity (relatedness), and career development (growth need).

All of the models of work motivation described above rely on a categorical understanding of motivation. They suggest that individuals potentially become fixated at a specific need level when that need is either not satisfied or if attempts to attain the higher need level have been frustrated in some way. For example, if work is not designed to provide identity, career development, and autonomy, workers will focus on physiological and safety issues. Researching the importance of individual needs at work suggests that needs once established and satisfied retain their salience for workers, even after they are satisfied (Herzberg *et al.* 1959). For example, work that is appropriately designed to accommodate workers' needs could impact their satisfaction. On the other hand, frustration and dissatisfaction can result if work is suddenly redesigned, so that workers used to participating in decisions and exercising individual discretion are denied this.

The content models of work motivation assume that individuals value some needs more highly than others. The variables identified in the traditional models of work motivation are difficult to measure in practice, so it is impossible to say categorically how valid they are. For example, a reward for work performance such as pay could satisfy both physiological and esteem needs since many work roles are afforded both status and prestige according to the amount of remuneration the position attracts. The amount of money a worker is remunerated for carrying out specific tasks has more to do with market conditions, such as a skill shortage and the employer's eagerness to attract that skill, than the performance of the person in that role.

There is also a belief that worker performance is based on either rewards offered by management or the threat of coercion. Theory *X* (McGregor 1960) refers to managers, who apply coercion in order to secure worker performance. Assumptions underlying Theory *X* are, as follows:

1. the average person has an inherent dislike of work and will avoid it if he or she can;
2. because of this human characteristic of dislike of work, most people are coerced, controlled, directed, threatened with punishment to get them to put forth adequate effort towards the achievement of organizational objectives;
3. the average person prefers to be directed, wishes to avoid responsibility, has relatively little ambition, wants security above all.

Alternatively, Theory *Y* (McGregor 1960) refers to managers who motivate people through rewards. Assumptions underlying Theory *Y* are, as follows:

1. the expenditure of physical and mental effort in work is as natural as play and rest;
2. external control and threat of punishment are not the only means for bringing about effort towards organizational objectives. The worker will exercise self-direction and self-control in the service of objectives to which he or she is committed;
3. commitment to objectives is a function of the rewards associated with their achievement;
4. the average person learns, under proper conditions, not only to accept but to seek responsibility;
5. the capacity to exercise a relatively high degree of imagination, ingenuity, and creativity in the solution of organizational problems is widely, not narrowly, distributed in the population;
6. under the conditions of modern industrial life, the intellectual potentialities of the average person are only partially utilized.

Theory *X* assumes that the basic needs of workers predominate; hence managers will bargain with workers (or their representatives) over basic working conditions and remuneration. Theory *Y* assumes that workers have rights in regard to satisfying social, esteem, and development aspects of their work in addition to basic needs.

10.4 Expectancy theories of motivation

Expectancy theories of motivation assume that workers value rewards in different ways depending on their personal and work situations. The assumption here is that workers expect that they have to perform to a standard if they are to achieve a performance outcome desired by the employer. The relationship between worker expectation and performance is drawn.

Knowing what comprises a desirable work performance depends on first, an understanding of the worker's expectation to perform (*expectancy*); secondly, the likelihood of receiving rewards exchanged for effort and labour (*instrumentality*), and thirdly, the value placed on the extrinsic and intrinsic rewards by the worker (*valence*). The motivational force that a specific job has for a worker is calculated if the valence, instrumentality, and expectancy (*VIE*) values are measured (Vroom 1964; Alderfer 1972).

An important aspect of work motivation is effort. Effort is modified by the worker's capacity to carry out tasks, which includes physical and emotional attributes, skill capacity commensurate with tasks, as well as the characteristics of the task. Task characteristics include factors such as how predictable a job is in terms of carrying out the task, dealing with the client/customer, and making a decision. The amount of control and support workers can muster influences their level of effort. For example, workers maximize their effort when they understand what has to be done in the job, have the knowledge and ability to carry it out, and feel happy about doing the job. If they are further supported by co-workers and supervisor, their effort is assured.

Effort also depends on how willing workers are to allow a supervisor to direct or instruct them, and how much work will tax them physically and emotionally. A particular type of effort is required when workers have to work in dangerous, dirty, unpredictable, strenuous, stressful jobs that involve shift work and other similar demands. For example, most workers working in mines, on oil rigs, high-rise buildings and bridges deal with additional health and safety problems in their workplaces that impinge upon their work efforts.

The worker invests work effort in the job in expectation of rewards. The exchange of effort for rewards is referred to as the 'effort bargain' which is difficult to measure in practice, and therefore anticipate, in any specific work situation (Baldamus 1961). Effort and rewards are difficult dimensions in designing work. First, effort is difficult to quantify because no one can predict in advance how much effort a person will contribute to a situation since effort depends on a person's physical and emotional well-

being. For example, a worker may be very willing, but personal or work factors can prevent a person from contributing their maximum effort. Secondly, most work conditions are specified in advance. However, other job rewards such as personal fulfilment and satisfaction are difficult to specify in advance. For example, the worker may expect the job to provide personal fulfilment but finds that the tasks are very dissatisfying and subsequently, unrewarding. The uncertainty of effort coupled with not knowing how rewarding a job will be, makes the effort-bargain between employer and worker tenuous, and frequently unequal between workers.

The link between productivity and work satisfaction is inconclusive. Productivity is determined by managerial strategies targeted towards increasing efficiency through technological change, while work satisfaction depends more on the workers' perceptions of an equitable workplace.

10.5 Core characteristics of work

Working out the way in which performance contributes to or detracts from positive approaches to work, including productivity, is achieved partially through understanding the essential characteristics of work. According to the job characteristics model (Hackman and Oldham 1980), there are five dimensions central to work:

1. *skill variety*: the extent to which work demands the use of different skills and knowledge;

2. *task identity*: the extent to which work requires the completion of a whole, identifiable piece of work;

3. *task significance*: the extent to which workers feel their work is worthwhile;

4. *autonomy*: the extent to which work allows the worker to use discretion and control over performance; and

5. *task feedback*: the extent to which a worker receives clear and direct information about task performance.

The job characteristics model suggests that workers experience three critical psychological states, when work is designed around the five dimensions. When work is designed appropriately three critical states are experienced by workers:

1. a sense of meaningfulness influenced by task variety, identity, and significance;

2. responsibility for work outcomes influenced by autonomy; and

3. knowledge of results of work activities influenced by the amount of feedback received from supervisors.

Based on research into work design, it is possible to identify a set of fundamental dimensions that continue to be the building blocks for work organization today. The way work is designed leads to skills either being complemented or replaced (Buchanan and Boddy 1982). Managers need to understand how work design decisions lead to worker adjustment and increased work involvement. Similarly, managers need to appreciate how some of their decisions lead to skill replacement, worker maladjustment, and ultimately exit, as when:

- worker skills and knowledge are not reflected in work tasks and responsibilities;
- workers are engaged in routine and repetitive work tasks;
- workers have little control over task, work pace, work flow, or resources including equipment;
- workers have limited understanding of equipment used by them.

Similarly, managers need to appreciate how some of their decisions lead to worker adjustment as when:

- workers use experience and judgement in performing work tasks;
- workers have essential data and information for doing their jobs;
- workers are trained and appropriately qualified for their job;
- the job enhances existing skills and capabilities of workers;
- workers are able to anticipate problems and either deal with the problem or advise supervisor;
- workers are able to provide useful feedback or results to co-workers and supervisors;
- workers are able to participate in decisions about product or service improvements.

When managers view work design from a *technical orientation*, this suggests that their social obligation to workers is low, and has a de-motivating effect on workers. Employers with a strong sense of social obligation to workers are less likely to engage in deskilling practices in the workplace (Anderson 1993). Work design programmes need to take into account the following factors that are associated with generating a sense of control and commitment, leading to a reduction in work distress, absenteeism, and turnover, and consequently are associated with an increased capacity to perform.

The issue of control and its analysis is critical for designing work as it concerns the degree and flow of decision-making and communication throughout the organization. Static hierarchies (functional and divisional forms) separate decision-making from real work and assume that workers actually performing work have neither the time nor the inclination to participate, monitor, or control decision-making. In other words, workers at the front line of work (i.e. involved in product or service delivery) lack the depth and breadth of opportunity required for making decisions. This type of organization is labelled centralized. Conversely, a decentralized organization is structured to facilitate communication, information, discretion, and decision-making processes throughout all parts of the enterprise. Responsibility for performance is designed into all positions, which provides increased opportunities for self-determination and advancement for individual and groups of workers.

The inclusion of *social orientation* in the analysis of work design ameliorates many of the problems associated with over-specialization, simplification, repetition, control of personal time, and an over-reliance on physical strength and endurance associated with a 'Taylorist' approach. Designing work with a social orientation attempts to include dimensions such as diversity, autonomy, significance, skill usage, participation, recognition, development, achievement, security, safety, and feedback into the workplace. Many of these dimensions concern worker control, that is, a person's capacity to determine his or her own performance. Self-determination is the key to ensuring that all these dimensions are designed into work.

10.6 **Decentralized work organization**

The extent to which management centralizes or decentralizes work activities concerns the trade-offs between regulating worker activities and performance and being customer-responsive. One way to balance this trade-off is through integrating work activities both vertically and horizontally.

1. *Vertical integration.* Decision-making is shared by management with workers about important aspects of their work organization providing:

(a) access to relevant tools for both making decisions and implementing them;

(b) responsibility to accept the consequences of their decisions;

(c) consistency of performance standards across individual workers and time;

(d) consideration of potential bias of performance standards;

(e) consideration of the accuracy of the information obtained from standards relating to performance;

(f) flexibility of standards to correct mistakes;

(g) compatibility of standards with workers' motivation and ethical values;

(h) worker participation in constructing new or additional standards;

(i) piloting of change before new, design aspects become fixed.

2. *Horizontal integration.* Skill diversity replaces repetitive and routine tasks and enhances skill usage by:

(a) enlargement of groups of work activities;

(b) use of work rotation;

(c) efficacy and skill enhancement through co-relationships;

(d) consultation;

Horizontal integration is more likely to lead to self-management, a central part of developing strategic capacity.

10.7 **Self-management**

The principle of self-management suggests that individual workers or groups are given a set of task objectives with minimal instructions about task methods. The task set is linked as closely as possible to the subunit goals in which workers or groups participate. Accompanying the broad task objectives is a set of performance standards that have been established, ideally through worker participation. Self-management means that workers require as much autonomy as possible to perform specified work processes or roles. Autonomy is a significant prerequisite in the delivery of effective customer service, and is derived from aspects of work such as work pace, the speed at which work is performed, and work methods (Hackman and Oldham 1980). Workers need to have some flexibility set within performance standards to decide how results are achieved. Subsequently within groups, members make decisions about *task diversity* (high or low), the number of different tasks that are grouped together; *task scope* (broad or narrow), the range and nature of knowledge and information required for a given group of tasks; and *task control* (high or low), and the amount of discretion a person has when performing work. Moreover, the balancing of these three dimensions contributes to how specialized or generalized work is.

Establishing work goals, standardization of output, as well as decentralization of control are important so that the subunit is guaranteed a degree of choice about whether and when to work, the allocation of workload, and work methods. Self-management requires additional capacities and skills on the part of workers with implications for extra on-the-job training and development. One key change to training will be a greater emphasis on social skills such as communication and negotiation and perhaps mediation for supervisors to facilitate decision-making processes at the subunit level. Work analysis under these conditions will need to specify:

1. *information input*: where and how workers and/or teams acquire the training and information needed for the job;

2. *cognitive processes*: the reasoning, decision-making, planning, and information-processing activities that are involved in performing the job;

3. *worker output*: the physical activities, tools, equipment, and devices used by the worker/team to perform the job;

4. *relationships with other workers/groups*: the nature of the link (e.g. interdependency) with other people required in performing the job;

5. *job context*: the physical and social contexts where the work is performed;

6. *other characteristics*: the activities, conditions, and characteristics relevant to the job not included under (1) to (5).

The principles of self-management are increasingly appropriate for all work situations even in situations where this may not seem to be so on first observation, such as those that require workers to adhere to fixed schedules and work-flow patterns due to technological processes. Under these conditions, work analysis usually takes the form of:

1. identifying and describing all elements of work;

2. identifying and describing all tasks;

3. specifying and describing all duties;

4. identifying and describing all positions;

5. identifying and specifying all assignments.

This type of work analysis is less information-rich and not useful as many of these prescribed work contexts are disappearing as businesses become more responsive to customers. Even where a strong focus on the technical orientation to work persists in a workplace, it is important to introduce some principles of self-management, such as participative decision-making, that allow workers to have some control over their work context. For example, instead of having operations management setting procedures and times, workers themselves require some input into establishing these at different points throughout the work schedule. Participation of this type often leads to reduction in errors, accidents, and similar incidents.

Self-management is fundamentally about enhancing coordination and empowerment to subunit or small groups by establishing within them greater control over their performance context.

10.8 **Team working**

Increasingly, evidence suggests that the use of teams, particularly those based on self-managing principles, contribute to performance effectiveness such as productivity improvement (Beekun 1989), cost efficiency, and performance effectiveness (Cohen and Ledford 1994). Teams usually consist of individuals who have a high degree of interdependency in task execution, decision-making, monitoring, or any combination of these. Team members work together on projects, work assignments, and share and/or exchange skills, knowledge, information to create

their own core competence. More often than not, authority is delegated to the team through a team leader to make decisions about work methods and performance and the allocation of resources within the team. The team as an organizational form is compatible within a dynamic network and less so within static hierarchies (see Ch. 8).

One of the tensions in designing work focuses on whether people work as individuals, in groups, or networks. Coordination becomes a key issue due to differences in goals, skills, knowledge, priorities, and interaction. Intergroup coordination is also an issue for similar reasons as well as differences in time horizons. Examples of teams such as *market group* comprise an output, a customer, and a place mix; whereas *matrix* suggests a cross-functional mix. Cross-skilling or multi-skilling indicates a skill, knowledge, and often a functional mix, usually among individuals but also groups.

The way work is organized depends on work-flow, process, scale, and social factors. *Work-flow interdependencies* are described as either pooled where resources are shared; sequential where the completion of a task leads into the doing of the next; or reciprocal in which tasks are exchanged (Thompson 1967). *Process interdependencies* occur when tasks are grouped to encourage interaction between various processes. For example, workers who share particular skills (specialists) are grouped together into a functional grouping such as marketing, production, finance, human resources, and so on. This functional grouping often operates at the expense of work flow coordination. A process can be social as well as technical, as in providing a service to a group of customers, or political such as a communication network. *Scale interdependencies* refers to cost efficiency. An enterprise may not want to decentralize totally. For example, certain functions, such as information services, will provide global support to the enterprise, while other core functions, such as human resource management, may be decentralized to subunits. *Social interdependencies* refers to the co-relationships and interactions necessary for the doing of work.

Designing work around function, whether it is by knowledge, skill, work process, or task, emphasizes process and scale interdependencies, often at the expense of work-flow interdependencies. Functional work design means that people and resources are pooled from diverse areas. Functional work design reinforces task specialization by establishing career paths for specialists within their skill domain and demarcation between different skill groups. Social interdependency is likely to be enhanced as people are more likely to share tasks, knowledge, skills, and interests. Functional specialization aids coordination within a subunit of the organization but not across the organization. Designing work around markets is based on sequential and reciprocal interdependencies performing all the functions for a specific set of products, services, customers, or places. Market specialization needs a greater focus in work design than it has had so far.

Most workers are capable or have the potential to perform a diverse range of tasks, hence the notion of multi-tasking (Delbridge *et al.* 1992). In teamworking, each member has a variety of skills relevant to the work process. The *residual performance capacity* of both individual workers and teams as a whole needs to be identified and harnessed as this is crucial to creating strategic capacity. Teamworking facilitates flexible work-flows, and is dependent on the following processes.

- Social support: Support from team members for each other is important. Teams are the building blocks of organizations. Management is most likely to enhance productivity if they target improvement efforts at team ownership.

- Team leader support: Team leaders need to demonstrate trust, respect, friendship, and a deep concern for the interests of team members (Michaels and Spector 1982). Both team leaders and members act as buffers against work distress, and increase the likelihood of the team staying intact and increasing team commitment.

- Safety: Satisfaction with physical conditions promotes the intention to stay within the team (Mobley 1982) and commitment.

- Job security: A lack of job security or where team members are threatened continuously with dismissal for poor performance is a vital factor in team commitment (Ashford *et al.* 1989).

- Equity: Team members need to feel that their work inputs (time, effort, experience) and outcomes (measurement of performance, rewards, incentives, and job design) are compatible and organized fairly.

All these factors are subject to managerial choice. The way the workplace and work practices are organized is crucial in achieving desired outcomes of high performance and commitment and increased productivity.

10.9 The training context

Management recognizes training as an essential dimension of designing and redesigning work, either through the need for massive improvements in skill levels and/or in facilitating work adjustment to organizational change. This recognition is leading to growth in *operational skills* training (especially in the use of data-based tools and techniques) and *self-management* in the development of personal communications and effectiveness, team skills (for leaders and members), negotiation, mediation and coaching skills, as well as process improvement and management techniques.

Effective training involves a change in performance and needs to be based on a set of training objectives. A training objective is a written statement of how individual workers or teams are expected to perform at the completion of the training programme. The training objective needs to include a statement of the quality or level of performance that is acceptable and agreed upon by management, team, and workers. Training objectives need to include a statement of workplace conditions under which workers are expected to perform the desired outcome. Evaluation of the training context and programme should be conducted by an independent practitioner who is familiar with the work context in which workers have to perform.

A *training needs assessment* is vital for the ongoing training and development of all workers:

1. Worker: Identify whether the issue is training, motivation, work design, or a combination of these. Determine the actual performance discrepancy. Decide whether the performance discrepancy is important. Decide whether the performance discrepancy is linked to deficits in knowledge, skill, or behaviour. Work out with individual workers or teams how the performance discrepancy is to be minimized. Establish the most effective course of action to correct the performance discrepancy in terms of managerial, team, and individual objectives. Identify who needs training: individual workers or teams. Ascertain whether teams/workers are prepared adequately to receive training. Ascertain whether prior training has been conducted in relation to this issue. If so, take this into account when conducting the new training programme.

2. Work analysis: Identify tasks that are leading to problems in performance. Identify deficits in knowledge, skills, and behaviour.

3. Training issue: Define the actual training need and put it into writing. Ascertain whether the issue is one of performance, technological change, customer-related, work redesign, new legislation, regulation or procedure, or skill/knowledge-related.

4. Organization: Link training objectives to sub-unit and business objectives. Allocate and state resources set aside for training. Identify the level of support for training in each subunit for individuals, teams, supervisors, and management.

10.10 The future of work design

Horizontal integration (see Sect. 10.6) is inevitable with the spread of business activities in time, place, and distance as management disperses production and distribution processes over distance, both nationally and internationally. These dimensions of place–distance–time limit the way managers and workers imagine how work can be done as well as the way they design business practices, organizations, communication technologies, and perceptions of travel behaviour. The future of work lies in understanding the design of the internal organization, work routines and capabilities, telecommunications and information technologies, together with the marketing context. It is important that strategic developments are grounded in this connection between organization, technology, and markets so that managers can identify the competitive advantage of their businesses.

The flexibility associated with information technologies presents a number of opportunities to develop new, more humane organizational forms and work practices leading to a higher quality of work life (Brewer 1993). Similarly, due to the rapid rate of all technological innovation, operational changes are inescapable and increasingly significant to the way organizations conduct their transport and logistics business. Although decentralized business activities and managerial practices have been conducted for some time, the emergence of new telecommunications technologies has radically enhanced management's capacity to distribute their work processes, leading to greater potential decentralization of the business process. Table 10.1 shows some technological capabilities offered by information technology.

Table 10.2 demonstrates the growing linkage capabilities of information technology and their implications for organizational design. For example, market changes in the airline industry led to code-sharing with service ramifications for those in the codeshare partnership. Cross-functions in logistics have led to services processes that integrate both the supply and value chain more efficiently and effect-

ively. A change in work processes and activities may also be necessary if new equipment is introduced or new products or services are designed. Within individual functions, teams may minimize parallel processes and facilitate reciprocal interdependencies. This discussion will continue in the last section of this chapter.

As information technology makes work and customer activities more location-independent, distributed work will prove a greater incentive for employers in creating flexible forms of work scheduling. Distributed work is the closest so far to realizing a 'virtual' work organization among managers, workers, and technology, enabling them to perform work which may be at variance spatially and temporally with each other. For example, distributed work opens up new work contexts, such as access to other organizations (e.g. network organizations and strategic partnerships), workplaces (e.g. home, car, telecentre), or work sites (e.g. customer service outlet) (Venkatesh and Vitalari 1992). However, it is easier for management to accept changes in individual jobs, i.e. allow exceptions, than it is to tolerate modifications in work group arrangements or in organizational control structures since such modifications intrude on managerial territory.

The choice to distribute work processes or not depends on management's *capacity* and *willingness* to operate and manage internal, inter-workplace and interorganizational relationships and communications in the broadest sense. *Capacity* refers to organizational flexibility in terms of restructuring operations, redesigning work, changing

Table 10.1 Technological capabilities offered by information technology

Communication capabilities of information technology	Organizational design benefits of enhanced communication
'Go anywhere' electronic mail, fax, and data interchange	Organizational functioning independent of time and space
Desktop video teleconferencing	Greater dissemination of information and expertise, especially remotely
'Groupware' applications	Enhancement of collaboration in time and space
E-commerce	Creation of co-relations within the enterprise and interorganizational relations

Source: Adapted from Nadler *et al.* (1992).

Table 10.2 Linkage capabilities of information technology

Linkage capabilities of information technology	Organizational design implications of IT linkage
Across organizational boundaries	Service processes
Across functions	Service processes that integrate the supply and value chain more efficiently and effectively
Within individual functions, groups, etc.	Enabling of parallel processes and facilitation of reciprocal interdependencies

Source: Adapted from Nadler *et al.* (1992).

technologies, and assisting people in relocating business activities to take advantage of transport and telecommunications networks (McKay 1988). *Willingness* is a function of managerial ideology, reflected in the design and implementation of information technology and associated work practices and content.

Despite the complexities of these responsibilities, the extent to which management can live up to them is often measured principally by financial outcomes, for example, cutting costs in the short term at the expense of organizational programmes that would make good business sense in the long term. In other words, a successful organization and leader is judged more often than not by financial success alone, defined narrowly as cost-cutting, more than any other outcome or aptitude.

10.11 Towards flexible work scheduling and redesign

It is important that redesigning work is complemented by flexible work scheduling (FWS). The emergence of FWS, principally telecommuting, the compressed work week, and flexitime, has implications for the way work is designed and the type of workers who benefit from it. FWS refers to the use of telecommunications and/or information technology to modify and/or replace the commute to the usual workplace by salaried workers, thereby providing them with flexibility such as improved choice about use of time and work location as well as blending work and home demands. These factors may have greater appeal for women workers, if it is accepted that family roles compete more strongly with work roles and time among women than men. Introducing FWS into the work design has far-reaching implications for the division of labour and how it structures the options for men and women to participate and benefit from it.

10.12 **Driving forces of FWS**

There are two driving forces underlying FWS, first, an increasing perception that information is a significant economic resource, and secondly, a need for greater flexibility in conducting business regardless of national, market, industry, or time boundaries (Salomon and Schofer 1988; Warf 1989). These forces lead to a requirement for organizational flexibility in the face of intense competition and increased labour costs, which are placing pressure on management to raise productivity, increase flexibility, and quality of outputs (Porter 1990). Distributed work is one way of addressing these initiatives providing management is prepared to redesign work to be compatible with FWS (Brewer 1993, 1994, 1995; Brewer and Hensher 1996; Harrison 1994).

Secondly, new telecommunications and information technology have radically changed an organization's capacity to distribute work processes, and hence, improved opportunities for FWS programmes. For example, problems, viewed as formidable in the past, that plagued the successful implementation of telecommuting, such as access to information and maintaining the customer interface, have been somewhat mastered today. With the increasing dispersal of business activities, FWS, and particularly telecommuting, are more relevant today than ever before (Gray et al. 1993) although some concern remains in terms of cost of access, security of information, and occupational health and safety issues for employees working remotely. More importantly, as information technology makes work and customer activities increasingly location-independent, distributed work will prove a greater incentive for employers in creating flexible forms of work scheduling.

However, the use of information for monitoring productivity and performance has become the new technical focus of management. The development of detailed management information systems (MIS), such as just-in-time (JIT) and total quality management (TQM), legitimate and make relevant new types of data collection and use by management (Conti and Warner 1993). Management information systems (MIS) approaches improve processes at sub-unit levels of the business. In other cases, processes are radically re-engineered across vertical departments at macro or strategic levels. Investments in automation, information systems, voice and data communication systems, as well as inventory control systems are growing rapidly as businesses urge for higher productivity, faster response times, and improved service and quality.

The problem is that many of these efforts are piecemeal or implemented in isolation from central flows within the organization and across the supply chain. For example, separate departments, with little or no cooperative planning and coordination often implement training and development, customer service, technology, and process re-engineering. As a result, business processes including services are either improved or rapid or low-priced or innovative, but rarely all four. Enhancement in one area of the business leads to a weakened competitive position in another. And distrust concerning subsequent change programmes grows throughout the organization.

10.13 **Analysis of future work design**

In the light of these problems, it is important to note that human resource (HR) strategy governs work design in a corporate setting. As previously discussed, the nature of the division of labour in its simplest form is an assignment of particular tasks to distinctive occupational groups who interrelate in certain ways. There are two issues worth exploring in relation to work design and FWS: first, what structures the division of labour; and secondly, how is the division of labour in work organizations today conducive to the implementation of FWS? Relying on past practices of work design may no longer be appropriate in the current context of distributed work if workers are not taking up the option to engage in FWS. The increasing participation of women in the workforce in all Western labour markets suggests that women, where they are the primary care givers in the home, may be more likely to engage in FWS than men. In short, the question is to what extent does work design impose a barrier on FWS?

10.13.1 Factors structuring the division of labour

First, a number of authors (e.g. Cavendish 1982; Game and Pringle 1983; O'Donnell 1984) have argued that a segregation rule persists in delimiting a sexual division of labour, and this may impact those workers who have access to FWS and those who do not. There is a strong notion in the literature that only certain tiers of the workforce such as managers and professionals are eligible for FWS (Christensen 1988a). In Australia, for example, approximately 52% of managers and administrators and 31% of professionals use some form of flexible start and finish times compared to 28% of clerical staff and 14% of sales personnel (ABS 1993). If the assumption is made that managers and professionals are 'best' suited to FWS, this may limit women's access given their representation in these groups, particularly managerial.

Handy and Mokhtarian (1996b) discuss the emergence of a two-tiered workforce structure comprising professional workers and support staff, and its relevance for FWS. They contend that a two-tiered workforce has implications for FWS in that each group may experience alternative work scheduling, differently. The two tiers relate to the degree of control or autonomy associated with each group of workers, with professional workers having more control than support workers do. This division correlates with the structure of the internal labour market in which

assumptions are made about the competencies of occupational groups based on their internal labour market value. To claim that different occupational groups have different capabilities or capacity for controlling their work is also an artificial barrier. Within a distributed work context, providing appropriate organizational restructuring has occurred, there is no plausible reason as to why one group of workers 'lower' in the managerial hierarchy should be tied to the workplace compared to any other. However, the rationale of distributed work is often accompanied by a decentralized organization structure based on *trust* between management and workers (Pratt 1997). Segregation may be based on trust of particular groups rather than in relation to individuals.

The assumption of a two-tiered workforce, within which managers make decisions about monitoring employees and productivity, is more to do with the power of groups defending their occupational boundaries than the way work is actually performed. It is a form of segregation, which separates 'lower-paid' workers (women) from 'higher-paid' workers (men). This assumption about occupational groups provides insight into this particular barrier on FWS. In other words, a decision being made about eligibility for participating in an FWS programme on the basis of an occupational label or hierarchical position seems to be a fundamental barrier that needs to be addressed in this debate.

Secondly, gendered thinking may be constructed and maintained by the assumptions of *place, distance, and time* which preserve the conventional allocation of work between men and women, managers and non-managers. Place, distance, and time are reflected in the way work is designed as shown in Table 10.3.

Table 10.3 reflects the conventional view of management where *place* is viewed in terms of the perceived need for the physical presence of workers, division of labour, and the allocation of work to different parts of the workplace and the ownership of work space such as a work station or office. Secondly, *distance* is viewed in terms of proximity in workplace relationships, such as face-to-face interactions among co-workers and the perceived need for con-

Table 10.3 The significance of place, distance, and time to worker and work organization

	Worker	Work organization
Place	Personal visibility/or physical presence in workplace	Division of labour, functional boundaries, and resource allocation
Distance	Proximity of interpersonal contact	Hierarchical control and direct supervision
Time	Amount of time invested at work is indicative of loyalty	Work standardization, amount of time devoted to reaching deadlines is associated with quantity of output and productivity

trol between supervisor and subordinate as well as work output. Finally, *time* is viewed in terms of standardizing work tasks as well as the amount of time spent at the workplace linked both to productivity and commitment.

10.13.2 **Place**

Work tasks have been designed contingent on workers, for example, receptionists, secretaries, customer service officers, being physically located in particular places at specific times. One of the key barriers in rethinking work design is the culture of 'presenteeism' (Welch 1998). Within conventional models of work design, workers are seen as being in a given context that is a 'position in time and place which is exactly definable' (Lenntorp 1976: 12), creating boundaries that become fixed and official. Often, this process leads to a separation of jobs allocated to women and to men. The presumption of *place* conceals an important dimension of being human, that is, people's capacity to both shape and reshape their contexts, contracting or expanding the boundaries of work performance. This capacity to interact with one's context is crucial in a distributed work context where work is no longer simply packaged as an individual job, represented by a job description and duty statement. Thinking of work as a process and not as a job potentially erodes conventional notions of the division of labour, which in practice (albeit unofficially) is increasingly blurred between occupational groupings and at a time when team working is considered as a corporate requisite for doing work. The rationale for introducing telecommunications

and information technology enables people to 'distribute' themselves (McLuhan 1964) and not be tied to place. For FWS to work well, place will be viewed as 'articulated moments in networks of social relations and understandings' rather than as fixed location (Massey 1993: 66). Communications technology potentially erodes territorial boundaries in the physical, although not in the political sense. The issue of boundary is important in terms of the distribution of personal capacity which will lead to workers questioning where they 'draw the line' in regard to their personal investment in the organization in terms of time, workload, and commitment. Moreover, the preoccupation with 'place' as a dimension of work design has led to the failure to exploit virtual reality and consider out-of-work place and out-of-work time. The idea of the detachment of the 'person' from the workplace and the integration of the person within communication networks challenges conventional models of work design.

Preoccupation with 'place' has important skill implications. As place of work becomes less 'visible' through telecommuting, the skills of maintaining the work context may become more visible through coordination, cooperation, and communication. Allowing for individual differences, these skills have been typically associated with women workers.

10.13.3 **Distance**

Just as distributing work has 'distance' connotations, so does people's capacity to distribute 'themselves' impinge on this notion. In the case of telecommuting, workers are able to distribute themselves, by maintaining intimate real-time contact with co-workers and business associates through an infrastructure of communication and information technologies, making connections potentially intimate. Under this scenario, the nature of distance is changing both in terms of place (i.e. located anywhere) and time (i.e. increased response rate) (Moss 1987: 536). As time and place have become 'undistanciated', this has implications for work redesign. Under conventional models of work design, social interaction and cooperation, regarded as essential elements in most jobs, depend on 'proximity'. More significantly, modifying proximity leads to changes in the power and authority relationships particularly between supervisors and workers. Power is thus increasingly based on accessibility to information not proximity. Consequently, supervisors lose their surveillance role of subordinates with a rise in personal autonomy for workers, which has implications for clerical and service operators who may work from home. Thinking of distance in terms of control, FWS, particularly telecommuting, is anti-hierarchical in that it reconfigures work through the communication-information infrastructure to be more 'horizontal' in nature and less vertical. Under these conditions, the managerial hierarchy conflates as does the distinction between a two-tiered, internal labour market structure whereby assumptions are made about the competencies of occupational groups based on their internal labour market value and subsequently marginalized within the organization.

Power based on accessibility may have gender-specific connotations. Women and men may express a different preference for controlling events. For example, a preference for control could be linked to a greater appreciation to telecommute so as to exercise greater influence over hours of the day between work and home. This type of influence also has implications for 'time'.

10.13.4 Time

Time is a critical issue in designing work. Time is usually conceived as physical in terms of observance of punctuality, deadlines, and is associated with quantity of work output. The investment of physical time is also transformed into an emotional investment in the enterprise and equated with a worker's commitment or loyalty to the organization. A significant oversight in work design is the psychological and cultural quality of time and its relationship to notions of career, work evaluation, and comparability, which also have specific implications for the way women and men approach work.

The quality of time mitigates against FWS. For example, in many Western nations including Australia, the shift in travel mode from public to private transport and to the car and drive alone has continued for the commute trip, as has the substitution in destinations from central city to suburban centres. Interestingly, the major move to drive alone has been by female workers (Gibbs *et al.* 1996). One explanation for this is the extent to which women, in particular, may have to engage in multi-tripping characterized by setting down and collecting family members, shopping, and attending to household business during their commute trip. In other words, FWS may not overcome the need to engage in tasks associated with multi-tripping and hence, may be a barrier on women taking up the option to engage in it.

10.14 Perceived barriers to FWS and its relationship to place, distance, and time

Place, distance, and time act as barriers in terms of job suitability, perceptions of productivity (and measurement), corporate policy, and the structuring of two-tiered, internal labour markets. The potential for work redesign to support FWS lies within examining and modifying managerial assumptions about place, time, and distance. To support this view a literature review was conducted to identify definitions and perceived barriers to adopting telecommuting.

10.14.1 Definitions

The distinguishing feature between telecommuting and a compressed work week (CWW) is that with telecommuting, telecommunications is used as a surrogate for transportation for either all of the commute trip or part thereof (Memmott 1963; Nilles 1975; Mokhtarian 1990; Bush 1990), and subsequently it is perceived as a tool for reducing work trips and vehicle kilometres travelled (Bernardino and Ben-Akiva 1996). In the case of the CWW an employee works a four-day week or a nine-day fortnight, reducing the commute trip by either one day per week or fortnight. Both telecommuting and CWW result in saved travel time, which is a bonus for workers. A second distinction between telecommuting and the CWW is that with the CWW there is a day off-duty when there is no official expectation that work will be performed at home, making it a more attractive option for workers to engage in educational, leisure, or family-related activities. CWW may have greater appeal for women who wish to have additional time for family-related activities.

Telecommuting and the CWW can be either official when an organization has a policy as part of their HR policy, which applies to all or part of the workforce; or unofficial, when there is an arrangement between individual workers and their supervisors. The presence or absence of a FWS policy

may lead to equity issues in terms of it favouring particular workers or occupational categories over others.

10.14.2 Perceived barriers

A survey of the telecommuting literature revealed over 20 articles focusing on the factors contributing to the decision to offer and accept telecommuting by both employers and employees (see e.g. Bernardino and Ben-Akiva 1996; Mahmassani *et al.* 1993; Mannering and Mokhtarian 1995; Mokhtarian *et al.* 1995; Mensah 1995). Almost without exception, the barriers to telecommuting are underpinned by assumptions of place, time, and distance. Specific interpretation of place, time, and distance are summarized in Table 10.4 as substantive barriers to telecommuting. The literature survey revealed that generally employers are more reluctant to adopt telecommuting than workers are.

If the potential role of FWS in work organizations is to be better understood, barriers, and hence facilitators, need to be investigated. Secondly, it is necessary to consider whether these barriers are more likely to prevent men or women from taking up the option to engage in FWS. To address these questions data from the greenhouse gas emissions (GGE) study of urban travel behaviour exploring the use of FWS as a substitution for travel were analysed. This is a unique Australian study conducted in six capital cities on the mainland (excluding Darwin and Tasmania) in 1994 by the Institute of Transport Studies (Hensher *et al.* 1994). The study provides a valuable data set for addressing the issues in the FWS debate. The sample was a stratified random sample of over 1,400 households.

Drawn from the GGE study, data in Table 10.5 shows respondents who currently engage in FWS with the support of company policy. Table 10.5 is interpreted by FWS type since some respondents

Table 10.4 Perceived barriers to telecommuting categorized as place, distance, and time

Place

- job suitability: separation of work tasks from workplace
- concern over data and information security
- frequent input and ready aceess to information currently available in the office
- access to telecommunications from home e-mail, voicemail, fax, Internet etc., and subsequent cost
- physical visibility of workers in the work-place and its relationship to performance recognition

Distance

- contact with co-workers, customers, managers
- ability to supervise employees
- division of work between home and workplace

Time

- amount of time devoted to work tasks and its relationship to work output and productivity
- productivity growth is more significant than potential cost savings

Table 10.5 FWS by company policy by gender

Gender	Work CWW			Work flexitime			Telecommute		
	Yes	No	Total	Yes	No	Total	Yes	No	Total
Men	80	40	120	148	31	179	23	30	53
Women	24	37	61	107	24	131	12	17	29
Total	104	77	181	255	55	310	35	47	82

Table 10.6 Experience with telecommuting from home

	Men	%	Women	%	Total frequency	Total %
Have telecommuted	37	5.1	32	6.0	69	5.5
Seriously considering	60	8.4	33	6.2	93	7.4
Not considering	621	86.5	466	87.5	1,087	87
Total	718	100.0	531	100.0	1,249	100.0

Table 10.7 Reasons for not engaging in telecommuting

Work design dimensions	Men	%	Women	%	Total	%
People contact	5	1.9	9	3.4	14	5.3
Supervisory control	3	1.1	0	0.0	3	1.1
Motivation—productivity	2	0.8	1	0.4	3	1.1
Facilities access	26	10.0	17	6.5	43	16.5
Job suitability	126	48.3	65	24.9	191	73.2
Total	166	63.6	95	36.4	261	100.0

Table 10.8 Reasons for not engaging in CWW

Work design dimensions	Men	%	Women	%	Total	%
Extra hours	13	8.0	12	7.4	25	15.3
Company policy	73	44.8	36	22.1	109	66.9
Workload	18	11.0	5	3.1	23	14.1
Job responsibilities	2	1.9	4	2.5	6	3.7
Total	106	65.0	57	35.0	163	100.00

checked more than one FWS strategy when asked about company policy.

Men are more likely to work in a company that supports some form of FWS compared to women. Except in the case of telecommuting, the majority of respondents take advantage of their company's policy for FWS.

Overall 24.8% of respondents' organizations support flexitime compared to 14.5% for CWW and 6.6% for telecommuting. This trend emphasizes the conservatism among employers about maintaining standard hours with either an extended period for early and late starts and finishes; or working a condensed week or fortnight rather than considering alternative work scheduling, such as telecommuting. A further 7.4% of the sample are seriously considering telecommuting but the majority (87%) is not, as shown in Table 10.6.

Table 10.6 does not depict a significant difference in telecommuting experiences between women and men although differences are observed across occupational categories (see Table 10.7).

10.15 Work design barriers to telecommuting and CWW

Out of the 261 reasons provided by respondents for not engaging in telecommuting, Table 10.7 shows that job suitability is the most likely perceived barrier to telecommuting (48.3%) followed by facilities access (10%). Of those respondents reporting job unsuitability, 79% are full-time workers and 43% are managers or professionals.

From the 163 reasons provided by respondents for not engaging in the CWW, Table 10.8 shows that company policy is the most likely barrier perceived by both men and women, followed by an inability to condense workload into a four-day or nine-day fortnight. While company policy is the reason cited for not engaging in the CWW, many respondents did not take advantage of FWS when company policy allowed for this (see Table 10.5).

Place, distance, and time, when translated into work practice choices, are perceived by both men and women as barriers to FWS in terms of job suitability and access to facilities to work from home in the case of telecommuting, and in the case of CWW, company policy.

10.16 Job suitability as a place barrier

Based on the GGE study, the concept of job suitability is a main barrier in thinking about telecommuting. The dominant feature of telecommuting is people working from home providing their *job* allows for this (Salomon 1994). There is a persistent view that telecommuting is feasible for specific occupational groups of workers only, which lends support to a tiered internal labour market where some workers are provided with access to benefits and others are not. An often quoted example is 'information workers' (US Department of Transportation 1993). Mokhtarian and Salomon (1996), in modelling the choice of telecommuting among a sample of predominantly information workers in San Diego, reported that job unsuitability allowed for 44% of the constraint on telecommuting. The reason for this persistent view is that, despite a distributed work context, work activities are still linked predominantly to workplace performance (or rather have not been redesigned within a distributed work context) due to issues of supervisory control, task output and productivity, information access and security, and interrelationships among co-workers and customers. As the majority of businesses today are based on information, consequently most workers are involved in information tasks and relationships. Appropriate telecommunications and information technology should allow most people to perform their work responsibilities from home or alternative work sites, at least for part of the working week.

Potential access to the 'information preserve' is immediate and boundaryless, fundamentally suggesting a need to redesign work. In practice, work is changing but management views may not be keeping pace with the changes and this is reflected in the work design in organizations. As with information work, the conditions of telecommuting are more uncertain than in the past so workers need to be able to respond to and counteract the unexpected. Telecommuting leads to the substitution of managerial prerogative by an 'information preserve', and may be a reason for management resistance to work redesign.

Job suitability is related to 'distance' in terms of proximity in workplace relationships, and the perceived need for control (surveillance) between supervisor and worker. Work design today implies certain structural outcomes, which conflict with the flexibility of FWS. For example, a job is defined in terms of a given span of control, fixed tasks, skills, and procedures, performed within standard working hours and conditions, most of which are perceived as inflexible. Conversely, in contrast to the past, work is rarely performed as a 'packaged job' today and instead is organized along lines of workflow, process, scale, and social factors. Work reflects a mix of dimensions including market focus, comprising an output, customer, and place mix, a cross-functional and/or cross-skilling mix. This implies changing spans of control, functions, career structures, work practices, and autonomy. However, the language of 'job' and its underlying assumptions remain conventional and mirror little of this flexibility in practice.

Using job suitability as a reason for promoting FWS or not, therefore, is not only an artificial constraint but also a real barrier to work redesign and hence, FWS. The conventional notion of 'job' is the single most significant barrier to FWS as well as the culture of 'presenteeism', which is usually linked to career opportunities, for example, promo- tion, or even just 'keeping the job'. Understanding these issues in work design will prove a significant way forward for removing them as a barrier to FWS.

10.17 Company policy as a distance barrier

The study findings show that company policy is a main barrier in thinking about telecommuting. The decision to engage in FWS is a complex one. Even the existence of a company policy masks the real bar- riers, which occur within the employment relation- ship itself (Welch 1998). The unwillingness of many employers to allow workers to take up the option (Handy and Mokhtarian 1996b; Sullivan et al. 1993) manifests itself in different ways. For example, while a company policy may provide for FWS, the option to take it up by workers may be constrained by the unbalanced power or interpersonal relationship between supervisor and worker, or because a super- visor does not perceive the benefits of FWS. In other cases, FWS works well without any policy or official decision-making to support it because people per- ceive that it is expeditious for a variety of reasons. Some surveys report that up to 21% of a person's work is already being performed at home (Gregg 1998).

There is no doubt that FWS requires support from flexible work design, that is not constrained by place, distance, and time as well as HR policy. There is a clear advantage when there is a coherent combin- ation of corporate policies, human resource man- agement strategies, and work practices (Guest 1987; Schuler and MacMillan 1984). When businesses dis- perse production and distribution processes over dis- tance, and work practices subsequently change, strategies need to be in place to allow workers to take advantage of the increased flexibility through work redesign and FWS.

10.18 Productivity as a time barrier

Productivity growth is central to the employer's decision whether or not to introduce FWS (Ber- nardino and Ben-Akiva 1996). In part the problem lies in management focusing on certain dimensions of work, for example, costs, profits, technological change in isolation to the exclusion of other, pos- sibly more important dimensions such as finding new ways of measuring productivity, effectiveness, or quality. However, there is still much ambiguity surrounding productivity measurement. Associated with this is the ability of management to restructure workplaces horizontally, promoting the teamwork and accountability necessary for distributed work processes to be effective. Access to training and appro- priate telecommunications are essential (Schweizer 1993) and may be denied to specific workers.

10:19 Towards flexible work scheduling through work redesign

The changing dynamics of business and distributed work are still not reflected in work redesign. Work is still largely conducted in the workplace, during standard work time in the proximity of co-workers and managers who are linked to each other by way of a hierarchy. If FWS provides workers with greater autonomy over their work, some supervisors may fear loss of control and this may affect particular categories of workers (e.g. clerical or service), primarily women. Further, the way work is designed reinforces the dimensions of place, distance, and time. This persistent pattern of work design contradicts distributed work processes, which essentially break down the barriers of *place, distance, and time*. Understanding this fact not only provides valuable insights into work redesign but also assists in identifying both the barriers and the facilitators in implementing FWS in workplaces.

Recent technological developments parallel those that have been occurring for over 20 years (Nilles 1975), suggesting that technology alone was not the only barrier to FWS. For example, problems that hamper telecommuting concern issues about the measurement and monitoring of costs and productivity together with management's fear of loss of control over employees which are as evident now as they were 20 years ago.

The current generation of workers is facing a new variant of work organization, raising new questions about assumptions of place, distance, and time in relation to work design. The essence of the problem now is that past assumptions of work organization focused on the *form* of work such as task standardization, observance of punctuality, and supervisory control, and ignored the *substance* of work such as the psychological quality of place, distance, and time. FWS places a greater emphasis on the *substance*

of work whereby place and distance are not as easily defined as they are in the conventional model of work design, and time becomes virtual reality. Under these conditions, FWS fundamentally changes the division of labour.

Place, distance, and time are key social rules in determining work design. Place, distance, and time form a set of assumptions that shape work and work relations and give them permanence. Consequently, work design is a robust system of social constraint on FWS. The existing definitions of place, distance, and time:

- are situated deep within organizational and work practices, making them less readily observable;
- reside within existing power bases (e.g. management and unions) in the workplace, and
- are linked to the worker's desire to protect their interests and job security.

It is time to re-define these critical work design dimensions in order to inject *real flexibility* into the workplace.

There are still many unanswered questions about FWS options and related barriers to access and implementation. However, there is little doubt that recent technological developments allow individuals and work groups to perform in several different settings. It is argued that these barriers contribute to the under-utilization of FWS options. Job suitability defined by the internal and external labour market is an important influence in terms of which workers will have access to telecommuting and which ones will be marginalized by taking up the option. It is important to develop a better understanding of the assumptions underlying work organization and labour market barriers and how these ultimately impact on travel behaviour to and from work.

10.20 **Workforce flexibility**

The increasing flexibility of labour markets and its implications is in line with the trend towards distributed work. That means that the average tenure in a particular job is falling. There are more part-timers, temporary workers, and contract workers in the employment mix in the enterprise than there used to be. Shorter employment tenures tend to be associated with low levels of training. The 1993 OECD *Employment Outlook* concluded that 'roughly, training increases with employment stability'. Low levels of training, in turn, may have negative implications for the broader competitiveness of an economy, and for its long-term capacity for growth.

Distributed work processes may lead employers to decide that, if their core of workers is on contract, that training will be wasted, and so the focus will be on enterprise-specific skills. It is assumed that gaining 'a competitive edge' contains an inherent fixed trade-off, in this case, the value of training versus its costs. On the one side of the trade-off are the business and social benefits that arise from training. On the other hand, is the business's financial investment in implementing training—costs that managers often perceive lead to higher prices and reduced competitiveness. However, management is operating in the real world of competition where they need to find innovative solutions to pressures of all sorts. Properly designed training programmes can trigger innovations that lower the total cost of products and services, or improve their value.

The objective is to help managers to break out of their existing pre-conceptions of what constitutes their business's competitive edge and to re-assess the perceived trade-offs, that is, to invest in workforce strategies rather than engage in cost-cutting strategies:

1. defining learning roles for individuals and groups to realize in the enterprise;

2. defining, measuring, and reviewing learning processes outside the formal training arena;

3. adopting new management practices which emphasize interpersonal and organizational skills needed by enterprises that are part of 'prior learning'—this has an important advantage for women;

4. examining selection processes that are biased towards general appearance and personality which have little to do with skills, qualifications, experience, or the ability to learn;

5. breaking down a masculine culture that dominates the trades and skill training programmes;

6. avoiding numerical flexibility strategies of using part-timers and casuals to fill the gaps rather than investing in learning strategies;

7. extending staff training and development rights to women on maternity leave.

One of the competitive resources with which all nations have to find an innovative solution is its workforce. Governments around the world are developing policies as a way of developing a more flexible labour market encouraging business to commit to more flexible employment policies with an emphasis on training and education. One of the most notable statistics evident in a review of changes to labour force statistics over the past 30 years is the increasing participation of women. For example in Australia, the participation rate for all women in the workforce reached 53.7% in 1998 (ABS 1998). At the same time, there has been a radical shift in employment by industry with a marked fall in employment in manufacturing industries and increase in service sector jobs, particularly in the retail industry and in tourism. Part-time jobs now make up around one-quarter of all jobs, with three-quarters held by women. Most part-time positions are located in the periphery of the organization. Also striking is persistent segregation by gender in the labour market in most Western countries. The majority of women are employed in service industries, mainly in the occupations of clerks and salespersons, and with a small segment in the trades. Most men are located in management of trades and labouring work. Women are also concentrated in the industries where part-time work is most abundant. Industries most likely to invest in training are mining and the public sector.

A more flexible labour market needs a more flexible training market. In some cases, the market has forced businesses to recognize the value of becoming 'learning companies' and of empowering workers who each add much greater value to the business than they did before. This trend is valuable. A flexible training market might be the beginning of a solution to the problems posed by flexible labour markets. Management needs to work out the learning gap within their own enterprise. How big is the learning gap? What needs to be done, and by whom, in order to capture and translate learning from tough challenges into effective management action? (See Chapter 9.)

10.21 **A concluding case study: LOGSYNCO**

This case study provides the reader with a chance to reflect on some of the issues discussed in this chapter.

LOGSYNCO is a company based in the Road Transport sector. The previous chief executive officer of LOGSYNCO, Ian Simons, had shocked the organization by his unexpected, early retirement. At first, the resignation remained a secret. A generous early retirement package was quietly made with Simons, who was due to leave within four weeks of the announcement. Two weeks later, the senior promotions committee was advised of this development. A further announcement to staff was made soon after.

The senior promotions committee held their first meeting after the shock announcement. As the committee began to disperse at the conclusion of their meeting, Pru Davis, the chairperson of the senior promotions committee, asked Mark Calgar, the financial director, to remain behind. Davis had noted during the meeting that Calgar had remained silent throughout. Davis revealed to Calgar that the board of directors had already indicated who Simons's successor would be. Further, that the preferred successor, Dave Adler, had already been approached and indicated that he would accept the offer of the position of CEO. The news came as no surprise to Calgar as he had suspected all along that senior management would have someone in mind, and all that remained for the committee to do was endorse their decision. Since Calgar had been a member of the senior promotions committee, most of the decisions made by this group were merely 'rubber stamping'. *Two weeks later, Adler was offered the appointment and accepted it.*

Adler, as the new chief executive officer, observed that LOGSYNCO was now confronting a tougher, competitive phase in the business with increased costs in resources and labour. Part of this was due to the nature of LOGSYNCO's business, multi-manufacturing lines, regional warehousing, and distribution for the group. Adler knew that the logistics systems had to be upgraded and integrated with other members of LOGSYNCO's international business if the local division was to survive. Adler established three task forces: a global supply chain committee, a materials requirement planning (MRP) committee, and a human resource planning (HRP) committee.

In regard to HRP, the committees reported that HRP at LOGSYNCO, including work design, training, and teamworking, was ad hoc and fragmented. In particular, the training budget was focused on rewarding subunits and ignoring those where skill development was lacking. In discussing all these matters with the human resources manager, Adler learnt from her that there were considerable tensions between the human resources unit and other departments in LOGSYNCO.

10.21.1 **A new approach for human resource planning for the future**

Adler knew that the situation required urgent rethinking and restructuring of LOGSYNCO. He recognized that he would have to win initially the commitment of each of the line managers. Although sales were what Adler knew best, he appreciated that he would have to become familiar with all operations in LOGSYNCO. After one intensive week of meetings with each of the line managers, and absorbing a massive amount of information from reading internal documents, Adler spent the weekend mapping out the new approach. The new approach was characterized by the following objectives:

1. The complex circumstances facing LOGSYNCO, such as regulatory, economic, efficiency, and safety, required a continuous scanning of environmental factors, both external and internal.

2. Line managers had to be viewed as essential to business and HRP. It was vital that these two strategies were integrated right through to operator level.

3. The human resources unit would be an active participant in coordinating all aspects of HRP within LOGSYNCO. An advertisement was placed immediately for a human resources director reporting directly to the chief executive officer. The human resources director would be responsible for identifying key human resource management (HRM) issues and problems and for ensuring the link between business and HRP. The human resource director would be responsible for providing expertise in these areas but line managers would ultimately be accountable for HRP for their departments. The human resource director would coordinate the recruitment and selection programme throughout LOGSYNCO, ensuring that equal employment opportunity (EEO) principles were applied without exception. In the future, all positions regardless of seniority would be advertised externally and internally.

4. Until the human resource director was recruited, Adler would incorporate HRM into his role, thereby ensuring senior management commitment to the new approach.

On the following Monday, Adler called a meeting of all line managers. He tabled his new approach. He requested each line manager to take the first steps towards HRP. Adler presented them with a list of criteria:

1. HRP was to be used as a tool in planning, budgeting, and control;

2. line managers had to base an HR forecast on an analysis of their own situations;

3. a forecast period of two years was required;

4. the plan had to be simple and logical without using sophisticated models;

5. productivity was central to HRP.

Adler presented each manager with a set of indicators for their work organization as follows:

- business objectives for the subunit for the next forecast period;

- current internal workforce: full-time, part-time, casual, contract;

- resources to support current commitments;

- productivity measures;

- recent productivity changes;

- workload pressures;

- changes in workload: quantitative and qualitative;

- predicted turnover;

- future resource requirements.

The benefits for LOGSYNCO

1. Senior management, including the chief executive officer, can see quantitative and qualitative changes in human resources required to ensure the development of LOGSYNCO.

2. The magnitude and timing of the future demand and supply of skills can be identified.

3. The effects of productivity enhancements can be seen.

Table 10.9 Strategy development for flexible work organization

Objectives	How?	How?	Implement	Training
Develop human resource management (HRM) strategy	Define and explain HRM link to business strategy	Communicate with senior management and supervisory support	Articulate commitment to flexibility in work design	Identify skills, knowledge, and abilities and develop training programmes
Internalize HRM practices within the enterprise	Incorporate into other business initiatives	Create and suport relationships and networks	Expand and refine HR department roles	Assess training needs as well as experiences, and acceptance of practices
Sustain the commitment	Communicate internally about the issues	Promote flexibility externally	Implement accountability measures	Evaluate work environment and modify activities continuously

4. Anticipated turnover and mobility can be identified.

5. Training needs can be evaluated and resources allocated more effectively and equitably.

6. Communication within departments can be integrated now that all line managers are participating, including the research and development manager. Such integration of functions and information will impact on product development initiatives.

The next step that Adler took was to request the implementation of a strategy development for enhancing flexibility of all aspects of the work organization.

Since the 1980s, management have been seeking to introduce substantial positive changes in the work environment of their businesses. Table 10.9 assists managers in developing a strategy for introducing flexibility into their places of work.

Readers should now seek to:

- define and interpret the problems outlined in the case;

- set goals for problem-solving;

- utilize principles outlined in the chapter;

- draw upon their own learning (i.e. their 'theories-in-use') (Argyris 1990);

- reinterpret the problem;

- appreciate constraints;

- prescribe resolution processes and consequences of each;

- decide upon a course of action.

Discussion issues for Chapter 10

1 Describe the primary characteristics of a technical orientation to work design. Why has a purely technical approach lost its appeal in organizations?

2 People need to perform work that provides them with autonomy and diversity. Develop an argument to support this statement. Then build an argument to refute it.

3 Which of the core work dimensions are more significant in workplaces today? And in 20 years time?

4 Describe how teams (or integrated work groups) differ from other forms of work design. What are the advantages and disadvantages of each approach?

Knowing your people

11.1 Introduction

Chapter 10 promoted the argument that the future of work lies in understanding the design of the internal organization, work routines and capabilities, telecommunications (TCT) and information technologies (IT) together with the marketing context. The flexibility associated with information technologies presents a number of people-related challenges. There are no easy solutions. The essential flexibility of the technologies means that IT and TCT need to be implanted in the cultural organization of the workplace to achieve a competitive blending of worker commitment, performance, and high quality customer service. One of the main effects of new IT and TCT is the significant decline in the cost and time of storing, processing, and transmitting information. This price reduction has in turn influenced the way the supply chain is managed, including the operation and distribution of services and, subsequently, of work itself.

These developments are reshaping work, skill, and organizational structures (see Chs. 8 and 10), presenting two key challenges for managers. The first challenge concerns the way people will adjust to these technological changes and associated work redesign. The second challenge is associated with the need to maximize the total capacity of the transport and logistics business through performance capability.

11.2 First challenge: maximizing people's capacity

The primary task of managers is to direct business along efficient and effective lines. For managers to ensure that the organization is efficient and profitable often means that the interests of workers play a secondary role to the interests of management, customers, and key stakeholders, such as shareholders. For example, the interests of workers are often downplayed in the interests of maximizing efficiencies, cutting costs, and delivering effective customer service. The cutback process frequently results in a reduction in staff training, the absence of incentives, loss of staff, and the failure to communicate and provide information to workers about what is happening.

What are worker interests and why are they so important in the managing of worker commitment? Worker interests are expectations, goals, and needs that they hold in relation to the work they perform. Mostly, workers want to carry out work they enjoy, use skills that they have learnt, receive appropriate rewards in exchange for effort, undergo training, and be provided with good opportunities for future work and working conditions, including balancing home and work demands. Management is instrumental in providing these opportunities to satisfy worker interests but has to address what is perceived as a fundamental dilemma of answering to shareholders and addressing the demands of the workforce. The difference between worker and managerial interests points to the conflict within the manager-worker relationship, that is, managers have more control over responding to workers' demands than workers themselves. One way to resolve this problem is for management to coopt workers by providing them with more control over the transport and logistics task.

Survival of the transport and logistics business depends on the cooperation of the workers, and is more likely to exist when worker interests are addressed. It is just not good business sense for management to ignore worker interests. The interests of people in the workplace are dynamic and continuously influenced by internal and external circumstances. It is important for managers to appreciate that the interests of managers and workers change over time, and so does the nature of conflict. The interests of workers, such as higher wages, diminish in times of economic downturn but are replaced by requests for less tangible benefits such as additional training, greater participation in managerial processes, or similar. When worker interests are completely ignored by management, workers seek to address them either overtly through confronting management directly or appealing to some form of industrial representation to address their interests in the workplace, or covertly, through seeking some means to redress the perceived imbalance between effort, reward, and opportunity.

Managers do have choice over the nature and degree of conflict that emerges in their relationship with workers. The purpose of this section is to examine how managers contribute to the emergence of cooperation and conflict, and how this influences worker commitment as shown in Figure 11.1.

Managing commitment is about overcoming the fundamental conflict in the manager-worker relationship. The real difference may lie not so much in the business direction as in the strategies and tactics used to achieve business goals. Managers have a responsibility to develop a relationship with workers based on consent rather than conflict, if they are to operate a successful transport and logistics business. Gaining the consent of workers is a complex process

but ultimately worth it, if the organization is to work efficiently and with a minimum of conflict.

11.2.1 Conflict

'Managerial prerogative' is based on the assumption that managers have more authority to exercise control in the workplace than workers. As a consequence of managerial prerogative, managers expect to and are required to organize work in terms of what is to be done, who is to perform it, how it is to be performed, when and where it is to be performed. Essentially, this means that managers control key decision-making about recruitment and selection, establishing work priorities, directing the acquisition and distribution of resources as well as rewards. Static hierarchies preserve this form of control by traditional reporting lines between management and workers.

The major reason why direct supervision is obsolete is due to the increase in complexity of work, skills, and technological change in the workplace, as well as the fact that today work is often performed outside the 'boundaries' of the enterprise. The increase in workplace complexity means that competent workers are recruited and developed, capable of exercising judgement and control over their task domains, which often goes under-utilized in the organization. These workers, because of their skills, knowledge, and ability, are able to make more appropriate decisions in relation to work processes, thereby increasing business outcomes such as productivity and quality and, particularly, customer service. If managers are to retain highly skilled workers who are loyal to the organization, power needs to be distributed in the workplace more equitably between managers, supervisors, and workers. An equitable distribution of power can simply mean the right to be consulted, advised, and informed about workplace and organizational changes. In other words, managers have to erode some of their prerogative in order to maximize this resource. However, if managers are not prepared to consider a redistribution of power, workers will continue to struggle for it.

The unequal distribution of power between man-

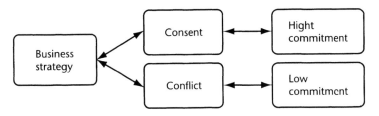

Fig. 11.1 The interrelationship of strategy, conflict, and commitment

agers and workers is the basic cause of the conflict between them. Conflict occurs when workers pursue their own interests within the organization and, in so doing, exert upward influence on management. Managers are dependent on workers, who in the day-to-day work situation actually have considerable control over processes that lead to increasing productivity, quality of output, minimizing costs and waste, as well as contributing to the climate and culture of the workplace. The capacity of workers to respond negatively to a managerial decision that they disagree with cannot be overlooked by managers since the worker response influences these organizational outcomes. It is important to understand the extent of potential control and choice which workers have in pursuing their interests in the workplace.

However, if management designs work in such a way that it does not reflect worker interests and instead emphasizes hierarchy and control, it leads to feelings of antagonism and frustration for workers. Worker frustration leads to disobedience, a challenge to managerial authority; submission; blame; and anger. In short, the worker response will be to resist 'managerial prerogative' and find ways around it. Given the potential control of workers over output coupled with a negative response, the outcome for the organization is poor and if allowed to continue could prove to be disastrous for the work context. It is in management's interests to take into account the concerns of workers. After all, addressing worker interests is more likely to lead to consent.

11.2.2 Consent

Committed workers are more productive, take more initiative, and thereby help to create a more competitive advantage for the organization. In considering the phenomenon of managing worker commit-

ment, two perspectives have to be taken into account: 'the perspective of the individual attempting to use organisations for the fulfilment of his or her needs (interests), and the perspective of the manager attempting to use human resources optimally to fulfil organisational needs (interests)' (Schein 1977). When workers become committed to a specific work organization, their actions demonstrate:

- an internalization of managerial strategy which management have set as the business objectives;

- a continuing willingness to work for the organization, and

- little desire to seek out an alternative employer (Kraut 1975).

There are two major issues for managers to consider in regard to developing consent. First, under what circumstances are workers prepared to commit to the work organization? Secondly, how does the design of jobs influence the commitment of workers? (Chapter 10 addresses the second question.)

As far as the strategic resources of the organization are concerned, there has been a gradual shift in managerial focus away from valuing capital and tangible assets towards assessing the benefits of the contribution of people to organizations. Simply stated, managers influence the type of contribution or response they receive from people. In other words, the way workers respond is based on their interpretation of how they are controlled by management. When workers are given flexible control by management, their response to management is positive. Conversely, rigid or overly bureaucratic forms of control lead to a negative response from workers. Managerial strategy and the worker response do not occur in isolation from each other, and result in a relationship based on consent and conflict as depicted in Figure 11.1 above.

11.2.3 **Worker commitment**

A person's commitment to an organization is a complex process to unravel. Commitment is higher at some stages in a person's work cycle and lower at others. For example, a person recently graduated from school and starting their first position is usually very enthusiastic about performing to the best of his or her ability. The new recruit is said to have high self-engagement to the organization. Self-engagement is a person's willingness to acquire and maintain an attachment emotionally and morally with a particular organization, the strength of which varies from individual to individual. However, after a period of time spent working in a specific context, most people's enthusiasm is moderated as they move into the maintenance phase of their work lives.

Generally, workers feel a degree of uncertainty about their organizational membership, both in terms of their relationship to management and their work group. Feelings of uncertainty increase as the labour market becomes more unpredictable and work permanency is less likely. Workers are prepared to trade some degree of personal freedom for the benefits of self-engagement. There are five interests that form the basis of maintaining the self-engagement, that is, the attachment of workers to the organization:

(*a*) identification;
(*b*) trust;
(*c*) investment of personal resources and effort;
(*d*) participation;
(*e*) equity.

(*a*) Identification

When identification occurs, workers think, feel, or act in accordance with their understanding of their work and their organization. Thus, identification is considered in two ways: a sense of feeling at one with their work and a feeling of belonging to the organization. Once identification with work occurs, workers accept values, attitudes, and actions that are significant to them but are principally those of the organization (Turner 1982). It is through the process of identification that workers learn to adjust to their work contexts. For example, when management articulates the value of customer service to workers, provides strategies for achieving this as well as incentives for delivering quality service, workers' capacity to deliver a higher quality of customer service is enhanced. In this example, worker identification contributes to the achievement of what management desires.

Identification with work: Most workers want to feel worthwhile, useful and valued by their employing organization. If work is designed so that it is clearly delineated, varied, creative, and somewhat autonomous (Hackman and Oldham 1980), workers feel at one with their work. The process of designing work that incorporates all these characteristics is not a simple task and is discussed in Chapter 10.

Identification with the organization: When work is designed to provide the worker with status and influence, a worker's attachment to the organization is strengthened. The attachment to the organization is based on the recognition and status associated with the worker's official position in the hierarchy.

(*b*) Trust

The basis of organizational engagement is trust.

Without the general trust that people have in each other, society itself would disintegrate, for very few relationships are based entirely upon what is known with certainty about another person, and very few relationships would endure if trust were not as strong as or stronger than rational proof or personal observation. (Simmel 1978: 179)

Trusting people involves risk-taking because a person can never predict in advance whether trust in another is misplaced or not. To trust means that a person acts in relation to others as if they know how they will respond, even though their future actions cannot be predicted in advance. People distrust others when they act in good faith and their expectations of the other's interests or actions are violated, resulting in both negative personal and organisational outcomes. (Hobbes 1978)

Increasingly in organizations today managers are having to move people from centring on 'low trust work'—that is, where the discretionary power of the worker is low—to 'high trust work'—where the worker has to make a range of decisions about making a product or delivering a service (Fox 1974). New work structures require responsible workers who can trust managers and co-workers, and in turn be trusted by them. Trust is important because in a flexible organization there is less control over information and knowledge and external relationships and hence increased influence for workers.

Gone are the days when work was standardized and routinized and performed by workers with narrow, specialist skills. The new image is one of flexible design, multi-skilling, and committed workers to meet the demands of customers and clients. Meeting such demands is no longer assumed to be predictable. In addressing changing needs of clients and customers, managers require workers to be cooperative beyond the limits of their explicit employment contract or agreement.

Trust is displayed according to the way workers are socialized into the organization. The conditions that lead to trust are best ensured, at least initially, in relatively limited ranges of 'social activity' or interaction. For example, a work group needs to be cohesive, disclose information, and be concerned about the diverse interests of its members. Work practices and communication processes are important in maintaining a high sense of trust in the workplace. A lack of trust leads to an attitude of self-interest and weakens the ability among individual workers to develop value orientations of service, loyalty, and a sense of commonality. Trust is an important factor in creating a social and collaborative relationship among workers and consequently is important for the development of affiliative processes such as team work in the workplace.

Trusting management implies that workers have faith in the ability of managers and supervisors to make sound decisions that create a range of work opportunities for them and, at the same time, protect their jobs. Individual workers are more likely to accept managerial strategies when they experience trust in relationships with managers and supervisors. Also, trust implies that there is some relationship between what managers say and how they act in the organization. For example, if the rhetoric used by management includes a concern for worker welfare, but managers' actions do not reflect ways of ensuring worker welfare, this creates a contradiction for workers that leads to mistrust.

(c) Investment of personal resources

A worker's decision to invest personal resources into their job and organization is dependent on first, their prior orientation to the employing organization; and secondly, their dynamic orientation to the organization (Watson 1986).

Prior orientation to the organization: Workers approach a new organization with a set of expectations about what it will be like to work there. For example, workers are recruited on the basis of their personal resources such as skill, knowledge, and experience, which they expect to use in the course of carrying out their jobs. For example, when workers are skilled in carrying out specific tasks, they expect to exercise discretion over their task domain. If supervisors or unnecessary rules block their discretion, skilled workers experience frustration and hostility. The resources which workers bring to their work organization include:

- education;
- skill development;
- personal sacrifices made to get and retain the job; and
- physical capacity to carry out work tasks.

When managers prevent workers from making an appropriate contribution to their work organization based on their education, previous training, and other personal resources, workers experience frustration. The frustration experienced by workers influences their willingness to invest further effort in their work. The most likely outcome is a reduced work effort from workers.

Dynamic orientation to the organization: A dynamic orientation (Watson 1986) refers to the ongoing relationship which the worker experiences with the enterprise, evident in the worker's attitudes. The relationship is dynamic because workers are continuously evaluating their work experiences and relationships. For example, when work is going well for the worker, the worker's attitude is positive. Conversely, when work is going poorly for the worker, the worker's attitude is negative. A dynamic orientation begins from the time the worker commences work with an organization, and continues throughout their lifetime with that organization.

The worker orientation is also influenced by the changing nature of work, organizational restructuring, or changed personal circumstances of the worker, both inside and outside the organization (Watson 1986). The nature of this ongoing orientation to the organization determines whether workers continue to contribute effort towards the achievement of managerial strategy. Work effort comprises four aspects:

1. a worker's emotional and physical energy to withstand the pressures of the job;

2. a worker's willingness to surrender a degree of autonomy to supervisors and management;

3. the time invested in the job by a worker; and

4. risk-taking behaviours associated with physical safety, social status, and credibility within and outside the organization.

The effort a worker is prepared invest in performance depends on a 'cost-benefit analysis' that is conducted as part of the dynamic orientation of the worker to the employing organization. Each of the aspects listed above—that is, emotional and physical energy, willingness to surrender autonomy, time investment, and risk-taking behaviours—have costs and benefits attached to them. A person's perceptions and attitudes determine the cost and benefits as well as rewards offered by management. In other words, each worker weighs up the costs of continuing to contribute effort to their work in the light of received benefits. If the benefits consistently outweigh the costs, workers continue their contribution

to the organization. If the opposite is true, workers will probably withdraw effort.

For example, a worker who consistently performs beyond what is expected by management but is not acknowledged by management over a period of time for making an extra effort, will experience frustration. The costs of investing effort are assessed as too high in this case. However, if the same worker feels that her remuneration and other incentives received outweigh the frustration experienced, she will continue to invest a higher work effort. The cost-benefit analysis is a trade-off between the estimation of the contribution of effort and the value of outcomes. This example demonstrates that it is important for managers to clarify for workers the types of behaviours they value as well as the rewards. The explanation of appropriate behaviours and rewards is vital for maintaining and increasing worker effort, and ultimately, their commitment.

(*d*) Participation

Participation is the ability of workers to involve themselves in decision-making processes that influence their performance and the long-term survival of the organization. For participation to eventuate, management needs to demonstrate first, legitimate modes of participation and secondly, rewards for worker participation. If there are no legitimate means for worker participation and/or little reward, this lowers worker commitment.

(*e*) Equity

Equity refers to the association made by workers between the distribution of rewards and resources among other individuals and groups in the organization in relation to their effort and performance. These outcomes are evaluated against the contributions made by other workers and the outcomes received by them. Workers compare themselves not only with co-workers but also with similar categories of workers working in different organizations and industries. If a worker believes that a co-worker puts in less effort but receives equal or greater rewards, this is viewed as inequitable and lowers the worker's commitment to the organization.

The way in which people respond to the unequal distribution of rewards and resources depends on their perception of procedural justice (Folger and Konovsky 1989). Perceptions of procedural justice depend on how individual workers view the methods or procedures established by management, in particular, to allocate resources and rewards within the organization. When certain workers or work groups are favoured over others by managers without a clear difference in their contribution to the organization, this is perceived as potentially inequitable by those who are least favoured. For example, when managers are eligible for rewards which non-managerial workers are presumed to be not entitled to receive due to organizational policy, this creates not only an equity gap but also a status differential between the two groups. The effect of equity gaps and status differentials is that they reduce the effort of the non-managerial workers and lead to heightened conflict within the workforce as a whole, and not just among those directly affected. The extent to which a situation is perceived as potentially inequitable depends on the general attitude of individual workers and whether these are positive or negative. When individual workers feel that, in general, they are treated fairly by management, they are less likely to see one-off situations, which result in inequity, as inequitable.

A sense of 'fair play' results in people seeing the relationship between management and themselves as one built on social exchange rather than one based on self-interest. Relationships based on social exchange are characterized by obligations founded on reciprocal trust and equity that result in the worker feeling the obligation to perform competently in their work (Organ 1988). A relationship based on reward exchange is limited to more explicit contractual obligations (Blau 1964), characterized by the worker feeling that 'I'm paid to do this specific job, no more and no less'. As long as feelings of equity and trust are maintained in the workplace, individual workers become less concerned about maximizing personal compensation as their sole reason for working, and are even more interested in contributing to work and the enterprise as a whole. Trust, equity, and the acknowledgement of workers'

performance by management result in social exchange. When social exchange is the basis of the employment relationship, individual workers are more likely to identify managerial interests as complementing their own.

11.2.4 Alternative work responses

The business culture serves to reflect whether managers value worker effort and investment, whether workers are acknowledged and participate in the organizational processes, and also the extent to which there is a climate of equity and trust. When the experience of work for the worker comprises a balance between identification, trust, investment, effort, participation, and equity, the probability of worker commitment increases. If this is not the case, the worker demonstrates an alternative response to commitment. Alternative responses include compliance, voice, and resistance (Hirschman 1970). Compliance, voice, and resistance represent responses by workers who find that the costs of commitment to their jobs and/or organizations outweigh the benefits.

11.2.4.1 Compliance

Compliance occurs when workers are observed as behaving correctly, such as obeying managerial directives and conforming to rules, procedures, and managerial objectives. Compliance is not a form of worker commitment but a response which workers use to protect themselves from criticism by managers, or from being or feeling threatened or embarrassed by their supervisors or peers. In that sense, compliance is a defensive mechanism and in aggregate can lead to a defensive organization. While compliant workers appear to be conforming to the intentions of managers, they are essentially distancing themselves from the organization. One example of workers distancing themselves from their organization includes a reduction of effort and a minimization of personal investment in the performance of their work. In other words, the attachment of 'distanced' workers to the organization is low relative to the committed worker. Creating distance between themselves and the work organization allows workers to engage in risk-taking behaviours at work. Compliant workers prefer to play it safe (Argyris 1990). Playing it safe is a defence that protects workers from confronting management with their own ideas, opinions, and actions. Clearly, it is not in the interests of management if workers play it safe in terms of their relationship to their work and the customer. For example, workers who carry out the work will not raise problems and issues. The lack of communication about workplace-based issues between management and workers means that error detection and correction is blocked, ultimately affecting productivity and quality. Defence mechanisms, such as playing it safe, also function to shield workers from feelings of shame or guilt associated with their continuing lack of commitment.

A further form of compliance exists when workers idealize their supervisors and find it difficult to act independently of them. The problem of recognizing idealization as compliance is that dependent workers are frequently viewed as obedient workers, often with high and unrealistic expectations of their supervisors. When the supervisor acts outside the scope of the workers' expectations, this has a negative impact on the worker that manifests itself in worker resistance rather than compliance.

A similar response occurs when workers hold unrealistic views of the workplace that cannot be implemented readily. Often management creates these unrealistic views when they refer to future organizational outcomes. When the future outcomes are not realized and this results in no increase in rewards, or, as is increasingly the case, loss of positions, workers become disenchanted and disengage from the organization. Another example of a utopian view is when workers are looking for a quick fix to organizational problems that can only be corrected over a long period of time (Kets de Vries and Miller 1984).

Compliant workers often seek and identify faults within the work processes without taking responsibility for correcting the problem themselves. Instead, the compliant worker devises ways to avoid

the problem. For example, avoiding problems results in a worker becoming apathetic, by not bringing work problems to the attention of supervisors or neglecting their responsibilities. A further form of compliance is when workers only see the negative aspects of the organization and de-emphasize the positive.

11.2.4.2 Voice

Voice provides an opportunity for workers to inform managers about their intentions, desires, grievances, to make suggestions for alternative managerial strategies, and to participate in organizational processes of change. In other words, workers who believe that what they say is listened to and acted upon by management, use voice. When workers are listened to, they feel valued. For example, if a worker believes that managers are concerned about reducing costs due to inefficiencies in work processes, and correcting these, they will continue to bring these issues to the attention of management. However, if past experience shows that managers do not act on worker reports of inefficiencies and similar problems, voice will be stymied. Some workers believe that managers will not listen to them and so fail to voice their grievances. Other workers may wish to voice but do not know how to use it.

However, workers who 'voice' discontent are not willing merely to conform. Conformity results in compliance, not commitment. Commitment is a complex phenomenon and cannot be equated merely with worker obedience or a decision to remain with a specific employer. A decision to remain with a current employer often has more to do with workers deciding whether or not they are better off in regard to current opportunities in the labour market, loss of benefits, friends, and fear of risking a new employer (Kraut 1975).

Voice occurs out of a desire by workers to improve work situations and conditions. However, manager and workers will frequently disagree over what constitutes improvement in the workplace. For example, workers may wish to modify work practices because they believe this will result in improved performance. In this case, management will focus on the costs involved in changing work practices and whether the results are commensurate with costs. When costs outweigh potential enhancements, proposed changes will not occur.

The importance of 'voice' is that it presumes workers' willingness to remain loyal to the organization, providing they see that they have some opportunity to have their interests heard by management (Burawoy 1979), or to exert some form of control over their work situation. In other words, 'voice' relies on a reasonably high degree of trust and respect between management and workers such that each party is acting with integrity. Voice also presumes that official communication channels are developed in order for workers to advise management about issues of improvement or discontent. The decision by workers to use voice rather than to neglect an issue demonstrates trust in management as well as their potential commitment. 'Voice' can be threatening to managers and perceived as a form of rebellion, that is, if managers view it simply as workers challenging managerial goals and values for the sake of it, rather than seeing it as a positive step for change.

The use of voice also depends on a cost-benefit analysis. The cost of voice for workers is that they appreciate it is threatening to managers to hear that people are frustrated at work or are aggrieved by management. Some managers perceive voice as a form of rebellion. When managers label voice as rebellion or resistance, this misrepresents the sincerity of workers who are prepared to use voice in order to suggest improvements to management, thereby providing evidence of being interested in the concerns of the organization. The cost of voice for the worker in this case is the fear of managerial reprisal. To ensure that voice takes place, management need to demonstrate that the threat of reprisal does not exist.

For managers and workers, the greater the sum of benefits of voice over costs, the greater the likelihood that a worker will use voice rather than resort to exit. Although exit is often not desirable for managers or workers, it is a likely outcome because there is no legitimate avenue for workers to use voice. Voice is an alternative to exit. However, if voice is denied workers, resistance is a likely outcome.

11.2.4.3 Resistance

Resistance arises when workers seek to exert influence either directly or indirectly over management and/or their immediate supervisors. One example of this type of influence is manipulation, whereby the attempt to exercise influence and the intent of the exercise is concealed from the other party, such as the withholding or concealing of information. Worker resistance is a general category incorporating a range of 'exit' options for the worker.

Exit can be either an overt or covert worker response. Overt forms of exit include sabotage, such as work stoppages, strikes, sudden resignations, and early retirement or unintended sabotage such as lack of knowledge or skills that prevent workers from working efficiently. Whistle-blowing is a further form of worker exit. The whistle-blower is a worker who becomes outraged morally or politically about a managerial strategy. The whistle-blower usually marshals support from other workers in order to maximize his or her influence over management.

Covert forms of exit include the 'taking of sickies' or other forms of absenteeism. Some types of occupational illness such as work distress and similar emotional symptoms, as well as selected physical symptoms, are also examples of covert exit. A further form of exit is a devaluing of and, subsequently, a disregard for managerial strategy. When workers disengage covertly, they perceive that the personal or collective costs are lower than those of either overt exit or voice.

A precursor of exit is the introduction of change or work redesign leading to a modification in a person's position, work practices, or workplace. Change experienced by workers in their workplace leads to anxiety or fear as they encounter new threats and constraints on their personal freedom. Fear and anxiety, when felt by a number of workers, accumulates quickly leading to voice, followed by exit. Exit is a last resort for most workers. For example, exit is precluded as an option for workers due to the financial as well as psychological investment in their work.

11.3 Second challenge: developing business capacity and performance capability

The capability of workers provides the roots for the total business capacity and, ultimately, the competitiveness of an organization. The capability of the business to produce, serve, and flourish over time relies on the ability of individual workers and teams to adjust and influence events within and outside the organization successfully. A significant part of the development of this capacity is how individuals learn to manage the difficulties they inevitably experience in the workplace.

The *Macquarie Dictionary* defines capacity as 'the ability to hold, receive, store or adjust'. In a people management sense, it is most frequently viewed as the aggregate performance output of the workforce and their overall productivity. The question for management is how this is achieved and at what level of capacity. Capacity is a comparative term in that it is the amount of inputs (acquisition, maintenance, development) available relative to output requirements at a particular time. Consequently, if a given business has a high capacity, it is assumed that

this is relative to inputs as well as the period of time over which it has been sustained. It is clear from reading Chapters 9 to 11 that capacity is related to the flexibility of organization and work design.

Measuring people's capacity is typically achieved through some form of work measurement and standards so as to:

- schedule work and allocate capacity through some form of scheduling;

- motivate the workforce through compensation, rewards, and incentives, and measure their performance in some way;

- benchmark performance internally and externally.

First, performance depends on a person's ability to perform specific work tasks. Secondly, as already discussed, effort is an important aspect of the worker's capacity to perform. The characteristics of the task, such as its predictability, whether routine or complex, and the amount of control, support, and

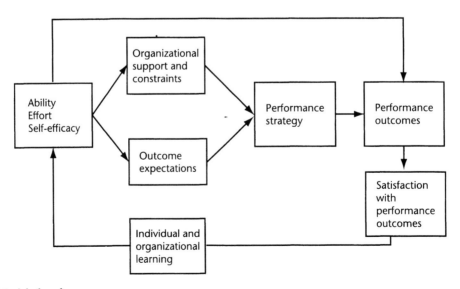

Fig. 11.2 Model of performance

Source: Based on Vroom (1964) and Bandura (1977).

training workers have over their performance also influences their level of effort. Individual workers are more likely to maximize effort when they understand what has to be done in their role, have the knowledge and ability to carry it out, and feel happy about performing the tasks. Effort is closely associated with discretion. The more discretion that individuals have over their work and its design, the less ambiguous they find it because they feel that they know what is going on. More importantly, they feel a greater sense of responsibility over work-related decisions (Stewart 1982).

11.3.1 Rewards

The expenditure of effort is also linked to rewards. The person invests work effort in the performance of work, expecting some kind of reward or incentive in return. Most work-related rewards are linked to pay, incentives (e.g. bonus), and working conditions, and are usually known by everyone in advance of carrying out the work. Other rewards, such as personal fulfilment, achievement, or skill enhancement, are unknown to the incumbent, and are difficult to expect in advance of commencing work in a particular organization. For example, sometimes workers expect their positions to provide personal fulfilment and find that the tasks are very dissatisfying, and subsequently, unrewarding. The uncertainty of worker effort coupled with not knowing how rewarding work is going to be, makes the employment relationship between manager and worker tenuous, and frequently inequitable. This has important implications for making the effort–reward bargain less implicit whenever possible. In other words, it is incumbent on management to be as explicit as possible about the employment contract.

Thirdly, self-efficacy refers to a person's belief that they have the capacity (skills, expertise, etc.) to meet the demands of the work. Workers with personal efficacy believe that high performance in one work situation is likely to be followed by similar levels of performance. Workers who are dubious about their capabilities draw back from performing tasks of complexity (Bandura 1988). As self-efficacy is associated with expectations, it influences workers' commitment to task and organizational goals and the way they interpret feedback from those in authority (Gist et al. 1991). Workers with high personal efficacy are more likely to perceive negative feedback as positive. For example, when a supervisor and co-worker recommends changes to work performance, the worker is more likely to respond positively by adjusting performance in the desired direction.

Self-esteem is an important dimension of personal efficacy. Self-esteem is present when workers feel good about themselves; that is, capable, successful, and worthy. It is conducive to performing well at work, being significantly associated with effort and the quality and quantity of output (Ellis and Taylor 1983). In the work context, self-esteem is contingent on how workers are perceived, valued, and acknowledged by others, particularly those in authority. Workers with high self-esteem are less likely to comply with instructions without thinking, and act deferentially. Conversely, they are more prone to work harder in response to negative feedback and contribute to team effort. Self-esteem is not necessarily attributed to a person's continuing disposition. Task complexity and variety, dealing with others, autonomy, feedback, task identity, friendship opportunities, and so on are more important in determining self-esteem than are the personalities of others in the work context (Gerhart 1987).

Understanding self-esteem is also related to performance feedback that influences a person's capacity to carry out tasks and to relate to other workers (Simpson and Boyle 1975). For example, when workers employ specific skills, they also require some understanding of what level of standard they should perform to. Other workers observing the skill performance derive knowledge of skill performance from the person's self-appraisal as well as the evaluation. Sometimes these appraisals are official, such as in performance management programmes, while at other times they are unofficial, such as the worker seeing that they have solved the problem, or a supervisor providing on-the-job feedback to workers, which is important in minimizing anxiety.

Self-esteem is based on a reasonable or better evaluation by the person of their capacity, that is, whether they are competent or not, their level of performance success across a range of situations, and their relationships with other workers. When there is a reasonable evaluation in terms of competency, success, and interpersonal skills, a person derives some degree of satisfaction from this. The degree of satisfaction is related to the person's level of self-esteem. Satisfaction derived from feeling competent, acting successfully, and the ability to get on with workers relates to fulfilling specific needs that most workers have such as achievement, power, social interaction, rewards, and career development. When these needs are fulfilled, a person has an expectation that this will continue. Workers become dissatisfied, frustrated, and uninterested, and ultimately disengage, when this expectation is not realized.

The capacity of workers to exercise initiative is strongly influenced by their self-esteem. Personal initiative is encouraged through the wider use of discretion. Work that is designed to encourage workers to take initiative or use their discretion reinforces such actions when exhibited by individual workers voluntarily. For example, when workers make decisions which impact the quality of their output and this is acknowledged by supervisors, it reinforces a similar response from them on subsequent occasions. Work also needs to be designed to ensure that workers are involved in setting aims and devising strategies that they can implement in their workplace. Self-management promotes worker responsibility and results in workers taking on a higher workload. An example of this is when workers are able to set their own performance targets and measure their outcomes against these goals.

What individuals achieve in their job frequently occurs spontaneously and cannot be specified in advance (Watson 1986). Actions that are spontaneous cannot be predicted and consequently cannot be written into work protocols and procedures. It is this spontaneity of action by individuals that is so vital to the performance of the organization and its subunits. A better link between spontaneous and required behaviours needs to be achieved in work design to support and not impede spontaneity of worker action.

The performance climate of any work unit is the most difficult to change as it requires commitment from as many stakeholders as possible, including senior management right through to workers in the 'front line' of the organization. Attempting to introduce performance improvement into a work unit is futile if workers are hostile to or complacent about the issues at hand. As stated previously, achieving performance improvement requires unit members to be involved directly in assessing the situation for themselves. Assessment means perceiving a need for performance improvement at the outset even if *not* agreeing with what direction this needs to take.

11.3.2 Performance management

Performance management often starts with some type of performance assessment, which, particularly in the case of individual workers, is often based on 'cause–effect attributions'. The attribution process is activated by an incident of either 'good' (e.g. success of a new service implementation programme) or 'poor' performance (e.g. missed deadline, errors, absenteeism). Supervisors attribute the success or failure of the performance based on three cues:

- *consensus*: compares this episode of performance by a worker with performance from a similar cohort;
- *distinctiveness*: compares this episode of performance by a worker with performance from the same person on previous situations;
- *consistency of observed behaviour*: compares performance over time for a similar task (Kelley 1973).

These attributions are based on behaviour associated with internal factors such as effort, ability, commitment, and/or external factors such as opportunity and difficulty of task. External attributions tend to be made when the worker:

- has little prior history of poor performance on similar tasks;
- performs other tasks effectively;
- is performing as well as other workers who are in a similar situation;

- performs poorly and this has few serious consequences;
- regrets and learns from the poor performance;

or when

- the supervisor is dependent upon the worker for their own success;
- there is evidence indicating external causes (Yukl 1989).

In summary, performance is essentially multidimensional. Performance comprises learned knowledge such as principles, rules, facts (Kanfer *et al.* 1994), operational knowledge and skill, commitment, that is, the choice to expend effort, the choice of what level of effort to expend, and the decision to persist in the expenditure of the chosen level of effort, ability, intention to act, and action. Performance is contingent on support from supervisors, for example, providing direction, relating immediate work to business strategy, workload, as well as from co-workers, for example, contributing effort and generalized norms of support (e.g. equity, training) prevailing in the organizational context.

Performance management is central to self-management (discussed in Ch. 10). Performance management is a process whereby current performance is observed and reviewed for the purpose of its future enhancement. The following criteria make up performance management:

- performance objectives and standards;
- performance appraisal criteria;
- long-term or short-term business focus;
- merit and equity;
- skill acquisition;
- work evaluation criteria;
- degree of decentralized decision-making.

Figure 11.3 provides the steps involved in planning performance improvement.

Performance appraisal usually occurs after the worker has been working in a position. There are several factors that are essential for workers to understand prior to their initial performance at work. These factors are outlined in:

- performance aims;
- performance standards;
- methods used to measure performance outcomes;
- timeliness of performance;
- durability of performance;
- visibility of performance.

Data for performance review usually start with the position specification, the position (or job) description, and the supervisor's expectations of a desirable performance level. Having this kind of data available suggests that an analysis of the position has been conducted. In addition, workers actually performing in the position can provide information relating to overall competence. All this information is used to create performance standards. Performance standards are characterized by four factors:

- *specific*: attributes, skills, quantity of performance, for example duration;
- *competence*: performance is categorized into minimum, moderate, maximum;
- *accountability*: level of responsibility, discretion, and authority;
- *evaluation*: quality, error detection.

As already stated, an appropriate performance appraisal programme is instrumental in promoting worker commitment, and managing current and future worker performance. When workers receive direct feedback on their performance from managers, performance expectations are stated clearly by them, and performance is related to task objectives, it is easier for workers to direct their performance towards agreed goals. Addressing the four questions assesses this link between performance objectives and work practices:

- How well did the worker perform?
- Are workers able to meet performance requirements?
- Is support forthcoming from supervisor to aid worker performance?
- How can workers improve performance?

When supervisors and workers address these four

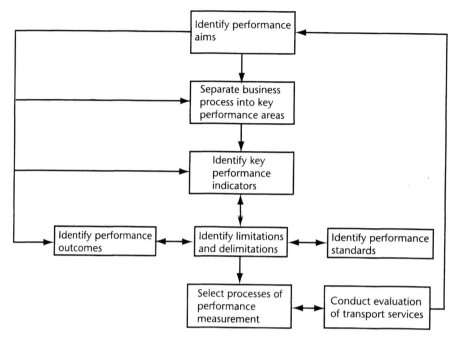

Fig. 11.3 Planning performance

Source: Based on Lovelock (1992).

questions, they are interested not only in complying with performance expectations but also wanting to demonstrate their goodwill. When a discrepancy occurs between actual and desired performance, several issues are addressed:

- Is there a simpler way of achieving desired results?
- Does the person's potential match the job requirements?
- Is the original training appropriate?
- Does the person use the skill often enough to develop competence?
- Has sufficient feedback on performance been provided in the past?

The potential factors contributing to the differences between desired and actual performance need to be assessed. First, the problem needs to be described accurately. For example, is the problem a shortfall in skill or knowledge of the worker, or does it lie in a lack of information or supervisory support? Secondly, the problem also needs to be viewed in terms of its importance to work outcomes.

A performance management system needs to be based on one or more of the following.

1. Critical incidents that demonstrate examples of effective and ineffective performance on a representative sample of workers/teams need to be recorded. For example, a customer contacted the company to find out why her goods had not arrived on time. A manager reviewing performance would use this as an example of negative performance. It should be shared with workers in a small group or subunit to discuss ways of minimizing these types of complaints.

2. Performance dimensions using five or seven-point scales (e.g. preparing for duty, communication, work adaptability) are derived from a large sample of critical incidents and are evaluated by a range of 'experts' including workers, teams, managers, unions, and consultants. Experts must receive training in rating performance. For example, suppose management wanted to evaluate how workers had performed three months

Table 11.1 A behaviourally anchored scale for rating workers skill retention

Scale	Sample of performance behaviours
5	Carries out task to minimum safety requirements, checks equipment before proceeding, communicates defects to shift supervisor; checks activities from previous shift before commencing work, communicates well within work group, able to pass on skill to other shift members
4	Carries out task to minimum safety requirements, checks equipment before proceeding, communicates defects to shift supervisor; checks activities from previous shift before commencing work
3	Carries out task to minimum safety requirements, checks equipment before proceeding, communicates defects to shift supervisor
2	Carries out task to minimum safety requirements, checks equipment before proceeding
1	Carries out task to minimum safety requirements, performance errors still detected

after attending a training programme. Conventionally, raters would evaluate each person's skill retention on a scale from 1 (definitely no skill retention) to 5 (full skill retention). Unfortunately, this type of scale leads to ambiguities as to what is meant by 'no skill retention' and 'full skill retention'. These types of generalized ratings rely on raters' impressions of workers' personalities. To minimize this problem, judgements and opinions of 'experts' are used to develop specific examples of performance, which serve to anchor each point on a rating scale (see Table 11.1). Behaviourally anchored rating scales can be communicated directly to workers and provide an excellent source of feedback to workers who are interested in improving their performance.

3. A performance process which has increased in popular use over the last few years is peer review, that is, having the members of an intact work group review and assess each other's performance. This process is achieved by using critical incidents, behaviourally anchored scales, or team objects. Team objectives are passed on to the work group by managers or developed in consultation with them using the business strategy as the benchmark. Team objectives are used as the standard by which the work group's (and its members') performance is assessed. An example of team objectives could include 'to improve the speed of fulfilling orders'.

4. Quantifiable indicators of performance need to be identified and measured. These quantifiable indicators need to measure quality and quantity. Quantifiable performance indicators must be based on objective feedback about the workflow process itself, for instance, flow charts, Pareto charts, and control charts. A flow chart provides the specific steps for performing a particular process such as handling a customer's telephone inquiry (see Fig. 11.4). A Pareto chart demonstrates the frequency of critical incidents that are either positive or negative. Figure 11.5 shows the frequency of customer complaints and the description of the complaint. A control chart allows the supervisor to manage either the sub-unit's performance or individual workers. Figure 11.6 demonstrates the orders fulfilled in 1998 compared to previous and projected years. Quantifying performance in this way provides an objective measure and allows both management and workers the opportunity to analyse the source of the problem in the case of negative performance and the source of accomplishment in the case of a positive performance. These forms of feedback provide continuous feedback to workers and teams. Performance indicators must be based on areas over which workers/teams have direct influence and not system or structural factors that are outside their control. Structural or system factors need to be managed strategically by the

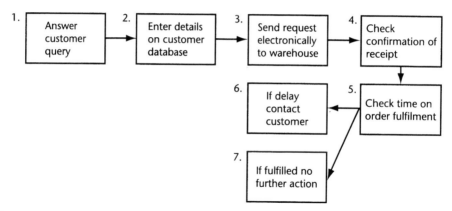

Fig. 11.4 Flow chart: handling a customer's telephone enquiry

Fig. 11.5 Pareto chart: frequency of customer complaints

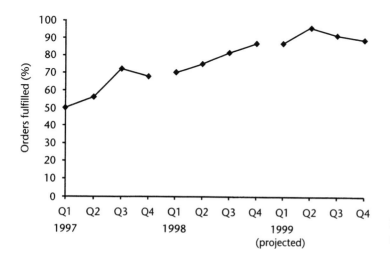

Fig. 11.6 Control chart: management of order fulfilment

senior management with feedback from supervisors.

5. An appeal system must be in place for workers and teams who consider that performance has been unfairly evaluated.

6. Feedback on performance outcomes needs to:

- allow workers to monitor the discrepancy between their performance and the goals they have established and to adjust their output accordingly (i.e. specific to actual performance behaviour);

- be critical so as to inspire co-workers to higher performance;

- act as a performance standard giving the group control over both the group's standards and performance;

- be informational, that is, supporting autonomy and promoting competence. Examples of feedback that are negative are task-contingent rewards, deadlines, threats of punishment, surveillance, and supervisor–worker evaluations.

11.4 **Planning performance improvement**

For most organizations, performance involves a puzzle, that is, if an organization succeeds on one performance indicator (e.g. increasing market share), to what extent is this achievement related to other performance indicators? Secondly, to what extent does the performance realization of a subunit contribute to overall productivity in the organization? Assessing performance fit between the overall organization, subunits, and the individual is achieved by understanding the process outlined in Table 11.2.

Performance improvement programmes are frequently designed and experienced as a 'bureaucratic' process in that an external agent such as legislators, politicians, or consultants imposes the dimensions onto a particular organization. For example re-engineering, widely lauded for its performance improvement outcome, is often introduced in a bur-

eaucratic fashion, with management starting blindly down one road with little reflection about its impact on workers, stakeholders, and customers, their values and interests. When re-engineering does not lead to the desired performance outcomes, the technique is viewed as a failure and passed over for the next 'improvement programme'. When it works in another context, either because it was understood differently and therefore implemented more effectively, or because the industrial climate was more accommodating, it is touted as a success. And so performance improvement programmes are replicated over and over again, either without much success or with little understanding of reasons for their success or failure.

Organizations that have attained mature businesses have been found to be most successful in their

Table 11.2 Analysing organizational performance

Auditing	Compare design, operations, and workers
Specifying key internal and external relationships	Identify key coordination devices
Comparing performance norms	Philosophy, methods, style, and values
Contrasting benefits versus risk	Resistance to change, turnover, issues, and problems

efforts to perform well on several indicators concurrently, which suggests that it takes time to learn how to do several things well at once. In comparison to mature businesses, organizations in start-up mode tend to be smaller and less hierarchical and consequently may perform differently.

In attempting to address these questions, it is important to appreciate the role that coordination plays within organizations. In addition to coordination, performance monitoring, reconciling diverse sources of performance information (customers, coworkers, performance management, and organizational learning) is also significant.

The prognosis for performance improvement is based on an examination of issues that present a current and/or future impact on organizational performance. Issues include political crises, emerging or declining competitors, market fluctuations, changing legislation and regulations, industrial and legal matters. Issues are perceived as either universal, affecting all organizations and industries; or specific, affecting selected organizations and industries, technical, or social. The way these issues are perceived and managed is outlined in Figure 11.7.

Performance management is contingent on the assessment of internal and external pressures. Coordination of external boundaries is pertinent when external pressures, emanating from the business context, are high and internal pressures are low. Coordination is required when both sets of pressures are high. In this case the business needs to become customer responsive as outlined in Figure 11.8.

To achieve a multi-management and customer-responsive position, a number of factors need to be addressed:

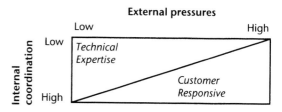

Fig. 11.8 Managing the high-performing transport business

- market access;
- services and products;
- capital access;
- technology;
- supply chain networks;
- resources;
- workers;
- business name, image, and reputation;
- economies of scale and scope;
- diversification.

A problem-solving process is required to analyse each of the above factors:

- determine key organizational factors central to the business or service;
- specify current and future performance levels;
- identify the time period for performance improvement;
- gauge stakeholders' interests and commitment;
- design the intervention;

	Internal business requirements	
		Low pressures	*High pressures*
External business context	*Low pressures*	Negligible management work	Internal relationship management: employees and units
	High pressures	External boundary management	Multi-process management

Fig. 11.7 Coordinating organizational performance

- ascertain quantitative and qualitative changes in workload in the future;

- predict the influence of workload changes on the internal workforce;

- formulate criteria for achievement of performance modification;

- estimate the impact of workload and workforce changes on productivity;

- approximate workforce trends, for example, attrition, retirement, and so on;

- provide a planned forecast.

11.5 A concluding case study: Performance Plus

This case study provides the reader with a chance to reflect on some of the issues discussed in this chapter.

Performance Plus is a shipping company and a subsidiary of a large multinational company based in Sydney. Performance Plus is facing the need for greater cultural and managerial flexibility than it has had in the past due to new competitive trends in Europe, Asia, and developing countries. Michael Farrow runs the Sydney-based operation. Performance Plus conducts a business planning approach worldwide with each director of a subsidiary organization developing a plan that includes business strategies and an annual operating budget. The business plan from each subsidiary organization is submitted to head office. This planning system has been operating for the last decade. Each year, the senior management executive based in head office noted that the managing directors of each subsidiary business had under-estimated their business performance. The discrepancy was attributed to the fact that the managing directors had consistently over-estimated their profits in their annual management reports to the executive group in head office.

To clarify the problem, the head office executive in London called a management meeting, and all managing directors of subsidiary organizations throughout the world were requested to attend. The managing directors and the senior management group from head office assembled together to explain and understand the rationale of the business planning model for Performance Plus. A team of management

consultants was hired to present a state-of-the-art model of business planning. The senior management group insisted that each director of a subsidiary comply with the business planning guidelines outlined by the management consultants at the London meeting. Further, consultation and agreement from each of the subsidiary directors were sought at the conclusion of the management meeting. It was explained that a rational planning model would be used to ensure that an accurate picture for the next year was forecast by each of them.

However, what did not emerge at the London meeting was that the annual over-estimation of profits by the directors occurred because they believed that over-estimation was essential to negotiating a realistic operating budget each year. One of the main reasons for the continuation of profits being over-estimated was that specific programmes such as research and development and management training, which were standardized throughout the corporation, relied on central funding. As a consequence of this form of negotiation, the management executive had less funding for centralized activities. Ultimately, the practice of over-estimating profits rebounded on the subsidiary organizations. Research and development and management training had contracted severely in the last two years. Instead of linking this trend with the process of budgeting, the directors of the subsidiaries saw the reduction in research and development and management training as reflecting the philosophy and lack of commitment of senior management. The view held by the managing directors was that head office did not value research, development, or management training.

A cycle of distrust developed throughout the organization characterized by an 'us' and 'them' approach. The 'us' was the subsidiary managers and the 'them', the management executive. The managing directors of the subsidiary organizations felt that the management executive would never see it their way, and would continue to cut their budgets. In order to counteract this, the directors of the subsidiary companies continued to report higher profits than were actually earned. While this strategy camouflaged the actual state of affairs for a further twelve months, the management executive uncovered the deception. Instead of calling a second meeting, a group of international management consultants was recruited to ascertain the reasons why the subsidiary organizations continued with the practice of over-estimation of profits. When the directors learned that the management consultants had been hired, they became further suspicious of the executive's intentions. An extraordinary meeting was called by Michael Farrow to be held in the Sydney. All managing directors in the South-East Asian, African, and Pacific regions were invited to attend the Sydney meeting. The team of management consultants at that meeting tabled a report. The executive summary included the following features:

A   *The current situation between Head Office and its subsidiaries is characterized by mistrust, evidenced by the over-estimation of profits.* The managers had learnt to play the 'budgeting game' constructed by Head Office. Subsequently, the outcome was fragmented, demonstrated by an 'us and them' approach. At the moment, little integration nor indeed open communication was possible between Head Office and the subsidiary organizations. Each party acknowledged the existence of a problem, but each attributed the cause of the problem to the other party. The problem now had negative implications for the business.

B   *The style of management is centralized, formal, and authoritarian.* Performance evaluation is based largely on quantitative aspects of the business such as cost. Risk-taking is guarded with limited delegation to the subsidiary managers. The response of management was tight cost control, reactive, conservative, more interested in changing products rather than processes, rewarding seniority and tenure rather than merit.

C   *The major concern for managers* in Performance Plus centred on business stagnation, lack of an inter-subsidiary network allowing head office to negotiate with one subsidiary at the expense of another, loss of incentive for middle managers in terms of salaries and training and its effect on product development.

D   *The priorities for managing change in the future include:*

1. introducing a global supply chain;
2. autonomy and control for line managers over their subsidiaries;
3. an integrated organizational communication and information orientation;
4. a greater degree of participation and involvement in head office activities by line managers;
5. creative organizational norms or standards;
6. high performance and improved productivity;
7. emphasis on new technology utilization;
8. improved quality of work life for middle managers;
9. emphasis on research and development;
10. emphasis on opportunity and risk-taking;
11. informal, work groups, high networking among workers and subunits within each of the subsidiaries.

Staffing the new structure

All management positions were open and advertised. Present incumbents were required to compete with new applicants for these positions. The criteria for the management posts were demanding, including risk-taking, leadership, team playing, and motivating. A recruitment company was hired to conduct the interviews and 100 managers were hired with 45% recruited from outside Performance Plus.

With the new management team in place, a major

programme was designed to communicate Performance Plus's new strategy and aims. The programme was in video format and was used in team meetings in each major subsidiary to explain philosophy and operating policies and to establish local business targets for divisions within subsidiaries.

Through this type of communication programme, Performance Plus established the agenda for the business worldwide. Key divisions were identified within each subsidiary and team leaders were appointed for each. Each team leader focused their efforts on their operations and was responsible for:

- customer-based divisional strategies;
- divisional results and profitability;
- day-to-day management of profit centres within each division;
- human resource management and development within the division.

Performance management

Performance Plus moved from a functional to a divisionalized structure so that people at the 'front line' of the organization became more involved in all facets of the business. Prior to the changes described above, business functions were organized into distinct units and any integration between them occurred only at senior management level.

The immediate strategy by Performance Plus management was to introduce new performance objectives aimed at increasing profitability, quality of projects and project management, and customer service. The changes included workplace reforms, implementation of improved financial and operating systems, and the provision of enhanced services. To this end, Performance Plus devised a performance management programme for the whole organization. This programme required that each worker and his or her team leader establish three performance-related objectives each financial year:

- redefining what business or businesses to be in (or what to hold on to or acquire);
- enhancing the company's public image and reputation through better relations with customers,

suppliers, shareholders, and the general public through more socially responsible actions such as implementing a trade waste strategy and project risk management including an occupational health and safety programme;

- improving organizational effectiveness through worker commitment and teamwork, less friction, and less diversion of human effort towards non-productive activities;
- providing better opportunities for workers to realize their potential capabilities;
- improving the capacity of people to anticipate or respond to market opportunities, as well as changes in industrial and legislative environment;
- introducing merit-based promotion, new selection processes based on psychometric measurements, performance measures, and standards, as well as disciplinary and exit procedures;
- strengthening specific organizational values such as job satisfaction and security, personal development, involvement, and quality;
- introducing new technology to reduce obsolescence;
- emphasizing occupational health and safety as integral to work practice;
- focusing on total quality management and continuous improvement central to each project;
- creation of client service teams to maintain regular contact with current clients and regular clients.

The human resources (HR) strategy has been decentralized with line management taking over the responsibility for personnel, work design, training and development, quality management, and occupational health and safety. The HR group provides advice and assistance with implementation of programmes.

Team leaders have full accountability for the projects managed by them, which means that they receive more timely information and feedback for making decisions. The success of a project depends on the competence of the project team. Each part of the project varies in the nature of the work, the different skills involved, and the responsibilities of team members.

Training

One major change was to reorientate training. A new strategy was implemented which targeted skills aimed at developing client relationships (both internal and external), flexible and innovative attitudes. Skill exchange programmes were used to increase on-the-job learning. Specific indicators for competency were introduced as well as performance agreements which contained training objectives. A multi-disciplinary advisory team was established to investigate problems and issues arising in the workplace.

Worker benefits

Performance Plus surveyed staff regarding a range of non-financial benefits and work and family initiatives. Dependent care emerged as high on their list of priorities. In Sydney, for example, a pilot programme for childcare was established including three childcare centres. Five days' family leave was introduced. Sick leave arrangements were also modified to allow people to take unlimited sick leave. An affirmative action strategy designed as a best practice programme (BPP) has also been implemented (see Ch. 10, esp. Table 10.4).

Performance Plus found that conventional performance systems failed to provide sufficient responsiveness from both managers and workers. There was a tendency for each to blame the other prior to the change. Performance systems in which workers share a degree of the risk and the benefits of the business facilitate responsiveness, competence, and accountability.

Flexibility was designed into managerial and work processes so that people continued to adjust to changing competitive conditions and were able to assess a situation quickly (see conclusion of case study in Ch. 10). The ability to implement decisions under conditions of uncertainty is critical in addressing change. It is important to develop this capacity among organizational constituents by developing competencies through increased training, and requesting managers to link competencies to key business areas.

Readers should now seek to:

- define and interpret the problem outlined in the case;
- set goals for problem solving;
- utilize principles outlined in the chapter;
- draw upon their own learning (i.e. their 'theories-in-use') (Argyris 1990);
- reinterpret the problem;
- appreciate constraints;
- prescribe resolution processes and consequences of each;
- decide upon a course of action.

Discussion issues for Chapter 11

1 Discuss several reasons for worker restrictions on output.
2 What are the basic tenets of equity theory? Describe the process by which perceptions of equity or inequity result.
3 According to expectancy theory, what contributes to motivation? Is this similar or different to factors that contribute to performance?
4 Describe the major influences on *voice*? Is *voice* an important process for management to encourage or not?
5 What tangible steps should be taken to ensure that an organization has a highly motivated and high-performing workforce? Use practical examples to demonstrate your points.

References

Abelson, P. W. (1987), *The Economic Evaluation of Roads in Australia*, Sydney: Australian Professional Publications.

Aberle, D. F. (1962), 'A note on relative deprivation theory', in Thrupp, S. L. (ed.), *Millenial Dreams in Action: Essays in Comparative Study*, The Hague: Mouton.

Adams, J. S. (1965), 'Inequality in social exchange', in Berkowitz, L. (ed.), *Advances in Experimental Social Psychology*, ii, New York: Academic Press.

Adler, P. S., and Cole, R. F. (1993), 'Designed for learning: A tale of two auto plants', *Sloan Management Review*, 34: 85–94.

Ajzen, I., and Fishbein, M. (1980), *Understanding Attitudes and Predicting Social Behaviour*, Englewood Cliffs, NJ: Prentice Hall.

Aldag, R. J., and Brief, A. P. (1975), 'Some correlates of work values', *Journal of Applied Psychology*, 60: 757–60.

Alderfer, C. P. (1972), *Existence, Relatedness and Growth*, New York: The Free Press.

Aldrich, H. E. (1986), *Population Perspectives on Organisations*, Uppsala: Acta Universitatis Upsaliensis.

Allen, W. B., and Liu, D. (1995), 'Service quality and motor carrier costs: an empirical analysis', *Review of Economics and Statistics*, 77/3: 499–510.

Anderson, C. (1993), 'Corporate social responsibility and worker skills: an examination of corporate responses to work place illiteracy', *Journal of Business Ethics*, 12/4: 281–92.

Anderson, N. R., and King, N. (1991), 'Managing innovation in organisations,' *Leadership and Organization Development Journal*, 12/4: 17–22.

Andrews, K. R. (1971), *The Concept of Corporate Strategy*, Homewood, Ill.: Dow-Jones-Irwin.

Ansoff, H. I. (1965), *Corporate Strategy*, New York: McGraw-Hill.

Anthony, P. D. (1977), *The Identity of Work*, London: Tavistock Publications.

Arendt, H. (1958), *The Human Condition*, Chicago: University of Chicago Press.

—— (1971), *The Life of the Mind, Volume One: Thinking*, California: Harcourt Brace Jovanovich.

Argyris, C. (1977), 'Organisational learning and management information systems', *Accounting, Organisations and Society*, 2/2: 13–29.

—— (1982), 'The executive mind and double loop-learning', *Organisational Dynamics*, 11/2: 5–22.

—— (1986), 'Skilled incompetence', *The Harvard Business Review*, 64/5: 74–9.

—— (1990), *Overcoming Organisational Defences: Facilitating Organisational Learning*, Boston: Allyn and Bacon.

—— (1993), 'Education for leading-learning', *Organisational Dynamics*, 21/3: 5–17.

—— and Schon, D. (1978), *Organisational Learning*, Reading, Mass: Addison-Wesley.

Ashford, S. J., Lee, C., and Bobko, P. (1989), 'Content, causes, and consequences of job insecurity: a theory-based measure and substantive test', *Academy of Management Journal*, 32/4: 803–29.

Australian Bureau of Agricultural Economics (ABARE) (1989), *Projections of Energy Demand and Supply—Australia 1989–90 to 1990–2000*, Canberra: ABARE.

Australian Bureau of Statistics (ABS) (1993), *Working Arrangements Australia*, Aug. 1993, Catalogue No. 6342.0, Canberra: Australian Government Printing Office.

—— (1996), *Employer Training Expenditure Survey*, 6353.0, Education and Training Section, Australian Bureau of Statistics, ACT.

—— (1998), *Labour Force Australia*, May 1998, Catalogue No. 6202.0, Canberra: Australian Government Printing Office.

Austroads (1994), 'Cost of personal travel', Sydney: Austroads.

Axelrod, R., (1976), *Structure of Decision: The Cognitive Maps of Political Elites*, Princeton: Princeton University Press.

Baldamus, W. (1961), *Efficiency and Effort*, London: Tavistock Publications.

Bandura, A. (1977), 'Self-efficacy: toward a unifying theory of behavioural change', *Psychological Review*, 84: 191–215.

—— (1988), 'Organisational applications of social cognitive theory', *Australian Journal of Management*, 13: 137–64.

Barnard, C. (1938), *The Functions of the Executive*, Cambridge, Mass: Harvard University Press.

Barnett, W. P., and Burgelman, R. A. (1996), 'Evolutionary perspectives on strategy', *Strategic Management Journal*, 17: 5–19.

Barney, J., (1986), 'Strategic factor markets; expectations, luck and business strategy', *Management Science*, 32: 1231–41.

Baron, J. N. (1984), 'Organisational perspectives on stratification', *Annual Review of Sociology*, 10: 37–69.

Bass, B. (1985), *Leadership and Performance Beyond Expectations*, New York: The Free Press.

Bates, J. (1987), 'Measurement of travel times values and opportunity cost from a discrete-choice model: A Comment', *Economic Journal*, 97/384.

Bateson, G. (1972), *Toward an Ecology of the Mind*, New York: Ballantine.

Batsell, R. R., and Louviere, J. J. (1991), 'Experimental analysis of choice', *Marketing Letters*, 2/3: 199–214.

Baumol, W. J., Panzar, J. C., and Willig, R. D. (1982), *Contestable Markets and the Theory of Industry Structure*, New York: Harcourt Brace Jovanovich.

Baxter, B. (1982), *Alienation and Authenticity: Some Consequences for Organised Work*, London: Tavistock Publications.

Beehr, T. A., and Newman, J. E. (1978), 'Job stress, employee health, and organisational effectiveness: a facet analysis, model and literature review', *Personnel Psychology*, 31 (winter) 665–99.

Beekun, R. I. (1989), 'Assessing the effectiveness of sociotechnical interventions: antidote or fad?' *Human Relations*, 47: 877–97.

Beesley, M. E. (1992), *Privatization, Regulation and Deregulation*, London: Routledge.

—— (1997), 'Rail: the role of subsidy in privatisation', in, Beesley, M. E. (ed.), *Regulating Utilities: Broadening the Debate*, London: Institute of Economic Affairs Readings 46: 237–86.

—— Gist, P., and Glaister, S. (1983), 'Cost benefit analysis and London's transport policies', *Progress in Planning*, 19, part 3: 169–269.

—— and Hensher, D. A. (1990), 'Private tollroads in urban areas: some thoughts on the economic and financial issues', *Transportation*, 16/4: 329–42.

—— —— (1992), *Managerial Efficiency, Regulation and Directional Training in the Public Sector*, Institute of Transport Studies, Graduate School of Business, The University of Sydney, Feb.

—— and Kettle, P. B. (1986), 'Devising business strategy for railways', *Transportation*, 13/1: 53–84.

Ben-Akiva, M. E., and Lerman, S. R. (1985), *Discrete Choice Analysis: Theory and Application to Travel Demand*, Cambridge: MIT Press.

Bennathan, E., and Walters, A. A. (1979), *Port Pricing and Investment Policy for Developing Countries*, World Bank Research Publication, New York: Oxford University Press.

Bennis, W. G. (1966), *Changing Organisations*, New York: McGraw-Hill.

Berger, J., Zelditch, M., Anderson, B., and Cohen, B. P. (1972), 'Structural aspects of distributive justice: a status value formulation', in Berger, J., Zelditch, M., and Anderson B. (eds.), *Sociological Theories in Progress*, ii Boston: Houghton Mifflin.

Bernardino, A., and Ben-Akiva, M. (1996), 'Demand for telecommuting—modeling the adoption process', *7th WCTR Proceedings*, 1: 241–53.

Bhat, C. R. (1995), 'A heteroscedastic extreme value model of intercity travel mode choice', *Transportation Research*, 29B/6: 471–483.

—— (1996), 'An endogenous segmentation mode choice model with an application to intercity travel', *Transportation Science*, 31: 34–48.

—— (1998), 'Accommodating variations in responsiveness to level-of-service variables in travel mode choice modeling', *Transportation Research*, 32A (Sept.), 495–507.

Bion, W. R. (1961), *Experience in Groups and Other Papers*, London: Tavistock.

Blau, P. (1964), *Exchange and Power in Social Life*, New York: Wiley.

Blauner, R. (1967), *Alienation and Freedom*, Chicago: University of Chicago Press.

Block, P. (1987), *The Empowered Manager*, San Francisco: Jossey-Bass.

Blood, M. R. (1969), 'Work values and job satisfaction', *Journal of Applied Psychology*, 53: 456–9.

Bly, P. H., and Webster, F. V. (1981), 'The demand for public transport: part I: the changing environment in which public transport operates', *Transport Reviews*, 1/4: 323–51.

Booz, Allen, and Hamilton Inc. (1985), 'Diversification: a survey of European Chief Executives', *Executive Summary*.

Borys, B., and Jemison, D. B. (1989), 'Hybrid arrangements as strategic alliances: theoretical issues in organisational combinations', *Academy of Management Review*, 14: 234–49.

Boulding, K. (1970), *Beyond Economics: Essays on Society, Religion and Ethics*, Ann Arbor: Ann Arbor Paperbacks.

Bouwen, R., and Fry, R. (1988), 'An agenda for managing organisational innovation development in the 1990s', in Lambrecht, M. (ed.), *Corporate Revival*, Leuven: University Press, 153–72.

Bovy, P., Orfeuil, J. P., and Zumkeller, D. (1993), 'Europe: a heterogeneous "single market" ', in Salomon, I., Bovy, P., and Orfeuil, J. P. (eds.), *A Billion Trips a Day: Tradition and Transition in European Travel Patterns*, Dordrecht: Kluwer Academic Publishers, 21–32.

Bower, G. H. (1976), 'Experiments on story understanding and recall', *Quarterly Journal of Experimental Psychology*, 28: 511–34.

Brewer, A. M. (1993), *Managing for Employee Commitment*, Melbourne: Longman.

—— (1994), *The Responsive Employee: the Road Towards Organisational Citizenship*, Sydney: Allen and Unwin.

—— (1995), *Change Management: Strategies for Australian Organisations*, Sydney: Allen and Unwin

—— and Hensher, D. A. (1996), 'Organisational structure, work organisation and flexible work arrangements and their impact on travel behaviour: identifying key linkages and establishing a research agenda', *New International Perspectives on Telework: From Telecommuting to the Virtual Organisation*, Brunel University, London, 31 July–2 Aug.

—— —— (1998), 'Distributed work and travel behaviour: the dynamics of interactive agency choices between employers and employees', prepared for the 8th International Conference on Travel Behaviour Research, Austin, Texas, Sept. 1997.

Brindle, R. E. (1992), 'Transport and land use: a "neo-modern" approach', *Proceedings of the 16th Australian Road Research Board Conference*, part 6: 111–36.

Brockner, J. (1988), *Self-Esteem at Work: Research, Theory and Practice*, Lexington, Mass: Lexington Books.

Brown, M. H. and Hosking, D. M. (1986), 'Distributed leadership and skilled performances as successful organisation in social movements', *Human Relations*, 39: 65–79.

Bruzelius, N. S., Jensen, A., and Sjostedt, L. (1996), 'Swedish rail policy: a critical review', in Hensher *et al.* (1996).

Buchanan, D., and Boddy, D. (1982), *Organisations and the Computer Age*, Farnborough, Hants: Gower.

—— and McCalman, J. (1989), *High Performance Work Systems: The Digital Experience*, London: Routledge.

Buchanan, G. (1975), 'To walk an extra mile', *Organisational Dynamics*, 3/4: 67–80.

Bullock, R. J. (1983), 'Participation and pay', *Group and Organisation Studies*, 8: 127–36.

Burawoy, M. (1979), *Manufacturing Consent*, Chicago: University of Chicago Press.

Bureau of Industry Economics (BIE) (1994a), *International Performance Indicators Overview*, Research Report 53, Canberra: Australian Government Publishing Service (AGPS), Feb.

—— (1994b), *International Performance Indicators: Coastal Shipping*, Research Report 55, Canberra: AGPS.

—— (1994c), *International Performance Indicators: Aviation*, Research Report 59, Canberra: AGPS.

—— (1995), *Waterfront 1995*, International Benchmarking Report 95–16, Canberra: AGPS.

Bureau of Transport and Communication Economics (BTCE) (1993a), *Waterfront Reform*, BTCE Report, Canberra: AGPS.

—— (1993b), *Costs of Reducing Greenhouse Gases in Australian Transport*, Canberra: AGPS, Nov.

—— (1995), *Greenhouse Gas Emissions from Australian Transport*, Report 88, Canberra: AGPS.

—— (1996), *Transport and Greenhouse: Costs and Options for Reducing Emissions*, BTCE Report 95, Canberra: AGPS, ch. 2.

Burns, T. (1974), 'On the rationale of the corporate system', in R. Marris (ed.), *The Corporate Society*, New York: Wiley.

Burrell, G., and Morgan, G. (1985), *Sociological Paradigms and Organisational Analysis*, London: Gower.

Bush, W. R. (1990), 'Telecommuting: the case of research software development', *Technological Forecasting and Social Change*, 37/3: 235–50.

Business Review Weekly (1994), 'For industrial efficiency, try asking the workers', 11 June.

Calfee, J., and Winston, C. (1998), 'The value of automobile travel time: implications for congestion policy', *Journal of Public Economics*, 69: 83–102.

Carroll, S., and Tosi, W. (1973), *Management by Objectives*, New York: Macmillan.

Cavendish, R. (1982), *Women on the Line*, London: Routledge and Kegan Paul.

Caves, D. W., Christensen, L. R., and Tretheway, M. W. (1984), 'Economies of density versus economies of scale: why truck and local service airline costs differ', *Rand Journal of Economics*, 15/4: 471–89.

Chadwick, E. (1859), 'Research of different principles of legislation on competition for the field as compared with competition with service', *Journal of the Royal Statistical Society*, Series A, 22: 381–92.

Channon, D. (1982), 'Industrial structure', *Long Range Planning*, 15/5: 3–17.

Charles, J. (1981), 'Approaches to teleconferencing justification—towards a general model', *Telecommunications Policy* (Dec), 296–303.

Child, J., and Smith, C. (1987), 'The context and process

of organisational transformation', *Journal of Management Studies*, 24: 565–93.

Christensen, K. E. (1988*a*), 'Conclusion: directions for the future', in Christensen (1988*b*).

—— (ed.) (1988*b*), *The New Era of Home-Based Work*, Colorado: Westview Press.

Christopher, M. (1998), *Logistics and Supply Chain Management: Strategies for Reducing Cost and Improving Service*, 2nd edn., London: Pitman.

Cobb, A. T. (1984), 'An episodic model of power: towards an integration of theory and research', *Academy of Management Review*, 9/3: 482–93.

—— and Margulies, N. (1981), 'Organisational development, a political perspective', *Academy of Management Review*, 6: 45–59.

Cohen, D., March, J. G., and Olsen, P. (1972), 'A garbage can model of organisational choice', *Administrative Science Quarterly*, 17/1: 1–25.

Cohen, S. G., and Ledford, G. E. (1994), 'The effectiveness of self-managing teams: a quasi-experiment', *Human Relations*, 52: 13–43.

Conger, J. A., and Kanungo, R. N. (1988), 'The empowerment process: integrating theory and practice', *Academy of Management Review*, 13/3: 471–82.

Conti, R., and Warner, M. (1993), 'Taylorism, teams and technology in "re-engineering" work organisation', *New Technology, Work and Employment*, 8: 31–46.

Coombe, D. (1996), 'Induced traffic: what do transportation models tell us?' *Transportation*, 23/1: 83–101.

Cosgrove, D., Gargett, D., and Viney, P. (1989), 'Simple demand equations for the short-term forecasting of air passenger movements', paper presented at the Annual Meeting of the Economic Society of Australia, Adelaide, July.

Cox, W., Kraus, J., and Mundle, S. (1997), 'Competitive contracting of transit services: Denver experience', paper presented at the 5th International Conference on Competition and Ownership in Land Passenger Transport, Leeds, UK, May 1997.

—— and Van de Velde, D. (1998), 'Franchising and tendering: Workshop 3', *Transport Reviews*, 18/4: 334–7.

Cyert, R. M., and March, J. G. (1963), *A Behavioural Theory of The Firm*, Englewood Cliffs NJ: Prentice Hall.

Dahl, C. A. (1986), 'Gasoline demand survey', *Energy Economics*, 7/1: 67–82.

Darley, J. M., and Latane, B. (1968), 'Bystander intervention in emergencies: diffusion of responsibility', *Journal of Personality and Social Psychology*, 8: 377–83.

Davies, P., Hill, C., and Gerlach, T. (1989), 'Virginia Fastoll—vehicle identification for non-stop toll collection', paper presented at the 5th World Conference of Transport Research, Yokohama, 8–14 July 1989.

Davis, S. M. (1984), *Managing Corporate Culture*, Cambridge, Mass.: Ballinger.

Deal, T., and Kennedy, A. (1982), *Corporate Cultures: The Rites and Rituals of Corporate Life*, Reading, Mass.: Addison-Wesley.

De Borger, B., Wouters, S., Mayeres, I., and Proost, S. (1996), 'Social cost pricing of urban passenger transport', in Hensher *et al* (1996), 385–93.

Deci, E. L. (1975), *Intrinsic Motivation*, New York: Plenum.

De Jong, G. C. (1989), 'Some joint models of car ownership and car use', unpublished Ph.D. thesis, Department of Econometrics, University of Amsterdam.

Delbridge, R., Turnbull, P., and Wilkinson, B. (1992), 'Pushing back the frontiers: management control and work intensification under JIT/TQM factory regimes', *New Technology, Work and Employment*, 7/2: 97–106.

Demsetz, H. (1968), 'Why regulate utilities?' *Journal of Law and Economics*, 11/1 (April) 55–66.

Denny, M., Fuss, M., and Waveman, L. (1981), 'The measurement and interpretation of total factor productivity in regulated industries, with an application to Canadian Telecommunications', in Cowing, T. G., and Stevenson, R. E. (eds.), *Productivity Measurement in Regulated Industries*, New York: Academic Press, 179–218.

De Rus, G. (1990), 'Public transport demand elasticities in Spain', *Journal of Transport Economics and Policy*, 24/2: 189–201.

DeSerpa, A. C. (1971), 'A Theory of the Economics of Time', *Economic Journal*, 81: 828–45.

Dess, G., and Davis, P. (1984), 'Porter's generic strategies and determinants of strategic group membership and organisational performance', *Academy of Management Journal*, 27: 467–88.

Deutsch, M. (1985), *Distributive Justice: A Social-Psychological Perspective*, New Haven, Conn.: Yale University Press.

DeVany, A. S., and Walls, W. D. (1997), 'Open access to rail networks', *Transportation Quarterly*, 51/2: 73–8.

Dickson, J. W. (1983), 'Beliefs about work and rationales for participation', *Human Relations*, 36: 911–13.

DiMaggio, P. J., and Powell, W. W. (1983), 'The iron cage revisited, institutional isomorphism and collective rationality in organisational fields', *American Sociological Review*, 48: 147–60.

Dobes, L. (1995), 'Greenhouse gas emissions in Australian transport in 1900 and 2000', *Bureau of Transport and Communication Economics Occasional Paper 110*, Department of Transport, Canberra.

Dodgson, J. S. (1983), 'Benefits of subsidising bus fare reductions', *House of Commons Third Report from the Transport Committee*, Bus Subsidy Policy, HC 285, London: HMSO, Evidence, 86–94.

—— (1996), 'Railway privatisation and infrastructure charging', in Hensher *et al.* (1996), 409–21.

—— (ed.) (1988), *Bus Deregulation and Privatisation: An International Perspective*, London: Gower.

Doganis, R., and Graham, A. (1987), 'Airport management: the role of performance indicators', Transport Studies Group, Polytechnic of Central London, London.

—— Lobbenberg, A. and Graham, A. (1995), 'The economic performance of European airports', Research Report 3, Department of Air Transport, College of Aeronautics, Cranfield University.

Doi, M., and Allen, W. B. (1986), 'A time series analysis of monthly ridership for an urban rail rapid transit line', *Transportation*, 13/3: 257–69.

Domberger, S., Hensher, D. A., and Wedde, S. (1993), 'Competitive tendering policies in the public and private sectors', *Australian Journal of Public Administration*, 52/4 (Dec.), 401–11.

—— Meadowcroft, S. A., and Thompson, D. J. (1987), 'The impact of competitive tendering on the costs of hospital domestic services', *Fiscal Studies*, 8/4: 39–51.

Domencich, T., and McFadden, D. (1975), *Urban Travel Demand*, Amsterdam: North-Holland.

Donnelly, W. A. (1983), 'The regional demand for petrol in Australia', *Economic Record*, 58/163: 317–27.

Downs, A. (1962), 'The law of peak-hour expressway congestion', *Traffic Quarterly*, 16: 393–409.

—— (1992), *Stuck in Traffic: Coping with Peak-Hour Traffic Congestion*, Washington: The Brookings Institution.

Drollas, L. P. (1984), 'The demand for gasoline: further evidence', *Energy Economics* (Jan.), 71–82.

Dufetel, L. (1991), 'Job evaluation: still at the frontier', *Compensation and Benefits Review*, 23/4: 53–67.

Dunn, W. N. (1981), *Public Policy Analysis: An Introduction*, Englewood Cliffs, NJ: Prentice Hall.

Edwards, R. (1979), *Contested Terrain: The Transformation of the Workplace in the Twentieth Century*, New York: Basic Books.

Elliott, W. (1992), 'Peak-hour road charges for Southern California: has their hour come round at last?' *Transportation Quarterly*, 46/4: 517–28.

Ellis, R., and Taylor, M. (1983), 'Role of self-esteem within the job search process', *Journal of Applied Psychology*, 68: 632–40.

Emery, F., and Trist, E. (1965), 'The causal texture of organisational environments', *Human Relations*, 18: 21–32.

England, E. (1967), 'Personal value systems of American managers', *Academy of Management Studies*, 21/1: 88–115.

Etzioni, A. (1968), *The Active Society*, New York: The Free Press.

Evans, A. (1990a), 'Are urban bus services natural monopolies?' *Papers of the Australasian Transport Research Forum*, 15/1: 251–68.

—— (1990b), 'Competition and the structure of local bus markets', *Journal of Transport Economics and Policy*, 24/3 (Sept.), 255–82.

Fairhurst, M. H., and Morris, P. J. (1975), 'Variations in the demand for bus and rail travel up to 1974', London Transport Executive Report R210, London Transport.

Fels, A. (1992), 'Towards a national competition policy', paper presented at the Conference on Industry Economics, Graduate School of Business, The University of Sydney, 5–6 July 1992.

—— (1995), 'Competition policy and law', paper presented at a workshop on infrastructure planning, Hanoi, Dec.

Festinger, L. (1957), *A Theory of Cognitive Dissonance*, Evanston, Ill.: Row, Peterson.

Fineman, S. (1993), 'Organisations as emotional arenas', in Fineman, S. (ed.), *Emotion in Organisations*, Newbury Park, Calif.: Sage, 9–35.

Finnveden, B. (1997), 'Improvement of the environment by purchasing bus transport services', paper presented at the 5th International Conference on Competition and Ownership in Land Passenger Transport, Leeds, UK, May 1997.

Flanagan, A., and Marcus, M. (1993), 'The secrets of a successful liaison', *Avmark Aviation Economist*, 10 (Jan.–Feb.), 20–3.

Folger, R. (1986), 'Rethinking equity theory', in Bierholf, H. W., Cohrn, R. L., and Greenberg, J. (eds.), *Justice in Social Relations*, New York: Plenum Publishing Corporation.

—— and Konovsky, M. A. (1989), 'Effects of procedural and distributive justice on reactions to pay raise decisions', *Academy of Management Journal*, 32: 115–30.

Foresster, J. W. (1971), 'Counter-intuitive behaviour of social systems', *Technological Review*, 73.

Forinash, C. V., and Koppelman, F. S. (1993), 'Application and interpretation of nested logit models of intercity mode choice', *Transportation Research Record*, 1413: 98–106.

Forsyth, P. J. (1980), 'The value of time in an economy with taxation', *Journal of Transport Economics and Policy*, 14/3 (Sept.), 337–62.

Fox, A. (1974), 'Industrial sociology and industrial relations', in Flanders, A. (ed.), *Collective Bargaining*, London: Penguin.

Frankena, M. W. (1983), 'The efficiency of public transport objectives and subsidy formulas', *Journal of Transport Economics and Policy*, 17: 67–76.

Frank Small and Associates (1994), *Insights into Community Attitudes towards RTA Activities*, Sydney: Roads and Traffic Authority, Apr.

Freeman, R. E. (1984), *Strategic Management, a Stakeholder Approach*, Boston: Pittman/Ballinger.

French, W. (1969), 'Organisation development: objectives, assumptions, and strategies', *California Management Review*, 12 (winter), 34–45.

Fromm, E. (1941), *Escape from Freedom*, New York: Farrar & Rinehart.

Frost, P. J., Moore, L. F., Louis, M. R., Lundberg, C. C., and Martin, J. (eds.) (1985), *Organisational Culture*, Beverly Hills, Calif.: Sage Publications.

Game, A., and Pringle, R. (1983), *Gender at Work*, Sydney: Allen and Unwin.

Gannon, C., and Shalazi, Z. (1995), *The Use of Sectoral and Project Performance Indicators in Bank-Financed Transport Operations*. Discussion Paper, Environmental Sustainable Development, Report TWU 21, Washington: The World Bank.

Geertz, C. (1973), *The Interpretation of Cultures*, New York: Basic Books.

Gerhart, B. (1987), 'How important are dispositional factors as determinants of job satisfaction? Implications for job design and other personnel programs', *Journal of Applied Psychology*, 72/3: 366–73.

Gerson, E. M. (1976), 'On quality of life', *American Sociological Review*, 41 (Oct.), 793–806.

Gibbs, P. G., Brotchie, J., Hensher, D., Newton, P., and O'Connor, K. (1996), *The Journey to Work: Employment and the Changing Structure of Australian Cities*, Australian Housing and Urban Research Institute, Research Monograph No. 3, Brisbane: University of Technology.

Giddens, A. (1979), *Central Problems in Social Theory*, London: Macmillan.

Gillen, D. W. (1977), 'Estimation and specification of the effects of parking costs on urban transport mode choice', *Journal of Urban Economics*, 4/2: 186–99.

Gist, M. E., Stevens, C. K., and Bavetta, A. B. (1991), 'The influence of self-efficacy and training condition on retention of learning', *Personnel Psychology*, 42: 837–61.

Glaister, S. (1981), *Fundamentals of Transport Economics*, Oxford: Basil Blackwell.

—— (1983), 'Some characteristics of rail commuter demand', *Journal of Transport Economics and Policy*, 17/2: 115–32.

—— (1984), 'The allocation of urban transport subsidy', in LeGrand, J., and Robinson, R. (eds.), *Privatisation and the Welfare State*, London: George Allen and Unwin.

—— (1987), 'Can the value of transport subsidy be measured?' in Harrison, A., and Gretton, J. (eds.), *Transport UK 1987 Policy Journals*, Newbury, Berks., 64–70.

—— and Lewis, D. (1978), 'An integrated fares policy for transport in London', *Journal of Public Economics*, 9: 341–55.

Goleman, D. (1995), *Emotional Intelligence: Why it Can Matter More than IQ*, London: Bloomsbury.

Golob, T., Kitamura, R., and Long, L. (eds.) (1997), *Panels in Transport Planning*, Boston: Kluwer Scientific Publishers.

Gomez-Ibanez, J. (1997), 'Estimating whether transport users pay their way: the state of the art', in Greene *et al.* (1997), 149–72.

Goodstein, L. (1983), 'Managers, values and organisational development', *Group and Organisational Studies*, 8/2: 203–20.

Goodwin, P. B. (1988), 'Evidence on car and public transport demand elasticities, 1980–1988', *Transport Studies Unit Paper 427 (revised)*, University of Oxford, June.

—— (1992), 'A review of new demand elasticities with special reference to short and long run effects of price changes', *Journal of Transport Economics and Policy*, 26/2: 155–69.

—— (1995), 'The case for and against urban road pricing', *London: House of Commons Transport Committee, Third Report*, ii, Minutes of Evidence, London: HMSO, 49–64.

—— (1996), 'Empirical evidence on induced traffic: a review and synthesis', *Transportation*, 23/1: 35–54.

—— Hallett, S., Kenny, F., and Stokes, G. (1991), *Transport: The New Realism*, Report Transport Studies Unit, University of Oxford, London: Rees Jeffrey Road Fund.

—— and Jones, P. M. (1989), 'Road pricing: the political and strategic possibilities', Transport Studies Unit Reference 4/40, University of Oxford, report prepared for the ECMT Round Table 80 meeting on Systems of Infrastructure Cost Coverage (Road Pricing, Principles and Application), Paris, Feb.

Graham, A., and Dennis, N. (1993), 'Factors affecting airport performance', paper presented at the Regional Science Association International British Section, 24th Annual Conference, 1–3 Sept. 1993.

Granovetter, M. (1986), 'Labour mobility, internal labour markets, and job matching: a comparison of the sociological and economic approaches', in Kalleberg, A. L. (ed.), Research in Social Stratification and Mobility, V, Greenwich, Conn.: JAI.

Gray, B., Bougon, M. G., and Donnellon, A. (1985), 'Organisations as constructions and destructions of meaning', Journal of Management, 2: 83–98.

Gray, M., Hodson, N., and Gordon, G. (1993), Teleworking Explained, New York: John Wiley.

Greenberg, J. (1987), 'A taxonomy of organisational justice theories', Academy of Management Review, no. 12: 9–22.

Greene, D. L. (1989a), Energy Efficiency Improvement Potential of Commercial Aircraft to 2010, Report published by the Oak Ridge National Laboratory for the US Department of Energy, Oct.

—— (1989b), CAFÉ or PRICE?: An Analysis of the Effects of Federal Fuel Economy Regulations and Gasoline Price on New Car MPG, 1978–89, Report published by the Oak Ridge National Laboratory for the US Department of Energy (contract DE-AC05–84OR21400), Oct.

—— (1989c), 'Motor fuel choice: An econometric analysis', Transportation Research, 23A/3 (May), 243–55.

—— and Hu, P. S. (1984), 'The influence of the price of gasoline on vehicle use in multivehicle households', Transportation Research Record, no. 988: 19–24.

—— Jones, D. W., and Delucchi, M. (eds.) (1997), The Full Costs and Benefits of Transportation, Berlin, Springer-Verlag, 281–314.

—— and Roberts, G. F. (1984), 'Fuel consumption for road transport in the USA—a comment', Energy Economics, 6/2: 145–7.

Greene, W. (1997), Econometric Analysis, New York: Macmillan.

Gregg, L. (1998), 'Humanity in the workplace: when work/family becomes an HR issue', Credit Union Executive, 38/5: 32–8.

Grey, A. (1975), Urban Fares Policy, Farnborough: Saxon House Books.

Grinyer, P. H., and Spender, J. C. (1979), 'Recipes, crises and adaptation in mature businesses', International Studies of Management and Organisation, 9/3: 113–23.

Guest, D. E. (1987), 'Human resource management and industrial relations', Journal of Management Studies, 24/5: 503–21.

Gwilliam, K. M., Nash, C. A. and Mackie, P. J. (1985), 'Deregulating the bus industry in Britain—the case against', Transport Reviews, 5/2: 105–32.

Hackman, J. R., and Oldham, G. R. (1980), Work Redesign, Reading, Mass.: Addison-Wesley.

Hammant, J. (1995), 'Information technology trends in logistics', Logistics Information Management, 8/6, Bradford.

Hammer, M., and Champy, J. (1994), Reengineering the Corporation: A Manifesto for Business Revolution, Sydney: Allen and Unwin.

—— and Stanton, S. A. (1995), The Reengineering Revolution: A Handbook, New York: Harper Business.

Hammond, J., and Morrisson, J. (1996), The Stuff Americans are Made of, London: Macmillan.

Handy, C. (1978), Gods of Management: How they Work, and Why they will Fail, London: Souvenir Press.

—— (1989), The Age of Unreason, London: Hutchinson Business Press.

—— (1986), Understanding Organisations, Harmondsworth: Penguin.

—— (1994), The Age of Paradox, Cambridge, Mass.: Harvard University Press.

Handy, S. L., and Mokhtarian, P. L. (1996a), 'Forecasting telecommuting: an exploration of methodologies and research needs', Transportation, 23: 163–90.

—— —— (1996b), 'The future of telecommuting', Futures, 28/3: 227–40.

Harrison, B. (1994), 'The dark side of flexible production', National Productivity Review, 13: 479, 501.

Harrison, E. E. (1987), The Managerial Decision-Making Process, Boston: Houghton-Mifflin.

Harrison, R. (1972), 'How to describe your organisation', Harvard Business Review, 5/1: 119–28.

Hau, T. D. (1992), 'Congestion charging mechanisms: an evaluation of current practice', World Bank, Infrastructure and Urban Development Department, Washington, Mar. (mimeo).

Henderson, B. D. (1989), 'The origin of strategy', Harvard Business Review (Nov.–Dec.), 139–43.

Hensher, D. A. (1977), Valuation of Business Travel Time, Oxford: Pergamon Press.

—— (1986), 'Sequential and full information maximum

likelihood estimation of a nested logit mode choice model', *Review of Economics and Statistics*, 68/4: 657–67.

Hensher, D. A. (1987), 'Productivity efficiency and ownership of urban bus services', *Transportation*, 14/4: 209–25.

—— (1988*a*), 'Behavioural and resource values of travel time savings: a bicentennial update', *Australian Road Research Journal*, 19/3 (Sept.), 223–9.

—— (1988*b*), 'Some thoughts on competitive tendering in local bus operations', *Transport Reviews*, 8/4: 363–72.

—— (1988*c*), 'Productivity of privately owned and operated local bus services', in Dodgson (1988).

—— (1989*a*), 'Private financing of transport infrastructure: a discussion paper', report prepared for the NSW Ministry of Transport, Nov. (mimeo)

—— (1989*b*), 'Competitive tendering in the transportation sector', lecture presented at a workshop on Competitive Tendering and Contracting Out, held at the Graduate School of Management and Public Policy, University of Sydney, 14 Oct. 1988, *Economic Papers*, 8/1 (Mar.), 1–11.

—— (1993), 'Socially and environmentally appropriate urban futures for the motor car', *Transportation*, 20/1: 1–19.

—— (1994), 'Stated preference analysis of travel choices: the state of practice', *Transportation*, 21/2: 107–34.

—— (1996), 'The role of roads in the urban community', report prepared for Austroads, Sydney.

—— (1997), 'Behavioral value of travel time savings in personal and commercial automobile travel', in Greene *et al.* (1997), 245–80.

—— (1998), 'Extending valuation to controlled value functions and non-uniform scaling with generalised unobserved variances', in Gärling, T., Laitila, T., and Westin, K. (eds.), *Theoretical Foundations of Travel Choice Modeling*, Oxford Pergamon, 75–102.

—— Barnard, P. O., Milthorpe, F. W., and Smith, N. C. (1989), 'Urban tollways and the valuation of travel time savings', *Economic Record*, 66/193 (June), 146–56.

—— —— Smith, N. C., Milthorpe, F. W., and Battellino, H. C. (1988), 'Very fast train feasibility study: step one of stage one', Final Report, Transport Research Group, School of Economic and Financial Studies, Macquarie University

—— Battelino, H., Milthorpe, F. and Raimond, T. (1994), 'Greenhouse gas emissions and the demand for urban passenger transport: data requirements, documentation and preparation. Report 4', Institute of Transport Studies, Sept.

—— and Beesley, M. E. (1989), 'Contracts, competitive bidding and market forces: recent experience in the supply of local bus services', *Australian Economic Papers*, 29 (Dec.), 236–45.

—— —— (1997), 'Markets, government and environmental policy issues for public transit', invited position paper prepared for the 5th International Conference on Competition and Ownership in Land Passenger Transport, Leeds, UK, May 1997, *Journal of Public Transport*, 4/1: 81–99.

—— and Bradley, M. (1993), 'Using stated response data to enrich revealed preference discrete choice models', *Marketing Letters*, 4/2: 139–52.

—— and Bullock, R. (1979), 'Price elasticity of commuter mode choice', *Transportation Research*, 13A/3: 193–202.

—— and Daniels, R. (1995), 'Productivity measurement in the urban bus sector', *Transport Policy*, 2/3 (July), 179 94.

—— and Greene, W. H. (1999), 'Specification and estimation of nested logit models', Institute of Transport Studies, The University of Sydney, June.

—— Hooper, P. G., Robinson, R., and Everett, S. (1998), 'Transport and the environment', in Hens, L., and Devuyst, D. (eds.), *Environmental Management*, London: Routledge, 258–80.

—— and Johnson, L. W. (1981), *Applied Discrete-Choice Modelling*, London: Croom Helm.

—— King, J., and Oum, T. H. (eds.) (1996), *World Transport Research*, iii, Oxford: Pergamon Press.

—— Louviere, J. J., and Swait, J. (1999), 'Combining sources of preference data', *Journal of Econometrics*, 89: 197–221.

—— and Milthorpe, F. W. (1989), 'The externality benefits of public transport subsidies', Report prepared for the Ministry of Transport and the Urban Transit Authority of NSW, Transport Research Centre, Macquarie University, Sydney

—— and Prioni, P. (2000), 'Measuring service quality and evaluating its influence on the cost of service provision', *Journal of Public Transport*, 5/3.

—— and Raimond, T. (1996), *Estimation of Public Transport Fare Elasticities in the Sydney Region*, Research Paper No. 7, Independent Pricing and Regulatory Tribunal of New South Wales, Sydney, Oct.

—— and Smith, N. C. (1986), 'A structural model of the use of automobiles by households: a case study of urban Australia', *Transport Reviews*, 6/10: 87–111.

—— —— Milthorpe, F. W., and Barnard, P. O. (1992), *The Dimensions of Automobile Demand*, Amsterdam: North Holland.

—— and Waters, W. G. II (1994), 'Light rail and bus priority systems: choice or blind commitment?' in Starr Macmullen, B. (ed.), *Research in Transportation Economics*, iii, Greenwich: JAI Press, 139–62.

—— and Young, J. (1990), 'Fuel demand forecasts and long term elasticities of demands', *Occasional Paper 103*, Bureau of Transport and Communication Economics, Canberra: AGPS, Feb., 102.

Hepburn, S. (1994), 'A simple model for estimating vehicle operating costs in urban areas', *Road and Transport Research*, 3/2: 112–19.

Herzberg, F., Mausner, B., and Snydeman, B. B. (1959), *The Motivation to Work*, New York: Wiley.

Heschtera, C. (1997), 'The reform of the Austrian state policy on local and regional land passenger transport market', Paper presented at 5th International Conference on Competition and Ownership in Land Passenger Transport, University of Leeds, July.

Hill, C. W. (1990), 'Co-operation, opportunism, and the invisible hand: implications for transaction cost theory', *Academy of Management Review*, 15: 500–13.

Hilmer, F. G., Raynor, M. R., and Taperell, G. Q. (1993), *National Competition Policy*, Report of the Independent Committee of Inquiry, Canberra: AGPS.

Hirschman, A. O. (1970), *Exit, Voice and Loyalty: Responses to Decline in Firms, Organisations, and States*, Cambridge, Mass.: Harvard University Press.

Hobbes, T. (1978), *Man and Citizen*, Atlantic Highlands: Humanities.

Hofstede, G. (1984), *Culture's Consequences: International Differences in Work-Related Values*, Beverly Hills, Calif.: Sage.

Houghton, J. T., Callander, B. A., and Varney, S. K. (1992), *Climate Change 1992, The Supplementary Report to the Intergovernmental Panel on Climate Change*, World Meteorological Organization/United Nations Environment Programme, Cambridge: Cambridge University Press.

Hrebiniak, L. and Alutto, J. (1972), 'Personal and role-related factors in the development of organisational commitment', *Administrative Science Quarterly*, 17: 555–73.

Huse, E. (1966), 'Putting in a management development program that works', *California Management Review*, 9: 73–80.

Isabella, L. A. (1990), 'Evolving interpretations as a change unfolds: how managers construe key organisational events', *Academy of Management Journal*, 33/1: 7–41.

Jackson, S. E., and Dutton, J. E. (1988), 'Discerning threats and opportunities', *Administrative Science Quarterly*, 33: 370–87.

—— and Schuler, R. S. (1985), 'A meta-analysis and conceptual critique of research on role ambiguity and role conflict in work settings', *Organisational Behaviour and Human Decision Processes*, 36: 16–78.

Janis, I. (1972), *Victims of Groupthink*, Boston: Houghton Mifflin.

—— (1989), *Crucial Decisions, Leadership in Policy Making and Crisis Management*, New York: Free Press.

—— and Mann, L. (1977), *Decision Making*, New York: The Free Press.

Jara Diaz, S. R. (1982), 'The estimation of transport cost functions: a methodological review', *Transport Reviews*, 2: 257–78.

—— (1988), 'Multioutput analysis of trucking operations using spatially disaggregated flows', *Transportation Research*, 22B 3: 159–71.

—— (1998), 'A general micro-model of users' behaviour: the basic issues', in DeOrtuzar, J., Jara Diaz, S., and Hensher, D. A. (eds.), *Travel Behaviour*, Oxford: Pergamon Press.

Johanson, J., and Mattsson, L. G. (1988), 'Internationalisation in industrial systems—a network approach', in Hood, N., and Vahlne, J. E. (eds.), *Strategies in Global Competition*, New York: Croom Helm, 287–314.

Johnson, G. (1987), *Strategic Change and the Management Process*, Oxford: Basil Blackwell.

Joy, S. (1991), 'Options for port pricing', Report prepared by Hyland Joy and Wardrop for the Port of Melbourne, Port Pricing Steering Committee, Melbourne, Jan.

Kanfer, R., Ackerman, P. L., Murtha, T. C., Dugdale, B., and Nelson, L. (1994), 'Goal setting, conditions of practice, and task performance: a resource allocative perspective', *Journal of Applied Psychology*, 79/6: 826–35.

Kanter, R. M. (1989), 'Becoming PALs: pooling, allying, and linking across companies', *Academy of Management Executive*, 3/3: 183–93.

Karasek, R. A. (1979), 'Job demands, job decision latitude and mental strain: implications for job redesign', *Administrative Science Quarterly*, 25 (June), 285–309.

Karpin Report (1995), *Enterprising Nation: Renewing Australia's Managers to Meet the Challenges of the Asia-Pacific Century*, Report of the Industry Task Force on Leadership and Management Skills, Canberra: AGPS.

Kay, J. A. (1987), 'Public ownership, public regulation or public subsidy?' *European Economic Review*, 31: 343–5.

Kelley, H. H. (1973), 'The process of causal attributions', *American Psychologist*, 107–28.

Kemerer, B., and Arnold, V. A. (1993), 'The growing use of benchmarking in managing cultural diversity', *Business Forum* (winter/spring), 38–40.

Kennedy, D. (1996), 'London bus tendering: a welfare balance sheet', *Transport Policy*, 2/4: 243–9.

Kets de Vries, M. F. R., and Miller, D. (1984), *The Neurotic Organisation: Diagnosing and Changing Counterproductive Styles of Management*, San Francisco: Jossey-Bass.

Kimberly, J. R. (1981), 'Managerial innovation', in Nystrom, P. C., and Starbuck, W. H. (eds.), *Handbook of Organisational Design*, Oxford: Oxford University Press.

King, J. (1996), 'Economic significance of high speed rail', Proceedings of the 17th Australasian Transport Research Forum, Auckland, New Zealand, Aug.

King, M. (1996), 'New Zealand railways case study', in Kopicki, R., and Thompson, L. S. (eds.), *Best Methods of Railway Restructuring and Privatisation*, CES Discussion Paper No. 111, World Bank, 101–36.

King, S. P. (1997), *Access Pricing under Rate-of-return Regulation*, Discussion Paper No. 366, Centre for Economic Policy Research, Canberra: The Australian National University, May.

Kirzner, I. M. (1997), 'Entrepreneurial discovery and the competitive market process: an Austrian approach', *Journal of Economic Literature*, 35/1: 60–85.

Klaassen, L. H., Vogelaar, H., and Wagenaar, S. (1984), 'Allocating subsidies to public transport: some theoretical and practical considerations', *Transport Reviews*, 41: 43–72.

Klein, B., and Leffler, K. B. (1981), 'The role of market forces in assuring contractual performance', *Journal of Political Economy*, 89/4: 615–41.

Kluckhohn, C., and Murray, H. (1949), *Personality*, New York: A. A. Knopf.

Kolsen, H. M. (1991), 'Options for port pricing', Report no. 2, prepared for the Port of Melbourne, Port Pricing Steering Committee, Melbourne, Feb.

—— (1996), 'The new competition policy: problem areas in the transport sector', paper presented at Transport Policy Workshop, Institute of Transport Studies, 17 Sept.

—— Ferguson, D. C., and Docwra, D. E. (1975), *Road User Charges: Theory and Possibilities*, Occasional Paper No. 3, Canberra: Bureau of Transport Economics.

Kotter, J. P. (1995), 'Why transformation efforts fail?' *The Harvard Business Review* (Mar.–Apr.), 59–67.

Kouzes, J. (1998), 'Voice lessons', *Journal for Quality and Participation*, 21/1 (Jan.–Feb.), 64.

Kraft, G., and Domencich, T. A. (1972), 'Free transit', in Edel, M., and Rothenburg, J. (eds.), *Readings in Urban Economics*, New York: Collier-Macmillan, 231–54.

Kraut, A. I. (1975), 'Predicting turnover of employees from measured job attitudes', *Organisational Behaviour and Human Performance*, no. 13: 233–43.

Kvande, E. and Rasmussen, B. (1995), 'Women's careers in static and dynamic organizations', *Acta-Sociologica*, 38/2: 115–30.

Larsen, O. I. (1988), 'The toll ring in Bergen, Norway—the first year of operation', *Traffic Engineering and Control* (Apr.), 216–22.

Latham, G., and Yukl, G. (1975), 'A review of the application of goal setting in organisations', *Academy of Management Journal*, 18: 824–43.

—— and Locke, E. A. (1991), 'Self-regulation through goal setting', *Organisational Behaviour and Human Decision Processes*, 50/2: 212–47.

Lerner, A. C. (1992), 'Measuring performance of airport passenger terminals', *Transportation Research*, 26A/1: 37–45.

Lenntorp, B. (1976), 'A time-geographic simulation model of individual activity programmes', in Carlstein, T., Parkes, D., and Thrift, N. (eds.), *Human Activity and Time Geography*, London: Edward Arnold, 162–80.

Lerner, M. J. (1977), 'The justice motive in social behaviour: some hypotheses as to its origins and forms', *Journal of Personality*, 45: 1–52.

Lewin, K. (1951), *Field Theory in Social Science*, New York: Harper and Row.

Lindblom, C. (1958), 'The science of "muddling through"', *Public Administration Review*, 29: 79–88.

Lippitt, R., Watson, J., and Westley, B. (1958), *The Dynamics of Planned Change*, New York: Harcourt, Brace and World.

Litman, T. (1997), 'Using road pricing revenue: economic efficiency and equity considerations', *Transportation Research Record*, 1558: 24–8.

—— (1999), 'Generated traffic: implications for transport planning,' Victoria Transport Policy Institute, Victoria, British Columbia, June, 21 pp.

Louviere, J. J., and Hensher, D. A. (1983), 'Using discrete choice models with experimental design data to forecast consumer demand for a unique cultural event', *Journal of Consumer Research*, 10/3: 348–61.

—— —— (1996), 'Stated choice methods and analysis: a short course', Portland State University, Portland, June.

—— —— and Swait, J. (2000), *Stated Choice Methods: Analysis and Applications in Marketing, Transportation and Environmental Valuation*, Cambridge: Cambridge University Press, 697 pp.

Loveday, P. (1993), 'Review of household telephone interviews: December 1992', Transport Study Group, Roads and Traffic Authority, Sydney, June.

Lovelock, C. H. (1992), *Managing Services: Marketing,*

Operations, and Human Resources, 2nd edn., Englewood Cliffs, NJ: Prentice Hall.

Luk, J., and Chung, E. (1997a), *Public Acceptance and Technologies for Road Pricing*, ARR 307, Melbourne: ARRB Transport Research.

——— ——— (1997b), 'Induced demand and road investment—an initial appraisal', *Research Report ARR299*, Vermont South, Victoria: ARRB Transport Research Ltd. Feb., 31pp.

Lukes, S. (1974), *Power: A Radical View*, London: Macmillan.

Lyles, M. A., and Schwenk, C. R. (1992), 'Top management, strategy and organisational knowledge structures', *Journal of Management Studies*, 29: 155–74.

McAfee, R. P., and McMillan, J. (1987), 'Auctions and Bidding', *Journal of Economic Literature*, 25: 699–738.

McClelland, D. (1961), *The Achieving Society*, Princeton: Van Nostrand.

McFadden, D. (1974), 'The measurement of urban travel demand', *Journal of Public Economics*, 3: 303–28.

——— (1979), 'Quantitative methods for analysing travel behaviour of individuals: some recent developments', in Hensher, D. A., and Stopher, P. R. (eds.), *Behavioural Travel Modelling*, London: Croom Helm.

McGrath, R. (1994), 'Organisationally induced helplessness: the antithesis of empowerment', *Quality Progress*, 27/4: 89–92.

McGregor, D. (1960), *The Human Side of Enterprise*, New York: McGraw-Hill.

McGuire, J. B., Sundgren, A., and Schneeweis, T. (1988), 'Corporate social responsibility and firm financial performance', *Academy of Management Journal*, 21/4: 854–72.

McKay, R. (1988), 'International competition: its impact on employment', in Christensen (1988b), 95–113.

Mackie, P. J. (1984), 'Competition in the bus industry', *Public Money*, 3/2 (June).

McLuhan, M. (1964), *Understanding Media: The Extensions of Man*, New York: McGraw-Hill.

Madan, D. B., and Greenhout, R. (1987), 'Modelling travel mode choices for the Sydney work trip', *Journal of Transport Economics and Policy*, 21/2: 135–9.

Maddala, G. (1983), *Limited Dependent Variable and Qualitative Variables in Econometrics*, New York: Cambridge University Press.

Mahmassani, H. S., Yen, J. R., Herman, R., and Sullivan, M. (1993), 'Employee attitudes and stated preferences toward telecommuting: an exploratory analysis', *Transportation Research Record*, 1413: 31–41.

Malekzadeh, A. R., and Nahavandi, A. (1988), 'Acculturation in mergers and acquisitions', *Academy of Management Review*, 13/1: 79–90.

Mannering, J. S., and Mokhtarian, P. L. (1995), 'Modeling the choice of telecommuting frequency in California: an exploratory analysis', *Technological Forecasting and Social Change*, 49: 49–73.

March, J. G. (1976), 'The technology of foolishness', in March, J., and Olsen, J. (eds.), *Ambiguity and Choice in Organisations*, Bergen: Universitetsforlaget.

Martin, J., Sitkin, B., and Boehm, M. (1985), 'Founders and the elusiveness of a cultural legacy', in Frost, P. J., Moore, L. F., Louis, M. R., Lundberg, C. C., and Martin, J. (eds.), *Organisational Culture*, Beverly Hills, Calif.: Sage, 99–124.

Maslow, A. H. (1954), *Motivation and Personality*, New York: Harper.

Massey, D. (1993), 'Power-geometry and a progressive sense of place', in Bird, J. *et al.* (eds.), *Mapping the Futures: Local Cultures, Global Change*, London: Routledge, 59–69.

Mathieu, Y. (1997), 'Citizen's network: about utopia and myopia', Paper presented at the 5th International Conference on Competition and Ownership of Land Passenger Transport, University of Leeds, July.

Mayo, E. (1933), *The Human Problems of an Industrial Civilisation*, New York: Macmillan.

Mayworm, P., Lago, A. M., and McEnroe, J. M. (1980), 'Patronage impacts of changes in transit fares and services', Report No. 135–1, prepared for the Office of Service and Methods Demonstration, US Department of Transportation, by Ecosometrics Inc., Maryland, USA.

Memmott, F. W. (1963), 'The sustainability of communications for transportation', *Traffic Engineering*, 33: 20–5.

Mensah, J. (1995), 'Journey to work and job search characteristics of the urban poor: a gender analysis of survey data from Edmonton, Alberta', *Transportation*, 1–19.

Meyer, J. P., Paunonen, S. V., Gellatly, I. R., Goffin, R. D., and Jackson, D. N. (1989), 'Organisational commitment and job performance: it's the nature of the commitment that counts', *Journal of Applied Psychology*, 74: 152–6.

Meyer, J. W., and Rowan, B. (1977), 'Institutionalised organisations: formal structure as myth and ceremony', *American Journal of Sociology*, 83: 340–63.

Meyerson, D. (1991), ' "Normal" ambiguity? A glimpse of an occupational', in Frost, P. J., Moore, L. F., Louis, M. R., Lundberg, C. C., and Martin, J. (eds.), *Reframing Organisational Culture*, Newbury Park, Calif.: Sage, 131–44.

Meyerson, D. Weick, K. E., and Kramer, R. M. (1991), 'Swift trust and temporary groups', in Kramer, R. M., and Tyler, T. R. (eds.), *Trust in Organisations: Frontiers of Theory and Research*, Thousand Oaks, Calif.: Sage.

Michaels, C. E., and Spector, P. E. (1982), 'Causes of employee turnover: a test of Mobley, Griffeth, Hand and Meglino Model', *Journal of Applied Psychology*, 67: 237–42.

Miles, R. E. and Snow, C. C. (1978), *Organisational Strategy, Structure, and Process*, New York: McGraw-Hill.

—— —— (1984), 'Fit, failure and the hall of fame', *California Management Review*, 26/3: 10–28.

Mill, J. S. (1974), 'Consideration on responsible government', *Utilitarianism, On Liberty & Considerations on Responsible Government*, London: Dent.

Miller, D. (1987), 'Strategy making and structure: analysis and implications for performance', *Academy of Management Journal*, 30: 7–32.

Mintzberg, H. (1973), *The Nature of Managerial Work*, New York: Harper and Row.

—— (1979), *The Structure of Organisations*, Englewood Cliffs, NJ: Prentice Hall.

—— (1983), *Structure in Fives, Designing Effective Organisations*, Englewood Cliffs, NJ: Prentice Hall.

—— and McHugh, A. (1985), 'Strategy formation in adhocracy', *Administrative Science Quarterly*, 30: 160–87.

—— and Waters, J. (1982), 'Tracking strategy in an entrepreneurial firm', *Academy of Management Journal*, 25: 465–99.

Mitchell, T. R. and Beach, L. R. (1990), '"Do I love thee? Let me count . . . " Toward an understanding of intuitive and automatic decision making', *Organisational Behaviour and Human Decision Processes*, 47: 1–20.

Mobley, W. H. (1982), *Employee Turnover: Causes, Consequences and Control*, Reading, Mass.: Addison-Wesley.

Mohr, L. B. (1982), *Explaining Organisational Behaviour*, San Francisco: Jossey-Bass.

Mokhtarian, P. L. (1990), 'A typology of relationships between telecommunications and transportation', *Transportation Research Record A*, 24A/3: 231–42.

—— Handy, S. L., and Salomon, I. (1995), 'Methodological issues in the estimation of the travel, energy and air quality impacts of telecommuting', *Transportation Research Record A*, 29A/4: 283–302.

—— and Salomon, I. (1996), 'Modeling the choice of telecommunting 2: a case of the preferred impossible alternative', *Environment and Planning A*, 28: 1859–76.

Monson, T. C., Hesley, J. W. and Chernick, L. (1982), 'Specifying when personality traits can and cannot predict behaviour: an alternative to abandoning the attempt to predict single act criteria', *Journal of Personality and Social Psychology*, 43: 385–99.

Moore, J. F. (1996), *The Death of Competition: Leadership and Strategy in the Age of Business Ecosystems*, New York: Harper Business.

Morgan, G. (1986), *Images of Organisation*, London: Sage.

Moss, M. L. (1987), 'Telecommunications, world cities and urban policy', *Urban Studies*, 24: 534–46.

Mowday, R., Porter, L. W., and Steers, R. M. (1982), *Employee-Organisation Linkages, the Psychology of Commitment, Absenteeism, and Turnover*, Orlando, Fla.: Academic Press.

Mueller, C., Wallace, J., and Price, J. (1992), 'Employee commitment', *Work and Occupation*, 19/3: 221–36.

Nadler, D. A. (1987), 'The effective management of organisational change', in Lorsch, J. W. (ed.), *Handbook of Organisational Behaviour*, Englewood Cliffs, NJ: Prentice Hall, 358–69.

—— Gerstein, M. S., and Shaw, R. B. (1992), *Organisational Architecture: Designs for Changing Organisations*, San Francisco: Jossey-Bass.

—— and Tushman, M. (1989), 'Organisational frame bending, principles for managing reorientation', *Academy of Management Executive*, 1: 194–204.

Nash, C. A. (1982), *Economics of Public Transport*, London: Longman.

—— (1996), 'Rail privatisation in Britain', Institute for Transport Studies, The University of Leeds.

—— (1997), 'Rail privatisation in Great Britain', paper presented at the 5th International Conference on Competition and Ownership in Land Passenger Transport, Institute for Transport Studies, University of Leeds, May.

—— and Dodgson, J. (1996), 'Rail sector issues: workshop 3', *Transport Reviews*, 16/4: 277–84.

National Association of Australian State Road Authorities (NAASRA) (1984), *The NAASRA Roads Study*, various reports (Technical Reports T-8, T-10, Study Reports R-2, R-4), Sydney: NAASRA.

National Road Transport Commission (NRTC) (1992), *Discussion Paper on Heavy Vehicle Charges*, Melbourne: NRTC.

Neilson, E. H., and Rao, M. V. H. (1987), 'The strategy-legitimacy nexus, a thick description', *Academy of Management Review*, 12: 523–33.

Neutze, M. (1995), 'Funding urban infrastructure through private developers', *Urban Policy and Research*, 13/1: 20–8.

Nicholson, N., Rees, A. and Brooks-Rooney, A. (1990), 'The cultural deconstruction of innovation', in West, M. A., and Farr, J. L. (eds.), *Innovation and Creativity at Work*, London: Wiley.

Nijkamp, P., and Pepping, G. (1998), 'Meta-analysis for explaining the variance in public transport demand elasticities in Europe', *Journal of Transportation and Statistics*, 21, 1: 1–14.

—— Rienstra, S., and Vleugel, J. (1997), 'Long-term scenarios for surface transport', *International Journal for Environment and Pollution*, 7/3: 305–26.

Nilles, J. M. (1975), 'Telecommunications and organisational decentralisation', *IEE Transactions of Communications*, 23/10: 1142–7.

Nisbett, R. and Ross, L. (1981), *Human Inference: Strategies and Shortcomings of Social Judgement*, Englewood Cliff, NJ: Prentice Hall.

Nonaka, I., and Takeuchi, H. (1995), *The Knowledge-Creating Company: How Japanese Companies Create the Dynamics of Innovation*, New York: Oxford University Press.

Nystrom, N. C. and Starbuck, W. H. (1984), 'To avoid organisational crisis, unlearn', *Organisational Dynamics* (spring), 53–65.

Obeng, K. (1985a), 'Bus transit cost, productivity and factor substitution', *Journal of Transport Economics and Policy*, 19/2: 183–203.

—— (1985b), 'Variables affecting bus transit productivity', *Proceedings of the Transportation Research Forum*, 26/1: 302–10.

O'Donnell, C. (1984), *The Basis of the Bargain*, Sydney: Allen and Unwin.

Okada, H. (1994), 'Features and economic and social effects of the shinkansen', *Japan Railway & Transport Review*, 3 (Oct.), 9–16.

Olson, D. and Tetrick, L. E. (1988), 'Organisational restructuring', *Group and Organisation Studies*, 13: 374–88.

O'Reilly, C. A., Caldwell, D. F., and Barnett, W. P. (1989), 'Work group demography, social integration and turnover', *Administrative Science Quarterly*, 34: 21–37.

Organ, D. W. (1988), *Organisational Citizenship Behaviour: The Good Soldier Syndrome*, Lexington, Mass.: Lexington Books.

Organization for Economic Cooperation and Development (OECD) (1993), *OECD Employment Outlook*, Paris: OECD.

Ouchi, W. A. (1981), *Theory Z: How American Business can Meet the Japanese Challenge*, Reading, Mass.: Addison-Wesley.

Oum, T., Waters II, W. G., and Yong, J. (1992), 'Concepts of price elasticities of transport demand and recent empirical evidence', *Journal of Transport Economics and Policy*, 26/2: 139–54.

—— Tretheway, M. W., and Waters II, W. G. (1992), 'Concepts, methods and purposes of productivity measurement in transportation', *Transportation Research*, 26A/6 (Nov.), 493–505.

—— and Waters II, W. G. (1996), 'A survey of recent developments in transportation cost function research', *Logistics and Transportation Review*, 32/4 (Dec.), 423–63.

Parkhe, A. (1991), 'Interfirm diversity, organizational learning, and longevity in global strategic alliances', *Journal of International Business Studies*, 22/4: 579–601.

Peirson, J., and Vickerman, R. (1997), 'Environmental effects of transport: a model of optimal pricing and investment for the UK', *International Journal of Environment and Pollution*, 7/3: 343–56.

Perrow, C. (1972), *Complex Organisations: A Critical Essay*, Glenview, Ill.: Scott, Foresman.

—— (1984), *Normal Accidents: Living with High Risk Technologies*, New York: Basic Books.

Pettigrew, A. M. (1985), *The Awakening Giant: Continuity and Change in Imperial Chemical Industries*, Oxford: Basil Blackwell.

—— (1990a), 'Longitudinal field research on change, theory and practice', *Organisational Science*, 3/1: 120–38.

—— (1990b), 'Studying strategic choice and strategic change, a comment on Mintzberg and Waters, "Does decision get in the way?"' *Organisational Studies*, 11/1: 6–11.

Pfeffer, J. (1981), *Power in Organisations*, Marshfield, Mass.: Pitman.

—— (1982), *Organisations and Organisation Theory*, London: Pitman.

—— and Salancik, G. R. (1978), *The External Control of Organisations: A Resource Dependence Perspective*, New York: Harper and Row.

Philips Industries (1987), 'PREMID: how microwaves can make custom production profitable', Stockholm: Philips Industries.

—— (1988a), 'Automatic charging for tolls', System Information (Industrial Automation) Brochure, Norway: Philips Industries.

—— (1988b), 'PREMID toll road installation in Alesund, Norway', unpublished memorandum, Norway: Philips Industries.

Piore, M., and Sabel, C. (1984), *The Second Industrial Divide: Possibilities for Prosperity*, New York: Basic Books.

Pisano, G. P. (1997), *The Development Factory*, Cambridge, Mass.: Harvard Business Review Press.

Polanyi, M. (1966), *Tacit Dimension*, London: Routledge Kegan Paul.

Popper, M., and Lipshitz, R. (1998), 'Organisational learning mechanisms: a structural and cultural approach to organisational learning', *Journal of Applied Behavioural Science*, 34/2: 161–79.

Porter, M. E. (1985), *Competitive Strategy*, London: Collier Macmillan.

—— (1990), *The Competitive Advantage of Nations*, New York: The Free Press.

—— (1996), 'What is strategy?' *Harvard Business Review* (Nov.–Dec.), 61–78.

—— and Van der Linde, C. (1995), 'Toward a new conception of the environment-competitiveness relationship', *Journal of Economic Perspectives*, 9/4 (fall), 97–118.

Posner, B., Kouzes, J., and Schmidt, W. (1985), 'Shared values make a difference: an empirical test of corporate culture', *Human Resource Management*, 24: 293–309.

Potter, S., and Enoch, M. P. (1997), *Regulating Transport's Environmental Impacts in a Deregulating World*, Buckingham: Open University.

Powell, W. W. (1987), 'Hybrid organisational arrangements: new form or transformational development?' *California Management Review*, 67–87.

Prahalad, C. K. and Hamel, G. (1993), 'Strategic intent', *International Review of Strategic Management*; 4: 63–87.

Pratt, J. H. (1997), 'Why aren't more people telecommuting? Explanation from four studies', *Transportation Research Record*, No. 1607: 196–204.

Preston, J. (1991), 'Explaining competitive practices in the bus industry: the British Experience', *Transportation Planning and Technology*, 15/ 2–4: 277–94.

—— (1993), 'Competition policy and the British bus industry: the case of mergers', in Talvitie, A., Hensher, D. A., and Beesley M. E. (eds.), *Privatisation and Deregulation in Passenger Transport, Proceedings of the 2nd International Conference*, Finland: Auranen Publishers Ltd., 99–115.

Price, J. L., and Mueller, C. W. (1986), *Absenteeism and Turnover of Hospital Employees*, Greenwich, Conn.: JAI.

Prioni, P., and Hensher, D. A. (2000), 'Measuring service quality and evaluating its influence on costs of service provision', *Journal of Public Transport*, 5/3.

Quinn, J. B. (1980), *Strategy for Change: Logical Incrementalism*, Homewood, III.: Irwin.

—— (1992), *Intelligent Enterprise*, New York: The Free Press.

Quinn, R. E., and McGrath, M. R. (1985), 'The transformation of organisational cultures: a competing values approach', in Frost *et al.* (1985), 315–34.

RAMIS (1992), '1992 community research—attitudes to RTA activities', Programming Strategy Branch, Roads and Traffic Authority, Sydney, Aug.

—— (1993), *1993 Community Research—Attitudes to RTA Activities*, Corporate Strategy Development Branch, Roads and Traffic Authority, Sydney, Sept.

Ray, S. C., and Hu, X. (1997), 'On the technically efficient organisation of an industry: a study of U.S. airlines', *Journal of Productivity Analysis*, 8/1: 5–18.

Revans, R. (1980), *Action Learning: New Techniques for Management*, London: Blond and Briggs.

Riggs, M. L. (1989), Cited in Jex, S. M. and Gudanowski, D. M. (1992), 'Efficacy beliefs and work stress: an exploratory study', *Journal of Organisational Behaviour*, 13: 509–17.

Ring, P. S. and Van de Ven, A. (1992), 'Structuring cooperative relationships between organisations', *Strategic Management Journal*, 13: 483–98.

Roads and Traffic Authority (1992), 'Vehicle operating costs program (VEHOP), Sydney: RTA of NSW.

Roberts, N. C., and King, P. J. (1989), 'The stakeholder audit goes public', *Organisational Dynamics*, 17: 63–9.

Robinson, G. S., and Wick, C. (1992), 'Executive development that makes a business difference', *Human Resource Planning*, 15/1: 63–76.

Rodgers, R., and Hunter, J. E. (1991), 'Impact of management by objectives on organisational productivity', *Journal of Applied Psychology*, 76/2 (Apr.) 322–336.

Rogers, E. M., and Shoemaker, C. F. (1971), *Communication of Innovations: A Cross-Cultural Dynamics*, New York: Wiley.

Ross, J., and Staw, B. M. (1986), 'Expo 86: an escalation prototype', *Administrative Science Quarterly*, 31: 274–97.

Rothwell, R. (1977), 'Generating effective corporate innovation', *Technology Review* (Oct.–Nov.), 27–33.

Rouse, P., Putterill, M., and Ryan, D. (1997), 'Towards a general managerial framework for performance measurement: comprehensive highway maintenance application', *Journal of Productivity Analysis*, 8/2: 127–49.

RTA Teleworking Pilot Project (1993/94), 'Teleworking: a flexible opportunity', Roads & Traffic Authority NSW.

Saffold, G. S. (1988), 'Culture traits, strength, and organisational performance: moving beyond "strong" culture', *Academy of Management Review*, 13.

Salancik, G. R., and Pfeffer, J. (1977), 'Who gets power and how they hold on to it: a strategic contingency model of power', *Organisational Dynamics*, 5: 3–21.

—— —— (1978), 'A social information processing approach to job attitudes and task design', *Administrative Science Quarterly*, 23: 224–53.

Salomon, I. (1994), 'How much telecommuting should we count on? A forecast for Tel-Aviv in 2020', *Transportation Research Record*, 1463: 26–34.

—— and Schofer, J. (1988), 'Forecasting telecommunications—travel interactions: the transportation manager's perspective', *Transportation Research*, 22A/3: 219–29.

Sauer, J., and Anderson, N. (1992), 'Have we misread the psychology of innovation? A case study from two NHS hospitals', *Leadership and Organisation Development Journal*, 13/2: 17–21.

Savage, G. T., Nix, T. W., Whitehead, C. J., and Blair, J. D. (1991), 'Strategies for assessing and managing organisational stakeholders', *Academy of Management Executive*, 5/2: 61–75.

Schein, E. H. (1977), 'The individual, the organisation, and the career: a conceptual scheme', Hackman, J. R., Lawler, E. E. and Porter, L. (eds.), *Perspectives in Behaviour in Organisations*, New York: McGraw-Hill.

—— (1992), *Organizational Culture and Leadership*, 2nd edn. San Francisco: Jossey-Bass.

Schimek, P. (1996), 'Gasoline and travel demand models using time series and cross section data from the United States', *Transportation Research Record*, 1558: 83–9.

Schipper, L., Steiner, R., Josefina, F., and Dolan, K. (1993), 'Fuel prices and economy: factors affecting land travel', *Transport Policy*, 1/1: 6–20.

Schon, D. (1987), *Educating the Reflective Practitioner*, San Francisco: Jossey-Bass.

Schuler, R., and MacMillan, I. (1984), 'Gaining competitive advantage through human resource management practices', *Human Resource Management*, 23: 241–55.

Schultz, A. (1967), *Collected Papers*, The Hague: Martinus Nijhoff, 2: 11.

Schutz, W. (1958), *A Three-Dimensional Theory of Interpersonal Behaviour*, New York: Rinehart.

Schwartz, H. S. (1990), *Narcissistic Process and Corporate Decay: A Theory of the Organisation Ideal*, New York: New York University.

Schwartz, S. (1974), 'Awareness of interpersonal consequences, responsibility denial, and voluntarism', *Journal of Personality & Social Psychology*.

—— (1975), 'The justice of need and the activation of humanitarian norms', *Journal of Social Issues*, 31/3: 111–36.

Schweizer, S. (1993), 'Increasing profitability through distributed network teaming', *Telecommunications*, 27/3 (Mar.), Americas edn., 52–7.

Scott, W. R. (1987), *Organisational Rational, Natural and Open Systems*, Englewood Cliffs, NJ: Prentice Hall.

Selznick, P. (1949), *TVA and the Grass Roots*, Berkeley: University of California Press.

Seneviratne, P. N., and Martel, N. (1991), 'Variables influencing performance of air terminal buildings', *Transportation Planning and Technology*, 16: 3–28.

—— —— (1994), 'Criteria for evaluating quality of service in air terminals', *Transportation Research Record*, 1461: 24–30, Transportation Research Board, Washington.

Senge, P. M. (1990), *The Fifth Discipline: The Art and Practice of the Learning Organisation*, New York: Doubleday/ Currency.

Senna, L. A. (1994), 'The influence of travel time variability on the value of time', *Transportation*, 21/2: 203–29.

Shapiro, C. (1983), 'Premium for high quality products as returns to reputation', *Quarterly Journal of Economics* (Nov.), 659–79.

Shepherd, L. E. (1972), 'An econometric approach to the demand for urban passenger travel', *ARRB Proceedings*, 6/2: 214–51.

Shepherd, W. G. (1984), 'Contestability vs Competition', *American Economic Review*, 72: 1–15.

Silverman, D. (1971), *The Theory of Organisations*, New York: Basic Books, 45.

Simmel, G. (1978), *The Philosophy of Money*, London: Routledge.

Simon, H. A. (1976), *Administrative Behaviour*, 3rd edn., New York: The Free Press.

—— (1978), 'Rationality as process and product of thought', *American Economic Review*, 68: 1–16.

Simpson, C. K., and Boyle, D. (1975), 'Esteem construct generality and academic performance', *Educational and Psychological Measurement*, 34: 897–904.

Small, K. A., and Kazimi, C. (1995), 'On the costs of air pollution from motor vehicles', *Journal of Transport Economics and Policy*, 29/1: 7–32.

—— and Song, S. (1992), 'Wasteful commuting: a resolution', *Journal of Political Economy*, 100/4: 888–989.

—— Winston, C., and Evans, C. A. (1989), *Road Works: A New Highway Pricing and Investment Policy*, Washington: The Brookings Institution.

Smircich, L. (1983a), 'Concepts of culture and organisational analysis', *Administrative Science Quarterly*, 28: 339–58.

—— (1983b), 'Studying organisations as cultures', in Morgan, G. (ed.), *Beyond Method: Strategies for Social Research*, Beverly Hills, Calif.: Sage.

—— and Stubbart, C. (1985), 'Strategic management in an enacted environment', *Academy of Management Review*, 10/4: 724–36.

Smith, A. (1776), *The Wealth of Nations*, London: Random House.

Smith, I. (1997), '10 years of JR operation—the explicit and implicit aims of JNR privatization', *Japan Railway and Transport Review* (Sept.), 39–45.

Smith, K. G., Guthrie, J. P., and Chen, M. J. (1989), 'Strategy, size and performance', *Organisational Studies*, 10/1: 63–81.

Starbuck, W. H., and Hedberg, B. L. (1977), 'Saving an organisation from a stagnating environment', in Thorelli, H. B. (ed.), *Strategy and Structure = Performance, The Strategic Imperative*, Bloomington, Ind.: University Press.

Stewart, R. (1982), 'A model for understanding managerial jobs and behaviours', *Academy of Management Review*, 7: 7–14.

Stopford, M. (1988), *Maritime Economics*, London: Unwin Hyman.

Storey, J., and Sisson, K. (1989), 'Looking to the future', in Storey, J. (ed.), *New Perspectives on Human Resource Management*, London: Routledge.

Strathman, J. G., Dueker, K. J., and Davis, J. S. (1994), 'Effects of household structure and selected travel characteristics on trip chaining', *Transportation Review*, 23–45.

Strauss, A. (1978), *Negotiations*, San Francisco: Jossey-Bass.

Stumpf, S. A., and Hartmann, K. (1984), 'Individual exploration to organisational commitment or withdrawal', *Academy of Management Journal*, 27: 308–29.

Sullivan, M., Mahmassani, H. S., and Yen, J. R. (1993), 'Choice model of employee participation in telecommuting under a cost-neutral scenario', *Transportation Research Record*, 1413: 42–8.

Sweeney, J. L. (1984), 'The response of energy demand to higher prices: what lessons have we learned?' *American Economic Association Papers and Proceedings*, 74/2 (May), 31–7.

Talley, W. K. (1988), *Transport Carrier Costing*, New York: Gordon and Breach.

Taplin, J. H. E. (1982), 'Inferring ordinary elasticities from choice or mode-split elasticities', *Journal of Transport Economics and Policy*, 16: 55–63.

—— (1997), 'A generalised decomposition of travel related demand elasticities into choice and generation components', *Journal of Transport Economics and Policy*, 31: 183–91.

—— Hensher, D. A., and Smith, B. (1999), 'Imposing symmetry on a complete matrix of commuter travel elasticities', *Transportation Research*, 33B: 215–32.

Taylor, F. W. (1964), *Scientific Management*, New York: Harper and Row.

Texas Transportation Institute (1997), 'Urban roadway congestion—1982 to 1994', i: Annual Report, Austin, Texi University of Texas.

Thompson, J. D. (1967), *Organisations in Action*, New York: McGraw-Hill.

Thompson, L. S. (1997), 'World Bank support for developing railways of the world', *Japan Railway and Transport Review* (June), 4–15.

Tichy, N. (1983), *Managing Strategic Change, Technical, Political, and Cultural Dynamics*, New York: Wiley.

—— and Devanna, M. A. (1986), *The Transformational Leader*, New York: John Wiley & Sons.

—— and Ulrich, D. O. (1984), 'The leadership challenge—a call for the transformational leader', *Sloan School of Management*, 26: 58–71.

Tirole, J. (1986), 'Hierarchies and bureaucracies: on the role of collusion in organisations', *Journal of Law, Economics and Organisation*, 2: 181–214.

Tretvik, T. (1992), 'The toll road alternative: variations in choice behaviour and values of time', paper presented to the 6th World Conference on Transport Research, Lyon, France, 29 June–3 July 1992.

Truong, T. P., and Hensher, D. A. (1985), 'Measurement of travel times values and opportunity cost from a discrete-choice model', *Economic Journal*, 95/378: 438–51.

—— —— (1986), 'Valuation of travel time savings from a direct experimental approach', *Journal of Transport Economic and Policy*, 19/3 (Sept.), 237–61.

Turner, J. C. (1982), 'Towards a cognitive redefinition of the social group', in Tajfel, H. (ed.), *Social Identity and Intergroup Relations*, Cambridge: Cambridge University Press.

Turner, R. P., and White, P. R. (1991), 'Overall impacts of local bus deregulation in Britain', *Transportation Planning and Technology*, 15: 203–29.

Tye, W. B. (1984), 'Ironies in the application of the inverse elasticity rule to the pricing of U.S. postal services', *Logistics and Transportation Review*, 19/3: 245–60.

—— (1990), *The Theory of Contestable Markets: Applications to Regulatory and Antitrust Problems in The Rail Industry*, New York: Greenwood Press.

—— and Leonard, H. B. (1983), 'On the problems of applying Ramsey pricing to the railroad industry with uncertain demand elasticities', *Transportation Research*, 17A/6: 439–50.

United Nations (1992), *United Nations Framework Convention on Climate Change*, New York: United Nations.

US Congress (1991), *Changing by Degrees: Steps to Reduce Greenhouse Gases*, Office of Technology Assessment, Government Printing Office, Washington: US, Feb.

US Department of Transportation (1993), 'Transportation implications of telecommuting', Washington, Apr.

Vaes, T. (1982), 'Forecasting petrol consumption', paper Q3 presented at the Passenger Transport Research Corporation Annual Summer Conference, Warwick University, Sept.

Vaill, P. (1982), 'The purpose of high-performing systems', *Organisational Dynamics* (autumn) 23–39.

Van de Velde, D. M., and Sleuwaegen, L. I. E. (1997), 'Public transport service contracts: searching for the optimum', *International Journal of Transport Economics*, 24/1: 53–74.

Van de Ven, A. H. (1986), 'Central problems in the management of innovation', *Management Science*, 32: 590–7.

—— and Huber, G. P. (1990), 'Longitudinal field research methods for studying processes of organisational change', *Organisational Science*, 1/3: 213–19.

Venkatesh, A. and Vitalari, N. P. (1992), 'An emerging distributed work arrangement: an investigation of computer-based supplemental work at home', *Management-Science*, 38/12 (Dec.), 1687–1706.

Verhoef, E., Nijkamp, P., and Rietveld, P. (1996), 'The trade-off between efficiency, effectiveness, and social feasibility of regulating road transport externalities', *Transportation Planning and Technology*, 19/3–4: 247–64.

Vickrey, W. (1974), 'Direct and rebuttal testimony', Filed on behalf of the United States Postal Service before the Postal Rate Commission, Docket No. R74–1

Viegas, J., and Macário, R. (1997), 'Public transport regulation as an instrument of urban transport policy', paper presented at the 5th International Conference on Competition and Ownership in Land Passenger Transport, University of Leeds, May.

Virley, S. (1993), 'The effect of fuel prices increases on road transport CO_2 emissions', *Transport Policy*, 1/1: 43–8.

Vroom, V. H. (1964), *Work and Motivation*, New York: Wiley.

Walter, G. A. (1985), 'Culture collisions in mergers and acquisitions', in Frost *et al.* (1985).

Walters, A. A. (1968), 'The economics of road user charges', *World Bank Staff Occasional Paper No. 5*, Baltimore: Johns Hopkins University Press.

Walton, R., and McKersie, R. (1965), *A Behaviour Theory of Labor Negotiations*, Beverly Hills, Calif.: Sage.

Wang, C. S. J., and Friedlaender, A. F. (1984), 'Output aggregation, network effects and the measurement of trucking technology', *Review of Economics and Statistics*, 66/2 (May), 267–76.

Wardman, M., Whelan, G. A., and Toner, J. P. (1994), 'Diverting inter-urban car users to rail: results from a revealed preference mode choice model', Institute of Transport Studies Working Paper 423, University of Leeds, Sept.

Warf, B. (1989), 'Telecommunications and the globalisation of financial services', *The Professional Geographer*, 41/3: 257–71.

Warner, S. L. (1962), *Stochastic Choice of Mode in Urban Travel: A Study in Binary Choice*, Evanston, Ill.: Northwestern University Press.

Waterson, M. (1988), *Regulation of the Firm and Natural Monopoly*, Oxford: Basil Blackwell.

Watson, T. (1986), *Management, Organisation and Employment Strategy*, London: Routledge, Kegan and Paul.

Webster, F. E. (1992), 'The changing role of marketing in the corporation', *Journal of Marketing* (Oct.), 1–17.

Webster, F. V., and Bly, P. H. (1982), 'The demand for public transport: part II: supply and demand factors of public transport', *Transport Reviews*, 2/1: 23–46.

Weick, K. E. (1979), *The Social Psychology of Organising*, Reading, Mass.: Addison-Wesley.

Welch, J. (1998), 'Eli Lilly finds flexibility is hard to instil', *People Management*, 4/10: 13–15.

Welch, J. A. and Nayak, P. R. (1992), 'Strategic sourcing: a progressive approach to the make-or-buy decision', *Academy of Management Executive*, 6: 23.

Westin, R. B. (1974), 'Predictions from binary choice models', *Journal of Econometrics*, 2/1: 1–16.

Williamson, O. E. (1987), *Antitrust Economics*, Oxford: Basil Blackwell.

Windle, R. J. (1988) 'Transit policy and the cost structure of urban bus transportation', in Dodgson (1988).

Withey, M. J., and Cooper, W. H. (1989), 'Predicting exit, voice loyalty and neglect', *Administrative Science Quarterly*, 34/4: 521–39.

Wood, R. F., and Locke, E. A. (1990), 'Goal setting and

strategy effects on complex tasks', in Locke, E. A., and Latham, G. P. (eds.), *A Theory of Goal Setting and Task Performance*, Englewood Cliffs, NJ: Prentice Hall, 293–319.

Yukl, G. A. (1989), *Leadership in Organisations*, London: Prentice-Hall.

Zaltman, D., Duncan, R., and Holbek, J. (1973), *Innovations and Organisations*, New York: Wiley.

Zaskind, S., and Costello, T. W. (1962), 'Perception: implication for administration', *Administrative Science Quarterly*, 7: 218–35.

Index